Integrated Advertising, Promotion, and Marketing Communications

Integrated Advertising, Promotion, and Marketing Communications

Kenneth E. Clow
University of North Carolina at Pembroke

Donald Baack
Pittsburg State University

Prentice
Hall

Upper Saddle River, New Jersey 07458

Library of Congress Cataloging-in-Publication Data

Clow, Kenneth E.
    Integrated advertising, promotion, and marketing communications / Kenneth E. Clow,
Donald Baack.
      p. cm.
    ISBN 0-13-017578-1
    1. Communication in marketing. 2. Advertising. I. Baack, Donald. II. Title.

HF5415.123.C58 2001
659.1—dc21

                           2001034371

Acquisitions Editor: Bruce Kaplan
Assistant Editor: Anthony Palmiotto
Editorial Assistant: Melissa Pellerano
Media Project Manager: Cindy Harford
Marketing Manager: Shannon Moore
Marketing Assistant: Kathleen Mulligan
Managing Editor (Production): John Roberts
Production Editor: M. E. McCourt
Permissions Coordinator: Suzanne Grappi
Associate Director, Manufacturing: Vincent Scelta
Production Manager: Arnold Vila
Design Manager: Patricia Smythe
Designer: Kevin Kall
Interior Design: David Levy
Cover Design: Ox and Company
Associate Director, Multimedia Production: Karen Goldsmith
Manager, Print Production: Christy Mahon
Full-Service Project Management: Carlisle Communications, Ltd.
Printer/Binder: Courier

Credits and acknowledgments borrowed from other sources and reproduced, with
permission, in this textbook appear on appropriate page within text (or on page 615).

10 9 8 7 6 5 4 3 2 1
ISBN 0-13-017578-1

To my sons Dallas, Wes, Tim, and Roy who provided encouragement and especially to my wife, Susan, whose sacrifice and love made this textbook possible.

–Kenneth E. Clow

I would like to dedicate my efforts and contributions to the book to my wife Pam, children, Jessica, Daniel, and David, and grandchildren, Danielle and Rile.

–Donald Baack

Brief Contents

Contents

chaptereight
> **Advertising Media Selection   254**

chapternine
> **Advertising Design: Theoretical Frameworks and Types of Appeals   296**

chapterten
> **Advertising Design: Message Strategies and Executional Frameworks   336**

*T*he best way to learn integrated advertising, promotions, and marketing communications is with an integrated learning package. The best way to teach integrated advertising, promotions, and marketing communication is with an integrated teaching package.

We wrote this book and created the supplements because we thought the current teaching and learning materials fall short of the integration that is paramount with this course. Teaching supplements sometimes work with the text the student has, which is progress. But what about the student? For this particular course, students are often given textbooks and sometimes study guides. The textbooks are colorful, but they are linear, and the study guide is just another add-on piece that is not carefully integrated. This leads to a curious situation. While they are being asked to learn the value of integrated communications, students are not offered an integrated learning package.

The primary goal of this project is to do more than simply provide a textbook with a few extra supplements. Students must have a range of fully integrated learning materials that takes them beyond the textbook. Professors must have a range of fully integrated teaching supplements.

the student integrated learning package

To learn this material properly, students must first have a text that engages them. Next, students must go outside of the text and learn by doing.

The text has many features designed to grab the student's interest.

Lead-in vignettes

Each chapter begins with a vignette that is in some way related to the topic being presented as well as ideas found in other chapters. The majority of the vignettes revolve around success stories in companies students will recognize, such as Starbucks and Papa John's Pizza. Others are designed to attract reader interest by being somewhat quirky, such as the discussion of subliminal advertising techniques (Chapter Eight) and the use of white space in ads (Chapter Nine).

Business-to-business marketing concepts

A large number of marketing students are likely to find that they eventually will hold jobs that emphasize sales to other businesses. Why not highlight a topic likely to be of great interest to them? Therefore, a business-to-business component has been added to nearly every aspect of this text. Examples, cases, text illustrations, and Internet exercises all incorporate this element. We even include a complete exploration of the business component in Chapter Six, Business-to-Business Buyer Behaviors.

International marketing discussions

Students typically are curious about the greater world around them. Yet, international issues often are an add-on toward the end of chapters. While there are some separate discussions of international issues, this book also features international examples where they mesh naturally with the material being presented. Further, international cases are incorporated with others, and Internet materials also lead students to discover a more integrated approach to advertising, promotions, and marketing communications both at home and abroad.

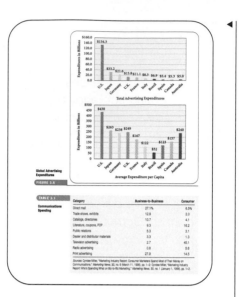

Communication action boxes

Students need to know how to apply concepts. In each chapter, two key illustrations of the subject matter are presented in Communication action boxes. They include business-to-business, consumer, and international examples, as well as illustrations from actual firms. In addition, interviews with members of the marketing/advertising field are presented in some of these boxes. The interviews add depth and a "real world" feel to the materials presented in the chapters.

Implications for decision makers

Students want to know how to apply concepts to make decisions. At the conclusion of each chapter, a short bulleted presentation is given, relating key chapter ideas to various decision makers. These sections are not simple reviews of the subject matter. They assist in the integration of materials by helping students "think like marketing managers" in various jobs and positions in the field.

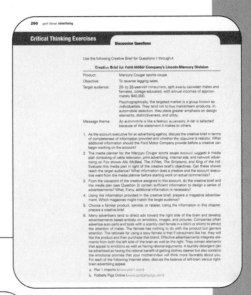

Key terms glossary

Students need appropriate review material in the text. In the end-of-chapter materials, a glossary of key terms and their definitions is provided. The terms are displayed in the order in which they appear in the chapter. When combined with the textbook's index, there is ready access to each new term that is presented.

Discussion and critical thinking exercises

Also, in the end-of-chapter materials, several short scenarios and cases are presented to help students review chapter concepts and apply them in various settings. Internet exercises lead students to individual Web sites to assess the quality of the advertising or Web page. Innovative approaches, such as asking students to prepare and evaluate various kinds of advertisements and advertising campaigns, are also suggested.

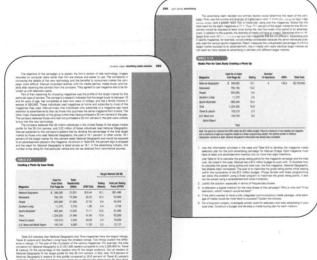

Application exercises

At the conclusion of each chapter, two application exercises are provided. These cases are fictitious, and assist student learning by providing plausible scenarios that require thought and review of chapter materials in order to be successfully completed. As a result, they help students conceptually understand individual chapter components as well as larger and more general marketing issues.

This is not all. The text forces students to grapple with the material by driving them outside of the text to learn by doing. This is done in two key ways.

Integrated learning experiences

At key points in each chapter the text guides students to the Internet where they can access information that ties into the subject matter and also provides additional materials beyond what is in the text. These places are marked in the book and are also highlighted on the Instructor's Teaching CD-ROM. This makes it possible for the instructor to go directly to a Web site while using PowerPoint slides. Also, the professor will have access to additional Internet resources. This unique feature brings the power of the Web directly into the classroom. It also contributes a wealth of supplementary information to course materials.

Integrated Learning Experience

One beneficial tool that can be used to help determine an IMC advertising budget is to examine expenditures of other firms within and in other industries. The Advertising Age Web site at www.adage.com provides information about advertising spending levels. Access the Ad Age Dataplace, and review the 100 leading national advertisers. This section contains information about ad spending by brands, companies, product categories, and in the various media.

stop!

Building Your IMC Campaign exercises

Near the conclusion of each chapter, students are given an exercise that leads them to develop their own IMC program, from start to finish. Each exercise helps students apply chapter theories to their products and IMC program, and they build upon each other. Suggested products are generic in nature, including bottled water, an ink pen, a perfume or cologne, an Internet service, and a customer service.

Building an IMC Campaign

Developing a Brand Name and an Image Management Program

Advertising PlanPro

One of the major challenges your product and company faces is brand equity. People may not perceive any great difference between items; therefore, a strong brand name is vital to success. If the product or service is part of larger company operations, the image of that firm also plays a key role as you develop your IMC campaign. The Web site www.prenhall.com/clow or access the Advertising Plan Pro disk that accompanied this textbook provides an exercise to help you create an effective brand and a positive image for the firm. Remember, your firm's image is important not only domestically but also in the international arena.

Advertising PlanPro

Advertising Plan Pro

As a part of this IMC Campaign Building, students can use a professional advertising planning software program, produced by Palo Alto software. We feel so strongly about this program that we have included it in the back of every student copy of the text, at no extra charge. This software can be used for the campaign, and then can be used by the student for other courses and after graduation. We think this is a great value for the student.

Thus, the student is given an integrated learning package by having a text that engages, opportunities to go beyond the text and learn by doing Internet exercises and building an IMC campaign, and a professional piece of software to make the task easier.

the instructor integrated teaching package

T*he best way to teach integrated advertising, promotions, and marketing communications is with an integrated teaching package. We have authored all of the supplements except the videos to make sure everything works together. And with the videos, we have taken an active role in their development. Here are the instructor supplements:*

PowerPoint CD-ROM
The PowerPoint presentation features print advertisements, logical content builds (through animation), discussion questions, Web links, and over 45 digitized TV commercials and recorded interviews with marketing experts. The print ads not only include ads from the text but also approximately 45 additional ads. These elements are not simply collected or included; they are integrated. Advance to a slide, visit some of the Web sites included, watch a video clip, and then answer questions about what was viewed on the Web sites and in the video. The print advertisements are accompanied by questions or captions relating them to the concepts presented in the text. Stop signs point to integrated learning experiences where links take the class to an interesting web site. And at the end of every chapter's PowerPoint set, as in the textbook, there is a slide for building an IMC campaign.

Web site
The interactive portal contains chapter objectives, faculty resources, and links to company sites referenced in the text. Study guide questions for each chapter can be assigned, and students can e-mail results—complete with a grade report—directly to instructors. The Companion Web site also includes details and information to direct students through the process of building their IMC campaign, and can serve as an alternative for those who cannot use Advertising Plan Pro for whatever reason. On the faculty side, the PowerPoint slides, Instructor's Manual, and other resources may be accessed.

Instructor's Manual
We prepared this resource to provide comprehensive support and suggestions for instructors. A complete outline for each chapter includes keywords and definitions, important themes, and references to text figures. Review questions, discussion questions, and application questions are all answered thoroughly by the authors, and chapter-opening vignettes are explained. A separate IMC section offers guidance and solutions to the Building an IMC Campaign activities.

Test Bank

We created numerous true-false and multiple-choice questions to help evaluate student understanding of chapter concepts. Approximately ten short-answer questions for each chapter are included. All answers include page references so that instructors can provide feedback to students. The test bank is also available in electronic format. Test Manager software helps instructors create tests of varying difficulties, question styles, and lengths. The program also includes a user database, where student records can be kept. A course database allows an instructor to conveniently access all of his or her courses, and a test database provides a place to store completed tests for editing and later use.

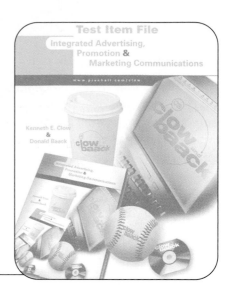

▲

Instructor's Resource CD-ROM

The IR-CDROM contains additional materials for instructors to bring into class, including figures from the book, a version of the electronic test bank, and some advertisements not found in the text.

◄

► Advertisement Transparencies

In order to provide many illustrations of important chapter concepts, the Advertisement Transparencies contain 75 print advertisements for instructors to display in class, approximately 50 not found in the text.

▼

The Prentice-Hall advertising video library

Those who adopt the text will have access to video segments, approximately one for each chapter in the text. Video segments cover such things as the Got Milk campaign, the WNBA, NASCAR, NIKE, and Starbucks.

ORGANIZATION OF THE TEXTBOOK

One of the most difficult problems many firms experience is simply being heard in a cluttered marketplace. The past decade has introduced numerous new ways to vend products, and many new venues to promote those items. The secret to an effective advertising, promotions, and integrated marketing communications program is to develop the one clear voice that will be heard over the din of so many ads and marketing tactics. Meeting this challenge involves bringing together every aspect of the firm's marketing efforts.

PART ONE

Chapter One presents a basic model of communication and describes how it applies to marketing products and services. An overview of the entire IMC approach is presented with the analogy of a baseball as a guiding theme. The baseball has an inner core (Section Two: The Integrated Communications Foundation), twine wrapped around the core (Section Three: Advertising), a cover (Section Four: The Promotional Mix), and is held together by seams (Section Five: Communications Tools).

Chapter Two describes the ethical, legal, and social responsibilities that apply to the course. Various criticisms of the profession are outlined and discussed.

PART TWO

These four chapters represent the core of an advertising and promotions program. They are vital steps in understanding the nature of the marketplace and the processes by which purchase decisions are made.

Chapter Three outlines the first step to developing an IMC model, which is the promotions opportunity analysis program. Market segmentation in consumer and business-to-business settings is also presented.

Chapter Four states the importance of a quality brand name and describes various kinds of brands and logos. Also, the nature of image management is detailed.

Chapter Five reviews the steps of the consumer buyer behavior process. Individual decision-making models are noted. Tactics to influence buyers are also described.

Chapter Six is a presentation of buying decisions made in business-to-business situations. The roles played by members of the buying center are discussed. Methods that can be used to reach individual members are suggested.

PART THREE

The actual advertising program is a major component of the IMC approach. Therefore, four chapters are devoted to explaining advertising in detail, incorporating the viewpoints of the advertising agency account executive, media planners and buyers, creatives, and the company seeking the assistance from the agency.

Chapter Seven describes the overall process of managing an ad campaign. Selection criteria to be used in choosing an agency are provided.

Chapter Eight reviews the various media, including their advantages and disadvantages. Methods for choosing media are also described. Considerations of reach and frequency are also discussed.

Chapter Nine analyzes the various kinds of appeals that can be used in actual ads. Sex, fear, rational approaches, and others are noted. Advantages of each type of appeal are given.

Chapter Ten completes the advertising model by explaining the individual executional frameworks that are available. Also, tactics for discovering the effectiveness of a campaign are noted.

PART FOUR

A fully integrated marketing communications approach requires the inclusion of the other parts of the program. Many customers are convinced to make purchases through the use of methods besides advertisements. This is especially true in the business-to-business arena. As a result, the other parts of the promotions mix are analyzed in this section.

Chapter Eleven details the various kinds of trade promotions that can be used. Advantages and costs of each are defined.

Chapter Twelve notes the connection between consumer promotions, advertisements, and effective IMC programs. Again, benefits and costs are noted.

Chapter Thirteen examines the natures of personal selling and sales management. To fully integrate a marketing program requires the careful training of sales representatives. Incentives and managerial approaches are described in this chapter.

PART FIVE

The "seams" that tie together a complete IMC program involve other important marketing activities as well as the assessment of the success of the company's efforts. The final section of the textbook provides key information regarding other elements of the marketing program.

Chapter Fourteen portrays the importance of quality public relations efforts. Individual sponsorship programs are noted in light of their contributions and costs.

Chapter Fifteen explains how new technologies make it possible to more carefully develop and analyze a market. Techniques for developing and utilizing databases are also described.

Chapter Sixteen gives special attention to Internet marketing and e-commerce programs. This unique new form of marketing must also be integrated with other company activities.

Chapter Seventeen is the assessment chapter. Managers who are faced with major accountability issues require quality methods for analyzing the effectiveness of their programs. This chapter describes the available tools.

ACKNOWLEDGMENTS

We would like to thank the following individuals who assisted in the development of this text through their careful and thoughtful reviews:

Craig Andrews, Marquette University

Ronald Bauerly, Western Illinois University

Mary Ellen Campbell, University of Montana

Les Carlson, Clemson University

Newell Chiesl, Indiana State University

John Cragin, Oklahoma Baptist College

J. Charlene Davis, Trinity University

Steven Edwards, Michigan State University

P. Everett Fergenson, Iona College

James Finch, University of Wisconsin – La Crosse

Thomas Jensen, University of Arkansas

Russell W. Jones, University of Central Oklahoma

Dave Kurtz, University of Arkansas

Monle Lee, Indiana University – South Bend

Ron Lennon, Barry University

Charles L. Martin, Wichita State University

Robert D. Montgomery, University of Evansville

S. Scott Nadler, University of Alabama

Ben Oumlil, University of Dayton

Melodie R. Phillips, Middle Tennessee State University

Don Roy, Middle Tennessee State University

Elise Sautter, New Mexico State University

Janice E. Taylor, Miami University

Robert L. Underwood, Bradley University

Robert Welch, California State University – Long Beach

While there were many individuals who helped us with advertising permissions we want to thank a few who were especially helpful. We want to thank Ethel Uy of the Bozell Advertising Agency for helping us obtain the "Got Milk" advertisements, Erin Flowers who assisted with a number of Proctor & Gamble products, and Cynthia Miller who not only assisted us with a number of Bijan advertisements but also gave us insights into the work of creatives. A special thanks goes to Kerri Martin of BMW Motorcycles and Gretchen Hoag of Publicis Technology for taking time to share with us their thoughts concerning their work and the IMC process.

On a personal note, we would like to thank Leah Johnson, who gave us the opportunity to write this book and prepare the other materials. Bruce Kaplan, our current editor, has rendered insightful opinions and given us a great deal of quality direction as the project moved forward. We would also like to thank the entire Prentice-Hall production team led by John Roberts and Mary Ellen McCourt, and the supplements team led by Anthony Palmiotto, who have been so helpful and pleasant as we finalized this project. We want to thank Lynn Steines of Carlisle Publishers Services for leading the page layout work.

Kenneth Clow would like to express a personal thank you to Rena Hill, the departmental secretary in the School of Business at the University of North Carolina at Pembroke for her assistance and patience, to Audra Harris for her valuable contribution as a graduate assistant, and to Celena Robins for her work as a student employee. A special thanks goes to Dallas, Wesley, and Tim Clow, Ken's sons, for their constant encouragement and support.

Donald Baack would like to express appreciation to Mimi Morrison for her continual assistance in all of his work at Pittsburg State University. Henry Crouch has been most gracious in his role as department chair for Management and Marketing. Also, Christi Leewright has been an excellent source of help in her role as grad assistant. Dan Baack, his son, also contributed to this work.

We would like to especially thank our wives Susan Clow and Pam Baack for being patient and understanding during those times when we were "swamped" by the work involved in completing this book. They have been very supportive and enthusiastic throughout the entire process.

Integrated Advertising, Promotion, and Marketing Communications

› Integrated Marketing Communications

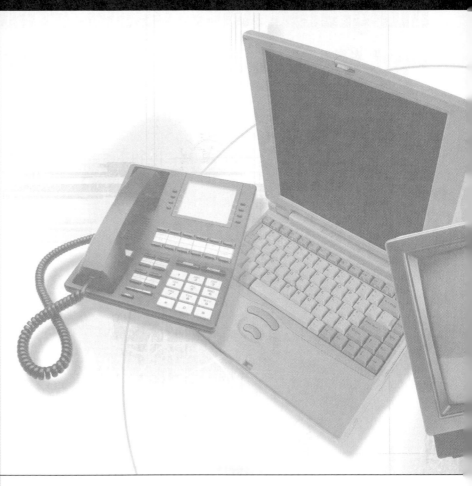

▶ CHAPTER OBJECTIVES

Recognize the critical role communication plays in marketing programs.

Review the nature of the communication process.

Apply a communications model to marketing issues.

Discover the nature of a totally integrated advertising and marketing communications approach.

Expand the concept of integrated marketing communications to the global level.

PAPA JOHN'S PIZZA:
An Integrated Marketing Communications Approach

Would you recognize a Papa John's Pizza sign from a distance? Many people would, given the distinctive green and red emblem and logo, which is designed to attract attention and place the store in a flattering light.

Papa John's began as a small, one-store operation that evolved out of the need to rescue a failing tavern. Quick success meant expansion to four stores in two years and 23 stores in five years. Currently, Papa John's plans to complete more than 2,000 units with over $1 billion in sales, in a mature industry most felt was saturated with competitors.

chapter one

In order to survive in a highly competitive marketplace, Papa John's needed to develop a distinctive voice. One clear message was needed to permeate every aspect of the business, including hiring decisions, selection of locations, and all business strategies and tactics.

At the strategic level, each of the Big Three pizza companies—Pizza Hut, Domino's, and Little Caesar's—holds a distinct niche in the market. Pizza Hut offers menu variety and a dine-in atmosphere; Domino's emphasizes 30-minute delivery, and Little Caesar's focuses on price. To establish a contrasting theme, Papa John's strongly centers its efforts on *quality,* including the overall theme of "Better Ingredients, Better Pizza." Owner John Schnatter makes a

concerted effort to keep his product "simple, consistent, and focused," by making personal visits to as many locations as possible each year.

In selecting locations, Papa John's tries to purchase prime real estate in prominent locations and then counts on its bright signs and logos to attract attention. As one manager in the organization stated, "We think the customer cares where a store is." The effort to find choice locations reemphasizes quality in every aspect of the organization's operation.

Papa John's hires employees based on their compatibility with an overall organizational attitude. Individuals are selected who are "warm, friendly, and nice," according to one human resource officer. As Susie Southgate-Fox, vice president of human resources, put it, "We can teach people about food and wine, and how to carry things, but we can't teach someone how to be warm and friendly. These people are not just serving food. They make the difference in whether someone will return to this restaurant."

The pizza itself is the major locus of the quality campaign. The ingredients are developed by key centralized commissaries that provide fresh dough and sauce, with a careful eye on consistency and quality. The final product always includes a small tub of garlic butter and two hot peppers with each pie, which promotes the perception that the customer is getting "more bang for the buck," according to Gerry Durnell, editor and publisher of *Pizza Today*. Papa John's patrons expect quality at a reasonable price. There are no in-store salad bars that add to costs, and the menu is limited to pizza, breadsticks, cheese-sticks, and soft drinks.

The Papa John's story is reprinted on the walls of many of its stores. Take-home menus not only circulate to retail customers but also find their way into other businesses, where employees can use them to order a quick, high-quality lunch. The menus have the same colors and logo as the store signs and delivery vehicles that carry the product to homes and other businesses. The hats and uniforms workers wear also carry the logo and emphasize the theme.

Advertisements, employees, locations, logos, hats, uniforms, take-home menus, delivery vehicles, suppliers, and the product itself all combine to form an integrated advertising and marketing communications theme emphasizing quality. The theme clearly works, as witnessed by the firm's phenomenal growth and astounding success. Customers know what they're getting when they dial up Papa John's Pizza.

In the future, Papa John's intends to continue its long-term expansion plans by opening more than 1,000 international units, beginning with stores in Mexico and Canada. Even so, the goal still remains to provide quality. As owner-manager Schnatter states, "I demand consistency so the consumer is not confused."[1]

overview

The global marketplace consists of an increasingly complex arena of competitors within a rapidly changing international environment. New companies are formed on a daily basis, from small businesses, to Internet-based operations, to expanding global conglomerates originating from major takeovers and mergers. At the same time, a wide variety of venues beckon company leaders to invest their advertising and marketing dollars. From approaches as simple as using billboards to methods as complex as establishing global Web sites, the number and ways to reach out to customers continually increases.

In the face of these sophisticated and cluttered market conditions, firms try to be heard. They attempt to speak with clear voices about the natures of their operations and the benefits associated with the firm's goods and services. With so many choices available, and so many media bombarding potential customers with messages, it is vital that what should be communicated is reaching buyers in a consistent and coherent manner.

Two important consequences emerge from this turbulent new marketing context. First, the issue of *accountability* is a primary concern to advertising agencies and for company leaders that hire those agencies. Currently, company leaders recognize that they cannot spend unlimited dollars on marketing and advertising programs. The funds must be spent wisely, and marketing managers increasingly demand *tangible results* from their advertising efforts. A coupon program, contest, rebate program, or advertising campaign must yield measurable gains in sales, brand awareness, or customer loyalty in order to be considered successful.

The second issue, which is tied to the first, is a change in the nature of the job of **account executive** in advertising agencies and marketing companies. With increasing demands for accountability, the advertising or marketing account manager is now on the hot seat. He or she must respond to the more careful scrutiny placed on individual marketing efforts. As a result, the increased responsibility has generated a new job description for the account manager. Rather than simply serving as a go-between working with the people who prepare commercials and the company, the account manager is increasingly expected to be involved in the strategic development of the marketing plan and to make sure efforts are garnering tangible results.

Another person facing increased accountability is the brand or product manager. The **brand manager** is responsible for the management of a specific brand or line of products. When sales of a brand slow down, it is the responsibility of the brand manager to find ways to boost them. He or she also must coordinate efforts so that every marketing endeavor used to promote the brand speaks with one voice. The brand manager must work diligently to make sure the advertising agency, the trade promotion specialist, the consumer promotion specialist, and any other individual or agency involved conveys the same message to customers. The brand manager must be a master at organizing the activities of many individuals while integrating each marketing campaign.

Previously, creatives were often the most visible individuals in promotional efforts. **Creatives** are the individuals who develop the actual advertising and promotional campaigns. Most creatives are employed by advertising agencies. Others work within individual companies or as freelancers. Creatives have seen their roles change as well, particularly in this era in which attracting attention to a company, product, or service is such a difficult task. Creatives are being asked to contribute to the strategic marketing direction of the firm, to develop effective advertisements, and to share accountability (in both rewards given as bonuses and lost accounts when campaigns fail) with the account manager.

This new partnership between account executives, brand managers, and creatives moves many advertising and marketing agencies into the realm of developing totally integrated communications programs in order to succeed. As the field evolves, this trend toward a more integrated approach to all advertising and marketing communications efforts can be expected to continue. This textbook is devoted to explaining marketing communications from the strategic perspective of the decision makers both inside and outside the firm. Various topics are viewed from the vantage point of the key individuals involved, such as the account manager, brand manager, creative, media buyer, and even the Web master, with careful consideration of every chapter's accountability issues.

In this first chapter, the nature of an integrated advertising and marketing communications program is examined. First, communication processes are described. This process builds the foundation for an integrated marketing program. Then, a totally integrated marketing communications program is outlined. Finally, the integrated marketing communications process is applied to global or international operations, generating the term *GIMC,* or global integrated marketing communications.

communication and IMC programs

Communication is defined as transmitting, receiving, and processing information. This definition suggests that when a person, group, or organization attempts to transfer an idea or message, the receiver (another person or group) must be able to process that information effectively. Communication occurs when the message that was sent reaches its destination in a form that is understood by the intended audience.[2] A model of communication is shown in Figure 1.1.

An illustration can be useful in demonstrating the communication process used to market a variety of goods and services. Assume someone plans to buy a new pair of athletic shoes. The **senders** are companies that manufacture and sell shoes. New Balance, Asics, Reebok, and Skechers all try to garner the customer's attention. In most cases, these firms hire advertising agencies to construct messages. An

The Communication Process

FIGURE 1.1

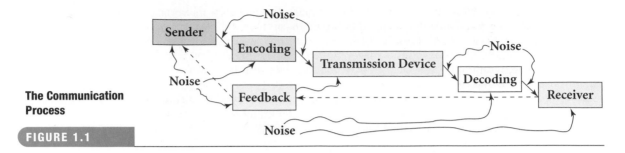

account manager serves as a major contact between the shoe company and the ad agency. In other situations the firm may have its own in-house marketing group.

Encoding the message is the second step in the communication of a marketing idea. Someone must take the idea and transform it into an attention-getting form, through an advertisement or some other verbal or nonverbal medium. An advertising *creative* usually performs this role. The shoe advertisements shown are examples of encoding.

Messages travel to audiences through various **transmission devices.** The third stage of the marketing communication process occurs when a channel or medium

Various advertisements for shoes.
Courtesy of New Balance Athletic Shoes Inc.
Photograph by Paul Wakefield.; ASICS Tiger
Corporation.; Reebok International.; Skechers USA Inc.

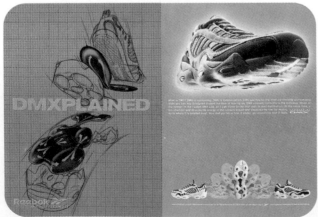

delivers the message. The channel may be a television carrying an advertisement, a billboard, a Sunday paper with a coupon placed in it, or a letter to the purchasing agent of a large retail store.[3] The shoe ads were transmitted through various magazines.

Decoding occurs when the message touches the receiver's senses in some way. Some consumers will hear and see a television ad. Others will handle and read a coupon offer. It is even possible to "smell" a message. A well-placed perfume sample may entice a buyer to purchase both the magazine containing the sample and the perfume being advertised. Those interested in purchasing shoes pay closer attention to advertisements and other information about shoes such as the brands being offered.

Study the shoe advertisements, then answer the following questions:

1. Which advertisement attracts your attention the most? Why?
2. Which advertisement is the least appealing? Why?
3. How important is the brand name in each ad? Why?
4. What is the major message of each individual advertisement?
5. What makes each advertisement effective or ineffective?
6. Discuss the pros and cons of each advertisement with other students.

Those who discussed the advertisements with other students probably discovered that the same advertisement was interpreted differently by each member of the group. In other words, the message that was decoded may not have been the same one the various companies meant to send. Quality marketing communication occurs when customers (the **receivers**) decode or understand the message as it was intended by the sender. In the case of the shoe ads, effective marketing communications depends upon receivers getting the right message and responding in the desired fashion (shopping, buying, telling their friends about the shoes, etc.).

Examining the Web sites listed in the Integrated Learning Experience provides additional insights into how each company encodes its messages. A comparison of the materials on the Web sites with the shoe advertisements should lead to the conclusion that the two messages go together. If they do not, the IMC program is not completely developed or fully integrated.

Integrated Learning Experience

How do companies integrate their ads with their Web sites? Access each of the following company Web sites, and compare the appearance and content of the Web site to the shoe advertisements shown both on the site and in this book. Using the communication model presented in Figure 1.1, examine how well they communicate to consumers accessing their site.

Reebok (www.reebok.com)
New Balance (www.newbalance.com)
Asics (www.asicstiger.com)
Skechers (www.skechers.com)

Consumers are not the only ones who see advertisements such as these. Other receivers include retail outlets (Sears, JC Penney, Foot Locker) that may carry the product (See Table 1.1). An intensive advertising campaign on behalf of a product can heighten a store's interest in carrying and selling the offering of a given manufacturer. In some situations, this effort encourages the retailer to advertise jointly with a producer. This develops a dual set of senders preparing messages for customers (receivers).

There are other difficulties in making certain marketing communications efforts efficient and effective. In Figure 1.1, notice that **noise** interferes with the communication process. Noise is anything that distorts or disrupts a message. It can occur at any stage in the process. Examples of noise are shown in Figure 1.2.

TABLE 1.1

Internet Sites of Selected Retail Outlets

Sears Canada (www.sears.ca)

J.C.Penney (www.jcpenney.com)

Foot Locker Australia (www.footlocker.com.au)

Shoe Carnival (www.shoecarnival.com)

Aardvark Shoe Mall (www.aardvarkshoes.com)

Feedback takes the forms of purchases, inquiries, complaints, questions, visits to the store, and "hits" on a Web site. Each indicates the message has reached the receiver and that the receiver is now responding.

The most common form of noise in the marketing communication process is **clutter.** Modern consumers are exposed to hundreds of marketing messages per day. Most are tuned out. Clutter includes:

- Eight minutes of commercials per half hour of television and radio programs
- A Sunday newspaper jammed with advertising supplements
- An endless barrage of billboards on a major street
- The inside of a bus or subway car papered with ads
- Web sites and servers loaded with commercials

Account managers, creatives, brand managers, and others involved in the marketing process must effectively utilize the communications model displayed in Figure 1.1. They constantly must work to make sure that the proper audiences receive their messages, while encountering as little noise as possible. In the case of athletic shoes, increases in market share, sales, and brand loyalty are common outcomes the marketing team tries to achieve.

Between Individuals
- Age
- Gender
- Social status
- Personality

Between Companies
- Poor selling techniques
- Unfocused advertising
- Poor media choices
- Failure to find correct contact persons

Within Companies
- Poor downward flow (orders, procedures)
- Poor lateral flow (communication between departments)
- Poor upward flow (computers, telephone systems, intranet systems)
- Information not stored for future use or poor retrieval system

Barriers to Communication

FIGURE 1.2

Communication with consumers and other businesses requires more than simply creating attractive advertisements. In the next section, the nature of a fully developed Integrated Marketing Communications program is described. An effective IMC process integrates numerous marketing activities into a single package, making it possible for companies to reach their target markets and other audiences more effectively.

integrated marketing communications

An integrated marketing communications program is based on the foundation provided by the communications model. Some marketing scholars argue that the integrated marketing communications (IMC) approach is a recent phenomenon. Others suggest the name is new, but the concept has been around for a long time. They note that the importance of effectively coordinating all marketing functions and promotional activities has been described in the marketing literature for many years.[4]

Although IMC programs have been described in several ways, the consensus is to define them as follows: **Integrated marketing communications** is the coordination and integration of all marketing communication tools, avenues, and sources within a company into a seamless program that maximizes the impact on consumers and other end users at a minimal cost. This integration affects all of a firm's business-to-business, marketing channel, customer-focused, and internally directed communications.

Before further examining the IMC concept, it is helpful to consider the traditional framework of marketing from which it originated. The **marketing mix** is the starting point for such an analysis. As shown in Figure 1.3, promotion is one of the four components of the mix that contains another series of marketing functions. Traditionally, promotional activities include advertising, sales promotions, and personal selling activities. The sales promotion area normally includes both sales and trade promotions, with sales promotions aimed at end users or consumers of goods and services and trade promotions directed toward distributors and retailers. Within the context of promotions, some add direct-marketing and public relations programs, as depicted in Figure 1.3. Others include them within the three major components of advertising, sales promotions, and personal selling.

An IMC plan begins with the development and coordination of the marketing mix, elements of prices, products, distribution methods, and promotions. This textbook primarily deals with the promotions component of the marketing mix. Keep in mind, however, that to present a unified message the four elements of the marketing mix must blend together.

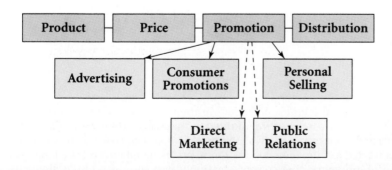

Traditional Marketing Mix

FIGURE 1.3

▶ Situation analysis

▶ Marketing objectives

▶ Marketing budget

▶ Marketing strategies

▶ Marketing tactics

▶ Evaluation of performance

The Marketing Plan

FIGURE 1.4

an integrated marketing communications plan

Integrated marketing begins with the development of a master marketing plan. The marketing plan is the basis of the total integrated communication design. The plan provides for the coordination of efforts in all components of the marketing mix. The purpose of the plan is to achieve harmony in relaying messages to customers and other publics. Planning also should integrate all key promotional efforts, which in turn keeps the company's total communication program in synch.

Figure 1.4 lists the primary steps required to complete a marketing plan. The first step is a *situational analysis,* which is the process of examining factors from the organization's internal and external environments. The analysis identifies external environmentally-generated marketing problems and opportunities; internal company strengths and weaknesses are also considered during this step. When the situation is fully understood, the second step is to define primary *marketing objectives.* These objectives normally are spelled out in the areas of sales, market share, competitive position, and desired customer actions. Based on these marketing objectives, a *marketing budget* is prepared and *marketing strategies* are finalized. The marketing strategies include the ingredients of the marketing mix plus all positioning, differentiation, and branding strategies the firm wants to use. From these strategies, *marketing tactics* emerge to guide the day-by-day steps necessary to support marketing strategies. The final step in the marketing plan is the *evaluation of performance.* These six steps are similar to those prescribed by management strategists attempting to integrate all company activities into one consistent effort. When properly designed and followed, they provide guidance to company leaders and marketing experts as they try to make certain the firm's total communications package is fully integrated.

Once the marketing plan has been established, the firm can prepare its integrated marketing communications program. This textbook's prime goal is to demonstrate this process. Developing an IMC program is similar to constructing a baseball. First, the cork or center becomes the basis for the rest of the ball. Then string is wound around the cork, followed by the leather shell. Finally, lacing holds the leather together. Figure 1.5 illustrates this view of the IMC model.

IMC components

Figure 1.5 outlines the topics presented in the remainder of this textbook. A brief description of each aspect of IMC follows. Chapter 2 identifies some *ethics and social issues* in marketing. Part of the overall message that a firm sends to consumers is related to how the organization treats its members and the larger society. A portion of any marketing communications plan should include elements that

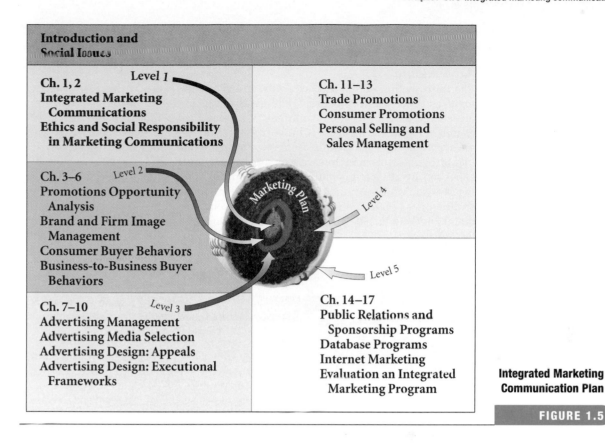

Integrated Marketing
Communication Plan

FIGURE 1.5

confront ethical and social concerns. Chapter 2 addresses the ethical, moral, legal, regulatory, and social responsibility issues that marketers encounter.

The foundation

The next section of this text builds the foundation for an effective IMC. Chapter 3 describes the *promotional analysis* part of an IMC plan. A promotional analysis identifies all target markets of the communications program. Consumer market segments often are distinguished by demographics, income, social class, and other psychographic variables. Business markets also can be segmented by understanding their demographics and end users and by determining which benefits they expect from a given firm's products or services.

In Chapter 4, *firm and brand image* issues are discussed. At this point, marketing executives attempt to understand what kinds of brand and firm images are currently being projected and decide whether or not atempts should be made to modify these images. Each message sent and every activity performed by a company has an impact on the firm's image. Everything from commercials, to logos, to letterhead, to publicity affects a company's image, as do the activities of sales representatives and repair departments. All communication efforts designed by the marketing department or an advertising creative should reinforce the desired image.

Chapter 5 outlines the nature of *consumer buyer behaviors*. The steps of the purchasing process can be used to explain how individuals make choices. Marketers need to identify which motives lead to purchase decisions and which factors affect those decisions. Then, effective communication programs indicate the manner in which company efforts can influence consumers.

Chapter 6 identifies *business-to-business buyer behaviors*. Knowing how to reach purchasing managers and other decision makers within target businesses is another critical element in the development of a totally integrated communications plan. Discovering viable business-to-business marketing opportunities plays a vital role in maintaining a fully developed IMC program.

Advertising

The third section of this text is devoted to advertising issues. *Advertising management,* as described in Chapter 7, addresses the major functions of advertising and directs the general path the company will take. Media selection and advertising design (Chapters 8 through 10) involve matching the message, media, and audience, so that the right people see and/or hear the ads. Many appeals can be used, including those oriented toward fear, humor, sex, music, and logic. These should be conveyed by attractive, credible, likable, authoritative sources. Effective advertising is based on the foundation built by understanding consumer buyer behaviors and business buyer behaviors. Advertising must reinforce or project a specific brand and firm image, which evolves out of the marketing plan at the center of the IMC process.

communication action

Wendy's Misses the Mark—Then Hits a Winner

"Where's the beef?" A series of commercials sponsored by Wendy's during the 1980s featured this slogan. The commercials were highly popular and even rated as the decade's best by some advertising analysts. The phrase was so well-known that one presidential candidate even asked another, "Where's the beef [in your campaign]?" during one of the debates. Unfortunately, the impact for Wendy's was marginal. When consumers were asked who sponsored the ads, most attributed them to Burger King. The clever slogan and Clara Pellar, the elderly woman who starred in the commercials, overshadowed the message and created interference. Thus the impact on sales was negligible.

This outcome demonstrates one type of advertising noise. In this case, it shows how an ambiguous transmission device can fail to achieve a complete transfer of the desired message to the audience. In essence, Wendy's may have missed the mark with this ad.

In 1982, Wendy's switched to featuring its CEO, Dave Thomas, as the pitchman. Thomas was able to demonstrate a self-effacing honesty that made his name and Wendy's nearly synonymous. At the time, the company had been drifting in a number of different ways. The food line had expanded to include breakfast; people were not sure what they were getting.

The refocus, with Thomas in the forefront, was a return to a simpler menu and a renewed focus on clean restaurants, high-quality food, and reasonable prices. The approach succeeded. Thomas has since performed in over 500 commercials and has won numerous awards as an entrepreneur and restaurateur. Theresa Howard of *Nation's Restaurant News* summarizes the success this way: "While all things surrounding Thomas on a set are fake, he is not. His integrity, charisma, and true commitment to basics continues to come through in each series of commercials."

The theme "quality is our recipe" drives Thomas. He believes one thing for certain—that he knows how to make a good hamburger. When that burger is served in a clean store, by friendly people, at a good price, customers are satisfied and they come back for more. This quality message permeates the entire organization, and as a result Dave Thomas has carefully built a solid IMC plan in his organization.

Sources: "Dave Thomas: Building a Better Burger," *Sales & Marketing Management,* 145, no. 5 (May 1993), pp. 52–53; Theresa Howard, "James Near," *Nation's Restaurant News,* NRN Fifty: Profiles in Power (January 1995), pp. 155–56; Louise Kramer, "Pioneer of the Year: Dave Thomas," *Nation's Restaurant News,* 29, no. 40 (October 9, 1995), pp. 152–54; Theresa Howard, "Will the Real Dave Thomas Please Stand Up?" *Nation's Restaurant News,* 30, no. 39 (October 7, 1996), p. 30.

The use of a consumer promotion by Papa John's. Courtesy of Papa John's International.

The promotional mix

The next level of activity includes the more traditional marketing elements of trade promotions, consumer promotions, and personal selling. When marketing managers carefully design all of the steps taken up to this point, the firm is in a better position to integrate consumer and trade promotions in conjunction with personal selling tactics. Messages presented in the advertising campaign can be reinforced in the trade and consumer promotions. *Trade promotions,* as described in Chapter 11, include contests, incentives, vendor support programs, and other fees and discounts that help the retailer promote the product. *Consumer promotions* are directly oriented to end users and include coupons, contests, premiums, refunds, rebates, free samples, and so forth. The advertisement for Papa John's pizza illustrates the use of consumer promotions. Consumer promotions are the subject of Chapter 12. Chapter 13 reviews *personal selling* techniques. The goal is to fully integrate all communications so that advertising messages are repeated and reinforced by the sales staff.

Communication tools

The last step (or outside layer of the baseball shown in Figure 1.5) in an IMC Program includes more tactical types of promotions. These include public relations efforts, sponsorship programs, database programs, and Internet marketing, plus the evaluation of integrated marketing programs. To take advantage of the total IMC concept, it is important to include *public relations* events and *sponsorship programs,* which are described in Chapter 14.

New forms of technology have generated tremendous new IMC opportunities for firms. The Internet and databases should become essential parts of the integrated communications program. The use of *database programs* (Chapter 15) allows firms to better target their customers. *Internet marketing* (Chapter 16) and a firm's Web site also are significant aspects of the total operation.

The last chapter (17) in this textbook explains how to *evaluate an integrated marketing program.* It is vital to make decisions about how a communication

The Internet is an important communication tool for companies such as WeddingChannel.com.
Courtesy of Wedding Channel.com.

program will be evaluated *prior to* any promotional campaign so materials may be designed accordingly. This makes a promotional evaluation process similar to the leather lacing on a baseball. It holds everything together and drives the entire IMC process as much as does developing the core business plan. Fully integrated marketing requires a careful linkage between planning and evaluation processes; one cannot occur without the other.

Refining the IMC program

It is important to realize that Integrated Marketing Communications is more than a plan or a simple marketing function. IMC should be an overall organizational process. To be successful, every part of the marketing operation must be included. Organizations that have not developed an IMC approach will discover that it takes time to get things established. A study by American Productivity & Quality Center of Houston of the best integrated marketing firms indicates that four stages are involved in cultivating an integrated marketing communications system.[5]

The first stage is to identify, coordinate, and manage all forms of external communication. The objective is to bring all of the company's brands and strategic business units or divisions under one umbrella. During this stage of IMC development, the firm needs to be sure all advertisements, brochures, and promotional materials use the same logos, colors, and themes, as was the case in the Papa John's Pizza program noted at the beginning of this chapter. Effort must be made to coordinate all advertising and public relations activities. These programs should be integrated with sales promotions, direct-marketing efforts, and all other external marketing programs.

In the second stage, the firm's goal must be to extend the scope of communication to include everyone touched by the organization. Thus, all external communications should mesh with internal messages sent to employees and departments. External contacts made during public relations events or with outside advertising agencies must be consistent with what is being communicated internally. This spreads the IMC umbrella over all the groups that have contact with the firm and includes employees along with every external organization, such as distributors, retailers, dealers, product package designers, and so forth.

Technology comes to the forefront in the third stage. Firms begin to apply information technology to their IMC programs. Databases must be developed summarizing each customer's activities, purchases, and interactions with the company. This step is critical to the development of an IMC program because now customer input is being gathered. This vital information becomes part of the overall IMC decision-making process.

Courtesy of PhotoEdit. Photograph by Michael Newman.

The last stage of IMC development occurs when the organization treats IMC as an investment and not a departmental function. Firms reaching this stage, such as Dow Chemical, FedEx, and Hewlett-Packard, take these databases and use them to calculate and establish a customer value for each of their customers. The companies recognize that not all customers are equal. In contrast to a typical marketing program designed to win customers by sending the same marketing message to each one, Dow Chemical, FedEx, and Hewlett-Packard are able to allocate sales and marketing communication resources to those customers with the greatest potential for return, based on previous calculations of customer values. This process helps them understand each customer's worth and treat each individual as a unique customer.

Other noteworthy aspects of IMC programs emerged from the American Productivity & Quality Center's study.[6] The best companies worked hard at developing both interpersonal and cross-functional communications. Not only was communication opened up within the typical marketing department, but communication lines were opened between the marketing department and other functional departments. Every employee in the company became a part of the communication and customer orientation.

To make sure that customer input is obtained outside of compiling databases, the best IMC companies involved customers in their planning processes. Consumer goods companies invited consumers and business-to-business firms invited target members of other businesses. As a result, the potentially adversarial relationship between buyers and sellers was replaced with a cooperative, "let's work together" mentality.

The final facet present in successful IMC companies was their understanding of the natures of their customers. These firms took the stance that customers should be considered customers of the whole company, not just the SBU, operating division, or outlet in which they are doing business. Seeing a patron as a customer of the total company encourages the cross-selling of goods and services. This approach allows a firm such as ServiceMaster, which provides janitorial services to various companies, to cross-sell various pest control and lawn services to those same organizations. This mode of thinking suggests selling across countries when the firm is a multinational operation. Thus, a customer who buys from Hewlett-Packard in the United States is an excellent prospect in other countries where both companies are operating businesses. When firms think in these terms, they are able to spend marketing dollars wisely. When company leaders fail to grasp this concept they often spend additional marketing dollars in order to gain new customers.

Integrated Learning Experience

The American Productivity & Quality Center has uncovered many leading-edge practices in the areas of sales, marketing, and integrated communications. Examine what it considers to be the best practices under the "Sales and Marketing at APQC" section at (www.apqc.org). Also examine the Web sites of Dow Chemical (www.dow.com), FedEx (www.fedex.com), and Hewlett-Packard (www.hp.com) to see why the American Productivity & Quality Center considers them excellent examples of firms using the IMC approach.

stop!

communication**action**

An excellent example of an integrated marketing communications program is provided by the software systems engineering division (SESD) of Hewlett-Packard. This group initiated its IMC process through workshops designed to help HP's employees better understand the dilemmas faced by its customers. These workshops were directed by representatives from sales, product marketing, engineering, and customer support departments within HP. Each had a different perspective of the customer and provided valuable input into the various dilemmas faced by end users. The team approach allowed everyone to see the customer from a more holistic perspective.

Based on input from these departments, a creative strategy emerged with a strong focus on customer needs. The theme "we understand" was adopted. HP's marketing emphasis centered on the idea that members of the company understood the issues, pressures, and constraints that software developers faced. Knowing about unrealistic deadlines, hidden-code errors, and other problems and how to cope with these issues was the key. HP's leaders believed they could solve transition problems for customers by moving to object-oriented programming and simultaneously developing multiple applications of company software. The theme was integrated into all of HP's marketing programs. It was launched in an advertising campaign, then reinforced in three direct mailings. The same message was used in trade show handouts and displays. HP's Web site was redesigned around the same principle.

The "we understand" idea served as an umbrella that all marketing strategies and tactics would then utilize. The integrated approach allowed HP to speak with one voice regardless of the communication method customers encountered when they contacted the firm. This more fully integrated program was more than just the theme, however. It began with effective communication within and built outward to the point where HP's end users (other business) could see and experience a real difference in the products and services that were being provided.

Source: P. Griffeth Lindell, "You Need an Integrated Attitude to Develop IMC," *Marketing News,* 31, no. 11 (May 26, 1997), p. 6.

the value of IMC plans

Why are IMC programs so crucial to marketing success? Figure 1.6 shows several items that are linked to the increasing importance of integrated advertising and marketing communications programs. The major force compelling firms to seek greater integration of advertising and marketing communications is *information technology.* Computers, the World Wide Web, and telecommunications are swiftly moving the world into ank information age where businesses and most consumers have access to an abundance of marketing information. The challenge for marketers in the future is not gathering information, but rather sifting through an avalanche of statistics, ideas, and messages and putting them together in a format company leaders can use. When this is accomplished, businesses leaders are better able to make intelligent, informed decisions about how to market products.

Technology makes it possible not only for companies to study customers but also for customers to study companies. In addition, quality information technology provides numerous other advantages and opportunities.

> Development of information technology
> Changes in channel power
> Increase in competition (global competitors)
> Maturing markets
> Brand parity
> Integration of information by consumers
> Decline in effectiveness of mass-media advertising

Factors Affecting the Value of IMC Programs

FIGURE 1.6

Information technology

Technology allows instant communications between business executives and their employees, even when workers are dispersed throughout the world. Through computer technology, huge amounts of data and information about customers can quickly be gathered. Advanced statistical software helps analyze these data files in a matter of hours or even minutes. Because of the connections between financial (credit card, banking) and business firms, purchasing data can easily be collected. Using this information, demographic and psychographic information about consumers can be correlated with the items they buy, when they make purchases, and where they make purchases. Marketers can quickly determine who is buying a company's products and identify the best communication channels to reach those customers.

In the past, predicting the purchasing behaviors of consumers was accomplished by using test markets, attitudinal research, and intention-to-buy surveys. Although these methods are excellent means of obtaining information about consumers, they often are slow, costly, and sometimes inaccurate.

The introduction of the new Coke by the Coca-Cola Company shows how consumer preferences for a product in a lab setting do not necessarily mean they will purchase the item when it is on the market. In that incident in the 1980s, Coca-Cola spent $4 million and interviewed almost 200,000 consumers. The company's blind taste tests indicated that the new Coke was preferred over Pepsi by as much as 8 percent of the sample, and the new Coke was chosen over the old Coke by a 55 percent to 45 percent margin. Even loyal Coke drinkers selected the new flavor when they did not know what they were trying. Further, when the drinks were identified as the new Coke and the old Coke, the preference for the new Coke was 61 percent to 39 percent. All of the research pointed to a strong preference for the new formula. Unfortunately, when the new Coke was actually introduced, sales were high during the first week and then quickly plummeted amid a backlash of customers demanding the old formula. Within four months, the old Coke was back, sold as "Classic Coke." Marketers at the time knew their methods were not infallible. They were aware that they needed to keep refining techniques used to understand consumer buyer behaviors, and new information technologies were helpful in the process.[7]

Today, predicting purchase behavior is more accurate because of the development of the UPC (universal product code) bar coding system and point-of-purchase systems. This technology was originally used to help control and evaluate inventory requirements. With computer scanning of every sale, retailers have been able to develop an inventory control system that did not rely as heavily on human counting of merchandise. Stockrooms were reduced and, in some cases, eliminated altogether as retailers shifted from stocking merchandise to selling merchandise.

A Visa advertisement encouraging consumers to book vacations over the Internet.

Changes in channel power

Technological developments also served as catalysts for changes in channel power.[8] Typical market channels are:

Producer → Wholesale → Retailer → Consumer

and

Producer → Business Agent → Business Merchant → Business User

With the advancement of the World Wide Web and information technology, the power is expected to shift more to the consumer.[9] Currently, consumers can obtain information about products and services from their homes or businesses and purchase almost anything over the Internet. For example, the VISA advertisement (on the next page) encourages consumers to book hotel rooms, air travel, and car rentals over the Internet. The sale of products through the Internet has grown at tremendous rate. In fact, beginning in 1997 these sales doubled three years in a row. In 1998, the Internet generated over $300 billion worth of business in the U.S. economy alone. Sales of books, automobiles, and other goods and services account for approximately 1 percent of the GDP in the United States.[10]

To illustrate the impact of this change on the channel members, suppose an individual is in the market for a new stereo. First she goes to the Internet and searches for information. She then identifies several possible brands and narrows them down to three. Next she travels to a local mall and investigates the three brands. Asking questions of the salesclerks helps her gather additional product information. Going home, she then logs onto the Web sites of the three manufacturers to learn about warranties and company policies. Having gathered sufficient information to make a decision, she can utilize Internet sources or a catalog to finalize the purchase either via the Web or by telephone. Within three days, the new stereo arrives complete with a money-back guarantee if she is not satisfied.

The same process applies to business-to-business purchasing activities. Buyers who shop on behalf of organizations, and other company members seeking business-to-business services, will be able to tap into the same resources (Web sites, databases) to help them make purchasing decisions. The same type of shift in channel power is likely to take place in the business-to-business sector.

Increases in competition

Information technology has dramatically changed the marketplace in other ways. Consumers can purchase goods and services from anywhere in the world. Competition no longer comes from the company just down the street—it can come from a firm 10,000 miles away that can supply a product faster and cheaper. People want quality, but they also want low price. The company that delivers on both quality and price gets the business, regardless of location, because advancements in logistics make it possible for purchases to arrive almost anywhere in a matter of days.

In this type of mature market, the only way one firm can gain sales is to take customers away from another firm. Integrating advertising and other marketing communications becomes extremely important in such an environment. Advertising alone is not enough to maintain sales. This situation is further complicated for manufacturers when retailers hold stronger channel power and control the flow of merchandise to consumers. In that situation, manufacturers have to invest in trade promotions (dealer incentives, slotting allowances, discounts, etc.) to keep their products in various retail outlets. Further, in order to encourage retailers to promote a manufacturer's brand or prominently display it for consumer viewing requires even greater promotional dollars. Manufacturers also must invest heavily in consumer promotions to keep end users loyal to their companies and encourage them to purchase their brands, because they know that the more they promote their own products, the more attractive those products become to retailers.

At the same time, retailers, equipped with scanner data, are quick to pull the plug on promotions that don't work.[11] To gain prominence for a product at the retail level requires a manufacturer to coordinate all advertising, trade promotions, and sales promotions as part of a larger integrated marketing communications effort. Retailers must also focus on IMC efforts to maintain customer loyalty to their stores and to maintain positive relationships with manufacturers. The net result is a strong case for the importance of understanding and creating a quality IMC program, at every level of the marketing chain.

Brand parity

The increase in national and global competition has resulted in multiple brands being available, and many of these products have nearly identical benefits for consumers. When consumers believe that many brands offer the same set of attributes, the result is called **brand parity.** From the consumer's perspective, this means shoppers will purchase from a *group* of accepted brands rather than one specific brand. When brand parity is present, quality is often not a major concern because consumers believe there are only minor quality differences among brands. If consumers view quality levels of products to be the same, they often base purchase decisions on other criteria such as price, availability, or a specific promotional deal. The net effect is that brand loyalty has experienced a steady decline.[12] This decline in brand loyalty is partly due to the proliferation of product choices.

In response, marketers must generate messages in a voice that expresses a clear difference. They must build some type of perceived brand superiority for their company and its products or services. They must convince consumers that their product or service is not the same as the competition's. A quality IMC program is, in part, designed to help regain the benefits of a strong brand name.

Integration of information

In today's marketplace, consumers have a variety of choices regarding how they interpret information sent by a firm. There are many ways in which consumers can integrate the information they receive about various goods and services.[13]

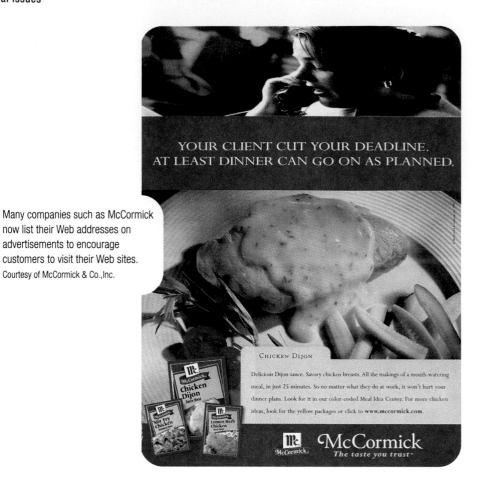

Many companies such as McCormick now list their Web addresses on advertisements to encourage customers to visit their Web sites.
Courtesy of McCormick & Co.,Inc.

Consumers now have the opportunity to obtain additional information. They may go to the Internet and read about companies and their competitors. Realizing this, many companies now list their Internet addresses on their advertisements to encourage consumers to visit their Web sites. In the McCormick's ad notice their address www.mccormick.com. The Web site contains additional information about McCormick seasonings along with ideas and recipes for consumers. Web users can discuss products and companies in chat rooms with other consumers to get other viewpoints. They may travel to a retail store and discuss various options with a salesclerk or consult independent sources of information such as *Consumer Reports.*

It is logical to conclude that because consumers integrate information they receive, marketers should also be concerned about integration. Company leaders need to make sure that every contact point projects the same message. **Contact points** are the places in which a customer may interact with or acquire additional information about a firm. These points may be direct or indirect, planned or unplanned. An effective IMC program seeks to establish a consistent message about the nature of the company, its products, and the benefits that result from making a purchase from the organization.

Decline in the effectiveness of mass-media advertising
In the past decade, the influence of mass-media advertising on the public has dramatically declined. Inventions such as the VCR and cable television now make it possible for consumers to watch programs without commercials. They can record

---

Positive Responses

▶ **Get amused by the ads (26%)**

▶ **Sit and watch commercials (19%)**

Negative Responses

▶ **Get annoyed at the number of ads (52%)**

▶ **Get up and do something else (45%)**

▶ **Switch channels (39%)**

▶ **Talk to others in the room (34%)**

▶ **Turn down the sound on TV (19%)**

▶ **Read (11%)**

▶ **Use the computer (5%)**

Viewer Activities during TV Commercials

Source: Jennifer Lach, "Commercial Overload," *American Demographics,* (September 1999), Vol. 21, No. 9, p. 20.

FIGURE 1.7

---

shows and zap out advertisements. Using the remote while watching television means it is likely that, during the commercial, the consumer is surfing through other channels to see what else is on. Thus, many television advertisements are not seen, even by people watching a particular program. In a recent survey conducted by Roper Starch Worldwide, only 19 percent of viewers stated that they watch commercials during a program. Figure 1.7 identifies the results of this Roper research. The rise in popularity of cable TV and satellite dishes means consumers have a wider variety of viewing choices. As a result, the number of people tuned to the major national networks has declined.[14] To help overcome this problem, it is vital to integrate all market communications with advertising tactics.[15]

Many firms use advertising agencies to assist in their marketing efforts, therefore it is helpful to examine how these agencies have addressed the issue of IMC. Until 1970, almost all advertising agencies focused only on the advertising aspect of marketing. Currently, many advertising agencies are spending substantial amounts of time assisting clients in the development of integrated marketing communication programs.[16] In addition to developing advertisements, many advertising agencies help create consumer promotion materials and direct-marketing programs, along with other types of marketing communications. As integration within a company occurs, more advertising agencies are working across a company's strategic business units to carefully integrate and coordinate every aspect of the marketing effort.

Integrated Learning Experience

Information is one key to developing a successful integrated marketing communications program. Two valuable sources for marketers are the Web sites of Roper Starch Worldwide at www.roper.com and Brandera at www.brandera.com. By accessing the "In the News" section along with the press releases, you can read recent consumer research reports prepared by Roper Starch Worldwide. Although many research projects are proprietary, others have been released to the public and are available to you. At the Brandera.com Web site, in the "Daily Digest" section, the Brandera staff provides a brief synopsis and critique of recent news events in marketing. The division of these sections into three categories—creatives, marketers, and advertisers—makes it possible to keep up with recent news events in each specific area.

stop!

globally integrated marketing communications

The same trend that exists among advertising agencies in the United States also occurs in the international arena. Instead of being called IMC, however, it is known as GIMC, or a globally integrated marketing communications program.[17] The goal is still the same—to coordinate marketing efforts. The challenges are greater due to larger national and cultural differences in target markets.

In the past, marketers could employ two different strategies for global companies. One was to *standardize the product and message* across countries. The goal of this approach was generating economies of scale in production while creating a global product using the same promotional theme. The language would be different, but the basic marketing message would be the same.

The second approach to global marketing was called **adaptation.** Products and marketing messages were designed for and adapted to individual countries. Thus, the manner in which a product was marketed in France was different than in Italy, India, or Australia.

The GIMC approach is easier to apply when a company has relied on the **standardization** method; however, GIMC can and should be used with either adaptation or standardization.[18] To reduce costs, careful coordination of marketing efforts should occur across countries. Even when a firm uses the adaptation strategy, marketers can learn from each other. Members of every company's marketing department should not feel like they have to reinvent the wheel. Synergy can occur between countries. More important, learning can occur. As telecommunications continue to expand, contacts between peoples of different countries are much more frequent, even when inadvertent. A commercial targeted for customers in France may be viewed by citizens of Spain because of satellite technologies. It is advisable to transmit a consistent theme, even when there are differences in local messages.

In terms of marketing, perhaps the best philosophy to follow is "think globally but act locally." As noted previously, in order to fully utilize the power of GIMC, marketing messages should be designed with a global theme in mind, so the same general message is heard throughout the world. At the same time, when marketers design or encode messages for local markets, they need to have the freedom to tailor or alter the message so that it fits the local culture and the target market. In other words, Pepsi may wish to portray a global image around a theme of "Generation Next," but how the final message is conveyed to each country often varies. Development of a GIMC is the final extension to an IMC plan. With its completion, companies are able to compete more effectively both at home and abroad.

implications for marketing professionals

Marketing Account Executives

Become acutely aware of accountability issues. Account executives must be able to justify *how* money is being spent. Therefore, three things are important:

1. Make sure that all marketing efforts focus on an integrated theme.
2. Establish clear-cut marketing objectives in the area of communication.
3. Recognize the difference between short-term outcomes (immediate sales, coupon redemptions, Internet "hits") and longer-term brand equity and company image issues. *Both* are vital components in the marketing success of a firm over time.

Remember that because account executives are being held accountable, they also tend to hold more power. Effective use of this power would include:

1. careful selection of creatives who will stay focused on company themes, objectives, and desired outcomes.
2. realistic expectations when campaigns are designed, so that they don't "oversell" anticipated outcomes.
3. precisely-tuned measurement instruments that provide clear information about success and failure rates for individual marketing communications campaigns.

Be reminded of several points from the communications model:

1. How the communications process works.
2. What can go wrong (clutter, poor media selection, etc.).
3. Ways to overcome clutter and send a clear, coherent message to all concerned.

Reconsider the total IMC approach:

1. Note that it is a building process that begins with an effective overall marketing plan.
2. Conceptualize advertising as part of the IMC program, and fit other marketing activities together with ads to construct a more powerful approach to the promotions part of the marketing mix.
3. Discover ways to incorporate IMC efforts to make better internal company contacts (employees, other department heads, management teams, etc.).
4. Watch for shifts in channel power. When customers have clearly established the ability to make decisions by seeking information on their own (through Web sites, personal visits, responses to advertisements, etc.), the account executive must rethink methods to reach consumers that keep the company at the forefront as they make purchase decisions.
5. Focus on ways to make an IMC message a global message. This involves keeping a theme intact while adapting that theme to the requisites of individual countries and cultures.

SUMMARY

A new era is evolving in the fields of advertising, promotions, and marketing communications. Marketing departments and advertising agencies, as well as individual account managers, brand managers, and creatives are encountering stronger pressures to be accountable for expenditures of marketing communications dollars. Company leaders expect tangible results from promotional campaigns and other marketing programs. As a result, new partnerships form between account executives, creatives, and the companies that hire them. The duties of the account manager have expanded in the direction of a more strategically oriented approach to the advertising and marketing communications. Those preparing to become advertising or promotions professionals must be aware of both accountability issues and the new aspects of these jobs.

Communication is transmitting, receiving, and processing information. It is a two-way street in which a sender must establish a clear connection with a receiver. Effective communication is the glue holding the relationship between two firms together. When communication breaks down, conflicts, misunderstandings, and other problems may develop between those same organizations.

The components of the communication process include the sender, an encoding process, the transmission device, the decoding process, and the receiver. Noise is anything that distorts or disrupts the flow of information from the sender to the receiver.

In the marketing arena, senders are companies seeking to transmit ideas to consumers, employees, other companies, retail outlets, and others. Encoding devices are the means of transmitting information, and include advertisements, public relations efforts, press releases, sales activities, promotions, and a wide variety of additional verbal and nonverbal cues sent out to receivers. Transmission devices are the media and spokespersons who carry the message. Decoding occurs when the receivers (customers, retailers, etc.) encounter the message. Noise takes many forms in marketing, most notably the clutter of an overabundance of messages in every available channel.

Integrated marketing communications takes advantage of the effective management of the communications channel. Within the marketing mix of products, prices, distribution systems, and promotions, firms that speak with one clear voice are able to coordinate and integrate all marketing tools. The goal is to have a strong positive impact on consumers, businesses, and other end users.

The components of a complete IMC program are explained in this chapter, which serves as a guide for most of this textbook. From the development of a marketing plan, the IMC program expands to include ethics and social issues; a promotional analysis program; brand and firm image management; understanding of consumer and business-to-business buyer behaviors; advertising; other traditional marketing activities such as trade promotions, consumer promotions, and personal selling, as well as tactical promotions; and the completion of the evaluation process, which begins the planning process again.

IMC plans are vital to achieve success. Reasons for their importance begin with the explosion of information technologies. Changes in channel power have shifted from manufacturers, to retailers, and in the future to consumers. Firms must adjust in order to maintain a strong market standing, and IMC programs can assist in this effort. New levels of competition drive marketers to attempt to better understand their customers and be certain those end users are hearing a clear and consistent message from the firm. As consumers develop a stronger sense of brand parity, whereby no real differences in product–service quality are perceived, marketers must reestablish a situation in which their brand holds a distinct advantage over others. This is difficult, because consumers now can collect and integrate information about products from a wide variety of sources, including technological outlets (Internet Web sites) and interpersonal (sales reps) sources. Quality IMC programs help maintain the strong voice companies need to be certain their messages are heard. An additional challenge is the decline in effectiveness of mass-media advertising. IMC helps company leaders find new ways to contact consumers with a unified message.

When a firm is involved in an international setting, a GIMC, or globally integrated marketing communications system, can be of great value. By developing one strong theme and then adapting that theme to individual countries, the firm conveys a message that integrates international operations into a more coherent package.

The majority of this text explains the issues involved in establishing an effective IMC program. The importance of business-to-business marketing efforts is noted, because many firms market their wares as much to other companies as they do to consumers. Successful development of an IMC program should help firms remain profitable and vibrant, even when the complexities of the marketplace make these goals much more difficult to reach.

REVIEW QUESTIONS

1. Define communication. Why does it play such a crucial role in business?

2. What are the parts of an individual human communications model?

3. Who are the typical senders in marketing communications? Who are the typical receivers?

4. Name the transmission devices, both human and nonhuman, that carry marketing messages. How can the human element become a problem?

5. Define clutter. Name some of the standard forms in marketing communications.

6. Define integrated marketing communications.

7. What are the four parts of the marketing mix?

8. What steps are required to write a marketing plan?

9. Describe a promotional analysis.

10. Describe firm and brand image.

11. What are the three main components of advertising?

12. How has the growth of information technology made IMC programs so important for marketing efforts?

13. What reasons were given to explain the growth of IMC plans and their importance?

14. What is channel power? How has it changed in the past few decades?

15. What is brand parity? How is it related to successful marketing efforts?

16. What is a GIMC? Why is it important for multinational firms?

17. What is the difference between standardization and adaptation in GIMC programs?

18. How has the job of an advertising account executive changed? How has the job of a creative changed? How has the job of a brand manager changed? How do the three jobs interact in this new environment?

KEY TERMS

integrated marketing communications   the coordination and integration of all marketing communication tools, avenues, and sources within a company into a seamless program that maximizes the impact on consumers and other end users at a minimal cost. This affects all of a firm's business-to-business, marketing channel, customer-focused, and internally oriented communications.

creatives   individuals who develop advertising and promotional campaigns.

communication   transmitting, receiving, and processing information.

sender   the person(s) attempting to deliver a message or idea.

encoding processes   the verbal (words, sounds) and nonverbal (gestures, facial expressions, posture) cues that the sender utilizes in dispatching the message.

transmission device   all of the items that carry the message from the sender to the receiver.

decoding   takes place when the receiver employs any set of his or her senses (hearing, seeing, feeling, etc.) in the attempt to capture the message.

receiver   the intended audience for a message.

feedback   information the sender obtains from the receiver regarding the receiver's perception or interpretation of a message.

noise   anything that distorts or disrupts a message.

clutter   exists when consumers are exposed to hundreds of marketing messages per day, and most are tuned out.

marketing mix   consists of products, prices, places (the distribution system), promotions.

brand parity   occurs when there is the perception that most products and services are essentially the same.

contact points   the places in which a customer may interact with or acquire additional information about a firm.

adaptation   occurs when products and marketing messages are designed for and adapted to individual countries.

standardization   when a firm standardizes its products and market offerings across countries with the goal of generating economies of scale in production while using the same promotional theme.

ENDNOTES

1. Carolyn Walkup, "John Schnatter," *Nation's Restaurant News,* 31, no. 4 (January 1997), pp. 182–84; Zachary Schiller, "Papa John's: From a Broom Closet in a Bar to 485 Pizza Restaurants," *Business Week* (May 23, 1994), p. 94; Carolyn Walkup, "People—The Single Point of Difference—Hiring Them," *Nation's Restaurant News,* 30, no. 4 (October 6, 1997), pp. 106–8; Nancy Brumback, "Moving Up," *Restaurant Business,* 96, no. 8 (April 15, 1997), pp. 94–97.

2. Donald Baack, "Communication Processes," *Organizational Behavior,* Ch. 13 (1998), pp. 313–37.

3. David Gianatasio, "Too Bad for Converse," *Adweek, Eastern Edition,* 39, no. 3 (January 19, 1998), p. 3; Mark Tedesci, "The End of an Era?" *Sporting Goods Business,* 31, no. 3 (February 4, 1998), p. 24.

4. James G. Hutton, "Integrated Marketing Communications and the Evolution of Marketing Thought," *Journal of Business Research,* 37 (November 1996), pp. 155–62.

5. Don Schultz, "Invest in Integration," *Industry Week,* 247, no. 10 (May 18, 1998), p. 20.

6. Ibid.

7. Robert M. Schindler, "The Real Lesson of New Coke: The Value of Focus Groups for Predicting the Effects of Social Influence," *Marketing Research,* 4, no. 4 (December 1992), pp. 22–27.

8. Based on Don E. Schultz, "The Inevitability of Integrated Communications," *Journal of Business Research,* 37 (November 1996), pp. 139–46.

9. Ibid.

10.   "Internet Economy Generates $300 Billion in Revenue," *The Robesonian* (June 10, 1999), p. 8.

11.   Kathleen Kerwin, "Kicking the Rebate Habit," *Business Week,* no. 3383 (August 1, 1994), pp. 28–29; Douglas Lavin and Oscar Suris, "No Rebate on That New Car? Just Wait a Month," *Wall Street Journal, Eastern Edition,* 225, no. 22, (February 1, 1995), p. B1.

12.   Adam Shell, "Brand Loyalty? Fuggedaboudit!" *Adweek,* Eastern Edition, 38, no. 19 (May 12, 1997), p. 40.

13.   Based on Schultz, "The Inevitability of Integrated Communications."

14.   Patricia Sellers, "Winning Over the New Consumer," *Fortune* (July 29, 1991), pp. 113–24; Jennifer Lach, "Commercial Overload," *American Demographics,* 21, no. 9 (September 1999), p. 20.

15.   P. Griffith Lindell, "You Need an Integrated Attitude to Develop IMC," *Marketing News,* 31, no. 11 (May 26, 1997), p. 6.

16.   Don E. Schultz and Philip J. Kitchen, "Integrated Marketing Communications in U.S. Advertising Agencies: An Exploratory Study," *Journal of Advertising Research* (September–October 1997), pp. 7–18.

17.   Stephen J. Gould, Dawn B. Lerman, and Andreas F. Grein, "Agency Perceptions and Practices on Global IMC," *Journal of Advertising Research* (January–February 1999), pp. 7–26.

18.   Ibid.

19.   Laura Petrecca, "Agencies Urged to Show the Worth of Their Work," *Advertising Age,* 68, no. 15 (April 14, 1997), pp. 2–3; Joseph A. Tradii, "Get the Most from Your Agency," *Marketing News,* 28, no. 22 (October 24, 1994), p. 4; Pete Millard, "Gauging Ad Success: Bean Counters Eclipse Agency Creatives," *Business Journal Serving Greater Milwaukee: Marketing Resource Guide,* 14, no. 29 (April 18, 1997), p. 4; Robert L. Gustafson, "Better Leaders Make Better Account Execs," *Indianapolis Business Journal,* 16, no. 15 (March 4, 1996), p. 15; John Bissell, "Agency Creatives: A Strategic Resource?" *Brandweek,* 39, no. 19 (May 11, 1998), p. 18.

Building an IMC Campaign

Pick Your Product

An effective integrated marketing communications program involves pulling together the thoughts and ideas described in each of the 17 chapters of this book. To help you understand how the process unfolds, the assignment is to pick a product to promote and then use the concepts presented in each chapter to develop an IMC program. Here are your product choices:

- Individual-size bottled water
- A new ink pen
- Chopsticks
- A baseball
- A perfume or cologne
- A purse
- An errand running and reminder service
- An e-trade service for NASDAQ stocks

Visit the Prentice-Hall Web site that has been built for this campaign exercise at www.prenhall.com/clow or access the Advertising Plan Pro disk that accompanied this textbook.

In addition to picking a product, in this chapter's exercise you will be asked to relate your product to the communications model described in Chapter 1, along with other basic IMC concepts.

Critical Thinking Exercises

Discussion Questions

1. The marketing director for a furniture manufacturer is assigned the task of developing an integrated marketing communications program to emphasize the furniture's natural look. Discuss the problems the director may encounter in developing this message and in ensuring that consumers understand the message correctly. Refer to the communication process in Figure 1.1 for ideas. What type of noise may interfere with the communication process?

2. Referring to Exercise 1, assume the director wants to develop an integrated marketing communications program emphasizing a theme focused on the furniture's natural look. This theme applies to all of their markets, that is, both retailers and consumers. Using Figure 1.4 as a guide, briefly discuss each element of the integrated marketing communications plan and how to incorporate it into an overall theme.

3. The marketing director for a manufacturer of automobile tires wants to integrate its marketing program internationally. Should the director use a standardization or adaptation approach? How could the company be certain that its marketing program would effectively be integrated among the different countries where it sells tires?

4. Look up each of the following companies on the Internet. For each company, discuss how effective its Web site is in communicating an overall message. Also, discuss how well the marketing team integrates the material on the Web site. How well does the Web site integrate the company's advertising with other marketing communications?

   a. Revlon (www.revlon.com)
   b. Reebok (www.reebok.com)
   c. J.B. Hunt (www.jbhunt.com)
   d. Trans World Airlines (www.twa.com)
   e. Steamboat Resorts (www.steamboatresorts.com)

Marketing Mini-CDs

APPLICATION EXERCISE I

Craft-tech Technologies was on the verge of a major expansion. The company's management team invested heavily in compact disk technology and created what they believed was a viable product for the mini-CD marketplace. Company leaders were certain mini-CDs soon would outsell the traditional-size version, giving them inroads into numerous markets, including the

- Music industry
- Computer industry
- CD player market (both Walkman and larger versions for home use)

The company's president, Merv Watson, contacted a full-service advertising agency. Merv asked the agency manager, Susan Ashbacher, to describe the meaning of full service. Susan responded, "We will take care of every aspect of your company's integrated marketing communications program. We'll either prepare the material ourselves, or outsource it and manage the process."

Merv was still confused. "What exactly does that mean?" he asked.

Susan handed him a worksheet (Figure 1.8). She responded, "We will sit down with you and figure out your company's primary message. Do you want to represent yourself as a

▌ Company logo

▌ Product brand name and company name

▌ Business cards

▌ Letterhead

▌ Carry home bags (paper or plastic)

▌ Wrapping paper

▌ Coupons

▌ Promotional giveaways (coffee mugs, pens, pencils, calendars)

▌ Design of booth for trade shows

▌ Advertisements (billboards, space used on cars and busses, television, radio, magazines, and newspapers)

▌ Toll free 800 number

▌ Company database

▌ Cooperative advertising with other businesses

▌ Personal selling pitches

▌ Characteristics of target market buyers

▌ Characteristics of business buyers

▌ Sales incentives provided to sales force (contests, prizes, bonuses and commissions)

▌ Internal messages

▌ Company magazines and newspapers

▌ Statements to shareholders

▌ Speeches by company leaders

▌ Public relations releases

▌ Sponsorship programs

▌ Web site

Items to Be Included in an IMC Program

FIGURE 1.8

high-quality leader in technology? Or is your focus more toward this particular product, and how you serve that niche better than anyone else? What we'll ask you to do is define yourself, and then we'll help you develop a marketing program to get that message out."

Merv studied the worksheet. He was amazed to see all of the items listed. Noting his interest, Susan said, "Every single thing on that page should speak with the same voice. Every one of your customers, from businesses to end users, should know your main message. Your customers should buy from you because they have confidence in your brand. We want to make sure you stand out. After all, it's pretty crowded out there in the world of technology."

Merv hired Susan, and the process began. The IMC program was to integrate a marketing plan to other businesses, individual users, and international markets.

1. What image or theme should Craft-tech Technologies portray?

2. Design an IMC approach and state how it will affect all of the items shown in Figure 1.8.

3. Choose another product or service. Consider every IMC aspect of that product or service as you read the following chapters.

Jenny Burns finished high school in the late 1980s. She had no real interest in college. She loved fashion, style, and "glamour." Moving out on her own meant trying to find a job that would accommodate her love of trendy things. She settled on being a hairstylist. After taking all the courses and gaining her cosmetology license, Jenny worked for two years at an independent salon, which went out of business when the owner developed health problems.

After careful deliberation, and with some help from an SBI loan, Jenny opened her own salon on the outskirts of Grand Lake, in Oklahoma. The building boom had just taken over the area, and she was convinced she would make a good living because of the growing population and bustle of activities present, especially in the summertime.

The new business, "Jenny's Hair Salon," was started. She used newspaper advertisements, radio spots, and coupons in a local advertising pamphlet to announce her grand opening. Her location was visible and accessible to residents of the major town near the lake, Grove, Oklahoma. Unfortunately, there was no quality sign maker in town, so Jenny had to rely on a portable flashing sign to present the name of her business.

When the business opened, Jenny was able to attract a solid clientele, because she was one of only two salons in town. The other business tended to attract the "blue hair" crowd, leaving Jenny with both younger women and some younger men. She was able to convince some people in the community to bring their children to her salon, although she used only word of mouth to entice them.

Two major problems made Jenny's Hair Salon less profitable in later years. The first was increasing competition. Stores such as Wal-Mart added salon outlets, and one chain, Perfect Cuts, attracted both customers and new graduates of the nearest cosmetology school.

The second problem was Jenny's inability to pay competitive wages. Her best workers left for "greener pastures," even though they often spent their last days on the job at Jenny's Salon in tears, wishing they could stay. Jenny is considering adding new specialties, such as tanning booths, massage, manicures, and pedicures to her lines, but knows these will increase her overhead and the wages she would have to pay.

Most of all, Jenny is uncertain about her best target market. She spends her time cutting hair rather than developing a coherent marketing scheme. She knows winters are her worst time of year, because tourists are scarce and locals, who are mostly retirees, tend to stay home due to inclement weather or patronize the other nonchain salon.

Jenny needs to attract and keep some high-quality hairstylists and entice some of her former customers back into the fold. She knows customer loyalty to her main stylists made her business much more successful in the early years.

1. How can Jenny succeed in this increasingly competitive environment?
2. Would an IMC program be helpful to Jenny? Why or why not?

CHAPTER OBJECTIVES

Review the concepts of morals, ethics, and social responsibility.

Examine the social issues that critics raise about marketing and advertising.

Study the role governmental regulation plays in marketing communications.

Recognize the role industry regulation plays in marketing communications.

Learn from the positive responses generated by socially responsible companies including cause-related marketing and green marketing.

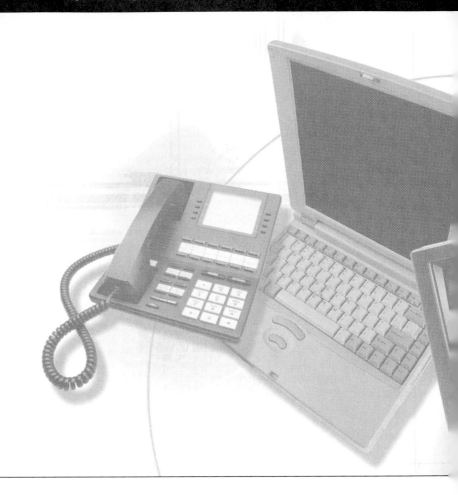

ALCOHOL AND MINORS:
Ethics, Marketing Communications, and the Brewing Industry

By the age of 18, the average American teen has viewed over 100,000 beer commercials. Critics of the brewing industry and of marketing agree: Many beer commercials are designed to encourage underage drinking and build brand loyalty (or brand switching) among a population which is not even supposed to use the product.

These critics point out that teens can develop an addiction to alcohol within a few months, because they are less developed physically, mentally, and emotionally. Binge

drinking particularly concerns those already frustrated with the brewing industry.

The alcohol industry spends $2 billion per year on advertisements and promotions. About one-third of this amount is spent on television advertising, usually broadcast during sporting events. Research indicates that young males strongly respond to ads featured during football, baseball, and basketball games, or as part of an auto racing telecast.

By using the common themes of sexuality and social acceptance in their advertising, brewers can target some of a teenager's most compelling needs. The Stroh's Swedish Bikini team, attractive models selling Budweiser, and other spots with intriguing people doing interesting things while holding a bottle or can of beer logically encourage underage viewers to consider partaking in alcohol to be socially desirable. Humor is also attractive to teens and is found in such commercials as the Coors "Hey Beer Man" ads.

Further evidence of the effect of beer commercials is even more troubling. A surprising number of children cite alcohol commercials, such as the ones for Red Rock Cider and Carling Black Label Beer, as being among their top 10 favorite television ads.

As a result, the brewing industry is walking a thin line. Too many missteps and the federal government may become more involved. Currently, alcohol producers are supposed to voluntarily make certain they aim marketing messages at adults. The Federal Trade Commission recently surveyed eight brewers about their marketing practices and tactics, in the effort to guarantee that target audiences are over 21 years old.

The beer industry has responded in some positive ways. Budweiser sponsors a series of "Know When to Say When" ads, along with others discouraging underage drinking. Coors ran a series of ads featuring comic actor David Spade, making a point to attack and discourage underage drinking.

Critics say this is simply not enough. With Joe Camel advertisements having been banned because of their unhealthy influence on children, opponents of alcohol openly wonder what difference there is between a camel and a frog, or any of the other animals and animated logos shown in TV commercials and on Internet Web sites. Apparently not enough. One survey of 800 children by the Cambell Mithum Esty ad agency revealed that Budweiser's frogs and lizards were number one in popularity in a pool of 240 spots, which included ads for Barbie and McDonald's. These ads are every bit as effective as were the Spuds MacKenzie spots of the 1980s, which included merchandising (stuffed animals, T-shirts) and other spin-offs so directly oriented toward children that the Surgeon General eventually asked Budweiser to stop.

Drunk driving, diminished performance in school, health problems, and death can easily accompany underage drinking. Is it ethical for marketing communications experts to continue to deny they are influencing young people? Should they be more socially responsible? As a young college student, your present view may be very different from what it might be when your own children reach the age of 16.[1]

overview

Many people in United States currently debate national ethics and morals. These major societal arguments are present in the political arena, in which "character" accusations permeate many national, statewide, and local elections. Ethical and moral controversies exist in the areas of gun control, taxation, welfare, sexual orientation, family values, and a wide variety of other topics. These issues are examined from a variety of political, social, and religious perspectives.

It is not surprising that in such an environment strong concerns about marketing and communication would surface. The media have come under attack because of their handling of stories such as the death of Princess Diana and the Monica Lewinsky affair. Many complain that even network news has become "tabloid journalism." Remember, however, that profit-seeking companies buy the commercials and sponsor these news programs as well as other shows. Several criticisms exist concerning the shows these companies sponsor and the commercials they use to entice buyers during these programs.

As marketers encounter greater demands for accountability from their clients and other company leaders, they can be tempted to resort to less ethical practices that may yield quicker results (sales, recognition, etc.). At the same time, a company's long-term success is generally associated with acting responsibly in its marketing practices. Thus, this chapter, about both ethical issues and legal responsibilities, fits well into a presentation of how to build a successful integrated marketing communications program.

In this chapter, moral, ethical, and social responsibility questions are addressed. These concepts are first examined at the individual level, when feelings about "right" and "wrong" are present. Next, marketing programs, advertising campaigns, and other promotional activities receive scrutiny. Legal and regulatory agencies which deal with ethical issues are also reviewed. Finally, overall company actions in both the areas of avoiding wrongdoing as well as promoting positive changes in society are described.

In the end, it is impossible to provide a "cookbook" to guide each person making ethical or moral choices. There cannot be a simple checklist of acceptable and unacceptable behaviors for each organization and its leaders. Instead, these issues are presented and discussed to help identify problem areas along with approaches to dealing with them. Hopefully, this analysis will serve as a meaningful frame of reference as you consider ethical debates both as a consumer now and as a marketing professional later in life.

morals and ethics

The first and most important level of concern in any discussion of ethics is the personal level. Any ethical action boils down to what one person did or did not do, individually or as part of a decision-making group. Thus, it is vital to understand personal issues at the beginning.

Morals are beliefs or principles that individuals hold concerning what is "right" and what is "wrong." Morals direct people as they make decisions about everything from dating behaviors, to work activities, to family life, and beyond. A person also may express moral feelings about what companies do. For example, numerous citizens believe the United States should neither conduct business with China nor give that country "most favored nation" status in trade because of the violations of human rights which routinely take place there. The feeling that it is wrong to buy from firms that employ and exploit child labor is another expression of moral outrage in a marketing situation.

Moral concerns are not just expressed by consumers. Employees in companies and their leaders are aware of ethical situations. Members of production crews, human resource departments, and marketing teams generally want to be involved in work-related activities they believe are morally defensible or right. In fuzzy or ambiguous situations, people become uncomfortable and look for guidance, trying to do the right thing.[2]

Ethics are principles that serve as operational guidelines for both individuals and organizations. They help establish boundaries regarding acceptable and unacceptable conduct, because these behaviors are related to moral feelings about right and wrong. Many leaders in organizations strongly assert that they wish to act ethically. To help them find the moral high ground when they encounter ethical dilemmas, leaders employ two methods to guide their decision-making processes: (1) ethics education and (2) codes of ethics.

Ethics education
One way to address ethical matters is by increasing levels of education for company employees. Ethics education programs concentrate on three processes:

1. Enhancing awareness of the existence of ethical problems
2. Attempting to completely define each problem as it occurs
3. Giving thorough consideration to all aspects of an ethical problem and reaching a reasonable resolution

A considerable amount of work has been completed in the area of ethics education. Books about corporate ethics have been in libraries and bookstores for many years. Specialized scholarly journals are also available, and numerous centers for business ethics have been established. These organizations provide support to individuals seeking to resolve ethical dilemmas on the job. At least 16 such centers have been started since 1990, and their numbers are likely to increase. Several universities have created endowed chairs in business ethics to encourage further writing and research, and accrediting agencies for business schools also emphasize the crucial role ethics education plays in a quality business curriculum.[3]

Ethics education is a positive force in business but does not address every situation. Currently, ethics education focuses largely on higher levels of corporate leadership. To expand the impact of this kind of program, education about ethical behaviors must be tailored to all members of an organization, from top to bottom.

Codes of ethics

A second approach to dealing with ethical matters is using a code of ethics as a guide. A **code of ethics** is the formal and official codification of acceptable and unacceptable responses to ethical dilemmas. Both the leadership and the members of an organization should approve these codes. Many companies have established codes as part of their formal charters or in policy statements. Many occupational groups adopt codes of ethics as well. For example, the American Bar Association and the American Medical Association have extensive codes describing professional and ethical conduct. The American Marketing Association also has its own code of ethics.

To construct a code of ethics involves an extensive examination of company practices. Attention is usually centered around behaviors in four areas:

- Those things that are likely to produce compromising situations
- Times when previous organizational decisions have produced negative consequences
- Industries or companies that have been subjected to calls for a higher standard of conduct than present practice dictates
- Areas of operation of great public or societal concern[4]

Examples of general ethical practices are provided in Figure 2.1. A code must be strongly enforced to be effective. If it is not, the firm or profession sends the message that it lacks the will to back its convictions. Not confronting a violation of one

Examples of General Ethics Codes

FIGURE 2.1

> In your interactions with customers, act in a way that is consistent with the principles of fairness, concern, mutual respect, and professionalism.

> Respect the rights of individual employees regarding employment practices, compensation, performance evaluations, and privacy.

> Honor property rights by treating the organization's property as if it were your own and by giving due credit for ideas created by workers and peers.

> Behave in a way that will promote the organization's desire to be a model citizen of the community, the country, and the world.

of the elements of Figure 2.1 can cause the entire ethical fabric of a firm to begin to unravel.

Ethical issues are complex and difficult. They are also important to individuals, groups, and society. Ethical education and codes of ethics provide some assistance in dealing with many of these predicaments. In the following section, more specific ethical issues in marketing are surveyed.

Integrated Learning Experience

To encourage proper conduct, the code of ethics of the American Marketing Association (AMA) guides member activities and decision-making processes. This code of ethics can be found at www.ama.org in the "About Us" section. Read the AMA's code of ethics to determine if these guidelines are sufficient to encourage ethical behavior or if the code is too specific.

stop!

ethical issues in marketing communications

Over the years, several advertising and marketing communications messages have generated accusations about the integrity of the profession. Some improper actions have led to new laws and regulations. In this section, various social and ethical concerns about IMC are described from the viewpoints of individual consumers and special-interest groups. In each case, the complaint is stated along with a response from the marketing communications perspective. In the next section, a discussion of the legal and regulatory aspects of advertising and marketing communications is provided. The goal is to present a complete picture of the ethical issues associated with IMC.

Some of the major criticisms leveled against companies with powerful marketing communications programs are displayed in Figure 2.2. As shown, these criticisms

- Marketing causes people to buy more than they can afford.
- Marketing overemphasizes materialism.
- Marketing increases the costs of goods and services.
- Marketing perpetuates stereotyping.
- Marketers create offensive advertisements.
- Marketing creates advertisements linked to bad habits and intimate subjects.
- Marketers use unfair tactics.
- Marketers prepare deceptive and misleading advertisements.
- Advertising professional services is unethical.
- Advertising to children is unethical.
- Salespeople use deceptive practices.

Ethical Issues in Marketing

FIGURE 2.2

center on what messages are sent, how they are sent, and target markets for various advertisements. Each is then discussed in greater detail.

Marketing causes people to buy more than they can afford

Marketing critics voice the concern that advertising and other marketing communications efforts persuade individuals to purchase goods and services they do not need and cannot afford. It is true that millions of marketing dollars are spent to influence purchase decisions, and sometimes people buy more than they should. Overuse of credit cards and business credit heightens this problem.

The question remains, however, whether marketers are the cause. Perhaps some of the blame should be assigned to credit companies that allow people to borrow more than they should to finance their purchases. In any case, the problem has been created by more than just marketing and finance departments. Overspending is epidemic in society. People seeking immediate gratification tend to live beyond their means, and the relatively easy escape offered by filing for bankruptcy makes matters worse. Unfortunately, critics point an accusatory finger toward marketing managers, arguing that they offer consumers luxurious goods and services that are out of their price ranges and entice them to create personal financial problems as a result.

Marketing overemphasizes materialism

Closely tied to the notion that people buy too many goods and services is the criticism that marketing has created a materialistic society. The debate centers on one issue: Has the marketing of goods and services created an attitude of materialism, or has marketing merely responded to the materialistic desires of society?

Underlying this argument is the assumption that materialism is wrong. In response, those who defend this aspect of free enterprise suggest that materialism, like many other things, is only bad if carried to an extreme. In comparing third world countries with the United States and other high-consumption cultures, it is easy to show how materialism has, in some fashion, created a positive impact on society and the standard of living people enjoy.

Marketing increases the costs of goods and services

Another reason people find fault with advertising and marketing communications is that it increases the cost of merchandise. Indeed, advertised goods do cost more and allow producers to charge higher prices. At the same time, a good has both tangible and intangible aspects. A baseball cap purchased at a discount store may cost only $4, whereas one with the emblem of a college or professional sports team may be priced at $10 or more. Both shade the buyer's eyes, but one has additional psychological value.

Those who defend marketing point out that choice is the key variable. Those who wish to spend less can and do. Those who buy products for prestige as well as function should be entitled to spend money as they wish.

Marketing perpetuates stereotyping

Some critics of advertising believe that negative stereotypes of women and minorities are common in marketing. They argue that many advertisements still portray women as the weaker gender whose primary responsibility is to care for the children and the home, or as sex objects. The elderly are often depicted as dumb and helpless. Individual critics suggest that various ethnic minorities are often portrayed as being inferior to whites.

Although many of these problem areas exist to some degree, in recent years marketing experts and advertising agencies have made giant strides to correct stereotyping. The question remains as to whether stereotyping still truly exists. On the one hand, marketers clearly try to identify specific demographic groups and sell

Mr. Magoo, and Men as Bimbos

Views about political correctness and cultural sensitivity issues can go to extremes. For instance, many visually impaired and blind people vehemently complain about the movie *Mr. Magoo.* They argue that it portrays blind people as foolish, dumb, and unwise. Mr. Magoo blunders into any number of problems through his ignorance, and the blind community believes better, more positive role models are available. Producers of the film counter that it is simply a lighthearted comedy, that Mr. Magoo is a kind and helpful soul who is a sympathetic figure, and that he wins in the end, so what's the problem?

A second group is more specifically concerned with IMC activities. Group members assert that the only "safe" group left to attack is white males. Consequently, white men are the only "bimbos" left in commercials: They can be stupid, dim-witted, and silly, and no one complains. This group, the Anti–Men–as–Bimbos League, argues that white men should have the same protections of political correctness other groups have. The group intends to boycott products and services using advertising that ridicules white men. Apparently, IMC experts must consider every demographic group before constructing an ad in which one person enlightens another.

to them. Some people consider this to be a form of stereotyping. Marketing professionals counter by stating that advertising to various demographic groups is simply trying to appeal to specific target markets, and if they offend those in the market, their products or services won't sell. To reach specific market segments effectively requires speaking in the language of the target group, and, if it appears to be phony or manipulative, it fails.

Marketers create offensive advertisements

Many citizens believe that advertisements are becoming more offensive. Sex and nudity are the most troubling and controversial issues. For example, critics have highly disparaged Calvin Klein for the level of nudity and sexual suggestiveness in various advertisements. More recently the company has been cited for the manner in which children are used in ads. Calvin Klein has a history of pushing sex and nudity to the limit.

The original objections occurred when 15-year-old Brooke Shields appeared in an advertisement saying, "nothing comes between me and my Calvins." Soon after, viewers protested another Calvin Klein television ad featuring underage girls being asked about their bodies. Some subscribers were offended by a series of magazine ads featuring partially clothed young models posed in sexy and suggestive ways to expose their underwear. Many magazine editors refused to run the print advertisements and some television stations objected to the television commercials. The FBI investigated Calvin Klein to see if the models featured in the ads were indeed 18 years old. Faced with this strong outcry, the television ads were pulled.

Later, in an attempt to sell children's underwear, Calvin Klein decided to prepare a large billboard in Times Square to accompany a series of magazine advertisements. Many people viewed the billboard promoting a new line of underwear as a form of child pornography. The billboards were designed to show two 6-year-old boys arm wrestling and two girls about the same age jumping on a sofa. All were only to be clad in underwear. Based on public opinion and strong objections from conservative groups, psychologists, and even the mayor of New York, Calvin Klein

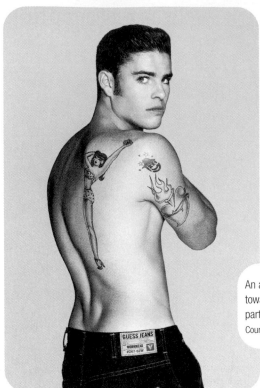

An advertisement directed toward females using a partially nude male. Courtesy of Guess?, Inc.

An advertisement directed toward males using sexual suggestiveness. Courtesy of Guess?, Inc.

canceled the proposed billboard advertisements.[5] At the same time, sex sells. What is offensive to one individual or group may not be to another. In a nation that proclaims freedom of speech and expression, this is a sticky issue. Company leaders must decide on a comfort level when it comes to advertisements emphasizing sexuality or utilizing nudity. The ultimate judges, however, are consumers and how they respond to the content of ads.

Marketing creates advertisements linked to bad habits and intimate subjects

Many products that people buy simply aren't good for them. For example, alcohol and tobacco have a negative impact on many persons, and on society as a whole, as discussed in the opening to this chapter. This had led some activists to object to advertising these items. Others condemn the marketing of personal products such as condoms and feminine hygiene items.

Again, the issue is one of free speech and free enterprise. So long as a firm is not violating the law (e.g., selling to minors), then the company should have the same rights to market individual goods as any other organization has. Those who defend current marketing practices say that even private commodities, such as bras, underwear, feminine hygiene, and jock itch remedies, must be granted the same protections under the law as razors, pens, and pencils.

Where limits are prescribed, such as the restrictions placed on hard liquor and cigarettes, firms must comply. The actual content of restrictions has begun new debates. Sponsorship programs such as the Virginia Slims tennis tour and the Marlboro racing cup have come under congressional scrutiny, because sportscasters

An advertisement for Cruex jock itch medication. Courtesy of Novartis Consumer Health Inc.

must state the names of the products in order to report results from matches. This form of wrangling over appropriate outlets for names of products is sure to continue into the future. The next major area of contention will likely be Internet advertising.

Marketers use unfair tactics

A sensitive ethical issue in advertising concerns the tactics marketers use when products or services are of a highly personal nature. Some find these approaches to be objectionable. For example, one tactic used to promote goods is to stress the idea that happiness depends on physical attractiveness.[6] Appearance is a critical issue to many women; therefore, it is unfair to create an advertisement that feeds on insecurities about looks. To illustrate, consider the various ads for weight loss programs. Most display both "before" and "after" pictures, with the woman looking forlorn in the "before" photo while the "after" shot depicts a much happier person.

Weight Watchers employs a different advertising approach. The company uses Sarah, Duchess of York, to illustrate the positive impact of losing weight. Weight Watchers also emphasizes that with this plan you can still eat foods that you crave.

Companies also offer consumers who are unhappy with their looks services such as abdominoplasty (tummy tuck), electrolysis (hair removal), breast enhancements, and liposuction. All of these programs depend on dissatisfaction with one's body image. Critics say these efforts create unrealistic goals about personal appearance and cause people to examine self-worth in an unfair, shallow, and sexist manner.

Recently, men have been drawn into the arena. Hair coloring products, hair transplants, face-lifts, penile enlargement programs, and Viagra advertisements all rely on worries about virility to sell their goods. The question becomes this: Is marketing responding to the wants and desires of society and the preoccupation some individuals have with their personal appearance, or is marketing taking advantage of a person's insecurities? This debate rages on, especially when America is graying (and doesn't like it) and its youth suffers far too often from bulimia, anorexia, and other eating disorders.

A Weight Watchers advertisement designed to illustrate the positive benefits of losing weight. Courtesy of Weight Watchers International Inc.

Marketers prepare deceptive and misleading advertisements

Another criticism of marketing communications' messages is that they are too often deceptive and misleading. Certainly some companies and marketing firms are guilty of this offense. As a result, the government has stepped in, passed laws, and created regulatory agencies to keep these practices from occurring regularly.

At the same time, members of the marketing community are quick to point out that deceptive and misleading ads are rare. It is not in a firm's best interests to create deceitful advertisements. In the long run, consumers realize they have been cheated and do not purchase products. In addition, negative publicity and bad word of mouth can force a firm out of business. Therefore, some instances of deceptive and misleading marketing communications do occur, the free market system normally punishes firms that consistently use this type of advertising. Governmental regulators also do their part to hold down the number of incidents. Lawsuits tend to further discourage such unethical practices.

Advertising professional services is unethical

Many citizens are frustrated when professionals such as attorneys, dentists, and physicians advertise their services. In a sense, these ads can appear to be forms of "ambulance chasing." On the other hand, marketers who help professionals vend their services are simply filling a need and doing what the law allows. They would suggest that only individual judgment and professional standards should be the guide, rather than seeking a total ban on advertising by professionals.

Advertising to children is unethical

Advertising to children is an especially controversial area of marketing. By the time a youngster is three years old, he or she can recognize the golden arches of McDonald's. Kids also may have learned other brand names such as Pepsi, Pizza Hut, Campbell's Soups, and Toys "R" Us. By the time they are in junior high, many teens have become so brand conscious that they believe they can wear only certain brands of jeans and shoes to be accepted by their peers.

Several strong advocacy groups oppose the current freedom companies have to advertise to children, especially preschoolers, and work diligently to curtail these advertising programs. The most radical groups want ads directed at children to be banished completely, because they believe children lack the mental ability to inter-

Advertising to children is an especially controversial area of marketing. Courtesy of Corbis/Stock Market. Photograph by Tom & DeeAnn McCarthy.

pret advertisements correctly. They contend that marketers take advantage of a child's inability to weigh evidence and make an informed decision. Other groups do not promote eliminating advertising to children, but do want it limited and regulated. At the other extreme are First Amendment advocates who feel any type of regulation would be an infringement of constitutional rights.

Recently, school violence has heightened this debate, particularly in the area of marketing graphic video games and cartoons to minors and children. Greater government intervention may be expected to follow, especially if school shootings and other acts of violence continue.

Salespeople use deceptive practices

For many consumers, the statement "salespeople cannot be trusted" applies to more people than just car salesmen. From the business-to-business perspective, many buyers feel that every salesperson will say and promise anything to make a sale. Often the relationship becomes almost adversarial, pitting buyers against sellers.

While it is true that some salespeople do use dishonest and misleading statements to sell, most do not. It is not in their best interests to do so. Even car salespeople rely on word of mouth communications from current customers and repeat business. Consumers will punish dishonest companies by making purchases elsewhere and filing complaints with agencies such as the Better Business Bureau. The long-term benefit of being honest far outweighs the short-term benefits of high-pressure, dishonest sales tactics.

For the business-to-business sector, more serious ethical issues include gifts and bribery. To influence sales, purchasing agents and other members of the buying center are often the recipients of gifts, meals, entertainment, and even free trips. From a personal ethics standpoint, many concerned leaders question accepting personal gifts that are designed to influence business decisions. The International Olympic Committee wrestled with this problem when it chose Salt Lake City for the Winter Olympics. Exorbitant gifts may have swayed the selection process.

Closely tied with the issue of receiving gifts is one that is even more complex and difficult. In many countries, it is common practice to offer bribes to obtain government permits and business contracts. Without them, permits and business contracts are not granted or are very difficult to obtain. In Germany and France, the government actually allows companies to write off bribes as tax deductions. Dealing with these ethical issues is a major concern for business-to-business operations and businesses operating in the international environment.[7]

In summary, Figure 2.2 presents the concerns many people have about the advertising and marketing communication profession. Those at one extreme believe current marketers are high-tech "snake-oil" salespeople. Those who take a moderate view suggest that society must be careful to balance issues such as free speech and free enterprise with the immense power of the media. Those at the other extreme push for an unregulated industry based on the First Amendment guarantee of free speech.

There would be little dispute that the social impact of advertising and marketing communication is huge. Every consumer is bombarded by dozens of messages each day. Business firms are inundated by ads from other companies trying to garner their attention. Consequently, government, private citizens, marketers, and companies themselves must work toward solutions that both guarantee liberties and protect individual consumers (see Figure 2.3).

Remember, some things may be legal but still be perceived by a large segment of society as unethical. One reason for the high level of social concern about advertising and marketing is that these activities serve such a crucial boundary-spanning role between a firm and its customers. In addition, promotions are probably the

Ethics and Social Responsibility in Marketing Communications Require a Balancing of Interests

FIGURE 2.3

most highly visible component of the marketing mix. These ingredients provide ample opportunity to attract criticism.

When considering ethical issues, keep in mind that individuals, groups, states, nations, and societies differ in their beliefs about what constitutes ethical and unethical behaviors, and about what should be considered legal or illegal. Still, in most cultures, there are two extremes to consider. At one extreme are firm's behaviors that are viewed as unethical by only a few individuals because they do not have a serious impact on society. At the other extreme are more serious unethical behaviors that do have a long-lasting and potentially serious impact on both individuals and the larger society.[8] The second area gives rise to laws and regulatory agencies, as well as self-imposed industry regulations, which are the subjects presented in the upcoming sections of this chapter.

stop!

Integrated Learning Experience

Calvin Klein has been criticized for the content in some of its ads. Using a search engine such as Yahoo!, type in Calvin Klein to locate Web sites that discuss the company. Access several of these sites, and read about its more controversial ads. What is your opinion of Calvin Klein's approach to advertising? Do you support its freedom to advertise in this manner or has it gone too far? Should it be restricted by either regulatory agencies or private sanctions? As a contrast, use a search engine to locate Web sites that discuss Guess and also examine its official Web site at www.guess.com. What similarities do you see in the advertisements of the two companies? What differences?

regulating marketing communications

Over the years, the federal government of the United States has passed a great deal of legislation designed to keep companies from taking advantage of consumers. These laws pertain to food quality, fair interest rates and collateral arrangements, the legal rights of workers, protection of minors, and a variety of additional measures. Various states also regulate matters such as cleanliness in restaurants and provide assistance to individuals who are injured by products or company operations. Many of these statutes also create regulatory agencies to oversee enforcement. In this section, governmental actions are reviewed in the areas of legislation and regulation of company marketing practices.

Unfair and deceptive marketing practices

Federal laws have been enacted and the courts have worked in conjunction with various regulatory agencies to guard consumers from unfair and deceptive marketing communication practices. These laws also protect businesses from unfair and deceptive marketing communications by other businesses.

Deceptive or false advertising liability can stem from many types of marketing communications including advertising on billboards, in mailings, in corporate literature, on labels, on packaging, through oral and written communications by salespeople or salesclerks, and in Internet Web site materials. Numerous ordinances have been enacted to defend consumers from wrongful practices. Other laws have established regulatory agencies for enforcement.

At the federal level the **Lanham Act,** originally passed in 1947, prohibits false and misleading advertising. A firm can violate the act even when the company did not expressly intend to deceive. An advertisement or communication is deemed to be deceptive or misleading when

1. A substantial number of people or the "typical person" is left with a false impression or misrepresentation that relates to the product.

2. The misrepresentation induces people or the "typical person" to make a purchase.

These conditions lead to the conclusion that a violation has occurred. Both individuals and businesses can sue under the Lanham Act. In the case of a business versus business lawsuit, the competing firm must show either infringement of a trademark or false advertising.[9]

A recent court case demonstrates the extent of the Lanham Act's reach. Patrick Fish sued the Wendy's hamburger chain for $30 million in U.S. District Court in Syracuse, New York, for false advertising and misleading marketing practices. Fish claimed Wendy's had misrepresented its veggie pitas as vegetarian food in statements by employees and in its nutritional guide. Specifically, Fish, who was a vegetarian, purchased a veggie pita only after workers in a Wendy's restaurant assured him it contained no meat or animal products of any kind. Later he discovered that the dressing used in the pita contained gelatin made from animal products. As a result of the court action, Wendy's has taken gelatin out of the recipe for the veggie pita and recalled all of the company's nutritional guides.[10]

Deception versus "puffery"

Before going any further into a discussion about misleading advertising, it is important to point out that firms can use what is called "puffery" in their advertisements and messages. **Puffery** exists when a firm makes an exaggerated claim about its products or services, without making an overt attempt to deceive or mislead. Terms normally associated with puffery include words such as *best, greatest,* and *finest.* Therefore, it is acceptable to state that a company's tacos are the best in town. Courts and the regulatory agencies view these statements as puffery and believe that consumers expect firms to use them routinely in their advertisements. The ad becomes false or deceptive if it states the company's tacos contain more meat than the competitor's, when they do not. Such a statement would be difficult to prove and would probably lead to objections by the competition. Notice the Tree Top advertisement. Saying Tree Top apple juice is "twice as good" is considered puffery and would be acceptable.

Obviously quite a bit of gray area exists when a claim about a false or misleading statement is made. Consequently, lawsuits are filed and governmental agencies are forced to address complaints and violations of the law. These agencies strongly affect individual marketing practices as well as other company actions.

An advertisement for Tree Top apple juice with the claim that it is "Twice as Good." Courtesy of Tree Top Inc.

Governmental regulatory agencies

Numerous governmental agencies serve as watchdogs to monitor for potential violations of the law, some of which are only partially related to marketing. For example, the Food and Drug Administration (FDA) regulates and oversees the packaging and labeling of products. The FDA also monitors advertising on food packages and advertisements for drugs, yet its primary responsibilities are ensuring food quality and drug safety.

The Federal Communications Commission (FCC) has authority over television, radio, and the telephone industry. The primary responsibility of the FCC is to grant (and revoke) operating licenses for radio and television stations. The FCC also has jurisdiction over telephone companies. The FCC does not have authority over the content of advertisements transmitted by mass-media. Further, the FCC does not control which products may be advertised. The organization is, however, responsible for monitoring advertising directed toward children. Under FCC rules, TV stations are limited to twelve minutes per hour of children's advertisements during weekdays and ten and one-half minutes per hour on weekends.[11]

The U.S. Postal Service (USPS) watches over all mail-type marketing materials. The USPS also investigates mail fraud schemes and other fraudulent marketing practices. The Bureau of Alcohol, Tobacco and Firearms (BATF) rules when the sale, distribution, and advertising of alcohol and tobacco are at issue. Ordinarily, the governmental agency that examines incidents involving deceptive or misleading marketing tactics is the Federal Trade Commission (FTC). These agencies are listed in Figure 2.4. The next section examines the FTC in greater detail.

> ▶ Food and Drug Administration (FDA)
>
> ▶ Federal Communications Commission (FCC)
>
> ▶ U.S. Postal Service (USPS)
>
> ▶ Bureau of Alcohol, Tobacco and Firearms (BATF)
>
> ▶ Federal Trade Commission (FTC)

**Governmental
Regulatory Agencies**

FIGURE 2.4

the federal trade commission

The most powerful federal agency with jurisdiction over marketing communications is the **Federal Trade Commission**, or FTC, which was created in 1914 by the passage of the Federal Trade Commission Act. The act's original intent was to create an agency to enforce antitrust laws and protect businesses from one another. It had little authority over advertising and marketing communications except when an advertisement would be considered unfair to the competition and therefore restrict free trade.

In 1938, Congress passed the Wheeler-Lea Amendment to increase and expand the authority of the FTC. The agency then had the ability to stop unfair or deceptive advertising practices and to levy fines when necessary. The law also granted the FTC access to the courts to enforce the law and ensure that violators abide by FTC rulings.

How investigations begin

Various types of complaints can trigger an FTC investigation. These include problems noticed by:

- Consumers
- Businesses
- Congress
- The media

Each can raise questions about what appears to be an unfair or deceptive practice. Most investigations by the FTC are confidential at first, which protects the agency and the company being investigated. If the FTC believes a law has been violated, a **consent order** is issued. If company leaders sign the consent order, they have agreed to stop the disputed practice without admitting guilt. Most FTC investigations end with the signing of a consent order.

An example of this process involves the Automotive Breakthrough Services (ABS) company. The FTC issued ABS a consent order, requesting that the company discontinue advertisements for its ABS/Trax system brakes. The ads claimed the brakes were as effective as factory-installed antilock brakes. While investigating the complaint, the FTC concluded that the advertiser's claims about the brakes were not supported by competent and reliable scientific evidence. The FTC was especially insistent that ABS neither claim nor even vaguely suggest that its brakes provided the same benefit as factory-installed antilock brakes.[12]

If a consent agreement cannot be reached, the FTC issues an **administrative complaint.** At that point a formal proceeding similar to a court trial is held before an administrative law judge. Both sides submit evidence and render testimony. At the end of the administrative hearing, the judge makes a ruling. If the judge feels a violation of the law has occurred, a *cease and desist order* is prepared. The order requires the company to stop the disputed practice immediately and refrain from similar practices in the future. If the company is not satisfied with the initial decision of the administrative law judge, the case can be appealed to the full FTC commission.

The *full commission* holds hearings similar to the those before administrative law judges. Rulings are made after hearing evidence and testimony. Companies not satisfied with the ruling of the full FTC commission can appeal the case to the U.S. Court of Appeals and further to the highest level, the U.S. Supreme Court. The danger for companies that appeal cases to the court of appeals is that consumer redress can be sought at that point. This means companies found guilty of violating laws can be ordered to pay civil penalties.

Court actions

Occasionally, the FTC uses the court system to stop unfair and deceptive advertising and communications practices when a company violates FTC cease and desist orders. For example, an ongoing case began in 1974 involving the National Talent Associates (NTA) organization. The FTC issued a complaint against National Talent Associates (NTA) claiming the company misrepresented its ability to place children as models and entertainers with professional acting jobs. In 1975, the company agreed to a consent order, which prohibited NTA from misrepresenting NTA's services. NTA agreed in the consent order to disclose specific information to customers about NTA's placement rates and to allow customers a three-day cooling-off period after signing their contracts. In 1979, NTA agreed to pay $25,000 in civil penalties for violation of the consent order. Again in 1985, the FTC found National Talent Associates in violation of the consent order and the company agreed to pay $150,000 in civil penalties.

In 1999, National Talent Associates was in court once again for violations of the consent agreement and was ordered to pay $160,000 in civil penalties. More importantly, the court has permanently prohibited NTA from making the claim to customers about any expertise to judge people's suitability as models, actors, and entertainers or to provide them with job placement. The FTC also prohibited NTA from making any in-home or in-office sales presentations until it satisfactorily instituted reforms of sales presentations made by company members that would prevent future violations of the FTC's ruling.[13]

In a more drastic step, members of the Federal Trade Commission immediately went to court to stop the practices of the company Screen Test USA. The FTC viewed Screen Test USA as a bogus front used to sell expensive modeling services. The FCC believed that Screen Test USA promised individuals easy access to professional modeling and acting jobs. Screen Test USA then persuaded consumers to purchase an assortment of products and services by representing itself as run by experts and professionals, when in fact they were not.[14] The FTC obtained a temporary injunction order from a federal judge in New Jersey. The injunction effectively stopped Screen Test USA's operation by freezing assets and appointing a receiver pending the final hearing. In that instance, the FTC believed the violations to be so serious that a consent decree was not sufficient and immediately took the case to the courts instead.

Corrective advertising

In more severe instances of deceptive or misleading advertising, the FTC can order a firm to prepare **corrective advertising.** These rare situations occur only when the FTC feels that discontinuing a false advertisement will not be a sufficient remedy. When the FTC concludes that consumers believed the false advertisement, it can require the firm to produce corrective ads to bring consumers back to a neutral state. The goal is for consumers to once again hold beliefs they had prior to the false or misleading advertisement.

The FTC utilized corrective advertising following an advertisement presented by Volvo Cars of North America. This television ad showed cars placed in a row being destroyed by a monster truck as it ran over them, except for a Volvo. Upon investigation, the FTC learned that the Volvo car had been altered with steel bars to prevent it from being crushed. The FTC concluded that the ad would cause consumers to believe that Volvo was a safer automobile than it actually was. As a result, the FTC deemed it necessary for Volvo not only to discontinue the advertisement, but also to run a series of new ads explaining how the car had been altered to obtain the effect in the advertisement.[15]

Trade regulation rulings

The final type of action the FTC takes is called a **trade regulation ruling.** These findings implicate an entire industry in a case of unfair or deceptive practices. Normally the commission holds a public hearing and accepts both oral and written arguments. The commission then makes a ruling that applies to every firm within an industry. As with other FTC rulings, decisions can be challenged in the U.S. Court of Appeals.

In 1984 and again in 1994, the FTC investigated pricing practices within the funeral home industry and subsequently issued a trade regulation ruling. The ruling requires funeral homes to provide an itemized list of funeral goods and services that state both the price and a detailed description of the product or service. As part of the itemization, the ruling requires all funeral homes to disclose the following four statements to consumers: (1) Consumers have the right to select only the goods and services they desire. (2) Embalming is not always required by law. (3) Individuals desiring cremation of a loved one can use alternative containers for the remains. (4) The only fee a consumer can be required to pay is the nondeclinable basic service fee.[16] A trade regulation ruling is designed to keep firms in industries from conspiring or colluding to become involved in the kinds of misleading or deceptive practices that also occur in individual companies.

communication action

Exxon's High-Octane Mistake

Recently, the FTC required Exxon to issue corrective advertisements as part of a consent decree. Exxon had been advertising that using its higher-octane premium gasoline lowers maintenance costs because the higher-octane fuel burns cleaner and leaves fewer engine deposits. The FTC ruled this claim was unsubstantiated and ordered Exxon to stop making the claim. The FTC also ordered Exxon to correct consumers' views about the gasoline. Exxon was compelled to run a series of 15-second advertisements stating that regular gasoline, not high octane, was the right fuel for most cars. Exxon was also required to distribute consumer information about octane levels at its stations nationwide. This brochure stated that a consumer's car would not benefit from using a higher-octane gas than what the vehicle's owner's manual recommended.

Sources: "Exxon, FTC Reach Advertising Agreement," *National Petroleum News,* 89, no. 9 (August 1997), p. 18; "Exxon to Launch Corrective Ads," *Oil Daily,* 47, no. 181 (September 19, 1997), p. 7; "FTC Finalizes Exxon Settlement," *Federal Trade Commission* (September 17, 1997), www.ftc.gov/opa/1997/9709/exxon.htm.

Substantiation of marketing claims

FTC rules cover every aspect of marketing communications. Regardless of the type of communication, the FTC prohibits unfair or deceptive marketing communications. Marketers must be able to substantiate claims through competent and reliable evidence. If companies use endorsers, these statements must be truthful and represent their experiences or opinions. If they use expert endorsements, these statements must be based on legitimate tests performed by experts in the field. All claims must reflect the typical experience that a customer would expect to encounter from the use of product or service, unless the advertisement clearly and prominently states otherwise.[17] Kleenex used actual touch tests by consumers as evidence that its brand was softer. The company then used engineering or lab tests to show that Kleenex tissue is made with 24 percent more cottony, soft fiber.

One of the keys to FTC evaluations of advertisements and marketing communications is the idea of **substantiation.** Firms, such as Kleenex, must be able to substantiate (e.g., prove or "back up") any claims made. Failure to do so can result in some form of FTC action.

For example, the FTC issued a consent order to Fitness Quest, Inc. because of the company's failure to substantiate claims of weight loss made regarding their exercise gliders and abdominal devices. Fitness Quest suggested that its exercise gliders would burn calories at the rate of 1,000 per hour, burn three times more calories than walking, and burn nearly twice the calories of cross-country skiing. The FTC ruled the company could not substantiate any of those claims. The rationale for the decision against Fitness Quest was partially based on the test that

An advertisement by Kleenex Cottonelle using a substantiated claim. Courtesy of Kimberly-Clark Corporation. The illustrated advertisement, all copyrights thereto and rights to the trademarks appearing therein are the property of Kimberly Clark Corporation and used with its permission.

the claim must reflect the typical experience that a customer would expect Fitness Quest used testimonials of consumers in its advertisement; these testimonials demonstrated how effective the gliders and abdominal exercise devices were in helping a person lose weight. The FTC, however, ruled that the testimonials did not reflect what the typical or ordinary person could expect from the use of the equipment.[18]

Up to this point, more of the "wrongs" of marketing have been described than the "rights." In other words, companies can accomplish much more than merely trying to refrain from doing bad things. They can make positive strides to improve local communities and the larger society. The next section defines and describes the concept of social responsibility, allowing marketers to go far beyond merely avoiding trouble.

Integrated Learning Experience

The primary federal agency responsible for regulating advertising is the Federal Trade Commission (FTC). The FTC's Web site (www.ftc.gov) provides considerable information to consumers and businesses. The "Consumer Protection" section contains laws and regulations that are designed to protect customers. The "Formal Actions, Opinions, and Activities" section contains the information discussed in this part of the textbook. It also lists cases filed with the FTC. A great deal of information is provided for each case, including the complaint, the agreement or stipulated final order, concurring or separate statements by FTC commissioners, and the official news release. News releases can also be found in the "News Releases, Publications, and Speeches" section. Spend some time reviewing the different cases filed with the FTC to discover examples of the concepts discussed in this section.

stop!

social responsibility

Social responsibility is the obligation an organization has to be ethical, accountable, and reactive to the needs of society. This definition suggests that socially responsible firms undertake two things: (1) eliminating negatives and (2) doing positives. Figure 2.5 outlines some of the general areas in which firms can become more ethical and reactive to society's needs.

In general, business experts agree that socially responsible firms are more likely to thrive and survive in the long term. Companies engaged in positive activities generate quality publicity and customer loyalty. Firms that work strongly toward

Image-Destroying Activities	Image-Building Activities
▶ Discrimination	▶ Empowerment of employees
▶ Harassment	▶ Charitable contributions
▶ Pollution	▶ Sponsoring local events
▶ Misleading communications	▶ Selling environmentally safe products
▶ Deceptive communications	▶ Outplacement programs
▶ Offensive communications	▶ Support community events

Examples of Socially Responsible Activities

FIGURE 2.5

reductions in unfair practices, pollution, harassment, and other negative activities are more likely to stay out of court, and they suffer fewer negative word-of-mouth comments by dissatisfied consumers.

In spite of these benefits, some individuals and firms still attempt to cheat customers. Therefore, who should be responsible for maintaining an environment in which socially responsible firms are the most likely to succeed? The question generates considerable debate among politicians, businesspeople, and citizens. Three competing points of view are: (1) the invisible hand, (2) the governmental duty, and (3) the enlightened management perspectives. Each reflects a different philosophy about the nature of free enterprise.

The invisible hand of the marketplace

Economist Milton Friedman is one of the strongest proponents of the invisible hand view, based on the work of Adam Smith. This perspective suggests that socially responsible firms must generate profits and use their resources wisely to meet the needs of owners and shareholders. As long as the firm stays within the laws provided by the nation, the company can openly compete for customers and sales. Both the government and consumers will punish any deception and fraud. Consequently, this view asserts that there should be a minimal level of governmental intrusion in the marketplace, leaving firms to compete as freely as possible.

Governmental duty

After Watergate and other violations of the public's trust occurred in the 1960s and 1970s, a growing consumerist movement emerged. These concerned citizens (including Ralph Nader) demanded that the government become more involved in business and take responsibility for protecting the public through more carefully constructed laws and greater regulation by agencies. This view maintains that companies are more interested in profits than in public well-being. Therefore, the government must try to keep individuals from being harmed by company practices that raise profits but hurt the country, such as by polluting the environment and defrauding consumers.

Enlightened management

Ethical managers can balance the firm's need for profits with society's desire for protection. An ethical manager will make careful judgments that reflect the best interests of all stakeholders. Consequently, those who argue for an enlightened management approach to social responsibility believe that the great majority of company leaders will be ethical, responsible, and, in general, do the right thing when confronted with an ethical dilemma.

For example, James Burke, past president of Johnson & Johnson, ordered the recall of all Tylenol capsules from the market when a few incidents of product tampering (the famous "Tylenol poisonings") occurred. The net effect was an $80 million loss, but the long-term goodwill generated by the decision extended to both consumers and governmental agencies, and still serves as a role model for supporters of ethical management approach.[19]

All three perspectives contain important arguments about the nature of social responsibility. The government, individual consumers, and company leaders must all serve as watchdogs to make sure unethical practices are punished rather than rewarded. Further, companies that promote positive and beneficial actions should be rewarded and continue to prosper over time. The next section describes two methods used to keep firms socially responsible: to eliminate negative IMC practices through the use of industry regulation and to improve a company's standing by doing positive things.

Integrated Learning Experience

Social responsibility is expected of firms in today's marketplace. Most consumers demand that companies act in a responsible manner. To aid businesses in this endeavor, an organization called Business for Social Responsibility (BSR) has been created. Its mission is to help firms become commercially successful in ways that demonstrate to consumers that they have respect for ethical values, people, communities, and the environment. Access the BSR Web site at www.bsr.org to find the possible benefits of joining this organization.

stop!

industry regulation of negative marketing practices

It is clear federal regulatory agencies cannot oversee all industry activities. Although various industry regulatory agencies have no legal power, they can reduce the load on the FTC and the legal system. Many allegations or complaints about unfair and deceptive advertising and marketing communication are handled and settled within the industry system. Although each industry has its own system of regulating marketing communications, the three most common are: (1) the Better Business Bureau, (2) the National Advertising Division, and (3) the National Advertising Review Board (Figure 2.6).

The Better Business Bureau is a resource available to both consumers and businesses. Consumers and firms can file complaints with the bureau about unethical business practices or unfair treatment. The bureau compiles a summary of all charges leveled against individual firms. Customers seeking information about the legitimacy of a company or its operations can contact the bureau. The bureau gives them a carefully worded report that will raise cautionary flags when a firm has received a great number of complaints, and reveals the general nature of customer concerns. The Better Business Bureau is helpful to individuals and businesses that want to make sure they are dealing with a firm that has a low record of problems.

Complaints about advertising or some aspect of marketing communications are referred to the National Advertising Division (NAD) of the Better Business Bureau for review. The role of the NAD is to discover the real issue. The NAD collects information and evaluates data concerning the complaint to determine whether the advertiser's claim is substantiated. If it is not, the NAD negotiates with the business to modify or discontinue the advertisement. If the firm's marketing claim is substantiated, then the complaint is dismissed.

Individuals and companies both can file complaints about unfair ads. Sometimes, however, they do not receive the ruling they are seeking. For example, General Motors filed a complaint with the NAD challenging a set of TV, print, and Internet advertisements by Ford Motor Company. In these comparative ads, Ford claimed that the Ford Expedition was the "best in class." GM claimed these ads were deceptive because in their conclusions, Ford had not compared the Explorer to GM's Chevrolet Suburban. GM claimed the Suburban was in the same sport

▶ **Better Business Bureau**
▶ **National Advertising Division (NAD)**
▶ **National Advertising Review Board (NARB)**

Industry Regulation

FIGURE 2.6

utility class as the Ford Explorer. In its investigation, the NAD found Ford's advertisements to be substantiated and ruled against GM. The rationale was based on GM's own advertisement which positioned the Suburban in a different class than the smaller Yukon and Tahoe. It was the Yukon and Tahoe that Ford used as comparison vehicles (the class).[20]

When a complaint is not resolved by the NAD or the advertiser appeals the NAD's decision, it goes to the National Advertising Review Board (NARB). The NARB is composed of advertising professionals and prominent civic individuals. If the NARB rules that the firm's advertisements are not substantiated, it then orders the firm to discontinue the advertisements. This is very similar to the consent order by the FTC, but is issued by this private advertising board. If the business firm being accused refuses to accept the NARB ruling, then the matter is turned over to the FTC or an appropriate federal regulatory agency.

The NARB has been involved in numerous business versus business disputes. For instance, Minute Maid orange juice was ordered to modify its ads because the ad copy claimed that consumers preferred Minute Maid to Tropicana by a 2–1 margin. Tropicana originally lodged the complaint about the ad and won when it was heard by the NAD. Minute Maid disagreed with the NAD ruling and appealed to the NARB. Minute Maid complained that the decision by the NAD placed an unnecessary and unfair burden on comparative advertising because all claims relative to a competitor must be substantiated. The NARB supported the NAD decision and forced Minute Maid to comply with the ruling.[21]

The NARB does not always rule in favor of the firm or consumer making the complaint. For example, MCI objected to AT&T's advertising claim that calling 1-800-CALL-ATT always costs less than MCI's 1-800-COLLECT. MCI filed a complaint with the NAD that was referred on to the NARB. Unfortunately for MCI, the NARB ruled that AT&T did not need to modify its advertisement because the pricing claim was substantiated.[22]

Occasionally the NARB will reverse a ruling by the NAD. FedEx lodged a complaint about the U.S. Postal Service's advertisements. FedEx wanted the U.S. Post Office to disclose in its comparative advertisements that Priority Mail neither tracks nor guaranteed its packages as do both FedEx and UPS. The NAD had originally ruled that the U.S. Postal Service did have to make such a disclosure in ads comparing Priority Mail to shipments by UPS and FedEx. The NARB reversed the NAD ruling saying the U.S. Postal Service did not have to make such disclosures.[23]

The NARB seldom refers a case to the Federal Trade Commission. In fact, such an action has been taken only four times in the last 25 years. The last was a case dealing with Winn-Dixie, which made direct price comparisons with competitors. The NARB found that Winn-Dixie was using prices that were sometimes up to 90 days old. The NARB ruled that any price comparisons made in an advertisement by Winn-Dixie must use prices that are no more than seven days old. The decision to forward the case to the FTC was made when Winn-Dixie refused to modify its ads and accept the NARB ruling.[24]

These industry-based actions are designed to control the marketing communications environment and prevent legal actions by either the courts or a regulatory agency. Effective management, however, should become proactive rather than reactive. Company leaders should work to create an image of a socially responsible firm rather than a firm that must constantly be watched by consumers and regulatory agencies. The next section looks at proactive methods firms can use to create a positive image.

stop!

Integrated Learning Experience

The National Advertising Division of the Better Business Bureau actively investigates accusations of false and deceptive advertising. News from the NAD can be found under the "News and Alerts" section of the Better Business Bureau Web site at www.bbb.com. Look through the large number of cases handled by the NAD over the past few years. Pick out a few of interest and examine how these cases were handled. Also find examples within the press releases that demonstrate the concepts presented in this textbook.

positive and socially responsible marketing activities

In general, positively oriented and socially responsible firms can couple the goal of being a beneficial force in society with the goal of attracting customers and generating loyalty. To do so, companies need to:

1. Identify areas in which they can make a positive difference.
2. Make local media aware of efforts to enhance the chances of positive publicity.
3. Inform employees with the goal of having them report the company's good deeds to their families, friends, and neighbors.
4. Invest in advertising to highlight company efforts.

Company-friendly publicity and advertising efforts often generate goodwill in the community. For example, each fall the Jerry Lewis Muscular Dystrophy

On its Web site, Papa John's highlights community involvement in causes such as the Juvenile Diabetes Foundation's Walk to Cure Diabetes. Courtesy of Papa John's International Inc.

Telethon portrays a wide variety of firms in a highly favorable light. These companies donate profits over the Labor Day weekend to the charity, enhancing sales and building customer loyalty. Smaller companies can sponsor little league baseball or soccer programs, or support YMCA/YWCA facilities. Others can help with community cleanup efforts and other charitable activities.

Marketing is, in part, building a strong company image. Being socially responsible and marketing those efforts can help build an effective image for the firm. Long-term odds of success improve when company leaders take the time to identify how their organizations can improve the lives of employees and members of the community. Two examples of altruistic marketing activities are (1) cause-related marketing and (2) green marketing.

Cause-related marketing

Cause-related marketing is the support of a social cause that a firm generates through financial transactions with its customers. In most cases, firms donate a certain percentage of their income or profits to a specific nonprofit cause. Some of the more famous examples of these include the Ronald McDonald House; Avon's "Race for the Cure," which supports the Breast Cancer Coalition; and AT&T's Save the Children foundation. Another approach firms can use is to become involved in cause-related gift programs for not-for-profit organizations, such as the United Way.

Cause-related marketing can benefit a firm's overall image. Approximately 83 percent of consumers report having more positive images of companies that support causes they care about. Seventy-four percent indicate they believe it is worthwhile for a company to engage in some form of cause-related marketing. This represents an increase of 66 percent between 1993 and 1999. Most Americans believe individual companies should have a positive impact on the marketplace, the environment, and the community. Many consumers are willing to support firms that show they care about consumers and the world in which they live. When price and quality are equal, 76 percent of Americans said they would switch to a brand they believed was associated with a good cause. During National Breast Cancer Awareness month, one in four women purchased a product or service directly linked to breast cancer awareness, and close to 50 percent could identify at least one corporate sponsor.

Rather than becoming involved in national causes, Wal-Mart tends to sponsor local events such as providing scholarships to local students and cleaning up a river at San Marcos, Texas. Wal-Mart's involvement with the Children's Miracle Network is shown in a recent advertisement.

Carefully selected causes have a positive impact on a firm's sales. For example, in the 1980s when American Express raised $1.7 million for the restoration of the Statue of Liberty, sales for American Express increased by 28 percent during the campaign.[25]

The impact can be even greater if the firm can find a way to utilize its products and services in the program. Recently Sprint PCS undertook a cause-related effort that was featured in articles in the *New York Times, New York Post,* and in other places. Rather than simply donating money, Sprint PCS supplied fifty 911-equipped digital wireless phones to CabWatch. The CabWatch system is one in which cab drivers are trained to spot and report potential crimes in progress. The free publicity had a positive impact on both Sprint's sales and the organization's public image.[26]

Cause-related market is a viable approach for many companies to become more socially active. A second approach is known as green marketing.

Green marketing

Green marketing is the development and promotion of products that are environmentally safe. When asked, consumers strongly favor the idea of green marketing. They indicate support for companies selling biodegradable products such as laundry detergents and trash bags and endorse the recycling of paper, aluminum cans,

A Wal-Mart advertisement highlighting a social cause. Courtesy of Wal-Mart.

and other materials. Normally, green marketing programs generate positive publicity and word of mouth for a company. In fact, a firm may actively advertise green products, such as when Ray O Vac utilized Michael Jordan to promote a new line of rechargeable batteries.

At the same time, the truth of the matter is that currently only 10 percent of the U.S. population are truly strong supporters of environmentally safe products. Most people give only lip service to protecting the environment, and few actually make purchase decisions based on the criteria of being environmentally safe.[27]

One of the major reasons that green marketing did not initially catch on was poor product quality and higher product prices. Originally, recycled paper looked gray and was inferior to regular paper. It also cost more. Early versions of environmentally safe fabric softeners clogged washing machines. The perception grew that green marketing meant inferior products for a greater price.

The question becomes this: Should marketers seek out the 10 percent of the U.S. population who are true green marketers? The majority of consumers are either apathetic or just don't care about the environment. The 10 percent, called True-Blue Greens, tend to be well educated and financially well-off consumers. They are often politically and socially active and are the opinion leaders in their communities. These consumers may have considerable influence on others. Unfortunately, the down side of this group is that it is willing to pay only 7 percent more for an ecologically friendly product.

A second group of environmentally aware individuals are known as Greenback Greens. They make up only 5 percent of the population but are willing to pay up to 20 percent more for an environmentally safe product. This group is not as active politically or socially as the True-Blue Greens. The more disturbing news to green marketers is that this group is steadily declining in numbers.

Beside these two groups, the only hope lies in a group called the Sprouts. They make up 33 percent of the population and have expressed concern about the environment. Again, however, their support is based on price. They must be convinced that ecologically friendly products are of the same quality as other products, and the price cannot be more than 4 percent higher.

Consequently, to increase the size of the green market requires firms to produce levels of quality in their environmentally safe products at prices comparable to their nongreen counterparts. Many company leaders believe it will be well worth the effort. When supported by the government and other social leaders, green marketing may become a strong positive force in the business world.

One bright spot for green marketing is the U.S. federal government, which spends over $200 billion annually for goods and services. In 1993, President Clinton signed an executive order directing the EPA to develop guidelines for federal agencies to help them seek out and purchase environmentally safe products.

A company may not need to develop green products to be socially conscious. Those who render services can do so in a professional and ethical manner and seek to help the community in some other way. The key to becoming an effective and socially responsible company is to look at "both sides of the coin" and make a concerted effort to reduce negative practices while emphasizing positive outcomes.

stop!

Integrated Learning Experience

Cause-related marketing is as important in other countries as it is in the United States. Not-for-profit organizations and social agencies can use this tool to address social issues with the help of corporate funds and resources. Contributing companies benefit from the publicity and patronage of customers who support a particular cause. Access the Cause Related Marketing (CRM) Web site of the United Kingdom at www.crm.org.uk. Notice the companies that have received awards for their CRM work as well as the benefits they received. Examine the case study information as well as the press releases. What role do you see cause-related marketing playing in a company's integrated marketing communications plan? For a different perspective, access the National Charities Information Bureau (NCIB) Web site at give.org. The mission of NCIB is to promote informed giving by corporations to charities.

implications for **marketing professionals**

Marketers

Consider the following while reviewing ethical and social issues:

1. Start in your own backyard. Make sure you are not doing anything that violates personal moral standards.

2. Get help when needed. Codes of ethics and other codes of conduct can be combined with ethics education to build a stronger moral base from which to proceed.

3. Do honorable work. Stay away from the mind-set of "not getting caught" or "right up to the edge." Don't give even a hint of impropriety. Long-term benefits of actively avoiding legal and ethical problems far outweigh any short-term gains.

Study regulatory agencies. Bear in mind the two kinds of responsibilities that account executives carry:

1. The responsibility to build sales and profits, reward shareholders, and build a strong and loyal customer base.

2. The responsibility to keep the organization out of legal trouble. This includes violations of the law as well as potential lawsuits. Although no company is immune

to being sued, each can work diligently to avoid "exposure" by staying away from questionable practices.

Be proactive about being positive:

1. Seek out situations in which the company can have a positive impact on the local community, from lending facilities to neighborhood cleanup programs to the development of products and services with beneficial aspects to them.
2. Make sure employees know about any positive social campaigns that the company undertakes. Include as many employees as possible in each effort.
3. Identify ways to promote the company's more positive aspects and activities, without being too heavyhanded.
4. Be as creative as possible in doing positive things.

SUMMARY

Ethics, morals, and issues surrounding social responsibility have become major forces in business in the United States. Those involved with integrated marketing communications should be aware that many individuals distrust the marketing profession, for a variety of reasons.

Those who work in the field are likely to express their desire to act in a moral, professional, and ethical manner. To help them reach this goal, ethics education and codes of ethics provide some guidelines for behavior.

At the same time, to enforce fair standards in the areas of advertising and marketing communications, a number of governmental agencies are ready to take action when needed. These include the Federal Trade Commission (FTC), Food and Drug Administration, Federal Communications Commission, and others. Each tries to keep unfair marketing activities from taking place. The FTC is the major overseer for marketing communications and gives special effort to stopping unfair or deceptive practices. In conjunction with the courts, the FTC and other governmental agencies regulate the majority of companies and industries in the United States. The FTC regulates cases of fraudulent practices targeted at individual consumers as well as conflicts between businesses. Through the use of consent orders, administrative complaints, cease and desist orders, and full commission hearings, the FTC makes its findings and rulings known to the parties concerned. Court actions and corrective advertising programs are utilized in more severe cases. Trade regulation rulings apply when an entire industry is guilty of an infraction.

Social responsibility is the obligation an organization has to be ethical, accountable, and reactive to the needs of society. Socially responsible firms eliminate negative practices and seek to be proactive in the area of positive actions on behalf of consumers, employees, and the larger society. To assist in the effort, industry-oriented regulatory agencies can gain voluntary compliance when complaints are filed. These include the Better Business Bureau, the National Advertising Division of the Better Business Bureau, and the National Advertising Review Board.

Four guidelines help reduce the risk of creating a false or deceptive marketing communication:

1. Marketers must be aware of the *substantiation* rule of the Federal Trade Commission. Any factual claims made in an advertisement or marketing communication must be documented through reliable scientific evidence. The substantiation test is especially important in comparative advertising. Any comparisons made with a competitor's product or service must be well documented. Using independent third-party or neutral sources of information such as *Consumer Reports* reduces chances of a lawsuit by the competition.
2. When an advertisement refers to the performance of *product tests,* make sure the tests are unbiased, objective, scientific, statistically sound, and conducted by experts in the field.
3. Be certain any *claims* made would be experienced by a *normal or typical consumer* using the product in a normal, typical fashion. If the company claims that using a piece of exercise equipment creates a firmer stomach, it must be sure these results occur under normal circumstances with a typical person. Any testimonials or endorsements used in an advertisement must meet this typical person test or a disclaimer must be provided stating the results were unusual or not ordinary.
4. When *price comparisons* are made, do not distort prices. Be absolutely sure comparisons are made with comparable products and that they are the same-size container, especially when prices are being compared. Prices should be obtained from the same time period, in approximately the same location, and in the same type of store. Comparing prices to those of companies in other states can have serious repercussions.[28]

To reduce the risk of both lawsuits and investigations by the NAD or FTC, marketers should be extremely careful when designing advertisements and marketing communications. Accusations of false, misleading, or deceptive advertising not only are costly in terms of direct legal costs, but the negative publicity can adversely affect a firm's image and cause customers to purchase from competitors.

Positive activities associated with social responsibility include sponsorship of charitable events, assistance to those in need, and many other programs. These efforts generate goodwill, positive publicity, and long-term customer loyalty. It is important to find ways to get customers to notice good deeds. Local media events and company advertisements can help guarantee that people know the company is inclined to do community service projects that benefit all concerned.

In the area of marketing, one specific program is to develop and sell items labeled green marketing products, or those that are better for the environment. Although there has been some reluctance to buy these goods because of poor quality and high prices in early versions, some customers are willing to make the effort. Companies that respond provide an example of a positive social force in a marketing program.

Integrated advertising and marketing communications programs design *messages* to consumers about products, services, and other activities. One strong message an IMC approach can convey is that the company's leaders and its employees have a strong desire to remain ethical and moral in what they do. Managers who want to "walk the walk and talk the talk" of social responsibility should be willing to make the effort to help their companies become a positive social force, rather than just "neutral" vendors of goods and services.

REVIEW QUESTIONS

1. Define morals. Are "right" and "wrong" absolute concepts? Why or why not?
2. Define ethics. How are ethics related to morals?
3. What are the key components of quality ethics education programs?
4. What is a code of ethics? What general principles should be included in such a code?
5. What are the major criticisms leveled against marketing communications programs? Are these criticisms legitimate? Why or why not?
6. When does an ad or message become false or misleading, according to the Lanham Act of 1974?
7. What is puffery? Should a company use a great deal of puffery in its ads? Why or why not?
8. What role does the FDA play in marketing communication?
9. What roles does the FCC play in marketing communication?
10. What role does the U.S. Postal Service play in marketing communication?
11. What are the steps of a Federal Trade Commission investigation of a claim of false or misleading advertising?
12. What is a consent agreement?
13. What is a trade regulation ruling? How is it different from other FTC rulings?
14. What does the term *substantiation* mean? How does a company know it has met the substantiation test in an advertisement?
15. Define social responsibility. Describe the invisible hand, governmental duty, and enlightened management perspectives regarding social responsibility.
16. What three industry regulatory agencies seek voluntary compliance in the area of marketing communications?
17. What is cause-related marketing? Green marketing? Are these approaches worth the effort? Why or why not?

KEY TERMS

morals   beliefs or principles that individuals hold concerning what is "right" and what is "wrong."

ethics   principles that serve as operational guidelines for both individuals and organizations.

code of ethics   the formal and official codification of acceptable and unacceptable responses to ethical dilemmas.

Lanham Act of 1947   prohibits false and misleading advertising.

puffery   when a firm makes an exaggerated claim about its products or services, without making an overt attempt to deceive or mislead.

Federal Trade Commission   the most powerful federal agency with control over marketing communications.

consent order   issued when the FTC believes a law has been violated. If company leaders sign the consent order, they have agreed to stop the disputed practice without admitting guilt.

administrative complaint   a formal proceeding similar to a court trial is held before an administrative law judge regarding a charge filed by the FTC.

corrective advertisements   ads that bring consumers back to a neutral state, so that consumers once again hold beliefs they had prior to being exposed to a false or misleading advertisement.

trade regulation rulings   findings that implicate an entire industry in a case of unfair or deceptive practices.

substantiation   firms must be able to prove or "back up" any claims made in their marketing communications.

social responsibility   the obligation an organization has to be ethical, accountable, and reactive to the needs of society.

enlightened management   occurs when ethical managers balance the firm's need for profits with society's desire for protection.

cause-related marketing   the support of a social cause that a firm generates through financial transactions with its customers.

green marketing   the development and promotion of products that are environmentally safe.

ENDNOTES

1. Judy Monroe, "Alcohol and Ads: What Effect Do They Have on You?" *Current Health,* 21, no. 26 (November 1994), p. 2; "How Kids Respond to TV Beer Commercials," 126, no. 2635, 1997, p. A-4.; Claire Beale, "Kids Get a Taste for Beer Ads," *Marketing* (May 20, 1993), p. 6; Alan E. Wolfe and Greg W. Prince, "Federal Flak, Stroh Suit Once Again Demonstrate It Isn't Easy Being Beer," *Beverage World,* 110, no. 1504 (November 30, 1991), pp. 1–6; Alicia Mundy, "Troubles Brew for Booze," *Mediaweek,* 8, no. 31 (August 10, 1998), p. 8; "Wrong Gig for Bud Ads," *Advertising Age,* 70, no. 15, p. 20.

2. C. E. Watson, *Managing with Integrity* (New York: Praeger Publishers, 1991); W. C. Frederick and L. E. Preston, eds., *Business Ethics: Research Issues and Empirical Studies* (Greenwich, CT: JAI Press, 1996).

3. AACSB, "Achieving Quality and Continuous Improvement Through Self-Evaluation and Peer Review," *Standards for Accreditation: Business Administration and Accounting,* 1993, p. 17.

4. E. L. Cass and F. G. Zimmer, eds., *Man and Work in Society* (New York: Van Nostrand Reinhold, 1992).

5. Andy Newman, "Calvin Klein Cancels Ad with Children Amid Criticism," *New York Times* (February 18, 1999), p. 9; Suzanne Fields, "Calvin Klein Ads Again Use Kids and Sex to Sell," *Philadelphia Business Journal,* 18, no. 4 (March 5, 1999), p. 47; Kirk Davidson, "Calvin Klein Ads: Bad Ethics, Bad Business," *Marketing News,* 29, no. 23 (November 6, 1995), pp. 11–12.

6. D. Kirk Davidson, "Marketing This 'Hope' Sells Our Profession Short," *Marketing News,* 32, no. 15 (July 20, 1998), p. 6.

7. Brian Marchant, "Bribery and Corruption in the Business World," *Credit Control,* 18, no. 7 (1997), pp. 27–31.

8. Marion Wheeler, "Tourism Marketing Ethics: An Introduction," *Ethics in Tourism* (May 31, 1999), www.meb.co.uk/services/conferen/jan98/cit/paper2-1.htm.

9. James A. Calderwood, "False & Deceptive Advertising," *Ceramic Industry,* 148, no. 9 (August 1998), p. 26.

10. "Fish Claims Wendy's Deceived," *Marketing News,* 32, no. 16 (August 17, 1998), p. 1.

11. Doug Halonen, "30% Disobey Kids Ad Limit," *Electronic Media,* 17, no. 10 (March 2, 1998), p. 3.

12. "FTC Upholds Charges: Automotive Breakthrough Services, Inc. Ordered Not to Use Term 'ABS' to Market Add-on Brakes," *Federal Trade Commission* (September 30, 1998), www.ftc.gov/1998/9809/abs.htm.

13. "FTC Wins Permanent Injunction Against Talent Broker," *Federal Trade Commission* (June 7, 1999), www/ftc.gov/opa/1999/9905/talent4.htm.

14. "Bogus 'Talent Scouts' Use Smoke Screen to 'Screen Test' Consumers," *Federal Trade Commission* (May 27, 1999), www.ftc.gov/opa/1999/9905/screen.htm.

15. R. Serafin and G. Levin, "Ad Industry Suffers Crushing Blow," *Advertising Age,* 61, no. 47 (November 12, 1990), pp. 1, 3.

16. "FTC Reviews Funeral Rules," *Federal Trade Commission* (April 30, 1999), www.ftc.gov/opa/1999/9904/fun-rule.rev.htm.

17. Jack Redmond, "Marketers Must Be Familiar with FTC Guidelines," *Inside Tucson Business,* 5, no. 51 (March 18, 1996), pp. 18–19.

18. Ibid.

19. Donald Baack, *Organizational Behavior* (Houston, TX: Dame Publications, 1998, Ch. 3, p. 27.

20. "NAD Rules in GM, Ford Ad Dispute," *Advertising Age,* 68, no. 35 (September 1, 1997), p. 32.

21. "Minute Maid Complains, but NARB Forces Change," *Advertising Age,* 68, no. 15 (April 14, 1997), p. 51.

22. "AT&T Wins NARB Case over Collect Call Ads," *Advertising Age,* 68, no. 8 (February 24, 1997), p. 2.

23. "Priority Mail Ads Win NARB Appeal," *Advertising Age,* 68, no. 6 (February 3, 1997), p. 38.

24. "NARB Sends Winn-Dixie Complaint to FTC," *Advertising Age,* 67, no. 52 (December 23, 1996), p. 2.

25. Kevin Rademacher, "Cause-Related Marketing Popular with Consumers," *Inside Tucson Business,* 8, no. 52 (March 22, 1999), p. 18; Becky Edenkamp and Myra Stark, "Brand Aid: Cause Effective," *Brandweek,* 40, no. 8 (February 22, 1999), pp. 20–21.

26. Edenkamp and Stark, ibid.; David Kratz, "In Cause-Related Marketing, Make the Product the Means of Giving," *Public Relations Tactics* (May 1999), p. 13.

27. This discussion based on Tibbett L. Speer, "Growing the Green Market," *American Demographic* (August 1997), www.demographics.com/publications/ad/97_ad/9708_ad/ad97082.htm.

28. Based on discussion by Richard Goff, "False Advertising Can Provoke Severe Penalties," *Pacific Business News,* 35, no. 34 (November 4, 1997), p. 26.

29. This fictional case is based in part on information from the following source: Outi Usitalo, "Marketing Ethics," *Business and Leadership Ethics* (May 31, 1999), www.meb.co.uk/services/conferen/jun98/bale/uusitalo.html.

Building an IMC Campaign

Create an Ethical and Moral Framework

Consider the product you chose to market this semester from the list provided at the end of Chapter 1. The item may seem fairly harmless, but ethical and social issues may still affect the company and its operations. Each is governed in some way by the regulatory agencies described in Chapter 2. At the Web site for this book, an exercise asks you to consider all of the criticisms of marketing to see if any apply to the organization that produces your product. Also, review governmental and industry regulations that affect the advertising and promotion of the product. Finally, you need to recognize aspects of social responsibility. Visit the Prentice-Hall Web site at www.prenhall.com/clow or access the Advertising Plan Pro disk that accompanied this textbook to build an the ethical, legal, and moral framework for your product. Bear in mind that you may have both domestic and international outlets.

Critical Thinking Exercises

Discussion Questions

1. Identify an advertisement that is offensive or in bad taste. What makes the ad offensive? How can it be changed so it is not in bad taste?

2. Children are one of the primary purchasers of video games. To entice them, many manufacturers advertise the level of violence in the game. Historically, more violent games sell better than less violent games. Should video game manufacturers be allowed to advertise a game's level of violence? Should the advertising of video games be regulated? Why or why not?

3. One intent of deregulating the telephone industry was to break up AT&T to allow consumers a choice. When consumers dial 10-10-345 to make long-distance calls, they believe they are using Lucky Dog Telephone Company. What they don't know is that Lucky Dog is owned by AT&T. Is it unethical for AT&T to disguise its ownership of Lucky Dog? After a complaint by MCI, the FTC ruled that Lucky Dog does not have to indicate it is owned by AT&T. Was this a fair ruling? Why or why not?

4. Although consumers verbally endorse the idea of green marketing, most are unwilling to support it with purchases. What strategies should the government undertake to encourage firms to move more toward green marketing? Or, should government stay out of the issue? Should the government do anything to encourage consumers to use green products? Why or why not? What else must be done to encourage firms and consumers to become more involved in protecting the environment?

5. Look up the following Internet Web sites. Identify the companies that are sponsoring non-profit causes. What is your evaluation of these Web sites? How beneficial is the sponsorship to the various companies?

   a. John Hopkins Aids Services (http://hopkins-aids.edu)

   b. Breast Cancer Awareness Crusade (www.avoncrusade.com)

   c. National Denim Day (www.denimday.com)

   d. World Walk for Breast Cancer (www.worldwalkfoundation.com)

   e. World Wide Fund for Nature (www.panda.org)

   f. Ronald McDonald House Charities (www.rmhc.com)

Fred and Red's Import Meats[29]

Fred and Johnny "Red" Johnson discussed a troublesome discovery, just as the Christmas season was about to begin. Their import meat business generated its largest profits during the holidays. As a result, Fred and Red weren't inclined to do anything that might cut into their sales. The problem was, they weren't sure which of their alternatives would best satisfy their customers and their supplier.

The two young entrepreneurs (Fred was 25, Red was 31) had been grocery store employees for several years, working in a major store in Minneapolis, Minnesota. During their breaks, they had long talks with various department managers. These coworkers revealed an exciting piece of information: Import meats have the luxury of generous markups, because many customers are willing to pay premium prices for exotic foods or tastes from their homelands.

Within a few months, the Johnsons had written a business plan, applied for a Small Business Institute loan, and begun operations. They ordered meats from all over the world. The company started as a small corner shop, but quickly Fred and Red expanded into mass-mailing catalog sales and Internet-based orders. They started by developing target markets in major northern and midwestern cities, including Omaha, Kansas City, Fargo, and Chicago. Sales and profits rose steadily.

One of their best-selling items was meat from Finland. The population base, as well as tastes in the region, created a strong demand. Fred and Red established a strong relationship with Bjorkland meats and even met their counterparts on a business junket to Scandinavia. Both firms were highly satisfied with the arrangement.

While examining news from foreign Web sites, Red came across a controversial item. He read that the Finnish people prefer to buy Finnish foods, especially meat, because of strong concerns about how animals have been fed and how they are transported. Finnish people worry about the animal's living conditions and, most importantly, controls for animal diseases. Mad cow disease in England had spiked interest in this issue.

A consumer group had ascertained that the country-of-origin laws in Finland allow local supermarkets to place the Finnish country-of-origin label on any meat that has been sliced, marinated, or in any way processed in the store. Thus, the meat may have come from another country with more liberal laws and yet be marked Finnish just because the local store sliced and packaged the meat. Although nothing is illegal about this practice, it would certainly be considered unethical if the intent of the label were to mislead the consumer into believing the meat was of Finnish origin.

Bjorkland foods regularly marinated, spiral sliced, and repackaged meats for delivery to Fred and Red's store in the United States. The Johnsons worried that they might somehow have violated truth-in-packaging and advertising laws by selling meats labeled as Finnish, when in fact the only thing Finnish about them was they were cut up, packaged, and shipped from Finland.

The Johnsons also worried about customer reactions if they found out the real nature of the product. Fred and Red also didn't like the idea of accusing their friends, the Bjorklands, of anything unethical, because the company clearly had not violated Finnish law.

Fred considered contacting the FTC and the FDA, but Red talked him out of that idea, stating there was no point in "inviting trouble." They also thought about printing a small disclaimer in their catalog ads and on their Web site, noting the Finnish law and what it meant about their product, but worried word of mouth might lead to a strong reaction to both their Finnish meats and their other offerings. Time was running short, and they needed to make a decision.

1. What role might governmental intervention play in this case?

2. What ethical issues are involved in this scenario?

3. What should Fred and Red do? Defend your answer in social, ethical, moral, and legal terms.

**APPLICATION
EXERCISE II**

Clara Morrison was contemplating a major expansion to her small herbal business. In the past few years her sales had risen dramatically, and she was certain that in the short term she would be able to sustain the purchase or rental of a new freestanding retail building. The major question became: What is the future of the herbal industry?

Prior to the 1980s, small-time producers had grown and sold herbs. Health food stores and alternative medicine shops carried a limited number of items. Many Americans believed herbs were something produced and vended by Oriental traders, especially Chinese. There was a mystic element associated with them, and the image was enhanced by TV programs such as *Kung Fu* in the 1970s.

Alternative health magazines often promoted herbs as cures that had been "forgotten" when modern medicine emerged. For example, in the Old West in the United States, one of the more common treatments for a bee sting was to cover the area with a piece of moist tobacco. Burn plants also were commonly used when someone was injured. As these and several other more noteworthy forms of nonprescription medicines became famous, the door swung wide open for other merchants.

In the 1990s, Clara's small operation began to boom. In the beginning she had sold herbs out of her house. She ordered her products from catalogs, marked them up, and sold them to friends and others interested in "old-fashioned" cures. When her business expanded for the first time, she rented a small part of a corner cluster shopping mall to sell vitamins and herbs.

Competition changed the nature of Clara's business during the 1990s. First, people began to express interest in magnets, pyramids, and other unproven yet highly popular health procedures. Various practitioners claimed they could improve a person's health by redirecting the flow of energy through the body, simply by moving their hands over the person. As a result, alternative health care became a lucrative and fast-growing industry.

Clara was troubled by some of the criticisms of her vocation. She had always known that herbs are not regulated by the Food and Drug Administration. As long as the product did not injure a patron, it could be sold without proving any medical claims. Therefore, the herbal industry heavily relies on testimonial evidence, rather than double-blind tests with a normal and placebo group over a series of years, which are required of actual medicines.

Clara also knew that the amount and quality of the herb varied greatly from producer to producer. Some companies provide very little actual content, and in others the amount per bottle or dispenser varied greatly. Many of the supplements Clara sold triggered serious safety questions. For example, the testosterone products used by weight lifters such as androsteindione had been linked to several negative side effects. Other herbs routinely used by various customers had resulted in harmful drug interactions when people took them along with prescription medicines. Unfortunately, because pharmacists do not know when people take herbs, the chances for dangerous side effects rose.

At the same time, Clara knew that if she did not keep up with the times, others would push her out of business. Consequently, she sold magnets; pyramids; herbs; vitamins; Oriental books about shakras, acupuncture, and acupressure; as well as various other food supplements. She gave referrals to those seeking therapeutic massage, ear candling, and numerous other services, which she knew could be incorporated into her own business if she had more retail space.

Clara also knew she could not guarantee that someone might take her products and neglect regular health care procedures. She was greatly upset when a friend told her of being diagnosed with breast cancer. Instead of following up the surgery for removal of the tumor with chemotherapy or radiation, Clara's friend chose to take additional herbal supplements, against the passionate advice of the physician on the case.

Consequently, Clara wondered what to do about expanding her business. It seemed, from all outward appearances to be a legitimate practice to sell the products and services her store offered. A variety of her customers reported that they had greatly benefited from aromas, magnets, and other unproven approaches. Just that day one man had told her that aromas helped to make his tinnitus much more bearable. Against this backdrop, Clara looked at several high-traffic locations that would undoubtedly provide her with more inquiries, increased sales, and improved profits.

1. Have you ever purchased an herbal remedy or taken part in some form of alternative medicine? What enticed you to try the product or service?
2. Should herbs and food supplements be regulated by the FDA? Why or why not?
3. What should Clara do? Is she the right person to run the Herbal Shoppe, or should she simply sell it to someone with fewer doubts?

> ## Promotions Opportunity Analysis

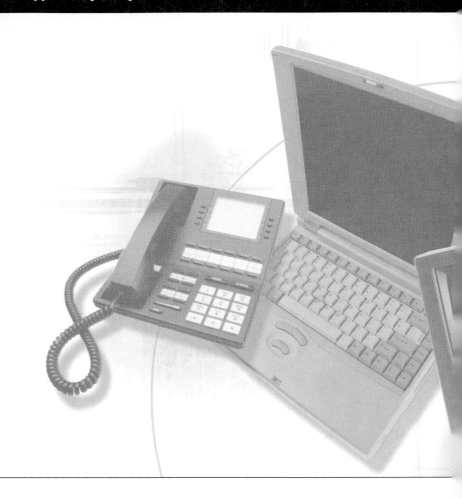

▶ **CHAPTER OBJECTIVES**

Recognize the steps in preparing a promotions opportunity analysis, along with the key activities involved.

Comprehend the relationship between a company's promotional efforts, the efforts of the competition, and the opportunities and threats that result from these two activities.

Understand the role market segmentation plays in marketing communications programs.

Study the characteristics of various forms of consumer market segments.

Become aware of business-to-business segmentation programs.

Expand IMC in communications and promotions to the global level.

THE HALLMARK DIFFERENCE:
Sending "The Very Best" to New Target Markets

Hallmark Cards has a long-standing tradition of excellence in the greeting card industry. In its early years, the firm developed and stood on the theme, "For people who only want to send the very best." The "very best" extended to the quality of cards, the types of employees who were hired, and a variety of promotional tactics, including the *Hallmark Hall of Fame* television series. Hallmark outlets, found in both freestanding locations and in retail malls, are clean, well lit, upscale, and provide a variety of products beyond cards. Keepsakes, wedding

items, and other specialty goods blend together to rein-force the theme of quality.

The greeting card business, however, has changed dra-matically in the past 30 years. To keep pace, Hallmark has reanalyzed its approach to the marketplace to continue its growth pattern and record of success. As a result, Hallmark Cards, as a company, provides an excellent example of an effective integrated marketing communications program.

First, humorous cards with lighter, less sentimental messages offered the opportunity to expand sales. In response, Hallmark created the highly successful Shoebox Greetings line. Seizing the chance to be both funny and dis-tinctive, Hallmark hired highly creative and productive writ-

ers to prepare punch lines on a daily basis. The line, launched in 1986, stresses variety and originality.

A second challenge came from specialty stores such as Factory Card Outlet and Card$mart. To meet this threat, Hallmark entered the "alternative" card market, whose cards offer offbeat humor and inspirational messages. They often result in impulse buys. To be noticed, these cards are displayed in prominent locations. Hallmark entered the business-to-business market by selling cards to other retail stores, such as drugstores and discount retailers. Hallmark used the Expressions brand to create 10 alternative card lines in 1998 alone. When particular cards work well, the verses and other artistic components are reproduced in more conventional cards. Keeping current is one key in the alternative card market. Consequently, the Expressions brand reaches the marketplace quickly and offers cards featuring recent events.

To strengthen its position in non-Hallmark retail outlets, the firm competes with both products and prices. The company also points to the ambience in-store cards give to retail outlets, heightening the store's colors and image. Because cards carry a large markup, they retain significant retail space in many locations. Walgreen's regards Hallmark cards as a major draw to complement its drugstores, cosmetics, and photofinishing departments.

As an additional attraction for company retailers outside of Hallmark's own stores, the company offers point-of-purchase-generated information to retail outlets. By collecting information about Hallmark purchases, the company provides demographic information and other sales data to companies that agree to carry Hallmark products, making them high-tech partners in understanding consumers who shop in various places.

Recently, Hallmark began another aspect of integrating its communications program by carefully studying consumers. Company executives discovered local preferences for certain types of cards. Through data mining, Hallmark's analysis determined which cards sell best in each type of outlet. Hallmark has established databases to hold information regarding sales transactions, customers, promotions and their effectiveness levels, product profitability figures, and other information. Hallmark understands its customer base more clearly as a result. Shoppers are more satisfied with the products, and the company has been able to customize promotional activities and reduce unnecessary inventories.

Hallmark also entered the international arena, with major operations on nearly every continent. Hallmark products are sold in at least 40 other nations, including China, Hong Kong, Germany, Brazil, Australia, Greece, and smaller countries. Besides greeting cards, the company sells calendars, gifts, gift wrap, ribbons, stationery, and party goods. Among the first to be established was business in Japan in 1966.

Finally, recognizing the influence of technology, Hallmark has developed a "Touch Screen Greeting" card, which enables customers to create individualized cards at an automated outlet. This form of card development allows consumers to express their own creative impulses on a high-markup card. It also allows Hallmark to compete with the "Create-A-Card" program of American Greetings, which made competitive inroads by starting a computerized version first. These technologically-based greeting cards entice an entire new set of buyers, especially men and younger consumers in their teens and early twenties, who are more familiar with computers in general.

One goal of an IMC program is to identify opportunities and threats in the environment. By doing so, Hallmark has been able to create a competitive advantage in the marketplace. Also, company strengths and weaknesses are highlighted. Hallmark has been able to take advantage of its high-quality image to appeal to customers and retailers. Consequently, the company has been able to build on a strong past and work toward a more lucrative future, even as competitive pressures intensify.[1]

overview

Individual customers and businesses receive a myriad of promotional materials every day. From pens marked with logos, to letterhead embossed with a company's mission statement, to calendars containing both advertisements and tear-off discount coupons, consumers and businesses encounter marketing materials in an increasing variety of ways. These marketing contacts do not occur by accident. At some point, a marketing official decided to distribute pens or calendars or the printing department was asked to design letterhead. Beyond the world of advertising

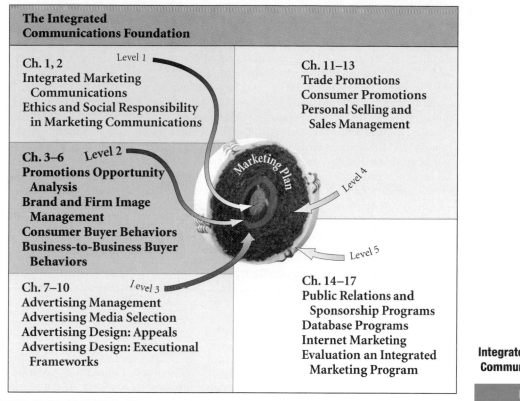

The Integrated
Communications Foundation

Ch. 1, 2   Level 1
Integrated Marketing
   Communications
Ethics and Social Responsibility
   in Marketing Communications

Ch. 11–13
Trade Promotions
Consumer Promotions
Personal Selling and
   Sales Management

Ch. 3–6   Level 2
Promotions Opportunity
   Analysis
Brand and Firm Image
   Management
Consumer Buyer Behaviors
Business-to-Business Buyer
   Behaviors

Marketing Plan

Level 4

Level 5

Ch. 7–10   Level 3
Advertising Management
Advertising Media Selection
Advertising Design: Appeals
Advertising Design: Executional
   Frameworks

Ch. 14–17
Public Relations and
   Sponsorship Programs
Database Programs
Internet Marketing
Evaluation an Integrated
   Marketing Program

**Integrated Marketing
Communication Plan**

FIGURE 3.1

and personal selling, successful marketing efforts occur because *someone identi-fied an opportunity to make a quality contact with a customer.* IMC is a program designed to help find the places to make those contacts and to present the customer with a well-defined message spoken in a clear voice by a firm.

This chapter describes the nature of a promotions opportunities analysis. The purpose of this IMC function is to identify customers and competitors in the marketplace to reveal new promotional opportunities. When these new opportunities are discovered, a company can build on its overall message by structuring it to fit the needs of various target markets. An effective promotional analysis causes the firm to specify which audiences and markets the company intends to serve. Locating key market segments helps company leaders more accurately define who they are trying to reach with their IMC programs.

In this section, target markets and promotional opportunities are studied first. Next, they are linked to the processes of firm and brand image maintenance. Finally, consumer buyer behaviors and business-to-business buyer behaviors are examined. All of these activities are key components in planning an effective IMC program, as shown in Figure 3.1.

the marketing plan

The process of building an integrated marketing communications program begins with the construction of a quality marketing plan. That is, IMC commences with a plan to develop and coordinate the elements of the marketing mix. The four parts of the marketing mix (the prices, products, distribution methods, and promotions the company uses) should blend together to present a unified message on the firm's behalf. This marketing plan is the inner core of Figure 3.1. The purpose of the plan is to achieve a harmony in relaying messages to customers and other publics.

promotions opportunity analysis

Once the overall marketing plan is established, the firm is ready to seek out new promotional opportunities. A **promotions opportunity analysis** is the process by which marketers identify target audiences for the goods and services produced by the company. People are different and have unique uses for various products. The same is true for businesses. These special features are especially pronounced in global markets; therefore, communication to each group requires distinct and somewhat customized approaches. An effective promotional analysis means making quality decisions about what approach or appeal to use for each set of customers.

A promotions opportunity analysis must accomplish two objectives: (1) determine which promotional opportunities exist for the company, and (2) identify the characteristics of each target audience so a coherent advertising and marketing communications message can reach it. The more a marketer knows about an audience, the greater the chance a message will be heard, understood, and result in the desired outcome (a purchase, increased brand loyalty, etc.).

The five steps in developing a promotions opportunity analysis are:

1. Conduct a communication market analysis
2. Establish communications objectives
3. Create a communications budget
4. Prepare promotional strategies
5. Match tactics with strategies

Figures 3.2 and 3.3 show the steps of planning the overall marketing program as well as the steps of planning for a promotions opportunity analysis. The upcoming sections describe the planning process in greater detail.

communication market analysis

The first step of preparing a promotions opportunity analysis is to undertake a communication market analysis. A **communication market analysis** is the process of discovering the organization's strengths and weaknesses in the area of marketing communication, and combining that information with an analysis of the opportunities and threats present in the firm's external environment. This process is quite similar to a managerial approach called SWOT analysis (strengths, weaknesses, opportunities, threats). The primary difference is that instead of looking at the environment from a company-wide or strategic business unit (SBU) perspective, the analysis is done from a communication angle.

A communication market analysis typically has five components:

- Competitive analysis
- Opportunity analysis

Planning Processes

FIGURE 3.2

IMC Plan
1. **Situational analysis**
2. **Establish marketing objectives**
3. **Create marketing budget**
4. **Prepare marketing strategies**
5. **Match tactics with strategies**

> **Promotions Opportunity Analysis**
> ❱ **Conduct a communication market analysis**
> ❱ **Establish communication objectives**
> ❱ **Create communications budget**
> ❱ **Prepare promotional strategies**
> ❱ **Match tactics with strategies**

**Promotions
Opportunity Analysis**

FIGURE 3.3

- Target market analysis
- Customer analysis
- Positioning analysis

These five ingredients are studied together rather than sequentially. Each contributes key information to be used in evaluating the marketplace.

Competitive analysis

A **competitive analysis** identifies major competitors. The objective is to discover who the competition is and what they are doing in the areas of advertising and communication. First, the marketing tactics being used by the competition must be identified to comprehend how they are attacking the marketplace. A consumer integrates information from a variety of sources into his or her knowledge structure. As a result, it is important to know what potential customers see, hear, and read about the competition.

Each company should clearly designate its competitors. For example, if Seattle Office Interiors designs an IMC program aimed at the upper end of the office furniture market, then in its competitive analysis Seattle Office Interiors needs to know which other firms target these upper-end customers. If Seattle Office Interiors establishes a marketing program aimed at the low-end office furniture market, it would have a different set of competitors. Although there may be some overlap of competitors in the two markets, the company should have a clear idea of its particular market when this activity is completed. The same approach would be used for international markets, even though competitors could be domestic or global.

After making a list of all of the competing firms, the company can continue its competitive analysis by collecting *secondary data*. The first items to look for are statements made by the competition about themselves. Sources of secondary data about competitors can be found in:

- Advertisements
- Promotional materials
- Annual reports
- A prospectus for a publicly held corporation
- Web sites

The idea is to obtain as much information as possible about the competition, including what they say to their own customers.

The next task is to study what *other people* say about the competition. Marketers should read trade journals and visit vendors and suppliers who have dealt with the competition or who have read the competition's literature. The library may yield news articles and press releases about competitor activities. The importance of this step is vital to find out how other companies close to the competition view them. It also provides a sense of how they see a given company in comparison with the competition.

Another part of an analysis of the competition is *primary research.* In the retail business, it is helpful to visit competing stores to see how they display merchandise and observe their store personnel dealing with customers. For businesses other than retail, marketers can talk to salespeople in the field to obtain additional information about the competition. They also can talk to channel members such as wholesalers, distributors, and agents.

Opportunity analysis

The next part of the communication market analysis is an **opportunity analysis.** This means watching carefully for new marketing opportunities by examining all of the available data and information about the market. Some helpful questions in conducting an opportunity analysis follow.

1. Are there customers that the competition is ignoring or not serving?
2. Which markets are heavily saturated and have intense competition?
3. Are the benefits of our goods and services being clearly articulated to our customers?
4. Are there opportunities to build relationships with customers using a slightly different marketing approach?
5. Are there opportunities that are not being pursued, or is our brand positioned with a cluster of other companies in such a manner that it cannot stand out?

An opportunity analysis reveals communication opportunities that can be exploited. These opportunities exist when there are unfilled market niches, when the competition is doing a poor job of meeting the needs of some customers, or when the company has a distinct competence to offer.

Target market analysis

A third component of the communication market analysis is the **target market analysis.** This stage requires the marketing department to recognize the needs of various consumer and business groups. Company marketers must define the benefits customers are seeking and determine the ways in which they can be reached. The company also must decide which promotional appeals will work.

The questions asked during a target market analysis are similar to those posed in the opportunity analysis. These questions can help recognize needs of the target market that no one is fulfilling or instances in which the competition is doing a poor job. Once a company understands the general target market, it can appraise various customers within that market. Target markets are often carefully specified as part of the *market segmentation* process, discussed in detail later in this chapter.

Customer analysis

The logical extension to examining a target market is to conduct a **customer analysis.** When thinking about customers, keep in mind the three types of customers to study:

1. Current company customers
2. The competition's customers
3. Potential customers who may become interested in purchasing from a particular company

An analysis of customers reveals their interpretations of the organization's advertisements and its other marketing communications. The point is to know what works within each customer base. It is helpful to ascertain how customers perceive individual advertisements as well as what they think about the larger company. Service Metrics (see advertisement) examines a firm's Web site from the customer's perspective and, more importantly, compares the Web site to the competition. This type of analysis identifies all of a firm's communication avenues.

Part of a customer analysis may include an analysis of a firm's Web site from the customer's perspective. Courtesy of Service Metrics.

Positioning analysis

Part of a communications analysis is examining the position a firm has relative to its competition. Positioning is the perception created in the consumer's mind regarding the nature of a company and its products relative to the competition. The quality of products, prices charged, methods of distribution, image, communication tactics, and other factors create positioning. Chapter 4 fully describes positioning issues. At this point, it is necessary simply to determine the company's position to make sure company leaders desire it. A problem exists when customers view the firm's position differently than the manner in which the company sees itself.

In summary, phase one of a promotional opportunities analysis is the completion of a communication market analysis. The tasks involved: (1) competitive analysis, (2) opportunity analysis, (3) target market analysis, (4) analysis of customers, and (5) positioning analysis are all interrelated. Target markets determine the competition, the customers, the position, and help reveal opportunities. Therefore, all of the tasks must be completed using an integrated approach to understanding what is happening in the marketplace, both for the company and its competition.

An example of an effective communication market analysis process is the recent success of the Yoplait Company. Yoplait manufactures yogurt in Australia. Frozen yogurt and frozen dairy desserts have experienced a phenomenal growth in sales in Australia in the past decade. In conducting a competitive analysis, Yoplait discovered no one was fully serving the yogurt market. Yoplait's primary competitors—Miam, Dany, Vigneur, and Fruche—all focused on frozen desserts. The rationale for a lack of interest in frozen yogurt was that Australians did not eat many frozen dairy products. In 1985, the consumption of frozen dairy products by Australians was 0.5 kg per person, compared to 16 kg per person for Europeans.

As Yoplait further investigated the market, it detected two factors company leaders believed would spur growth in the yogurt market. First, a heavy postwar immigration program brought many other nationalities and cultures into Australia, with different eating habits than those of Australians. Second, Australia's population was growing older. As people age they tend to become more health conscious. Yoplait believed this could help them create greater interest in yogurt.

Yoplait knew its competition and identified a growing target market (an opportunity). The product was originally produced in twin packs. Each pack held approximately two cups of yogurt. Through their target market analysis, Yoplait learned that the twin pack was too small for many families. As a result, the firm introduced a six-pack version.

The next step was to further investigate the needs of its customers. In doing so, Yoplait learned that, as company marketers suspected, health concerns primarily were causing individuals to become interested in yogurt. Yoplait introduced a low-fat version and a diet-lite version, both sweetened with NutraSweet. The firm marketed the low-fat version as a no-cholesterol yogurt, emphasizing its healthful aspects.

A new group of customers emerged when children began eating yogurt. As a result, Yoplait focused some promotions on young people. The features of these ads differed from those targeted at older people.

By analyzing its target market and opportunities, Yoplait designed advertising messages to create a successful position of being *a healthy new snack alternative for young and old alike.* By seizing upon what the analysis revealed as an opportunity, Yoplait now holds a 33 percent share of the yogurt market in Australia.[2]

An effective communication market analysis lays the foundation for the development of communication objectives, the next step of a promotions opportunities analysis. A poor analysis results in something similar to shooting at a target with a

To assist in a communications market analysis, commercial firms such as Dow Jones Interactive can help gather information. Courtesy of Factiva–Dow Jones Interactive.

blindfold on. It is nearly impossible to find the target, and the chances of hitting the bull's eye are very slim indeed. As illustrated in the Dow Jones interactive advertisement, such firms as Kellogg, Merck, and Ford use comprehensive commercial intelligence services to improve the accuracy of their promotions opportunity analysis.

establishing marketing communications objectives

The second step of a promotions opportunity analysis is to identify objectives. Communication objectives help account executives and advertising creatives design effective messages. Figure 3.4 lists some of the more common objectives found in profit-seeking organizations.

A communications plan is often oriented toward a single objective. It is possible, however, for a program to accomplish more than one goal at a time. For example, Dennis Max's Unique Restaurant Concepts of Boca Raton, Florida, gave a 10 percent discount to its frequent-diner members from May through October. The primary goal of this promotion was to increase customer traffic at its six restaurants during the "off" season. The catch to the discount was that it could only be used at one of the company's other restaurants, not where it issued. This encouraged customers to visit other locations in Dade and Palm Beach counties. Because the discounts could be accumulated, this encouraged repeat purchases.[3] This promotion reached three goals from Figure 3.4:

- Building customer traffic
- Reinforcing purchase decisions (rewarding them)
- Encouraging repeat purchases (at other locations)

Logical combinations of communication objectives found in Figure 3.4 and methods to accomplish them exist. For example, advertising is an excellent means of developing brand awareness and enhancing a brand's image. Further, increasing sales can be accomplished through price changes, contests, or coupons. The key is to match the objective to the medium and the message.

The process of defining and establishing communications objectives is a crucial element of promotional opportunities analysis. Without clearly specified objectives, the company can quickly drift off course or lose its focus on the overall IMC program. Objectives serve as reminders of what the firm tries to do with its communications to various customers.

- ❯ **Develop brand awareness**
- ❯ **Increase product–service category demand**
- ❯ **Change customer beliefs or attitudes**
- ❯ **Enhance purchase actions**
- ❯ **Encourage repeat purchases**
- ❯ **Build customer traffic**
- ❯ **Enhance firm image**
- ❯ **Increase market share**
- ❯ **Increase sales**
- ❯ **Reinforce purchase decisions**

Communication Objectives

FIGURE 3.4

Methods of Determining the Marketing Communications Budget

▶ Percentage of sales

▶ Meet the competition

▶ "What we can afford"

▶ Objective and task

FIGURE 3.5

establishing a communications budget

The third step of a promotions opportunity analysis is preparing a communications budget. Companies use several methods to develop these budgets. Four are listed in Figure 3.5.

The percentage of sales method

One common approach to setting the communications budget is the **percentage of sales method.** Companies using this form prepare their communications budgets for coming years based on either: (1) sales from the previous year or (2) anticipated sales for the next year. A major reason for using this format is its simplicity, which makes it relatively easy to prepare. Yet the percentage of sales approach also has problems. First, this type of budget tends to change in the opposite direction of what may be needed. That is, when sales go up, so does the communications budget. When sales decline, the communications budget also declines. In most cases, the communications budget should be the opposite: It should be increased during periods of declining sales to help reverse the trend. Further, during growth periods the communications budget may not need to be increased. The second major disadvantage of this method is that it does not allocate money for special needs or to combat competitive pressures. Therefore, many marketing experts believe the disadvantages of the percentage of sales method tend to outweigh its advantages.

The meet-the-competition method

Some firms use the **meet-the-competition** method of budgeting. The primary goal of this form of budgeting is to prevent the loss of market share. It is often used in highly competitive markets where rivalries between competitors are intense.

The potential drawback to meet-the-competition budgeting is that marketing dollars may not be spent efficiently. Matching the competition's spending does not guarantee success, which means market share can still be lost. The concept to remember is that it is not *how much* is spent, but rather *how well* the money is allocated and how effectively the marketing campaign works at retaining customers and market share.

The "what we can afford" method

A third type of budgeting is the "**what we can afford method.**" This technique sets the marketing budget after all of the company's other budgets have been determined. Money is allocated based on what the company leaders feel they can afford.

This method suggests management does not really see the benefits of marketing. Instead company leaders may view marketing expenditures as nonrevenue-generating activities. Newer and smaller companies with limited finances often use the what we can afford approach.

The objective and task method

The final form is the **objective and task method.** To prepare this type of communications budget, management first lists all of the objectives it intends to pursue during the year, then calculates the cost of accomplishing each objective. The communications budget is the cumulative sum of the estimated costs for all objectives.

Many marketing experts deem the objective and task method the best method of budgeting because it relates dollar costs to achieving specific objectives. Unfortunately, it is the least used, primarily because it takes longer to prepare than many of the other approaches. For a company such as Procter & Gamble, which offers hundreds of products, producing a budget based on objectives for each brand and product category would take many hours; other methods are faster and simpler. Not surprisingly, in the business-to-business sector, over 60 percent of the companies set their marketing budgets using the what we can afford method. Less than 10 percent use the objective and task method.[4]

Budgeting expenditures

When a budget is finalized, the company has specified how much it intends to spend on each of the major communications tools. Media advertising normally accounts for 25 percent of a communications budget. Trade promotions receive about 50 percent, and consumer promotions on average about 25 percent. These percentages vary considerably from industry to industry.[5] Consumer product manufacturers spend more on trade promotions directed toward retailers. Service companies tend to spend more on media advertising. Budgets also vary by product types. For example, for dolls and stuffed toys, the average expenditure on media advertising as a percentage of sales is about 15 percent, whereas for bakery products expenditures on media advertising represent only 3 percent of sales.[6]

The United States leads the world in marketing communications expenditures. Figure 3.6 lists the top ten countries in advertising expenditures and amounts spent per capita. In the United States, annual expenditures in advertising totaled $134.3 billion. This translates to $438 for every man, woman, and child. A distant second is Japan at $33.2 billion and $263 per person. Germany, the United Kingdom, and France round out the top. To better understand the discrepancy between dollars spent on communications in the United States as compared to the rest of the world, consider the following: The next nineteen countries spend a total of $146.3 billion combined, as compared to $134.3 billion in the United States. This means that 48 percent of all advertising dollars in the top twenty countries of the world is spent in the United States.[7]

Allocations of business-to-business firms are not the same as those of consumer-oriented firms. Business-to-business expenditures also vary by industry. Marketing spending by consumer goods and services companies tends to be a higher percentage of sales revenues than in business-to-business companies.[8] Table 3.1 highlights some other major differences between business-to-business firms and consumer firms. Notice that print ads are the primary method business-to-business companies use. Consumer firms are more likely to utilize television advertising.

How do business-to-business advertisers allocate their budgets? Approximately 20 percent of all business-to-business ads emphasize or promote the corporate image. In contrast, 80 percent focus on specific products or services.[9] The major goals of many business-to-business advertisements are to create awareness of new products or brands and/or to heighten awareness of the company. Many advertising creatives believe it is difficult to design effective business-to-business advertisements because they don't have the creative freedom possible with consumer advertisements. Also, because most business ads are print ads in trade journals, the flexibility of television and radio advertisements is not available.

Many firms have marketing programs aimed at both consumers and businesses. For example, Revlon produces television and print ads directed to consumers, but it also directs trade promotion dollars toward retailers. On average, companies spend about 30 percent of their total communications budgets marketing to other businesses. In some industries, such as services, the percentage is much higher (70 percent). In some technology-based industries, business-to-business allocations account for as little as 13 percent of the total marketing budget.[10]

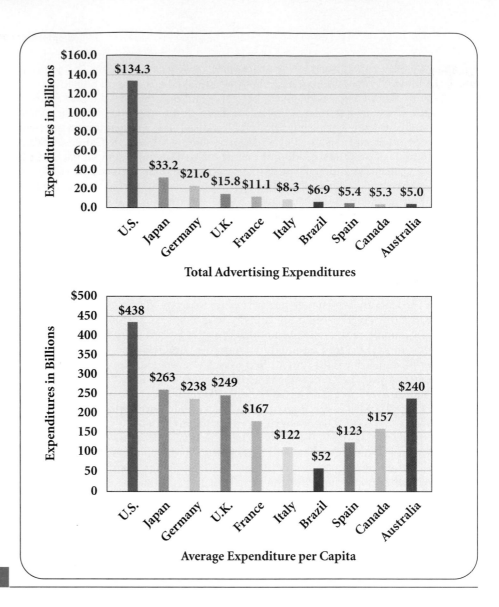

Global Advertising Expenditures

FIGURE 3.6

		Total Advertising Expenditures	
U.S.	$134.3		
Japan	$33.2		
Germany	$21.6		
U.K.	$15.8		
France	$11.1		
Italy	$8.3		
Brazil	$6.9		
Spain	$5.4		
Canada	$5.3		
Australia	$5.0		

	Average Expenditure per Capita
U.S.	$438
Japan	$263
Germany	$238
U.K.	$249
France	$167
Italy	$122
Brazil	$52
Spain	$123
Canada	$157
Australia	$240

TABLE 3.1

Communications Spending

Category	Business-to-Business	Consumer
Direct mail	27.1%	6.5%
Trade shows, exhibits	12.9	2.0
Catalogs, directories	10.7	4.1
Literature, coupons, POP	9.3	16.2
Public relations	5.3	3.1
Dealer and distributor materials	3.3	1.3
Television advertising	2.7	45.1
Radio advertising	0.8	5.6
Print advertising	27.9	14.5

Sources: Cyndee Miller, "Marketing Industry Report: Consumer Marketers Spend Most of Their Money on Communications," *Marketing News,* 30, no. 6 (March 11, 1996), pp. 1–2; Cyndee Miller, "Marketing Industry Report: Who's Spending What on Biz-to-Biz Marketing," *Marketing News,* 30, no. 1 (January 1, 1996), pp. 1–2.

In this business-to-business advertisement, Servicesoft reinforces its corporate image while promoting its interactive e-mail system.
Courtesy of Servicesoft Inc.

When the budgeting process is complete, company leaders should believe they have wisely allocated funds to increase the effectiveness of the marketing communications program. Although specific dollar amounts and percentages vary, the overall goal remains the same—to achieve the marketing objectives as established by the plan.

Integrated Learning Experience

One beneficial tool that can be used to help determine an IMC advertising budget is to examine expenditures of other firms within and in other industries. The Advertising Age Web site at www.adage.com provides information about advertising spending levels. Access the Ad Age Dataplace, and review the 100 leading national advertisers. This section contains information about ad spending by brands, companies, product categories, and in the various media.

stop!

prepare promotional strategies

The fourth step of a promotions opportunity analysis program is to state the general communication strategy for the company and its products. **Strategies** are sweeping guidelines concerning the essence of the company's marketing efforts. Strategies provide the long-term direction for all marketing activities.

An excellent example of a general communications strategy is the marketing efforts of Mountain Dew. The primary market for Mountain Dew is teenagers and young adults. As a result, communications efforts are directed to that market using slogans such as "Do the Dew" to "Been There Done That" and so forth. Action-oriented commercials featuring higher-risk activities are designed to attract younger people (and the young at heart) who are more willing to take "risks" in the products they sample and adopt. The overall theme of the Mountain Dew communications program guides all other activities.

It is critical that the company's communication strategies mesh with its overall message. Both must be carefully linked to the opportunities and threats identified by a communication market analysis. Communications strategies should be directly related to established objectives and must be reachable using the allocations available in the marketing and communications budgets. Once strategies have been implemented, they are not changed unless major new events occur. Only dramatic changes in the marketplace, new competitive forces, or new promotional opportunities should cause companies to amend their strategies.

Matching tactics with strategies

Tactics are the things companies do to support overall promotional strategies. Tactics include promotional campaigns designed around themes based on strategic objectives. For example, the Kellogg company seeks to enhance sales of some cereals by designing unusual features for certain holidays, such as Halloween and Christmas Rice Krispies.

Tactics do not replace strategies, nor should they distract consumers from the consistent message or theme the company is trying to create. At the same time, they add excitement or interest to what the company is ordinarily doing. Holiday promotions, anniversary sales, and a wide variety of other events can be the basis for a promotional effort. Methods used in tactical campaigns include:

- Advertisements based on the major theme or a subtheme
- Personal selling enticements (bonuses and prizes for sales reps)
- Sales promotions (posters, point-of-purchase displays, end-of-aisle displays, freestanding displays)
- Special product packaging and labeling
- Price changes

Besides the methods of communicating with consumers and sales reps who offer the products, companies are able to add other enticements. The items which may be included in tactical efforts include:

- Coupons
- Gift certificates
- Purchase bonuses (a second product attached to a first)
- Special containers (e.g., holiday decanters or soft drink glasses)
- Contests and prizes
- Rebates
- Volume discounts (larger-size packages, buy one, get one free promotions, etc.)

The Gold Bond advertisement shown on the next page uses a manufacturer's coupon to encourage people to purchase the product. The creative use of the snowy, winter scene highlights the product benefits of Gold Bond.

The more creative the campaign, the better the chance the company can overcome clutter and become recognized in the marketplace. Companies often conduct these campaigns during crucial holidays seasons, when marketing efforts are at their peak. The Christmas season is the key for many firms. For hotels and resorts, summer sales are vital. Each company leader must decide the best times to launch tactical campaigns and rely on the expertise provided by creatives to garner the interest and attention of end user customers and other businesses.

When a promotions opportunity analysis is complete, company leaders and the marketing department should have a grasp of the organization's marketing situation, along with specific information about internal strengths and weaknesses in

Unlike ordinary lotions, only Gold Bond...

- Moisturizes
- Soothes & Protects Cracked Skin
- Relieves Dry, Itchy Skin

PROTECT Your Skin With Gold Bond.

A creative message strategy is combined with the marketing tactic of a coupon to stimulate sales of Gold Bond Medicated Body Lotion. Courtesy of Chattem, Inc.

the promotions area. Also, opportunities present in the environment along with any threats to the communications program. They must study and understand the organization's competition to the greatest degree possible. Target markets must be defined and budgets set. Then, the marketing leaders of the company can establish strategies and tactics to guide efforts to reach specific marketing objectives and performance targets.

The next section describes in greater detail two key ingredients of the promotional opportunities analysis process. The first is the study of market segments and methods to identify viable segments for the company to target. The second is to extend promotional opportunities analysis to global or international markets.

market segmentation

IMC experts use **market segmentation** to identify specific purchasing groups based on their needs, attitudes, and interests. A **market segment** is a set of businesses or group of individual consumers with distinct characteristics. Market segmentation efforts are of great value in completing a promotions opportunity analysis. These advantages include:

1. Helping marketers identify company strengths and weaknesses as well as opportunities in the marketplace
2. Working toward the goal of matching what the firm does best with the most enticing sets of customers
3. Clarifying marketing objectives associated with individual target markets
4. Focusing budgeting expenditures or consumer groups and business segments more precisely
5. Linking company strategies and tactics to select groups of customers

Thus, segmentation is an excellent example of taking a traditional marketing concept and adding an IMC approach in order to build brand loyalty and improve the odds of success for a marketing plan.

For a market segment to be considered a viable target for a specific marketing communications campaign, it should meet the following tests:

- The individuals or businesses within the market segment should be similar in nature, having the same needs, attitudes, interests, and opinions. This means persons or businesses *within* the segment are *homogenous.*
- The market segment differs from the population as a whole. Segments are distinct from other segments and the general population.
- The market segment must be large enough to be financially viable to target with a separate marketing campaign.
- The market segment must be reachable through some type of media or marketing communications method.

Marketers engaged in research spend considerable resources and amounts of time working to identify quality market segments. These groups are specified in two general areas: (1) consumer markets and (2) business-to-business markets. The following section describes each of these segments in greater detail.

market segmentation by consumer groups

In many instances, end users are the primary target market for a firm's offerings. Effective IMC programs help the company identify sets of consumers who are potential buyers and who have things in common, such as attitudes, interests, or needs. These consumer market segments include the seven listed in Figure 3.7.

As shown, the first method of segmentation is by demographic variables. **Demographics** are population characteristics. Typical demographic segmentation variables which are useful in IMC programs include gender, age, education, income, race, and ethnicity. Consumer market segmentation approaches to demographic groups are based on the idea that people with distinguishable characteristics have different needs. Companies create products and services to meet the needs of individual demographic segments. They also tailor messages to those specific groups. At the same time, to meet the requirements of a successful IMC program, these products and messages must fit with the overall voice of the organization so that consumers receive consistent messages. Brief presentations of various demographic groups follow.

Segments based on gender
The first major way to classify customers is by gender. Males and females purchase different products, buy similar products with different features (e.g., deodorants), buy the same products for dissimilar reasons (stereos, televisions), and buy the same products after being influenced by different kinds of appeals through different media.

Women constitute a major market, especially as the number of working women trying to establish successful careers continues to rise. Nearly 70 percent of the

▶ **Demographics**
▶ **Psychographics**
▶ **Generations**
▶ **Geographic**
▶ **Geodemographics**
▶ **Benefits**
▶ **Usage**

Methods of Segmenting Consumer Markets

FIGURE 3.7

women in the workforce express concerns about balancing work and family. This worry has led to a change in how many companies market their products to women. Goods and services that offer convenience, flexibility, and independence are in demand, and marketing appeals using these hooks have been successful. At the same time, many working women do feel a certain need to reward themselves. Consequently, numerous women also are willing to indulge in purchases of CDs and other perks or seek out services including health spas and beauty salons to obtain these rewards.[11] Notice the three ways Bijan projects itself to women in their advertisement.

When Rogaine's hair loss treatment lost sales to Merck's Propecia, Upjohn decided to look at the female market for Rogaine in order to boost sales. The goal was to reach women in their twenties and thirties, before they begin losing hair. Recognizing this would be a difficult challenge and that the appeal used for men would not work for females, Rogaine joined with Paul Mitchell to develop a strong, integrated marketing program. Rogaine's decision to team up with Paul Mitchell was based on several ideas. First, having the Rogaine brand name on a Paul Mitchell product would add credibility. Second, regular beauty salon customers tend to spend more on hair care products. Third, women who regularly use a salon have confidence in and follow the advice of their hairstylists.

The television and radio advertisements were aimed at women 20 to 40 who were style-conscious, pro-active, and interested in taking control of their looks. The women want to prevent or stop hair loss before it occurs rather than afterward. The television spots resembled Paul Mitchell commercials and used the CEO of Paul Mitchell, John Paul DeJoria, as spokesperson. Both the broadcast ads and the print ads used the theme "Think ahead." Prior to the television, radio, and print ads, Pharmacia and Upjohn invested in trade advertising to encourage beauty salons to

An advertisement by Bijan targeted to females.
Courtesy of Bijan Fragrances, Inc.

stock the female version of Rogaine as a complete treatment kit. The kit included the Paul Mitchell Rogaine and a Paul Mitchell shampoo and conditioner. Upon its introduction, the product was available at over 90,000 salons.[12]

Marketing to females does not stop with products oriented to women. For example, a study by Goldhaber Research Agency found that women have an enormous impact on the spending habits of men. This survey revealed that men who are sports fans will attend 57 percent more sporting events if their wives are also sports fans, compared with men who are avid sports fans but their wives are not. The number of times a man attends a professional sporting event is directly related to his spouse's attitude toward sports. Therefore, to boost attendance, many professional sports teams realize they need to market to women. This approach can have a double impact. First, more women will attend sporting events, and second, men who are zealous sports fans will attend more games.[13]

It didn't take long for BMW Motorcycles to recognize that women exert a considerable amount of influence on purchase decisions for luxury touring motorcycles. When conducting research related to the launch of a new model, the K 1200 LT (Luxury Tourer), one consumer explained that, "If mama ain't happy, nobody's happy." Couples most often use luxury touring motorcycles for long-distance touring. This became an important factor in the development of the cycle and in creating its market position. The K 1200 LT has heated seats and backrests, with separate controls for both the passenger and the rider. This was because a man tends to look at a motorcycle in terms of style, horsepower, torque, and handling. A female passenger has other concerns, notably comfort.

Consequently, BMW Motorcycles took what was learned from this research and made sure to market the motorcycle with two target audiences in mind: men as the primary purchasers and women as the decision-making influencers. Each was an important part of the promotional campaign.[14]

An advertisement for milk based on nutritional benefits directed to women. Courtesy of Bozell Worldwide, Inc.

communication**action**

Milk, Mothers, and Children

Part of the goal of segmenting the market is to specify what kind of appeal to use in advertisements and other types of marketing communications. For several years the California Milk Processing Board has run a series of advertisements with the theme "Got Milk?" to stimulate purchase of milk. The primary theme of the series was a deprivation strategy showing various individuals without milk at a critical time, such as right after eating a batch of chocolate chip cookies with nothing to wash them down. The board believed a deprivation strategy would be more successful than a health message about milk, which had been used in the past.

As part of a promotions opportunity analysis, a national research study indicated that children would drink twice as much milk if their mother also drank milk. The study revealed that the primary reason women ages 25 to 49 drink milk is for the calcium, which they believe helps prevent osteoporosis later in life. Based on this information, the board hired the advertising agency Goodly, Silverstein & Partners to create a new advertisement tying a health message about calcium with the deprivation theme. The resulting ad shows a mother urging her children to drink milk. They complain they want soda and argue that Mr. Miller, an elderly neighbor doesn't need to drink milk. At that point, the children look out the window and see Mr. Miller gardening. When he starts pushing a wheelbarrow, his arms fall off. The children immediately slurp down large glasses of milk.

Source: Alice Z. Cuneo, "New 'Got Milk?' Tactic: Got Health?" *Advertising Age,* 70, no. 17 (April 19, 1999), p. 32.

An advertisement for milk based on nutritional benefits directed to men. Courtesy of Bozell Worldwide, Inc.

A BMW Motorcycle ad targeted toward men as the primary purchasers and women as the decision-making influencers. Courtesy of BMW of North America, LLC. © 1999 BMW of North America, Inc. All Rights Reserved. The BMW trademark and logo are registered. This advertisement is reproduced with the permission of BMW of North America, Inc. for promotional purposes only.

Some messages are directly targeted at men, because the products are masculine (aftershave) or because more men will use the product (e.g., athlete's foot remedies). Appeals aimed only at men speak in a different tone than do more general ads and messages. Notice the advertisement for milk that is directed toward men and how it differs from the one aimed at women.

Segments based on age

A second demographic method to segment consumers is by age. Marketing campaigns target children, young adults, middle-age grown-ups, and senior citizens. Often they combine age-related factors with other demographics such as gender. Logical combinations with other segments is a common approach. For example, older women may be primary targets for specific types of vitamins and other age-related products. Further, young working women with children are more likely to notice ads for conveniences (ready-made foods and snacks, quick lube oil change facilities, etc.). Other groups may buy vitamins, snack foods, and change their oil, yet individual segments can be targeted with messages that reach their particular sets of needs.

Children have a major impact on the purchasing decisions of their parents. Appeals to children can tie several items together, including advertisements, merchandise based on the ads, and selections from other media. For example, children attracted to the *Star Wars* films can buy toys, see the movie, and witness advertisements using the *Star Wars* theme, such as when Burger King, KFC, and Taco Bell all combined to sponsor a campaign.

Besides children, another age-based demographic group that appeals to many firms is seniors, defined as individuals over age 55. In the past, all seniors were treated as one market and tended to be stereotyped in ads. Often they were pictured as elderly grandparents or as feeble but avid gardeners. Several firms discovered that many seniors lead active lives and many are not gardeners. Nearly 60 percent are volunteers, and many have begun dating following the loss of a spouse. More than 25 percent in the 65 to 72 age group still work and 14 million seniors care for grandchildren.[15] In segmenting seniors, at least four different groups exist (see Figure 3.8).[16] In marketing to seniors, it is important to realize that they are not one group. Ads must be targeted to more specific groups within the senior citizen category.

Healthy Indulgers (18% of the people over the age of 55)

This group has experienced the lowest level of traumatic life events such as retirement, death of a spouse, or chronic illness. These individuals tend to resemble their younger counterparts, the baby boomers. However, the primary difference is that the healthy indulgers are better off financially and more settled in their careers.

Healthy Hermits (36%)

These individuals have experienced at least one major life event (normally the death of a spouse). Healthy hermits have withdrawn from society and tend to isolate themselves from others.

Ailing Outgoers (29%)

These people have experienced major health problems. At the same time, they tend to maintain positive self-esteem and are active in life. They acknowledge their physical limitations but continue to live active lives.

Frail Recluses (17%)

These individuals have experienced major health problems and adjusted their lifestyles. They tend to become more spiritual and less active socially.

Source: Rick Adler, "Stereotypes Won't Work with Seniors Anymore," *Advertising Age* (November 11, 1996), Vol. 67, Issue 46, p. 32; George P. Moschis, "Life Stages of the Mature Market," *American Demographics* (September 1996), p. 44–47; "The Ungraying of America," *American Demographics* (July 1997), pp. 12, 14–15; Faye Rice.

Segmentation of Senior Citizens

FIGURE 3.8

Segments based on income

Income is an important demographic segmentation variable for many goods and services. Spending is normally directed at three large categories of goods: (1) necessities, (2) sundries, and (3) luxuries. Lower levels of income mean consumers purchase mostly necessities, such as food, clothing, cleaning supplies, and so forth. With increased income, households can buy more items categorized as sundries: those things that are "nice to own," but not necessary. Sundries include televisions, computers, CD players, other similar goods. Vacation spending also is a sundry expenditure. Luxuries are things most people cannot afford or can afford only once in a lifetime, unless the family is a high-income household. Luxuries include yachts, expensive automobiles, extravagant vacation resorts, and other high-cost goods and services. Marketers work closely with creatives to tailor messages to various income groups and to select media that match those groups. Also, certain income categories view specific television programs. In the 1980s, the highly successful television programs *Cheers* and *Hill Street Blues* originally did not achieve ratings to keep them on the air. Marketing research indicated, however, that persons of above average earnings (with more disposable income) tended to watch the programs, a factor that highly enticed certain advertisers. The programs survived and eventually achieved wider audiences.

Segments based on ethnic heritage

By the year 2010, most Americans will be nonwhite. Currently, most advertisements and marketing communications tend to be written from a white, Anglo-Saxon perspective. This represents both an opportunity and a threat: an opportunity for

A Skechers advertisement featuring a multi-ethnic approach. Courtesy of Skechers USA Inc.

companies able to adapt their messages to other cultures and heritages. It may be a threat to those that do not.

Ethnic marketing is more than spending money with ethnically owned radio stations or hiring ethnically owned advertising agencies. It is more than translating an advertisement from English into Spanish. It is more than including African Americans or Asian Americans in advertisements. Successful ethnic marketing requires understanding various ethnic groups and writing marketing communications that speak to their cultures and values.

The three major ethnic groups in the United States are African Americans, Hispanics, and Asian Americans. African American economic power exceeds $400 billion annually. Hispanic sector purchases are in excess of $300 billion. In addition, a large number of immigrants are arriving from India and Pakistan. Another large group is coming from the Middle East and Eastern European countries. Each ethnic group contains multiple subgroups. Within the Asian community are individuals of Korean, Japanese, Filipino, Vietnamese, and Chinese descent. The Hispanic community is made up of individuals from Latin America, Mexico, Cuba, and Puerto Rico.

Although different in many ways, several common threads exist among these ethnic groups. They all tend to be more brand loyal than their white counterparts. They value quality and are willing to pay a higher price for quality and brand identity. They value relationships with companies and are loyal to those that make the effort to establish a connection with them.

To market effectively to ethnic groups, it is important to develop new creative approaches that respect America's ethnic differences while also highlighting its similarities. Achieving this requires advertising and marketing agencies who understand the subtleties of multiculturalism. Becoming involved in sponsorships of minority and ethnic events goes a long way toward establishing ties with specific ethnic groups. Indications are strong that ethnic consumers reward companies that invest in them. In addition to sponsorships, becoming involved in ethnic community groups and civic and trade associations should prove beneficial.[17]

Ethnic marketing is similar in some ways to global marketing. It is important to present one overall message that is then tailored to fit the needs and values of various groups. Successfully achieving this integration of the overall message with characteristics of individual cultures should result in valuable gains in loyalty to a company and its brands, and diversify the markets the company can effectively serve.

Psychographics

Demographics are easy to identify but do not always explain why people buy particular products or specific brands, or what type of an appeal should be used to reach them. To assist in the marketing effort while building on demographic information, psychographic profiles have been developed. **Psychographics** emerge from patterns of responses that reveal a person's attitudes, interests, and opinions (AIO). AIO measures can be combined with demographic information to provide marketers with a more complete understanding of the market to be targeted.[18] The Communication Action Box "Psychographics and Technology" presents an example of marketing psychographic segmentation.

*communication***action**

Psychographics and Technology

With the rapid development of multimedia technology, a company called Odyssey conducted pyschographic research to help the company develop a marketing program. Instead of one market, Odyssey's marketing team discovered six unique market segments with distinct attitudes about technology. Odyssey found that consumers may have identical demographic characteristics but differ greatly in how they view multimedia technology. Understanding the six different segments allowed Odyssey to create advertising and marketing themes to appeal to each segment. The six segments that Odyssey identified are:

1. *New Enthusiasts.* These households like to be on the cutting edge of technology and are eager to purchase the most recent version. This group also tends to have high incomes and higher levels of education.

2. *Hopefuls.* These households also like to be on the cutting edge of technology but lack the financial means to make extensive purchases. They are concerned that a new technology may be too difficult to use.

3. *Faithful.* These households are not eager to try new technologies but, more importantly, are not averse to trying something new.

4. *Oldliners.* These households are not interested in new technologies. Finances also concern this group.

5. *Independents.* These individuals have higher incomes and higher educational levels, but do not value television or any other new form of technology. They are not eager to try new things.

6. *Surfers.* These households are ambivalent about new technologies and tend to be cynical about business and privacy issues. They have above-average incomes and are able to afford technology, but don't trust it.

Each segment clearly requires a distinct advertising appeal. In this case, similar people have differing psychological attitudes and needs for a product, even though the product itself is the same for each group.

Source: Marilyn A. Gillen, "Tracking Multimedia's Fragmented Audience," *Billboard,* 106, no. 10 (March 5, 1994), p. 60.

TABLE 3.2

Generational
Marketing

Born	Cohort Name	Generation	Size (millions)	% of Population
1912–1921	Depression cohort	GI generation	13	5%
1922–1927	World War II cohort	Depression generation	11	4
1928–1945	Postwar cohort	Silent generation	41	17
1946–1954	Boomers I cohort	Woodstock generation	33	14
1955–1965	Boomers II cohort	Zoomers generation	49	21
1966–1976	Generation X cohort	Baby busters generation	41	17
1977–1994	Generation Y cohort	Echo boom generation	35	15

Sources: Based on Berna Miller, "A Beginner's Guide to Demographics," *Marketing Tools* (October 1995), pp. 54–61; Faye Rice, "Making Generational Marketing Come of Age," *Fortune* (June 26, 1995), pp. 110–12; Geoffrey E. Meredith and Charles D. Schewe, "Marketing by Cohorts, Not Generations," *Marketing News,* 33, no. 3 (February 1, 1999), p. 22.

Segments based on generations

Beyond using gender, age, income, ethnic heritage, education, or other demographic variables for segmentation, many marketers embrace the idea of generations or cohorts. This approach does not entail obtaining psychographic information to enrich the demographics, but does possess some of the richness of the psychographics. The concept behind this method of segmentation is that common experiences and events create bonds between people beyond those based merely on age.

Segmentation based on generations notes that as people experience significant external events during their late adolescence or early adulthood, these events impact their social values, attitudes, and preferences. Based on similar experiences, these cohorts of individuals develop common preferences for music, foods, as well as other products. They also tend to respond to the same types of marketing appeals. Based on this idea, seven cohorts or generations have been identified. Table 3.2 lists these cohorts along with the generation in which they belong, the estimated size of the segment, and the percent of the U.S. population.

A closer look at one of the groups, Generation X, illustrates generational segmentation. The aggregate income of this cohort is estimated at $1.8 trillion. From a marketing perspective, however, Generation X consists of three subgroups: (1) college and graduate students, (2) up-and-coming professionals, and (3) young married couples. All three subgroups have grown up with television and been saturated with advertising. Therefore, a more integrated approach will be necessary to reach them.

The most effective medium for Generation X is the Internet, not television. This cohort group averages 9.3 hours per week surfing the Internet, more than any other cohort group. Approximately 43 percent of this group is interested in music sites on the Web. Another 43 percent enjoys on-line games. An additional large segment is interested in sports sites. Integrating the Internet with television advertising can further increase the impact on this group.

Volkswagen has been very successful marketing to Generation X. First, VW has a Web site designed to interest them. Volkswagen links its Web site to others' sites, such as Snow Country, Smart Money, and Rolling Stone. Because Generation Xers have an interest in not-for-profit social organizations, VW has chosen to be one of the sponsors of Lilith Fair. In designing its television ads, Volkswagen uses music enjoyed by Generation X. One set of ads takes a fiction–fantasy approach. Another ad consists of a laid-back, more casual approach: Two young men drive around town in their VW. They pick up a sofa from someone's trash, discover it has an awful smell, and eventually discard it again. The ad is set to the tune "da da da," with no copy about Volkswagen itself.[19]

Segmentation by geographic area

Another form of segmentation is by geographic area or region. This method is especially useful for retailers who want to limit marketing communications programs to specific areas. It also helps a company conduct a direct-mail campaign in a target area. The primary disadvantage of this approach is that everyone in a geographic area receives the marketing communication or is exposed to the advertisement, regardless of their interest in the product or service. Geographic segmentation does not allow a firm to focus in on a more specific target market containing only those most likely to make purchases.

Geographic segmentation should be reserved for more basic products (restaurants, foods) or items of specific interest to a region. For example, *Sports Illustrated* now offers "Championship Editions" in limited geographic regions when college football or basketball teams win national championships. These editions were very successful in states such as Nebraska, Tennessee, Kentucky, and Florida in the 1990s.

Geodemographic segmentation

A hybrid form of geographic segmentation allows companies to enrich geographic approaches to segmentation. This new form of segmentation, called geodemographics, combines census data with psychographic information. This method is more powerful in targeting a firm's customers because it combines census demographic information, geographic information, and psychographic information into one package.

Geodemographic segmentation is especially beneficial for national firms that want to conduct a direct-mail campaign or use a sampling promotion. Normally, it is too expensive and unwise to mail a sample to every household in America. Through geodemographics, a firm can send samples to the households that match the profile of a target market. For instance, colleges and universities use geodemographics to locate zip codes of communities that match their student profiles.

One firm PRIZM (Potential Rating Index by Zip Marketing) specializes in geodemographics. PRIZM has identified 62 different market segments in the United States. The company has categorized every zip code within the United States. The concept behind PRIZM is that zip codes represent neighborhoods containing people with more uniform characteristics. Consumers tend to be attracted to neighborhoods consisting of people similar to themselves. Recognizing that more than one market segment may live within a zip code, PRIZM identifies the top market segments within each zip code.

For example, a PRIZM coded map of downtown Jackson, Mississippi, identifies two primary clusters. The more predominant is the "Southside City" residents. This cluster is mainly young and elderly African Americans employed in low-paying blue-collar jobs. They tend to have lower levels of formal education, rent apartments, and read sports and fashion magazines. The second cluster within downtown Jackson is labeled as the "Towns and Gowns" neighborhoods. Towns and Gowns inhabitants also rent apartments, but members tend to be college graduates with better-paying white-collar jobs. This group likes to ski, reads beauty and fitness magazines, and uses ATM cards heavily.[20]

Geodemographic marketing has been expanded to the Internet. Adfinity, designed by Intelligent Interactions, allows an advertiser to direct specific ads to Web users based on user-defined demographics. Often, when users visit Web sites, they provide their names and addresses along with other demographic information to gain access. While the user is surfing a site, Adfinity's software can access the user's file in order to place a targeted ad on the page. To extend its power and effectiveness, Adfinity formed a strategic alliance with PRIZM. When a user accesses a Web site, the user is matched with data from the 62 PRIZM clusters. Based on the lifestyle and interests of that cluster, messages are sent to the user that match. For example, if the person is from the cluster "Executive Suites," then an advertisement about jazz or business books may appear, because people in the Executive Suites cluster tend to prefer those items.

Benefit segmentation

Benefit segmentation focuses on the advantages consumers receive from a product rather than the characteristics of consumers themselves. Demographics and psychographic information can be combined with benefit information to better identify segments. Then, the company can seek to further understand each segment's consumers.

Benefit segmentation has been used in the fitness market. Regular exercisers belong in one of three benefit segments. The first group, called "winners," do whatever it takes to stay physically fit. This segment tends to be younger, upwardly mobile, and career oriented. The second group, "dieters," exercise to maintain weight control and physical appearance. This group tends to be females over the age of 35. They are primarily interested in reliable wellness programs offered by hospitals and weight control nutritionists. The third group, "self-improvers," exercise to feel better and to control medical costs.[21] Understanding that individuals exercise for different reasons provides excellent material for a fitness center to design a marketing program.

Benefit segmentation can be very helpful in understanding what customers seek from a product. By tying these benefits to demographic and psychographic data, companies use this information to design targeted messages for each market segment.

Usage segmentation

The final type of consumer segmentation is based on customer usage or purchases. The goal of usage segmentation is to provide the highest level of service to a firm's best customers while promoting the company to casual or light users. Usage segmentation is also designed to maximize sales to all user groups.

For example, Thrifty PayLess is a chain of 158 drugstores in the Los Angeles area. Thrifty PayLess turned to usage segmentation to increase sales, gather information on the best promotional techniques, and gain new market information. To reach these objectives, the 158 stores were first organized into four clusters: (1) mid–downscale urban, (2) metro elite, (3) upper middle suburbs, and (4) upscale suburbs.

Next, Thrifty PayLess identified heavy shoppers and created customer profiles for each cluster. The marketing team retained a research firm to provide additional information about the neighborhoods in which company stores were located. Heavy shoppers were identified as individuals who shopped in Thrifty PayLess on a weekly basis. Research indicated that nearly 45 percent of Thrifty PayLess's heavy users came from households earning less than $25,000 annually. Further, 30 percent of the heavy users belonged to households earning less than $15,000. The larger the household and the younger the children in the household, the more likely they were to be heavy shoppers. These heavy shoppers had higher-than-average unemployment rates and a significant number had female heads of households. Most had blue-collar jobs and most rented houses or lived in apartments.

The next step was to gain lifestyle and media information about heavy users. The researchers discovered that Thrifty PayLess heavy shoppers were 37 percent more likely than the average Los Angeles family to visit Magic Mountain, 29 percent more likely to jog or run, 91 percent more likely to play soccer, 32 percent more likely to play softball, and 6 percent more likely to attend a Los Angeles Dodgers baseball game. Thrifty PayLess heavy shoppers were not big newspaper readers; however, they were 14 percent above the average in daytime TV viewing. Their primary viewing habits focused on MTV, HBO, auto racing, and wrestling.

Armed with this information, Thirfty PayLess developed an advertising and promotional campaign to target its heavy shoppers. The ads increased the purchases by current heavy shoppers. Further, others who fit the heavy shopper profile became more likely to witness PayLess advertisements and to begin shopping there.[22]

Many companies can identify heavy users by utilizing their own databases. With bar code scanners, point-of-sale systems, and credit, debit, transaction cards data, in-house marketers can accumulate a wealth of information about their customers. Most companies are learning that between 10 percent and 30 percent of their customers generate 70 percent to 90 percent of their sales. Instead of using firms such as PRIZM to create customer clusters, firms develop their own customer clusters from their own databases. They place customers in clusters based on common attitudes, lifestyles, and past purchase behaviors. This technique offers a business the following advantages:[23]

1. A meaningful classification scheme to cluster customers based on a firm's actual customers.

2. The ability to reduce large volumes of customer data down to a few concise, usable clusters.

3. The ability to assign a cluster code number to each customer in the database. Each number is based on the customer's actual purchases and other characteristics (address, amount spent, credit versus cash, etc.).

4. The capacity to measure the growth and migration of customers over time and from one cluster to another, which allows for the evaluation of marketing programs.

5. The capability of using a database to develop multiple clusters based on different benefits or usages.

Not all businesses have such extensive databases. For these types of businesses, several companies sell and provide consumer databases. These consumer databases can be linked to a customer's records through a name, address, or social security number. These commercial databasees contain typical information such as the household's income, the ages of household members, the length and type of residence, information about car ownership, and telephone numbers.

In summary, there are many ways to segment a consumer market. Each has advantages and disadvantages. The best methods depend on the circumstances of the company. In choosing a segmentation approach, a marketer should use the method that provides the best information and that helps in designing the best integrated marketing communications package. Remember, it is important to match the company's goods and services to its overall message and also to fit the message to the needs of various market segments, as shown in Figure 3.9. As the figure indicates, all three components must blend together and build upon one another in order to have an effectively integrated plan for the IMC program.

Integrated Learning Experience

For consumer markets, a leading geodemographic firm is Claritas. Go to its Web site at www.claritas.com and access the "Analysis & Segmentation" section. From there you can type in your zip code to see what lifestyle groups live near you. Compare the Microvision information, with 48 lifestyle groups, to the PRIZM lifestyle information, with 62 groups. Gen-X Press at www.genxpress.com is a leading developer of marketing solutions for Generations X and Y consumers. Another valuable tool is American Demographics at www.marketingtools.com. What information and articles does American Demographics provide to assist in understanding a particular market segment?

stop!

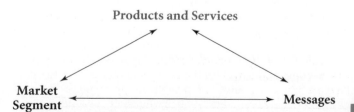

FIGURE 3.9

business-to-business segmentation

Some approaches to segmentation used to differentiate consumers can also be used to define business-to-business markets. There are also differences. Figure 3.10 lists the various ways of segmenting business-to-business markets. Keep in mind that, as with consumer markets, the primary goals of segmentation are to provide better customer service and to group homogeneous customers into clusters to enhance the marketing effort.

Segmentation by industry

The first method of segmentation is to decipher which industries contain potential customers. To do so, many firms use the NAICS (North American Industry Classification System) code. The NAICS code is replacing the SIC (Standard Industrial Classification) coding system. Firms can target specific industries such as construction (23) or wholesale trade (42). They also can segment within a specific category. For example, NAICS codes health care and social assistance services as 62. A company that manufactures health-related products can divide the market into four segments based on the subsections. These four market segments are:

621   Ambulatory Health Care Services

622   Hospitals

623   Nursing and Residential Care Facilities

624   Social Assistance

If these segments are too broad, a company breaks each segment down into smaller subcomponents. For example, Ambulatory Health Care Services includes physicians, dentists, chiropractors, and optometrists.

The NAICS divides the economy into 20 broad sectors instead of the 10 used by the SIC system and uses a six-digit code rather than the SIC four-digit code. The six-digit code allows greater stratification of industries and provides greater flexibility in creating classifications. The federal government records corporate information and data using the NAICS, making it a logical system to choose for identifying market segments.

Segmentation by business

A second method of segmentation is by the type of business served in a business-to-business relationship. This approach is similar to the NAICS system. Also, it identifies various targets within a business, such as "low-end" versus "high-end" companies, in which low-end firms purchase lesser quality or reduced-price items. Business segmentation allows the marketing firm to tailor the same product or service to individual business customers.

Methods of Segmenting Business-to-Business Markets

- NAICS/SIC code
- Type of business
- Size of business
- Geographic location
- Product usage
- Purchase decision process
- Customer value

FIGURE 3.10

Segmentation by size

Another segmentation approach for businesses is by size of customers. The rationale for this method is that large firms have different needs than do smaller companies and therefore should be contacted in a different manner. For instance, the marketing effort often focuses on the other company's purchasing department when the firm is large. For smaller firms, the owner or general manager often makes the purchase decisions.

Recently Harris Bankcorp, Inc. decided to invest money into a major marketing campaign directed toward small to midsize companies. Harris Bankcorp defined small to midsize companies as firms with revenues from $5 million to $25 million. The goal was to boost a 15 percent market share of the 15,000 firms in this market segment to 50 percent. To accomplish this objective, Harris Bancorp designed a series of financial services specifically for companies of that size. The company built branch banks closer to the areas where these customers operated and extended operating hours for their convenience. For many of the businesses, it meant taking the banking business to their place of business. Through aggressive advertising and a dedicated sales staff, Harris Bankcorp captured a much larger share of the midsize business market.[24]

Segmentation by geographic location

As with consumer segmentation, geographic segmentation of businesses can be a successful tactic. This approach especially benefits businesses whose customers are concentrated in geographic pockets such as the Silicon Valley area of California. It works for other firms as well. When the Applied Microbiology firm developed a new antimicrobial agent, it needed to market it to dairy farmers. The traditional agricultural marketing and distribution channel required to launch such a new product nationally was estimated at $3 million. Such a traditional marketing plan involved national advertising in agriculture magazines plus recruiting sales agents and brokers to introduce the product.

Instead, Applied Microbiology used geodemographics, which combined geographic areas with demographic and psychographic data. Applied Microbiology used geodemographics to find areas with larger dairy herds consisting of 1,000 or more cows per ranch. These farmers were contacted for two reasons. First, large dairy farmers who adopted would buy greater quantities of the product. Second, Applied Microbiology believed that the larger farmers were opinion leaders who would influence smaller farmers, thereby causing them to adopt the product.

The company mailed several separate direct-response pieces offering discounts and samples of the new product to larger farms. After sales started rising, Applied Microbiology asked farmers for testimonials. These testimonials were extremely powerful and the company incorporated them into new direct-marketing pieces. One brochure contained three testimonials and validation of the product by Cornell University. After a dairy farmer adopted the product, direct-marketing pieces were sent to farmers in the surrounding area. Not only did this method bring excellent results, the marketing costs were one-third of the traditional approach. Using geodemographics cost only $1 million, not the traditionally required $3 million expenditure.[25]

Segmentation by product usage

Business markets can be segmented by how the product or service is used. Many services (financial, transportation, shipping, etc.) have a variety of uses for distinct customers. For example, in the hotel industry, a major source of revenue is booking business events and conferences. A hotel or resort may segment the business market based on various types of events. Single-day seminars require only a meeting room and refreshments. A full conference may involve renting rooms for lodging, preparing banquets, furnishing meeting rooms, and planning sightseeing excursions. By segmenting the market based on the use of the hotel's facilities and staff, a

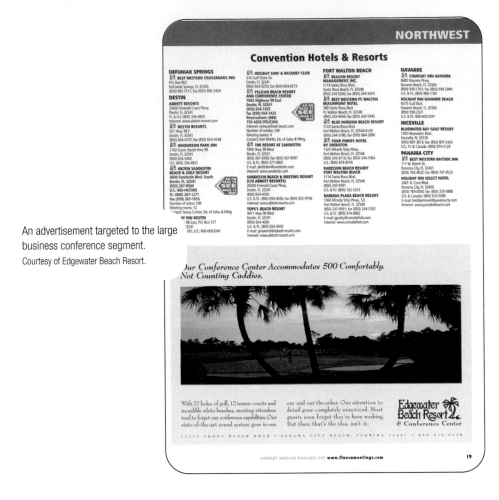

An advertisement targeted to the large business conference segment.
Courtesy of Edgewater Beach Resort.

manager can prepare marketing materials that address the needs of each specific type of conference. The advertisement by Edgewater Beach Resort is an example of this type of approach.

Segmentation by purchase decision process

Another approach to business segmentation addresses the purchase decision process, which consists of three segments: (1) first-time prospects, (2) novices, and (3) sophisticates.[26] Each segment has specific requirements and may be convinced to purchase through different kinds of marketing tactics.

First-time prospects are companies that have never purchased a particular product or service but have started evaluating vendors. *Novices* are first-time customers who have made a recent purchase of the product or service. *Sophisticates* are companies that have already purchased the product and are ready to rebuy or have just made repeat purchases.

The key to taking advantage of this form of segmentation is understanding the needs of each segment. First-time prospects want someone to care for them. They are nervous and unsure of themselves, because they have never purchased the particular product or service. They tend to rely on sales reps who know and understand their businesses. Buyers want someone they can trust. They do not want someone who talks industry jargon and cannot relate to them. Because of these needs, first time prospects often prefer buying directly from the manufacturer. With no experience to utilize in making decisions, first-time buyers are hesitant to use catalogs or direct mail and prefer not dealing with a distributor.

Novices have recently purchased the product or service and seek different benefits as a result. They are more likely to have overcome feelings of uncertainty and a lack of trust. Novices are concerned with improving product utilization. They desire manuals and hot lines that answer questions as well as dependable service. Many novices are ready to buy from catalogs and distributors. The key for this business segment is to provide strong customer support.

Sophisticates have experience with purchasing the product so they are looking for a relationship. They evaluate the track records of vendors and are especially concerned about how quickly a vendor can react to an emergency. They are also interested in customization of a product or service and want a company that will work with them specifically and not just sell standardized components. Sophisticates are also very concerned about costs. They are willing to buy from catalogs and distributors as long as the product or service is customized to their needs.

Developing a marketing campaign using this segmentation approach requires careful attention to the appeal. For first-time prospects, the firm emphasizes trust and its long history in the marketplace. Salespeople are extremely important. Advertising and direct marketing are likely to be ineffective. For novices, the marketing appeal must switch to customer service. Salespeople are not as important with this group. The company uses advertising and direct-marketing techniques. With the last group, sophisticates, direct marketing is very successful. Price and customization are the keys to selling to this group. Although salespeople can be used, telemarketing accomplishes the same results with lower costs.

Segmentation by customer value

The last method of business segmentation is based on customer value. This method of segmentation is much easier for business-to-business firms to utilize than it is for consumer businesses, due to the availability of in-depth data about each business customer. A more concise value can be assigned to each individual business through sales records and other sources of data and information. This method of segmentation is illustrated by the Application Exercise, Commercial Consolidated, at the end of the chapter.

In summary, when choosing the communication objective, it is important to decide what the desired response should be. Sometimes a company wants its customers to quickly purchase a product or service. In others, marketing managers try to persuade customers that their product is better than the competition's. For other companies, the goal is to convince a retail store to allocate more shelf space for certain products. The desired response should be based on the communication market analysis discussed in the previous section.

Integrated Learning Experience

The North American Industry Classification System (NAICS) developed by the federal government is available at www.census.gov/epcd/www/naics. html. It is also available at the Industrial Who's Who Web site at www.industrialwhoswho.com. This Web site does not provide the NAICS information but does offer SIC codes for comparison. It also lists the various manufacturing categories and information about companies within each one.

implications for GIMC programs

As first presented in Chapter 1, globally integrated marketing communications (GIMC) programs are vital for international firms. The world consists of many different languages and cultures. Brand names, marketing ideas, and advertising campaigns devised for one country do not always translate correctly to another. Consequently, understanding the international market is essential. Figure 3.11

> Understand the international market

> A borderless marketing plan

> Thinking globally but acting locally

> Local partnerships

> Communication segmentation strategies

> Market communications analysis

> Solid communication objectives

Successful Globally Integrated Marketing Communications Tactics

FIGURE 3.11

highlights the ingredients of successful globally integrated marketing communications plans.

Recognizing the many cultural nuances throughout the world is one key. This does not mean that different marketing campaigns must be developed for each country and each cultural group within a country. Still, marketers must understand the region and its culture in order to tailor messages to individual areas.

A borderless marketing plan suggests that the firm should use the same basic marketing approach for all of its various markets. At the same time, it allows each subsidiary the freedom to determine how to implement that marketing plan. This presents the opportunity to maintain a theme while targeting the message carefully.

The same idea applies to the concept of thinking globally but acting locally. The same basic message is used throughout all markets, but how it is presented specifically within a given country may vary.

Another key to a successful GIMC is developing local partnerships. Local partners can be marketing research firms or advertising firms that are familiar with the local language and culture. These partnerships sometimes are formed by hiring someone from a particular country with a full understanding of the market. Such a person is sometimes referred to as a **cultural assimilator.** It is also vital that the chosen individual has a clear understanding of the English language or the language of the parent firm and the parent firm's business.

As with domestic markets, segmentation is critical. The goal is to design a communications package that effectively communicates to all the market segments. Care must be given to identify target markets within other countries, using one or more of the tactics described in the consumer and business-to-business segmentation programs outlined earlier in this chapter.

A well-designed market communications analysis process is a key factor in the success of a GIMC program. Marketing managers must identify strengths and weaknesses of local competitors and places in which opportunities exist. They must also develop an understanding of how their own firms are perceived in the international marketplace.

Finally, solid communication objectives based on an effective market communication analysis greatly improve the chances that a GIMC program will be successful. Linguistics is a major hurdle to overcome. Translating an English advertisement into another language requires expertise, because exact word translations often do not exist. For example, the slogan of Ruth's Steak House, "We sell sizzle as well as steaks," could not be translated into Spanish, because there is no equivalent word for *sizzle*. Therefore, the translator found a Spanish idiom conveying a similar meaning in order to solve the problem.

The promotions opportunity analysis process is difficult in international settings, however, it is crucial in creating an effective GIMC. Language, culture, norms, beliefs, and laws all must be taken into consideration in the development of the

GIMC program. Literal translation of a commercial's tagline may not be acceptable within a given culture. Laws concerning advertising and promotions vary by country. Further, cultures view ideas and objects differently. These differences must be considered when designing an integrated program. Also, remember that humor is especially difficult to move across cultures and languages.

Without a solid market communication analysis, international communication programs have a high chance of failing. On the other hand, one good thing about international markets is that many of the communication objectives are the same. In all countries, marketers must make consumers aware of their product or service. Marketers must break through local clutter and garner the attention of their audience. They must be able to communicate ideas effectively about their product or service. They also must present the product or service using emotions and imagery that will speak effectively to the target audience. And finally, they must somehow find a way of persuading their target audience to purchase the product or service.

implications for marketing professionals

Brand and Promotions Managers

Recognize the connection between planning processes and evaluation processes. Planning begins only after reviewing and analyzing previous efforts. This leads the brand and promotion managers to ask the following questions about previous marketing communications and campaigns:

1. What was done right?
2. What was done wrong?
3. What are the company's strengths and weaknesses?
4. Did the last campaign (or previous promotional efforts) change this company's strengths and weaknesses?

When conducting a promotions opportunity analysis, the brand and promotion managers must be aware of the following items:

1. What the competition is doing (and plans to do, if that can be discovered)
2. What opportunities are present in the environment
3. How to integrate current company objectives into the overall IMC approach
4. What kinds of promotional strategies are in place
5. Alternative tactics that help support the company's strategies

When examining potential new market segments, consider the following criteria:

1. Contribution to sales
2. Contribution to profits, including how much should be spent to induce sales and revenues from the segment
3. Potential for growth of the segment
4. Potential to build company and brand loyalty in the segment
5. Potential for competition from other firms seeking to capture the same segment
6. The ability to match the firm's message to the particular attitudes and needs of the segment
7. The possibility of combining segments or designing similar appeals to segments
8. Other short- and long-term implications of designing promotional efforts toward the segment

Appraise global markets using the same criteria that were used for local target markets.'

Be reminded of *accountability* concerns. Both short- and long-term objectives should be identified through tangible measures of success. These measures include

1. Sales
2. Campaign results such as coupons redeemed, catalog orders, Web site hits, telephone (800 number) orders, and so forth
3. Reduced complaints
4. Unsolicited statements of loyalty or favorable comments by consumers
5. Recognition in the marketplace (brand awareness)
6. Other objectives measured by market research including postpurchase questionnaires, telephone interviews, chat room information from a Web site, ratings of programs containing company commercials, and so on.

SUMMARY

A promotions opportunity analysis is the process by which marketers identify target audiences for the goods and services produced by the company. It consists of five steps: conduct a communication market analysis, establish communications objectives, creating a communications budget, preparing promotional strategies, and matching tactics with strategies. Along the way, marketing managers must conduct a competitive analysis, an opportunity analysis, a target market analysis, a customer analysis, and a positioning analysis.

Market segmentation is identifying sets of business or consumer groups with distinct characteristics. Segments must be clearly different, large enough to support a marketing campaign, and reachable through some type of media. Consumer groups that can be segmented include those identified by demographics. These are gender, age, income, and ethnic heritage. Markets can also be segmented using psychographic, generational, and geographic delineations. Geodemographic segmentation combines demographic, psychographic, and geographic information together. Other methods to categorize consumers are by the benefits they receive from products or services and by the ways they use products.

Business-to-business segmentation can be accomplished by targeting business customers by industry, business type, size of the company, geographic location, usage, purchase decision processes, and customer value calculations. Marketing managers need to spend sufficient time specifying both consumer and business market segments, because all other promotions opportunity analysis processes are tied to the identification of key customers.

Globally integrated marketing communications efforts must also be linked to promotions opportunities analysis programs. National differences, cultural concerns, language issues, and other challenges must be viewed in light of the target markets an individual company intends to serve.

A promotions opportunity analysis program is the first step in developing a complete IMC package. Based on an overall marketing plan, company leaders gather information and generate decisions regarding target markets and marketing opportunities. They proceed to develop a further understanding of the company's image, and dig deeper into the process of revealing key consumer and business buyer behaviors. They should address their message and theme to mesh with the overall IMC plan. This stage is a foundation stage in an IMC program. A solid marketing plan and promotional analysis program help the company build the rest of the IMC plan and greatly increase the chances that marketing messages will reach the right audiences. This leads to increased sales, customer loyalty, and a stronger long-term standing in the marketplace.

REVIEW QUESTIONS

1. What is a promotions opportunities analysis? Why is it a critical part of a company's marketing effort?

2. How are the components of an IMC plan comparable to the steps of a promotions opportunities analysis planning process?

3. What are the five parts of a promotions opportunities analysis planning process?

4. What common marketing communications objectives do firms establish?

5. Name and describe four types of communications budgets. Which is best? Why?

6. What is a strategy? Give an example of a promotional strategy.

7. What are tactics? How are they related to strategies?

8. Give some examples of tactics companies can use to support promotional strategies.

9. Define demographics. How are they used to segment consumer markets?

10. How can firms take advantage of target markets by gender?

11. What generational cohorts have marketing experts identified?

12. What problems are associated with segmented markets by geographic areas?

13. What are geodemographics? Why have they been so successful in defining marketing segments?

14. Describe usage segmentation and benefit segmentation.

15. What are the common business-to-business market segmentation concepts?

16. What is a NAICS approach to segmentation? Why is it better than the old SIC format?

17. Describe a usage segmentation approach in a business-to-business setting.

18. Describe a segmentation approach based on company size.

19. How does the idea of a promotions opportunities analysis fit with a GIMC program?

KEY TERMS

promotions opportunity analysis the process by which marketers identify target audiences for the goods and services produced by the company.

communication market analysis the process of discovering the organization's strengths and weaknesses in the area of marketing communication, and combining that information with an analysis of opportunities and threats that are present in the firm's external environment.

competitive analysis the identification of competitors in the marketplace.

opportunity analysis watching carefully for new marketing opportunities.

target market analysis the examination of the target market to recognize specific needs.

customer analysis studying three distinct types of customers—current company customers, the competition's customers, and potential customers—who may become interested in purchasing from a particular company.

positioning creating a perception in the consumer's mind regarding the nature of a company and its products relative to the competition.

percentage of sales method a form of communications budgeting in which budgeting is based on the communications budget from the previous year or anticipated sales for the coming year.

meet the competition a method of communications budgeting in which the primary rationale is to prevent the loss of market share, which occurs in highly competitive markets where rivalries between competitors are intense.

the "what we can afford" method a method of communications budgeting in which the marketing budget is set after all of the company's other budgets have been determined and communications monies are allocated based on what the firm feels it can afford to spend.

objective and task method a form of communications budgeting in which management first lists all of the objectives it wants to accomplish during the year and then allocates budget to meet those objectives.

strategies sweeping guidelines concerning the essence of the company's marketing efforts.

tactics the things companies do to support overall promotional strategies.

market segmentation identifying specific purchasing groups based on their needs, attitudes, and interests.

market segment a set of businesses or group of individual consumers with distinct characteristics.

demographics the study of population characteristics.

psychographics the study of patterns of responses that reveal a person's attitudes, interests, and opinions (AIO).

cultural assimilator a person who is familiar with the local language and culture of a given country who can help marketing efforts in that particular country.

ENDNOTES

1. Christy Edison, "Thinking Out of the (Shoe) Box," *Across The Board,* 36, no. 3 (March 1999), pp. 9–10; Mike Troy, "New Cards Alter Discount Convention," *Discount Store News,* 37, no. 16 (August 24, 1998), p. 35; Seth Mendelson, "Card Sharks," *Discount Merchandiser,* 38, no. 8 (August 1998), pp. 73–77; "Sell-through Is in the Details: Refined Assortments Tap Consumer Gold," *Discount Store News,* 37, no. 22 (November 23, 1998), pp. S5–S7; Mike Troy, "An Ideal Dose of Consistency," *Discount Store News,* 37, no. 23 (December 14, 1998), pp. 57, 74; Joe Dysart, "Getting the Most from your Greeting Card Department," *Drug Topics,* 137, no. 14 (July 19, 1993), pp. 48–50; Renee Covino Rouland, "Greeting Card Boutiques, Take Two," *Discount Merchandiser,* 35, no. 6 (June 1995), pp. 68–70.

2. Mike Slater, "Marketing Case Study," *Business Date,* 2, no. 4 (September 1994), pp. 5–7.

3. "Unique Adds a Twist to Frequent Dining," *Nation's Restaurant News,* 28, no. 22 (May 30, 1994), p. 12.

4. Bob Lamons, "How to Set Politically Correct Ad Budgets," *Marketing News,* 29, no. 25 (December 4, 1995), p. 6.

5. Scott Hume, "A Bit of Good News," *Adweek, Eastern Edition,* 44, no. 20 (May 16, 1994), p. 8.

6. "Schonfeld: Strong '98 Bodes Well for 1999," *Advertising Age's Business Marketing,* 83, no. 7 (July 1998), p. 6.

7. Juliana Koranteng and Normandy Madden, "Ranking of the Top Global Ad Markets," *Advertising Age International* (May 2000), pp. 17–20.

8. Cyndee Miller, "Marketing Industry Report: Consumer Marketers Spend Most of Their Money on Communications," *Marketing News,* 30, no. 6 (March 11, 1996), pp. 1–2; Cyndee Miller, "Marketing Industry Report: Who's Spending What on Biz-to-Biz Marketing," *Marketing News,* 30, no. 1 (January 1, 1996), pp. 1–2.

9. Laurie Freeman, "B-to-B Marketing Communication Budgets Grow 14.5% as Overall Spending Reaches $73 Billion," *Advertising Age's Business Marketing,* 84, no. 5 (May 1999), pp. S3–S4.

10. Matthew Martinez, "Reed Study Sees Where Ad Dollars Go," *Advertising Age's Business Marketing,* 82, no. 9 (October 1997), p. 46.

11. Cyndee Miller, "Study Dispels '80s Stereotypes of Women," *Marketing News,* 29 (May 22, 1995), p. 3.

12. David Goetzl, "Pharmacia's Rogaine Tries to Link Up with Paul Mitchell," *Advertising Age,* 70, no. 19 (May 3, 1999), p. 26.

13. Andy Bernstein, "Study: Women Vital to Pro Sports," *Denver Business Journal,* 50, no. 14 (December 4, 1998), p. 62.

14. Interview with Kerri Martin, brand manager of BMW Motorcycles, July 18, 2000.

15. Eick Adler, "Stereotypes Won't Work with Seniors Anymore," *Advertising Age,* 67, no. 46 (November 11, 1996), p. 32.

16. George P. Moschis, "Life Stages of the Mature Market," *American Demographics* (September 1996), pp. 44–47.

17. Alf Nucifora, "Ethnic Markets Are Lands of Opportunity," *Business Journal Serving Phoenix & the Valley of the Sun,* 18, no. 52 (October 16, 1998), p. 31; Steve Climons and David O'Connor, "Marketers Lose Out by Ignoring Ethnic Segments," *Advertising Age,* 70, no. 10 (May 10, 1999), p. 40.

18. Rebecca Piirto Heath, "Psychographics," *Marketing Tools* (November–December 1995), pp. 74–81.

19. Laura Koss-Feder, "Want to Catch Gen X? Try Looking on the Web," *Marketing News,* 32, no. 12 (June 8, 1998), p. 20.

20. Susan Mitchell, "Birds of a Feather," *American Demographics,* 17, no. 2 (February 1995), pp. 40–45.

21. Ronald L. Zallocco, "Benefit Segmentation of the Fitness Market," *Journal of Health Care Marketing,* 12, no. 4 (December 1992), p. 80.

22. "How Chains Cluster Stores and Find Sales Opportunities," *Drug Store News,* 18, no. 4 (March 4, 1996), p. 50.

23. Susan Pechman, "Custom Clusters: Finding Your True Customer Segments," *Bank Marketing,* 26, no. 7 (July 1994), pp. 33–35.

24. Julie Johnsson, "Harris' New Game Plan: A Middle-Market Run," *Crain's Chicago Business,* 21, no. 21 (May 25, 1998), pp. 3–4.

25. Gene Koprowski, "Bovine Inspiration," *Marketing Tools* (October 1996), pp. 10–11.

26. Thomas S. Robertson and Howard Barich, "A Successful Approach to Segmenting Industrial Markets," *Planning Review,* 20, no. 6 (November–December 1992), pp. 4–11, 48.

27. Shannon Dortch, "Going to the Movies," *American Demographics,* 18, no. 12 (December 1996), pp. 4–8.

28. Information for this fictional case was derived from the following articles: Sandy Berry and Kathryn Britney, "Market Segmentation," *Bank Management,* 72, no. 1 (January–February 1996), pp. 36–40; "Study Reveals Wide Use of Value-Added Cards," *America's Community Banker,* 6, no. 9 (September 1997), p. 43.

Building an IMC Campaign

Conducting a Promotions Opportunity Analysis for Your Product

Advertising PlanPro

Each of the products listed in Chapter 1 has various kinds of competitors. In order to build a complete and solid IMC program, it is important to begin by following each of the steps of the promotions opportunity analysis. Also, to succeed, you need to identify key target markets for your item. This includes both consumer markets and business-to-business opportunities. In addition, it will be important to consider the possible international customers as you proceed. Go to the Prentice-Hall Web site at www.prenhall.com/clow or access the Advertising Plan Pro disk that accompanied this textbook to develop a market analysis for your product by completing the exercise for Chapter 3.

Critical Thinking Exercises

Discussion Questions

1. Use a search engine to locate five companies on the Internet that sell swimwear. Do a competitive analysis of these five companies to find the type of products they sell, the type of promotional appeal they use, and the type of special offers they use to entice buyers. What type of advertising strategy would you use to sell swimwear over the Internet?

2. A promotions opportunity analysis of movie theaters reveals the primary moviegoer to be between 18 and 24 years of age. In 1986, 44 percent of the individuals in this age bracket went to movies frequently. Today, less than 34 percent are frequent moviegoers.[27] Conduct a customer analysis by interviewing five individuals between 18 and 24. Based on their responses, what suggestions would you make to movie theaters to reverse this declining trend?

3. Make a list of five consumer products or services segmented on the basis of gender but sold to both genders. Are there any differences in the product or service attributes? Are there differences in how they are marketed? What are those differences? Do you think using a different marketing approach has worked?

4. For each of the following products or services, identify the various benefits that consumers may derive from the product or service. Can you think of an advertisement or other marketing communication that has used the benefit as the central part of its appeal?
   a. Seafood restaurant
   b. Auto insurance
   c. Optometrist or eye care clinic
   d. Soft drink
   e. Aspirin or other pain reliever

5. Choose one of the following Internet companies. Access each company's Web site, and determine what segmentation strategy the firm uses? Describe who is the target market for the Web site. Using Figure 3.4 as a guide, what communication objective(s) do you think the company is trying to fulfill with its Web site?
   a. Axiom Greeting Cards & Calendars (www.axiom-web.com)
   b. Ty Beanie Babies (www.ty.com)
   c. American Health and Beauty Aids Institute (www.proudlady.org)
   d. Advanced Hardware Architectures (www.aha.com)
   e. Dr. James R. Romano (www.jromano.com)

**APPLICATION
EXERCISE I**

Johm Mulvaney had been a marketing account manager for many years. He left a private firm to take a position at a local bank, Commercial Consolidated. Bank officials concluded that because the marketplace for financial services had become so competitive, they needed an on-staff marketing executive to continually fine-tune the bank's advertising program. The company's headquarters were in John's hometown, only 12 blocks from his house. John saw the opportunity to make a "lifestyle" move while staying active in his chosen profession.

Once he was settled in, the first issue John pursued was a promotional analysis, focusing on various customers. His research indicated that in most banks, 10 percent to 20 percent of the small business accounts yield 80 percent to 90 percent of the bank's profitability. Upon being informed of this statistic, bank officials set the goal of moving some of the small businesses within the 80 percent, which were not currently profitable, to become more like the 10 percent to 20 percent.

John told the bank's leaders that he wanted to pursue a customer valuation segmentation approach, assigning each business a value related to the bank's level of profitability. To illustrate how this segmentation method works, John described the ways banks could market to small businesses. He noted that the first step in customer value segmentation is to identify the drivers that impact each business customer's profitability potential. For a bank providing financial services to small businesses, the primary value drivers are:

1. Deposit balances wherein interest and other revenues exceed requirements for servicing the account

2. Consistent fee income from sundry banking and financial services

3. Efficient lending practices emphasizing underwriting, approval, and processing of profitable loans

4. Targeted customer development focusing on building relationships leading to profitable transactions between the bank and the small business

5. Sales and service delivery programs that match the bank's profitability goals

John told Commercial Consolidated's management team that not all customers have the potential to be highly profitable accounts. He noted that by segmenting its small customers into customer value clusters, the bank could design different marketing programs for each segment to maximize effectiveness while minimizing marketing costs. He suggested putting a greater marketing effort into an account with high profitability potential than into one with low potential for profitability.

The marketing team decided to segment various small business customers along several dimensions. Codes placed in each customer's data file allowed for easy clustering. The team used seven characteristics to code the bank's small business customers. Account managers were given the following instructions for each account and its particular characteristics:

1. *Value segment.* Code the account based on how profitable it has been over the last 12 months. Codes range from highly profitable to unprofitable.

2. *Long-term value segment.* Code the account based on profitability potential for the next five years.

3. *Industry growth potential segment.* Code the growth potential of the industry in which the firm operates, from high-growth industry to negative anticipated growth.

4. *Industry position segment.* Relative to the industry, code the size of the firm from large to small within the same industry.

5. *Transaction frequency segment.* Code the business customers from high to low based on frequency of transactions with the bank over the past six months.

6. *Product propensity segment.* Code the business customers based on their propensity to purchase a 401(k) plan with the bank. This code would be based on the firm's size and growth characteristics, from high potential for a 401(k) to low potential.

7. *Creditworthiness segment.* The code indicates the businesses' relative credit risk.

This coding system allowed the bank greater flexibility in designing its marketing program. The codes identified customers with the highest profit potential based on these factors.

Commercial Consolidated's overall theme had always been focused on its "hometown" bank image. Advertisements and other promotions restated the message that dollars invested locally were more valuable to the community than those shipped to the home office of a competitor in another city or state.

Using this technique, a bank could assign customers to clusters based on loan usage. Another set of clusters could be developed for investment services. A bank could develop many different clusters with customers assigned to clusters based on their purchase behavior of that particular type of service.

From there the bank generated an aggressive marketing program including advertising, direct-mail pieces, and some personal visits to companies with high profit potential. Customers with a medium level of transaction frequency could be targeted to increase their transactions with the bank if their potential was high. The bank aimed the direct marketing program at its top 20 customers; advertising was designed to reach the next 100 customers (in terms of profit potential), and the remainder of the firm's advertising funds were spent on brand awareness commercials.

Next, individual consumers were segmented and targeted. The bank was most interested in increasing use of their highly profitable consumer credit card. To do so, it needed to understand the usage of the credit card. The bank's customer cluster analysis identified the following seven clusters:

1. *The uncommitted.* The newest users of the credit card, these individuals tended to use the card infrequently and make relatively small purchases. This cluster primarily consisted of retired persons and individuals with low incomes.

2. *Convenience users.* These customers used their cards frequently and normally paid off their balances at the end of each monthly billing cycle. This cluster tended to have below average assets and slightly less than average household income.

3. *Starting out.* This cluster was predominantly young adults with lower than average incomes and low assets. They tended to have high purchases and to carry moderate to high balances on their cards.

4. *Channel shoppers.* Some of the older cardholders, these individuals had the highest income levels and were primarily females or married couples. This cluster had a low level of delinquency, low service charges, and moderate card activity.

5. *Credit addicts.* The group had the longest tenure of cardholders in the bank. They had the highest credit limits, the greatest spending, and the highest payments due each month. This cluster was of average age with above average income.

6. *Cash driven.* As the cash-hungry cluster, these individuals tended to pay off account balances slowly, had moderate credit limits, and used the card frequently to garner cash advances. This cluster generally were younger males and other singles with low assets.

7. *Borderline.* The youngest of the clusters with the lowest card activity, these customers had a high delinquency rate and have low incomes.

Using the cluster information, the bank sought to expand revenues by targeting current customers. They developed specialty marketing communication pieces for each cluster. Based on the demographic and psychographic information from each cluster, marketing pieces were designed to elicit responses. This clustering information helped the bank prevent customer defections to the competition by meeting the needs of each individual segment. To maximize the success of the program, the firm's marketing team made sure that the correct services were matched with customer needs. This information was used to focus media and advertising strategies creating specific messages for specific customers.

Within a few months, bank profits had risen significantly. John received a healthy raise and concluded he had made a wise choice in moving to this particular organization.

1. Explain how the steps of a promotions opportunity analysis are present in this case.
2. Explain why John and Commercial Consolidated were so successful.
3. Based on information in this case, design a business-to-business print advertisement offering local businesses "loans" or "investment services." Where should the ad be placed? Why?
4. Choose one of the credit card customer clusters listed in the case. Design a print advertisement to reach this group. Where should the print ad be placed? What other marketing tools could be used with the print advertisement?

Mike's Real Estate

APPLICATION EXERCISE II

Mike Kelly, a lifelong resident of Fremont, Nebraska, had built a successful career in real estate by knowing everyone who mattered in his small community. Mike's Real Estate competed successfully against ReMax, Century 21, Realty Executives, and other firms that offered alternatives when people were ready to buy or sell a home or business.

Mike's business concept was simple. He hired only real estate agents who had been residents of Fremont for at least 10 years. He insisted on loyalty combined with an intense drive to make the real estate transaction as painless as possible for all concerned. Mike's activity in several local community events and charities gained name recognition for himself and his company.

Mike's firm developed one key advantage during the late 1980s. Prior to that time, all real estate companies had charged a fee of 6 percent of the sale price of a house to the seller. With inflation and other pressures, the larger chains raised that fee to 7 percent. Mike held the line at 6 percent. Even though Mike had experienced several unfriendly visits from local agents from other companies, complaining about the price difference, he held his ground. He knew these same agencies circulated rumors about his personal life (Mike was divorced), his lack of "professionalism," and other negative comments. The same was true for the sale of businesses. Mike charged 10 percent. Several realty companies had progressed to 15 percent. As a result, even with the unethical tactics used by the competition, based on price alone, Mike's Realty had an advantage accentuated by the personal attention given to clients.

As the new century began, however, the field changed. One major challenge was a shift in residents. Fremont had emerged partly as a "bedroom" community serving Omaha. In other words, many people lived in Fremont but worked in the city of Omaha. This gave realtors in Omaha an advantage, because they could provide listings and a retail site in both towns. Someone living in Omaha but seeking a more quiet, smaller community would probably first call a realtor in the city, meaning Mike had lost many potential customers.

The second most significant challenge was the Internet. The larger companies were able to post their listings worldwide through Web sites. A house or business could be shown to virtually anyone, anywhere. Even though Mike added a computer specialist to build his own site, the edge he had of being "local" was lost, and the difference in fees was not enough to be able to sell a house at a lower price, or to persuade a local seller to list with his company, rather than a national firm with worldwide exposure.

In the previous fiscal year, Mike's listings (houses for sale registered with his company) had declined by 20 percent. He was forced to cut his staff by one person. Fortunately, one of his agents had decided to move out of the area, so he did not have to actually fire someone. Meanwhile, he was getting fewer and fewer walk-in customers. His Internet "hits" were not very substantial. Many businesses simply ignored him when he asked about being the listing agent when they decided to sell.

Mike's costs were also rising, and his agents complained that they received less per sale than those in other companies. He began to worry that he might actually lose some of his staff. It was time to take action, but he wasn't sure what to do.

1. Is Mike's situation hopeless? Why or why not?
2. What should Mike do to increase his business and revenues?
3. What, if any, market segment still exists for Mike's Real Estate?
4. Outline a communication market analysis plan for Mike's Real Estate. For each step in the communication market analysis listed in Figure 3.3, identify how Mike's Real Estate should proceed.
5. What type of segmentation strategy should Mike pursue?

▶ **CHAPTER OBJECTIVES**

Understand the nature of a corporation's image and why it is important.

Develop tactics and plans to build an effective corporate image.

Discover the advantages of a quality logo.

Cultivate effective brand names, family brands, brand extensions, flanker brands, co-brands, private brands, brand equity, and brand recognition.

Recognize the importance of effective brand and product positioning, and utilize strategies to help establish a positive position.

Build quality damage control procedures, including both proactive and reactive responses to negative events or stories in the media.

IMAGE ISSUES:
Food Lion and ABC

In 1997, the Food Lion grocery chain won a well-publicized lawsuit against *ABC News*. The jury awarded $1,402 in compensatory (actual) damages and $5.5 million in punitive damages. Naturally, ABC appealed, and there has been no final judgment in the case. The question remains, however, whether Food Lion managed this sensitive image-related problem correctly.

The grocery chain grew rapidly during the late 1980s and early 1990s, expanding into numerous markets. Food Lion executives enjoyed the advantage of being a nonunion

chapter**four**

chain in a predominantly unionized industry, giving the company a competitive edge in labor costs. Over the years, a highly acrimonious relationship had developed between Food Lion and the United Food and Commercial Union workers, as numerous attempts to unionize Food Lion have taken place. The union charged Food Lion with violations of food-safety and -handling laws, discrimination in hiring, conspiracy to violate state wage and price laws, and libel and slander.

To make matters worse, ABC was "tipped" that Food Lion had many unsanitary food-handling practices occurring in their operations. The program *PrimeTime Live* investigated the chain by having two members of its staff apply to

work in a Food Lion store. Once hired, the two ABC employees videotaped various Food Lion operations using hidden cameras and microphones while on the job. What followed was a report showing workers at two stores tampering with expiration dates on meats and other products. Footage was aired depicting employees bleaching soiled chickens and selling cheese that had been gnawed by rodents. Interviews of former employees were conducted regarding management practices and mistreatment. Viewers saw the initial report on November 5, 1992.

Food Lion's sales and profits dramatically dropped following the telecast. Eighty-eight of its stores nationwide eventually closed. In response to the news report, Food

Lion tried to launch a public relations offensive indicating the opposite of what ABC had aired—happy employees and quality working conditions. Company leaders also filed suit against the network, arguing that the two "employees" had fraudulently gained employment by misrepresenting themselves on the application blank. Food Lion also contended that ABC had trespassed on its property. The jury agreed and ruled that ABC should pay the training costs of the two employees (the $1,402) and pay punitive damages for hurting Food Lion's reputation (the $5.5 million).

Food Lion also charged that the Giant Food, Kroger, Safeway, and Magruder's grocery chains engaged in similar practices. By attacking competitors, Food Lion was in essence challenging the union. Public charges and press conferences followed, each claiming the wrongdoing of the other.

Once the verdict was in, another round of publicity followed. In fact, *PrimeTime Live* revisited Food Lion asking questions about the ethical use of hidden cameras and First Amendment rights. Once again, video of the unsanitary food-handling practices was shown as part of the program. Food Lion stated that the attack on its company was being directed by the union, that the incidents were isolated but made to seem as if they were common practice, and that ABC had cost it over $200 million in sales. Food Lion reasoned that the company would not have been so successful initially had it routinely sold spoiled food.

In the end, Food Lion's image and reputation changed from being a low-cost competitor in the grocery industry to being a "sour grapes" company too busy pointing fingers to solve its own internal problems. More than spoiled food products were at stake—the firm's image had spoiled as well.[1]

overview

One of the most critical ingredients in the successful development of an integrated marketing communications plan is effective management of an organization's image. A firm's **image** is based on the feelings consumers and businesses have about an organization as well as evaluations of individual brands. Advertising, sales promotions, trade promotions, personal selling, and other marketing activities are all part of the larger umbrella of the firm's general image. If the image of either the organization or one of its brands becomes tarnished, sales revenues and profits often plummet, and rebuilding or revitalizing that image is a momentous task.

Developing and maintaining a quality image is one key responsibility being assigned to both brand managers and account executives at the agency level. Image has a "bottom line" that can even be assigned a value on accounting statements. Advertising managers and other marketing experts are expected to perform services that sell products in the short term and build image over time. Advertising creatives must think of both goals as they design individual ads and more elaborate campaigns.

In the overall IMC program, image first becomes a concern as part of the promotions opportunity process, (see Chapter 3). Image is connected to company strengths and weaknesses. A strong image can be combined with an opportunity discovered in the external environment to create a major strategic advantage for the firm. A complete analysis of a firm's image and the strengths of its individual brands can be connected to a forceful effort to make solid connections with end use consumers and business-to-business accounts. As part of the IMC planning process, image and brand ideas can be related to various consumer and business buyer behaviors, thereby establishing a consistent message with all of the individuals who may purchase a company's goods and services.

The first part of this chapter examines the many facets of managing a corporation's image. The second part addresses the issues associated with developing and promoting the various forms of brand names. Brand names and company logos (e.g., McDonald's arches, the Nike swoosh, etc.) are closely tied to a firm's image. The third part of this chapter presents market positioning strategies through brand and corporate image management. The fourth and final section of this chapter highlights techniques for minimizing the impact of negative events or bad press. As illustrated in the Food Lion vignette, organizations often experience assorted forms of negative press that can affect consumer perceptions of an organization's image.

the corporate image

Effective marketing communication begins with the establishment of a clearly defined corporate image. This image summarizes what the company stands for as how well its position has been established. Whether it is the "good hands" of Allstate Insurance or the "good neighbors" at State Farm Insurance, the goal of image management is to create a stable impression in the minds of clients and customers (in the case of insurance companies, helpfulness, safety, and security are most prevalent).

More important than what organizational officials believe about the company is what consumers believe about the company. Corporate names such as IBM, Apple Computers, General Motors, Nike, and Exxon all conjure images in the minds of consumers. Although the specific version of the image varies from person to person or business to business, the overall or most general image of a firm is determined by the conglomerate view of all publics. This image influences customers either positively or negatively as they make purchase decisions.

A State Farm advertisement informing consumers about the company's goal of making driving safer. Courtesy of State Farm Insurance Companies. © State Farm Mutual Automobile Insurance Company, 1999. Used by permission.

Components of a corporate image

Consumers see many things as they encounter a company or organization. The goods or services offered are only part of the total picture. For example, personal views associated with General Motors consist of evaluations of the vehicles the organization produces, the dealerships that sell them, the factories where vehicles are built, and the advertisements used to persuade customers. In addition, the corporation's image includes assessments of the employees who work at the company's headquarters, factories, and dealerships. In fact, the mechanic trying to repair a GM vehicle at a local Mr. Goodwrench garage may become a major part of a customer's specific image of General Motors. Every aspect of General Motors, from the literature provided to the finished products sold, is a component in GM's image.

Further, as shown in the Figure 4.1, a corporate image contains many invisible and intangible elements. A policy of a pharmaceutical or cosmetic company that prohibits animal testing becomes integrated into consumer attitudes toward the firm. Personnel policies and practices impact the firm's image, as Texaco recently learned when employee lawsuits regarding discrimination in hiring and promotion practices emerged. The business philosophies of Bill Gates at Microsoft and of Ross Perot at EDS affect the images consumers have of Microsoft and EDS, respectively. The beliefs and attitudes consumers hold concerning the country of Japan influence their viewpoints of firms such as Sony and Toyota. Further, negative events or attitudes, such as were recently revealed regarding relationships with black patrons of Denny's restaurants, can stain or damage long-term perceptions of a firm's overall image.

The role of a corporate image—consumer perspective

From a consumer's perspective, the corporate image serves several useful functions. These include:

- Assurance regarding purchase decisions of familiar products in unfamiliar settings
- Assurance concerning purchases where there is little previous experience
- Reduction of search time in purchase decisions
- Psychological reinforcement and social acceptance

A well-known corporate image provides consumers with positive assurance of what they can expect from the firm. A can of Coke or Pepsi purchased in

Tangible Elements

1. Goods and services sold
2. Retail outlets where the product is sold
3. Factories where the product is produced
4. Advertising, promotions, and other forms of communications
5. Corporate name and logo
6. Employees

Intangible Elements

1. Corporate, personnel, and environmental policies
2. Ideals and beliefs of corporate personnel
3. Culture of country and location of company
4. Media reports

Components of a Corporate Image

FIGURE 4.1

Anchorage, Alaska, has a comparable taste to one purchased in Liverpool, England, or Kuala Lumpur, Malaysia. McDonald's serves the same or similar value meals in San Francisco as the ones sold in Minneapolis or Paris. Consumers on vacation know that if they purchase a product from Wal-Mart in Texas, they can return it if defective to a local store in Toronto, Canada, or Mexico City, Mexico.

This assurance increases in importance when consumers purchase goods or services with which they have little experience. For example, consider a family on vacation. Often travelers in another state or country look for signs or logos of companies from their native area. Purchasing from a familiar corporation is perceived to be a "safer" strategy than purchasing from an unknown. Patronizing a hotel or restaurant that the consumer has never heard of will be seen as riskier than would be utilizing a familiar one. Vacationers from Brazil may never have stayed in a Holiday Inn, but because they have heard of the name, they feel it is a lower-risk alternative than staying in an unknown hotel.

A significant role that the corporate image plays for the consumer is the reduction of search time. Purchasing products from a familiar firm can save a consumer considerable energy. An individual loyal to Chrysler automobiles spends fewer hours searching for a new car than does one with no loyalty toward a particular automobile manufacturer. The same principal holds in purchasing low-cost items such as groceries. A great deal of search time is saved when a consumer purchases brands and items from the same corporation, such as Kellogg or Nabisco.

For many individuals, purchasing from a highly recognized company provides psychological reinforcement and social acceptance. The psychological reinforcement comes from the customer's feeling that he or she made a wise purchasing choice and that the product or service will perform well. The social acceptance is derived from the consumer's knowledge that many other individuals have also purchased from the well-known firm. More importantly, other people, such as family and friends, are likely to accept the choice.

The role of a corporate image—business-to-business perspective

Corporate image is a crucial element of the business-to-business marketplace. Purchasing from a well-known company reduces the feelings of risk that are part of the buying process. A firm with a well-established image makes the choice easier for business customers who often seek to reduce search time during the decision-making process. Also, a form of psychological reinforcement and social acceptance exists, because company buyers who make quality purchases receive praise from organizational leaders and others involved in the process. Once again, a strong company image or brand name can make the difference in a choice between competitors.

Brand image is especially important when expanding internationally. Foreign businesses are likely to feel more comfortable making transactions with a business from a different country with a established corporate image. Risk and uncertainty are reduced when the buyer knows something about the seller. Therefore, a company such as IBM or Nike can expand into a new country and more quickly gain the confidence of consumers and businesses.

The role of a corporate image—company perspective

From the viewpoint of the firm itself, a highly reputable image generates many benefits. These include:

- Extension of positive consumer feelings to new products
- The ability to charge a higher price or fee
- Consumer loyalty leading to more frequent purchases
- Positive word-of-mouth endorsements
- The ability to attract quality employees
- More favorable ratings by financial observers and analysts

A quality corporate image provides the basis for the development of new goods and services. When consumers are already familiar with the corporate name and image, the introduction of a new product becomes much easier, as long-term customers are willing to give something new a try. Customers normally transfer their trust in and beliefs about the corporation to a new product.

A strong corporate image allows a company to charge more for their products and services. Most customers believe they "get what they pay for," which means higher quality is often associated with higher prices. This, in turn, can lead to better markup margins and greater profits for the firm with a strong corporate image that can charge higher prices.

Further, firms with well-developed images have customers who are more loyal. A higher level of customer loyalty results in patrons purchasing more products over time. This is, in part, because less substitution purchasing takes place (such as when other companies offer discounts, sales, and other enticements to switch brands.)

Heightened levels of customer loyalty are often associated with positive word-of-mouth endorsements of the company and its products. These favorable comments about the firm help generate additional sales and attract new customers. Most consumers have more faith in the personal references they receive than in communication that comes from any form of advertising or promotion.

Another advantage of a corporate image is that it attracts quality employees. Just as consumers are drawn to strong firms, potential workers will apply for jobs at companies with solid reputations. Consequently, recruiting costs are reduced because of lower employee turnover, and fewer advertising expenditures are needed to entice new applicants.

An additional value of a strong corporate reputation is a more favorable rating by Wall Street analysts. A strong corporate image can also lead to more favorable evaluations by financial institutions. This is especially helpful when a company tries to get capital financing. Further, legislators and government entities tend to act in a more supportive manner toward companies with strong and positive reputations. Lawmakers are less inclined to pursue actions that may hurt the business. Regulatory agencies are less likely to investigate rumors of wrongdoing.

In summary, building a strong corporate image provides tangible and intangible benefits. Both customers and organizations benefit from a well-known firm that has an established reputation in the community or area it serves. Organizational leaders devote considerable amounts of time and energy to building and maintaining a positive organizational image. Companies expect advertising account managers and their creatives to help design marketing programs that take advantage of the benefits of a strong corporate image.

Integrated Learning Experience

Using Yahoo! Shopping, choose a product category. Look at the brands and the stores listed in that product category. Why were those particular brands chosen? Are any brands missing? How important is a well-known, well-established brand name to consumers? What about when the firm attempts to sell goods to another business?

promoting the desired image

Communicating the proper image is critical to an organization's success. Organizational leaders try to understand the nature of the company's current image in order to make sure that future communications that promote the image are successfully transmitted. Marketing experts should make sure all constituencies correctly discern the nature of the company's image. This includes customers, suppliers, and employees. In addition, other consumers, especially noncustomers of the firm, should be approached to ascertain their views of the company. Once those in the firm understand how others currently view them, they can make decisions about the image they wish to portray in the future.

In making decisions about the image to be projected, marketers should remember four things:

1. The image being projected must accurately portray the firm and coincide with the products and services being sold.

2. Reinforcing or rejuvenating a current image that is consistent with the view of consumers is easier to accomplish than is changing a well-established image.

3. It is very difficult to change the images people hold about a given company. In some cases, modifying or developing a new image simply cannot be done.

4. Any negative or bad press can quickly destroy an image that took years to build. Reestablishing or rebuilding the firm's image takes a great deal of time once its reputation has been damaged. This issue (repairing an image) is examined at the end of this chapter.

communication**action**

An Interview with a Brand Manager

Being an effective brand manager is a difficult task. One person who has taken the challenge is Kerri L. Martin, brand manager for BMW Motorcycles. We asked Kerri to describe her work. Here was her answer:

The responsibilities of my job as brand manager fall into two very different yet linked areas, strategic and tactical. While on one hand I'm responsible for leading the brand's long-term identity and strategic positioning, on the other hand I'm also responsible for guiding all tactical marketing consumer communications programs and materials. It's my job to assure that all communications that touch the consumer are integrated, speaking in one tone and voice, and visually complementary of each other.

Beyond this more general description, Kerri noted her main duties.

On a daily basis I could be involved in one or more of the following: new product launches, ad campaign marketing, media planning, point-of-purchase merchandising, co-op advertising, budgets, and general administration.

The company is quite attentive to the idea of developing a consistent theme to reach potential customers. Kerri stated it this way:

BMW Motorcycles are the Indisputable Mark of a Real Ride. [We] . . . broadly communicate, in powerful terms, the reality that the most passionate riders, real riders, recognize the extraordinary characteristics of the BMW motorcycle. It is not a "two-wheeled car," but the result of the finest motorcycle design and manufacturing in the world over the last 75 years. The end result is a motorcycle that offers true synchronicity between the rider and the machine.

Kerri reported that her department is acutely aware of the importance of brand management, brand development, and integration of brand strategies with an overall IMC approach. She described the process this way:

The building of a brand is a long-term proposition, not an overnight miracle. A brand is not just a logo, a unique product, or the latest ad campaign. Instead it is multi-dimensional and flows from a set of values. I believe that branding should be a company-wide focus that differentiates the product from its competition in both marketing communications and operations. At all sets in the relationship with your customer and contact points, you're building brand loyalty. In the long run, this loyalty becomes the backbone of your brand.

The IMC approach to brand development helps ensure stability in the process. At BMW, the firm reflects many of the ideas reported in Chapter 1 of this text. Listen to Kerri talk about its approach:

Today, more than ever in history, consumers are bombarded with marketing messages everywhere they go. Buy this, do this, visit us, go there, be here . . . it goes on and on. With such a crowded marketplace, marketers must be careful not to confuse customers any more than they already are. Thus, it's critical that a brand have one voice and communicate in that one voice in everything they do. With increased segmentation, you can no longer be all things to all people. Pick a USP (Unique Selling Proposition) and stick with it. It's important to be conscious of everything you put out there for the public to absorb, right down to the shirts that your event staff wear and the manner in which customers are treated when they call your customer service department to ask a question.

BMW Motorcycles works with the Merkley Newman Harty agency. The agency highlights a "governing brand idea," which is very similar to BMW's notion of a unique selling proposition. Although BMW uses Merkley Newman Harty as its "agency of record," Kerri stays highly involved in the brand management process.

I manage another handful of agencies which specialize in defined areas, such as events, collateral, the Internet, merchandising co-op program administration, telemarketing, and sales promotion. The key to successfully managing each of these agencies so that one brand message is consistently conveyed in all marketing efforts is communication. It's extremely important that each of these other marketing partners buys into and understands the brand positioning as thoroughly as our primary agency of record. Therefore, I spend a lot of time working closely with them on all projects and bring them up to speed quickly when there are new developments on our product offering, industry and consumer research, media direction, creative strategy shifts, and so forth.

Through Kerri's efforts and those of the staff at BMW and all of the agencies involved, the company has a strong brand name and maintains a strong position in the marketplace. If there is one thing to note, it may be that Kerri would remind every student reading this text that "EVERYTHING COMMUNICATES!"

Creating the right image

As mentioned previously, company leaders are often willing to spend substantial amounts of money to create the proper image for a firm. For example, when British Airways expanded into a low-cost operation and customers could buy tickets directly, the advertising department spent nearly $60 million to achieve the desired image. The outcome was the brand name *Go* for the subsidiary. At the same time, the firm tried to move away from close connotations with the country of Great Britain in its overall image management program. As a result, British Airways removed the U.K. flag from all its planes. British Airways' goal was to maintain the image of being a safe and secure method of travel, with easy access in the *Go* program.[2]

In contrast, Singapore Airlines accentuates its national identity by using the "Singapore Girl" in every advertisement. The image goal of Singapore Airlines is to stress quality service. Industry experts agree that although methods vary, the key for all airline images is to be simple, international, and easily translatable, emphasizing safety and security to reassure potential passengers.[3]

In each industry, the right image reaches all target markets and conveys a clear message about the unique nature of the organization and its products. This image must portray the nature of the firm accurately and logically fit with the products and services that organization offers. The advertisement for BMW Motorcycles is

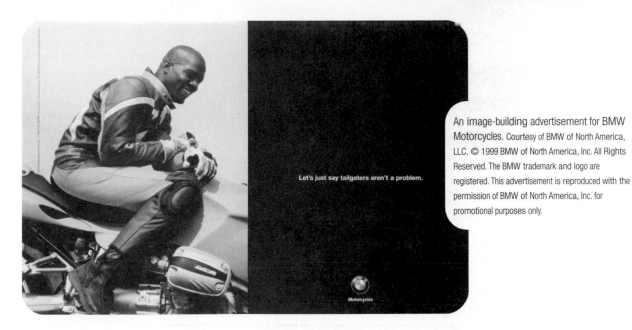

An image-building advertisement for BMW Motorcycles. Courtesy of BMW of North America, LLC. © 1999 BMW of North America, Inc. All Rights Reserved. The BMW trademark and logo are registered. This advertisement is reproduced with the permission of BMW of North America, Inc. for promotional purposes only.

designed to further the image that "BMW Motorcycles are the indisputable mark of a real ride," according to BMW brand manager Kerri Martin. The Communication Action Box contains more information about how Martin works to create the desired image for the BMW Motorcycles. Once the image is established, other promotions can be built around that reputation to increase long-term customer loyalty and future sales.

Rejuvenating an image

Reinforcing or rejuvenating a current image consistent with the view of consumers is easier to accomplish than is changing a well-established image. McDonald's discovered that projecting a more grown-up Ronald McDonald (playing golf and being involved in other more adult activities) did not radically change the overall image, which is primarily oriented toward children, nor did it help the company sell the Arch Delux line of hamburgers.

An example of an organization that has more effectively rejuvenated its image is Radio Shack. As technology has become more sophisticated, it has only become more "mystical" to a large number of consumers, and Radio Shack is in the business of technology. Therefore, it was important to demystify that technology for average people. The slogan "You've got questions, we've got answers" helps the company reach people who want the advantages of new technologies but are at the same time intimidated by them.

Rejuvenating an image helps a firm sell new products and can attract new customers. At the same time, reinforcing previous aspects of an image assists the company in retaining loyal patrons comfortable with the firm's original image. The key to successful image reengineering is to keep consistent with a previous image while at the same time building to incorporate new elements to expand the firm's target audience.[4]

Changing an image

It is very difficult to change the images people hold regarding a given company. Company leaders must carefully consider what they wish to change, why they wish to make a change, and how they intend to accomplish the task. Changing an image is most necessary when target markets have begun to shrink or disappear, or the firm's image no longer matches industry trends and consumer expectations.

Another competitor in the airline industry, the Soviet-owned Aeroflot, was aware of its poor safety image. Company officials decided to use humor to change this image, so they adopted a flying elephant as its symbol. This form of self-mocking is designed to let customers know Aeroflot has identified and is trying to fix any safety-related problems. Aeroflot's leaders then hope to move toward a more positive image in future years.[5]

Conveying an image to business customers

Officials from many companies believe corporate advertising sends important signals to other businesses. Image advertising helps build a reputation not only with the general public but also with other firms. Robert Worcester, chairman of MORI, a British market research group, reports that the more a company advertises, the more it is admired. Opinion Research Corporation, a U.S. firm, noted that "knowing a company very well" is a key reason to award new business. Therefore, image advertising is a crucial ingredient in business-to-business marketing. Stephen Greyser, from the Harvard Business School, states that corporate image advertising should be aimed at three constituencies: opinion formers (customers, politicians, investors), employees, and *other businesses*.[6]

stop!

Integrated Learning Experience

Web sites are an important element of a company's image. Access the Web sites of the following companies to get a feel for the image each company tries to project.

> www.kelloggs.com
> www.nabisco.com
> www.ibm.com
> www.bmwusacycles.com
> www.britishairways.com
> www.singaporeair.com

Is the image projected on the Web site consistent with the image portrayed in the company's advertisements? Several consulting firms specialize in helping businesses project a consistent image to their stakeholders. One such firm is Corporate Images, Inc. Access this Web site at www.corporate-images.com to see services that might be beneficial to a business attempting to establish a sound corporate image.

corporate names and logos

A corporate name is the overall banner under which all other operations occur. According to David Placek, president and founder of Lexicon, Inc., "The corporate name is really the cornerstone of a company's relationship with its customers. It sets an attitude and tone and is the first step toward a personality."[7] When AT&T spun off its $26 billion systems and technology business, company officials examined over 700 names including the acronym AGB, which stood for Alexander Graham Bell. The name Lucent Technologies was finally chosen because it conveyed the idea of something glowing with light, which executives at AT&T felt would be a better image going into the twenty-first century than an acronym such as AGB.[8]

A critical corollary to the corporate name is the corporate logo. Both must be carefully chosen, be compatible, and say the correct thing about the company. Most organizations spend millions of dollars on selecting and promoting corporate names and logos. For example, Taco Bell spends more money on its permanent media such as signs that carry its name and logo than it does on advertising.[9] Because consumers are flooded with hundreds of advertisements daily, corporate names and logos can aid in memory recall of specific brands and even specific advertisements. They help consumers in the retail store by making shopping easier and faster. Search time is reduced when consumers can look for specific corporate products that are easily identified by logos and names.[10]

Quality logos and corporate names should meet four tests. They should: (1) be easily recognizable, (2) be familiar, (3) elicit a consensual meaning among those in the firm's target market, and (4) evoke positive feelings.[11]

Logos are especially important for in-store shopping. Because pictures can be processed in the mind faster than words, corporate logos are easily recognizable by consumers. To be advantageous to companies, logo recognition must occur at two levels. First, consumers remember seeing the logo in the past. It is stored in memory, and when it is seen at the store, the memory is jogged. Second, the logo reminds consumers of the brand or corporate name. This reminder should elicit positive feelings regarding either the brand name or corporate manufacturer.

Successful logos elicit shared meanings across consumers. The notion that a logo can elicit a consensual meaning among customers is known as **stimulus codability.** Logos with high stimulus codability easily evoke consensually held meanings within a culture or subculture (such as the Prudential Rock). Logos with a high degree of codability are more easily recognized, such as Apple, General Electric, and Budweiser. Logos with a low degree of codability must spend more money on advertising so recognition comes through familiarity rather than the stimulus codability. For example, Nike spent a considerable amount of resources making its Swoosh recognizable to those in various target markets, because the Swoosh itself did not conjure any specific image of the firm early in its life.

Negative logos can hurt a firm's image. For example, the bad press aimed at Joe Camel and negative reactions associated with Procter & Gamble's moon and stars logos have caused some damage to the images of those two corporations.

In summary, image is an all-encompassing umbrella which projects the overall nature of the corporation. Firms seek to create the proper image, rejuvenate that image when necessary, change it in extreme circumstances, and extend it into all aspects of advertising, including plans to build stronger relations with other businesses. Corporate names and logos, brands, and the many components of an organization's operations, from manufacturing to service, all add up to the image of the firm, unless, of course, the firm is Sprite, because Sprite suggests that "Image is *Nothing,* Thirst is Everything!"

branding

Many of the characteristics and benefits of a corporate image apply to brands as well. The primary difference between the two is that of scope. **Brands** are names generally assigned to a product or service or a group of complementary products while a corporate image covers every aspect of the company. A company such as Procter & Gamble carries many brands such as Tide, Cheer, and Bold laundry detergents; Crest and Gleem toothpastes; and Old Spice, Secret, and Sure deodorants. As with a well-known corporate image, an effective brand name allows a company to charge more for its products, which in turn increases gross margins. Strong brands provide customers with assurances of quality and reduction of search time in the purchasing process.

In mature markets, few tangible distinctions exist between competing brands. If a substantial product improvement appears, competitors usually quickly copy it. Thus, only minor differences exist and in many product categories, even minor variations are hard to find. When brand names and labels are removed, consumers often find it difficult to distinguish between products.

If many competing brands are not really different, then why are there such a huge differences in market share? This primarily is due to the difference in what is **salient** for customers. A particular brand is salient for consumers if they are aware of the brand, have it in their consideration sets (things they consider when making purchases), regard the product and brand as a good value, buy it or use it on a regular basis, and recommend it to other consumers.[12] A brand name develops strength in the marketplace when many consumers choose the brand because they consider it salient, memorable, and noteworthy.

Developing a strong brand name

Developing a strong brand begins with discovering why consumers buy a brand and why they rebuy the brand. Questions to be asked include:

- What are the most compelling benefits?
- What emotions are elicited by the brand either during or after the purchase?
- What one word best describes the brand?
- What is important to consumers in the purchase of the product?

Once the answers to these questions are known, a company is ready to develop a stronger brand position.

Two important processes help establish stronger brand prestige. First, the brand name must be prominently promoted through repetitious type ads. Because of the colossal number of brands and the myriad of advertisements consumers encounter, repetition is essential to capture the individual's attention and to store the message in his or her knowledge structures. Second, the brand name must be associated with its most prominent characteristic.[13] For example, many consumers associate Crest with "cavity prevention." Coca-Cola seeks to associate its name with a product that is "refreshing." For Volvo, the impression is "safety." For BMW, it is "performance driving."

Brands develop histories. They have personalities. They include strengths, weaknesses, and flaws. Many brands produce family trees.

A **family brand** is one in which a company offers a series or group of products under one brand name. For example, Black & Decker has its name on numerous power tools. The advantage of a family brand is that consumers usually transfer the image associated with the brand name to any new products added to current lines. Thus, when Black & Decker offers a new power tool, it automatically assumes the

This advertisement by Ford is designed to convince consumers that the brand stands for "built tough." Courtesy of Ford Motor Company.

reputation associated with the Black & Decker name. These transfer associations occur as long as the new product is within the same product category. When additional products are not related to the brand's core merchandise, the transfer of loyalty may not occur as easily.

The goal of branding is to set a product apart from its competitors. Market researchers must seek to identify the "one thing" the brand can stand for, that consumers recognize, and that is salient to consumers. When these tasks are successfully completed, more powerful brand recognition occurs. Notice the Ford advertisement in this section. In developing the brand for its SUVs and trucks, Ford has tried to convey to consumers that its vehicles are durable and tougher than the competition's.

Once brand recognition is achieved, the next step is to prolong its success. The secret to a long brand life is finding one unique selling point and sticking with it. A company that attempts to change the concept associated with a brand often confuse consumers and, in the long run, hurt its overall corporate image.

An example of brand image confusion may be found in American Express's attempt to move into the discount brokerage business. American Express officials hoped to take advantage of a high-quality image associated with the company's credit card service through a highly visible and expensive advertising campaign. The clash between serving as a low-cost discount brokerage and a high-quality credit card service confused consumers, and low sales resulted even as overall stock purchases grew, especially for competing firms such as Charles Schwab and E*TRADE. Consequently, American Express pulled back and moved to lower-cost direct-mail and on-line advertising in the attempt to salvage the project. When the brand does not match the corporation's image, it becomes more difficult to succeed.[14]

Brand equity

A strong brand name gives businesses several advantages associated with what is called brand equity. **Brand equity** is the set of characteristics unique to a brand that allows the company to charge a higher price and retain a greater market share than would otherwise be expected for an undifferentiated product. Such strength provides power to the company as it deals with retailers. This power, in turn, leads to an improved position in terms of shelf space and displays. Brand equity also influences wholesalers by affecting what they stock and which brands they encourage their customers to purchase. Wholesalers often will stock several brands but place greater emphasis on high equity brands.

In business-to-business markets, brand equity often allows a company to charge a higher price. Equity also influences selections in the buying decision-making process. Products with strong brand equity are often selected over products with low brand equity or brands that firms know little about. The same scenario is present in international markets. Brand equity opens doors of foreign firms, brokers, and retailers and provides privileges that products with low brand equity cannot obtain.

Brand equity is a strong weapon that might dissuade consumers from looking for a cheaper product or for special deals or incentives to purchase another brand. Brand equity prevents erosion of a product's market share, even when there is a proliferation of brands coupled with endless promotional maneuvers by competitors. Additional benefits of brand equity are displayed in Figure 4.2.

Brand-name recognition and recall can be built through repetitive advertising. Building brand equity, however, goes beyond mere brand recognition. Kmart has a high brand recognition but has fallen behind Wal-Mart and Target in terms of brand equity. To build brand equity requires the following six steps.[15] The previous section discussed the first three:

1. Research and analyze what it would take to make the brand distinctive.
2. Decide what makes the brand unique.

1. **Allows manufacturers to charge more for their products**
2. **Higher gross margins**
3. **Provides power with retailers and wholesalers**
4. **Additional retail shelf space**
5. **Weapon against consumers switching due to sales promotions**
6. **Prevents erosion of market share**

Benefits of Brand Equity

FIGURE 4.2

3. Boldly communicate the unique selling point of the brand.
4. Spend no more than 30 percent of the communication budget on *driving sales,* which includes techniques such as coupons, sweepstakes, premiums, and price-off incentives.
5. Make domination the goal.
6. Deliver on the promise or uniqueness being communicated.

The first three steps cultivate brand recognition. The last three steps build brand equity. Brand equity cannot be built without brand recognition. To develop brand equity, a firm must create messages that express the product's unique selling point and establish strong, positive consumer feelings. The firm should spend only a small portion of its communications budget on sales-driven techniques (coupons, sweepstakes, premiums, and price-off incentives). Although these techniques increase sales, they tend to affect brand image adversely.

Brand equity involves *domination,* consumers' strongly held view that the brand is number one in its product category. Domination can take place in a geographic region or in a smaller product category or market niche. Domination is associated with any product benefit that consumers desire. In each case, the brand must be viewed as number one in some way by consumers. For instance, with toothpastes, the number-one cavity fighter is Crest. For automobiles, the number-one car in terms of safety is Volvo.

Perhaps the most critical aspect of brand equity is delivering on the promise. If Crest promotes itself as the cavity fighter, then it must deliver on that promise. Consumers have to believe that Crest does a better job of preventing cavities than does any other brand of toothpaste. Recently, Buick launched a massive campaign designed to displace Volvo's position by making Buick known as the safest automobile. Buick's attack on Volvo's "safety" position is based on the premise that Volvo is not delivering the highest degree of safety due to the firm's recent cost-cutting measures. Still, for Buick to become viewed as the safest automobile, the company must demonstrate that its cars have surpassed Volvo's safety record.

The Mazda automobile company is attempting to move its image away from being price based and toward being a producer of stylish designs in performance cars. In the effort to simplify and clarify this image, the firm focuses advertisements on the overall company name rather than on individual products, ending with the tag line "Mazda: Get in, be moved." The program extends from new-product introductions, to advertisements, to advice given in a handbook to local dealerships, each stressing the simple consistent message about the organization and its products. The ultimate goal is stronger brand equity, which will occur only if Mazda does indeed produce and deliver stylish performance cars.[16]

Integrated Learning Experience **stop!**

A major consulting firm that has been a leader in extending marketing knowledge is the Boston Consulting Group. Access this Web site at www.bcg.com. Under the "Branding" section, read about the Boston Consulting Group's current thinking on the subject. Two other firms that assist companies with branding are Lexicon Branding, Inc. at www.lexicon-branding.com and Corporate Branding at www.corebrand.com.

Brand extensions and flanker brands

To leverage the equity built in its brands, firms often enter new markets using a brand extension strategy. Figure 4.3 identifies the types of brand strategies firms can utilize. **Brand extension** is the use of an established brand name on products or services not related to the core brand. For example, Nike has been successful in extending its brand name to a line of clothing. Black & Decker has been somewhat successful in extending its brand name to a line of small kitchen appliances. Less successful was the brand extension of Singer in Europe from sewing machines to refrigerators, ranges, and televisions.

An alternative to brand extension is the development of flanker brands. A **flanker brand** is the development of a new brand by a company in a product or service category it currently has a brand offering. For example, Procter & Gamble's primary laundry detergents are Cheer and Tide. Still, the company has introduced a number of additional brands such as Ivory Snow. In total, P&G offers 11 different brands of detergents in North America; 16 in Latin America; 12 in Asia; and 17 in Europe, the Middle East, and Africa. Table 4.1 lists Procter & Gamble's various brands of laundry detergents, cosmetics, and hair care products. The company's marketing team introduced these flanker brands to appeal to target markets that

- **Family brands** a group of related products sold under one name.
- **Brand extension** the use of an established brand name on products or services not related to the core brand.
- **Flanker brand** the development of a new brand sold in the same category as another product.
- **Co-branding** the offering of two or more brands in a single marketing offer.
- **Ingredient branding** the placement of one brand within another brand.
- **Cooperative branding** the joint venture of two or more brands into a new product or service.
- **Complementary branding** the marketing of two brands together for co-consumption.
- **Private brands** proprietary brands marketed by an organization and sold within the organization's outlets.

Types of Brands

FIGURE 4.3

A Procter & Gamble ad featuring one of its flanker brands in the laundry detergent product category.
Courtesy of Procter & Gamble Company.

Procter & Gamble believed its main brand in each product category was not reaching. Thus, flanker brands can help a company offer a more complete line of products. This creates a barriers to entry for competing firms.

Sometimes a flanker brand is introduced when a company's leaders feel that offering the product under the current brand name may adversely affect the current brand. For example, Hallmark created a flanker brand known as Shoebox Greetings (described in Chapter 3's opening vignette). These cards sell in discount stores as well as Hallmark outlets, however, the Hallmark brand sells only in its named retail stores. Shoebox Greeting's cards are lower priced and allow Hallmark to attract a larger percentage of the market. Firms often use this type of strategy in high-end markets that want to compete in low-end markets. It is also used in international expansion. For example, Procter & Gamble sells Ariel laundry detergent in Latin America, Asia, Europe, the Middle East, and Africa, but not in North America. Offering different brands for specific markets is a common flanker brand strategy that helps a firm expand in an international market using more than its current brands.

stop!

Integrated Learning Experience

Brand extensions and flanker branding are common leverage strategies for large corporations. Access the following company Web sites. Examine their various product categories and the brands they offer in each category.

Marriott Hotels (www.mariott.com)
Procter & Gamble (www.pg.com)
Sara Lee Corporation (www.saralee.com)
VF Corporation (www.vfc.com)

TABLE 4.1

**Brands Sold by
Procter & Gamble**

Product Category	North America	Latin America	Asia	Europe, Middle East, and Africa
Laundry and cleaning brands	Bold	Ace	Ariel	Ace
	Bounce	Ariel	Bonus	Alo
	Cheer	Bold	Bounce	Ariel
	Downy	Downy	Cheer	Azurit
	Dreft	Duplex	Doll	Bold
	Dryel	InExtra	Ezee	Bonux
	Era	Limay	Gaofuli	Bounce
	Gain	Magia Blanca	Lanxiang	Dash
	Ivory Snow	ODD Fases	Panda	Daz
	Oxydol	Pop	Perla	Dreft
	Tide	Quanto	Tide	Fairy
		Rapido	Trilo	Lenor
		Rindex		Maintax
		Romtensid		Myth
		Supremo		Rei
		Tide		Tide
				Tix
Cosmetics	Cover Girl	Cover Girl	Cover Girl	Cover Girl
	Max Factor	Max Factor	Max Factor	Max Factor
	Oil of Olay			Ellen Betrix
Hair care	Head & Shoulders	Drene	Head & Shoulders	Head & Shoulders
	Mediker	Head & Shoulders	Mediker	Mediker
	Pantene Pro-V	Pantene Pro-V	Pantene Pro-V	Pantene Pro-V
	Physique	Pert Plus	Rejoy–Rejoice	Rejoy–Rejoice
	Rejoy–Rejoice		Pert Plus	Pert Plus
	Pert Plus		Vidal Sassoon	Vidal Sassoon
	Vidal Sassoon			

Co-branding

Locating Subway's Sandwich Shops in convenience stores, Little Caesar's in Kmart outlets, and McDonald's in Wal-Mart stores is a co-branding trend that has recently mushroomed. **Co-branding** can take three forms: ingredient branding, cooperative branding, and complementary branding. **Ingredient branding** is the placement of one brand within another brand, such as Intel microprocessors in Compaq computers. **Cooperative branding** is the joint venture of two or more brands into a new product or service. Study the advertisement featuring a cooperating branding venture by American Airlines, Citibank, and MasterCard in this section. **Complementary branding** is the marketing of two brands together to encourage co-consumption or co-purchases, such as Seagram's 7 encouraging 7-Up as a compatible mixer, or Oreo milkshakes sold in Dairy Queen stores.[17]

Co-branding succeeds when it builds the brand equity of both brands. For example, when Monsanto created NutraSweet, consumer trust was built by placing the NutraSweet logo on venerable brands consumers trusted, such as Diet Coke, Wrigley's Chewing Gum (Wrigley's Extra), and Crystal Light. The strategy worked so well that NutraSweet is now the standard of quality in the sweetener industry.[18]

Conversely, there can be risks in co-branding. If the relationship fails to do well in the marketplace, both brands normally suffer. To reduce the risk of failure, co-branding should be undertaken only with well-known brands. Co-branding of goods and services that are highly compatible generally will be less risky.

An example of cooperative branding.
Courtesy of Citibank.

Ingredient and cooperative branding tend to be less risky than complementary branding because both companies have more at stake and devote greater resources to ensure success. The Communication Action Box shows how General Electric uses co-branding to expand its own market and reach new markets.

communication**action**

Co-Branding Strategies at General Electric

General Electric spends a considerable amount of advertising funds working to build a positive corporate image through the slogan "We bring good things to life." This image helps establish GE in good standing not only with consumers but also with other businesses.

A recent development in GE's approach to growth occurred when the company began to take advantage of its strong business-to-business ties by co-branding with new partners. Three of these partners include Culligan, Calphalon, and Lenox.

GE produced a co-branded Water by Culligan Profile Performance refrigerator in the summer of 1997. The product offers a built-in Culligan water filtration system. Advertising features the names of both companies with the message accentuating quality-of-life and convenience issues.

Calphalon is a strongly established marketer of high-end cookware. GE co-produced and co-branded a new Profile Performance electric range designed to give consumers greater cooking flexibility and quality heating of foods through an oval-shaped burner. This top-line product is aimed at older consumers (over 45) with higher incomes ($80,000 or more per year).

Lenox and GE have co-branded the GE SureClean dishwasher, designed to maintain the quality of stemware and china. The consumer group being targeted is highly educated adults, ages 25 to 54, with incomes of over $100,000 per year. Lenox has been strongly protective of its brand and only was willing to co-brand with GE because of GE's strong brand equity.

The strength of GE's approach to co-branding begins with the well-established GE name. When coupled with producers holding equally strong corporate images, GE has been able to enter clearly identified segments of the larger market. The net result thus far has been effective targeting of market segments and growth in sales for both GE and the cooperating firms.

Sources: "Puffed Up," *The Economist* (March 21, 1998), p. 82; Tobi Elkin, "Brand Builders," *Brandweek* (February 2, 1998), pp. 16–18.

For small companies and brands that are not as well known, co-branding is an excellent strategy. The difficult task is finding a well-known brand willing to take on a lesser known product as a co-brand. Yet, if such an alliance can be made, the co-brand relationship often builds brand equity for the lesser known brand, as in the case of NutraSweet. Co-branding also provides access to distribution channels that may be difficult to obtain either because of lack of size or dominance by the major brands.

Private brands

Private brands (also known as *private labels*) are proprietary brands marketed by an organization and normally distributed exclusively within the organization's outlets. Over the last 50 years, private brands have experienced a roller coaster ride in terms of popularity and sales. To many individuals, private brands carry the connotation of a lower price and inferior quality. Historically, the primary audience for private labels was price-sensitive individuals. Not surprisingly, private labels often experience a growth in sales during recessions.

Over the past few years, several changes have occurred in the private brand arena, which Figure 4.4 summarizes. First, the quality levels of private label products have improved. In some cases, the quality is perceived to be equal to or better than that of national brands. For example, consumers perceive Nike's clothing merchandise and Gap's private label of clothing to be of excellent quality.

Second, although private labels still tend to be priced around 25 percent lower than national brands, some private labels are priced higher. These higher prices are due to the perceived increase in product quality.

A third major difference is that loyalty toward stores has been gaining while loyalty toward individual brands has been declining. Rather than going to outlets that sell specific brands, many shoppers go to specific stores. They are willing to

1. Improved quality

2. Priced 25% below manufacturer's brands

3. Loyalty toward retail outlets increased while loyalty toward specific brands decreased

4. Increase in advertising of private brands

5. Increase in quality of in-store displays of private brands

Changes in Private Brands

FIGURE 4.4

buy from the brands offered by that store. Because of this increase in store loyalty, many department stores and specialty stores see an opportunity to expand their private brands. Store displays of private brands are now as attractive as those of national brands.

The fourth change in private labeling is in the area of advertising. Because of the increase in the image of private labels, many firms now advertise their brands. Although most advertising is still done within the scope of the store's promotion, some advertising is being designed apart from the store. The purpose of this latter approach is to establish the name as a bona fide brand that can effectively compete with national products. Recently, Sears launched a series of advertisements featuring its Kenmore and Craftsman brands. The emphasis on Sears has been reduced to simply informing consumers where to purchase Kenmore and Craftsman items. Kmart heavily promotes its private lines of Chic, Jacyln Smith, Kathy Ireland, Expressions, Route 66, and Sesame Street. Wal-Mart now has 14 private labels of clothing alone, including labels such as Basic Image, Bobbie Brooks, Catalina, Jordache, and Kathy Lee.

Private labeling has exploded in the area of active lifestyle–related clothing. The successes of Nike, Reebok, and Adidas apparel lines have enticed another sports retailer to create a competing private label. Woolworth Company's Foot Locker, the world's largest active lifestyle and apparel store, has begun to market products under the Flo-Jo (Florence Griffith-Joyner) and Saucony brands. By creating fresh, original private label products, the store competes against other manufacturer brands. Retailers make higher margins from these lower-priced (but still premium) goods.

Some manufacturers have responded aggressively to the inroads made by private labels in the clothing industry. For example, Wrangler and Lee have increased their advertising budgets to restore their brand-name advantage and want to make sure they offer the proper mix of jeans to cooperating stores. They also sew more private label apparel for various retailers. Other partnerships between manufacturers and retailers looking to carry private brands will undoubtedly follow.[19]

Another approach manufacturers have taken to reduce the negative impact of private labels is to expand their own offerings. Sara Lee Corporation—which owns a number of branded apparel companies such as Bali, Playtex, Champion, Ocean, and Hanes—has expanded into the active wear market with the Hanes Sport casual collection. The surge in popularity of active lifestyle clothing has created an increase in sales of other related products such as the sports underwear featured in the advertisement. Hanes Sport manufacturers products for women, men, and children in order to slow the surge of private label entries into the market.

Integrated Learning Experience

Private labels are an important source of revenue for many retail stores and manufacturers. The Private Label Manufacturers' Association promotes manufacturers that produce private labels. From the Web site at www.plma.com, identify the press updates, store brands, and upcoming events that illustrate the importance of private labels for both retailers and manufacturers. To get a feel for how many private label manufacturers exist, access Private Label News at www.plnews.com, and study the various lists of private label manufacturers in the "Product Categories" section.

Brand management during recessions

A **recession** is a phase in which the gross national product (GNP) declines for two consecutive quarters. In most economies, a recession occurs once every four to five years. During a recession, brand managers face the issue of selecting an appropriate response. When the economy is in a slump, prices often rise, layoffs occur, and consumers curb spending. Marketing experts must decide if advertising budgets should be cut and money shifted to promotions that drive sales. Although this strategy may negatively affect profits, it normally prevents market share erosion.

Poor economic conditions do not affect all product categories equally. Luxury goods, such as real estate, furniture, and automobiles, may be strongly affected. Necessity goods, such as food, medicine, and gasoline, may not experience as strong of an impact. Manufacturers and retailers often encounter substitute buying. In other words consumers hunt for lower-priced alternatives. Thus, hamburger is purchased rather than steak, Kool Aid rather than Pepsi or Coke, and so forth, during slower economic periods.

The best approach for coping with a recession depends on a brand's product category. Also, the brand's unique selling point and position in the marketplace are factors. A brand that has promoted itself as the "cheapest" or "lowest-cost" alternative should not change during a recession. In fact, the firm may wish to emphasize such a position.

Building market share is difficult (although not impossible) during recessions, because consumers often become more choosy in their purchases. They are sometimes less willing to experiment and try new brands. Consumers tend to stick with brands they can trust and that provide them with a feeling of security. For example, Levi-Strauss normally projects its brand from a "value-added perspective," which helped it gain market share in Europe, the United States, and Asia during recent recessions.[20]

At the same time, during slow economic times, many companies try to gain on their competitors in terms of both market share and brand equity. In a recent recession, Levi-Strauss promoted itself as a choice that illustrated individuality and self-confidence. This approach often works during a recession because it bolsters an

Hanes Sport is one of many companies that has introduced new products into the active lifestyle wear market. Courtesy of Sara Lee Corporation.

individual's confidence that he or she made a solid decision during a time that the economy is slumping. Levi-Strauss also invested in targeted promotional activities including pop concerts and sponsorships that promoted a sense of belonging and feeling good. Both a sense of belonging and feeling good appear to be important to consumers during slower economic periods.[21]

Another way to gain a competitive advantage during a recession is to increase consumer awareness at a relatively low cost. Many companies cut advertising expenditures during poor economic times. As a result, various media make attractive offers to those willing to advertise. Recent studies in Japan, Asia, and the United States indicated that companies that increased advertising expenditures during recessions always gained in sales, market share, and operating profits. Recessions can be good times to attract new users and encourage brand switching. Because people need to feel secure during recessions, individuals are more willing to switch to a brand they perceive to be a lower risk. Effective advertising helps firms take advantage of this opportunity.[22]

positioning

Another important element in corporate and brand image management is its position. **Positioning** is the process of creating a perception in the consumer's mind regarding the nature of a company and its products relative to the competition. Position is created by variables such as the quality of products, prices charged, methods of distribution, image, and other factors. Positioning consists of two important elements: (1) It is established relative to the competition, and (2) it exists in the minds of consumers. Although a firms attempts to position its products through advertising and other marketing communications, consumers ultimately determine the position of the firm's products. To be effective, firms must either reinforce what consumers already believe about a product and its brand name or shift the consumer's view toward a more desirable position. The former strategy is certainly easier to accomplish than the latter. The goal of positioning is to find that niche in a consumer's mind that a product can occupy.

Positioning is vital for companies such as Procter & Gamble, VF Corporation, Sara Lee Corporation, and Campbell's Soups, because it helps prevent cannibalism among various brands within a product category. For example, Campbell's Soups produces five different types of V8 juice. The one pictured is marketed to individuals concerned about calories and fat content. Campbell's offers a low-sodium version of V8 for individuals on a low-sodium diet, a spicy hot version for consumers who want something with more taste or who need a mixer, and a calcium-enriched version for those who desire more calcium, potassium, or vitamins A and C.

Effective positioning can be achieved in seven different ways (see Figure 4.5). Although companies may try two or three approaches, such efforts generally result in confusing the customer. The best method is to use one of these approaches consistently.

An *attribute* is a product trait or characteristic that sets it apart from other products. Ultra Brite positions itself by the attribute that it makes teeth their brightest. Ultra Brite has chosen a different attribute (whitening) to make a distinction in the consumer's mind because other toothpastes focus more on cavity prevention. In the advertisement on the next page, Sony is promoting the attribute of its projector having a stronger light to its business customers.

Using *competitors* to garner a position in the consumer's mind is another common tactic, whereby one brand is contrasted to show the position of another. For example, in an effort to gain market share, Avis ran a series of advertisements comparing itself to Hertz. Avis admitted the company was not number one, then went on to explain the advantage that second place brought to consumers, because Avis was willing to "try harder" for business.

Use or application positioning involves creating a memorable set of uses for a product. Arm and Hammer has long utilized this approach in the attempt to con-

To prevent cannibalism, Campbell's Soups must position each version of its V8 juice for individual target markets.
Courtesy of Campbell Soup Company.

▶ **Attributes** a product trait or characteristic that sets the product apart from its competitors.

▶ **Competitors** contrasting a particular brand relative to a competing brand.

▶ **Use or application** positioning a brand based on a particular use or application.

▶ **Price–quality** using the price–quality relationship to set a product apart from its competitors.

▶ **Product user** distinguishing a product from its competitors based on who uses it.

▶ **Product class** identifying a particular product by the product class within which it wishes to compete.

▶ **Cultural symbol** identifying a product with a well-known cultural symbol.

**Positioning
Approaches**

FIGURE 4.5

vince consumers to use its baking soda as a deodorizer in the refrigerator. Arm and Hammer has also been featured as a co-brand in toothpaste, creating yet another use for the product.

Businesses on the extremes of the price range often use the *price–quality relationship.* At the top end, businesses emphasize high quality while at the bottom

A business-to-business advertisement positioned based on the product's attributes.
Courtesy of Sony Electronics, Inc.

end, low prices are emphasized. Hallmark Cards cost more but are for those who "only want to send the very best." Other firms seek to be a "low-price leader," with no corresponding statement about quality.

A *product user* positioning strategy distinguishes a brand or product by clearly specifying who might use it. Apple Computers originally positioned itself as the computer for educational institutions. Although this strategy helped it grow rapidly, Apple had a difficult time convincing businesses to use its computers in the business arena. Apple had done such a good job with their original positioning strategy that changing people's view was virtually impossible.

Sometimes firms seek to position themselves in a particular *product class.* Orange juice was long considered part of the breakfast drink product class. Years ago, those in the industry decided to create advertisements designed to move orange juice into a new product class, with slogans such as "it's not just for breakfast anymore." If this repositioning is successful, then consumers would consider orange juice at any time during the day. Such a move would be somewhat successful if orange juice is viewed as a "healthy" drink. On the other hand, if the product class is beverages, then orange juice suddenly competes with giants such as Pepsi and Coke and is much less likely to succeed.

The Kenmore appliance brand uses a similar strategy. By seeking to make Kenmore a distinct product class (appliances) separate from retail, Sears tries to take advantage of product class positioning.

Identifying a product with a *cultural symbol* is difficult but, if done successfully, can become a strong competitive advantage for a firm. Chevrolet uses this type of positioning strategy. Chevrolet is advertised as being as American as baseball and apple pie during the summer. Playboy has evolved into an entertainment empire by becoming a cultural symbol, albeit a controversial one. In its advertisement, Stetson attempts to identify its cologne with the American cowboy and the spirit of the West. The ad copy reads that "The attraction is legendary." The purpose of placing this ad in *Glamour* magazine was to entice women to purchase the product for the men in their lives.

Other elements of positioning

Brand positioning is never completely fixed and can be changed. For instance, Gillette, traditionally firmly entrenched with males, has recently launched a massive campaign to position itself in the women's market. The company distributes new products (the Sensor Excel razor and Satin Care shave gel) through direct-marketing efforts such as mailings to consumer homes and free samples in homeroom bags for 14- and 15-year-old girls at school. The positions of the women's products are to be established through ads asking "Are you ready?" with the tagline "Yes, I am!" Gillette designed the campaign to encourage women to view its products as a key part of being physically and psychologically ready for anything. This positioning supports the position of Gillette's men's razors, marketed through the "Best a man can get" slogan.[23]

Understanding how consumers view a product is important to successfully position it. Industry analysts discovered that many consumers perceived the Lexus automobile to be distant and cold. According to Scott Gilbert, co-chairman of Team One Advertising Agency, the Lexus had "been criticized at times for not having enough soul." Current ads, in response, are dedicated to communicating the emotional connection between a Lexus driver and his or her car.[24]

Brand positioning also applies to business-to-business marketing efforts. Crowne Plaza, a subbrand of Holiday Inn, has developed a positioning strategy for upscale business travelers based on attributes. The goal is to provide the services and amenities that business travelers desire along with those relevant to their jobs. At the same time, the company does not provide amenities that might be considered extravagant, so that the room can be charged to an expense account.[25]

The SubmitOrder.com ad positions the company as the business solution for those involved in e-Commerce. A visit to the firm's Web site at www.submitorder.

An advertisement by Stetson using the cultural symbolism of the cowboy as the positioning strategy.
Courtesy of J.B. Stetson Company.

com indicates the firm offers multiple services such as brand development, IT management, data mining, e-distribution services, and customer response services.

Effective positioning is important in the international arena and must be included in the marketing plan when a firm expands into other countries. The Communication Action Box illustrates how MTV successfully positioned the channel in each country into which the company expanded. Often the positioning strategy used in one country will not work in another. Marketing experts carefully analyze the competition as well as the consumers or businesses who are potential customers. After this analysis, the firm is better able to choose a positioning strategy. Although the positioning strategy may need to be modified for each country, the company's overall theme and the brand image should be consistent.

Finally, in positioning products, it is important to be sure that the positioning strategy chosen is relevant to consumers and provides them with a benefit they consider useful in decision making. Aunt Jemima learned the hard way that although the company itself occupied a unique, strong position in the marketplace, sales of frozen waffles, a new product, could not be based on one attribute, a resealable storage bag. The attribute was not important to consumers in the decision process. This was because the product itself, the waffles, had a poor taste relative to fresh waffles.[26]

Brand positioning is a critical part of image and brand-name management. Consumers have an extensive set of purchasing options, which means they can try products with specific advantages or attributes. Effective positioning, by whatever tactic chosen, increases sales and strengthens the long-term positions of both individual products and the total organization.

An advertisement for SubmitOrder.com featuring positioning by product class.
Courtesy of SubmitOrder.com Inc.

communication**action**

MTV is the only television channel currently available on every continent. The MTV image and brand not only is strongly identified with its operations in the United States but also has been launched into many other nations, some of which would not seem to be ideal candidates for a video music channel. For example, when the network expanded into India, executives positioned MTV to fit with the culture of the region by using not only internationally well-known sponsors such as Pepsi and Elle cosmetics but also local production companies including Filmi Fundas and Hipshakers. Also, programming featuring local musicians and a spoof of Hollywood known as Bollywood helped India-based network to succeed and build a major share of the market.

In Latin America, MTV also localized its services and displayed videos from native artists. This programming move helped the company gain a 25 to 30 percent share of the multichannel advertising business. In Singapore, MTV Networks Asia reaches more viewers than the competition through a network of terrestrial, satellite, and cable distribution systems. In each move, the company has managed to capture one key ingredient that specializes the image and brand to the geographic territory. In Asia, MTV began ads that used harsh language and featured a man wearing only a towel around his waist, straddling two large boxes, with a TV set showing the MTV logo between his knees. This "in-your-face" approach gained instant credibility with the audience.

Currently MTV is launching a network in Russia. Each time the company enters a new country, the network must fight the image and perception that MTV's shows will have too strong of an American flavor. Company officials believe that by thinking internationally but acting locally, they will succeed. There is wisdom in this approach, as MTV Europe, Asia, Latin America, India, Russia, and Brazil give them a combined audience of over 400 million households worldwide. The MTV brand has also expanded into products beyond the video network such as videotapes produced for in-home VCRs. Brand positioning must contain components designed to attract a general worldwide audience and then be modified, to whatever degree is possible, to more specific audiences of each country.

Sources: John Lannert, "MTV to Launch Russian Network," *Billboard* (April 18, 1998), pp. 37–38; "MTV International: A Billboard Tribute to the World's First Global Network," *Billboard* (September 13, 1997), pp. 49–66; Diane Goldner, "MTV Rocks Dial to Latin Beat," *Variety* (May 19–25, 1997), p. 22; Fara Warner, "MTV Shuffles Its Lineup: New President to Take Helm of Asian Operations," *Asian Wall Street Journal Weekly* (December 2, 1996), p. 10; Marla Matzer, "Lost in Translation: MTV Fashioned Instant Hip with Harsh Language," *Brandweek* (November 11, 1996), pp. 18–19.

damage control

As illustrated in the Food Lion case at the beginning of this chapter, corporate and brand images can be easily damaged by negative publicity. Strong images, which took years to build, may be destroyed in just a few months or even weeks. Not all negative press is generated by the media, as in the Food Lion situation. Sometimes negative publicity comes from word-of-mouth communication from one customer to another.

For example, consider the fate of Wells Fargo, which had built a strong reputation as a retail banking innovator. Wells Fargo was the first financial operation to replace traditional branch banks with supermarket outlets. The company was among the first to offer Internet banking, Wells Fargo established pilot banks to take advantage of "smart card" technology and pioneered small business loans through credit scoring and direct-mail offerings.

Wells Fargo purchased First Interstate Bancorp in an effort to facilitate continued growth. While reconfiguring the banking system from branch outlets to supermarket outlets, Wells Fargo tried to integrate the First Interstate facilities into the

Reactive Strategies

1. Crisis Management
2. Apology
3. Defense of innocence
4. Excuses
5. Justifications
6. Other explanations

Proactive Strategies

1. Entitlings
2. Enhancements
3. Social responsibility advertising
4. Internet interventions

**Damage Control
Strategies**

FIGURE 4.6

same program. The result was a sharp decline in customer service. The Wells Fargo image became tainted and customers started leaving. Gaining new customers became equally difficult. Word of mouth spread about the poor service that followed the acquisition. The image of being an innovative, service-oriented bank, which had taken Wells Fargo years to build, began to unravel quickly.[27]

Damage control in defense of an organization's image takes place in two ways: (1) reactive strategies and (2) proactive strategies (see Figure 4.6). Firms must react in two potential areas. The first occurs when the firm has made an error or caused legitimate consumer grievances. The second takes place when unjustified or exaggerated negative press appears.

Reactive strategies

Company leaders often must react to unforeseen events, because they cannot anticipate every possible contingency. In these instances, managers must work diligently to blunt the effects of unwanted bad publicity by every means possible. Crisis management and other techniques should be designed to help the firm cope with circumstances that threaten its image.

Crisis management

A crisis may be viewed as either a problem or an opportunity. Many times a crisis contains the potential to improve the firm's position and image. For example, PepsiCo recently encountered a series of charges of hypodermic needles being found in its products. The management team quickly responded with photographs and video demonstrating that such an occurrence was practically impossible, because the bottles and cans are turned upside down while empty before being filled with any soft drink. Next, footage of a con artist slipping a needle into a can was shown. This fast and powerful answer eliminated the negative publicity, and Pepsi was able, at the same time, to make a strong statement about the safety of its products. Pepsi's reaction was quite effective in dealing with this particular crisis. Unfortunately, company leaders sometimes manage only to make matters worse. The recent problem with tires made for the Ford Explorer is an example of a serious safety problem. Time will tell whether the recall of 6.5 million tires was sufficient to resolve the crisis and the damage done to the company's (Bridgestone's) image.

Crisis management involves either accepting the blame for an event and offering an apology, or refuting those making the charges in a forceful manner. Typically, the steps of crisis management are:

1. Advance preparation for any crisis (a crisis management team should be in place).

2. Recognize the crisis.

3. Contain the crisis.

4. Resolve the crisis.

5. Build an advantage from the crisis.

Apology strategies

Using an **apology strategy** is a reactive form of crisis management and damage control. If the end result of the investigation is the revelation that the firm is at fault, an apology should be offered quickly. A full apology contains five elements:[28]

1. An expression of guilt, embarrassment, or regret

2. A statement recognizing the appropriate behavior and acceptance of sanctions because of wrong behavior

3. A rejection of the inappropriate behavior

4. Approval of the appropriate behavior and a promise not to engage in the inappropriate behavior again

5. An offer of compensation or penance to correct the wrong

Apologies are most often used either in situations in which the violation is minor or ones in which the firm or person cannot escape being found guilty.

In the Food Lion story, author William Schecter suggests that the firm might have obtained a much better outcome if an apology strategy had been used. The company should have stated concern for the shoppers' well-being and launched a highly public investigation. If this had been done, customers may have been more forgiving and the firm's image might not have suffered so greatly.

Responding to negative publicity

Negative press causes leaders of companies to behave in the same ways as any person would to protect his or her own personal image. The tendency to protect one's self-image is called **impression management,** or "the conscious or unconscious attempt to control images that are projected in real or imagined social interactions."[29] In order to maintain or enhance self-image, individuals and corporations attempt to influence the identities they display to others. The goal is to project themselves in such a manner as to maximize access to and the visibility of positive characteristics while minimizing any negative elements.

Any event that threatens a person's self-image or desired identity is viewed as a predicament. When faced with such a predicament, individuals make concerted efforts to reduce or minimize the negative consequences. If the predicament cannot be avoided or concealed, then an individual engages in any type of remedial activity that reduces the potentially harmful consequences. Remedial tactics include the following:[30]

- Expressions of innocence
- Excuses
- Justifications
- Other explanations

An *expression of innocence* approach means company leaders provide information designed to convince others (clients, the media, government) that they were not associated with the event that caused the predicament. In other words, they say, "We didn't cause this to happen. Someone (or something) else did."

Excuses are explanations designed to convince the public that the firm and its leaders are not responsible for the predicament or that it could not have been foreseen. Thus, they should not be held accountable for the event that created the predicament (e.g., "It was an act of God. It was totally unavoidable").

Justifications involve using logic designed to reduce the degree of negativity associated with the predicament. Making the event seem minor or trivial is one method. Making the argument that the firm had to proceed in the way it did (e.g., "We pollute because if we don't we'll be out of business, and our employees will lose their jobs") is another form of justification.

Other explanations may be created to persuade individuals that the cause of the predicament is not a fair representation of what the firm or individual is really like. In other words, the case was the exception rather than the rule, and customers should not judge the firm too harshly as a result. (You will hear comments such as "This was a singular incident, and not indicative of the way we do business.")

Many times companies do not always use the best defense when choosing from these tactics. Food Lion, in an attempt to clear its image, decided to fight back by using the "excuses" approach by blaming ABC for unbiased and unfair coverage. Although consumers may have believed that ABC used unethical tactics in gathering the information, the excuse did not clear Food Lion of wrongdoing. In the long run, a more forthcoming approach may have been a wiser choice.

A few years before the Bridgestone problem, Firestone used the defense of innocence approach when charges were leveled that its tires tended to blow up, or explode. Firestone's leaders made the charge that a small segment of consumers was simply putting too much air in the tires, and that this was the cause of the problem. Although the tactic worked in terms of eliminating governmental and class-action suits against the firm, many customers switched their brand loyalties to other manufacturers. In essence, Firestone did not complete the task of managing the crisis and lost an opportunity. Had company leaders developed a different tactic, such as a tire pressure gauge giveaway, to instruct consumers on proper tire maintenance, it may have been possible to eliminate the negative effects of its defective products completely and turn the situation into something more positive.[31]

Integrated Learning Experience

Because of the potential damage bad press can cause a firm, a number of consulting firms have been created to offer crisis management expertise. Public Image Corporation at www.publicimagecorp.com is a full-service public relations agency. Lexicon Communications Corporation at www.lexiconcommunications.com is one of the leading crisis management firms. Access these two firms to see what they say about crisis management as well as what services they offer.

stop!

Proactive strategies

Rather than waiting until harmful publicity occurs and then reacting, many firms utilize proactive strategies to minimize the effects of any bad press. Such approaches may prevent negative publicity from starting in the first place. One method achieving these result comes from the proactive side of the impression management. These techniques are called entitlings and enhancements.[32] **Entitlings** are attempts to claim responsibility for positive outcomes of events. **Enhancements** are attempts to increase the desirable outcome of an event in the eyes of the public.

Entitling occurs when a firm associates its name with a positive event. For example, being the official sponsor of a U.S. Olympic team that wins a gold metal attaches the company's name to the athletic achievements of people who don't even work for the firm, yet the firm can claim responsibility for some aspect of the success.

Enhancements occur when a bigger deal is made out of something that is relatively small. For instance, many products now claim to be *fat free,* which makes it sound like they are diet foods. In fact, many fat-free products have just as many calories as do products that contain fat. At the same time, the fat-free label helps convince customers that the company tries to help them eat a more healthy diet and watch their weight at the same time.

Another method of proactive management is for companies to become involved in their local communities by participating in special events and supporting social causes. The rationale for this type of involvement is to build a "good neighbor" image. If a company constantly pushes the image of being a solid social citizen and neighbor, the public tends to view it in a more positive fashion and is less affected by any negative reports. Also, the media are not as quick to investigate any single consumer complaint they hear. Although these strategies will not overcome bad decisions, poor customer service, illegal or unethical behavior, they do help in some situations.

Social responsibility advertising is another proactive approach to damage control. A considerable amount of publicity exists about the dangers of drinking and driving. As a proactive method to reduce the impact of this kind of publicity, companies such as Anheuser-Busch actively advertise and promote "safe drinking." Ads paid for by Anheuser-Busch appeal to the public not to drink and drive and not to let minors consume alcohol. The goal of these ads is to convince consumers that despite the negative feeling some consumers have toward alcohol, Anheuser-Busch is a responsible corporation and does care about this country's social problems.

Internet interventions are another method of combating negative mouth-to-mouth communication. With the rise of the popularity of the Internet, a new forum for sharing negative word of mouth and spreading bad experiences has arisen: the chat room. Chat rooms provide an environment in which consumers from every part of the world can share horror stories. Because of freedom of speech and First Amendment rights, individuals even can put up Web sites that blast certain industries, companies, or brands.

In an effort to manage proactively what is being said about companies in chat rooms, many companies hire individuals to monitor them. When they see messages criticizing their company or proclaiming untruths, company representatives log into the chat room. They immediately identify themselves as company representatives and attempt to explain the company's viewpoint and correct misconceptions.

implications for **marketing professionals**

Brand Managers and Publicity Departments

Note the tricky relationship between a strong corporate image and bottom-line profits. Be aware that it is difficult to use numbers to express the value of an effective image in an era wherein accountability is such a major concern.

Recognize the value of the following items:

1. An identifiable company logo
2. A brand name that generates both recall and a favorable impression
3. Quality family brands
4. Brand equity
5. Effective use of private labels

Study the company's position and the position of each individual product. Use the attributes of price, competition, use, quality, users, product class, and cultural symbols to identify the positions the company and its products hold. Then, make decisions about the following issues:

1. Is this position where we thought we were?
2. Is this the position we want?
3. If we intend to change our position, where do we aspire to be?
4. Which tactics will move the company and its products to the correct, appropriate, or desired position?

Understand the bottom-line value to damage control. When unfavorable events occur, they affect accountability issues such as:

1. Sales
2. Complaints, lawsuits, legal action by the government
3. Profits
4. Long-term survival concerns

Develop programs to reduce the impact of unfavorable events. Avoid blame placing and work toward more positive responses.

1. Use reactive tactics when necessary.
2. Be as proactive as possible to reduce the potential for negative events and to blunt the impact when they occur.

SUMMARY

An effective integrated marketing communications plan must emphasize, as part of the program, an effective company or corporate image. This image consists of consumer and business-to-business feelings toward the overall organization as well as evaluations of each individual brand the firm carries. An image has both tangible and intangible components. Tangible ingredients include products, advertisements, names, logos, and services provided. Intangible elements consist of policies and practices that change or enhance the company's image in the consumer's mind. A well-developed and well-established image benefits both customers and the company in many ways.

Creating an effective image is a difficult task. It is important to know how all publics view the firm before seeking to build or enhance an image. Rejuvenating the image involves reminding customers of their previous conceptions of the company while at the same time expanding into a closely related area of concern. Once an image is strongly pressed into the minds of customers, it becomes difficult, if not impossible, to change.

A corporate name is the overall banner under which all other operations occur. The corporate logo accompanying the name is the symbol used to identify a company and its brands, helping to convey the overall corporate image. The firm's name and image are important not only to general customers but also to any firms that may make purchases from or conduct business with a manufacturer or service provider.

Brands are names given to products or services, or groups of complementary products. Effective brands give the firm an advantage, especially in mature markets containing fewer actual product or where service differences exist. Strong brands convey the most compelling benefits of the product, elicit proper consumer emotions, and help create loyalty. There are many versions of brands, including family brands, flanker brands, and co-brands. In each, brand equity is built by domination, or the recognition that the brand has one key advantage or characteristic.

Recently, private brands or private labels have become an important component in the success rates of both producers and retailers. Consumers now view private brands as having quality equal to or close to that of more famous manufacturer brand names. At the same time, customers expect price advantages in private label products. Consequently, effective management of brands and products includes creating a mix of offerings that both end users and retailers recognize as a beneficial range of choices.

Brand name management is crucial during recessions. Consumers may be more cautious about switching brands during slow economic periods. At the same time, firms that promote and emphasize key features (safety, low cost, confidence) may be able to build sales, create loyalty, and gain share during recessionary periods.

Positioning is the relative psychological location of the good or service as compared to its competitor's in the views of customers. Marketing managers must select a positioning strategy that highlights the best features of the company's products or services. Positioning is never fixed, because markets evolve over time. Positioning can be established with both the general public and business-to-business customers.

Damage control is the attempt to reduce the effects of either bad press generated by the media or negative word-of-mouth communications between customers. Both reactive and proactive responses are possible. The key to effective damage control is quality management of the impressions made by the firm, its employees, and the products sold. If these impressions are not positive, extensive and irreparable damage may be done to the firm's image and its long-range chances for success in the marketplace.

REVIEW QUESTIONS

1. What is meant by "corporate image"? What are the tangible aspects of a corporate image?

2. How does a corporation's image help customers? How does it help the specific company?

3. How will company leaders know they have created the "right" image for their firm?

4. What is a corporate logo? What are the characteristics of an effective corporate logo?

5. What is meant by the term *stimulus codability*?

6. What is the difference between a brand name and a corporation's overall image?

7. What are the characteristics of a strong and effective brand name?

8. What is the difference between brand equity and brand recognition?

9. Describe the use of brand extension and flanker brand strategies.

10. Name and describe three types of co-brands.

11. How has private branding, or private labeling, changed in the past decade?

12. Describe effective brand management during recessions.

13. What is product–brand positioning? Give examples of various types of positioning strategies.

14. Name the steps involved in effective crisis management.

15. What is an apology strategy? What are the steps involved?

16. What is impression management? How can it be used as a reactive damage control strategy? As a proactive approach?

KEY TERMS

image   overall consumer perceptions or end user feelings toward a company along with its products and services.

corporate logo   the symbol used to identify a company and its brands, helping to convey the overall corporate image.

stimulus codability   items that easily evoke consensually held meanings within a culture or subculture.

brands   names generally assigned to a product or service or a group of complementary products.

salient   when consumers are aware of the brand, have it in their consideration sets (things they consider when making purchases), regard the product and brand as a good value, buy it or use it on a regular basis, and recommend it to other consumers.

family brand   when a company offers a series or group of products under one brand name.

brand equity   a set of brand assets that add to the value assigned to a product.

brand extension   the use of an established brand name on products or services not related to the core brand.

flanker brand   the development of a new brand by a company in a product or service category it currently has a brand offering.

co-branding   offering two or more brands in a single marketing effort.

ingredient branding   a form of co-branding in which the name of one brand is placed within another brand.

cooperative branding   a form of co-branding in which two firms create a joint venture of two or more brands into a new product or service.

complementary branding   a form of co-branding in which the marketing of two brands together encourages co-consumption or co-purchases.

private brands   (also known as *private labels*) proprietary brands marketed by an organization and normally distributed exclusively within the organization's outlets.

recession   a phase in which the gross national product (GNP) declines for two consecutive quarters.

positioning   the process of creating a perception in the consumer's mind about the nature of a company and its products relative to the competition. It is created by the quality of products, prices charged, methods of distribution, image, and other factors.

apology strategy   a reactive form of crisis management and damage control.

impression management   the conscious or unconscious attempt to control images that are projected in real or imagined social interactions.

entitlings   attempts to claim responsibility for positive outcomes of events.

enhancements   attempts to increase the desirable outcome of an event in the eyes of the public.

Internet interventions   a method of combating negative mouth-to-mouth communication by entering chat rooms on the Internet to present the company's position on an issue.

FOOTNOTES

1. William Schecter, "Food Lion's 'Victory'—But at What Price?" *Public Relations Quarterly* (Spring 1997), pp. 20–21; Cornelius B. Pratt, "Food Lion Inc. vs. ABC News Inc.: Invasive Deception for the Public," *Public Relations Quarterly* (Spring 1997), pp. 18–20; Ryan Mathews, "Wrestling with the Lion," *Progressive Grocer* (June 1997), pp. 43–44; Ryan Matthews, "Can Five Wrongs Make One Right?" *Progressive Grocer* (June 1995), pp. 53–59; "Mystery Meat?" *Progressive Grocer* (June 1995), p. 16.

2. Alexandra Lennane, "Speaking for Themselves," *Airfinance Journal* (March 1998), p. 204.

3. Ibid.

4. Christopher Palmeri, "RadioShack Redux," *Forbes* (March 23, 1998), pp. 54–56.

5. Lennane, "Speaking for Themselves," p. 204.

6. "Puffed Up," *The Economist* (March 21, 1998), p. 82.

7. Paul McNamara, "The Name Game," *Network World* (April 20, 1998), pp. 77–78.

8. Ibid.

9. James R. Shennan Jr., "Permanent Media Can Generate a Long Lasting Image," *Hotel and Motel Management,* 201 (1986), p. 30.

10. David J. Morrow, "An Image Makeover," *International Business,* 5, no. 3 (1992), pp. 66–68.

11. Pamela W. Henderson and Joseph A. Cote, "Guidelines for Selecting or Modifying Logos," *Journal of Marketing* (April 1998), pp. 14–30.

12. Andrew Ehrenberg, Neil Barnard, and John Scriven, "Differentiation or Salience," *Journal of Advertising Research* (November–December 1997), pp. 7–14.

13. Chuck Pettis, "Making Ignorance an Opportunity," *MC Technology Marketing Intelligence* (February 1998), pp. 52–53; David Martin, "Branding: Finding That 'One Thing,'" *Brandweek* (February 16, 1998), p. 18.

14. Stephen E. Frank, "American Express Image Fails to Deliver Success for Its Discount-Brokerage Unit," *Wall Street Journal* (May 5, 1997), p. C1.

15. Marsha Lindsay, "Five Ways to Build Brand Equity," *Electrical World* (March 1998), p. 15.

16. Frank S. Washington, "Brand Advertising Pulls Consumers from the Clutter," *Auto Marketing* (April 6, 1998), p. S10.

17. Stephanie Thompson, "Brand Buddies," *Brandweek* (February 23, 1998), pp. 22–30.

18. Ibid. pp. 22–30.

19. Mark Henricks, "Private Labeling: Who Said the Stores Would Get Tired of Manufacturing. . .?" *Apparel Industry Magazine* (March 1998), pp. 20–28; Jeffrey Arlen, "Brands as Beacons," *Discount Store News* 47, no. 20 (October 26, 1998), pp. A8–A9.

20. Prashun Dutt, "Brand Management During Recession," *Asian Business* (May 1998), pp. 32–34.

21. Ibid.

22. Ibid.

23. Pat Sloan, "Gillette Bets $80 Mil on Women," *Advertising Age* (May 4, 1998), p. 63.

24. Kathy Tyrcr, "Lexus Makes an Emotional Appeal: New Team One Campaign Hopes to Dispel Cold, Distant Image," *Adweek,* Eastern Edition (September 8, 1997), p. 5.

25. "The New Address for the Savvy Traveler," *Lodging Hospitality* (April 1998), pp. 74–78.

26. Marc Schwimmer, "Relevance Is a Key, but Relative, Factor," *Brandweek* (January 12, 1998), p. 14.

27. Kenneth Cline, "The Devil in the Details," *Banking Strategies* (November–December 1997), pp. 24–31.

28. Marvin E. Shaw and Philip R. Costanzo, *Theories of Social Psychology,* 2nd ed. (New York: McGraw-Hill, 1982), p. 334.

29. Ibid., p. 329.

30. Ibid., p. 333.

31. Schecter, "Food Lion's 'Victory'—But at What Price?" pp. 20–21.

32. Shaw and Costanzo, *Theories of Social Psychology,* p. 334.

Building an IMC Campaign

Developing a Brand Name and an Image Management Program

One of the major challenges your product and company faces is brand equity. People may not perceive any great difference between items; therefore, a strong brand name is vital to success. If the product or service is part of larger company operations, the image of that firm also plays a key role as you develop your IMC campaign. The Web site www.prenhall.com/clow or access the Advertising Plan Pro disk that accompanied this textbook provides an exercise to help you create an effective brand and a positive image for the firm. Remember, your firm's image is important not only domestically but also in the international arena.

Critical Thinking Exercises

Discussion Questions

1. Dalton Office Supply Company has been in operation for over 50 years and was the predominant office supply company in its region during that time. Approximately 85 percent of Dalton's business is based on providing materials to other businesses. Only 15 percent comes from walk-in customers. Recently, low-cost providers such as Office Depot have cut into Dalton's market share. Surveys of consumers indicate that Dalton has an image of being outdated and pricey. Consumers did report that Dalton's customer service was above average. What image should Dalton project to regain its market share? Outline a plan to rejuvenate the company's image.

2. Henry and Becky Thompson plan to open a new floral and gift shop in Orlando, Florida. They want to project an image of being trendy, upscale, and fashionable. They are trying to decide on a name and logo. What should be the name of their company? What kind of logo should they develop?

3. Suppose Terminix Pest Control wants to expand through co-branding. To gather more information about Terminix, access its Web site at www.terminix.net. What type of co-branding would you suggest? Which companies should Terminix contact?

4. Look up one of the following companies on the Internet. Discuss the image conveyed by the Web site. What positioning strategy does it use? What changes or improvements could it make?

    a. Secret Sea Visions (www.secretsea.com)
    b. Union Pacific Railroad (www.uprr.com)
    c. Bicycle Museum of America (www.bicyclemuseum.com)
    d. Metro Dynamics (www.metrodynamics.com)
    e. Canyon Beach Wear (www.canyonbeachwear.com)

5. Research a company that has recently experienced some bad press. What negative things were said about the company? How did it handle the negative press? Did it handle the situation appropriately? Why or why not? What would you have done differently?

"For sale," read the sign in front on Dave's Scuba Shop. Dave Dishman, who loved his business, sadly had to admit that he could not continue operating with the kinds of losses he had been experiencing. He was left to ponder what had gone wrong.

From what he could tell, Dave's problems came in three areas: turnover, inconsistency, and bad public relations. He had tried to deal with all of the issues, but with no success.

The company began with a promising opening weekend. Dave set up shop on the south side of Arlington, Texas, with a small store containing basic scuba equipment items for sale and the offer to make repairs and provide routine maintenance for scuba gear. Early traffic through the store was encouraging, partly due to radio remote features of a local disk jockey, who was an avid diver.

In the first year, Dave sponsored a dive and also provided funds for a diving-for-charity event. He was trying to build a name for his store as the center of activity when it came to diving in the region. He posted billboards promoting his outlet as where the "best scuba gear and repair" could be found.

The first bad break came when Dave's key repairman, John, had to quit. John was a first-class repairman who took the time to do a job right. He never compromised on the quality of a repair, even if the store lost money on the deal. John's wife, who was their major source of income, had gotten a promotion, which meant they had to move. John's talent was easily transferred to another city. Consequently, he agreed to move on.

Dave tried three new maintenance and repair workers in the next six months. Two were male, one was female, and all three were unacceptable. There was either sloppy work to contend with or the work took too long. Dave had to soothe the feelings of many unhappy customers during that time period.

Since Dave couldn't find a good repair person, he decided to do all of the repair work personally. He hired a sales rep to run the front of the store. Mimi was an attractive snorkeling enthusiast. Her only drawback was a great interest in talking about diving rather than selling gear. She was not highly productive in terms of other chores, such as checking out the drawer or restocking shelves. Dave ended up spending longer hours at night fixing things in the "front room." He was also inclined to make mistakes when he was tired, meaning even some of his repairs were suspect.

Word around town was that customers would get an overpriced diving suit with marginal service at Dave's Scuba Shop. Business slowed, and Dave was forced to terminate Mimi, leaving him to run the entire operation himself. Mimi quickly began spreading rumors that Dave was a "jerk," not a good thing to happen in a tightly knit diving community.

Dave decided to try big discounts. He cut prices on all of his products and took out several ads showing how his products were comparably priced with those in major discount stores. To offset his margin losses on scuba equipment, Dave raised the price for his repairs. He soon was spending too much time on the sales floor and not enough in the repair room.

Finally Dave found a competent maintenance person. He could again focus on selling. He lowered the rates for his repair business, but word around town was that his was the highest price in the area.

Dave tried getting more involved in the diving community to offset the negative image Mimi was creating. He had some limited success, enticing a few former customers to come back.

By then Dave pretty well knew that there was insufficient demand to continue operations in the same way. He was at a loss about how to proceed. Before he could even offer a new program, his rent was three months' overdue and several suppliers had "cut him off" until he paid some back bills. He knew the store's credit rating was ruined. Even the utility companies were unhappy.

At that point, Dave had no choice. He had lost his investment and knew his store was about to become one of those nameless and faceless statistics of failed entrepreneurial ventures.

1. What image did Dave try to establish in his store?
2. What image did Dave's Scuba Shop end up projecting?
3. What could Dave have done to maintain and improve the image of his store and his company?
4. Could Dave's Scuba Shop have been salvaged? How?

The Candidate

APPLICATION EXERCISE II

Sheila Patterson wanted to make a career change. Sheila had been a paralegal for the past 10 years and decided to run for circuit clerk of Gastonia County in Illinois. The job essentially involved managing a group of individuals responsible for sending out tax forms and collecting county taxes on vehicles and property.

The trick to getting the job, however, was that Sheila would need to win an election. Local politics are among the most shady and divisive that take place, especially when a good-paying job is at stake. During other elections over the past decade, Sheila was aware that one candidate had seen her billboard ads changed from "Democratic" party to "Communist" party in the middle of the night by a rival. Another black candidate had reported to the media that someone had scrawled the word *nigger* on several campaign posters, and then used the sympathy and backlash vote to win a district election for city council.

The other main issue was name awareness. In the most recent election, a local police chief who had been fired for illegal activities at his last two jobs had his name splashed all over the media for several years. In spite of the negative news about his work habits, the man ran for county sheriff, counting on voters to remember his name and little more. The strategy worked, and the county now is run by a less-than-ethical law enforcer.

Sheila would be running against an incumbent whose primary advantages were that he had his name sent out on tax mailings every December, meaning he had strong name recognition, and that the gentleman was a member of the Republican party, the stronger political party in the area. She knew these two obstacles would be difficult to overcome.

Sheila's major edges in the race were that her opponent would be complacent and not campaign very hard (he had won three times previously) and that she had a major "war chest" to spend on the election. She had carefully raised funds for the past year and would be able to spend three times as much on campaign ads.

Sheila wasn't sure if being female would be an advantage or a disadvantage. In her focus groups, some felt the term *clerk* is readily associated with a female. Others believed that her opponent could capitalize on the management aspects of the job, which was most associated with males.

The primary question Sheila had was about image. She knew the crooked sheriff had won but still wasn't sure a bad image was better than no image at all. On the other hand, she was not sure what kind of image to promote. Her choices were, of course, to make a strong positive case about her skills and qualifications, or to go negative and claim her opponent simply was doing a poor job. There was some evidence that he was unpopular with his staff and that the state auditor had criticized some of his practices for being "sloppy" at best.

Still, Sheila knew the risks of going negative. First, she was divorced and had had a few minor brushes with the law over traffic tickets and reckless driving a few years ago. Her friends warned her that a negative campaign would make her look worse and damage her own image in what could turn into a tight race. At the same time, Sheila knew she only had six months to make people aware of her name and image, and to persuade them to vote against an incumbent, when many people vote only along party lines or for names they recognize.

1. What are the brand image issues in this case?
2. What kinds of ads should Sheila develop for this race?
3. Is there anything else Sheila could do to enhance her chances of winning?
4. Is "no image" better than a negative image in the politics of your hometown? Defend your reasoning with examples.
5. Based on the information given, develop a campaign theme to help Sheila win.
6. If the incumbent uses a negative ad campaign informing the public about Sheila's reckless driving charges and infers that she would also be a careless circuit clerk, how should she react? What type of damage control technique would be the most effective? Why?

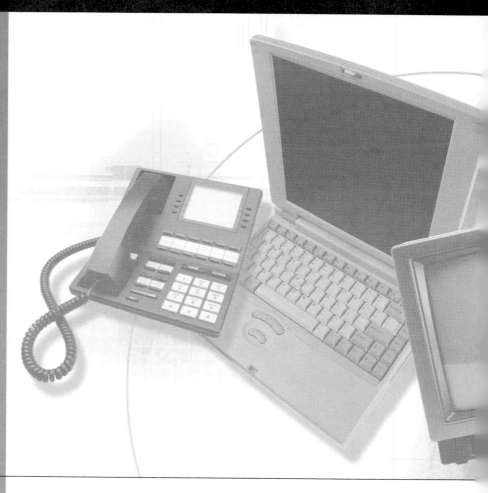

▶ **CHAPTER OBJECTIVES**

Learn how to take advantage of each stage in the consumer purchase decision-making process.

Target advertisements and other marketing communications to meet the emotional and logical needs of consumers.

Refine knowledge about how attitudes and values are reflected in buyer behaviors.

Discover the traditional factors that affect consumer purchasing decisions.

Understand how new trends in society affect purchasing processes.

STARBUCKS CREATES A NEW COFFEE CULTURE

Is it possible to convince ordinary Americans who routinely open three-pound "value" cans of coffee, shovel the grounds into a paper filter, push a button, and go about their business to suddenly change their ways? Will they be willing to spend $2 or more per day on the same item? Will this eventually evolve into a $1,400 per year habit of a *latte* and a *scone* each day? The answers to these questions, according to Starbucks, is "absolutely!"

Starbucks began as a coffee importing firm. Howard Schultz, an employee in the organization, toured Italy in the

early 1980s and watched as crowds of city dwellers began each morning with a stop at a coffee bar. Schultz tried to convince the owners of Starbucks to do something similar in the United States and was roundly rejected. Quitting the firm and launching out on his own quickly turned into a lucrative decision for Schultz. He raised money from a variety of investors and opened a café in Seattle using the name *Il Giornale.* Success came rapidly. Schultz wound up buying the original importing business and renaming his cafés Starbucks.

Within 15 years, Starbucks Coffee Company expanded to over 1,200 retail outlets. The firm achieved this remark-

able growth because of several key marketing ideas. The product itself, locations, employees, sourcing, and effective marketing communications all worked together to help the firm prosper in a saturated marketplace. The nonchalance of major competitors was also a factor.

The product itself, coffee, had been a rather banal commodity for most consumers. Purchase price was traditionally the primary decision variable. Starbucks needed to convince prospective buyers of the difference in its offerings. By studying the basics of coffee (flavor, acidity, and body), the company's leadership sought the best beans in the world. Then, other aspects of the product changed, including steaming milk and brewing coffee in a plunger pot. *espresso* is an acquired taste for most consumers. To reach the market, Starbucks offers it both straight and diluted in creamy drinks such as *caffe lattee,* which is *espresso* mixed with steamed milk and covered with a topping or milk foam. Other products include *cappuccino* and *caffe mocha.* When any one of these Starbucks products is sold, the basic ingredient, coffee, is never more than an hour old.

Locations are key ingredients in Starbucks's success. Cafés must be easily accessible on commuter routes and in other places where people can gather to socialize. In each café there are numerous enticements, including jazz music in the background and other merchandise to examine, such as stainless steel thermoses, commuter mugs, filters, natural hairbrushes for cleaning coffee grinders, and home *espresso* machines.

Starbucks attracts employees who enjoy coffee. They are retained through a variety of motivational programs including buy-in options. Workers are called *baristas,* Italian for "bar person." Starbucks continually encourages these *baristas* to provide high-quality, pleasant service to patrons. Extensive training helps ensure they become experts in all aspects of coffee vending. The company also insists on a diverse workforce reflecting the makeup of the local community.

Starbucks holds a major advantage of sourcing. The firm is vertically integrated and relies on quality suppliers from around the world. Each region grows beans with distinct flavors for coffee connisseurs, and Starbucks brings all of the flavors to a single location for purchase.

The most impressive aspect of Starbucks may be its marketing communications program. The firm had to convince price-conscious buyers to shift away from old purchasing decision rules in order to part with a great deal more money each day. Starbucks also needed to convince some consumers to develop a habit that, to many, seemed like a bad habit because of the caffeine involved.

To achieve these goals, Starbucks noted two primary target markets. The first was the younger, grunge-dominated Generation X types inhabiting the Seattle area. Many people of this generation found coffee shops to be an alternative to the bar scene and made purchases accordingly. Coffee-shop regulars tend to hang out for longer periods of time, reading, talking, and listening to the background music. Next, the baby boom generation became a target as people in their forties and fifties began consuming less alcohol and looking for other products with a degree of "snob appeal." Coffee became an excellent choice. The most loyal boomer customers can discuss coffees such as Jamaican Blue Mountain with as much sophistication as they used to describe wines such as Chateauneuf-du-Pape. Starbucks customers appear to agree that this more expensive but higher-quality coffee makes regular joe seem almost distasteful.

Coffee giants Maxwell House (owned by General Foods) and Folgers (owned by Procter & Gamble) simply ignored the potential of gourmet coffee. The idea of vending coffee in a café seemed so far-fetched to these firms that they did not view Starbucks as a threat, even as Seattle became known as "Latteland." Failing to see the growing market for whole bean coffee as a retail product led to lost market share. In 1990, gourmet coffee companies had a 13.5 percent share of the market. By 1991, the share was up to 17.1 percent. The trend has continued throughout the decade. Today Starbucks easily has as much name recognition and more brand loyalty than its major competitors.

Starbucks has continued to expand through business-to-business marketing efforts based on the strength of the company's name. New customers include United Airlines, the Holland America cruise line, Chicago's Wrigley Field, and a new alliance with Barnes & Noble bookstores. What started as essentially a small blip on the competitive radar is now a major force in the coffee industry. Consumers continue to happily part with extra dollars to support coffee habits that represent something far more complex than simply buying a beverage in the morning. Starbucks has created a whole new coffee culture.[1]

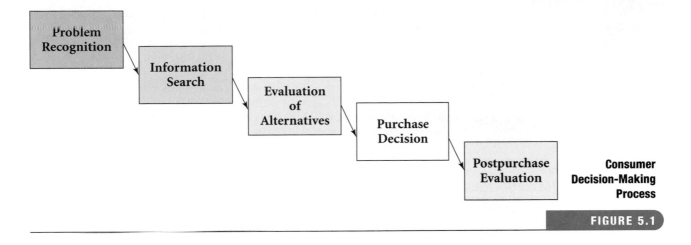

**Consumer
Decision-Making
Process**

FIGURE 5.1

overview

One of the most common practices present in the behavioral and social sciences is *modeling* various activities and behaviors. Marketing experts can utilize models to understand and manage a number of critical factors. Modeling helps researchers develop sophisticated approaches to effectively recognize and react to customer attitudes, preferences, and desires.

This textbook has already presented several models. Chapter 1 showed two models. One represented the communications process, and the second depicted an integrated marketing communications program. Chapter 2 described models of behavior as codes of ethics and approaches to social responsibility. Chapter 3 outlined a planning model. Chapter 4 used a model representing ways to respond to image-related issues.

In this chapter, another important marketing model appears. This one characterizes the processes consumers go through as they make purchasing decisions (Figure 5.1). The model is useful in explaining consumer buyer behaviors as well as recent factors that have affected the choices being made by individuals making purchases.

A primary goal of an integrated marketing communications program must be to develop an effective method of persuading consumers to purchase a particular product or service. Therefore, this chapter reviews *consumer buyer behaviors* from an IMC perspective. When consumer purchasing decisions are more fully understood, it becomes possible to develop better marketing communications programs.

consumer purchasing processes

Marketing managers constantly endeavor to influence consumer decisions. In an era in which they are directly accountable for results of individual campaigns, these marketing experts must carefully develop messages that will entice buyers to purchase the products being featured in a timely fashion. Therefore, it is helpful to step back and look at a traditional model of the process. Figure 5.1 highlights the five steps in the consumer decision-making process: (1) problem recognition, (2) information search, (3) evaluation of alternatives, (4) the purchase decision, and (5) postpurchase evaluation. A detailed analysis of each of these steps follows.

problem recognition

The first step in the consumer decision-making process is the recognition of a problem. A problem is present when a consumer's desired state is different than his or her actual state. In other words, it is the recognition of a need or a want. For instance, after a long day at work, a consumer might go home to look in the refrigerator for food. If there isn't any, then a need is present. Other times, food is in the refrigerator, but it is not the kind the consumer wants. Again, the consumer's current state is different than his or her desired state. In both situations, the consumer identifies a problem.

Recognition of a problem is not always a cognitive event, in which a person actively thinks about a need. Simply seeing and smelling cookies at a bakery triggers a reflex or desire to have them (a want). The consumer must then move forward to satisfy the need or want that exists.

information search

Once a need or want is recognized, the consumer conducts a search for information. This begins with an *internal search;* the consumer mentally recalls images of products that might fulfill or meet the need. Often, the individual remembers how the need was satisfied in the past. If a particular brand was chosen and the experience with that brand was positive, the consumer may repeat the purchase decision. When this happens, further evaluation of alternatives is not necessary. On the other hand, if the previous experience was not positive, the consumer will conduct a more in-depth internal search. Exposures to other brands from past experiences and memories are then considered.

There are many motives present in internal searches. Dissatisfaction with the last purchase is not the only reason an individual conducts a search. He or she may want to try a new brand or product for novelty or variety. For instance, a consumer who normally eats at Taco Bell decides to go to Hardee's instead because she wants to try something different. Further, a consumer expands an information search after hearing about a new or a different brand from a friend or because of a positive response to an advertisement.

When conducting the internal search, consumers utilize what is known as an evoked set. An **evoked set** consists of the set of brands a consumer considers during the information search and evaluation processes. The set does not normally contain every brand the consumer has experienced. The consumer often removes from the evoked set brands that have been tried that did not provide a positive experience. The consumer also usually eliminates brands he or she knows little about. During the information search process, the consumer reduces the number of brands to a subset he or she can mentally manage.

A major objective of creatives and brand managers is to make sure that a given brand becomes part of a consumer's evoked set. When the brand is part of the evoked set, the chances of its being purchased are greatly increased. High-quality, reasonably priced products and services, when accompanied by attractive and powerful advertising messages, greatly enhance the odds that the good or service will become a finalist in the purchasing decision. The Neutrogena advertisement shown on the next page uses "#1" four times to persuade consumers that Neutrogena is the number-one anti-wrinkle cream. If the ad accomplishes this, consumers who want an anti-wrinkle cream will recall Neutrogena as part of their evoked sets and may view the product as the first or best choice.

Following an internal search, consumers make mental decisions about *external searches.* If the customer has sufficient information internally, he or she moves on to the next step of the decision-making process: evaluating the alternatives. When the consumer feels uncertain about the right brand to purchase, an external search takes place.

External information comes from many sources. They include friends, relatives, expert consumers, books, magazines, newspapers, advertisements, exposures to public relations activities, in-store displays, salespeople, and searching the

A Neutrogena ad designed to convince consumers that the product should be their first choice when selecting an anti-wrinkle cream. Courtesy of Neutrogena Corporation.

Internet. The amount of time a consumer spends on an external search depends on four factors: (1) ability, (2) motivation, (3) costs, (4) and benefits.[2]

The first factor that determines how extensively a consumer searches for information is the *ability to search*. Ability depends on the person's educational level combined with specific knowledge of the product category and the brands being offered. An individual's level of education and his or her tendency to conduct external searches are closely connected. That is, educated individuals are more likely to spend time searching for information. They are also more inclined to visit stores prior to making a decision.

Consumers with extensive knowledge about individual brands and product categories can conduct more involved external searches. For example, someone who knows a great deal about cameras has a more sophisticated ability to examine information than does someone who knows little about cameras. In addition, a person with more comprehensive knowledge of a product area often collects additional data even when he or she is not in the market for the product.[3]

The degree to which an external search takes place also depends on the customer's level of motivation. The greater the motivation, the greater the extent of external search. Motivation is determined by the consumer's:

- Level of involvement
- Need for cognition
- Level of shopping enthusiasm

Individuals are motivated to search for information when their involvement levels are high. **Involvement** is the extent to which a stimulus or task is relevant to a consumer's existing needs, wants, or values. The more important a product is to a consumer, the more likely he or she will engage in an external search. The amount of involvement is based on several factors. The cost of the item is a primary concern. Also, the importance the item holds for the consumer is a key variable. Involvement may be enduring or situational. *Enduring involvement* occurs in a purchase situation that always is important to a consumer. *Situational involvement* is based on a particular temporary situation. For example, clothes for many male consumers may not be high-involvement decisions (low enduring involvement), but picking a tux for a high school prom is more likely to include greater levels of involvement (higher situational involvement).

Involvement increases when the purchase of a product helps the customer express a personal value. For instance, for some consumers, cause-related marketing, as described in Chapter 2, is important. There is value associated with the product purchased as well as value associated with the cause or charity the purchase supports. Under these conditions, involvement is more likely to be enduring.

The **need for cognition** is a personality characteristic an individual displays when he or she engages in and enjoys mental activities. These mental exercises have a positive impact on the information search process. People with high needs for cognition gather more information and search more thoroughly than do individuals with a lower need for cognition.

The search also depends on a person's enthusiasm for shopping. Customers who like to shop undertake a more in-depth search for details about products and services. Involvement, need for cognition, and enthusiasm for shopping determine the individual's motivation to search for information.[4]

The final factors that influence an information search are the *perceived costs* and the *perceived benefits* of the search. Higher perceived benefits increase the tendency to search. One benefit that a consumer often looks for while examining external information is the ability to reduce purchase risk. This means that by obtaining additional information a customer can lower the chances of making a mistake in the purchasing selection.

The cost of the search consists of several items:

- The actual cost of the good or service
- The subjective costs associated with the search, including time spent and anxiety experienced while making a decision
- The opportunity cost of foregoing other activities to search for information (e.g., going shopping instead of playing golf or watching a movie)

As would be expected, the greater the perceived subjective cost of the external information search, the less likely the consumer will conduct a search.[5]

The four factors that make up an external search (ability, motivation, costs, and benefits) are normally all considered at the same time. When the perceived cost of a search is low and the perceived benefit high, a consumer has a higher motivation to search for information. A consumer with a minimal amount of product knowledge and a low level of education is less likely to undertake an external search, because the consumer lacks the ability to find the right information.

From a marketing communication perspective, the search process is an important time to reach the consumer with information about a particular brand. The consumer's goal in making the effort to perform an external search is to acquire information leading to a better or more informed decision. The goal of marketers during this stage is to provide information that allows consumers to make the correct decision. Because consumers have not yet made the purchase decision, this is an ideal time for marketers to influence their decision-making processes. The key is to provide the right information at the right time, about costs, benefits, quality, price, image, and any other advantage the company can gain as consumers make comparisons between products. Marketing experts need to consider three additional concepts as they study the information search process: (1) attitudes and values, (2) information processing models, and (3) cognitive mapping.

Integrated Learning Experience

Consumers or businesses conduct external searches when they lack sufficient internal knowledge to make wise purchase decisions. Assume you have $50,000 to $70,000 to spend on a sailboat. Access the following four Web sites:

> www.multihulls.com
> www.yachtworld.com
> www.2hulls.com
> www.boatshow.com

Select a sailboat in your price range. Why did you select that particular brand? What features are attractive to you? Do you want to consider any additional information before making an actual purchase? Would you consider any other sources of information than these Web sites?

Attitudes and values

To fully understand the role of information processing in consumer purchasing decisions, it is helpful to review attitudes and values and how they relate to marketing communications. An **attitude** is a mental position taken toward a topic, person, or event that influences the holder's feelings, perceptions, learning processes, and subsequent behaviors.[6] From a marketing communications perspective, attitudes drive purchases. If a consumer has a positive attitude toward a brand, the propensity to actually purchase that brand is higher. If a consumer appreciates an advertisement, the probability of purchasing the product it features increases.

An attitude consists of three components: (1) affective, (2) cognitive, and (3) conative.[7] The *affective* component contains the feelings or emotions a person has about the object, topic, or idea. The *cognitive* component refers to a person's mental images, understanding, and interpretations of the person, object, or issue. The *conative* component is an individual's intentions, actions, or behavior. The most common sequence of events as an attitude forms is as follows:

$$\text{Cognitive} \rightarrow \text{Affective} \rightarrow \text{Conative}$$

In other words, a person first develops an understanding about an idea or object. In the case of marketing, these ideas center on the nature of the product or service. Thoughts about the product emerge from watching or reading an advertisement. They may result from exposures to information from other sources, such as the Internet or a friend's referral. Eventually, these thoughts become either positive or negative. Most people judge "crime" as "bad" and "helping others" as "good." Consumers make positive or negative evaluations about companies and their products and services. For instance, some consumers may have negative views of credit cards while others see them as helpful and convenient.

The affective part of the attitude is the general feeling or emotion a person attaches to the idea. In the case of goods and services, the product, its name, and other features all can generate emotions. For example, what are your emotional reactions to these goods and services?

- Cough medicine
- Diaper wipes
- Laxatives
- Baseball and apple pie
- *Sports Illustrated*'s annual swimsuit issue
- Condoms

What emotions does this ad for Pampers Wipes elicit? Courtesy of D' Arcy Masius Benton & Bowles Inc. © Procter & Gamble Productions, Inc. 1999. Photograph by Penny Gentjeu.

What emotions and thoughts emerge when you think about diaper wipes? Now, examine the Pampers diaper wipe advertisement shown in this section. What emotions does the ad solicit? Does the picture in the ad change your emotions? As you consider the items listed and this ad, some of your emotions or attitudes about them are relatively benign. Others are more strongly held. It is likely cough medicine does not evoke much of an emotional response, as compared to the swimsuit issue or condoms generate a much stronger reaction.

The decision and action tendencies are the conative part of the attitude. Therefore, if a person feels strongly enough about the swimsuit issue, he or she may cancel a subscription to *Sports Illustrated* or buy extra copies for friends. Many times attitudes are not held that strongly. Some may feel favorably about a topic, such as green marketing, yet not be moved to change their purchasing behaviors.

Attitudes can develop in other ways. An alternative process may be

Affective → Conative → Cognitive

In marketing, advertisements and other communications often appeal first to the emotions or feelings of consumers. The goal is to get a consumer to "like" a product and then make the purchase (the conative component). The cognitive understanding of the product follows. For example, a young woman may be exposed to a feminine hygiene product advertisement featuring soft, gentle images of nature that actually does not show the physical product. Still, the ad conjures favorable emotions. The person eventually purchases the product and finally learns more about it by using it and reading directions, instructions, and other information on the package or label.

Some attitudes result from a third combination of the components, as follows:

Conative → Cognitive → Affective

Purchases that require little thought, have a low price, or do not require a great deal of emotional involvement might follow this path. For instance, while shopping for groceries, a customer may notice a new brand of cookies on sale. The person may have never even seen the brand or flavor before but, because it is on sale, decides to give it a try. As the consumer eats the cookies, he or she develops a greater understanding of the product's taste, texture, and other qualities. Finally, the consumer reads the package to learn more about contents, including how many calories were devoured in one short gulp. Then the buyer finally establishes feeling toward the cookies that will affect future cookie purchases.

No matter which path is taken to develop attitudes, each component is present to some extent. Some attitudes are relatively trivial (e.g., "I like table tennis, even though I hardly ever get to play"). Others are staunchly held, such as "*I hate cigarette smoking!*" Both are associated with feelings toward things, including products in the marketplace, that may eventually result in behaviors (purchases).

Attitudes are shaped, in part, by an individual's personal values. **Values** are strongly held beliefs about various topics or concepts. Values contribute to attitudes and lead to the judgments that guide personal behaviors. Values tend to be enduring and normally form during childhood, although they can change as a person ages and experiences life.

Figure 5.2 lists some of the more common personal values that personality theorists recognize. Individuals hold these values to differing degrees. Factors that affect their impact on the person include the individual's personality, temperament, environment, and culture. These values will be discussed in greater detail in Chapter 8 in the context of advertising design. By appealing to basic values, marketers hope to convince prospective customers that their products can help them achieve a desirable outcome. At the same time, creatives know marketing communications are much more effective in changing a person's attitude about a product than they are in changing a consumer's value structure.

In terms of consumer decision-making processes, both attitudes and values help marketing experts. If a product or service can be tied to a relatively universal value, such as patriotism, then the firm can take advantage of the linkage to present a positive image of the product. The advertisement for Lucky Brand jeans uses the

▶ **Comfortable life**	▶ **Pleasure**
▶ **Equality**	▶ **Salvation**
▶ **Excitement**	▶ **Security**
▶ **Freedom**	▶ **Self-fulfillment**
▶ **Fun, exciting life**	▶ **Self-respect**
▶ **Happiness**	▶ **Sense of belonging**
▶ **Inner peace**	▶ **Social acceptance**
▶ **Mature love**	▶ **Wisdom**
▶ **Personal accomplishment**	

Personal Values

FIGURE 5.2

An advertisement designed to tap into patriotic values of consumers. Courtesy of LuckyBrandJeans.com.

slogan "Always America's favorite" and the fact that "every pair [is] American made" in the attempt to tie into the patriotism value. Lucky Brand further illustrates its desire to support America through the Lucky Brand Foundation logo with the idea that the foundation is "making a difference now."

Attitudes may also be helpful. For example, most people consider being put on hold to be a nuisance. Therefore, a marketing creative may be able to tap into that attitude and use it to present a product or service in a more favorable light. The manner in which individuals process such information further affects decisions and is described next.

Integrated Learning Experience

stop!

Almost everyone has an opinion about tattoos and body jewelry. Some attitudes are positive whereas others are negative. Few are neutral. Examine the following Web sites:

www.bmefreeq.com
www.tattoos.com
www.tattoospa.com
www.allsoulstattooing.com

Did these sites have any impact on your attitude toward tattoos and body jewelry? Which of the businesses would you be most inclined to patronize? What factors in the Web site affected or reinforced your attitude? To which of the personal values listed in Figure 5.2 does each Web site seem to appeal?

Information processing models

The ultimate goal of an integrated marketing communications program is to positively influence the attitudes of consumers and to persuade them to buy a particular good or service. A common tool used in simulating decision-making processes is the **elaboration likelihood model (ELM)**.[8] The ELM is based on the belief that individuals take the time to consider persuasive communication messages designed to change consumer attitudes.

Information processing occurs along two routes in an ELM. The first is the *central processing route*. When a consumer cognitively processes a message, giving a high degree of attention to message's major or core elements, then the pathway is the central processing route. For example, a core message from KFC is "We do chicken right!" Attitudes adopted through the central route (believing KFC does indeed do chicken right) are more firmly held, longer lasting, and resistant to change. Further, attitudes based on exposures to advertisements are excellent predictors of subsequent buyer behaviors. A young man or woman who has developed the attitude that Marines are indeed "The few, and the proud" is more likely to enlist.

The alternate route of processing the information is the *peripheral route.* Individuals follow this path when they pay attention to other, more marginal cues embedded in a communication message. In a television advertisement, peripheral cues can be music, actors, and the background (beach, mountains, forests). When a car salesperson attempts to persuade a customer to purchase an automobile, the peripheral cues include the salesperson's clothes, appearance, demeanor, and tone of voice.

Consumers using the peripheral route pay less attention to the primary message or argument, focusing instead on one or more peripheral cues. The attitude that develops is based on these peripheral cues. For instance, a person who dislikes André Aggassi may develop a negative attitude toward the product he endorses without even listening to or considering what he says about it. Attitudes formed by using the peripheral route tend to be less rigid, less resistant to change, and are poorer predictors of subsequent behaviors than are messages processed through the central route.

Two factors determine the route consumers choose : (1) motivation and (2) ability. Just as motivation impacts the information search itself, it also influences the manner in which information is processed. The more motivated an individual is to search for information, the greater the tendency to process the information using the central route. Highly motivated consumers pay closer attention to the core message argument of an advertisement or sales pitch than they do to peripheral cues.

The second factor, ability, is a consumer's intrinsic desire to use his or her cognitive skills. Individuals who enjoy thinking tend to cognitively process more of the elements of the environment around them. These people pay more attention to the primary message arguments in advertisements and are more inclined to use the central route to process marketing information.

Repetition is an important key when individuals process messages using the peripheral route. The more often a consumer sees a particular advertisement or marketing communication, the better the chance is that he or she will process the message argument. With a greater number of exposures to the same advertisement or communication, peripheral cues tend to become less important as customers attend more to the core message.

The elaboration likelihood model assumes consumers make rational purchase decisions, yet clearly not all purchase decisions are rational. Some purchase decisions are made on the spur of the moment and are highly irrational. They can be made because someone wants to "have fun" or to pursue a particular feeling, emotion, or fantasy. These behaviors are more accurately portrayed using the **hedonic, experiential model (HEM)**.[9] Hedonism is the tendency to maximize pleasure while minimizing pain. Following hedonic impulses often means ignoring longer-term consequences of behaviors while giving in to short-term pleasure.

Information processing using the HEM model uses the same two routes discussed previously: (1) the central route and (2) the peripheral route. The primary difference is in the appeal or content of the message argument. With the ELM approach, the consumer ordinarily pays attention to the elements of message argument pertaining to prices, company attributes, and product qualities or functions. With the HEM approach, the consumer pays attention to elements of the message related to emotions, feelings, fun, and new or unusual experiences. Price advantages and making wise purchases are less important.

Both the ELM and HEM methods of viewing consumer decision-making processes help marketing experts. Account managers direct creatives to focus on one type of appeal or another, based on the product type and target market. For example, one campaign selling life insurance may focus on a rational, cognitive element, with the message directed toward long-term financial security based on careful investments. The creative probably will develop a more serious and intellectual approach to such a campaign. A second campaign may emphasize the more emotional aspects of life insurance, such as showing love, care, and concern for family members. The creative, in that case, should probably design an ad with richer peripheral images, including music and set design elements.

Another important ingredient in understanding attitudes and persuasion is the connections people make when they recall events or things. Cognitive maps help explain the linkages individuals rely on as they think about various ideas.

Cognitive mapping

The manner in which consumers store information and relate that information to previous experiences and other memories can be explained by yet another model. Knowing how people store, retrieve, and evaluate information is a useful tool for companies developing marketing communications. Also, studying how memory works can assist marketers in designing effective advertisements and promotional campaigns.

Cognitive maps are simulations of the knowledge structures embedded in an individual's brain.[10] These structures contain a person's assumptions, beliefs, interpretations of facts, feelings, and attitudes about the larger world. People use their knowledge structures to help them interpret new information and to determine an appropriate response to fresh information or a novel situation. Figure 5.3 is a hypothetical cognitive map for an individual thinking about a Ruby Tuesday's restaurant.

Based on the cognitive structures illustrated in Figure 5.3, when this customer thinks about Ruby Tuesday's, she connects images of it to other restaurants offering fast food and others that provide dine-in services. In this case, the individual recognizes Ruby Tuesday's as a dine-in establishment. The consumer also believes that Ruby Tuesday's offers excellent service, but that the service is slow. Next, when the person thinks of slow service, her thoughts turn to Mel's Diner. When she thinks of excellent service, she also recalls Applebee's. Besides these initial linkages, other features of cognitive maps are present. These include:

Consumers use cognitive mapping to assess and evaluate information.
Courtesy of PhotoEdit.
Photograph by Mary Kate Denny.

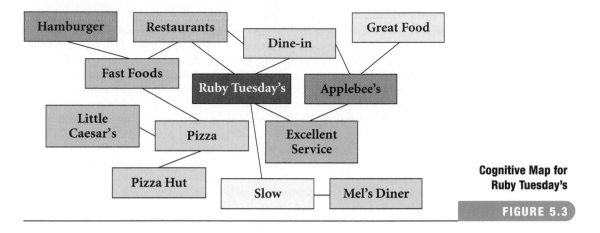

Cognitive Map for Ruby Tuesday's

FIGURE 5.3

- Levels and layers
- Factors that affect existing linkages
- Situations in which a message has no current linkages

Concerning *levels and layers,* remember that Figure 5.3 is a simplified form of a cognitive map. Cognitive structures contain many linkages and can exist on several levels. For instance, one level of cognition is the map with the linkages in Figure 5.3. At another level, the cognitive map is more spatial and conjures images of the actual physical location of Ruby Tuesday's along with the surrounding businesses. A third cognitive map (or another level) of Ruby Tuesday's considers the interior of the restaurant along with other linkages that occur at that level. The consumer can even have a cognitive map of Ruby Tuesday's oriented toward its employees and a relationship she had with an employee who is a friend. Therefore, cognitive processing occurs on many levels using highly complex mechanisms.

The second element of cognitive maps occurs when the person encounters a message with *linkages that already exist.* When consumers process these types of information as they view advertisements or read direct-marketing pieces, the result is often a multi-faceted set of reactions and responses. As a marketing communication item reaches a consumer, several options about how to handle the message surface. If the new information is consistent with current information, then the new information primarily serves to strengthen an existing linkage. For example, when a consumer views a Ruby Tuesday's ad promoting great service, the result may be that the ad will strengthen an existing belief, because the consumer already concluded that Ruby Tuesday's has great service.

A different response can occur in other situations including times when a *message has no current linkages.* For example, if a consumer sees an advertisement featuring Ruby Tuesday's seafood selection, and the consumer did not know that Ruby Tuesday's offers seafood, a different reaction occurs. In order for this information to remain in the consumer's mind and to become linked to Ruby Tuesday's, the customer must create a new linkage between previous Ruby Tuesday's images with other images of seafood.

Hearing something once usually is not enough to cause it to be retained in a person's memory because of the difference between short-term recall and long-term memory. The cognitive mapping process explains knowledge structures embedded in a person's long-term memory. Ordinarily, information is retained in short-term memory for only a few seconds. As stimuli reach an individual's senses, short-term memory processes them. Short-term memory can retain five to nine bits of information. These new messages are either soon forgotten or eventually added to long-term memory. When a message is repeated, an individual is more likely to remember it because it will be processed into long-term memory and fitted into previously developed cognitive maps.

As a result, when a company attempts to introduce consumers to a new brand, the advertisements and other marketing messages should repeat the name of the product several times during the presentation. This repetition improves the chances of its recall at a later time. To illustrate how this works, consider what happens when a person gives a phone number to a friend. To help remember it, the individual repeats the number several times to place it into longer-term recall.

Another way a consumer can process information is to link the message to a new concept. For example, if a consumer sees an advertisement from Ruby Tuesday's emphasizing that it has great food, but has never thought about the restaurant in terms of quality food, that linkage is not currently present. If the advertisement persuades the consumer, she may construct a linkage between Ruby Tuesday's and good food without even traveling to the restaurant. If she does not believe the message, she will ignore or forget the information, and no new linkage evolves. A third possibility is that the consumer recalls the advertisement at a later time and decides to try Ruby Tuesday's. If the food is great, then the link is established at that point. If it is not, the consumer continues thinking that Ruby Tuesday's does not offer good food.

From a marketing perspective, it is easier to strengthen linkages that already exist; adding new linkages or modifying linkages is much more difficult. Regardless of how the information is presented, repetition is important due to the limitations

communication**action**

Marketing to Continuing Caregivers

A new group of consumers has emerged as a target market for many organizations. These individuals are the continuing caregivers or "the sandwich generation." They care for their children and their parents at the same time. Continuing caregivers often provide care for parents longer than they do for children, because of increased life spans.

The typical continuing caregiver is female. These women are very difficult to reach with marketing messages because they do not have time to watch television or listen to the radio. Consequently, marketers try to reach them with alternate media.

Continuing caregivers tend to be creatures of habit. They patronize the same retail stores, not because they particularly like them, but because they know where merchandise is located. Time is critical to them, so they do not like to invest the energy it would take to learn a new store layout. Not surprisingly, sandwich generation customers prefer one-stop shopping where they can find items for themselves as well as for an aging parent or relative.

One method to reach continuing caregivers is through catalogs. Shopping at home is convenient and a time saver. As a result, people in this target market are likely to become active users of on-line services in the coming years.

Continuing caregivers are also value-oriented shoppers. Almost 75 percent said they would try a new brand if it was perceived as a good value. This group is also willing to pay a little higher for a proven brand and does not switch to another brand merely because it is cheaper. They are not status- or brand-conscious consumers, meaning brand names per se do not stimulate purchases. Rather, the perceived value of the brand drives the purchase. Therefore, marketing the concepts of value and convenience is most important to this group.

As the baby boom generation continues to age, more shoppers will find multiple family responsibilities to be part of their cognitive maps regarding purchasing choices and shopping locations. Effective IMC programs will reach them with supportive, sincere, and convenience-oriented messages.

Source: Laura Liebeck, "The Customer Connection: Continuing Caregivers," *Discount Store News,* 37, no. 20 (October 26, 1998), pp. 97–100.

of the short-term memory. Keep in mind that consumers are exposed to hundreds of messages a day. Only a few are processed into long-term memory. Chapter 8 describes this issue in more detail. Advertising techniques that can be used to get and hold a consumer's attention are presented at that point.

Cognitive mapping and persuasion techniques designed to change attitudes or tap into strongly held values are two key ingredients in any IMC program. It is important first to understand the needs and attitudes of the target market. Then, structure messages to fill those needs and to capture consumers' attention by exposing them to messages that will travel effectively through a core processing channel or peripheral channels, either through solid reasoning or alluring emotional appeals.

Further, creatives should attempt to design ads that reach the linkages consumers have already made between a product and other key ideas. For example, a longtime linkage existed between Cadillac and quality, as evidenced by the advertising and promotional phrase "This product is the *Cadillac* . . . [of all products in the market]." Common linkages exist between products and ideas such as quality, value, low cost, expense, fun, sex, danger, practicality, exotic, and many others. Carefully planned marketing campaigns look for linkages to entice the consumer to buy a given product and to believe in (or be loyal to) that product in the future. At that point, the company is ahead of the game as consumers consider their various purchasing alternatives.

Integrated Learning Experience

The two models of information processing discussed in this chapter are the elaboration likelihood model (ELM) and the hedonic, experiential model (HEM). Examine the Web sites:

> Fox (www.fox.com)
> Carnival Cruise Line (www.carnival.com)
> Merrill Lynch (www.ml.com)
> Intel (www.intel.com)
> Campbell Soup (www.campbellsoup.com)
> IBM (www.ibm.com)

For each site, which model is predominant in the processing of information? What peripheral cues does it provide? What is the purpose of the peripheral cues in each site?

stop!

evaluation of alternatives

The third step in the decision-making process is the evaluation of alternatives. Three models portray the nature of the evaluation process: (1) the evoked set approach (described earlier in chapter), (2) the multiattribute approach, and (3) affect referral.

The evoked set method

A person's evoked set consists of the brands he or she considers in a purchasing situation. Two additional components of evoked sets are part of the evaluation of purchase alternatives: (1) the inept set and (2) the inert set. The **inept set** consists of the brands that are part of a person's memory that are *not considered* because they elicit negative feelings. These negative sentiments are normally caused by a bad experience with a vendor or particular brand. They may originate from negative comments made by a friend or by seeing an advertisement that the potential customer did not like.

The **inert set** holds the brands that the consumer is aware of but the individual has neither negative nor positive feelings about the products. Using the terms from cognitive mapping, these brands have not been entered into any map or have only weak linkages to other ideas. The lack of knowledge about these brands usually eliminates them as alternatives. In other words, in most purchase situations, the only brands considered are those that are strongly present in the evoked set.

Procter & Gamble uses intense advertising to ensure that Head & Shoulders is part of a consumer's evoked set when considering hair care products. Courtesy of Procter & Gamble Company. © The Procter & Gamble Company. Used by permission.

Beyond the evoked set, individuals consider a variety of issues as they evaluate alternatives. A new model can simulate this process.

The multiattribute approach

In evaluating alternatives, one method consumers use is the multiattribute approach. The key to understanding this model is noting that consumers often examine sets of attributes across sets of products or brands. The multiattribute model assumes that a consumer's attitude toward a brand is determined by the

- Consumer's beliefs about a brand's performance on each attribute
- Importance of each attribute to the consumer[11]

The higher a brand is rated on attributes that are important to the consumer, the more likely it becomes that the brand will be purchased. Table 5.1 notes products along with some of the characteristics that affect their selection, each with potentially a lesser or greater value to individual consumers. An illustration of this concept is found in the Application Exercise "Buying a Television? It's Not That Simple" at the end of this chapter.

Affect referral

A third model used in the evaluation of purchase alternatives is known as **affect referral.** With this method, a consumer chooses the brand he or she likes the best. The individual does not evaluate the other brands and often does not even think about which attributes are important. Instead, the consumer simply buys the brand he or she likes. Toothpaste, catsup, soft drinks, and milk are some of the products

Product	Characteristics				
Computer	Price	Style	Service contract	Software	Memory–storage
Telephone	Price	Style	Speed dial	Caller ID	Cordless feature
Car	Price	Style	Safety	Room	Other features
T-bone steak	Price	Age	Fat content	Degree cooked	Seasonings
Sunglasses	Price	Style	UV protection	Durability	Prescription lenses
Sofa	Price	Style	Foldout bed	Stain resistance	Color
Credit card	Interest rate	Fees	Billing cycle	Access to ATM	Credit limit

Consider each item. Which characteristic is most important to you personally? Least important?

TABLE 5.1

The Multiattribute Model

consumers normally select using this method. The types of purchases are those with low levels of involvement and those made frequently.

Two things explain why consumers rely on affect referral. First, it saves mental energy. A quick choice is easier than going through the mental process of evaluating all the possible alternatives. Some purchases basically don't deserve much effort, and the affect referral model is useful in those situations.

Second, the multiattribute model may have been utilized previously. The person has already spent a great deal of time considering various product attributes, deciding which are most critical, and reaching a decision about the product with the greatest number of advantages. Therefore going through the process again would be "reinventing the wheel." For example, in purchasing jeans, a teenager may have spent considerable time evaluating styles, prices, colors, durability levels, and "fit" of various brands. After making the purchase, this consumer continues to purchase that same brand as long as the experience remains positive and reinforces the evaluation made.

Using one or more of these three processes (evoked set, multiattribute approach, or affect referral), the individual eventually completes the evaluation of alternatives. At that time, the person stores the knowledge for future use, and recalls it when the time comes to make a purchase, or moves immediately on to purchasing behavior.

the purchase decision

The fourth step in the consumer decision-making process is the purchase decision. Most of the time the consumer purchases the brand chosen during the evaluation of alternatives stage. Keep in mind that evaluations often occur at a retail store, and the purchase decision immediately follows the evaluation. Occasionally, however, the consumer makes a different purchase decision. There are several possible reasons for a shift away from the evaluation process. These include:

- A temporary change in the consumer's situation
- A desire for variety
- An impulse purchase
- An advertisement, consumer promotion, or some other marketing material
- The influence of a friend or relative

Each of these possibilities is briefly described next.

Situational changes

Consumers may not always buy the brands they evaluated as best because of changes in the situation at the time of the purchase. If they are short on money, they may choose a cheaper brand to "get them by" until they can afford their first choice. Or this may mean buying a smaller quantity just to tide them over (e.g., a 10 ounce bag of chips versus the 16 ounce size). If the weather is bad, they may purchase a brand from a store that is closer to avoid making a longer trip. When a store is out of their favorite brand, they may substitute another product or brand rather than going without. At times a sales promotion deal may influence them to buy a different brand, especially for low-cost or low-involvement items.

Desire for variety
A consumer will also purchase a different brand to satisfy an internal need for variety. Individuals tend to get tired of "the same old thing" and want something different as a result. Those who routinely drink Diet Coke occasionally buy a different brand—just to have something different.

Seeking variety does not mean an individual's attitude or past evaluation of various options has changed. Rather, the person decides to purchase an inferior brand merely for the sake of variety. The alternative purchase is essentially a one-time exception to a decision made previously.

Impulse decisions
The "best" alternative may sometimes be ignored in favor of an impulse buy. Impulse purchases normally occur at the store while the consumer is shopping. Some consumers view a product displayed and make an immediate decision to buy it. Candy bars, gum, and magazines usually are offered near checkout registers because consumers purchase these items as an impulse. In retail stores such as Wal-Mart or Kmart, other low-price items appear in the same place, including batteries, small toys, pens, pencils, and so forth.

Impulse purchases occur for more expensive items as well. Clothes are sometimes purchased in this manner. Further, when people travel on vacations, their pocket money essentially takes on a different value. Consequently, T-shirts, memorabilia, and other gift shop–type items become impulse buys. People also make impulsive decisions when Christmas shopping. Retailers are fully aware of the numbers and types of impulse purchases their customers make. Items that cause impulse buys usually are displayed at the front of the store, on center aisles, and in other key places.

Advertisements, consumer promotions, and other marketing materials
At times consumers may also alter purchasing decisions after seeing an advertisement or receiving some type of consumer promotion. For example, an individual writes "lunch meat" on a shopping list and will have a specific brand in mind while traveling to the store. On the other hand, when a person sees an ad, such as the Carl Budding advertisement with a 60 cent coupon, shown in this section, he or she may alter the purchase decision. If this coupon were placed at the store next to the lunch meat section, the change in purchase decision could occur at that instant.

The same is true for other marketing materials. A salesperson at a retail store could encourage a consumer to purchase a different brand of jeans than was intended. An outdoor sign for Wendy's viewed just as a person exits a highway could alter the person's restaurant choice.

The impact of friends and family
Finally, friends, relatives, and other people can alter purchases. At a restaurant, a person may conclude that a particular red wine is the best the restaurant offers and routinely purchases it. On another occasion, the same person, when out with business associates in a social setting, may be more inclined to order a more expensive wine in order to impress those associates. He may purchase the wine even though it is more expensive, but at the same time, in the consumer's mind, is inferior or not

Firms can use a consumer promotion to alter consumer purchase decisions.
Courtesy of Carl Buddig & Company.

the best-tasting choice. Consumers make similar decisions when they buy products because they know their parents will like them better, or to suit the needs and tastes of friends.

Remember, these four cases are the exceptions. Ordinarily a person who has thought about a decision and evaluated the alternatives chooses the best available option. Only unusual circumstances lead to differing purchasing decisions. Even then, the purchase process is not complete. One further item remains.

postpurchase evaluation

The final step in the consumer decision-making process is the postpurchase evaluation phase. During this time, a consumer evaluates of the purchase. This review is the comparison of what he or she expected with what actually occurred. If the product or service meets his or her expectations, then the shopper is satisfied. If the product or service does not meet those expectations, then the individual experiences dissatisfaction. Sometimes the reaction is not based on using the product but rather takes place immediately following the physical purchase.

In situations where there is high involvement, a socially visible purchasing experience, or if the product or service is expensive, consumers often experience doubt after purchases. This is known as **postpurchase cognitive dissonance.** This form of dissonance is most likely when the consumer has spent a substantial amount of time searching for information and evaluating the different alternatives. Because of the investment in time, money, and ego, it is natural for a consumer to question a decision. To reduce the tension or sense of disharmony associated with cognitive dissonance, consumers continue to pay attention to advertisements and other marketing materials. These communications, along with other endorsements and reassurances (including those made by the sales agent) can help the individual believe a good decision was made.

In making postpurchase evaluations, consumers often compare the brand they chose with those they did not. For example, if a consumer purchased a new stereo, undoubtedly several brands were evaluated before the purchase decision. It may have been a very tough decision, and the consumer could have viewed two or three brands as being just about equal to one another. After the purchase, the consumer could be exposed to numerous advertisements by the competitor and none by the firm selling the chosen brand. If so, this increases the level of dissonance.

It often costs a firm five to six times more to gain a new customer than to keep a current customer. Because of this, marketing executives work diligently to retain current customers. Consider the impact of postpurchase evaluations in the banking industry. In a national survey, 90 percent of the sample said they were satisfied or very satisfied with their bank. Seventy-six percent said they were likely or very likely to recommend the bank to a friend. Word-of-mouth communication has a very strong impact on service purchases; consequently, having a friend recommend a bank can be instrumental in gaining new customers.[12]

The most intriguing part of the banking study, however, was that 51 percent of the respondents said they had recently switched banks. This suggests that even customers who appear to be satisfied may be motivated to switch. Why did they change banks? Common reasons given were because:

- The new bank had better operating hours and more convenient locations.
- The old bank changed personnel and banking policies frequently.
- The old bank let mistakes go uncorrected.
- Service charges were excessive at the old bank.
- The customer had not developed a relationship with the bank.

The fifth reason appeared to be the most critical to customers. The survey's respondents indicated they wanted banks that could be trusted and have their best interests at heart. The types of things that build a sense of trust and a more personalized attachment to the bank include:

- Calling customers by name
- Creating advertisements and promotions that communicate the ways the bank has the customer's interests at heart
- Encountering a brightly lit, comfortable physical environment
- Finding bank employees who answer questions and solve problems
- Receiving quick feedback when problems occurred

Although banking is a situation in which trust and a sense of security are key components, these same features apply to other services as well. Every type of organization, from a restaurant to an auto repair company, benefits when consumers believe they can trust the firm and its employees.

The importance of the postpurchase stage should not be underestimated. This step in the process is critical because it has a strong impact on future decisions. If a customer is satisfied, he or she is more likely to repurchase the brand in the future. If dissatisfaction occurs, a customer is more inclined to purchase another brand.

Also, consumers often talk to others about their purchases. A satisfied customer provides positive word-of-mouth communications to friends, relatives, and even strangers. Dissatisfied customers spread negative comments. These negative reports damage the firm's image and affect perceptions others develop about the product.

An effective integrated marketing communications plan addresses postpurchase evaluations and the potential for cognitive dissonance. Advertisements depicting satisfied customers giving positive testimonials serve this purpose. Comparative ads showing the advantages of the chosen brand over competing brands can be successful in reassuring customers. Phone calls by sales and customer service representatives may be used to reassure customers that they have made good purchase decisions and verify that all of their expectations were met. Direct-mail pieces can be designed to reach customers following a purchase. These items provide consumers with additional product information while reassuring them about the purchase. People like to believe they make quality decisions.

In summary, marketing professionals can take advantage of every step of the consumer purchasing decision-making process. First, they can both identify times when needs are likely to occur (problem recognition) and spur additional needs for products or services by making products appear attractive and desirable. Second, they can try to be certain that a given brand becomes part of the individual's evoked set as the consumer searches internally and externally for information. Third, they design messages to reach a salient information processing channel as the consumer evaluates alternatives. Fourth, they can develop final persuasion tactics for the key moments when the purchase decision is actually made, including the aesthetics of the store, the techniques the sales representative uses, and the ease of physically making the purchase (no waiting lines, credit availability, etc.). Fifth and finally, marketing communications must address postpurchase dissonance issues. Marketers constantly need to reassure customers that they have made wise choices with their dollars and decisions. Then, the IMC program works effectively in conjunction with the consumer's decision-making process.

the consumer buying environment

Utilizing the standard steps consumers employ to make purchasing decisions remains an effective tool for studying marketing communications. At the same time, the environment in which purchases are made rapidly changes and constantly evolves. It is important to examine these new features of the purchasing climate. In this section, two factors are examined. First, traditional factors that affect consumer buying decisions. Second, recent trends influencing purchasing habits.

traditional factors

To understand the consumer buying process, marketers should be reminded of the traditional elements of the buying environment. Purchases are often affected by the environment in which they take place. Figure 5.4 lists factors that impact buying behavior. Notice that the items are quite similar to those described in Chapter 3 as segmentation variables. This is because segmentation assumes individuals can be separated into homogeneous groups based on their buying behaviors. Each of the factors shown in Figure 5.4 will now be described in greater detail.

> ▶ **Demographics (age, gender, income, etc.)**
> ▶ **Heredity and home environment**
> ▶ **Family life cycle**
> ▶ **Life-changing events**
> ▶ **Cultural environment**
> ▶ **Social environment**
> ▶ **Situational environment**

Traditional Factors Affecting Consumer Purchasing Behavior

FIGURE 5.4

Demographics

Children under 13 represent 21 percent of the U.S. population. They spend nearly $24 billion annually on goods and services. In addition, children directly influence an additional $187 billion in family purchases. Children tend to spend 33 percent of their money on food and beverages, 28 percent on toys, and 15 percent on apparel. Many make their own purchasing decisions and can be influenced by various marketing communications. The goal of many companies (e.g., Coke and Pepsi) is to turn these young prospects into lifelong customers.

As children move into teenage years, many take on greater responsibilities at home to help parents who work. Some teenagers work part time to earn extra money. Peer pressure mounts as children grow into teenagers, affecting many purchase decisions. To reach these consumers, marketers must understand the changes that teenagers experience, both physically and psychologically. Advertising and other marketing communication tools can be used to reach this group, but the message must be tailored to them.[13]

At the other end of the age spectrum are senior citizens. This group consists of individuals who vary widely in their attitudes toward purchasing. They buy gifts for grandchildren as well as travel, leisure, and health products for themselves. In sum, every age is related to purchasing behavior, and as a result age can be used as means of segmenting the market and designing marketing communications.

Age is just one of the demographic variables that impacts purchase behavior. Marketing professionals should identify viable demographic market segments and create communications that appeal to those groups. The RCA ad in this section specifically targets a particular age group, teenagers.

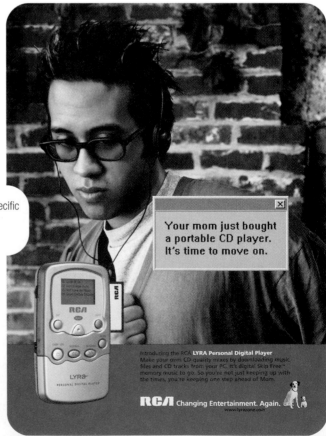

An advertisement targeted to a specific demographic group—teenagers.
Courtesy of RCA.

Heredity and home environment

Heredity and the home environment are important influences on an individual's purchasing behavior. Children often display purchasing behaviors similar to those of their parents and other family members. Many attitudes and values are transmitted at home, and become strongly held, potentially lifelong features of the consumer's personality.

For example, a common characteristic of baby boomers is a tendency to substitute money and gifts for emotional support. Working spouses facing intense time pressures use gifts and money to demonstrate their love for a child, rather than time and involvement. The children of baby boomers are now displaying the same type of behaviors as their parents. Thus, this phenomenon appears to be a learned behavior rather than an inherited one. Marketers can target goods, services, and messages to those affected by the guilt of not spending enough time with their kids, as well as other inherited and home environment issues.

Family life cycle

The family life cycle affects purchasing behaviors. Some relatively standard stages in the life cycle of the family include:

- Being single (bachelorhood)
- Newlyweds with no children
- First families (with young children)
- Full nest (with growing and teenage children)
- Empty nest (children have moved out)
- Remaining partner (following death of a spouse)

Each of these stages creates unique marketing opportunities. An example is shown in the Communication Action Box "Marketing to First Families."

An advertisement directed to first families and the arrival of a new baby.
Courtesy of State Farm Insurance Companies.
© State Farm Mutual Automobile Insurance Company, 1997. Used by permission.

communicationaction

First families are those in which couples have started having children. To qualify as a first family, the oldest child is still not a teenager. In this group, children are the central focus. First family parents are willing to buy their kids just about anything. In various surveys, 60 percent say they put the needs and wants of their children ahead of their own.

About 50 percent of first families have dual incomes. Although parents of young children are family oriented, they also are wrapped up in their careers. Almost 80 percent report that one key to happiness is being able to support their family financially.

The demands of providing for their children leads nearly 60 percent of first family parents to say they don't have enough leisure time. This compares unfavorably to the 44 percent of the population as a whole that desires more free time. Dual career families are the most likely to report they do not have enough time for rest and relaxation.

The dynamics of an involved family life combined with long hours of work lead first family parents to desire convenience and time-saving features from their products and services. Financial strains cause them to look for bargains and buy products they perceive to be better values. Reaching parents with marketing messages can often be a challenge. The average workweek for husbands is over 50 hours per week and for wives is 40 plus hours. Both must also spend time commuting. When they are at home, one or both parents are often involved in a child's activities, such as soccer, PTA, music lessons, parent–teacher conferences, and so forth.

Consequently, IMC programs must seek out the places to expose such parents to advertisements. Drive time radio spots and later night television programming offer some contacts. Creative companies often find places where these families' children will be to advertise to the adults. Bathroom walls in fast-food outlets, fences surrounding soccer fields, and billboards on well-traveled commuter routes may be keys to reaching these frazzled and busy members of the community.

Source: Robert Scally, "The Customer Connection: First Families," *Discount Store News,* 37, no. 20 (October 26, 1998), pp. 85–87.

Life-changing events

Life-changing events also influence consumer buyer behaviors. Some of the more prominent life changes that impact or modify purchasing behaviors include divorce, remarriage, death of a spouse, a spouse renewing or starting a second career, having a parent move into the home, and a major illness in a family member.

One of the main events that drastically affects purchasing behaviors is divorce and remarriage. Remarried divorcees represent about 10 percent of the population. These individuals tend to develop a new outlook on life that alters many things, including their purchasing patterns. This group, called *second chancers*, is usually between the ages of 40 and 59 and has a higher household income.

Second chancers are more content with life than are average adults. They tend to be happy with their new families but also have a different focus in life. They spend less time trying to please others and more time seeking fuller, more enriching lives for themselves and their children or spouse.

A few companies successfully market to second chancers. One is the IKEA company. IKEA launched a unique advertising campaign featuring a divorced woman and her daughter shopping for furniture. The ad notes that the ex-husband received most of the household goods in the divorce settlement. PreVision Marketing of Concord, Massachusetts used a list of newly divorced individuals to launch a marketing campaign directed toward them. The list also was an effective

Years ago, the only insurance a woman had was her husband.

These days, what kind of women need
to have life insurance?
  Women who manage companies.
  Women who manage households.
  Women who somehow manage.
  Women with children.
  Women with husbands.
  Women without husbands.
  If you think you may be one of them,
simply call your State Farm agent.

State Farm Understands Life.

State Farm Life Insurance Company (Not licensed in NY or WI) • State Farm Life and Accident Assurance Company (Licensed in NY and WI)
Home Offices: Bloomington, IL • www.statefarm.com

An advertisement directed to women, especially women without husbands. Courtesy of State Farm Insurance Companies. © State Farm Mutual Automobile Insurance Company, 1997. Used by permission.

way to find potential customers for a dating service. It also advertised hair coloring products. Divorcees, especially women, are more inclined to change hair color after a divorce than are women in the general population. In general, second chancers respond to marketing messages that convey the idea of getting back into the swing of things. This group, as a whole, has a tremendous amount of money to spend and is willing to buy quality products and services. Entertainment and vacation services especially appeal to this group.[14]

Each of these groups presents unique marketing opportunities. Care of the elderly, especially following the loss of a spouse, should spark a major increase in products and services as the baby boom generation continues to grow older.

Cultural, social, and situational environments
Other factors that shape consumer buying behaviors include the culture, social setting, and situational environment in which a consumer lives. For instance, a person near the ocean is more likely to develop a taste for seafood. Also, individuals often prefer food, clothing, and music that reflects their ethnic heritage. The cultural background in which a person is raised normally impacts purchasing choices.

Socially visible products such as furniture, automobiles, clothing, and housing affect other buyer behaviors. In one survey, 64 percent of a sample of teenagers said their friends had the greatest influence on clothing purchases, and that the influence was higher than that of parents or the media.[15] Social pressures can be just as great for many adults making clothing purchases. These socially conscious individuals buy clothes that they believe will be accepted and admired by their friends and other social contacts. The need for social acceptance is used to market a wide variety of products and services, ranging from things as minor as perfume or cologne to items as expensive and involved as vacations in the Bahamas.

Many situational factors affect purchasing behavior. These temporary factors change a consumer's thought processes just as a purchase is about to be made. For

> Products–services provide utility

> To satisfy physical needs

> To satisfy psychological needs

> To satisfy social needs

> To satisfy emotional needs

> To satisfy epistemic needs

**Common Reasons
Purchases Are Made**

FIGURE 5.5

example, something as simple as bad weather can change a person's behavior; the consumer avoids a trip that involves a great deal of driving or where access to the store is inconvenient. Further, a great tragedy or major news story, such as the death of John F. Kennedy Jr., caused many consumers to buy newspapers or magazines with additional information about the plane crash as well as books about the lives and times of the Kennedy family.

Other factors affecting purchases

In addition to the environment surrounding consumers, people buy various items for several other reasons. Consumer purchasing decisions are based on a number of factors, some of which are found in Figure 5.5. For example, people buy goods and services because of the utility present in those articles. **Utility** is the value or expected value associated with an item. A product has utility either directly (drinking Kool Aid to satisfy thirst and to get a sugar buzz) or indirectly (thinking that wearing the Tommy Hilfiger brand causes people to assume the consumer is well-off financially and has a strong sense of fashion). Services also have utility. For instance, an instant teller card from a bank has the utility of 24-hour access to cash, plus the ability to conduct other transactions when the bank is closed. People exchange money, in part, for the utility present in the goods and services they purchase.

Other reasons consumers purchase products or services include the drive to satisfy physical, psychological, social, and emotional needs. Few goods are purchased solely because of their physical attributes; a consumer does not purchase deodorant because of the chemicals in the product. Rather, the purchase is made to satisfy social needs, due to the fear that body odor offends others, and due to the belief that smelling good is attractive to others. Automobiles are purchased as much because of psychological issues as they are for their physical attributes.

To be effective in reaching consumers, marketing communication messages must go beyond physical descriptions of the product or service. Instead, messages should focus on the needs the product can satisfy. To illustrate this principle, consider an ad for chewing gum. Simply showing people munching on a given brand probably won't sell much product. Instead, chewing gum commercials emphasize fun, excitement, sexiness, love, romance, and so forth.

An epistemic need is the human desire to obtain knowledge. Some epistemic needs are related to novelty or curiosity. One might satisfy a certain curiosity about celebrities by touring a Planet Hollywood or Hard Rock Café facility. Planet Hollywoods and Hard Rock Cafés are filled with celebrity nostalgia and memorabilia. The Rainforest Café appeals to the concept of novelty because its unique atmosphere sets it apart from other dining spots. Restaurants currently can satisfy basic needs for knowledge by offering computer on-line services while people dine or sip a beverage. In each case, the marketing approach fits the product or service with the customer's desire for knowledge.

Nearly every purchase reflects one or more of the needs shown in Figure 5.5. Consequently, ads and other messages should tap into these items. A more in-depth discussion linking needs to communications is found in Part 3 (the advertising portion) of this textbook.

Integrated Learning Experience

Values and lifestyles (VALS) psychographic segmentation can be a valuable tool for marketers as they prepare their marketing materials. VALS puts adult consumers into eight mutually exclusive groups. Access VALS through the Business Intelligence Center at www.future.sri.com. Once at the VALS site, examine the characteristics of each of the groups. Then take the test to determine into which group you fit. How can VALS help marketers develop advertising messages?

new trends

To conclude this chapter on consumer buyer behaviors, it is important to note some of the more recent trends affecting purchasing patterns listed in Figure 5.6.

Changes in cultural values and attitudes

As mentioned previously, values and attitudes affect many purchasing decisions. Values tend to form during childhood and remain strongly held through life. At the same time, cultural values shift. Some of the attitudes and values shifting at a cultural level include those associated with:

- Sexual orientation
- Use of profanity in public arenas (television programs)
- Tolerance of nudity
- Living arrangements (unmarried couples)
- Views about the end of life, including assisted suicide and "do not resuscitate" orders
- Racial tolerance and acceptance of diversity in society

At that same time, there is considerable intolerance in a segment of society, as witnessed by the wide-ranging number of hate Web sites and paramilitary organizations flourishing throughout the country.

Values in a society continually change and are sometimes dichotomous. For example, as the median age of the population increases (the aging of the baby boom generation), modifications in values are readily evident. While being tolerant of sexuality and other more "liberal" concepts, millions of Americans are, at the same time, returning to more "traditional" values and embracing some form of religion or spirituality. After decades of materialism and self-indulgence, many baby boomers are searching for meaning. Even younger members of society are changing. Many have embraced greater levels of temperance in terms of drugs, alcohol, and sex.[16]

These new values are present in many purchasing decisions. For example, instead of sitting on a beach, some vacationers combine social responsibility with

> - **Changes in cultural values and attitudes**
> - **Time pressures and busy lifestyle**
> - **Cocooning**
> - **Indulgences and pleasure binges**
> - **Desire for excitement and fantasy**
> - **Emphasis on health**
> - **Clanning**

Recent Trends Affecting Consumer Buying Behavior

FIGURE 5.6

their time off by using vacation time to become involved in an altruistic activity. Others travel to places where they witness rain forests and various natural wonders without damaging them. The money they spend helps encourage national governments to preserve these places.

Many consumers increasingly value cause-related marketing. In situations wherein price and quality are perceived to be equal, 76 percent of consumers are willing to switch to a brand associated with a cause. Approximately 65 percent of consumers say they consider a company's involvement with charities or other good causes when purchasing a product.[17]

The restructuring of values in society presents three challenges for marketing experts. The first is to monitor for changes so that the company is aware of what is happening in society. The second is to create products and services compatible with changing values. The third is to design marketing messages that reflect and build on the values target markets and individual customers hold.

Time pressures

Active, busy life styles have had a dramatic impact on consumer behaviors. In one survey, 44 percent of the respondents stated that they would prefer additional free time over more money. Almost 60 percent indicated they have less leisure time now than in the past. This increased time pressure has resulted in a shifting of values and priorities. Consumers focus less on material possessions and more on experiences such as vacations, entertainment, events with friends and family, and dining out.[18]

Time pressures account for increases in sales of convenience items, such as microwave ovens, drive-through dry cleaning establishments, maid services, quick lube and oil change facilities, and one-stop shopping outlets, most notably Wal-Mart's Supercenters. People on the go utilize cell phones and answering machines to make sure they don't miss messages during their busy days.

Cocooning

One of the side effects of a busy and hectic lifestyle is cocooning. The stress of long hours at work with additional hours spent fighting commuter traffic has led many individuals to retreat and cocoon in their homes once they arrive. A major element of cocooning is making the home environment as soothing as possible. Evidence of cocooning includes:

- Major expenditures on elaborate homes
- Extensive and expensive sound systems
- Satellite systems with big-screen televisions
- Swimming pools, saunas, and hot tubs
- Gourmet kitchens with large dining rooms
- Decks and porches
- Moving to the country or to a gated theme community

At the same time, shopping, going out on the town, and even visiting with neighbors is out.[19] Many advertisements emphasize cocooning aspects of shops and services. Recently, Internet ads focused on the utility of shopping at home during the Christmas season to offer the consumer a method to avoid the hustle and bustle of the holidays.

Indulgences and pleasure binges

Some people handle stress through occasional indulgences or pleasure binges such as expensive dinners out and smaller luxury purchases. These produce feelings of comfort and reassurance. Pleasure binges also include "get-away" weekends in resorts and on short cruises. These self-rewarding activities make the consumer feel that all the work and effort is "worth it."

The implications for marketing experts are to note the indulgence aspects of products. For example, a long-time tag line for Preference by L'Oréal was "Because I'm worth it." More recently Clairol's Herbal Essence shampoo and conditioner commercials play to the emotions of pleasure and self-indulgence, with the "yes, Yes, YES!" approach.

Excitement and fantasy

Many people respond to stress through exciting adventures. From theme parks to virtual reality playrooms, consumers enjoy the mental relaxation of experiencing things that seem almost unreal. Many gambling establishments cater to these more exotic types of vacations. IMAX theaters generate a much more exciting experience than do normal movies. As the technology of fantasy continues to develop, more firms enter the marketplace to profit from consumer desires to "get away from it all."

Emphasis on health

The U.S. population continues to age. Two outcomes of this trend are a blossoming interest in health and maintaining one's youthful appearance. Many consumers manage their health by trying to develop a balanced lifestyle. Rather than total abstinence from fried foods, tobacco, or alcohol, many baby boomers and older adults try to limit them to reasonable levels. This includes a regular emphasis on nutrition, exercise, and staying active without feeling too guilty about an occasional overindulgence. To preserve a youthful appearance, some people turn to cosmetics and fashions to make them feel and look younger.

Marketers often create messages about the healthy aspects of products. These goods include vitamins, food products, exercise machines, stress management programs, and herbal remedies. Booming sales of all of these products indicate many people have a growing fascination with a healthy lifestyle.

Clanning

In spite of cocooning efforts, people still feel social needs. To maintain their social lives people occasionally visit friends and relatives. Also, many adults enjoy coffee or *cappuccino* at places such as Starbucks, as noted in the chapter-opening vignette. There, consumers socialize for limited periods while indulging in a low-cost perk.[20] A close circle of friends has replaced wide-ranging contacts and the elaborate social lives that were part of the youthful experiences of many baby boomers and members of Generation X.

Undoubtedly other new trends affect consumers. Each generation contributes new ideas and values that eventually end up in the marketplace and in communication messages selling various goods. Effective integrated marketing communications programs must be devoted to revealing these buying trends, and to preparing messages that speak to the attitudes, values, needs, desires, and expectations of consumers.

Integrated Learning Experience

A current trend for many companies is the development of marketing messages for specific demographic, ethnic, or lifestyle groups. This allows for a more targeted message than possible for the mass audience. Examine the www.women.com Web site. What information does this site provide about women's purchase behaviors? How do they differ from those of men? Because many times their lifestyles are different, marketing to individual ethnic groups may require a more individualized approach. For the Hispanic community, examine www.hisp.com, and for the African American community, go to www.targetmarketnews.com. The Web site www.planetout.com is for the gay and lesbian community. What clues does this Web site provide about the consumer behaviors of members of this group? What evidence do you see at these Web sites of recent trends affecting consumer behaviors (see Figure 5.6)?

stop!

implications for **marketing professionals**

The Marketing Team

Recognize the opportunities that the consumer buying decision-making process identifies. Structure the IMC program to take advantage of those opportunities. This means:

1. Knowing when consumers are likely to experience buying needs.
2. Knowing how to cause customers to feel those needs, and to recall the specific company's products when they experience those needs.
3. Designing ads and other messages that make it more likely that a given product or service will become part of a consumer's internal and external search for information.
4. Making the perceived benefits of finding the company greater than the perceived costs (in the consumer's mind).
5. Tying ads to widely held consumer attitudes and values.
6. Making sure ad information is consistent across potential central and peripheral route processing of the message.
7. Making sure, to whatever extent is possible, that the consumer links the firm's products and services to other positive thoughts as part of his or her cognitive mapping process.
8. Market products emphasizing key features that will show up as being important in consumer multiattribute assessments of goods and services.
9. Making it easy to complete the purchase once the consumer decides on the company. Don't lose sales because of credit snafus, products that can only be back ordered, or stores that are hard to find or access.
10. Providing all of the necessary postpurchase reassurance needed to keep customers happy and loyal to the company.

Remember that, in an era of increased accountability for outcomes, the consumer buying decision-making process is a key ingredient in success. This is because:

1. Purchases are about to be made, so the company must be ready when the customer is on the "hot spot."
2. A consumer can go through the whole process and then actually ignore his or her own choice under extenuating circumstances. Therefore, the company needs to reduce the odds of this happening and try to increase the odds that a consumer will buy its products–services on such a last-minute impulse.

Review all of the key factors that affect consumer purchases. Make sure ads meet those needs effectively.

Carefully study all of the newer trends affecting consumer purchases. Features that are increasingly important to many major target markets include:

1. The relationship between price and value
2. Distinctiveness
3. Convenient access to information (Web sites, noticeable ads)
4. Easy access when problems arise
5. Effective servicing
6. Ease of purchase, especially time-saving features

Make sure that the marketing department gets credit for successful campaigns linked to the consumer buying decision-making process. Collect evidence, such as:

1. Coupons redeemed
2. Internet hits
3. 800 or 880 calls
4. Postpurchase surveys
5. Overall sales figures and changes in sales following a campaign

SUMMARY

There are five steps to the consumer buying decision-making process. Marketing experts and especially creatives must be aware of each step and prepare effective communications that will lead most directly to the decision to buy.

In step 1, the consumer recognizes a want, need, desire, or force that entices him or her to seek out purchasing alternatives. Companies must identify ways to inspire these needs and to have the product readily available for customers who are ready to start looking or to actually make the purchase.

In step 2, the consumer searches for information, internally and externally. Marketing messages must be directed to placing the product or service in the consumer's evoked set of viable purchasing prospects. The more involved the customer feels in the search, the more likely the product will have a longer-lasting impact once it is purchased. Those with greater needs for cognition are attracted to the process of thinking through a decision. Those with a greater degree of enthusiasm for shopping spend more time analyzing the available alternatives. Customers consider the benefits and costs of searches and make more or less rational decisions about how extensively they will seek out information. The elaboration likelihood model explains rational consumer reactions to messages via either central or peripheral channels of thought. Central routes are more direct and focus on the key message. Peripheral cues include the music, setting, and more subtle elements of the message. A hedonic, experiential model utilizes central and peripheral routes but portrays situations in which purchase decisions are designed to pursue fun, pleasure, excitement, and other more pleasurable emotions.

In step 3, the consumer evaluates alternatives. Evoked sets, attitudes and values, and cognitive maps explain how an individual evaluates various choices. Evoked sets reveal which products "make the cut" and receive consideration. Attitudes and values predispose consumers toward some products and companies and away from others. Attitudes are constructed from thoughts, emotions, and behaviors, all of which can be utilized in designing effective ads and marketing messages. Cognitive maps help the customer link what the company says about itself with other experiences. Marketing experts must identify consumer attitudes and values that affect purchase decisions and make sure they do not offend prospects with their messages. Stronger ties can be built with customers when the product or service is favorably attached to strongly held attitudes and values.

In step 4, the consumer makes the purchase. In some instances the individual ignores a decision reached because of some extenuating circumstance. It is the job of the marketing department to eliminate as many of these extenuating circumstances as possible by making the purchase itself easy to complete.

In step 5, the consumer looks for affirmation that a quality purchasing decision was reached. The less reassurance, the greater the degree of postpurchase cognitive dissonance. Marketing experts should design elements of messages and other activities to help customers feel comfortable about the purchasing decisions they have made. It is much easier to retain current customers than to continually attract new ones.

A traditional view of the consumer buying environment suggests that markets can focus on demographic groups as target markets. Factors that routinely affect purchasing decisions include heredity and the home environment; the stage in the family life cycle; life-changing events; and the cultural, social, and situational environments surrounding the consumer. People buy things to receive the utility (value) present in the product or service. They also buy to fulfill or satisfy physical, psychological, social, emotional, and epistemic needs. Marketing experts tailor messages that match their products or services with specific consumer needs.

The new millennium presents a changing buying decision-making environment to marketers. New cultural values and attitudes, time pressures, and busy lifestyles influence what people buy, how they buy, and the manner in which they can be enticed to buy. Many families try to isolate themselves from everyday pressures by cocooning. They also try to escape through indulgences and pleasure binges, by finding excitement or fantasy, and by clanning to meet social needs. An aging baby boom population is more focused on lasting values and on health issues. Marketing can address these needs and lead customers to purchases based on them.

Understanding consumer buyer behaviors within chosen target markets helps the firm construct a more complete and integrated marketing communications program. Effective advertising identifies and meets the various needs, attitudes, values, and goals of consumers. In the future, there will be many new challenges to conquer. Successful companies continue to know their customers and find ways to reach them so that the right product meets the right need at the right time.

1. What are the five steps of the consumer buying decision-making process?

2. How can a marketing account manager take advantage of each step in the consumer buying decision-making process?

3. What is an evoked set? Why is it so important to the marketing department?

4. What is meant by the term *involvement* in the buying decision-making process? Why is it important to marketers?

5. What is the difference between an internal search and an external search?

6. Define attitude. What are the three main components of attitudes, and how are they related to purchasing decisions?

7. How do values differ from attitudes? Name some personal values related to purchasing decisions.

8. What is an elaboration likelihood model? What are its two main pathways, and how do they relate to consumer buyer behaviors?

9. How is the hedonic, experiential model different from the elaboration likelihood model?

10. Develop a cognitive map of your own mind about your most recent major purchase (car, stereo, computer, etc.).

11. What are the key features of the multiattribute approach to evaluating purchasing alternatives?

12. What is meant by affect referral? When is a person likely to rely on such a cognitive approach to evaluating purchasing alternatives?

13. Under what conditions might a person ignore his or her own reasoning processes when actually making a purchase?

14. What is postpurchase cognitive dissonance? Why is it so important to companies that have just sold their products or services?

15. What traditional factors, as described in this chapter, affect consumer purchasing decisions?

16. What new trends affect consumer buyer behaviors? Give an example of one that applies to your life.

17. Do time pressures affect college student purchasing decisions? If so, how?

18. Do college students cocoon? If so, how?

evoked set   consists of the set of brands a consumer considers during the information search and evaluation processes.

involvement   the extent to which a stimulus or task is relevant to a consumer's existing needs, wants, or values.

need for cognition   a personality characteristic an individual displays when he or she engages in and enjoys mental activities.

attitude   a mental position taken toward a topic, person, or event that influences the holder's feelings, perceptions, learning processes, and subsequent behaviors.

values   strongly held beliefs about various topics or concepts.

elaboration likelihood model (ELM)   A tool used in stimulating consumer purchase decision-making process focusing on more rational elements of the decision.

hedonic, experiential model (HEM)   A tool used in stimulating consumer purchase decisions that are spur of the moment and more irrational, based on wanting to "have fun" or to pursue a particular feeling, emotion, or fantasy.

cognitive maps   simulations of the knowledge structures embedded in an individual's brain.

inept set   part of a memory set that consists of the brands that are held in a person's memory but are *not considered*, because they elicit negative feelings.

inert set   part of a memory set that holds the brands that the consumer has awareness of but has neither negative nor positive feelings about.

affect referral   a purchasing decision model in which the consumer chooses the brand for which he or she has the strongest liking or feelings.

postpurchase cognitive dissonance   the feelings of doubt consumers experience after a purchase has been made.

utility   the value or expected value associated with an item.

compensatory heuristics   a purchasing decision model that assumes that no one single brand will score high on every desirable attribute and further that individual attributes vary in terms of their importance to the consumer.

conjunctive heuristics   a purchasing decision model that establishes a minimum or threshold rating that brands must meet in order to be considered.

phased heuristics   a purchasing decision model that is a combination of the compensatory and conjunctive heuristics models.

ENDNOTES

1. Len Lewis, "Coffee Culture," *Progressive Grocer,* 76, no. 11 (November 1997), pp. 20–22; "Starbucks Roasts the Competition," *Journal of Business Strategy,* 16, no. 6 (November–December), 1995; Kate Rounds, "Starbucks Coffee," *Incentive,* 167, no. 7 (July 1993), pp. 22–23; Ingrid Abramovitch, "Miracles of Marketing," *Success,* 40, no. 3 (April 1993), pp. 22–27; Jennifer Rose, "Starbucks: Inside the Coffee Cult," *Fortune,* 134, no. 11 (December 9, 1996), pp. 190–200.

2. Jeffrey B. Schmidt and Richard A. Spreng, "A Proposed Model of External Consumer Information Search," *Journal of Academy of Marketing Science,* 24, no. 3 (summer 1996), pp. 246–56.

3. Merrie Brucks, "The Effect of Product Class Knowledge on Information Search Behavior," *Journal of Consumer Research,* 12 (June 1985), pp. 1–15; Schmidt and Spreng, "A Proposed Model of External Consumer Information Search."

4. Laura M. Buchholz and Robert E. Smith, "The Role of Consumer Involvement in Determining Cognitive Responses to Broadcast Advertising," *Journal of Advertising,* 20, no. 1 (1991), pp. 4–17; Schmidt and Spreng, "A Proposed Model of External Consumer Information Search"; Jeffrey J. Inman, Leigh McAllister, and Wayne D. Hoyer, "Promotion Signal: Proxy for a Price Cut," *Journal of Consumer Research,* 17 (June 1990), pp. 74–81; Barry J. Babin, William R. Darden, and Mitch Griffin, "Work and/or Fun: Measuring Hedonic and Utilitarian Shopping Value," *Journal of Consumer Research,* 20 (March 1994), pp. 644–56.

5. Schmidt and Spreng, "A Proposed Model of External Consumer Information Search."

6. M. Fishbein and Icek Ajzen, *Belief, Attitude, Intention, and Behavior: An Introduction to Theory and Research* (Reading, MA: Addison Wesley, 1975).

7. Richard P. Bagozzi, Alice M. Tybout, C. Samuel Craig, and Brian Sternathal, "The Construct Validity of the Tripartite Classification of Attitudes," *Journal of Marketing,* 16, no. 1 (February 1979), pp. 88–95.

8. Discussion of the ELM based on Richard E. Petty and John T. Cacioppo, *Attitudes and Persuasion: Classic and Contemporary Approaches* (Dubuque, IA: William C. Brown, 1981); C. P. Haugtvedt and Richard E. Petty, "Personality and Persuasion: Need for Cognition Moderates the Persistence and Resistance of Attitude Change," *Journal of Personality and Social Psychology,* 63 (1992), pp. 308–19; Kenneth R. Lord and Myung-Soo Lee, "The Combined Influence Hypothesis: Central and Peripheral Antecedents of Attitude Toward the Ad," *Journal of Advertising,* 24, no. 1 (spring 1995), pp. 73–85.

9. Discussion of the HEM based on Veronika Denes-Raj and Seymour Epstein, "Conflict Between Intuitive and Rational Processing: When People Behave Against Their Better Judgment," *Journal of Personality and Social Psychology,* 66, no. 5 (May 1994), pp. 819–29; Morris B. Holbrook and Elizabeth G. Hirschmann, "The Experiential Aspects of Consumption: Consumer Fantasies, Feelings and Fun," *Journal of Consumer Research,* 9 (September 1982), pp. 132–40; Elizabeth G. Hirschmann and Morris B. Holbrook, "Hedonic Consumption: Emerging Concepts, Methods and Propositions," *Journal of Marketing,* 46 (summer 1982), pp. 92–101.

10. Discussion of cognitive mapping based on Anne R. Kearny and Stephan Kaplan, "Toward a Methodology for the Measurement of Knowledge Structures of Ordinary People: The Conceptual Content Cognitive Map (3CM)," *Environment and Behavior,* 29, no. 5 (September 1997), pp. 579–617; Stephan Kaplan and R. Kaplan, *Cognition and Environment, Functioning in an Uncertain World* (Ann Arbor, MI: Ulrich's, 1982, 1989).

11. Discussion of heuristics and multiattribute model based on William L. Wilkie and Edgar A. Pessemier, "Issues in Marketing's Use of Multiattribute Models," *Journal of Marketing Research,* 10 (November 1983), pp. 428–41; Peter L. Wright, "Consumer Choice Strategies: Simplifying vs. Optimizing," *Journal of Marketing Research,* 11 (February 1975), pp. 60–67; James B. Bettman, *An Information Processing Theory of Consumer Choice* (Reading, MA: Addison-Wesley, 1979).

12. Sugato Chakravarty and Richard Feinberg, "Reasons for Their Discontent," *Bank Marketing,* 29, no. 11 (November 1997), pp. 49–53.

13. Mike Troy, "The Customer Connection: 13–17," *Discount Store News,* 37, no. 20 (October 26, 1998), pp. 60–65.

14. Discussion of Second-Chancers based on Richard Halverson, "The Customer Connection: Second-Chancers," *Discount Store News,* 37, no. 20 (October 26, 1998), pp. 91–95.

15. Mark Dolliver, "Part-time Role Models," *Adweek,* Eastern Edition, 39, no. 44 (November 2, 1998), p. 20.

16. David B. Wolfe, "The Psychological Center of Gravity," *American Demographics,* 20, no. 4 (April 1998), pp. 16–19.

17. Becky Ebenkamp and Myra Stark, "Brand Aid: Cause Effective," *Brandweek,* 40, no. 8 (February 22, 1999), pp. 20–21.

18. "The Devotion Cycle," *Chain Store Age,* 75, no. 1 (January 1999), pp. 52–58.

19. Hester Cooper and Ann Holway, "Consumer Behaviour: The Seven Key Trends," *New Zealand Marketing Magazine,* 18, no. 2 (March 1999), pp. 27–30.

20. Ibid.

21. Schmidt and Spreng, "A Proposed Model of External Consumer Information Search."

22. Buchholz and Smith, "The Role of Consumer Involvement in Determining Cognitive Responses to Broadcast Advertising"; Schmidt and Spreng, "A Proposed Model of External Consumer Information Search"; Inman, McAllister, and Hoyer, "Promotion Signal"; Babin, Darden, and Griffin, "Work and/or Fun: Measuring Hedonic and Utilitarian Shopping Value."

Building an IMC Campaign

Inducing Consumers to Buy a Product

The products and services listed in Chapter 1 are mostly common items. For each one, some type of consumer decision-making process is involved in making a selection. To develop an effective IMC program for the product you selected to market, it is important to comprehend the manner in which a given brand is chosen as well as why one brand may be perceived as the top choice when a set of purchase alternatives appears. Go to the Prentice-Hall Web site at www.prenhall.com/clow or access the Advertising Plan Pro disk that accompanied this textbook to complete the exercise that helps you integrate consumer purchasing activities with the other elements of the IMC program that you already have completed.

Critical Thinking Exercises

Discussion Questions

1. In a study of compulsive buying behaviors among college students, a primary influence was the family. Often one or both parents were compulsive shoppers. Families that displayed other forms of dysfunctional behaviors such as alcoholism, bulimia, extreme nervousness, or depression produced children who were more inclined to exhibit compulsive shopping behaviors. Why do dysfunction behaviors among parents produce compulsive shopping behavior among children? Another component of compulsive buying behaviors is self-esteem. Again, self-esteem is partly inherited but also develops in the home environment.[21] How would self-esteem be related to compulsive shopping behaviors? What other influences other than family might contribute to compulsive shopping behaviors? If an individual has a tendency to be a compulsive shopper, what can (or should) be done?

2. Study the list of personal values presented in Figure 5.2. Identify the five most important to you. Rank them from first to last. Beside each value, identify at least two products or services you have purchased to satisfy those values.

   Gather in small groups of three to five students. Using the information from your list of values, discuss differences among members of the group. Identify how to design a marketing message to appeal to the top value from each person's list.

3. One recent approach used in reaching teenagers by Coca-Cola occurred in 1998. The firm distributed 55 million wallet-size "Coke cards" in various high schools and to college students at spring break parties. Individuals who purchased Coke with the card earned discounts at fast-food outlets, movie theaters, video stores, and theme parks. The real benefit to Coke was the ability to track purchasing information for 55 million teenagers and young adults. Why is this information valuable to Coke? Research has indicated that 10.3 percent of Coke's core customers account for 48.5 percent of its sales.[22] How can the information obtained from tracking Coke cards be used to convert teenagers to core customers? Why does Coke want teenagers to develop a loyalty to Coke at an early age?

4. Cultural values and norms constantly change. In groups of three to five students, discuss the cultural values and norms that have changed in the last ten years. Are these values and norms different from those held by most parents? If so, why? What caused these changes to occur?

5. Look at the following Web sites. Would consumers tend to use the ELM or the HEM approach in processing the information at the site? Is the product or service pro-

moted to satisfy physical, psychological, social, or emotional needs of consumers? If not, how does the site discuss the functional aspects of the product or service? Is the site designed to affect cognitive, affective, or conative elements of the consumer's attitude?

a. Kenneth Cole (www.kennethcole.com)

b. Starbucks (www.starbucks.com)

c. Cadillac (www.cadillac.com)

d. IKEA (www.ikea.com)

e. Baby Gap (www.gap.com/onlinestore/babygap)

Buying a Television? It's Not That Simple

Kelli is evaluating four console television brands. The multiattribute approach to processing information helps explain Kelli's final purchasing decision. In making this purchase, she bases her evaluation on five criteria: (1) quality of sound, (2) quality of picture, (3) style of cabinet, (4) other features, and (5) the price or value of the television. The importance ratings in Table 5.2 indicate that Kelli is most interested in the quality of the sound, because she gave it a 5 rating. Quality of picture and style of cabinet are next, with ratings of 4. Other television features and price are the least important to Kelli.

TABLE 5.2

Example of a Multiattribute Approach Evaluation of Console Televisions by Kelli

Attribute[b]	Importance[a]	Brand A	Brand B	Brand C	Brand D
Quality of sound	5	5	4	3	4
Quality of picture	4	3	4	4	5
Style of cabinet	4	4	5	2	3
Television features	3	3	3	5	4
Price of television (good value)	3	4	2	5	4
Compensatory Score[c]		74	71	69	76

[a] Ranked from 1 to 5 with 5 being highly important and 1 being unimportant.
[b] Each attribute is rated on a score from 1 to 5 with 5 being high performance and 1 being poor performance.
[c] Scores are cumulative sums of the importance rating times the brand evaluation.

The next column of numbers shows her evaluation of each attribute for each brand. In terms of quality of sound, Brand A was the best (Kelli gave it a score of 5). Brands B and D were next. The score of 4 each received indicates approximately equal sound quality. Brand C had the lowest sound quality and thus she gave it a score of 3.

After evaluating all the brands across all the criteria, Kelli will make a decision. There are different ways to calculate the brand with the highest score in Kelli's mind. One method is to multiply each attribute's importance rating times the corresponding evaluation for each brand. Summing these results in the scores is shown in the row labeled Compensatory Score. Using this method, she would choose Brand D because of its overall score. This method of evaluating alternatives is **compensatory heuristics.**

The compensatory heuristics method assumes that no one single brand scores high on every attribute and that individual attributes vary in importance. When considering several brands, consumers make trade-offs. Notice that, in Table 5.2, Kelli rates Brand A as having the best quality of sound, her most important product attribute. At the same time, Brand A has the worst quality picture and she ranked it lowest in terms of television features. Although Brand A had the best sound, it was not the best brand for Kelli because of the poor ratings on other attributes.

When Kelli considers Brand D, she concludes it has good sound, although the sound is not as good as in Brand A. Brand D does have the best-quality picture. In terms of price and television features, it is not the best but is still good. The worst rating Kelli gives Brand D is for the cabinet style. But even there, Brand C's cabinet style rating is lower. To get the best overall television, Kelli has to make trade-offs and choose the best one over all of the attributes evaluated. Consumers are not likely to draw a table like Table 5.2, but they go through a similar process mentally.

A second computational form Kelli can use to make her evaluation is called **conjunctive heuristics.** In this method, Kelli establishes a minimum or threshold rating. She considers only brands that meet the threshold, even when one product ranks high in individual criteria. Going back to Table 5.2, assume Kelli has mentally established a minimum threshold of 4. She discards a brand if it scores 3 or lower on any criterion important to her. Using this method, she would eliminate all five brands because of low scores on individual attributes.

Consequently, consumers can use an *iterative approach*. Quality of sound is most important to Kelli and so she starts there. She rated Brand C a 3, and because this is below the minimum, Kelli eliminates Brand C. Next, Kelli looks closely at Brands A, B, and D. All have good or excellent sound. Therefore Kelli goes to her next most important criterion—quality of the picture. She ranks both quality of picture and style of cabinet each with a "4" in terms of importance. Before Kelli can eliminate any more brands, she has to decide which of those two criteria is more important. Assuming that quality of picture is next, she would eliminate Brand A due to its rating below the threshold. Now Kelli has narrowed her choice to two models, Brand B and Brand D. The next attribute she considers is style of cabinet. Because Brand D is below the threshold, she eliminates it. Thus, she chooses Brand B because it is the only one left.

A fourth calculation can be made using a **phased heuristic** approach. This method is a combination of the others. Going back to Table 5.2, assume that Kelli eliminates any brand with a score lower than a 3 on any criterion. Notice Brand B's rating of 2 on price and Brand C's rating of 2 on style of cabinet. Kelli immediately discards them (Brand B because it is too expensive and Brand C because she does not like its cabinet). This leaves Brands A and D. To make the decision between these two brands, she can use the compensatory heuristic approach. Consumers often use a phased approach similar to this when they have many brands to evaluate. This method easily reduces the evoked set to a smaller and more manageable subset.

Buying a television isn't easy. The same mental gymnastics are part of many purchases. Marketing experts spend a great deal of time trying to make sure that the characteristics you value appear in their products, services, and marketing messages.

1. Go through Table 5.2 and make sure you can explain how Kelli makes her purchase decision, whether product A, B, C, or D is chosen, using the various heuristic models.

2. Construct a similar table for one of the following products:
   a. An automobile
   b. A night out for dinner
   c. A drinking establishment
   d. A new clothing outfit
   e. A spring break vacation

3. For each product listed in Question 2, identify a recent purchase. Explain the process you used to make the purchase decision. Which heuristic model did you use?

The Food Court

Chi-Hung Chien was about to begin an exciting new phase of life. Chi-Hung grew up in Taiwan, but came to the United States to get his education. During his college years, Chi-Hung fell in love with a local girl, married her, and applied for a permanent visa. Even though this meant leaving his family behind, Chi-Hung believed he could get home often enough to see family and friends while building a new life in America.

For the past seven years, Chi-Hung worked at a local Chinese restaurant. He studied the moves of the owners carefully while trying to apply the many things he had learned in college from his marketing major and management minor. Finally, an opportunity presented itself. The biggest shopping mall in town had an opening for a new restaurant in its food court. The Chien family took out its life savings, applied for a small business loan, and obtained additional funding from their parents in order to open the new KA-POW! restaurant.

Chi-Hung spent a great deal of time in the mall prior to making his decision to open his business. Having studied the five steps of the buying decision-making process in college, he was interested to see how they might apply in the mall. After all, there was a considerable amount of traffic through the food court. People stopped to buy soft drinks, snacks, and full meals. Some people ate with families. Junior high and young high schoolers would "hang out" for hours. Shoppers stopped for a quick bite to eat. Even old-timers visited the food court as part of their morning "mall walking" ritual. Most wanted coffee, but the opportunity existed to sell tea to some of these patrons.

The most interesting part of the mall food-buying experience was to watch as an individual entered the food court. Some clearly had their minds made up and traveled directly to the restaurant of their choosing, whether it was McDonald's, Dairy Queen, Sbarros, or Chick-Fil-A, these national chains had steady inflows of traffic. Some of the local outlets had more trouble enticing the quick visit. Spuds Are Us, a baked potato place, and a locally owned taco place had some regular customers, yet nowhere near the same number as McDonald's. Chi-Hung also knew many regulars were simply mall employees.

At the same time, Chi-Hung called numerous clients "wanderers." These shoppers would walk back and forth between shops, trying to decide what kind of food to buy. Several of the stores offered free small food samples to entice the customer to develop a stronger craving for a certain kind of food and make a purchase as a result.

The key seemed to be discovering how various consumer groups made food-buying decisions. Chi-Hung was convinced he could deliver a quality product at a competitive price, with solid service. He just wanted to make sure he knew his potential customers before they even got out of their cars in the mall parking lot.

1. Describe your buying decision-making process the last time you ate at a mall food court.
2. What decision criteria influence a family making a food court purchase? Would they be the same as those for mall rats?
3. Which group should Chi-Hung target, or should he try to sell to everyone?
4. Should KA-POW! offer takeout? Delivery? How else can the company sell additional products?
5. Design an attractive advertisement for KA-POW! using the cognitive → affective → conative approach to influencing consumer attitudes. How can you modify the ad to use the affective → conative → cognitive approach? How can you modify the ad to use the conative → cognitive → affective approach?
6. In a group of three students, design three different advertisements, each using a distinct approach to impact consumer attitude, compare the advertisements and discuss how each approach tries to influence consumer attitudes.

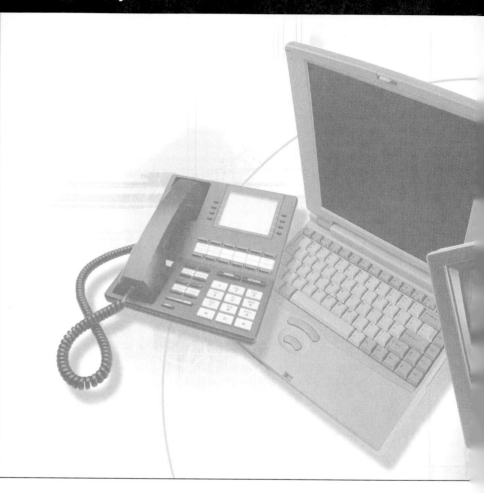

> **CHAPTER OBJECTIVES**

Identify the types of business buyers in the global marketplace.

Review the buying decision-making process and apply it to business-to-business marketing.

Recognize the challenges of dual channel (retail and business-to-business) marketing programs.

Understand the new environment facing companies that sell to other businesses.

INTEL BUNNIES:
The Next Generation In Brand Awareness

Quick, name all of the companies you can think of that sell microprocessors for computers, and the brand names of their products. If you are the typical consumer, you can identify one: Pentium. A few more sophisticated computer consumers may be able to recall one or two more, but in the next breath would probably report that the Pentium is "the best." How did Intel reach this point?

The staggering growth and success rate of the Intel Pentium brand can be traced to an increased demand for personal computers. The original Intel 486 name could not be

patented, because numbers are part of the description of the product's use. This "setback" caused Intel to develop a new brand name right at the time when everyone needed processors, but no one knew their names. The Pentium brand was advertised extensively both in the consumer retail market and in business trade publications directed toward computer manufacturers and software companies. Consumers began asking if the PCs they were about to buy have Pentium processors. At the same time, Intel formed a major alliance with Microsoft as Windows 95 was introduced. Suddenly Intel held a major advantage in the marketplace.

In 1994, a math expert discovered a flaw in one part of the Pentium processor. A second problem, named the "Wob Clobber Bug" was also revealed. What seemed like major obstacles, however, only added to name recognition of the Pentium processor. The company swiftly pointed out that the mathematical flaw would affect only a very small number of applications and just as quickly developed methods to overcome the Wob Clobber Bug problem. By the end of the year, what could have been a tremendous predicament had become an advantage because of the public admission of the problems and attempts to solve them, which bolstered consumer confidence in the company.

As the 1990s came to a close, users required newer, faster processors. Intel sought to continue its dominance in the marketplace by making sure both business customers and retail end users would ask for the Pentium part by name when purchasing computers. In 1997, Intel introduced "BunnyPeople," the workers producing the Pentium II processor. Soon, the Bunnies danced and traveled excitedly across the land in various advertisements and trade shows. These happy chip makers in shiny, colorful suits added humor and a human presence to a high-tech product. The program was so successful that the firm even authorized the manufacture of BunnyPeople dolls.

Two new issues confronted Intel following the introduction of BunnyPeople. One was an increasing insistence for privacy by some consumer groups. Intel designed the Pentium III in such a way that an ID number was easily garnered when the customer accessed the Internet. A boycott followed by a small number of customers who demanded better security from their computers. The company continues to address this issue.

Second, Intel had to move away from its "one size fits all" approach to processor design. Consequently, the company reorganized by the various types of business buyers it serves. Intel created four new business units to meet these needs: (1) the Consumer Products Group, (2) the Business Platform Group, (3) the Small Business and Networking Group, and (4) the Digital Imaging and Video Division.

The Consumer Products Group primarily targets the consumer desktop PC market. New products lines are emerging in this area, including TV set-top computing devices and PCs for automobiles. The Business Platform Group focuses on business computers, including PCs, network computers, NetPCs, workstations, and data security solutions for PCs. The Small Business and Networking Group addresses the needs of smaller companies. This group sells networking products, management software, business communications products, reseller products, and Internet services. The Digital Imaging and Video Division tries to tap a growing market in the audiovisual industry, especially related to stand-alone digital cameras.

The IMC advantage held by Intel began with a demand pull strategy, where it enticed consumers to ask for the Pentium processor by name when purchasing products. The primary message was that Intel offered the fastest and most sophisticated product. Brand recognition by both retail customers and business buyers increased through effective advertising in the early 1990s and grew when BunnyPeople added humor and personality to Intel's Pentium II and III products. By redeploying company resources at the turn of the century, Intel intends to continue to rule the market by carefully meeting the needs of various business buyers, while maintaining its primary image and message. Competitors face a major uphill battle to retake the turf currently held by BunnyPeople in colorful suits.[1]

overview

Many perceive marketing to be a "glamorous" profession. Students majoring in marketing think about designing various goods and services as well as creating innovative programs to move products from the manufacturer to the consumer, while making massive profits for the organization. When compared to the mundane "bean counting" tasks of accounting, or the routine aspects of human resource management such as recruiting and selection, marketing indeed can appear to be more exciting than other business vocations.

Further, advertising may seem like the most "glamorous" aspect of marketing. Creatives designing eye-catching, funny, sexy, or humorous ads appear to work in an alluring field. Advertising design classes are often among the most popular on college campuses, both in the communications department and in the marketing field.

The reality is, of course, that very few people actually get to write ad copy and record or shoot advertisements to be released on television, radio, or through another medium. The majority of people employed in the marketing area work at some other kind of job that is often just as challenging and rewarding.

One of the most vital tasks account executives and others in the field of marketing can perform is to *identify new buyers and new markets for existing goods and services.* Many firms recognize that competition is fierce for individual consumers. As a result, it makes good sense to seek out *other companies* willing to purchase much larger quantities of a company's products. Any effective IMC program must incorporate an in-depth analysis of potential business-to-business outlets the firm can cultivate.

In this chapter, four major items are presented. First, it defines the various types or categories of business-to-business buyers. Second, the major roles associated with making purchases, called the business buying center, are described. Third, the steps of the business purchasing processes are outlined and explained. Fourth, important new factors and issues in business-to-business sales are discussed.

Effective business-to-business sales increase a company's revenues. For some firms, sales to other businesses provide stability in sales figures by offering new markets in conjunction with retail sales efforts. For others, selling to other businesses is the company's primary or sole marketing function. In every case, effective management of communications messages begins with discovering how business buyers make decisions. Once these processes are understood, it is possible to select the proper message, media, and tools to reach these vital market segments.

types of business customers

Business customers purchase both goods and services. This section describes the various types of goods companies sell. The next section outlines the various services required by companies. Many firms buy both goods and services, and many business-to-business operations involve the sale of both goods and services. For the purposes of presentation, however, the two major categories (goods and services) are described separately.

There are two ways to address business customers buying products. The first is to list the types of products that a business would sell to another business. The second is to identify the different types of customers a business would try to reach. Both approaches offer insights into the nature of business-to-business marketing.

types of goods

The types of goods individual businesses purchase include: (1) major equipment, (2) accessory equipment, (3) fabricated and component parts, (4) process materials, (5) maintenance and repair parts, (6) operating supplies, (7) raw materials, and (8) products for resale.[2] Each represents a marketing opportunity and challenge for a company's IMC program.

Major equipment includes machinery, mainframe computers, product assembly machines, and robots. The price tag for this type of equipment is often fairly high. Many times servicing agreements accompany the sale. Such major purchases require financing arrangements (leases or payment plans) and lead buyers to carefully consider their options before making decisions. Upper management is often involved in the negotiations and the final purchase can take several months to complete.

Accessory equipment facilitates product usage along with basic company functions or operations. Items such as office equipment (coffee machines, calculators, computers, phones) and other goods (fire extinguishers, chairs) do not require service agreements or major financing packages. Visibility and reputation help companies that manufacture such items gain buyers, even though price and quality are still concerns. The ad for a Motorola product shown on the next page is designed to take advantage of the firm's strong name.

The pager being advertised by Motorola is an example of accessory equipment. Courtesy of Motorola, Inc. ©1999/Personal Communications Sector.

Fabricated and component parts are completed goods that can be identified, but are incorporated into another product. Air filters and spark plugs are component parts included in automobiles and lawn mowers. Pentium processors from Intel, as described in the chapter-opening vignette, fit in this category. When fabricated and component parts become integrated into a product, the firm that produces the final finished product often is referred to as an **original equipment manufacturer (OEM).** Quality and consistency are two major selling features for fabricated and component parts.

Process materials go into other products, but lose their identities when added to the final, finished good. Wire, cement, aluminum, steel, plastic, and other materials cannot be viewed or identified once they become part of the good. These materials must meet certain specifications (e.g., insulation values of wire, grades of steel) and are so standardized that price becomes a key factor in purchasing decisions. Relationships with vendors are critical to ensure the manufacturer's supply of process materials is never interrupted. This is especially important in international transactions because trust is often lower between the buyer and seller.

Maintenance and repair parts are needed to keep machines operating at peak efficiencies. They include oil, grease, replacement filters, and other maintenance-like items. Many times service providers vend these items, such as when a "lube and oil" outlet sells a particular brand of oil. Carburetors, gears, transmissions, and other more mechanical goods are repair parts. Repair and maintenance companies often sell parts (usually with a markup in price) as part of their repair services.

Operating supplies are the less expensive items companies need to conduct day-to-day operations. Everything from coffee to toilet paper to lightbulbs to toner for a copy machine is an operating supply. This category also includes office supplies such as typing paper and paper clips. Price and convenience in making the purchase are major selling features for these goods.

Raw materials are supplied by the agriculture, lumber, mining, and fishing industries. The wide variety of customers purchasing diverse forms of raw materials suggests the need for numerous types of marketing programs. Buying decisions vary based on location, standardization of the goods, and a variety of other factors. Often companies use distributors and agents because raw materials usually have a commodity status. The key for buyers is to find a vendor who can provide an uninterrupted supply of raw materials. One of the dangers companies face in buying raw materials in the international market is transportation. Although the raw materials may be cheaper, it is more difficult to assure that they will be delivered on time and in a continuous fashion. Storms and other natural phenomena as well as political unrest or turmoil may cause unexpected delays in shipments.

Products for resale are completed goods sold to end user consumers or other business entities. The product may travel through a wholesaler, distributor, or agent prior to being sold to a retail outlet or business. Other products are sold directly to the retailer. Manufacturers producing goods aimed at retail markets must understand consumer needs, create products that meet those needs, and develop strong alliances with the firms in the marketing channel that will handle or sell those products. Some manufacturers have begun to move away from the more traditional marketing channel and are selling directly to end user customers through Web sites, catalogs, 800 numbers, and other direct-marketing techniques.

Integrated Learning Experience

Accessing the "Business-to-Business" section of Yahoo! shows how many firms sell to other businesses. Unfortunately, many firms know little or nothing about these customers. Access the following web sites. What types of products do they sell and what types of businesses might buy these products? Also, examine the various brands and identify whether they are OEM manufacturers.

www.eastman.com
www.moruzzi.com
www.racemark.com
www.harman.com
www.delhi-industries.com
www.fkusa.com
www.dolch.com

types of customers

As many successful companies have discovered, business-to-business customers offer numerous lucrative outlets for goods and services. The previous section presented various types of business products. In this section, the different types of business-to-business customers are described in order to provide a second perspective into the nature of marketing to other companies. Also, Table 6.1 matches the products described in the previous section with the types of customers to be defined in this section. Potential customers of individual products can be placed into the following categories:

- Manufacturing customers
- Governmental customers
- Institutional customers
- Wholesalers and distributor customers
- Retail customers
- International customers

A brief discussion of each type of customer follows.

TABLE 6.1	Types of Customers				
Business Customers and What They Buy					

Types of products and services	Manufacturers	Government	Institutions	Wholesalers Distributors	Retail
Major equipment	✔	✔	✔	✔	✔
Accessory equipment	✔	✔	✔	✔	✔
Component parts	✔				
Process materials	✔				
Maintenance supplies	✔	✔	✔	✔	✔
Operating supplies	✔	✔	✔	✔	✔
Raw material	✔				
Operating services	✔	✔	✔	✔	✔
Professional services	✔	✔	✔	✔	✔
Products and services for resale				✔	✔

Manufacturers as customers

Selling to manufacturers requires a clear understanding of the production process and how it uses a material in completing a finished item. Meeting quality standards and other stringent specifications is essential. Marketing to manufacturers also requires an understanding of the manufacturer's customers.

For example, a manufacturer making an item for Delphi Energy has a better chance of making the sale when its marketing representatives understand Delphi Energy's business philosophy. Further, any company trying to sell process materials to Delphi Energy, which manufactures batteries, generators, and cruise motors, should also know that Honda is one of Delphi's major customers.

Manufacturers purchase many of the products noted in the previous section. Most of what they buy is used to create new goods. Component parts, process materials, and raw materials are elements of a finished product. Consequently, maintaining a continuous supply of materials is critical. Manufacturers cannot afford to have a supplier of raw materials fail to deliver on time, because delays may stop the assembly process and cost a producer thousands of dollars.

Governmental customers

Many goods and services are sold to various groups within the federal, state, or local government. Companies that sell to governmental agencies must understand that a bidding process often is involved. Clear specifications are spelled out by the agency regarding the characteristics of the product or service. Federal, state, and local government contracts can be quite lucrative, and a host of companies become interested when bids are taken for various goods or projects, such as a new government building. Companies selling to the government must develop specialized marketing techniques and have sufficient access to information to be successful. The government sector of the economy is very large. Governmental purchases account for 20 percent of the gross national product of the United States.[3]

Institutional customers

Another major source of revenue can be generated by selling to institutional buyers, those nonbusiness and not-for-profit organizations looking for goods and services. A large number of these kinds of organizations exists, including colleges and uni-

It's the new look.

The Pentium® II processor for a whole new style of computing.

intel.
The Computer Inside™

Many computer manufacturers purchase the Intel series of Pentium processors. Courtesy of Intel Corporation Museum Archives & Collection. Reproduced by permission of Intel Corporation. ©1998 Intel Corporation.

versities, hospitals, charitable organizations, churches, political parties, museums, unions, and others.

Institutional buyers require many of the same office supplies, fixtures, communication machinery (phones, faxes, computers), office equipment, clocks, intercom systems, and other products that profit-seeking firms use. The large number of not-for-profit organizations means this marketplace is quite lucrative. Marketing firms should not ignore the potential of these organizations when they select target markets. Many of these organizations use formal bidding processes similar to those utilized by governmental agencies.

communication action

Making Music

Manufacturers of musical instruments have experienced volatile periods of sales in the past decade. Several forces have changed the nature of the music business. One major factor is the number of children playing musical instruments. When numerous public schools began cutting back on music programs, sales to individual consumers as well as to local music stores declined. In fact, the number of small retail music stores dropped by 13 percent within a five-year period. These companies were the ones that had primarily marketed instruments to children, normally through rental or purchase agreements. Consequently, producers of musical instruments were among the first to feel the pinch of this trend.

A renewed interest in music, spurred by reports that musical training spurs intellectual growth and development, has created a stronger marketplace. Manufacturers of guitars, pianos, and other instruments noticed a resurgence in sales in the last five years. Current markets for musical instruments include:

- Small, independently owned music stores
- Grade schools, middle schools, high schools, and universities
- Large new music superstores, such as MARS and Guitar Center
- Individual buyers via the Internet and catalog sales

Instrument manufacturers must keep up with the technology of music. Computerization essentially allows for music makers of all ages to create home recording studios and to make a wide variety of sounds out of the same instrument.

The one remaining major competitive threat is resale firms that market used instruments.

Future markets for instruments include aging baby boomers interested in relearning an instrument, older adults taking up new hobbies, and the next generation of children. Reaching these groups will require careful marketing efforts to schools and institutions, to retail outlets, and through direct-marketing programs.

Sources: Robert Scally, "Striking a New Chord in a Mom and Pop Industry," *Discount Store News,* 37, no. 9 (May 11, 1998), pp. 70–82; Robert Scally, "Guitar Center Acquires a Friend," *Discount Store News,* 38, no. 11 (June 7, 1999), p. 10; Nakamura Akemi, "The Strings the Thing for Adults Learning Violin," *Japan Times Weekly International Edition,* 38, no.13 (March 30– April 5, 1998), p. 16; James Mammarella, "Grow Bix: Good as New," *Discount Store News,* 36, no 9 (May 5, 1997), pp. 72, 84.

Wholesalers and distributors as customers

Wholesalers or distributors can be divided into two types, agent and merchant. *Agent wholesalers* vend goods without taking title to them. They represent the manufacturer to other customers (retail outlets, other companies). *Merchant wholesalers* purchase and resell the item to other customers. Both are customers for manufacturers.

The power levels of both agent and merchant wholesalers have diminished, as more direct purchasing opportunities have become available (factory outlet stores, Internet direct purchases, etc.). At the same time, when companies sell to other businesses, these distributors can be helpful partners in the process.

Retail customers

Retailers are the customers of products marketed by manufacturers and wholesale distributors. Retailers also are customers for major equipment, such as computerized cash registers, accessory equipment, maintenance supplies, and operating supplies. Retailers are sometimes customers of other retailers, such as when a caterer buys flowers from a local florist. Many retail computer stores sell their products and services to other retail stores in a given community. Smaller retail outlets can stabilize sales when they are able to identify local businesses that purchase their products on a regular basis.

Retailers have formed new partnerships with manufacturers in many situations. Retail outlets provide valuable purchasing information to manufacturers, who in turn offer cooperative advertising, direct shipping, inventory control services, and price discounts to these outlets. Many manufacturers find retail outlets to be their lifeblood, because retailers are the key connection between the manufacturer and the consumer. As a result, retailers often hold considerable power.

As noted in Chapter 1, retailers have access to a tremendous amount of information about products that are selling and those that are not. Retailers also can collect information about success rates of promotions, price deals, and other marketing efforts. This gives retailers bargaining power in negotiations with various manufacturers and they can use it to create longer-term relationships with those same producers. This, in turn, affects relationships between retailers and wholesalers.

International customers

When a business develops international ties, a new series of markets and customers emerges. These include the groups shown in Table 6.2. Each provides a company with new markets for existing products. Within increased competition, international expansion no longer is an option for most companies; it is an essential part of survival.

Beyond the importers and exporters noted in Table 6.2, other businesses, governments of other nations, and institutions in other countries are viable markets for a firm's products. To be successful, firms expanding into the international arena must understand the cultures of the countries in which they are expanding. The buying process and the nature of acceptable practices vary from country to country.

TABLE 6.2

		TABLE 6.2
Importers	Firms purchasing goods from other countries, either for resale in their own retail outlets (e.g., Import Warehouse) or to other companies.	**Types of International Customers**
Exporters	Companies that specialize in finding international customers for goods and services. They provide shipping, billing, and other logistics, similar to domestic wholesalers.	
Retail outlets	Companies that buy directly from manufacturers in other countries.	
Other businesses	Firms using goods in the production of other goods, or as part of business operations.	
Governments	Products and services purchased by other nations.	
Institutions	Institutions (not-for-profit organizations, universities, etc.) that buy goods and services from international firms.	
Individual customers	Private individuals who buy goods and services directly from firms in other countries.	

Therefore, it is important to understand these unique customs to avoid offending potential international customers and to increase the odds of generating successful transactions.

In addition to products noted in this section, many firms offer services to other businesses. A review of service customers provides a more complete picture of all the outlets for business-to-business marketing efforts.

Integrated Learning Experience

Each business operates in a different environment. Many business categories have some type of organization available to assist individual firms within a specific product category. For example, beauty and barber shops can utilize the Beauty and Barber Supply Institute at www.bbsi.org. Go to this Web site to get a sense of how the organization tries to benefit its constituents. In the automotive industry, the Specialty Equipment Market Association at www.sema.org. is available. Go to the site to see the types of automotive suppliers this organization represents and how it can help both suppliers and automobile manufacturers. Sporting goods manufacturers can go to the Sporting Goods Manufacturer's Association Web site at *wwwsgma.com*. Notice the types of information provided on these Web sites and the benefits to a sporting goods manufacturer becoming a member of the SGMA.

stop!

Warehousing and shipping are examples of operating services provided to business customers.
Courtesy of The Image Works.
Photograph by David Lassman.

business-to-business services

Over the past 30 years, the fastest-growing part of the economy has been the service sector. Many business customers purchase these services. See Table 6.3 for examples of business services. The types of customers for services can be placed into four broad categories:

- Other companies that use a service per se
- Other companies that use services in bulk
- Other companies that use a service in conjunction with the sale of a product
- Other companies that use the service as part of another service

Each represents a major opportunity or target market for service providers. A brief discussion of each follows.

Companies using services

Numerous organizations take advantage of the services other companies provide. As a simple example, many firms utilize travel agencies to book airline tickets for employees making business trips. Many employees use company credit card accounts to pay for and record business expenses. Also, to entertain clients, numerous firms purchase "luxury boxes" at major stadiums hosting sporting events such as professional basketball, football, baseball, and so forth. Repair and maintenance services and building clean-up services are routinely provided by one company (such as ServiceMaster) to another. Two additional examples of services to other companies are: (1) operating services and (2) professional services.

Operating services are necessary to keep a company running smoothly. They include telephone services, Internet service, and utilities (e.g., water, gas, and electricity). In most cases, service agreements are reached with one vendor to provide operating services. Competition between providers can be intense, as in the case of long-distance telephone carriers. With the coming deregulation of the utility industry, business customers will have more bargaining power to control their utility costs. An in-house department or an outside vendor can perform other operating services such as janitorial and lawn care.

Professional services include accounting, legal, and consulting services. They may be purchased as a continuous service contract, on an as-needed basis, or by creating a retainer arrangement. Businesses that offer professional services must understand customer needs. Many firms believe specialization is key to winning professional contracts. It is difficult to provide professional services that meet the needs of all business customers.

The most rapidly expanding part of the professional services market is industry usage of the Internet. Firms can conduct market research and contact customers

TABLE 6.3

Types of Services

Banking and finance services	Health care services
Stock market services	Food services
Credit services	Repair and maintenance services
Insurance services	Laundry and uniform services
Educational services	Rental services
Travel services	Social services (drug and alcohol counseling)
Shipping services	Lawn and pest control services
Accounting services	Legal services
Computer services	Consulting services

SubmitOrder.com is one of the many business-to-business firms taking advantage of the Internet explosion.
Courtesy of SubmitOrder.com, Inc.

directly through Web sites and home pages. Some of these services can be rendered on-line. Internet marketing offers service providers a vast new set of potential customers.

SubmitOrder.com (see advertisement) is just one of many companies offering business-to-business services to Internet firms. SubmitOrder.com provides such services as information technology management, data mining, brand development, customer response services, and e-tail distribution services. SubmitOrder.com has distribution warehouses in Memphis, Tennessee, and Central Ohio. The company provides receiving, inventory management, picking, packing, shipping, and management of returned items for Internet businesses. By using SubmitOrder.com, an Internet business can concentrate on the retail side of the business and let the company take care of all of the shipping, distribution, and customer service aspects of the business.

Bulk services

A second manner in which services move from one organization to another is the sale of bulk services to employees. The classic example of this kind of service is insurance. Blue Cross provides essentially individualized health care insurance policies to employees in the organizations that purchase group coverage in exchange for a price discount. Life insurance packages, disability, liability, and other insurance programs are either provided to or sold to employees in other companies. Prescription cards represent a growing segment of this industry.

Anytime a company purchases a service for its employees or allows a company to sell the service to its employees, a new market exists for a service provider. Recently, several companies have purchased time from massage experts, who come into the plant and provide neck and shoulder massages for hardworking employees at their desks. The organization often pays for these services, recognizing that relaxed employees with less neck and back pain are likely to be happier and more productive on the job. Creative packaging of such bulk services can open markets

Ad advertisement for Buzzsaw.com, which offers e-commerce support in the construction industry. Courtesy of Buzzsaw.com Inc.

that never existed previously. Estate planning and retirement planning services are a growing portion of this category of providers. Even retailers offer services to businesses.

Services combined with products

When a company owns a fleet of cars or delivery trucks, it often tries to find a firm to provide services to accompany products. For example, one firm may develop a maintenance agreement relationship with another firm to service company cars driven by individual employees. Others use the services of auto auction companies when they are ready to discard older vehicles. Computer companies often vend software packages and service agreements along with the actual physical computer.

Other forms of services that accompany products in business-to-business relationships include financing packages for the purchase of goods, inventory counting, and inventory control when a manufacturer sells to a retailer or distributor, and the sharing of marketing information between two companies in a partnership. Thus, when a retailer agrees to share customer information with a manufacturer as part of selling the manufacturer's products, another market has developed combining products with services.

Services combined with other services

Many services are compatible with other services. For example, at the retail level it is quite common for a credit card company to sell life or disability insurance through credit card statements and other mailings. Many firms find it in their financial interests to create alliances with other service providers. Airlines routinely form relationships with hotels, travel agencies, and cruise ship operations. Internet companies have begun packaging tour programs together, featuring several services under one travel plan. For example, a financial institution may provide an organization with banking services as well as access to the stock market.

Connections and relationships between service providers expand rapidly. Hotels sell entertainment packages as part of the enticement to get people to stay with them. Several professional sports teams offer VISA and MasterCard programs, as does the Professional Golfers Association (PGA). Ingenious combinations of services spring up daily, often enhanced by Internet programs.

As mentioned previously, many companies sell both products and services to other businesses. Any target market analysis or promotions opportunity analysis, as described in Chapter 3, should identify all potential customer groups for products and services. In addition, marketing executives are able to recognize opportunities to link products and services together. One major new form of marketing involves creative integration of seemingly disparate offerings of two businesses into one product–service or service–service package. These include golf and credit cards, baseball tickets and credit cards, records with books, books with on-line bidding for goods, and so forth. The potential growth of services marketing represents a major opportunity for a wide variety of companies. To take advantage of these opportunities means carefully understanding how various firms purchase goods and services, the subject in the next section.

stop!

Integrated Learning Experience

A large number of companies operate in the international market, which means translation (of foreign language) services are in high demand. Using Yahoo!, first locate the "Business-to-Business" section. Next go to the "Translation Services" section. Notice the different languages listed. Choose one language, such as Russian, and then locate at least four translation firms. Which translator service should an international firm trying to expand to Russia use? Justify the selection.

business buying centers

How are business-to-business purchases completed? *People* still make purchase decisions, but, within a business organization, several individuals normally become involved. Further, corporate policies provide parameters and decision rules as purchases are made. Factors such as budgets, costs, and profit considerations often influence the final choice.

Business purchases seldom are made in isolation. With so many people involved, the decision-making process becomes much more complex. The group of individuals involved in the buying decision is called the **buying center.** As illustrated in Figure 6.1, the buying center consists of five different subsets of individuals playing various roles in the process. The five roles involved in the buying center are:

- Users
- Buyers
- Influencers
- Deciders
- Gatekeeper

Users are the members of the organization who actually use the product or service. When the product is office supplies, users are usually members of the secretarial staff. If the product is the tin used in the production of tin cans, users are the factory workers in the production facility. Computing staff members run mainframes and computers. In the Elekta ad on the next page, neurosurgeons are the users of the products, services, and treatment solutions offered by the company.

Buyers are the individuals given the formal responsibility of making the purchase. In larger organizations, buyers are either purchasing agents or members of the purchasing department. In smaller organizations, the buyer can be the owner or president of the company, a manager, or even a secretary.

Influencers are people who shape purchasing decisions by providing the information or criteria utilized in evaluating alternatives. Influencers often are formally appointed as part of a committee charged with selecting a vendor. In other firms, the process is more informal. For example, an engineer describes the specifications for a particular product that his or her department needs.

Deciders are the individuals who authorize decisions. They are often purchasing agents. In large organizations, a financial officer, a vice-president, or even the president of the company must finalize purchase decisions. Whoever agrees to allocate funds to complete a purchase is the decider.

The **gatekeeper** controls the flow of information to members of the buying center. Gatekeepers keep people informed about potential alternatives and decision rules being used. The gatekeeper also lets members know when certain alternatives

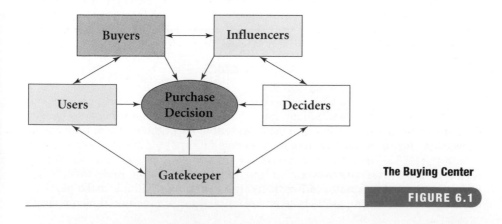

The Buying Center

FIGURE 6.1

Neurosurgeons who use the products, services, and treatment solutions Elekta offers are an important component of the buying center. Courtesy of Elekta Instruments Inc.

have been rejected. In some situations, it is not a specific individual who is the gatekeeper, but rather a *gatekeeping function* in which members notify each other regarding various events associated with the purchase.

Many times these five roles overlap. For example, the gatekeeper may also be the buyer. Often the purchasing department determines what information to give to members of the buying center. The department usually controls the amount of access a salesperson has to members of the buying center. Also, several individuals can occupy the same role, especially for large or critical purchases. It is not unusual for a variety of members of the organization to serve as influencers, because these roles usually are not fixed and formal. Roles change as the purchase decision changes.

The buying behavior process is unique in each organization. It varies within an organization from one purchasing decision to the next. Salespeople calling on a business must be able to locate members of the buying center and understand their roles in the process. These roles often change from one purchase situation to another, making the marketing task more difficult than one might expect.[4]

Integrated Learning Experience

The United Raw Material Solutions, Inc. is a business-to-business marketplace that brings together buyers and suppliers of textiles, petrochemicals, plastics, and electronic materials. Access this Web site at www.urms.com. Which members of the buying center are most interested in this Web site? How can the various members utilize this organization? How can suppliers use this Web site to reach various members of a buying center?

factors affecting members of business buying centers

The behaviors of each member in the buying center are influenced by a series of cultural, organizational, individual, and social factors.[5] These influences change the manner in which decisions are made and often affect the eventual outcome or alternative chosen. A discussion of these factors follows.

Organizational influences

Several organizational factors affect the ways in which individuals make purchasing decisions for a company. These organizational factors include the company's goals and its operating environment (recession, growth period, lawsuits pending, etc.). Decisions are further constrained by the organization's finances, capital assets, market position, the quality of its human resources, and the country in which the firm operates.

Some organizations have highly centralized purchasing programs. In those firms, a few individuals at the corporation's headquarters make most purchase decisions. Other individuals have only minimal influence on the purchase process. Other organizations are more decentralized. These firms grant various departments and individuals autonomy in making purchase decisions, and, as a result, those groups often seek advice and input from a variety of members of the company.

Studies of organizational decision making indicate that employees tend to adopt *heuristics*, which are decision rules designed to eliminate quickly as many options as possible. Company goals, rules, budgets, and other organizational factors create heuristics. One decision rule often employed is called *satisficing*, which means that when an acceptable alternative has been identified, it is taken and the search is completed. Rather than spending a great deal of time looking for an optimal solution, decision makers tend to favor expedience.[6]

Individual factors

At least seven factors affect each member of the business buying center: (1) personality features, (2) roles and perceived roles, (3) motivational levels, (4) levels of power, (5) attitudes toward risk, (6) levels of cognitive involvement, and (7) personal objectives.[7] (See Figure 6.2.) Each impacts how the individual interacts with other members of the center.

Regarding the issue of *personality*, a decisive person makes decisions in a manner different from one who vacillates. Confidence, extroversion, shyness, and other personality features affect both the person performing the decision-making role and others in the process. An aggressive "know it all" type affects the other members of a decision-making team, and such a personality feature does not always benefit the organization. An extrovert tends to become more involved in the buying process than a more introverted individual. The extrovert spends more time talking, and the introvert spends more time listening to sellers. The introvert might be too timid with salespeople and consequently may not ask important questions.

The *roles* people play are influenced by the many of the same factors that affect consumer buyer behaviors, including the individual's age, heredity, ethnicity, gender, cultural memberships, and patterns of social interaction. These role-playing ingredients affect how the individual interacts with others in the buying center.

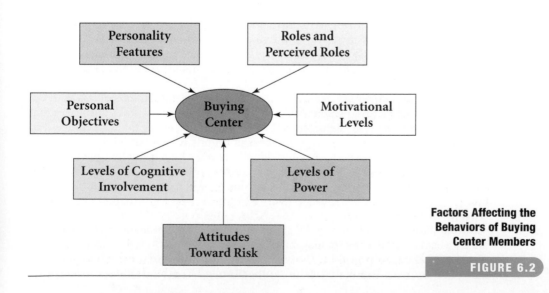

Factors Affecting the Behaviors of Buying Center Members

FIGURE 6.2

Remember, roles are socially constructed, which means people define how they intend to play roles as part of the negotiation process with others nearby.

It is not just the role itself which affects decisions. A person's perception of how the role fits into the buying center process and the overall organization is important. When a buying center member perceives the role as merely giving approval to decisions made by the boss (the decider), then the individual will not be an active member of the group. When members feel their inputs are important and wanted, they become more active. A person can believe his role is to provide information. Another might think he is supposed to play the devil's advocate. Someone else might perceive her role as being the person who synthesizes information provided by vendors and then relates it to the buying center to save the other members time. Roles and perceptions of roles are major factors determining how members of the buying center go about their business.

Motivation depends on how well the individual's goals match the organization's goals. If a factory foreman has a personal goal of becoming the vice-president of operations, that foreman is more likely to become involved in all purchasing decisions that affect his performance and that of his department. If a purchasing agent has been charged by the CEO to cut expenses, she may take a more active role to ensure cost-cutting selections are made. Many individuals also are motivated by needs for recognition. The goal of making successful purchasing decisions is to ensure that others recognize their efforts. They believe recognition is linked to getting promotions and pay raises.

A person's *level of power* in the buying process depends on his or her role in the buying center, official position in the organization, and the impact of the purchase decision on a specific job. When a particular purchase decision directly affects an employee, that person tries to gain more power in the buying process. For instance, a factory foreman has greater power within the buying center in the purchase of raw materials whereas the maintenance foreman has more power in the purchase of maintenance supplies. In these situations, both foreman strive to influence the decision that affects their area.

Risk is another factor that affects members of the buying center. Many vendors are chosen because buyers believe the choice has the lowest risk. Also, risk avoidance means firms tend to stay with current vendors rather than switching. In marketing to businesses, reducing risk is a major concern, especially when signing large contracts or when the purchase might affect company profits. People tend to think taking risks (especially when a failure follows) can affect performance appraisals, promotions, and other aspects of an individual's job.

Levels of cognitive involvement influence not only consumer buyer behaviors but also business buyers. Individuals with higher levels of cognitive capacity want more information prior to making decisions. They also ask more questions when interacting with a sales rep. These individuals spend more time deliberating prior to making a decision. Clear key message arguments are the important ingredients in persuading people with higher cognitive levels (as noted in the Chapter 5 discussion of consumer buyer behaviors).

Personal objectives are tied to motives, personality, perceptions of risk, and the other individual factors. Personal objectives can lead buyers to make purchases that help them politically in the organization, although not being the best choice. For example, if someone knows his or her boss is friends with a particular vendor, the buyer can choose that vendor even when others offer higher quality, lower prices, or both. Personal objectives can be tied to getting promotions, making rivals look bad, "brown nosing" a boss, or the genuine desire to help the organization succeed.

Cultural factors

Cultural patterns affect managerial styles as well as decision making processes. For many years, the Japanese management style normally included consensus-based decision making, in contrast to those of the United States and other cultures, which are often more individualistic and authoritarian. In a buying decision-making

Social interactions impact the way business purchase decisions are made. Courtesy of The Image Bank. Photograph by Anne Rippy.

process, a key boss in a U.S. company gathers input and then makes a decision and simply announces it. For many years, such a scenario was highly unlikely in Japanese firms, which tend to favor a more group-based approach. Therefore, marketing experts must carefully examine the culture in which the firm operates when developing a plan to reach members of the buying center.

Social factors

The final category of items that influence business buyer behaviors is a set of social factors. Consumers are social beings. The need for social acceptance is an important element in many purchases. Each member of the buying center has certain expectations of the buying group. These expectations, combined with the individual's desire to conform to them determine social interactions within groups.

Members of the buying center tend to adhere to group *social norms.* **Norms** are, in essence, rules of behavior regarding the proper way to behave in a group. In buying centers, one common norm is to act in a positive and friendly fashion. Another relates to understanding who is acting as the "leader" and who are the "followers" in the group. Norms affect language (cursing, use of titles, formality or informality), after-work socialization (happy hours, parties), and at-work interactions (who is invited to lunch). Norms strongly determine how problems are solved in buying centers as well as the ways in which individuals interact with one another.[8]

The buying center is a complex, interactive group of individuals. Members of the buying center serve different roles and may serve more than one role in a particular buying situation. In marketing to businesses, it is important to understand these dynamics. It is also important to recognize who is making decisions, how decisions are made, and what forces or factors may change decisions. By examining organizational, individual, and social influences, it is possible to design a communications program which will reach the key people at the right time.

types of business-to-business sales

The steps involved in the business-to-business buying process are quite similar to those individual consumers make in their purchase decisions. Before examining these steps, however, it is useful to study the types of purchase decisions. These fall into one of three categories: (1) straight rebuy, (2) modified rebuy, or (3) a new task.[9]

A **straight rebuy** occurs when the firm has previously chosen a vendor and wishes to make a reorder. This tends to be a routine process and involves only a few members of the buying center. Often the purchasing agent (buyer) and the users of the product are the only persons aware of a rebuy order. The user's role in this purchase situation is to ask the buyer to replenish the supply. The buyer than contacts the supplier and places an order. There is no evaluation of alternatives or information. Buyers often place orders electronically.

In making a **modified rebuy,** the company needs to consider and evaluate alternatives. A modified rebuy situation occurs for four different reasons. First, if a company's buyers are dissatisfied with a current vendor, they may want to look at other options. The greater the level of dissatisfaction, the greater the enticement to look for new possibilities.

Second, if a new company offers what is perceived by a member of the buying center to be a better buy, the purchase decision may be revisited. The new option may be a superior quality product or one offered at a lower price. Also, the terms of purchase may be more attractive with a different company. When the dependability of a new vendor is perceived as superior to the current vendor, the company may reconsider its previous choice.

A third reason for a modified re-buy occurs at the end of a contractual agreement. Many companies, as dictated by corporate policy, ask for bids each time a contract is written; this is true of most governmental and institutional organizations. The amount of time spent in the buying process depends on a comparison between the company's current vendor with other potential vendors.

The last modified rebuy situation takes place when a company purchases a product or service with which it has only limited or infrequent experience. For example, a company that purchases delivery trucks every five to seven years probably would make a modified rebuy, because many factors change over that amount of time. Prices, product features, and vendors (truck dealerships) change rapidly. Further, in most cases, the composition of the buying group will be different.

Modified rebuys occur when someone in the buying center believes it is worth reevaluating vendors based on new information. The decision to reconsider depends on the buying center individual's ability to influence other members of the group. Company policies also dictate modified rebuy procedures. Someone seeing an advertisement for Oracle may want to look into purchasing the software to enhance his or her e-business. The buyer and influencer in the modified rebuy situation may be impressed that Oracle is the world's second largest software company. Users would evaluate the quality of the software as compared to what they currently use.

In **new task** purchasing situations, the company buys a product or service for the first time and the product involved is one with which organizational members have no experience. This type of purchase normally requires input from a number of people in the buying center and a considerable amount of time is spent gathering information and evaluating vendors. In many cases vendors are asked to assist in identifying the required specifications.

Integrated Learning Experience

Access the business-to-business section of Yahoo! at *b2b.yahoo.com.* Pick one of the categories listed and work your way through the various levels to discover a specific set of products for sale. Find examples of products that would be considered modified rebuy situations for most companies and examples of new buy situations. Are any products shown ones that would be considered straight rebuy possibilities?

the business-to-business buying process

In new task purchasing situations, companies go through seven steps in the business-to-business buying decision process. The steps are similar to those consumers use as part of their decision-making process. The business-to-business steps are:

1. Identification of needs
2. Establishment of specifications
3. Identification of alternatives
4. Identification of vendors
5. Evaluation of vendors
6. Selection of vendor(s)
7. Negotiation of purchase terms

In new buy situations, companies go through all seven steps. In modified rebuy or straight rebuy situations, one or more of the steps are eliminated. A more in-depth examination of each of these steps follows.[10]

Identification of needs

Just as consumers identify needs (hunger, protection, social interaction), businesses also make purchases because of their needs. Companies identify a wide variety of needs. A review of the types of products sold to various companies, as described earlier in this chapter, suggests a myriad of needs for everything from raw materials to complete component parts. Needs also exist for many types of services, including financial, repair, maintenance, and others. Individual buyers and members of individual firms recognize company needs on a daily basis.

Many needs in the business world are created by derived demand. **Derived demand** is based on, linked to, or derived from the production and sale of some other product or service.[11] For example, the demand for steel is largely based on the number of cars and trucks sold each year. When the demand for vehicles goes down because the economy experiences a recession or downturn, the demand for steel also declines. Steel manufacturers find it difficult to stimulate demand because of the nature of derived demand. Derived demand is often associated with the raw materials used in the production of goods and services, such as steel, aluminum, concrete, plastic, petroleum products (e.g., jet fuel for airlines), construction materials, and so forth. Derived demand also exists for services. For example, demand for mortgage money directly depends on housing sales.

Companies selling products with derived demand properties often find their sales figures are volatile. Fluctuations and swings in demand are much more common because of the **acceleration principle**. When consumer demand for a product increases or decreases, drastic changes in the derived business demand also occur.[12] For example, if the demand for a consumer product increases, it can spark the demand for new equipment and new buildings as companies expand to handle increased production. Thus, a small increase in consumer demand of 10 percent to 15 percent can cause as much as a 200 percent increase in the demand for machines, equipment, and supplies needed to supply the higher demand. Unfortunately, a small 10 percent decrease in consumer demand can cause a complete collapse in business demand for machines and equipment. Small changes in consumer demand usually have much larger impact on demand for business goods and services that support it because of its derived nature.

Another helpful concept in understanding business needs is *joint demand.* Joint demand exists when similar demand forces influence component products. Recently, the strike of suppliers of transmissions to General Motors affected demand for all of the products used to build automobiles. Suddenly, orders to the suppliers of tires, radios, car seats, batteries, and other products used in the manufacture of automobiles were cut or stopped completely. If the supply of one component used in the manufacture of a product is delayed, reduced, or stopped, it infuences the demand for every component used in that product. In this case, a demand factor influencing GM also affected companies that supply GM with other component product parts.

As with consumer services, marketers can use various aspects of communication to help a firm recognize a need. For example, a Unisys advertisement could raise the question of whether a company effectively uses customer information to power its business. Seeing the ad, a company's leader may decide the firm needs more information about its customers and then contacts Unisys.

Establishment of specifications

Once a need has been recognized, if a straight rebuy choice is made, then an order is placed with the current vendor. Occasionally specifications need to be changed, but these are normally minor alterations. In modified rebuy situations, examination of specifications makes sure they are current and meet the company's needs. In new task purchases, more complete specifications will be established.

Experts formulate specifications. Engineers specify machinery specifications. When purchasing a new computer system, the company consults a computer expert (internal or external). Sometimes the expertise of a vendor is utilized. For example, for a new telecommunications system, a firm asks various vendors to help identify the specifications, because that technology changes so rapidly. In marketing to businesses, when a company asks a vendor to assist with the development of specifications, the vendor hopes its advice and counsel will gain it an advantage in winning the contract.

A company usually writes down the specifications and distributes them internally to those in the buying center. A firm also communicates to vendors, so that each can make a case for its particular version of the product or service. Simply meeting specifications is rarely enough to win the bid—often the company must provide other incentives or reasons to be chosen.

Identification of alternatives

In this third step, the business examines alternative ways of meeting the need identified in the first step. One primary issue is a choice about whether the product or service can be provided or created internally. Most of the time, it is necessary to go outside of the firm, though there are exceptions. Janitorial services can be provided by hiring a few employees or by a commercial service. A review of the goods and services detailed earlier in this chapter makes it clear most purchases are made from other companies. At the same time, a firm can develop an advantage, or grow by creating an in-house program or through expansion into a new line of services. For instance, Sears originally provided credit cards for use solely in its own retail outlets. Over time, however, the company developed the Discover card, moving Sears into a service line retail customers and other businesses use.

The primary task involved in identifying alternatives is to consider all of the ways to meet a need. Beyond considering if the product can be provided internally, a company could identify various methods to eliminate the need. For example, when developing credit alternatives for business-to-business e-commerce customers, a firm has three choices:

- Use in-house credit
- Not offer credit to e-commerce customers
- Hire an external firm such as ecredit.com to provide the service

Once this decision is made, the firm is ready to move on to the next step in the buying process.

Identification of vendors

When members of the buying center decide to pursue a supplier, potential vendors are identified and notified to see if they are interested in submitting bids. In most business situations, written, formal bids are required. A vendor's ability to write a clear proposal determines how successful it is in winning bids. Effective proposals spell out prices, quality levels, terms of payment, support services, and any other condition requested by the company looking to purchase goods.

One member of the buying center is normally chosen to compile files of vendors that submit proposals. The offers are circulated to all of the members of the buying center who have input into the final decision. Next, formal and informal meetings are held to discuss proposals as they arrive.

Evaluation of vendors

Evaluations of vendors normally occur at three levels. The first level is an initial screening of proposals. This process narrows the field of vendors down to three to five competitors. Often, the purchasing department performs the initial screening. Occasionally an engineer or user of the product assists.

The number of people from the buying center involved in the initial screening depends on the dollar value of the bid and how critical the product or service is to the firm's operation. As dollar values increase and the product becomes more critical, the number of individuals involved from the buying center involved also rises. Minor choices usually are left to a single individual.

The second level of evaluation occurs as the firm undertakes a vendor audit. An audit is especially important when members of the company want to develop a long-term relationship with a supplier. Vendors that are the primary sources for critical components or raw materials recognize that long-term bonds benefit both the vendor and the purchasing firm.

Members of the audit team normally include an engineer, someone from operations, a quality-control specialist, and members of the purchasing department. The goal of the audit is to assess potential suppliers about a series of items (see Figure 6.3). Most audits are conducted at the supplier's business site.

The third and final level of evaluation occurs when various members of the buying center share vendor audit information. At that time, firms consider purchase procedures, and for manufacturers it may require sharing production schedules with the vendor. Sharing information, such as the production schedules with suppliers, requires a degree of trust of the vendor.

Many of the concepts described in the previous chapter regarding consumer buyer behaviors apply to this stage of the business purchasing process. Members of the buying center who believe they are performing an "official" duty when making company purchases emphasize the central route of processing (from the Elaboration Likelihood Model described in Chapter 5). The primary message arguments provided by vendors are more likely to be processed and stored in the long-term memories of buying center members.

The peripheral route, however, cannot be ignored. A shoddy brochure or a poorly dressed salesperson creates an impression that is processed peripherally. Such an unflattering message can cause a member of the buying center not to consider the primary message argument. The reverse also can occur. Peripheral cues can cause a business buyer to pay more attention to a message when it hears or sees it being repeated, or when the sales rep is dressed professionally and the materials the vendor provides are exciting and enticing.

> ▶ **Production capability**
> ▶ **Quality-control mechanisms and processes**
> ▶ **Type and age of equipment used**
> ▶ **Telecommunication and EDI capabilities**
> ▶ **Capacity to handle fluctuations in orders**
> ▶ **Financial stability of the firm**
> ▶ **Number of competitors that purchase from the firm**

Typical Items Examined During a Vendor Audit

FIGURE 6.3

It is important to remember that vendors are people and members of the buying center are people. Attitudes, values, opinions, and first impressions influence evaluations made about vendors. Successful marketing means carefully designing all messages, including the bids and proposals, which can create favorable images in the minds of various business buyers.

Selection of vendor(s)

Once a firm has carefully studied all of the vendors and the bids have been considered, it is time to make a final choice. At this point it is critical that marketers recall that the members of the buying center face all of the individual, social, organizational, cultural, and political pressures discussed earlier. The final decision should be made based on a comparison of dollar value of the contract to the value offered by various vendors. In reality, however, politics and other forces often have a significant impact. Successful marketing requires an understanding of these forces.

A critical decision to be made at this point is whether to utilize one supplier or multiple suppliers. The advantage of using only one supplier is the ability to negotiate a lower price. Computer linkages with one company allow for continuous communication with the supplier and paperless billings. The disadvantage is that a company's entire production schedule is at the mercy of a single vendor. If the flow of a critical component is delayed or halted, the whole production process can come to a screeching halt.

Once the choice is made, there are still items to be completed before shipment begins, including negotiation of purchasing terms. Often, those companies not chosen are not notified until these other agreements are reached and finalized.

Negotiation of purchase terms

In most purchasing situations, negotiation of terms is merely a formality, because most of the conditions have already been worked out. Occasionally, however, changes are made at this point in a contract or purchase. These tend to be minor and are normally negotiated by the purchasing agent.

When the final agreement is set, goods are shipped or services provided. Assuming no further complications, the buying process is complete until the next cycle begins. At this point, firms that did not win the contract are notified. They may follow up and try to discover why they were not selected. It is in the best interests of the company to be as honest as possible, because future relationships with such companies may be possible. In the upcoming sections, two additional issues that impact business buyer behaviors are considered. The first is a review of the nature of dual channel marketing. The second is concerned with the buying community.

Integrated Learning Experience

Wholesalers are a major component of the supply channel. From the Yahoo! search engine, type "wholesalers." Note the large number of organizations and the various categories of wholesalers. Pick one cateogry and examine its wholesalers and distributors. Assume a purchase manager for a chain of grocery stores needs to locate wholesalers of vegetable and fruit produce. In Yahoo!, under "wholesalers" there is a category called "Food and Beverage" and one called "Produce." Select at least two viable vendors. Utilize the information in this section of the textbook to help the purchase manager make a buying decision.

dual channel marketing

When firms sell virtually the same products or services to both consumers and businesses, it is known as **dual channel marketing.**[13] Dual marketing channels arise for several reasons. Perhaps the most common scenario occurs when a product is first sold in the business market and then adapted to the consumer market.

New products often have high start-up costs including R&D expenditures, market research, and so forth. Businesses tend to be less price sensitive than are retail consumers. Thus it is logical to sell to them first.

As sales grow, economies of scale can be created. Larger purchases of raw materials combined with more standardized methods of production make it possible to attack the consumer market. The benefits of economies of scale entice manufacturers to sell products previously supplied to the business sector in the retail markets. Products such as digital cameras, calculators, computers, fax machines, and cellular phones first were marketed to businesses and then later to consumers. To make the move to the retail arena possible, prices have to come down and products need to become more user-friendly. For example, consumers can now have their photos put on a CD rather than obtain prints. The imaging technology developed by Kodak and Intel was first sold to various businesses, and now is being offered to retail customers. By forming an alliance with Intel, Kodak brought the cost down and developed economies of scale needed for the consumer market.

The service sector also has used the strategy of selling the first application to business then the second to consumers. Speech-controlled telephone dialing first was developed for businesses and is now is available to consumers using mobile phones.

Another type of dual channel marketing results from *spin-off sales.* Individuals who buy a particular product at work often have positive experiences and, as a result, purchase the product for personal use. This situation often occurs with computers and computer software. Favorable feelings about more expensive items can also result in spin-off sales. For example, a salesperson who drives a Buick LeSabre to work may like it so well that she buys one for personal use. Holiday Inn discovered that many of its private stays come from business-related spin-offs. Approximately 30 percent of Holiday Inn's business customers also stay with the chain on private vacations.[14]

Image concerns

Image issues are major concerns for marketers vending products in dual channel situations. As noted in Chapter 4, a firm's image is an important ingredient in successful marketing programs, for both business and retail customers. When a company sells virtually the same product to both markets, image transfer occurs. Marketers have to be extremely careful that the image they project in one market does not damage their image in the other market.

Any organization that sells to businesses must be wary of being considered incompetent or frivolous when it also sells consumer products. For example, Gateway

Approximately 30 percent of Holiday Inn's business customers also stay with the chain on private vacations. Courtesy of PhotoEdit. Photograph by Jeff Greenberg.

may have damaged its business image by its consumer marketing communication approach. Gateway adopted a Holstein cow as its mascot to promote sales to consumers. Unfortunately, this approach created problems for the firm's business-to-business marketing program. Large corporations became leery of the company after it began to paint its computer shipping boxes with the black and white Holstein design. They also were uncomfortable with a firm that allowed employees to work in jeans and T-Shirts. Gateway's image in the business-to-business market suffered further when the news stories about the company appeared showing the CEO leading a pep rally backed by rock bands and with other executives dressed as Holsteins.[15]

Differences versus similarities

In dual channel marketing, a primary decision to make is how to represent the product in each channel. The firm can either emphasize similarities between the two markets or focus on differences. Consumers and businesses looking for the same benefits and product features probably will see marketing messages quite similar in both channels. When consumers and business buyers value different product attributes or desire differing benefits, the marketing strategy develops more customized messages for the separate markets.

When there are substantial differences between the two channels, the typical tactics are to:

- Use different communication messages
- Create different brands
- Use multiple channels or different channels

In many instances the product attributes are the same, but the value or benefit of that attribute are different. Messages should focus on the benefits each segment can derive from the product. Cellular phones marketed to businesses can stress the area coverage and service options. For consumers, cell phone messages can center on the fashionable design of the product, its ease of use, or a lower price.

To avoid confusing individuals who may see both messages from the same producer, companies often utilize dual branding. For instance, when Black & Decker decided to launch a professional line of power tools, it used the DeWalt brand name. This avoided confusion with the Black & Decker name and prevented any negative image transfer from home tools to professional tools.

In most cases, business customers and consumers want the same basic benefits from products. In these situations, a single strategy for both markets is best. Tactics include:

- Integrating communications messages
- Selling the same brand in both markets
- Scanning both markets for dual marketing opportunities

There are two advantages to integrating consumer markets with business markets: (1) synergies and (2) economies of scale. Synergies arise from increased brand identity and equity. An image developed in the consumer market can then be used to enter a business market, or vice versa. Using one brand makes it easier to develop brand awareness and brand loyalty. A business customer who uses a company-owned American Express Card is likely to have a separate card from the same company for personal use.

Scanning both types of customers for new opportunities is an important part of dual channel marketing. For example, the firm Intuit, which sells the Quicken software, discovered that individuals who use Quicken at home also are willing to use a similar version for their small businesses. Capitalizing on this need or demand, Quicken added features such as payroll and inventory control to a business software package. At the same time, Quicken maintained its easy-to-use format. By finding business needs for a consumer product, Quicken adapted a current product and captured 70 percent of the small business accounting software market.[16]

communication**action**

Success at Dell

A company that has successfully integrated messages across the consumer and business markets is Dell Computers. Dell has accomplished this feat by using five demand generation channels:

- The field sales force
- Third-party business partners
- Retailers
- Telechannels
- The Internet

Dell uses its field sales force to reach major corporations, institutional customers, and governmental customers, which generates 65 percent of their total revenue.[5] To reach small and medium-size businesses, Dell uses third-party business partners, telechannels, and the Internet. To reach consumers, Dell uses retailers and the Internet. To further reduce its costs, once a business customer has been obtained, Dell encourages the customer to place additional orders either by telephone to inside salespeople or through a special premium Internet page Dell sets up for the business customer. The premium Internet page allows the business customer to order merchandise not normally available via the Internet.

Dual channel marketing is a key to Dell's success. Specializing its methods of reaching consumers has led to growth in sales. At the same time, Dell maintains its image across all markets: one of being a quality provider of various computers.

Source: Liam Hegarty, "Winning Marketing Strategies: How Dell Does It," *Fairfield County Business Journal,* 37, no. 48, (November 30, 1998), p. 7.

The importance of dual channel marketing should not be underestimated. A major competitive advantage can be cultivated when a producer or service vendor discovers items that can be sold in both markets. A complete IMC planning process includes the evaluation of potential business market segments as well as consumer market segments, as noted in Chapter 3. Firms that integrate messages across these markets take a major step toward reaching every potential user of the company's goods or services.

Marketing account executives must recognize differences between consumer purchases and business purchases. Although the purchasing processes are similar, those who make buying decisions vary and numerous factors may affect them. One example of the difference between consumer and business purchasing decisions is revealed by examining business buying communities.

the buying community

The buying community is an interlocking network of individual business owners and managers, trade organizations, social organizations, and firms that work for small and medium-size businesses. Small business owners use buying communities to obtain information pertinent to their businesses and their purchase decisions.

The buying community is an important link for small and medium-size businesses. Often these expert, reliable sources are other business owners who have made similar purchase decisions. Thus, the small business owner can go outside of his or her business to obtain information needed to make an informed decision. In these situations, the influencers of the decisions are other business owners. The buying community is normally utilized when a new task and modified rebuy decision is being made, not in straight rebuy situations.

The concept of a buying community is most important to smaller and medium-size firms. These companies tend to operate in different ways than larger organizations. Some of the primary differences are in the areas of identifying, evaluating, and selecting vendors. Decision makers in smaller organizations tend to have less expertise and experience than those in larger firms. Also, buying centers in small to medium-size companies are smaller, meaning that each member of the center must become more involved in the purchasing process. The risks associated with making purchasing decisions are often higher in smaller organizations. A bad decision can easily create a major financial crisis for the small company. Small and medium-size firms do not have the financial security to weather a poor decision that a large firm would have.[17] A buying community's expertise and advice especially helps smaller firms. A large number of companies are small to medium-size organizations. This makes the role of the buying community crucial to the economic well-being of many regions.

A recent survey demonstrates the value of the buying community. In a study of small business owners, the following sources of information were indicated as important:

- Members of the same business association, such as Kiwanis or Rotary (80 percent)
- Associates and speakers at business seminars (61 percent)
- Other business owners (34 percent)
- Business periodicals (3 percent)
- Local newspapers (4 percent)[18]

The problem with business periodicals and local newspapers is that they do not provide enough information to make any type of judgment. They may be important in terms of sparking an interest, but not in the evaluation stage of the buying process. Consequently, buying communities provide the information that smaller firms cannot obtain elsewhere.

The implications for business-to-business vendors are clear. First, the company needs to devote some of its IMC efforts toward key members of a buying community. Whenever possible, the firm should provide information and expertise to help smaller business owners and their purchasing departments. Communications in the form of brochures and help lines can assist smaller companies. The substantial number of small organizations currently operating makes them a viable market for many business-to-business vendors, especially those that take the time and make the effort to reach those companies directly.

Integrated Learning Experience

For the business community, being a member of the Chamber of Commerce presents the opportunity to network with other businesspeople. Access the U.S. Chamber of Commerce at www.uschamber.org. In addition to networking, what other benefits does the Chamber of Commerce provide? Access the Chamber Biz page, a resource for small businesses. Examine the information provided in the sections "Government," "Marketplace," and "BizCenter." What information is of value to small businesses? In addition to the Chamber of Commerce, memberships in organizations such as the Rotary and Kiwanis Clubs can be valuable resources. Access the Rotary Web site at www.rotary.org and the Kiwanis Web site at www.kiwanis.org. Which would be the best organization for a small business owner to join? Why?

business-to-business trends in the twenty-first century

One issue that continues to gain momentum in the marketing community is accountability (see Figure 6.4). Firms expect tangible results from the money they invest in marketing and advertising programs. As a result, account executives face growing pressures to ensure that dollars spent yield quick results. Firms expect account executives to understand their businesses as well as the many potential target markets

▶ Emphasis on accountability

▶ Importance of Web sites and Internet marketing

▶ Global branding

▶ Database mining

▶ Changes in methods of communication

▶ Focus on internal marketing communications

Business-to-Business Trends

FIGURE 6.4

that can be tapped. Expanding from business customers to consumers, or vice versa, is one way to respond to the increasing insistence on immediate results.

The second major trend is the expansion of e-commerce and increased Web-based marketing. One business executive recently noted that the electronic commerce revolution is probably doing more to integrate business-to-business marketing communications than any other marketing force. Engaging in Web-based commerce is no longer an option. Either firms must get involved, or it is likely that they will not stay in business.

Part of the e-commerce revolution is the creation of more effective Web sites. Web sites must be more than merely placing a catalog on-line. Sites need to be truly interactive, allowing business customers to gain information, product specifications, prices, and other key information. The Internet's technology saves time and money for both customers and vendors.

Another prominent trend is the development of global corporate brands. In the future, a firm's reputation and image will continue to be critical features of an IMC effort. As a result, companies must invest in brand image building projects. They should strive to convey a uniform message to business customers, retail customers, the financial community, and other publics. Part of this process includes establishing an effective global brand.

Database mining and integration in the business-to-business arena is another recent phenomenon affecting IMC programs. Firms can utilize the immense power of computers to access databases containing information about customers and prospects. Database mining searches identify buyer behavior patterns that can be matched with business communication programs. Additional analyses can be performed to segment business customers into target groups. Then a distinct appeal can be designed to reach each group. Eventually, companies will use information to customize messages to individual consumers, based on their needs and past purchase behaviors.

Use of alternative methods in communicating with customers also continues to expand. Many firms recognize that having salespeople call on customers is expensive and time-consuming. Personal calls have given way to other methods, including contacts by mail, telephone, fax, interactive Internet sites, and e-mail. Effective IMC programs integrate all of these methods to maximize company exposure while making it extremely easy for customers to contact the firm. They also allow marketers to bypass gatekeepers in other businesses. Getting to users, deciders, and influencers in the buying center increases the firm's chances of making a sale.

The final trend emerging as the twenty-first century begins is the growing importance of internal integrated marketing communications. *Internal marketing communications* efforts include creating, packaging, and delivering the organization's IMC marketing message (including its business-to-business components) to all employees of the organization. Employees must understand and believe in the firm's image and its marketing position. Employees need to comprehend what each company brand stands for and the benefits it offers consumers. Most importantly, each employee must believe in the company and its mission. Spending more time marketing internally produces more knowledgeable and dedicated employees, who will, in turn, seek the goal of providing excellent service to customers.[19]

implications for **marketing professionals**

Brand Managers and the Business-to-Business Sales Team

Know the business first. Account executives should be aware of the product type being sold along with the types of customers who may purchase the product.

1. Use Table 6.1 to help identify the types of product and customers the firm currently serves.
2. Examine all potential customers carefully to determine any potential markets the firm has not yet explored.

Study the nature of services that businesses provide to other business. Try to expand the firm's domain by taking advantage of these services. Ask these questions:

1. Are there new services the company could provide?
2. Are there services the company could add to make various products more attractive purchasing options?
3. Could the company link its products with the services provided by another firm to make both firms' offerings more enticing?
4. If the firm expands its service offerings, how can the company continue to speak with a clear voice and integrated marketing communications messages?

Before designing any communications effort, the account executive should work with the company's production department to identify all of the members of the buying center. Then the members of the team need to address and fine-tune communications.

Account executives and creatives should review the steps of the business buying process. Then, they should design messages to have an impact on key points in the process, depending the on the product and the buyer.

1. Modified rebuys require messages to entice businesses to take a long, hard look at their previous purchasing choices.
2. New task purchases offer the greatest opportunity to make an impression, including attracting attention to the vendor, the product, the terms of the sale, and any other advantage the company offers.

Account executives should help their clients understand all of the potential opportunities for dual channel marketing, while also making them aware of the following:

1. Times to sell products differently versus times when the need being filled is essentially the same across the two channels
2. Situations in which marketing in one channel might damage marketing efforts in the other
3. Methods to design messages that take advantage of the firm's strengths and brand equity and keep the overall voice clear and focused on the total company

Suggest all of the new venues to reach business customers, include e-trade, Internet programs, and database mining.

Note the value of global brands.

Make sure internal marketing messages match with those sent to external groups. Be certain employees and departments clearly recognize how the IMC program works, and how they can help to achieve the greatest levels of success.

Integrating business-to-business marketing programs into the overall IMC plan means many things. To compete both locally and globally, marketers must integrate marketing communication across all venues. This includes advertisements, public relations efforts, brand and firm image, and every other aspect of the IMC program. Rick Kean, executive director of the Business Marketing Association of Chicago recently said, "Integrated marketing is a term business marketers have used for years, but now it has emerged as a driving force in how companies are presenting themselves overall. There has to be a plan that puts everyone in a company on the same page; in this economy, no company can afford to have a fragmented message."[20] This includes speaking with a clear voice to both business and end user retail customers.

This chapter addresses business-to-business marketing concerns. The many potential markets available to firms desiring to sell products to other firms present a variety of opportunities to expand sales and stabilize revenues over time. The people who make purchases are members of the business buying center, which includes users, buyers, influencers, deciders, and gatekeepers. Each plays a key role in leading the firm to an eventual purchasing choice.

The types of purchases business buyers make can be divided into three types: (1) a straight rebuy, (2) a modified rebuy, and (3) new tasks. The best opportunity to reach a firm is when a new task purchase is being made. A company should, however, be willing to make competitive efforts to build its sales in all three situations, because the environment changes so rapidly. Products evolve, markets grow, competitors enter and leave the marketplace, and, as a result, firms that continually seek to identify business buyers stand ready when new opportunities appear.

The steps involved in business buying processes include: (1) identification of needs, (2) establishment of specifications, (3) identification of alternatives, (4) identification of vendors, (5) evaluations of vendors, (6) selection of vendor(s), and (7) negotiation of purchase terms. Careful understanding and input into each of the steps can improve the chances of a successful business-to-business transaction.

Dual channel marketing is vending goods and services to both consumers and businesses. Dual channels help firms develop economies of scale in production and other synergies in operations. It is important to maintain a consistent, positive image in both markets. Marketers must be careful that messages sent to one market do not present a negative image in the other. Firms must decide whether to highlight differences or similarities in products and the need requirements those products meet. When similarities are present, companies use consistent brand names and messages. When significant differences exist, firms must tailor messages to individual markets. At times, it is wise to establish separate brand names to sell in business and retail markets.

As the twenty-first century unfolds, increasing pressures for accountability may drive many companies to seek out business customers. Marketing in cyberspace makes it possible for marketing executives to reach other businesses efficiently and effectively. Global brands with consistent messages adapted to individual regions is one common approach to reaching new customers. Database mining helps vendors seeking to expand business-to-business operations. At the same time, IMC programs must communicate internally to employees and departments so that the firm can reach outward with a consistent, strong voice projecting the qualities and benefits of the firm's goods and services. Those companies that incorporate effective business-to-business components into their overall IMC plans stand a better chance of remaining successful in future years of operation.

1. Name the types of products that manufacturers may sell to other businesses.

2. What types of customers are there for manufacturing firms trying to enter the business-to-business marketplace?

3. What kind of company can successfully sell to governmental organizations? What special conditions apply to this type of marketing program?

4. Name five organizations that are examples of institutional not-for-profit customers in the business-to-business marketplace.

5. What types of services are sold in business-to-business settings? Give examples.

6. What customers do wholesalers serve? What customers do retailers serve? What business-to-business opportunities exist for wholesalers and retailers?

7. Name and describe the five members of a business buying center.

8. What types of organizational influences affect business buying decisions?

9. What kinds of individual factors affect members of business buying centers?

10. How would norms affect business buying decisions?

11. Name and describe the steps of the business-to-business buying process.

12. How are the steps of the business buying process similar to the consumer buying decision-making processes described in Chapter 5?

13. What is derived demand? Why is it important to business-to-business vendors?

14. Define straight rebuy, modified rebuy, new task. Which presents the best opportunity for a firm entering the business-to-business marketplace?

15. What is dual channel marketing? What special problems and opportunities are present in dual channel situations?

16. What is a buying community? Which types of firms does it best serve? Why?

17. What trends affect business-to-business marketing in the early part of the twenty-first century?

KEY TERMS

original equipment manufacturer (OEM) a firm that manufactures a final finished product using fabricated and component parts integrated into that product.

buying center a group of individuals involved in a company's buying decision-making process.

users members of the organization's buying center who actually use the product or service.

buyers the individuals from the buying center who are given formal responsibility for making the purchase, such as purchasing agents or members of the purchasing department.

influencers people from the buying center who influence purchasing decisions by providing the information or criteria utilized in evaluating alternatives.

deciders individuals from the buying center who authorize decisions, including purchasing agents, financial officers, a vice-president, or even the president of a company.

gatekeeper member of the buying center who controls the flow of information to members.

norms rules of behavior regarding the proper way to behave in a group.

straight rebuy a purchase that occurs when the firm has previously chosen a vendor and wishes to make a reorder.

modified rebuy a purchase that occurs when the company needs to consider and evaluate alternatives, even though the decision was made previously.

new task a purchasing situation in which the company is buying product for the first time and the firm has no previous product experience.

derived demand demand based on, linked to, or derived from the production and sale of some other consumer product or service.

acceleration principle when consumer demand for a product increases or decreases, drastic changes in the derived business demand also occur.

dual channel marketing when a firm sells virtually the same product or service to both consumers and businesses.

ENDNOTES

1. Eric Hausman and Kelly Spang, "Intel Unwraps New Strategy," *Computer Reseller News,* no. 767 (December 8, 1997), pp. 45–46; Kelly Spang, "Intel: We Will Be Everywhere," *Computer Reseller News,* no. 769 (December 22, 1997), p. 104; Anya Sacharow, "Intel Power," *Mediaweek,* 8, no. 4 (January 26, 1998), pp. IQ13–IQ15; Marcia Savage, "Intel Modifies Security Feature After Outcry," *Computer Reseller News,* no. 827 (February 1, 1999), pp. 83–84; Dayna Delmonico and Joel Shore, "Pentium-Based Servers Heat Up Market," *Computer Reseller News,* no. 650 (September 24, 1995), pp. 139–142; Joshua Piven, "Can Industry Stop Microsoft–Intel Jaggernaut?" *Computer Technology Review,* 15, no. 11 (November 1995), pp. 1–20; Booke Crothers, "Pentium Pro Errata Beginning to Surface," *Infoworld,* 17, no. 50 (December 11, 1995), p. 8.

2. Frank G. Bingham Jr. and Barney T. Raffield III, *Business Marketing Management* (Cincinnati, OH: South-Western Publishing, 1995).

3. Discussion based on Frederick E. Webster Jr. and Yoram Wind, "A General Model for Understanding Organizational Buyer Behavior," *Marketing Management,* 4, no. 4 (winter–spring 1996), pp. 52–57.

4. Ibid.; Patricia M. Doney and Gary M. Armstrong, "Effects of Accountability on Symbolic Information Search and Information Analysis by Organizational Buyers," *Journal of the Academy of Marketing Science,* 24, no. 1 (winter 1996), pp. 57–66; Rob Smith, "For Best Results, Treat Business Decision Makers as Individuals," *Advertising Age's Business Marketing,* 84, 3, (1998) p. 39.

5. Patricia M. Doney and Gary M. Armstrong, "Effects of Accountability on Symbolic Information Search and Information Analysis by Organizational Buyers," *Journal of the Academy of Marketing Science,* 24, no. 1 (winter 1996), pp. 57–66.

6. Herbert Simon, *The New Science of Management Decisions,* rev. ed. (Upper Saddle River, NJ: Prentice Hall, 1977).

7. Webster and Yoram Wind, "A General Model for Understanding Organizational Buyer Behavior"; Doney and Armstrong, "Effects of Accountability on Symbolic Information Search and Information Analysis by Organizational Buyers"; James A. Eckert and Thomas J. Goldsby, "Using the Elaboration Likelihood Model to Guide Customer Service-Based Segmentation," *International Journal of Physical Distribution & Logistics Management,* 27, no. 9–10, (1997), pp. 600–615.

8. P. F. Secord and C. W. Backman, *Social Psychology* (New York: McGraw-Hill, 1964); Marvin E. Shaw and Phillip R. Costanzo, *Theories of Social Psychology,* 2nd ed. (New York: McGraw-Hill, 1982).

9. Patrick J. Robinson, Charles W. Faris and Yoram Wind, "Industrial Buying and Creative Marketing," *Marketing Science Institute Series* (Boston: Allyn and Bacon, 1967).

10. Adapted from Webster and Wind, "A General Model for Understanding Organizational Buyer Behavior."

11. Eugene F. Brigham and James L. Pappas, *Managerial Economics,* 2nd ed. (Hinsdale, IL: Dryden Press, 1976).

12. Ibid.

13. Discussion of dual channel marketing is based on Wim G. Biemans, "Marketing in the Twilight Zone," *Business Horizons,* 41, no. 6 (November–December 1998), pp. 69–76.

14. Ibid.

15. P. Elstrom and P. Burrows, "Can Gateway Round Up the Suits?" *Business Week* (May 26, 1997), pp. 64–68.

16. Biemans, "Marketing in the Twilight Zone."

17. Discussion of small and medium-size firms based on Karen Maru File and Russ Alan Prince, "Emerging Critical Success Factors in Marketing to the Smaller Business: Issues and Trends from the U.S. Market," *International Journal of Bank Marketing,* 10, no. 5 (1992), pp. 19–25.

18. Ibid

19. Discussion of trends based on Laurie Freeman, "Technology Influences Top Trends for 1999," *Advertising Age's Business Marketing,* 84, no. 1 (January 1999), pp. 1–2; John Obrecht, "Speculations for the Millennium," *Advertising Age's Business Marketing,* 84, no. 6 (June 1999), p. 13; Laurie Freeman, "Agencies See 37 % Growth Amid B-to-B Revolution," *Advertising Age's Business Marketing,* 84, no. 7 (July 1999), pp. 1–2.

20. Richard L. Kaye, "Companies Need to Realize Internal Marketing Potential," *Advertising Ages' Business Marketing,* 84, no. 7 (July 1999), p. 13.

Building an IMC Campaign

Developing a Business-to-Business Component of an IMC Program

All of the products and services suggested in Chapter 1 have potential business buyers or must be marketed through a distribution channel. A complete and effective IMC program identifies those buyers and channel members who would purchase the product. Utilizing the tactics described in this chapter, you can develop a plan to induce members of the buying center to consider and eventually purchase the item, in both domestic and global markets. Go to the Prentice-Hall Web site at www.prenhall.com/clow or access the Advertising Plan Pro disk that accompanied this textbook and complete the Chapter 6 exercise for your product. Upon completing this stage of your IMC program, you have built a solid foundation from which to proceed in developing the other aspects of your marketing plan.

Critical Thinking Exercises

Discussion Questions

1. A member of the buying center for a large shoe manufacturer tries to purchase soles for shoes from an outside vendor (or vendors). Study the list of factors affecting buying center members in Figure 6.2. Discuss the effect of each factor on the roles of members in the shoe company's buying center. How does the factory foreman's role differ from the purchasing agent's role? How do these roles differ from the company president's role?

2. A purchasing agent for a clothing manufacturer is in the process of selecting a vendor (or vendors) to supply the materials to produce about 30 pecent of its clothes. The clothing manufacturer employs about 300 people. As the audit nears completion, what factors are most important to the purchasing agent?

3. A member of the buying center has been asked to gather information about possible shipping companies for international shipments. Go to the following Internet addresses. What companies have the most appealing Web sites? Beyond Internet materials, what additional information do they need to supply to the buying center in order to win the contract?
   a. ABC India Limited (www.abcindia.com)
   b. BDP International, Inc. (www.bdpint.com)
   c. Falcon Transportation & Forwarding Corp. (www.falcontrans.com)
   d. Global Freight Systems (www.globalfreightsystems.com)
   e. NTS Transport Services (www.ntstransport.com)

4. Access the Web site www.SubmitOrder.com. Suppose you want to sell a product over the Internet. Describe how SubmitOrder.com can assist your business venture. Discuss each service offered by SubmitOrder.com and how that would fit into an Internet venture.

Stirring Up Steamy Sales

APPLICATION EXERCISE I

Erin Snyder decided she was ready for the big move. After spending a dozen years in the publishing industry, Erin felt she had sufficient knowledge and the right kind of backing to begin her own imprint. She worked for a medium-size company that produced about 1,000 titles per year, and that largely served a female target audience in both its fiction and nonfiction books. What the company did not have, however, was a list containing romance novels.

Romance books constitute a major portion of the publishing industry. By 1998, projections were that romance novels generated $800 million in annual sales, or roughly half the mass-market paperbacks sold. Romance books are staples on best-seller lists. The typical reader buys between four and twenty books *per month*. The average reader is female, near the age of 40, and lives in a household earning $40,000 per year or more. Women read such novels for escape and because these books speak in a voice that is "by women, for women," according to one romance novel scholar.

Most literary critics dismiss the books as essentially trash or soft-core porn, with tragically poor levels of writing skill. Many follow a standard 200-page formula in which the heroine first rejects the suitor and then, by page 100, discovers he was indeed Mr. Right. Early versions used no profanity, no graphic sex, no infidelity, and no interracial sex. The great majority of the books have happy endings. Sex is consensual and pleasurable, and adultery normally is not part of the story, *The Bridges of Madison County* notwithstanding. (One successful romance author noted that *Bridges* is not truly a romance novel because of the adultery, and because the couple ends up apart. As she noted, "You can tell it was written by a man.") Some feminists are angry that women in romance novels are passive and often are the victims of violence. Also, the message seems to be that woman simply cannot get along in the world without a man.

In spite of these criticisms, the market continues to grow. Plots have become less formulaic and more complex, and topics have expanded to include alcoholism, depression, aging, and a variety of other issues. Erin felt her firm was in an excellent position to expand into the area, because her publisher had strong brand equity with female readers.

The romance novel market is stratified into a variety of customers and by several products. One method by which customers can be enticed is simple price. Wal-Mart began offering novels published by Zebra Books for $1.78 each in 1996. This approach gave these books a major advantage over the typical book, which sells for $5.99 to $7.99. Obviously the markup for such a product is low, and volume is the key.

At the other extreme in pricing are hardback or hardbound titles written by high-profile authors such as Danielle Steele. Markups are much higher, but so are "returns" of unsold books. The issue of returns is a key problem. Romance books have a shelf life of four to six weeks. Then, the company must absorb the cost of unsold books that are sent back by individual bookstores. Also, the advances paid to hardcover writers are prohibitive for smaller publishers. For example, Sandra Brown, a highly successful romance writer received over $10 million to write three books, beginning in 1997.

There are three levels of sexuality in romance novels. "Sweet" romances have pastel covers and sketchy descriptions of sex. About one-fifth simply end with a rapturous kiss in the marital bed. One specialty area in sweet romances are the so-called Christian romances, which constitute a viable and growing market. Christian romances are sold in both regular bookstores and Christian bookstores, giving them a wider distribution. "Sensual" romances are for middle-of-the-roaders. The hero and heroine in these books have mutually satisfying sex with lots of code words used to describe body parts and the actual act. Terms like "peaks of ecstasy" dominate sensual romances. "Spicy" titles contain more graphic descriptions. Anything goes in these novels, so long as the sex is consensual and occurs in the context of a committed relationship. Even bondage and whipping make it into spicy novels.

Erin prepared her proposal to the publisher stating reasons why the imprint could succeed. She began her presentation by noting the kinds of outlets that exist for romances. Although Zebra Books and the Kensington imprint had captured Wal-Mart, many other chain discount stores might carry books, including Kmart, Target, ShopKo, and Walgreen's. Book-of-the-month clubs present a viable outlet for some customers. Also, Erin's firm was well established with the major book wholesalers and warehouses, such as Barnes & Noble and Ingram. Internet sales through Amazon.com represented another outlet for the titles. Erin was convinced interactive Web pages for authors and series books offered great potential to build sales and customer loyalty to her company.

Erin knew the two keys to success in starting her imprint. The first was to attract quality authors so that she could build name recognition with them. She knew Harlequin books dominated the authors' list, and that the firm "owned" the writer's pen name for seven years, even if the individual chose to move to a new publisher. Erin decided she could attract authors through writer's conventions and contests.

The second key challenge was shelf space. Because the major publishers dominated the market, Erin needed "hooks" that would encourage retailers to buy from her imprint. This meant selecting the proper niche in terms of sexuality levels and price. She would have to be able to offer a series of products or stand-alone titles different from those currently on the shelves. Erin was looking forward to the challenge.

1. Discuss the business-to-business issues present in this case.
2. Discuss the concept of the buying center and how it relates to retailers and wholesalers who Erin would contact for the romance novels.
3. What venues should Erin's imprint pursue?
4. Is dual marketing a good option for Erin? What types of challenges would dual marketing present?
5. Would it be possible to develop romance novels for other target markets, using various demographics? If so, how?

Taking the Next Step in the Death Industry

APPLICATION EXERCISE II

Nancy Hines was always reluctant to tell people about the business she was starting, even though she was convinced it would be a valuable service people would appreciate. It also might be quite lucrative. Still, many of her friends viewed her work as maudlin, or worse.

For the past seven years, Nancy had been employed by a local newspaper as a reporter. Among her duties was preparation of the daily obituary column. She made phone calls to the local mortuaries, and they would provide the basic information for each newly deceased person. Then, Nancy would rewrite or edit the materials to fit the space requirement for the paper.

During the past year, however, the paper substantially cut down her duties. The standard of eight to 12 column inches to use for an obit was reduced to one or one and one-half column inches, which would normally contain about 80 words. The paper charged a fee for the family to have a complete obituary printed. In spite of initial objections from the community, the new system was soon in place, and Nancy was relieved of her duties for that area of the paper.

A close friend of Nancy's, Margo Youker, recently completed a series of courses in the area of e-commerce. Margo saw a great opportunity for the two of them to pursue. They established a new company, *Remembrances.com,* a Web site dedicated to the mortuary industry.

The "death industry," as it is known, has peaks and valleys, which are based on how many people die in any given month or year. Fees are collected for grave sites, cremations, embalming, caskets, memorial services, and limousine services for family members and the deceased (the hearse). Margo and Nancy believed they could add to the revenues of these companies by offering an additional service: a Web site for the family of the deceased.

The Web site would contain a full-length obituary, photos, directions to the church and grave site, and requests for memorial contribution allocations. It also allowed long-distance friends to send on-line notes and comments. The mortuary would provide a home page directing people to the site for each individual person. It also would set up links to the newspaper (for a fee) in which the newspaper would print the Web address as part of the short obituary. The text would appear as follows:

Fred Johnson, aged 83, died on Monday, June 6, 2000, from natural causes. He was a lifelong resident of Oxnard, California. He retired from Montgomery Ward in 1981. Further information may be obtained at *Remembrances.com.*

Nancy and Margo would sell their Web site service to individual mortuaries. They would charge a fee for each person, and the cost would be passed along to the family as part of the burial price. Nancy would manage the Web site, including writing full-length obits for each person. Margo would help with additional information and make sales calls. Their intention was to build a base of operations in Southern California and to expand outward from there.

1. Describe how various morticians could use the buying decision-making process as they considered a sales pitch from *Remembrances.com*.

2. Is this a dual-channel program? Should Nancy and Margo promote this service directly to potential patrons? If so, how?

3. Will this business succeed? Why or why not?

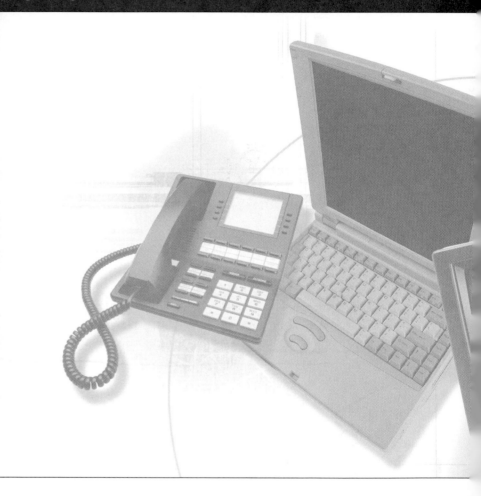

› Advertising Management

▶ **CHAPTER OBJECTIVES**

Understand the steps of an effective advertising management process.

Study the roles that the company's overall mission, its products, and its services play in advertising programs.

Recognize when to use an in-house advertising approach and when to go to an external advertising agency.

Review the steps of effective advertising campaign management programs.

Comprehend the functions performed by the advertising account manager and the advertising creative in preparing an advertising campaign.

IS THERE SUCH A THING AS "TOO YOUNG"?
Advertisers Tackle the Kid Market

One of the emerging marketing controversies is the extensive amount of advertising aimed at children. On the one hand, children represent a tremendous level of spending and buying power ($20 billion spent by persons under age 14 in 1997). On the other, critics complain that the tactics have become so subtle, and so invasive, that children have become pawns in a massive marketing game. Mary Pipher, clinical psychologist and author of *The Shelter of Each Other,* suggests that "No one ad is so bad, but the combi-

nation of 400 ads a day creates in children a combination of narcissism, entitlement, and dissatisfaction."

Ads to children utilize several tactics, including building brand awareness, using toys and other collectibles, developing tie-ins with movies and other children's programs, emphasizing memorable humor that entices purchases, and pressuring Mom and Dad by building expectations and demands by their kids. The major issues are whether children have the psychological capacity to make reasonable choices and if kids understand how they are being manipulated by various advertising campaigns.

Parents may be part of the problem. "Babies are the BMWs of the Nineties," explains one marketing expert.

What used to be a hand-me-down marketplace has turned into a $23 billion per year industry of indulgence for babies, featuring designer clothes, special furniture, and other baby baubles. Parents who postpone childbirth tend to have more disposable income and lavish some of these resources on infants, often aided by well-to-do grandparents. Consequently, companies such as Gap capitalize on the baby-as-doll trend by developing GapKids lines. It may not be surprising, then, that by the age of 10 many kids have highly refined tastes and strong brand preferences.

In response, advertisers look to venues such as *Sports Illustrated for Kids,* which attracts 8- to 14-year-old boys. A recent issue featured a two-page spread of the Chevy

Venture minivan. The goal is to cause these "backseat consumers" to beg their parents for a new mode of transportation, one that keeps up with the Joneses.

Other marketing appeals are directed at younger and older kids. For the very young, characters such as Barney and Ronald McDonald vend everything from food to toys to clothes. The long-term successes of the Trix Rabbit and Lucky the Leprechaun are tributes to the power of cartoon spokescharacters. The Taco Bell Chihuahua has great appeal for many kids. Also, the Bart Simpson "Nobody Better Lay a Finger on My Butterfinger!" campaign quickly turned the candy bar into one of the biggest sellers in the market. Further, kids love humor, making funny ads and other humor-based campaigns for adult products appealing to nontarget market young children.

At the other end of the spectrum, Marlboro gear and Camel dollars induce teenagers into the smoking marketplace, government protests notwithstanding. Even more benign products, such as Pepsi, vend heavily to teens. A recent "caps for merchandise" campaign heightened Pepsi's appeal to teenagers while raising sales.

Tie-ins with movies have also generated tremendous new business. Companies and their advertisers capitalize on the popularity of a film to sell T-shirts, fast food, toys, and a wide variety of other products.

With such a major marketplace available, and a wide variety of methods to reach kids, it is not surprising many companies and their advertising agencies have begun to believe it's best to "get them while they're young." The question is, is it marketing or exploitation? When your kids start asking to try beer, or nag you incessantly to buy high-priced designer gear, your thoughts on the subject may change.[1]

overview

The average person is exposed to more than 600 advertisements per day. As every marketing manager knows, people are bombarded with messages through an expanding variety of media. Television and radio have long been the staples of advertising programs, and they compete with newspaper and magazine ads, billboards, signs, direct-mail campaigns, and other traditional channels. Recently, the number of ways to contact customers has grown. Ads on the Internet, clothing lines with messages printed on them, telemarketing programs, and even messages heard while a consumer is on hold on the telephone create numerous new opportunities to contact potential customers.

This situation represents a tremendous challenge for marketers. A company simply cannot afford to prepare ads for every possible medium. Choices must be made, and messages must be of sufficient quality to give the company an advantage in a highly cluttered world, and a world in which people are becoming increasingly proficient at simply tuning ads out.

To be effective, an ad first must be noticed. Next, it must be remembered. Then, the message of the advertisement should incite some kind of action, such as a purchase, a shift in brand loyalty, or at least a spot in the buyer's long-term memory.

Part 3 of this text deals with the role advertising plays in a complete integrated marketing communications program. Figure 7.1 is a reminder of the overall IMC approach. The upcoming three chapters describe in detail the relationship between a company's advertising program and its IMC plan.

Three ingredients must be combined to create effective advertisements: (1) development of a logical advertising management scheme for the company, (2) carefully selection of media, and (3) thoughtful design of the advertisement. Selecting media and designing the actual advertisements go hand in hand: one cannot be performed without the other in mind. Actual discussions of these topics (media selection and advertising design) are presented in separate chapters. Still, it is important to remember that in reality both occur together. Only then will the ad

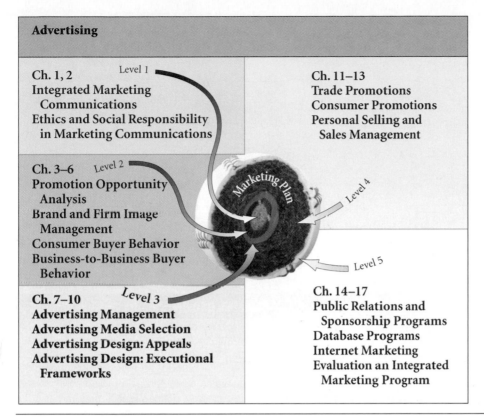

Advertising

Ch. 1, 2
Integrated Marketing
  Communications
Ethics and Social Responsibility
  in Marketing Communications

Level 1

Ch. 3–6   Level 2
Promotion Opportunity
  Analysis
Brand and Firm Image
  Management
Consumer Buyer Behavior
Business-to-Business Buyer
  Behavior

Level 3

Ch. 7–10
Advertising Management
Advertising Media Selection
Advertising Design: Appeals
Advertising Design: Executional
  Frameworks

Marketing Plan

Ch. 11–13
Trade Promotions
Consumer Promotions
Personal Selling and
  Sales Management

Level 4

Level 5

Ch. 14–17
Public Relations and
  Sponsorship Programs
Database Programs
Internet Marketing
Evaluation an Integrated
  Marketing Program

**An Integrated
Marketing
Communications Plan**

FIGURE 7.1

agency or creative department be able to create consistent, effective advertisements and promotional campaigns.

This chapter focuses on advertising management, which lays the groundwork for the total advertising program. Advertising campaign management is the process of preparing and integrating a specific advertising program with the overall IMC message. One key element in this process is to develop the message theme. The **message theme** is an outline of key idea(s) that the advertising program is supposed to convey. The message theme should match the company's overall marketing and IMC strategies. The message theme component of advertising is described in greater detail later.

Chapter 8 describes media selection. A series of important decisions must be made about which media to use in the advertising campaign. Logical combinations of media should match the message strategy as well as the design and desired appeal of the ad.

Chapters 9 and 10 describe the advertising design process. There are several primary decisions to be made at that time. They include deciding what leverage point to use, the major appeal in the advertising campaign, and the type of executional framework to use. A **leverage point** is the key element in the advertisement that taps into, or activates, a consumer's personal value system (a value, idea, or concept). The **appeal** is how to design the advertisement that attracts attention or presents information to consumers. Typical appeals include the use of humor, fear, sexual suggestiveness, logic, and emotions. The **executional framework** or theme explains how the message will be delivered. Some examples of executional frameworks include the slice-of-life approach, fantasies, dramatizations, and ads constructed using animation.

When these three tasks (message theme design, media selection, and advertisement design) have been integrated, the advertising account executive can make a better case that the IMC format has been followed. The firm speaks in one clear

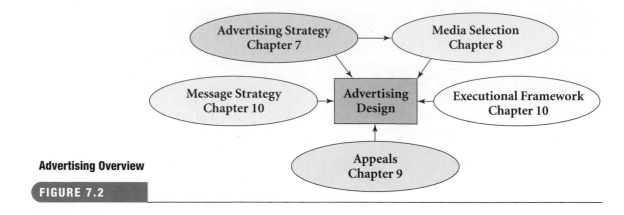

Advertising Overview

FIGURE 7.2

communication**action**

Colgate's IMC Program for Fresher Mouths

Colgate-Palmolive recently provided an example of an effective advertising strategy, when a new brand of toothpaste was introduced. The company used a two-tiered marketing strategy to launch its new Total brand. The first tier was a campaign aimed at end users. The second tier was a trade campaign focused on the retail channel and dentists. The goal was to capture a major share of the market.

Colgate's research identified its primary target as "orally aware" consumers with an above-average interest in oral health. These individuals are heavy users of toothpaste and other dental products and visit their dentists more often than average patients. For these consumers, Total has an ingredient called "Triclosan" that aids in the prevention of cavities, combats gingivitis, and fights plaque buildup. It also helps control tartar and reduces bad breath. No other toothpaste can offer all of these benefits in a single product. Not surprisingly, Total has a higher price, but Colgate was convinced that the target group for this product would be willing to pay a premium price to obtain these benefits.

Colgate invested $100 million to launch the Total brand. The money was divided among network and cable television advertising, print advertising in general-interest magazines, multiple freestanding inserts in newspapers, outdoor advertising on bus shelters, and postcards distributed in health clubs and coffee shops. Colgate's sales force worked diligently to cultivate the retail channel to get favorable store displays and in-store support. Colgate used 20 percent of the $100 million for a massive sampling push to its secondary target market, dentists, with the goal of encouraging them to introduce Total to their patients.

The result of Colgate's massive integrated marketing thrust were impressive. During the first six days of sales, a projected six-week supply of the product was sold. After just four months on store shelves, Total had captured a 10.6 percent share of the toothpaste market. At that point, Colgate shifted its advertising thrust from creating brand awareness to encouraging repeat purchases. Colgate exceeded its market share goal by integrating the consumer and business thrust with advertising and other promotional tools. The results could not have been obtained only by developing an advertising campaign, nor only by using sales promotions. To succeed, the company effectively integrated advertising into a consumer marketing plan combined with business-to-business tactics.

Source: Karen Benezra, "The Fragging of the American Mind," *Brandweek,* 39, no. 24 (June 15, 1998), pp. S12 – S17.

voice, and the message has a better chance of reaching and affecting key buyers, such as was the case in the Colgate Total toothpaste story told in the Communication Action Box. Figure 7.2 indicates how the elements of an advertising program fit together. As shown, many activities interact with one another, and all must match consistently with the strategy and appeals the company has in mind.

overview of advertising management

An **advertising management program** is the process of preparing and integrating a company's advertising efforts with the overall IMC message that already exists. An effective program consists of four activities, which combine to form the advertising management process. They are:

1. Review the company's activities in light of advertising management.
2. Select an in-house or external advertising agency.
3. Develop an advertising campaign management strategy.
4. Complete a creative brief.

The major principle guiding these four efforts is *consistency*. To be effective in developing successful advertisements, the company's products or services and methods of doing business need to match the form of advertising agency chosen, the strategy of the campaign, and the work of the advertising creative. The goal is to provide a coherent message that restates the image of the overall IMC program.

the role of advertising in the IMC process

Advertising is one component of integrated marketing communications, as shown in Figure 7.1. It is also part of the "traditional" promotions mix of advertising, sales and trade promotions, and personal selling. These functions, along with other activities such as direct marketing and public relations efforts, form the basis for communicating with individual consumers and business customers. The role advertising plays varies by company, products, and the marketing goals established by the firm. For some products and companies, advertising is the central focus, with the other components (trade promotions, consumer promotions, and personal selling) used to support various advertising campaigns. In other situations, advertising supports a national sales force and trade promotions programs. In the business-to-business sector, advertising often supports other promotional activities, such as trade shows and personal sales calls. In the consumer sector, the reverse is often true. Advertising usually is the primary communication vehicle in reaching consumers. Other promotional tools (contests, giveaways, special packages) are then used to support the advertising function. In both business-to-business and consumer promotions, the key to using advertising effectively is to see it as one of the spokes in the "wheel" of the promotional effort with the remaining "spokes" being the other components of the IMC approach.

Remember, an IMC program is more than just promotions and advertising tactics (as described in Chapter 1). Integrated communications include clear communications between departments as well as with outside customers and suppliers. IMC programs apply information technologies to develop databases that help everyone in the firm to understand customer needs and characteristics, including both business customers and end user consumers. Effective integrated communications programs mean that every facet of the organization works toward the goal of reaching customers with a clear, consistent message.

Within that framework, advertising plays a *major and vital role* in establishing effective communications. Therefore, a full section of this textbook is devoted to an explanation of how to prepare advertising campaigns and work with account executives, media buyers, and advertising creatives, with the goal of incorporating advertising into the IMC program in a manner designed to effectively and efficiently use all available promotional dollars. As advertising agencies and account managers feel growing pressures to produce tangible results, developing noticeable and measurable advertising results is the major challenge for the advertising agency and for the company itself.[2]

company activities in advertising management

Successful company leaders build their businesses by carefully tending to a few major activities. One key endeavor is to make sure the firm has a well-thought-out, clearly specified mission statement. The overall mission of an organization is a general outline of the company's direction and purpose. Many times, an IMC program is based on a similar statement of an overall objective. From there, members of the company can complete the following tasks:

- Identify potential customers.
- Build products and services to meet customer needs.
- Match the company's IMC process with its advertising management program.

These three efforts must be coordinated in order to mesh the company's message with its desired audience while vending various goods and services. Most firms have four general categories of *potential customers:* (1) end users, (2) other businesses, (3) institutions, and (4) governmental customers. Some even argue there is a fifth, international customers. Although marketing to consumers and businesses in another country offers unique challenges, most marketers see it is an extension of

SkyTel markets products to businesspeople. Courtesy of SkyTel Corporation.

these four general categories. As discussed in Chapter 3, it is important to designate which customers are being approached so that the company's messages are attractive to these target markets.

Products and services are designed, in part, with target markets and customers in mind. For example, the recent minivan boom in the automobile industry in not an accidental discovery. A large segment of the car-buying community is 30- to 50-year-old parents with higher levels of disposable income who need to haul around kids, groceries, sports equipment, and other more bulky items. The response to improved minivan design and heightened efforts to solicit business from well-to-do families is a phenomenal growth in sales of these vehicles, with large profit margins as a result. Similarly, in the business-to-business market, Motorola developed the PageWriter 2000X interactive communicator to meet the needs of business travelers. Motorola formed a partnership with Skytel, which also sells the device and the service. The SkyWriter advertisement featured in this section shows the product's advantage to a business person. The ad highlights the advantage of the SkyWriter over cell phones in the context of a restaurant, where using a pager does not disturb the atmosphere for other restaurant patrons.

IMC programs and advertising campaigns are much easier to integrate with clearly specified target markets and well-designed products and services. Thus, when the Discover Card is advertised, key customers are kept in mind as ads for this service are prepared. Effective IMC programs heavily rely on management teams defining the company's mission and aligning company activities into the same integrated, one-voice approach that speaks to all constituents. When these factors are pulled together effectively, the company can commence with more specific advertising projects.

choosing an advertising agency

The first step in developing an advertising program is choosing between an in-house advertising group and an external advertising agency. Many larger-size organizations have begun to house integrated communications and advertising programs within internal departments. Part of the reasoning is that internal organization members have a better sense of the company's mission and message. By hiring a few key marketing and advertising experts, many firms can develop effective advertising programs by outsourcing some of the functions, such as the writing, filming or recording, and editing the actual advertisement in addition to planning and purchasing media time (on television and radio) and space (in magazines, in newspapers, and on billboards). The disadvantage to this approach is that the company can go "stale" in its marketing efforts and fail to recognize other promotional or advertising opportunities. The department also may lack the expertise to carry out all of the necessary functions. Instead, the tendency may be to cut costs in developing ads rather than taking advantage of the knowledge and expertise that advertising agencies have to offer. This is especially true in the international arena, wherein a firm probably lacks the necessary understanding of language and customs, as well as key buyer behavior of the target market.

Certain firms have successfully moved away from advertising agencies. For example, Georgia Power became dissatisfied with the work of the Ogilvy & Mather agency and changed to an in-house department. General Electric also keeps most of its advertising work in-house.

Decision variables
In making the decision to use an external agency or in-house department, a firm considers the following five critical issues:[3]

1. Size of the account
2. Money that can be spent on media

3. Objectivity factor

4. Complexity of the product

5. Creativity issue

Concerning the *account size,* a small account usually is not attractive to an advertising agency, because it sees little opportunity for profit. Also, with regard to *money spent on media,* smaller accounts are less economically sound for the agency, because more money must be spent on producing advertisements rather than on purchasing media time or space. A good rule of thumb is called the 75–15–10 breakdown. That is, 75 percent of the money buys media time or space, 15 percent goes to the agency for the creative work, and 10 percent is spent on the actual production of the ad. For smaller accounts, the breakdown may be more like 25–40–35, where by 75 percent of the funds go to the creative and production work, and only 25 percent is spent on media purchases. Unless 75 percent of the company's advertising budget can be spent on media purchases, it may be wise either to do the work in-house or to develop contracts with smaller speciality firms to prepare various aspects of the advertising campaign.

An agency is likely to be more *objective* than is an in-house advertising department. The company, instead of an independent ad agency, pays creatives working for an in-house advertising department. Many times it is more difficult for in-house creatives to remain unbiased and to ignore the influences of others in the organization who may not fully understand the artistic aspects of advertising. The exception to this is advertisements for highly *complex* products. Agency members have a difficult time understanding more complicated products. To get them to understand often requires a considerable amount of time, which costs money. For complex products, in-house departments work best. For generic or more standard and simple products, ad agencies have more to offer.

The final issue to consider in choosing an agency versus performing the work in-house is *creativity.* Most agencies claim they have greater creativity than any in-house department has. Although they may, in-house departments are able to freelance with various creatives in the actual ad design process. The question, then, is how well the company's creatives or freelancers can perform as compared to an agency's creatives. For most firms, this is very difficult to judge.

Consequently, when the decision is made to utilize an external advertising agency, the company is committing substantial resources to the goal of expanding its audience through carefully designed advertising and communications programs. A brief review of the various types of agencies follows.

Integrated Learning Experience

Making the decision to use an external advertising agency as opposed to an in-house program for advertising or some aspect of the advertising function is difficult. Access the American Association of Advertising Agencies (AAAA) at www.aaaa.org. From the "News Releases" section, examine articles that may help identify the benefits of using an advertising agency. What types of articles are at this site? Go to the "Related Industry Association" section and examine the large number of related industry associations. Pick out three and further explore the industry the association serves. How can each one facilitate an integrated marketing communications program?

external advertising agencies

Company leaders have a variety of options when they decide to hire an advertising agency. All sizes and types of advertising agencies exist. At one end of the spectrum are the highly specialized, boutique-type agencies that offer only one specialized service (e.g., making television ads) or that serve one particular type of client. For example, G & G Advertising of Albuquerque, New Mexico, specializes in advertising to Native Americans, a market of an estimated 10 million people.[1] At the other end of the spectrum are the full-service agencies providing all types of advertising services as well as advice and assistance in working with the other components of the IMC model, such as sales and trade promotions, direct-marketing programs, and public relations events.

Individual advertising agencies provide a number of services for companies seeking to refine their IMC programs. They may include:

- Consulting and giving advice about how to develop target markets
- Providing specialized services for business markets
- Providing suggestions on how to project a strong company image and theme
- Supplying assistance in selecting company logos and slogans
- Preparation of advertisements
- Planning and purchasing media time and space

In addition to advertising agencies, there are other closely associated types of firms. *Media service companies* negotiate and purchase media packages (called "media buys") for companies. *Direct-marketing agencies* handle every aspect of a direct-marketing campaign, either through telephone orders (800 numbers), through Internet programs, or by direct mail. Some companies focus on either *sales promotions or trade promotions* or both. These companies assist in giveaways such as pens and calendars. They also provide assistance in making posters, end-of-aisle displays, and other attention-getting mechanisms. *Public relations* firms are experts in helping companies and individuals develop positive public images and are called in for damage control when negative publicity arises. In-house members of the organization can render these activities, just as an in-house marketing department can perform advertising and IMC programs. In both instances, company leaders must decide how they can complete these key marketing activities effectively and efficiently.

A recent trend in the advertising industry is that some agencies are getting larger by purchasing smaller firms. Still, although the top 500 agencies in the United States had billings (charges made to client companies) of $15 billion in 1998, this amount was only 13 percent of the total $116.25 billion in billings. Worldwide, the top 20 agencies generated billings of $25.63 billion, or 13 percent of the total $197.96 billion. This means there is still room for the small, dynamic advertising agency.

As would be expected, New York City is the capital of the advertising world. Big Apple agencies generated a total of $44.57 billion in 1997 in billings, which was 38 percent of all U.S. billings. In addition to being known as the capital of advertising, New York City is the home of the largest agency, Grey Advertising, which had billings of $2.82 billion in 1997.[5]

A second recent trend in advertising began over two decades ago. The Young and Rubicam Advertising Agency introduced its "whole egg theory." The concept of the whole egg theory was to move from selling a client's products to helping the client achieve total success in the marketplace. Achieving success requires integrating the marketing approach by offering a fuller array of services to both business and consumer clients. Thus, as client companies began to move toward more integrated marketing approaches, agencies such as Young and Rubicam captured more accounts. Such companies continue to succeed because they work with clients on every aspect of an integrated marketing plan.[6]

The decision to retain an advertising agency is largely based on the belief that the agency can provide important services and assistance. These services give the client firm an advantage in the marketplace. For instance, a high-quality advertising agency can help a firm create and build the type of strong image and brand name critical for survival in the twenty-first century. A strong brand name strengthens both consumer and business-to-business preferences for products. This in turn results in greater sales, lower marketing costs, and allows the producer to charge a price premium. Therefore, finding an advertising agency that can both create a strong brand name and increase brand sales is important for long-run success.

The Ford Motor Company recently decided to build on the company's brand name to achieve a greater level of success in the marketplace. To rejuvenate the Ford brand and new Focus automobile in Europe, Ford Motor Company asked both Young and Rubicam from the United States and the European agency Ogilvy & Mather Worldwide to prepare bids. Both advertising agencies worked for six months on presentations for Ford's European managers. Young and Rubicam won the $100 million Focus account and a $90 million corporate account. Ford was so impressed with Young and Rubicam's strategic thinking about the Ford brand and its work on the small budget models of the Puma and Cougar that it transferred four other model accounts (Ka, Fiesta, Explorer, and Windstar) from Ogilvy & Mather Worldwide to Young and Rubicam.[7] In this instance, the advertising agency of Young and Rubicam convinced Ford that it had the most effective program to help the organization succeed in the long run.

The process of choosing an advertising agency is difficult. The company's leaders must decide how much involvement the agency will have and how many functions the agency should be able to perform. The next step is to develop effective selection criteria to help company leaders make wise choices in the process of hiring an advertising agency.

stop!

Integrated Learning Experience

A number of agencies assist business organizations with integrated marketing communications programs. Whereas some firms try to provide a wide array of services, others are more specialized. Using the Council of Public Relations Firms Web site at www.prfirms.org, locate some local public relations firms. What type of services do these firms offer? Access the Promotion Marketing Association, Inc. at www.pmalink.com. What types of information does this site contain? How would this information benefit a business, a sales promotion firm, or an advertising agency trying to outsource the sales promotions aspects of its work? For outdoor advertising, access the Outdoor Advertising Association of America at www.oaaa.org. What type of information does this site contain? For direct-marketing firms, check the Direct Marketing Association site at www.the-dma.org. What information is useful to a business organization looking for help with a direct-marketing program?

choosing an agency

Choosing the advertising agency that best suits a company requires careful planning. Figure 7.3 lists the steps involved in this process. Additional information about each of these steps follows.

Goal setting
Before making any contact with an advertising agency, it is important to identify and prioritize various corporate goals. Goals provide a sense of direction for the company's leaders, for the agency account executive, and for the advertising creative. Each is more likely to be "on the same page" as preparation of the advertising campaign unfolds. Without clearly understood goals, it becomes virtually impossible to choose an agency, because company leaders may not have a clear idea what they want to accomplish. Unambiguous goals help ensure a good fit between the company and the agency.

Selection criteria
The second step in selecting an agency is to finalize the process and refine the criteria that will be used. Even firms that have experience in selecting agencies must establish the process and criteria in advance. The objective is to reduce biases that may enter into the decision process. Emotions and other feelings can lead to biased decisions that are not in the company's best interests. Although good chemistry

- ❱ Identify and prioritize corporate goals
- ❱ Develop agency selection process and criteria
- ❱ Initially screen firms based on credentials, size, capabilities, relevant experience, and conflict of interests
- ❱ Request client references
- ❱ Do background check with other firms and media agents
- ❱ Request written and oral presentation
- ❱ Meet creatives, media buyers, account executives, and other personnel that will work with account
- ❱ Select and draw up contract

Steps in Selecting an Advertising Agency

FIGURE 7.3

between the agency and the firm is important, this aspect of the choice comes later in the process, after the list has been narrowed down to two or three agencies.

Figure 7.4 lists some of the major issues to be considered as part of the selection process. This list is especially useful in the initial screening process, when the task is to narrow the field to the top five (or fewer) agencies.

The *size* of the agency is important, especially as it compares to the size of the company hiring the agency. If a large firm were to hire a small agency, the small agency may be overwhelmed by the account. A small firm hiring a large agency may find that the company's account might be lost or could be treated as being insignificant. A good rule of thumb to follow regarding the size of the agency is that the account should be large enough for the agency that it is important to the agency but small enough that, if lost, the agency would not be badly affected.

When Norwest Banks of Minneapolis acquired Wells Fargo of San Francisco, the size of the company tripled. Norwest's agency, Carmichael Lynch, was not large enough to handle the new larger company. According to Larry Haeg, "We needed the resources and services of a larger agency."[8] In this case, it was not a matter of the firm being incompetent, but rather that Norwest needed a wider variety of services and expertise when the company began to grow.

Relevant experience in an industry is the second type of evaluation criteria that companies use. When an agency has experience in a given industry, it better

- ❱ Size of the agency
- ❱ Relevant experience of the agency
- ❱ Conflicts of interest
- ❱ Creative reputation and capabilities
- ❱ Production capabilities
- ❱ Media purchasing capabilities
- ❱ Other services available
- ❱ Client retention rates
- ❱ Personal chemistry

Evaluation Criteria in Choosing an Ad Agency

FIGURE 7.4

In addition to the backstroke and the butterfly, I can perform a world-class chug-a-lug. With milk. It has protein for my muscles, plus essential vitamins and minerals like calcium and potassium. All of which help me get the one mineral every Olympian craves. Gold.

MILK

Where's *your mustache?*™

The milk industry is just one of the accounts handled by the Bozell Advertising Agency.

Courtesy of Bozell Worldwide, Inc.

understands the client firm, its customers, and the structure of the marketing channel. At the same time, it is important to be certain the agency does not have any *conflicts of interest.* An advertising firm that has been hired by one manufacturer of tires experiences a conflict of interest if the firm is hired by another tire company. Further, the agency should have relevant experience without representing a competitor. Such experience may be gained when an agency sells a related product or works for a similar company that operates in a different industry. For example, if an agency has a manufacturer of automobile batteries as a client, this experience is relevant to selling automobile tires. The agency should have experience with the business-to-business side of the market, so that retailers, wholesalers, and any other channel party is considered in the marketing and advertising of the product.

All of the milk advertisements in this textbook were created by Bozell. In addition to the milk advertisements, Bozell's clients include Datek Online, Bank of America, Unisys, Lycos, Excedrin, Jergens, and the pork industry. Notice that this list does not include competing firms within the same industry. Also note that Bozell's success in promoting milk led the pork industry to believe Bozell would have the right kind of expertise to promote pork products.

The initial screening process includes an investigation into each agency's *creative reputation and capabilities.* One method of judging an agency's creativity is to ask for a list of awards the company has received. Although awards do not always translate into effective advertisements, in most cases there is a positive relationship between winning awards and writing effective ads. Most creative awards are given by peers. As a result, they are good indicators of what others think of the agency's creative efforts. Assessing creative capabilities is very important when developing advertising campaigns for a different country in which the firm has limited experience.

Production capabilities and *media purchasing capabilities* of the agencies should be examined if these services are needed as the company prepares its advertising campaign. The information is gathered to be sure the agency has the desired capabilities. A firm needing an agency to both produce the television commercial and buy media time should check on these items as part of the initial screening process. Media buying skills are important. Questions the company should ask in this area include:

- Does the agency buy efficiently?
- Is the agency able to negotiate special rates and publication positions?
- Does the agency routinely get "bumped" by higher-paying firms, so ads do not run at highly desirable times?

This type of information can be difficult to obtain. The company hiring the agency must be persistent and engage in thorough research. Accessing each agency's Web page, reading annual reports, and searching for news articles about individual agencies can be helpful. Most ad agencies provide prospectus sheets describing their capabilities. These reports render some information about their media buying skills.

The final three selection criteria—*other services available, client retention rates,* and *personal chemistry*—are revealed as the final steps of selection take place. These criteria help make the final determination in the selection process.

Reference requests

Once the initial screening is complete, it is time to request references from those agencies still in the running for the contract. Most agencies willingly provide lists of their best customers to serve as references. A good strategy the company can use is to obtain references of firms that have similar needs. Also, when possible, it helps to obtain names of former clients of the agency. Finding out why they switched can provide valuable information. Often changes are made for legitimate reasons. Discovering an agency's *client retention rate* helps reveal how effective the firm has been in working with various clients. Poor service is not the only reason a firm switches advertising agencies. As noted in the case of Norwest Banks, the advertising agency was let go because it was too small to handle the increased size of Norwest.[9]

Background checks also provide useful information. This can be accomplished by finding firms that have dealt with each agency. Also, talking to media agents who sell media time provides insights as to how an agency buys time and deals with customers. Companies that have formed contracts with individual agencies for production facilities or other services are excellent sources of information. Background checks help the client company make sure the agency can provide quality professional services.

Oral and written presentations

The next step in the selection process is to request an oral and written presentation by the finalists. The agency should be willing to provide a formal presentation addressing a specific problem, situation, or set of questions. These presentations reveal how each agency would deal with specific issues that arise as a campaign is prepared. This helps client companies ascertain whether the agency uses tactics and methods that are acceptable.

Meeting key personnel

During the presentation phase, the opportunity exists to meet with the creatives, media buyers, account executives, and any other personnel who will be working with an account. *Chemistry* between employees of the two different firms is important. The client companies' leaders should be convinced that they will work well together and that they feel comfortable with each other.

In competing for the new Norwest–Wells Fargo account, the firm DDB was chosen over the incumbent agency, Carmichael Lynch, because Fargo executives believed DDB had greater strategic insights, a better range of services, higher-quality creatives, and offered a more thorough media plan. DDB was able to show how the agency intended to combine the strength of Wells Fargo's 150-year heritage with the excellent customer service qualities of Norwest. This presentation led to the decision to hire DDB. It came after Fargo executives listened to the presentations of both agencies and asked key questions about who would actually be working on the account.[10]

Whenever possible, a client company's leaders should visit the advertising agency's office as part of the evaluation process. Often agencies use people called "heavy hitters" to win contracts, but then turn the account over to other individuals in the agency after signing the deal. Visiting the agency's office provides an opportunity to meet every person who might work on the account. Talking with these individuals generates quality information about how the account will be handled. The visiting period also can be used to hammer out specific details, such as identifying the actual person(s) who will work on the advertisements, and either agreeing to the use of freelancers (independent contractors who provide various services) to work on the project or prohibiting the agency from using such individuals.

Selection and contract

The final step of the process is to make the choice and to notify all finalists of the decision. A contract is drawn up with the advertising agency to specify all terms and activities and letters are written to agencies that did not win the bid. Many times, these agencies contact the company seeking information about why they were not chosen. It is in the interests of both organizations to remain cordial and professional, even when a contract is not given, because they may do business in the future.

When the process has been completed, the agency and the company work together to prepare the advertising campaign. Along the way, the account executive plays a key role in the process, as does the advertising creative and media buyer. A brief review of the activities performed by these two individuals follows.

stop!

Integrated Learning Experience

The *Advertising Age* Web site at www.adage.com provides considerable information about advertising agencies that helps in understanding the selection process. In the "World Brands" section, look for the list of the top 25 advertising agencies. Using the search function, enter an advertiser and see what agencies are used in the various countries in which the advertiser operates. By clicking on "Summary Chart," you can find the primary advertising agencies that various firms employ. Locate the advertising agencies Procter & Gamble, Nestlé, and Coca-Cola use. Access the Web sites of these agencies to try to discover why these particular agencies were selected. Finally, select the "Account Action" section, which contains the accounts up for renewal or open to bid. Study the various companies looking for agencies and the type of agencies being considered.

the roles of advertising account executives

The **advertising account executive** is the key go-between for both the advertising agency and the client company. This individual is actively involved in soliciting the account, finalizing details of the contract, and selecting the creatives who will prepare the actual advertising campaign. Many times, the account executive helps the company refine and define its major message for an overall IMC program and provides other support as needed.

As noted throughout this textbook, advertising agencies and account executives are expected to produce measurable results. Whether the agency is marketing a 50-cent candy bar or a $40,000 car, the pressure for tangible results is present. Unfortunately, much of the impact of certain types of advertisements is not easy to measure. For example, brand image and brand equity are highly important but difficult to evaluate. This problem is further compounded when advertising agencies fail to effectively demonstrate what they have accomplished. In many cases the agency may be doing a good job but is unable to convince the company's leaders.

Clients always want to know if they are getting a good value for their investment. Most clients believe they don't have a clue in trying to understand the relationship between an agency's cost and its actual value to the company. Ron Cox, a vice-president at Wrigley Jr. Company, suggests that agencies update clients regularly on the work they are doing and the results obtained. These types of reports (called *stewardship reports*) help clients understand the process and the outcome more clearly. Updating clients on what is being done for them becomes more important as the amount being spent on advertising increases.[11]

Further, periodic reviews should be held to show that the agency is doing its work. These reviews need not be confrontational. To the client company, these updates represent the opportunity to evaluate how well the agency has done and also to become better acquainted with the personnel working on the account. As part of the process, the client firm can spend time with creatives as they work on the campaign. Client companies can also talk to media buyers, public relations experts, and others working on the account. In short, the account manager oversees the process in such a way that everyone involved feels comfortable and oriented toward the goal of creating an effectively integrated advertising campaign and marketing communications program.

The traffic manager works closely with the account executive. This person's responsibility is to schedule the various aspects of the agency's work to ensure the work is completed by the target deadline. See the Communication Action Box for more information about how the traffic manager serves an important link between the account executive and the creatives.

communication**action**

An Interview with a Traffic Manager

One individual who plays a key role in the media scheduling process is a traffic manager. Gretchen Hoag plays this role in her agency, Publicis Technology. We asked her to describe the job. She responded,

> I have many responsibilities, but my main purpose is to manage the workflow and ensure that all deadlines are met. Along with managing the process, I'm also in charge of maintaining project history, creating schedules, managing resources, setting up team meetings, prioritizing projects, training new employees about agency processes, setting up new clients, routing proofs, proofreading, and whatever else is needed to get the job done. One of the best things about my job is that I work closely with every team member within the agency. Not many people have the opportunity to work with so many different types of people, as I do.

We then asked Gretchen to describe a typical day at work. She replied,

> There is no such thing as a typical day in an ad agency no matter what your job is, but traffic managers probably have the least typical days of anyone. In traffic, you could spend the majority of one day creating schedules and the next routing and proofreading mechanicals, and the day after that opening up new jobs and attending kick off meetings. There are a few things that do remain constant, I always have paperwork to file, history to record in my databases, and team members to keep happy.
>
> Usually when it comes time to schedule a project, I create a basic outline of when I think the project can be completed. This is very difficult, because the artwork has not been concepted yet. I don't know if I'm scheduling for an illustration, stock photography, a photo shoot or a text only ad. So I have to guess.

With this client I guess the artwork will take about two weeks to complete. Once I have an outline completed, I talk with each of my team members to see if they agree with my schedule. Most importantly, I need to make sure my timing corresponds with media's timing. Once the team is in agreement on the schedule, I can create a formal estimate for the client. At this time the account team works with the client to ensure they can commit to the deadlines as well.

Of course all this guesswork changes once a concept has been chosen. Maybe we have to paint a backdrop, which will take the artist three weeks to complete before a photo shoot can happen. Or perhaps we are using stock photography, which will perhaps allow the schedule to be sped up a bit. This is where good juggling skills and flexibility come into play.

After a schedule has been approved, I evaluate all of my current projects and then work with the other traffic managers to see what jobs they have scheduled. We reevaluate each client's needs for each team member day-by-day. If one person in either the creative department or the production department is overwhelmed then we reassign work, or if everyone appears to be booked we can try to push schedules around or perhaps bring in freelance help. Occasionally, we can predict days or weeks when we will need extra help, like the week two art directors were going to be out of the office. Basically, we do whatever is humanly possible to get the job done as efficiently and cost effectively as we can, while maintaining the highest standards for our clients.

Ideally on a print project, I would like to schedule about four weeks for creative concepting, two to three weeks to simultaneously write copy and produce artwork, three to four days to build mechanical, and one week for color corrections. This will work for some of the product categories, because they have existing creative we can continue running until the new creative is completed. But there are some product categories that have media purchased and no existing creative work for. Given this information, we need to work on these jobs first and wait on the product categories we already have materials for. Before we can concentrate on the individual product categories, we have to go through a look and feel exercise.

Once the look and feel has been decided on, we can begin the product ads, which does not allow us much time. So, we have to crunch down what would normally take seven to nine weeks to three to four weeks. In order to do this, my creative team will present only concepts that we know we can produce in this short time frame. We also cut down on the time we can come up with ideas for the campaign and we beg for additional time from the publications to see if we can receive an extension on the material due dates. If our other clients also have jobs in the creative concepting stage, I may even need to bring in additional art directors and copywriters to work on the job.

Being a traffic manager makes her part of a larger team that also includes the account service people, clients, and creatives. Here is how Gretchen describes some of these relationships.

I work with the account service people very closely. They are the ones who are directly in front of the client representing the agency, so they play a very important role in the process. They filter through all the information from the client and pass the information on to me. I then pass the information on to the appropriate team members. I do this by meeting with all of my account service people at least once a day to be sure they are comfortable with the status of all their projects and to discuss any new information from the client.

Regarding the agency's clients, Gretchen told us,

The account team is responsible for maintaining the relationship with the client, which includes all contact with the client. However, my number and name has been passed on to many of our clients. I have been known to serve as backup when the account teams are out of the office. I also have been pulled into meetings and conference calls to explain schedules and to give technical explanations about color and film processes.

There are also involvements with other members of the marketing team, making the job of traffic manager more complex. Here's what Gretchen told us about other people at work:

I also have a close relationship with the creative and production teams. Let's face it, no one likes to be told what to do and how quickly it needs to be done, especially if the due date requires working on the weekend or staying past 5:00. And as a traffic manager, I am the person who has the distinct honor of relaying this kind of bad news. It is by far the hardest part of the job. But not all of our conversations are based on bad news. The creative and production departments depend on the traffic managers to help them to work uninterrupted, which is one reason why all information filters through us.

We asked her if she chooses the creatives who will work on an assignment. She replied,

Yes and no. Since I have such a close relationship with my creatives, I do recommend to the Creative Director who I would like to see working on a particular project. I would like to think I am really in-tune with how each team member within the department likes to work, what type of projects they thrive on, and more importantly, how much work each person can handle.

Finally, we asked her to describe her role in making sure that all the communication is integrated into a common theme. She said,

Here is another area where my role is limited. However, Publicis Technology is a real team environment. Generally speaking we were all hired for strengths in a particular area of expertise and you would not want to overstep those bounds, but if you are lucky enough to work in the kind of team environment, those boundaries are a little less clear. Everything we produce or show the client is a reflection on the entire agency, so we all feel ownership in the projects we work on. Every client has a creative team member who is what we call a brand guardian. The brand guardian's responsibility is to maintain that particular client's standards. We also have an editor on staff, who is responsible for proofing all work against the client's style sheet. The account team reviews work against the strategic and creative briefs. I review all work against my own knowledge and client notes and records that I maintain. So really all team members are looking out for the client's best interests. My main role is to point out any issues that may be found to the other team members to determine how we would like to address the issue and to make sure that all recommended changes are made.

the roles of creatives

Creatives are the persons who actually develop and produce advertisements. These individuals are either members of advertising agencies or freelancers. Some smaller companies provide only creative advertising services without becoming involved in other marketing programs and activities. Creatives may appear to hold the "glamour" jobs in advertising, because they express their talents in the advertisements they produce. At the same time, creatives face long hours and work under enormous pressures to design ads that are effective and produce results that client companies and marketing account managers want. The role of the creative is discussed in the section on creative briefs later in this chapter.

advertising campaign management

Managing an advertising campaign is the process of preparing and integrating a specific advertising program in conjunction with the overall IMC message. An effective program consists of five steps. The steps are similar to the planning processes described in Chapter 3. The steps of **advertising campaign management** are:

1. Review the communication market analysis.
2. Establish communication objectives consistent with those developed in a promotions opportunity analysis program.
3. Review the communications budget.
4. Select the media in conjunction with the advertising agency.
5. Review the information with the advertising creative in the creative brief.

The advertising program should be consistent with previous activities performed as part of the IMC program. This helps to make sure the firm presents a clear message to key target markets, and advertising efforts can then be refined to gain the maximum benefit from the promotional dollars being spent. A review of the steps involved is next.

communication market analysis

In the first phase of planning, the account executive studies what the company's communication market analysis reveals (see Chapter 3). The *competitive analysis* identifies the firm's major competitors. The *opportunity analysis* reveals where the firm can best focus its advertising and promotional efforts by discovering company strengths along with opportunities present in the marketplace. The *target market analysis* identifies key target markets. The *customer analysis* suggests how the firm's previous marketing communications efforts have been received by the public as well as by other businesses and potential customers. A *positioning analysis* explains how the firm and its products are perceived relative to the competition. The value of reviewing the communication market analysis is in focusing the account executive, the creative, and the company itself on key markets and customers, while helping them understand how the firm currently competes in the marketplace. Then the team is better able to establish and pursue specific advertising objectives.

For the purposes of advertising, two important items are outlined as part of the communication market analysis:

1. The media usage habits of the target market
2. The media utilized by the competition

When analyzing customers, knowing which media they use is vitally important. For example, teenagers watch many hours of television and listen to the radio. Only a small percentage reads newspapers and newsmagazines. Various market segments have differences in when and how they view various media. For example, older blacks watch television programs in patterns quite different from older Caucasians. Males watch more sports programs than females and so forth. In the business-to-business market, knowing which trade journals or business publications the various members of the buying center most likely read is essential for the development of a print advertising campaign. Engineers, who tend to be the influencers, have different media viewing habits than do vice-presidents, who may be the deciders. Discovering which media reach a target market (and which do not) is a key component in a communication market analysis and an advertising program.

Further, studying the competition reveals how other firms attempt to reach customers. Knowing how other firms contact consumers is as important as knowing what they say. An effective communication market analysis reveals this information, so that more effective messages and advertising campaigns can be designed.

Integrated Learning Experience

Part of a communication market analysis is understanding the media usage habits of consumers and their attitudes toward the various media. An excellent source of information in Canada is the Media Awareness Network at www.media-awareness.ca. Review the types of information available at this site. In the "Media Industries" section, examine the news archives. Find articles that relate to media usage to help a firm better understand its target market's media usage habits. What types of information are in the other sections such as "Media Issues" and "News"?

stop!

communication and advertising objectives

The second step of advertising planning is to establish and clarify advertising and communication objectives. Several advertising goals are central to the IMC process. Some of these goals are listed in Figure 7.5. A discussion of each individual goal area follows.[12]

Building brand image

One of the most important advertising goals is to build a global brand and corporate image. These, in turn, generate brand equity. As discussed in Chapter 4, brand equity is a set of characteristics that makes a brand more desirable to consumers and businesses. These benefits can be enhanced when we combine effective advertising with quality products and services. Higher levels of brand equity give the company a distinct advantage as consumers move toward purchase decisions.

Advertising is a critical component in the effort to build brand equity. Successful brands have two characteristics: being (1) "top of mind" and (2) the consumers' "top choice." When consumers are asked to identify brands that quickly come to mind from a product category, one particular brand is nearly always mentioned. That name has the property of being a **top of mind brand.** For example, when asked to identify fast-food restaurants, McDonald's almost always heads the list. The same is true for Kodak film and Campbell's Soups. This is true not only in the United States but also in many other countries. The term **top choice** suggests exactly what the term implies: A top choice brand is the first or second pick when a consumer reviews his or her evoked set of possible purchasing alternatives.

Part of building brand image and brand equity is developing brand awareness, and advertising is the best method to reach that goal. Brand awareness means the consumers recognize and remember a particular brand or company name when they consider purchasing options. Brand awareness, brand image, brand equity are vital for success.

In business-to-business marketing, brand awareness is often essential to being considered by members of the buying center. It is important for business customers

- ▶ **To build brand image**
- ▶ **To inform**
- ▶ **To persuade**
- ▶ **To support other marketing efforts**
- ▶ **To encourage action**

Advertising Goals

FIGURE 7.5

Campbell's Soups builds on its brand name to sell a new product.
Courtesy of Campbell Soup Corporation.

to recognize the brand name(s) of the various products or services a company sells. Brand awareness is especially important in modified rebuy situations, when a firm looks to change to a new vendor or evaluates a product or service that has not been purchased recently. In new buy situations, firms spend more time seeking prospective vendors than they do in modified rebuys. Consequently, brand equity is a major advantage for the firm who has such recognition. Further, many firms have increased their importing and exporting activities. As a result, developing recognized and accepted global brands has become an increasingly important part of many marketing programs.

Providing information

Besides building brand recognition and equity, advertising serves other goals. For example, advertising often is used to provide information to both consumers and business buyers. Typical information for consumers includes a retailer's store hours, business location, or sometimes more detailed product specifications. Information can make the purchasing process appear to be convenient and relatively simple, which can entice customers to finalize the purchasing decision and travel to the store.

For business-to-business situations, information from some ads leads various members of the buying center to consider a particular company as they examine their options. This type of information is the most useful when members of the buying center are in the information search stage of the purchasing process. For high-involvement types of purchases, wherein members of the buying center have strong vested interests in the success of the choice, informative advertisements are the most beneficial. Low-involvement decisions usually do not require as much detail.

In marketing to both consumers and other businesses, information can help those involved reach a decision. Information is one component of persuasion, another objective of various advertising programs.

Persuasion

One of the most common goals of advertising programs is persuasion. Advertisements can convince consumers that a particular brand is superior to other brands. They can show consumers the negative consequences of failing to use a particular brand. Changing consumer attitudes and persuading them to consider a new purchasing choice is a challenging task. As described later on, advertisers can utilize several methods of persuasion. Persuasive advertising is used more in consumer marketing than in business-to-business situations. Persuasion techniques are used more frequently in broadcast media such as television and radio than in print advertising.

Supporting marketing efforts

Another goal of advertising is to support other marketing functions. For example, manufacturers use advertising to support trade and consumer promotions, such as theme packaging or combination offers. Contests, such as the McDonald's Monopoly promotion, require extensive advertising to be effective. Retailers also use advertising to support their marketing programs. Any type of special sale (white sale, buy-one-get-one-free, pre-Christmas sale) needs vigorous advertising to attract customers to the store. Both manufacturers and retail outlets use advertising in conjunction with coupons or other special offers. Del Monte placed a 30 cent coupon in the advertisement shown below. The ad highlights a smaller-size container with a pull-top lid. These features match the ad's target market: senior citizens. The magazine outlet in which the ad ran was *Modern Maturity*. Manufacturer

An advertisement for Del Monte vegetables directed to senior customers by offering a price-off coupon offer. Courtesy of Del Monte.

coupons are regularly redeemed at grocery stores (sometimes at double their face value), and in-store coupons are part of many retail store print advertisements. When ads are combined with other marketing efforts into a larger, more integrated effort revolving around a theme, the program is called a **promotional campaign.**

Encouraging action

Many times firms set motivational types of goals for their advertising programs. Television commercials that encourage viewers to take action by dialing a toll-free number to make quick purchases are examples. Everything from Veg-A-Matics to CDs and cassettes are sold using action tactics. More recently, infomercials and home shopping network programs heavily rely on immediate consumer purchasing responses.

Action-oriented advertising is heavily used in the business-to-business sector. The goal is to generate sales leads. Many business advertisements provide a Web address or telephone numbers that buyers can use to request more information or move toward a purchase more easily.

The five advertising goals of building image, providing information, being persuasive, supporting other marketing efforts, and encouraging action are not separate ideas. They work together in key ways. Image and information are part of persuasion. Thus, when Barnes & Noble announces its Internet sales program, the firm's image combines with the information provided to persuade on-line book buyers to consider it rather than Amazon.com. The goal of encouraging action is often part of supporting other marketing tactics. The key advertising management objective is to emphasize one goal without forgetting the others.

the communications budget

Once the company, account manager, and creative agree upon the major goals of the advertising campaign, a review of the communications budget is in order. In Chapter 3, various methods for establishing budgets were described, including the following methods:

- Percentage of sales
- Meet the competition
- "What we can afford"
- Objective and task

After the total dollars allocated to advertising have been established, account managers and company leaders agree to uses for the funds. This includes the media to be utilized (television versus newspaper versus billboards). Also, however, the *manner of distribution* must be arranged. Three basic tactics include:

- Advertising the most when sales are at peak seasons
- Advertising the most during low sales seasons
- Level amounts

Firms that advertise during peak seasons such as Christmas are emphasizing sending out the message when customers are most inclined to buy. Since consumers are on the "hot spot," this approach makes sense for some products. For example, Weight Watchers, Diet Centers, and others advertise heavily during the first two weeks of January. Many New Year's resolutions include going on a diet. In fact, in January 2000, Monica Lewinsky was introduced as the new spokesperson for the Jenny Craig weight-loss program.

Advertising during peak seasons can be accomplished in two ways. The first is a **pulsating schedule of advertising.** This schedule involves continuous advertising with bursts of higher intensity (more ads in more media) during the course of the year, most notably during peak seasons. Companies can also utilize what is called a **flighting** approach or schedule, where ads are presented only during peak times, and not at all during off seasons.

The firms that decide to advertise the most during slow sales seasons are essentially oriented toward "drumming up business" when people do not regularly buy. In retail sales, slow seasons occur during January and February. Some companies advertise more during those periods to sell off merchandise left over from the Christmas season.

Many marketing experts believe it is best to advertise in level amounts, particularly when a product purchase is essentially a "random" event. This approach is a **continuous campaign schedule.** For example, many durable goods, such as washing machines and refrigerators, are purchased on an "as needed" basis. A family ordinarily buys a new washing machine only when the old one finally breaks down. Consequently, level advertising increases the odds that the buyer will remember a given name (Maytag, Whirlpool, General Electric). Also, there is a better chance that consumers will be exposed to ads close to the time they are ready to make purchases.

In any case, the objective should be to match the pacing of advertisements with the message, media, and the nature of the product or service. Some media make it easier to advertise for longer periods of time. For instance, billboards are normally posted for a month or a year. They can be rotated throughout a town or city to present a continuing message about the company or its products. Budgetary constraints must also be incorporated into the strategies and tactics used in the advertising program.

media selection

The next step of advertising management is to develop strategies and tactics associated with media selection, refining intent of the message, and development of the actual campaign with specific ads. It is crucial to develop consistent messages that match with various media. Media buys are guided by the advertising agency or media agency, the company, and the creative. In the next chapter, the advantages and disadvantages of all relevant media are described. Also, the expanding number of usable media is described. They should complement the IMC program. When media selection is performed carefully, and messages are designed to fit with those choices, the chances for success greatly increase.

For example, Monster.com hired the Mullen advertising agency to create the definitive promotional campaign for a new on-line job search site. The primary goal of the campaign was to increase brand awareness, so that Monster.com would become the first brand Americans think of when they are ready to change jobs, that is, top of mind. When the process began, most job searchers had little brand awareness regarding any specific company or brand. Most viewed all Internet job search sites as being essentially equal. The only differentiation that was apparent among the sites was the number of job or resumés listed.

If the goal of high brand awareness could be reached, Mullen would then work toward enhancing Monster.com's brand image. To heighten brand awareness, Mullen recommended Monster.com advertise on the Super Bowl. Although spots on the Super Bowl telecast are quite expensive (almost $2 million per spot), the program would provide Monster.com with a large audience.

The most critical task facing Mullen Agency was to design an effective message. To be successful, the advertisement had to break through the clutter of the ads and garner the viewers' attention. Monster.com used an emotional appeal designed to touch people dissatisfied with their current jobs and wanted to work for companies that would treat them right. Instead of focusing on items such as job listings, Monster.com presented the image of a firm that cares about people and finds them good jobs with quality companies. The ads resulted in increases in job searches of 2,604 percent, and new posted resumé listings grew by 472 percent.[13]

The Monster.com experience demonstrates the effective use of an advertising plan. The firm was aware of the potential market and of the activities of competitors. The company set the goals of increased brand awareness and a positive brand image and worked within a budget to buy airtime on the Super Bowl. The strategies and tactics (media choice combined with tone of advertisements) matched with the overall IMC plan by developing a message with the greatest meaning for the target audience. Advertising management is part of the overall IMC scheme. When effectively coordinated, a company develops a major advantage in the competitive arena. These coordination efforts are largely guided by a creative brief, which is the final step of the campaign program to accompany producing the actual advertisements.

stop!

Integrated Learning Experience

Media selection is an important component in a successful IMC program. A resource that contains considerable information about various media is Responservice at www.responservice.com. The Times-Group promotes it as the advertising, media, and marketing one-stop shop. From its menu, examine all the different sections available and the types of information within each section. How can a firm use this information in the development of an IMC plan?

the creative brief

In preparing advertisements, creatives work with a document called a creative strategy or creative brief. The components of a creative brief are provided in Figure 7.6. Using this instrument, the creative takes the information provided by the account executive and is expected to produce an advertisement that conveys the desired message in a manner that will positively impact potential customers. Details about each element of the creative brief are provided next.

The objective

The first step in preparing the creative strategy is to identify the objective of the advertisement. Possible objectives include:

- Increase brand awareness
- Build brand image
- Increase customer traffic
- Increase retailer or wholesaler orders
- Increase inquiries from end users and channel members
- Provide information

The creative must understand the main objective before designing an advertisement, because the primary objectives guide the design of the advertisement and the choice of an executional theme. An ad to increase brand awareness prominently

The Creative Brief

FIGURE 7.6

> ▶ **The objective**
> ▶ **The target audience**
> ▶ **The message theme**
> ▶ **The support**
> ▶ **The constraints**

Soft on sinks.
Brutal on bacteria.

Antibacterial Soft Scrub.
Soft Scrub Cleanser kills 99.9% of household germs and bacteria, while it cleans and removes stains. Yet, it's as kind as ever to your surfaces.

Use only as directed. ©1998 The Clorox Company.

An advertisement for Soft Scrub designed to enhance the brand's image by displaying the product prominently. Courtesy of The Clorox Company.

displayes the *name* of the product. An ad to build brand image can display the *actual product* more prominently as in the Soft Scrub advertisement shown in this section.

The target audience

A creative should know the target audience. An advertisement designed to persuade a business to inquire about new computer software will be different than a consumer advertisement from the same company. A business advertisement focuses on the type of industry and the project member of the buying center who will see it. The more detail that is known about the target audience, the easier it is for a creative to design an effective advertisement.

Target market profiles that are too general are not very helpful. Rather than specifying males, ages 20 to 35, more specific information is needed (e.g., males, 20 to 35, college educated, professionals). Other information such as hobbies, interests, opinions, and lifestyles makes targeting an advertisement even more precise. Notice that the Playtex advertisement on the next page is designed for young females who enjoy playing sports and have an active lifestyle. This additional information was needed to create an advertisement that appeals to this particular market segment of females.

The message theme

The message theme is an outline of key idea(s) that the advertising program is supposed to convey. The message theme is the benefit or promise the advertiser wants

It's true. Pads feel so much like diapers.

With Playtex Gentle Glide all you feel is comfortable.

Yes, even the thinnest pads can give you this weird, uncomfortable feeling, like you're wearing a diaper. Who needs protection like that? Playtex Gentle Glide tampons give you a more comfortable way to deal with your period. They have a unique design that adjusts to comfort fit. So whatever you do the only thing you feel is totally comfortable!

So **comfortable** you can't even feel them.

Visit our website at www.playtextampons.com

An advertisement for Playtex using additional target market profile information to design a message directed to teenage and young adult females. Courtesy of Playtex Products, Inc.

I never get bent out of shape over a few vampires. And with fat free milk on my tray, there's a good chance I never will. It has calcium to help prevent osteoporosis. So have a nice tall glass. It's easier to keep your neck out of a vampire's reach if you can stand up straight.

got milk?

An advertisement by the milk industry illustrating the importance of maintaining a consistent theme over time. Courtesy of Bozell Worldwide, Inc.

to use to reach consumers or businesses. The promise or unique selling point should describe the major benefit the product or service offers customers. For example, the message theme for an automobile could be oriented toward luxury, safety, fun, fuel efficiency, or driving excitement. The message theme for a hotel could focus on luxury, price, or unusual features, such as a hotel in Paris, France, noting the ease of access to all of the nearby tourist attractions. The message theme should match the medium selected, the target market, and the primary IMC message to be effective.[14]

Notice the advertisement by the milk industry featuring Sarah Michelle Gellar. The theme of milk providing the calcium needed for strong bones is consistently used in a number of "got milk?" advertisements, as is the visual display of the white mustache. Although the model and context change, the theme is consistent.

Message themes can be oriented toward either rational or emotional processes. A "left-brain" ad is oriented toward the logical, rational side, which manages information such as numbers, letters, words, and concepts. Left-brain advertising is logical and factual and the appeals are rational. For example, there are logical features which are part of the decision to buy a car (size, price, special features). At the same time, many cars are purchased for emotional reasons. The right side of the brain deals with the emotions. It works with abstract ideas, images, and feelings. A car may be chosen for its color, sportiness, or other less rational reasons.

Most advertising is either right-brained or left-brained. Effective advertising is produced when there is a balance between the two sides. Rational, economic beings have difficulty defending the purchase of an expensive sports car such as a Porsche. Many product and service purchases are based on how a person feels

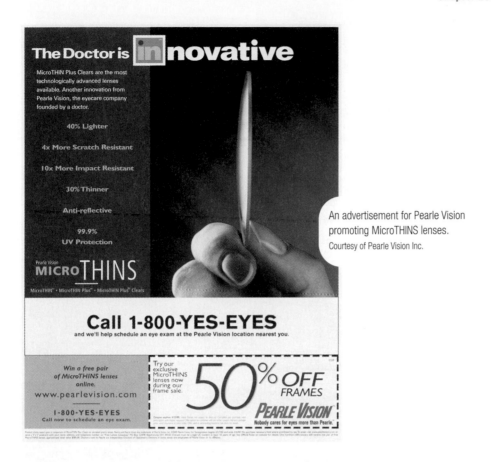

An advertisement for Pearle Vision promoting MicroTHINS lenses.
Courtesy of Pearle Vision Inc.

about the product or service combined with rational information.[15] More complete information about the message theme is provided in Chapter 10.

The support

The fourth component of the creative strategy is the support. **Support** takes the form of the facts that substantiate the message theme. A pain reliever advertising claim of being effective for arthritis may support this point by noting independent medical findings or testimonials from patients with arthritis. Notice the support claims Pearle Vision makes in its advertisement. The microTHINS are 30 percent thinner, 40 percent lighter, 4 times more scratch resistant, 10 times more impact resistant, anti-reflective, and have 99.9 percent UV protection. The creative needs these supporting facts to design effective advertisements.

The constraints

The final step in the development of a creative strategy is identification of any **constraints.** These are the legal and mandatory restrictions placed on advertisements. They include legal protection for trademarks, logos, and copy registrations. They also include disclaimers about warranties, offers, and claims. For warranties, a disclaimer specifies the conditions under which they will be honored. For example, tire warranties often state they apply *under normal driving conditions with routine maintenance,* so that a person cannot ignore tire balancing and rotation and expect to get free new tires when the old ones wear out quickly. Disclaimer warranties notify consumers of potential hazards associated with products. For instance, tobacco advertisements must contain a statement from the Surgeon General about the dangers of smoking and chewing tobacco. Disclaimers about offers spell out the terms of financing agreements, as well as when bonuses or discounts apply. Claims identify the exact nature of the statement made in the advertisement. For example,

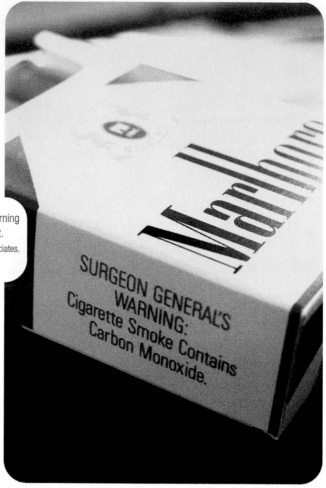

This Surgeon's General's warning is an example of a constraint.
Courtesy of Woodfin Camp & Associates.
Photograph by C. Nacke.

nutritional claims must contain a statement about the size of serving or other information that makes it clear how many nutrients are actually in the product.

After these steps have been reviewed, the creative brief is complete. From this point forward, the message and the media match, and actual advertisements can be produced. Effective creative briefs focus everyone involved on both the IMC message and the current intent of an advertising campaign. This, in turn, gives companies better chances of reaching customers with messages that return measurable results and helps guarantee the success of both the company and the advertising agency.[16]

implications for **marketing professionals**

The Marketing Team

The agency should study the client's paperwork. It will help in designing ads and IMC programs. This includes:

1. Mission statements
2. Goals
3. Past history (through magazine articles, minutes of meetings, etc.)
4. Past advertisements and other marketing activities
5. Advertisements of the competition

The agency should carefully match the "pitch" used to gain new clients with the needs and identities of prospective firms.

Be aware of the relative advantages an external advertising agency holds over in-house programs.

Remember the selection criteria companies use to choose advertising agencies. An agency should solicit client companies where a built-in advantage is present because the agency has the characteristics a company desires. The company, in return, should make certain the agency is being clear about what it offers.

Build the capacity to provide as many marketing activities as possible. If the company cannot provide them directly, work diligently to construct a list of freelancers who are partner organizations, so that the firm can serve as a quality contact point for all types of marketing efforts, including:

1. Direct-marketing campaigns of all types
2. Sales and trade promotions
3. Public relations efforts
4. Advertising campaigns

Build an effective work force through

1. Hiring quality creatives
2. Establishing strong bonds with current creatives
3. Recruiting regularly at schools and universities as well as other places where quality creatives may be found in future years

Company leaders should expect advertising agencies to help them work through every aspect of an advertising campaign, from goal setting, to media selection, to creative briefs, to the actual advertisements, to methods for measuring effectiveness.

Both client companies and advertising agencies can build relationships with media buyers or media agencies that will be contracted to purchase media time (on radio and television) and space (in print media).

SUMMARY

Effective advertising requires matching a noticeable message with appropriate media. Like a company's business cards, stationery, and brochures, a firm's commercials spell out the organization's identity and image. The IMC approach makes certain all of these elements speak with the same voice so that customers can understand clearly the nature of the company, its products and services, and its methods of doing business.

This chapter reviews the advertising management process. Effective advertising is more likely to occur when the firm has a well-defined mission statement and targets its energies in the direction of creating goods or services to meet the needs of a target market. Then an integrated marketing communications program can build on the central theme pursued by those in the firm.

Advertising management begins with deciding whether an in-house department or group should develop advertisements or to retain an external advertising agency. When choosing an external agency, the company's leaders establish clear steps to lead to the best chance that the optimal agency will be selected. The steps include: (1) spelling out and prioritizing organizational goals, (2) carefully establishing quality

selection criteria, (3) screening firms based on those criteria, (4) requesting references from firms that are finalists, (5) performing background checks, (6) requesting a written and oral presentation from the finalist agencies, (7) making an on-site visit to get to know those in the agency, and (8) offering and finalizing a contract.

Common selection criteria used in selecting agencies include: (1) the size of the agency matching the size of the company, (2) relevant experience, (3) no conflicts of interest, (4) production capabilities, (5) quality creative capabilities, (6) suitable media purchasing skills, (7) other services that can be rendered as needed, (8) client retention rates, and (9) a good chemistry between those in the company and those in the agency. Carefully utilizing these criteria increases the odds of a fit and match between the company and the agency, which heightens levels of success.

Within the advertising agency, the account manager performs the functions of soliciting accounts, finalizing contracts, and selecting creatives to prepare advertising campaigns. Account executives are go-betweens who mediate between the agency and the client company. Account executives also help client organizations refine their IMC messages and programs.

Creatives prepare advertisements, and are guided by the creative brief. This document spells out: (1) the objective of the promotional campaign, (2) the target audience, (3) the message theme, (4) the support, and (5) the constraints. The message theme is an outline of the key idea(s) that the program is supposed to convey. The constraints are any warranties, disclaimers, or legal statements that are part of various advertisements.

The creative, account executive, and company should agree about which media to use in a campaign. Media are selected based on costs, types of messages, target market characteristics, and other criteria which will be discussed in detail in Chapter 8. The creatives then complete the final elements of the ad, and the campaign is then prepared.

Advertising management is an important ingredient in the success of an integrated marketing communications program. Quality ads that garner the attention of the target audience, make a key memorable point, and move the buyer to action are difficult to prepare. At the same time, company officials and market account executives know that designing effective ads with tangible results is a challenging but necessary activity. It is important to go through every step of the process carefully, to help the company achieve its marketing goals in both the short and long term.

REVIEW QUESTIONS

1. What is a message theme? What role does a message theme play in an advertising campaign?

2. Define advertising management. What are the four main steps involved?

3. What is the relationship between advertising and the overall IMC process?

4. What three main company activities are part of the advertising management process? What role does the company's mission play in this process?

5. What criteria can be used to help a company decide between an in-house advertising group and hiring an external advertising agency?

6. Besides advertising agencies, what other types of organizations play roles in the communication process?

7. What steps should be taken in selecting an advertising agency?

8. What evaluation criteria should be used in selecting an advertising agency?

9. How important is interpersonal chemistry in selecting an advertising agency?

10. Describe the role of an advertising agency account executive.

11. Describe the role of an advertising creative.

12. What are the steps of an advertising campaign management process? What other process in this textbook is similar in nature?

13. Describe the elements of a creative brief.

KEY TERMS

message theme   an outline of key idea(s) that the advertising program is supposed to convey.

leverage point   the key element in the advertisement that taps into, or activates, a consumer's personal value system (a value, idea, or concept).

appeal   how that leverage point and executional theme combine to attract attention, through humor, fear, sexual suggestiveness, rational logic, or some other method.

executional framework   how the message will be delivered (musically, visually, verbally, written statements, etc.).

advertising management program   the process of preparing and integrating a company's advertising efforts with the overall IMC message.

advertising account executive   the key go-between for both the advertising agency and the client company.

creatives   the persons who actually develop and produce advertisements.

top of mind brand   the brand that is nearly always mentioned when consumers are asked to identify brands that quickly come to mind from a product category.

top choice   the first or second pick when a consumer reviews his or her evoked set of possible purchasing alternatives.

promotional campaign   combining advertisements with other marketing efforts into a larger, more integrated effort revolving around a central idea or theme.

pulsating schedule of advertising   continuous advertising with bursts of higher intensity (more ads in more media) during the course of the year, most notably during peak seasons.

flighting schedule of advertising   a schedule in which companies present ads only during specific times and not at all during off-seasons.

continuous campaign schedule of advertising   when the company advertises in level amounts because product purchases are essentially "random" events.

support   the facts that substantiate the unique selling point.

constraints   the legal and mandatory restrictions placed on advertisements. They include legal protection for trademarks, logos, and copy registrations.

advertising campaign management   the process of preparing and integrating a specific advertising program in conjunction with the overall IMC message.

ENDNOTES

1. "Hey Kid, Buy This!: Is Madison Avenue Taking 'Get 'Em While They're Young' Too Far?" *Business Week* (June 30, 1997), pp. 62–67; Lisa Gubernick and Marla Matzer, "Babies as Dolls," *Forbes* (February 27, 1995), pp. 78–82; Becky Ebenkamp and Bruce Miller, "Who's Kidding Whom?" *Brandweek*, 40, no. 14 (April 5, 1999), p. 20; Karen Benezra, "The Fragging of the American Mind," *Brandweek*, 39, no. 24 (June 15, 1998), pp. S12–S17.

2. Based on Charles F. Frazier, "Creative Strategies: A Management Perspective," *Journal of Advertising*, 12, no. 4 (1983), pp. 36–41.

3. Al Ries, "Should Your Ads Be an Inside Job?" *Sales and Marketing Management*, 147, no. 2 (February 1995), pp. 26–27.

4. "Ad Firm's Focus: Native Americans," *Editor & Publisher*, 132, no. 28 (July 10, 1999), p. 28.

5. R. Craig Endicott, "Leading U.S. Shops Top $15 Billion in Revenue," *Advertising Age*, 70, no. 17 (April 19, 1999), pp. 1–4.

6. Beth Snyder and Laurel Wentz, "Whole Egg Theory Finally Fits the Bill for Y&R Clients," *Advertising Age*, 70, no. 4 (July 25, 1999), pp. 12–13.

7. Ibid.

8. James Zoltak and Aaron Baar, "Norwest–Wells Fargo to DDB," *Adweek,* Western Edition, 49, no. 19 (May 10, 1999), p. 50.

9. Ibid.

10. Ibid.

11. Laura Petrecca, "Agencies Urged to Show the Worth of Their Work," *Advertising Age,* 68, no. 15 (April 14, 1997), pp. 3–4.

12. Robert J. Lavidge and Gary A. Steiner, "A Model for Predictive Measurements of Advertising Effectiveness," *Journal of Marketing,* 24 (October 1961), pp. 59–62.

13. "Mullen," *Adweek,* Western Edition, 49, no. 28 (July 12, 1999), p. 13A.

14. Henry A. Laskey and Richard J. Fox, "The Relationship Between Advertising Message Strategy and Television Commercial Effectiveness," *Journal of Advertising Research*, 35, no. 2 (March/April 1995), pp. 31–39.

15. Tim J. Williams, "A Whole-Brain Approach to Advertising," *Marketing News,* 29, no. 9 (April 24, 1995), p. 4.

16. Michael Alvear, "On the Spot," *Mediaweek*, 8, no. 13 (March 30, 1998), pp. 26–28.

17. Ibid.

Building an IMC Campaign

Constructing an Advertising Program

You must make a key choice about advertising the product and company you selected. Is an in-house approach best or will you utilize an advertising agency? How can you make sure your advertising campaign matches the overall theme of your IMC program? How much money is budgeted for the campaign? What type of budgeting strategy will be used? These and other questions are raised in the Chapter 7 exercise for an IMC campaign. Go to the Prentice-Hall Web site at www.prenhall.com/clow or access the Advertising Plan Pro disk that accompanied this textbook to begin the process of developing your ads. Among the items to prepare at this stage are the communication market analysis and the creative brief, which will guide the rest of your advertising program.

Critical Thinking Exercises

Discussion Questions

Use the following Creative Brief for Questions 1 through 4.

Creative Brief for Ford Motor Company's Lincoln-Mercury Division

Product:	Mercury Cougar sports coupe.
Objective:	To reverse lagging sales.
Target audience:	25- to 35-year-old consumers, split evenly between males and females, college educated, with annual incomes of approximately $40,000.
	Psychographically, the targeted market is a group known as *individualists.* They tend not to buy mainstream products. In automobile selection, they place greater emphasis on design elements, distinctiveness, and utility.
Message theme:	An automobile is like a fashion accessory. A car is selected because of the statement it makes to others.

1. As the account executive for an advertising agency, discuss the creative brief in terms of completeness of information provided and whether the objective is realistic. What additional information should the Ford Motor Company provide before a creative can begin working on the account?

2. The media planner for the Mercury Cougar sports coupe account suggest a media plan consisting of cable television, print advertising, Internet ads, and network advertising on Fox shows *Ally McBeal, The X-Files, The Simpsons,* and *King of the Hill.* Evaluate this media plan in light of the creative brief's objectives. Can these shows reach the target audience? What information does a creative and the account executive want from the media planner before starting work on actual commercials?

3. From the viewpoint of the creative assigned to this account, do the creative brief and the media plan (see Question 2) contain sufficient information to design a series of advertisements? What, if any, additional information is necessary?

4. Using the information provided in the creative brief, prepare a magazine advertisement. Which magazines might match the target audience?

5. Choose a familiar product, service, or retailer. Using the information in this chapter, prepare a creative brief.

6. Many advertisers tend to direct ads toward the right side of the brain and develop advertisements based entirely on emotions, images, and pictures. Companies often advertise auto parts and tools with a scantily clad female in a bikini or shorts to attract the attention of males. The female has nothing to do with the product but garners attention. The rationale for using a sexy female is that if consumers like her, they will like the product and then purchase that brand. Effective advertisements integrate elements from both the left side of the brain as well as the right. They contain elements that appeal to emotions as well as having rational arguments. A laundry detergent can be advertised as having the rational benefit of getting clothes cleaner but also contains the emotional promise that your mother-in-law will think more favorably about you. For each of the following Internet sites, discuss the balance of left-brain versus right-brain advertising appeal.

    a. Pier 1 Imports (www.pier1.com)

    b. Potbelly Pigs Online (www.potbellypigs.com)

   c. Dark Dog (www.darkdog.com)

   d. Athletic Women (www.athleticwomen.com)

   e. Cheers Australia (www.cheersaustralia.com)

   f. American Wilderness Gear (www.awigear.com)

7. You have been asked to select an advertising agency to handle an account for Red Lobster, a national restaurant chain. Your advertising budget is $30 million. Study the Web sites of the following advertising agencies. Follow the selection steps outlined in the chapter. Narrow the list down to two agencies and justify your decision. Then choose among the two agencies and justify your choice.

   a. DDB Worldwide (www.ddbn.com)

   b. Leo Burnett (www.leoburnett.com)

   c. BBDO Worldwide (www.bbdo.com)

   d. BADJAR Advertising Pty Lfg (www.badjar.com)

   e. Anderson Lucas Advertising (www.aladv.com)

   f. Underground Advertising (www.grounderground.com)

   g. Grey Advertising (www.grey.com)

   h. Bozell Advertising (www.bozell.com)

8. A marketing manager has been placed in charge of a new brand of jeans to be introduced into the market. The company's corporate headquarters is in Atlanta, and the firm's management team has already decided to use one of the local advertising agencies. Two primary objectives to use to choose an agency are: (1) the agency must have the capability to develop a strong brand name, and (2) the agency must be able to help with business-to-business marketing to place the jeans into retail stores. Access Atlanta Ad Agencies at www.AtlantaAdAgencies.com. Follow the steps outlined in the chapter to narrow the list down to three agencies. Then design a project for each agency to prepare as part of an oral and written presentation to the company's marketing team.

How to Win (and Lose) an Advertising Account[17]

APPLICATION
EXERCISE I

Being selected to manage a major advertising account is a difficult but enriching process. For instance, consider the case of Atlanta-based Charter Behavioral Systems. Charter is the largest provider of alcoholism and depression treatment services in the United States. The goal was to select an agency to handle a $20 million television advertising account. Charter identified some basic goals and developed a selection process that included the criteria to use in the screening process. The six agencies identified for initial screening were McCann Erickson, BBDO, Rubin Postaer, Carat ICG, Tauche Martin, and Bates USA. The initial screening process was based on the following items:

- Size

- Capabilities

- Credentials and references

- Documented experience and past successes

   Tauche Martin was dropped from the list because they were too small. Although the management team at Charter believed the staff at Tauche Martin consisted of some very bright people, the size of the account would have overwhelmed them. Bates USA was rejected because Bates's major client was Korean. A recent lag in Asian economy caused the leaders of Charter to fear that Bates might be forced to close its Atlanta office if Charter lost its Korean client. Charter eliminated another agency based on reference checks. From television station reps to media buyers, the consistent word was "run!" At the end of the initial screening process, two agencies remained: Rubin Postaer and Carat ICG.

Rubin Postaer is a $550 million Los Angeles–based full-service agency. The firm is known primarily for work with Honda, Charles Swab, and *Discover* magazine. Carat ICG is a $600 million agency with clients such as Ameritech, Midas, Primestar and DHL Worldwide.

To decide between Rubin Postaer and Carat ICG, each was asked to make a final presentation addressing a series of 10 questions. They were further instructed to think of it as a "mock buy" in the Atlanta market. The companies were asked to provide their projected list of media buys and the rationale for the buys. The most challenging aspect of the final presentation requirement was a round table discussion with at least five of the agency's media buyers. Although each agency's management team could be present, the managers were told not to answer questions posed to the buyers.

Carat ICG included employees in the final presentation who were not going to be part of the account team. Although Charter's management team felt that it was flattering to have Carat ICG's chairman present for the three-hour presentation, Charter believed ICG's approach was more a sales presentation than a mock media buy.

ICG demonstrated a solid command of the strategies the agency believed Charter should use in the Atlanta market. Unfortunately, ICG skimped on some logistical details. Charter's leaders also thought that when ICG presented the mock buy, its representatives were quick, superficial, and had not spent a great deal of time laying out a total approach. On the positive side, ICG's senior vice-president Jim Surmanek led the agency's presentation. Surmanek, the author of a media textbook, knew the media issues extremely well. In the final evaluation, Charter concluded ICG clearly was superior at developing an advertising strategy. The agency's recommendations highlighted the company's deep understanding of Charter's business.

On the other hand, Rubin Postaer made a presentation using employees who would be servicing the account. Chairman, Jerry Rubin, did not attend the meeting although he did meet with Charter's management briefly to assure them of his commitment. Charter felt Rubin Postaer made a serious mistake during the presentation. The presentation team did not bring in a buyer for the direct-response media. ICG did. At the same time, Rubin's vice-president of spot buying, Cathleen Campe, grasped quickly what was most important. Campe flew in buyers from Chicago, New York, and Los Angeles to assist in the presentation. These buyers spoke often, expressing their views. Charter concluded that Rubin was more powerful in "branding" its media style with a label called *active negotiation*. Rubin's basic philosophy was that the toughest negotiations begin after buying the media time. Rubin made the claim that the agency was willing to spend more time monitoring media purchases than making the actual purchases. This advantage was substantiated by all of the references.

1. Which agency should Charter Behavioral Systems hire? Justify your answer.
2. Should Carat ICG do anything differently the next time company representatives make a presentation? Why or why not?
3. Should Rubin Postaer do anything differently the next time the firm makes a presentation? Why or why not?
4. Should "fuzzy" variables such as trust and confidence be the deciding factor in choosing an advertising agency? Why or why not?

More Than Pots 'n Pans

Sophia Rushmore enjoyed challenges. Early in life she conquered the challenge of become a gourmet chef. She had held positions at some of the finest restaurants on the West Coast, preparing nouveau food as well as spectacular desserts. After 20 years in the business, she decided it was time to capitalize on her reputation and tackle a new aspect of the restaurant game, the equipment side.

Most people probably don't stop to consider the many items sold to restaurants. Everything from tables and chairs, booths, ovens and stoves, cooking equipment (pots and pans), silverware, cloth napkins and paper napkin dispensers, lighted menu panels, table candles, wine racks, glasses, cups, plates, and an endless variety of products are sold to both ongoing restaurants as well as new ventures.

Turnover is high in the food industry. Places come and go. It is not unusual for the same location to house four or five different types of restaurants over a 10-year period due to business failures. Each time, some of the equipment is sold to the new owner, but there is a constant demand for products to individualize the business.

Sophia raised venture capital from some of her favorite customers and former employers. She developed a kind of middle-person business that purchased all types of items from various manufacturers and then resold them to restaurants in packages. Her company created a paper catalog listing all of the products it could access and deliver and then posted the catalog on the Internet. She began by targeting new and ongoing businesses in southern California, most notably Los Angeles, San Diego, and Anaheim. Her goal was to expand the business northward over a period of five years.

Sophia personally trained the sales force. She selected an upscale name for her venture, "Accents by Sophia," hoping her new clients would respond to her reputation in the kitchen. Her company motto was "friendly, courteous, professional service to restaurants of every size and taste."

Trade shows are the staple of the food industry. Sophia established a strong presence at them. She had her life story published in a book, so she could give away free autographed copies at her display. Promotional giveaways are part of the trade show game. Sophia needed to develop her own unique set to bring attention to her business. Orders and expressions of interest at a show were followed up by phone calls, personal visits, and e-mail notes by the sales force, as quickly as possible.

The final part of Sophia's new venture was to construct an advertising campaign to support her personal selling, direct mail, Internet, and promotional (trade show) efforts. Sophia had a variety of choices because she lived in a major media center, Los Angeles, Becoming established in this highly competitive marketplace was the next big step for Accents by Sophia.

1. Should Sophia hire an external agency or do the work in-house?
2. How should she spend the money for her campaign? Which media should she buy?
3. What should be the primary goal of her advertising campaign?
4. Prepare a creative brief that Sophia could provide to an advertising agency.
5. Access Los Angeles Ad Agencies at www.LosAngelesAdAgencies.com. Follow the steps outlined in the chapter to select an advertising agency for Sophia. Justify the selection.

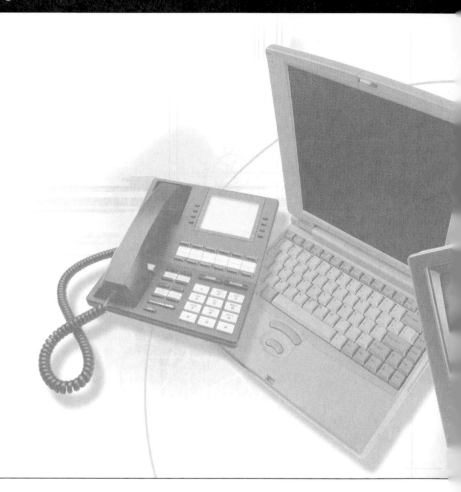

▶ **CHAPTER OBJECTIVES**

Master the process of
creating a media strategy.

Understand the roles media
planners and media buyers
play in an advertising
program.

Utilize reach, frequency,
continuity, impressions, and
other advertising objectives
in the preparation of an
advertising program.

Study and incorporate the
advantages of various media
in developing an ad program.

Recognize the value of an
effective mix of media in an
advertising campaign.

SUBLIMINAL SEDUCTION:
Does It Really Work?

Perhaps you've heard the story: During the first run of the
movie classic *Lawrence of Arabia*, the protagonist is forced
to cross a parched desert. A few enterprising movie theater
owners decided to flash the words *Drink Coca-Cola* across
the screen using single photo frames. These images moved
by so quickly that they were seen, and not seen, at the same
time. Subconsciously, the individual sees the message.
Consciously, it does not make an impression. According to
the sponsors of the program, more cola was sold. This technique is now known as "subliminal advertising."

chapter**eight**

Several issues emerged from this experiment. First, some sources claim that the event never really took place, that it simply was made up to capture greater attention for the movie. Second, a debate ensued about the ethics of manipulating people in such a subconscious fashion. And third, a new form of advertising was born.

In 1973, Wilson Bryan Key detailed the pervasiveness of this approach in his book *Subliminal Seduction*. Key argues that sexual imagery is found in practically every print advertisement. Naked bodies, couples making love, genitals, and other images are embedded in ice cubes, hairstyles, background images (clouds, trees), and everywhere else they can be placed. At that time, Bryan believed advertisers carefully structured strong psychological messages of love, affirmation, lust, and other emotions in ads to generate stronger appeal.

The unconscious mind allegedly processes this information and integrates it with more conscious thoughts. Someone possibly acts on cues without recognizing them, especially when they tie into deeply held emotions and feelings.

More recently, "Subliminal Man" became a regular feature on *Saturday Night Live*. Kevin Nealen, who played the character, imposed messages on unsuspecting women, bosses, and others to get his way. And, of course, it worked like a charm.

There is little doubt subliminal cues are used in today's advertisements. From the positioning of cigarettes (erect for males interacting with females), to body positioning, to the use of keywords (*tastes* looks quite a bit like *testes*), advertisers embed messages in print ads. The question becomes, do these techniques work? Even though little evidence supports subliminal cues, companies continue to use them.

New types of subliminal techniques include the use of scents. Product research indicates a person is more likely to buy a product in a room with an alluring appeal. Retail stores, packaging companies, and even casinos now scent key areas in hopes of leading a person to a buying decision. One bank even scents the money dispensed from its automatic teller machines!

People are willing to subliminally affect themselves. Self-help videos containing affirming messages ("You are a winner!" "You will succeed!" etc.) are available. Pictures featuring the same types of under-the-surface cues can also be purchased.

Companies spend a great deal of time and effort making sure cereals crunch at the appropriate levels, that dials and knobs feel sturdy and well built, and that packages produce attractive images. Perfume bottles and cologne containers are notoriously sexual.

As the use of blatant sexuality in advertising rises (e.g., Victoria's Secret television ads), will these more subtle techniques be necessary? Will they work? It is possible advertising companies know more than they're telling.

Some would say the brave new world of 1984 is here. Big brother moves and guides us with subliminal clues, and we don't even know it. You, the informed consumer, can make a game out of finding the subliminal messages in the ads, packages, labels, scents, and whispered words that are now part of your everyday life.[1]

overview

If a tree falls in the forest, and no one is present, does it make a sound? This philosophical question has been around for many years. In the world of advertising, one common problem is that many "trees" fall as unheard and unseen advertisements. Successful marketing account executives help a firm identify target markets and then find media that reach the members of those markets, in both retail situations and business-to-business marketing efforts. Once they identify the right media, creatives design clever, memorable, exciting, and persuasive advertisements to help convince customers to purchase products.

This chapter is devoted to helping you become a more savvy marketing expert by explaining the nature of advertising media selection. The topics include:

- The nature of a media strategy
- Media planning processes and the roles of the media planner and buyer
- Advertising objectives
- Media choices based on the advantages and disadvantages of each medium
- Media selection in business-to-business and international settings

Development of an advertising campaign within the framework of an integrated marketing communications program is the most important function an advertising agency can provide. Client companies depend on cost-effective ads to attract customers and entice them into purchasing various goods and services. The goal is to build a firm's image and to reach a larger consumer base. Advertising media selection is an important element in the success of any advertising program. A review of the elements of selection process follows.

media strategy

One of the most important ingredients in matching an advertising campaign with the overall integrated marketing communications program is to prepare an effective media strategy. A **media strategy** is the process of analyzing and choosing media for an advertising and promotions campaign. The strategy must take into account several factors as it is put together. These factors, which should have been specified in a creative brief (see Chapter 7) include: (1) the objective of the campaign, (2) the target audience, (3) the message theme (the key message to be conveyed to target markets), and (4) other constraints and considerations, such as the overall IMC objectives, legal restrictions, and so forth. These guidelines help the advertising creative, account executive, media buyer, and company representatives decide which media to use for a given campaign. They also must look for logical combinations of media for advertising messages.

The average consumer reads or looks over only nine of the more than two hundred consumer magazines on the market. A radio listener usually tunes in to only three of the stations available in a given area. Television viewers watch fewer than eight of the thirty-plus stations available by cable or satellite, and average network prime-time ratings have declined by more than 30 percent over the last decade. Simply finding the right places to speak to potential customers is an increasingly challenging task (see the Communication Action Box "Out with the Old: In with the New").

Also, to make the account executive and media buyer's jobs more difficult, prices for advertisements have not gone down and often have risen. Client budgets for advertising have not kept up with inflation, yet they have increased their demands for results and accountability. The marketing team faces many difficulties as they seek to provide the right media outlets for the company.

Recently, Porsche Cars North America altered its media strategy. The objective was to expand the company's customer base to include new, younger car buyers while still appealing to its loyal Porsche owners. To accomplish this goal, Porsche made the decision to retain the content and message of various advertisements. In conjunction with Porsche's advertising agency, Carmichael Lynch of Minneapolis, a specific media strategy was designed to reach younger prospects in the outer target markets. Porsche's media strategy included:

- More advertising space purchased in lifestyle magazines
- Expansion of direct-mail programs
- Regional television advertising campaigns

Most of Porsche's advertising dollars went for print advertisements in car-buff magazines. Television advertisements were placed in regional markets rather than national spots. The marketing team viewed buying national advertising as highly inefficient for Porsche, because most of the company's customers are located in specific regions.[2] The idea of this change in media strategy was to target new consumers more effectively and to find ways to speak directly to these prospective new sports car owners.

Once the media strategy is in place, other aspects of media selection can proceed. The first step is to prepare a thorough media planning program using the general advertising methods and objectives.

media planning

Media planning begins with a careful analysis of the target market. One method of addressing media planning is to approach it from the customer's viewpoint. The idea is to plot the choices in media that a specific, defined target market might experience through the course of a typical day.[3] For example, this list can include the examples in Figure 8.1.

communication**action**

To be successful in advertising in today's global market, many firms must change their view of advertising. The old advertising model had three distinct components. The first was the idea that a "mass-market" exists and can be reached through effective broadcast advertising. Second, the old model suggests that segmentation based on demographic factors such as age, income, gender, and education is sufficient to create effective ads. Third, with enough repetition and reach to the mass-markets, favorable impressions can be made. An analysis of the typical advertising budget using the old model shows the majority of advertising dollars spent on network television aimed at a mass-audience with the goal of building brand equity, whereby the consumer believes a given product or company has a distinct advantage in the marketplace. This perspective concludes that increased brand awareness is the key, because it eventually leads to a high level of brand equity. Therefore, advertisers felt regional and local advertising were not necessary and they were not interested in other media channels.

A revised view of advertising suggests a mass-appeal type ad is not likely to be effective. Further, merely knowing a target market's demographic makeup is not sufficient, and using only network television does not automatically result in brand awareness, brand equity, and brand loyalty. The new method of advertising campaign development is based on the idea that it takes a more integrated approach based on an in-depth understanding of the target market. In addition to demographics, it is essential to know the members of a target market's lifestyles, how these consumers think and what their opinions are, to have a solid grasp on the nature of their media habits.

This new approach emerged when consumers became more sophisticated as they gained access to more outlets. More clutter creates a highly refined ability to tune out ads and messages. To counter this tendency, the advertising agency chooses spots, magazine placements, newspaper sections, Internet links, and billboard locations based on the customer's strongest interests. In those situations, the individual is more likely to listen to, watch, or read an ad and actually process the information. The old method is simply "zapped" too easily, as consumers become increasingly better at ignoring mass-appeal approaches.

Source: Gary Blake, "Tune In to the New Face of Advertising," *Franchising World*, 26, no. 5 (September–October 1994), pp. 8–10.

Specific details of this type can be extremely valuable in developing the media strategy. Demographics such as age, sex, income, and education are not enough to determine the media habits of a person in a target market. Discovering viewing patterns of customers means companies can design messages to appeal to key consumers and make them available at the times and locations for key consumers to receive them.

Several individuals are involved in media planning. In addition to account executives and creatives, most agencies utilize **media planners** and **media buyers.**[4] In smaller agencies, the media planner and media buyer can be the same person. In larger companies, they usually are different individuals. A discussion of the main tasks performed in these positions follows.

Media planners

Media planners provide extremely valuable functions. The primary job of the media planner is to formulate a program stating where and when to place adver-

- A favorite wake-up radio station or one listened to during the commute to work
- A favorite morning news show or newspaper
- Trade or business journals examined while at work
- A radio station played during office hours at work
- Favorite computer sites accessed during work
- Favorite magazines read during the evening hours
- Favorite television shows watched during the evening hours
- Internet sites accessed during leisure time
- Shopping, dining, and entertainment venues frequented

Examples of Times Workers Are Exposed to Advertisements

FIGURE 8.1

tisements. Media planners work closely with creatives and account executives. It is important for the creative to know which media will be used, because the choices have such a large impact on how advertisements are designed. Thus, television ads are designed differently than are radio or newspaper ads.

One of the primary tasks of the media planner is to conduct research to match the product with the market and media. If a product's target market is 18- to 25-year-old males with college degrees, who love the outdoors, then the media must have a high percentage of its audience in the 18- to 25-year-old, male, college-educated, outdoor category. Thus, it is no accident that a fishing magazine contains advertisements for a bass boat and fishing gear next to articles about the summer feeding habits of bass and other fish. A successful media planner identifies these ideal locations for the client's advertisements. For example, the advertisement for New Balance running shoes was placed in *Runner's World* near an article about running. The media planner formulates a media plan spelling out the best way to reach the client's customers.

Part of the media planner's research is devoted to gathering facts about various media, such as the circulation rates and demographic groups each medium reaches. Besides demographic information, media planners want to know something about the lifestyles, opinions, and habits of each medium's audience. For instance, the audience for television shows may be quite different than those of radio stations and magazines. Careful research improves the chances of selecting appropriate media for the campaign.[5]

Media buyers

After the media are chosen, someone must buy the space and negotiate rates, times, and schedules for the ads. This is the work of the media buyer. Media buyers stay in constant contact with media sales representatives. They should have a great deal of knowledge about rates and schedules. Media buyers also look for special deals and tie-ins between different media outlets (e.g., radio with television, magazines with the same owner, etc.).

To ensure promotional dollars are spent wisely, it is best to involve the media planner and the media buyer with the creative and the account executive in the design of an advertising campaign. Each plays a critical role in the development of an integrated marketing communications program. The challenge of coordinating the efforts of these individuals intensifies when they are from different companies.

The size of the advertising agency or media buying firm alone does not ensure effective media purchases. Although it would seem logical to assume that larger

An advertisement featuring New Balance shoes that was placed in *Runner's World* magazine. Courtesy of New Balance Athletic Shoes Inc. Photograph by Paul Wakefield.

agencies have the clout to dictate lower prices from media outlets, this is not true. There is little connection between the size of an advertising firm and the prices it can negotiate. In fact, in one study the differences in media costs were based on the time the actual purchase was made (closer to the day the ad was to run) rather than the size of the agency.[6] Other major factors in cost differences are knowledge of the marketplace and the ability to negotiate package deals. Spot television media plans vary by as much as 45 percent in the price of the spot. For example, a media plan costing one firm $10 million can cost another firm $15.3 million. Radio time slots vary by as much as 42 percent and national print ads by as much as 24 percent.[7]

More importantly, differences in effectiveness of advertising are often related to:

- Quality media choices (the right ones) made by each agency
- Creativity
- Financial stewardship ("bang" for your advertising buck)
- Agency culture and track record
- Computer systems to analyze data
- Relationships between the agency and the medium's sales representative

Thus, the negotiated price is only one element in the success of an advertising program. Effectiveness in advertising is also determined by quality of the selections made by the marketing team and the content of the ad itself. Media should be selected and purchased with specific advertising objectives in mind. These goals assist marketing team members in choosing the right media and combining them effectively to achieve the desired results.

advertising objectives

In selecting media, it is important to review the communications objectives established during the development of the IMC program. These objectives guide media selection decisions as well as the message design (see chapter 9). Seven concepts or technical terms used in media objectives:[8]

- Reach
- Frequency
- Gross rating points
- Effective rating points
- Cost
- Continuity
- Impressions

These ingredients are the key features of an advertising program. **Reach** is the number of people, households, or businesses in a target audience exposed to media vehicle or message schedule at least once during a given time period. A time period is normally four weeks. In other words, how many targeted buyers did the ad reach? A country and western radio station is more likely to reach someone wanting to buy a cowboy hat. An ad in *Business Week* is more likely to reach a member of the buying center seeking financial services for a business.

Frequency is the average number of times an individual, household, or business within a particular target market is exposed to a particular advertisement within a specified time period, again, usually over four weeks. Or, how many times did the person see the ad during the campaign? A regular viewer sees the same ad shown each day on *Hollywood Squares* more frequently than an ad shown once on *Who Wants to Be a Millionaire?*, even though the Millionaire program has a far greater reach.

Gross rating points (GRP) is a measure of the impact or intensity of a media plan. Gross rating points are calculated by multiplying a vehicle's rating by the frequency or number of insertions of an advertisement. GRP give the advertiser an idea about the odds of the target audience actually viewing the ad. By increasing the frequency of an advertisement, the chances of a reader of the magazine seeing the advertisement will increase. It makes sense that an advertisement in each issue of *Time* over a four-week period is more likely to be seen than an advertisement that appears only once during that time period.

Cost is a measure of overall expenditures associated with an advertising program or campaign. Another useful number that can be calculated to measure a program's costs is its **cost per thousand (CPM)**. CPM is the dollar cost of reaching 1,000 members of the media vehicle's audience. The cost per thousand is calculated by using the following formula:

$$\text{CPM} = (\text{Cost of media buy} / \text{Total audience}) * 1{,}000$$

Table 8.1 shows some basic cost and readership information. The first three columns of the table provide the name of the magazine, the cost of a four-color full-page advertisement, and the magazine's total readership. The fourth column contains a measure of the CPM of each magazine. Thus, the cost per thousand (CPM) for *National Geographic* is $16.44. This means that it takes $16.44 to reach 1,000 *National Geographic* readers. Notice the CPM for *Sports Illustrated* is $71.11 and for *Travel & Leisure*, $83.09. Even though the readership of *Travel & Leisure* is the lowest, its CPM is the highest of all eight magazines. In terms of cost per thousand readers, the best buy is *Southern Living*, at only $1.98 per thousand.

Another cost calculation can be made besides CPM. One critical concern is the cost of reaching a firm's target audience. Therefore, a measure called the **cost per rating point (CPRP)** was developed. The cost per rating point is a relative measure of the efficiency of a media vehicle relative to a firm's target market. **Ratings** measure the percentage of a firm's target market that is exposed to a show on television or an article in a print medium. To calculate the cost per rating point, the formula is

$$\text{CPRP} = \text{Cost of media buy} / \text{Vehicle's rating}$$

Hypothetical Media Plan Information for Select Magazines

Magazine	Cost for Four-Color Full Page Ad	Total Readership (000s)	CPM Total	Target Market (20M)	
				Rating (Reach)	Cost per Rating Point (CPRP)
National Geographic	$ 346,080	21,051	$16.44	16.1	$21,496
Newsweek	780,180	15,594	50.03	12.2	63,949
People	605,880	21,824	27.76	9.4	64,455
Southern Living	11,370	5,733	1.98	2.4	4,738
Sports Illustrated	965,940	13,583	71.11	10.5	91,994
Time	1,324,282	21,468	61.69	15.9	83,288
Travel & Leisure	183,216	2,205	83.09	2.3	79,659
U.S. News and World Report	100,740	8,929	11.28	8.3	12,137

Table 8.1 ratings were generated for potential buyers of a 35 mm camera (see the Application Exercise at the end of this chapter). The table shows the CPRP for *National Geographic* is $21,496. This is the average cost for each rating point or of each 1 percent of the firm's target audience (35 mm camera buyers). Not all readers of a magazine are part of the firm's target market. The CPRP more accurately measures an advertising campaign's efficiency than does CPM. Notice that the CPRP is the lowest for *National Geographic, Southern Living*, and *U.S. News and World Report.*

CPRP provide a relative measure of reach exposure in terms of cost. For example, it costs $21,496 to reach 1 percent, or 200,000, of the 20 million in this firm's target market using *National Geographic*. To reach 1 percent, or 200,000, using *Sports Illustrated* costs $91,994. To reach 1 percent, or 200,000, using *Southern Living* costs only $4,738. Because *Southern Living* is so efficient, why wouldn't a media planner just do all of the advertising in that magazine? The answer lies in the rating for *Southern Living*. Advertising in only that magazine reaches just 2.4 percent of the target audience, meaning 97.6 percent of the target market does not read *Southern Living*. Thus, another magazine or media outlet is necessary to reach them. This example explains why diversity in media is essential to reach a large portion of a firm's target market.

Continuity is the exposure pattern or schedule used in the ad campaign. The three types of patterns used are continuous, pulsating, and discontinuous. A continuous campaign buys media time in a steady stream. For instance the Skechers ad shown on the next page uses a continuous schedule if the company buys ad space in specific magazines over a period of one to two years. By rotating the advertisement, readers do not become bored with one particular ad. A firm that uses a pulsating schedule (see Chapter 7) always maintains some minimal level of advertising but increases advertising at periodic intervals. For instance, a retailer such as JCPenney may advertise some throughout the whole year but will increase advertising in small, short bursts around holidays such as Christmas, the day after Thanksgiving, Memorial Day, Labor Day, Mother's or Father's Day, and Easter. The goal of pulsating advertising is to take advantage of consumer interests in making more purchases or buying special merchandise during holidays. For instance, the BLOCKBUSTER advertisement just prior to Christmas encouraged consumers to purchase a BLOCKBUSTER gift card. A discontinuous campaign schedule places advertisements at special intervals with no advertising between. For example, a ski resort can use discontinuous advertising by running ads during the fall and winter seasons with none during the spring and summer.

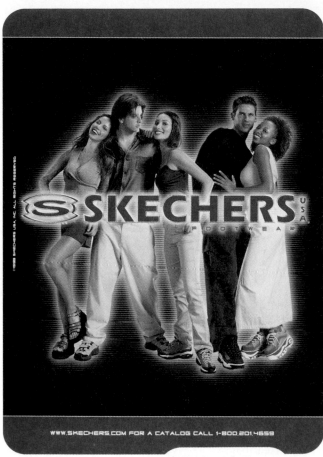

A Skechers advertisement promoting shoes. Courtesy of Skechers USA Inc.

A Christmas advertisement by BLOCKBUSTER promoting a gift card as the "perfect holiday gift." Courtesy of Blockbuster Entertainment Group.

The final objective advertisers consider is the concept of *impressions.* The number of **gross impressions** is the total exposures of the audience to an advertisement. It does not take into consideration what percentage of the total audience may or may not see the advertisement. Table 8.1 indicates the total readership of *National Geographic* is 21,051,000. If six insertions were placed in *National Geographic,* multiplying the insertions by the readership would yield a total of 126 million impressions.

Integrated Learning Experience

stop!

A major supplier of media research information is Nielsen Media Research. Access its Web site at www.nielsenmedia.com. Go to the "Who We Are and What We Do" section. After reading this, go to "Ratings 101" to learn about the terms Nielsen uses and how it determines ratings. The "What TV Ratings Really Means" section provides information about what ratings mean. The "Services" section presents information about the services Nielsen's offers. Why would this data be important in media planning? For the Internet, the Nielsen organization provides current information about top banner ads, top advertisers, and Web usage. Access this information from the main page under the heading "Hot Off the Net." In Canada, a valuable source of information about radio and television markets is BBM Bureau of Measurement at www.bbm.ca. Study the statistical tidbits presented (in the "Get Data" section) about Canadian radio and television markets.

achieving advertising objectives

One basic issue facing advertisers is how many times a person must be exposed to an ad before it has an impact on that consumer. Most agree that a single exposure is not enough. Deciding on what is the actual number inspires a great deal of debate. Some argue it takes three exposures whereas others say as many as ten. The basic rule, developed by Herbert Krugman, states it takes a minimum of three exposures for an advertisement to be effective. This is the *three-exposure hypothesis*. Most media planners have followed it for quite a while.[9]

Many advertisers believe three exposures are not enough to create an impression in the consumer's mind, because of the amount of clutter that exists. Clutter also can affect the types of objectives firms try to accomplish. For instance, increasing brand awareness may be easier than building brand image, because attention getting is easier than capturing someone's interest long enough to make a point about the firm's image. Also, a well-known brand that is the first choice of the majority of consumers can accomplish its objective with fewer ad exposures than a less well-known brand.

Seeking to discover the minimum number of exposures needed to be effective is based on two concepts: effective frequency and effective reach. **Effective frequency** refers to the *number of times* a target audience must be exposed to a message to achieve a particular objective. **Effective reach** is the *percentage of an audience* that must be exposed to a particular message to achieve a specific objective. Implied in the concept of effective reach is that some minimum number of exposures exists.

Both effective frequency and effective reach are crucial factors. Too few exposures means the advertiser will fail to attain its intended objectives. On the other hand, too many exposures wastes resources. The goal is to discover the optimal reach and frequency mix to accomplish the intended objectives without experiencing diminishing returns from extra ads. The challenge appears when consumer differences are considered. It may take three exposures to an advertisement to impact one consumer but ten for another. Differences in interests, personalities, and exposures to the media outlets chosen all influence individual consumers.

Other elements can enhance effective frequency and effective reach. They include the size and placement of ads. A small magazine advertisement will not have the same impact as a larger ad. In television advertising, a spot in the middle of an ad sequence usually does not have the same impact as those at the beginning and end of the series. If a firm is using 15-second television ads, effective frequency may require six exposures compared to only four if they use longer 45-second spots.

Another important factor that affects these objectives is the number of different media a particular advertising campaign uses. Generally, a campaign involving two types of media, such as television and magazines, has greater effective reach than a campaign using only one medium, such as magazines only. Media mixes will be described in detail later in this chapter.

Recency Theory

A new theory concerning reach and frequency challenges the traditional three-exposure hypothesis. This approach, called Recency Theory, suggests that a consumer's attention is selective and focused on his or her individual needs and wants.[10] The traditional three-exposure hypothesis is based on the *intrusion value* of advertisements and the idea that advertisements can make an impact on an audience regardless of individual needs or wants. **Intrusion value** is the ability of media or an advertisement to intrude upon a viewer without his or her voluntary attention.

Recency Theory states that consumers use selective attention processes as they consider advertisements. They give attention to messages that might meet their needs or wants. The closer, or more recent, an ad is to a purchase, the more power-ful the ad will be. Also, when a consumer contemplates a future purchase of the product being advertised, it becomes more likely that the consumer will pay atten-tion to and react favorably toward the ad. For example, a member of a buying cen-ter from a business that is in the market for a new copier notices advertisements about copiers. Someone not in the market for a copier ignores the same ad. The same is true in consumer markets: An individual needing a new pair of jeans notices clothing ads, especially ones that deal with jeans.

Recency Theory notes that advertising is a waste of money when ads reach individuals who are not in the market for a particular product and who do not need the product. Advertisers must give careful attention to targeting ads to individuals who want or need a firm's goods and services. In other words, advertising life insur-ance to teenagers wastes promotional funds. At the same time advertising supple-mental health insurance to the elderly on social security is highly likely to be noticed and have a profound impact on that target market.

One difference in Recency Theory is the idea that one ad exposure is enough to affect an audience when that person or business needs the product being promoted. Additional exposures actually may be a waste of money. The advertising strategy that matches recency theory spreads the message around using a variety of media, each one providing only one exposure per week or time period. In the case of sell-ing supplemental health insurance to the elderly, magazines such as *Senior Living*, televisions spots on local news and weather programs, and newspaper ads close to the obituary section can quickly reach the target audience in a cost-effective man-ner. Such an approach, which maximizes reach, accomplishes more than increas-ing frequency.

In the business-to-business arena, application of Recency Theory means ads should appear in a number of outlets rather than running a series of ads in one trade journal. Many times, a number of individuals who are members of the buying cen-ter. Each has different interests and training. To make sure each one sees the ad, placing ads in all of the journals that might contact a given buying center member is important. To facilitate the purchasing process for a company seeking to buy an audioconferencing system, the media buyer purchases space in trade journals, human resource journals, sales journals, and business journals to effectively reach various members of the buying center. Recency Theory suggests that one exposure might be enough for each member, because the member is looking for information and ready to help make a purchase decision. To reach business personnel while traveling, Polycom recently placed an advertisement in the Delta Airline's *Sky* magazine, because of the higher odds that more than one buying center member might see the ad while flying with Delta.

Integrated Learning Experience

Achieving advertising objectives normally requires blending various media in an advertising plan. Access Benchmark Communications at www.bmcommunications.com. Examine the information provided about traditional media, including newspapers, radio, and television. After examining each of the major media, look at the "Web Site Creation and Design" section. How can Benchmark Communications tie a firm's Web site into the traditional advertising media (newspapers, radio, and television)?

gathering evidence of success

Technology has made it easier to define effective reach and effective frequency. For instance, a business placing an advertisement in a business journal such as *Inc.* or *Business Week* can gain access to research tallying the number of responses to the advertisement. Then the business can track the impact of the message. If the objective

A business advertisement for Polycom. Courtesy of Polycom Inc.

were to increase inquiries about a product by 10 percent, the business can see how many direct inquiries were made before and after the ad runs. If the ad appears in successive issues of a magazine, it can be relatively easy to track increases in inquiries associated with each successive issue.

A business also can hire professional media research firms to track the reach of the advertisement. The research firm develops measures of how other businesses responded. Such firms provide information about whether the ad affected the buying decision and if members of the buying center remembered seeing the ad. Although these methods are not foolproof, they do provide better information than does an educated guess or past experience. Actual records kept over time can become valuable assets in determining effective frequency and effective reach.

Once the media buyer, media planner, account executive, and company leaders agree about basic objectives of the advertising campaign, they can select the actual media. Marketing experts consider each medium's distinct pros and cons. They also consider logical (and illogical) combinations of media. The next section examines media that an advertising program can use, leading to the final selection of media for the company's campaign.

media selection

In this section, various forms of advertising media are described. As noted earlier, effectively mixing media is an important part of designing quality advertising. In order to do so, the advantages and disadvantages of each individual medium must be understood so that an advertising campaign uses successful combinations.

Television

Choosing appropriate television advertising outlets is not easy, because there are so many options. Companies must carefully select those programs and channels most likely to reach their target audiences. Table 8.2 lists the advantages and disadvantages of television advertising. As shown, television offers advertisers the most extensive coverage and highest reach of any of the media. A solitary advertisement can reach millions of viewers simultaneously. Even though ads are quite expensive, the cost per contact is relatively low. This low cost per contact justifies spending $2 million for a 30-second spot on the Super Bowl, which continues to be the most costly television program. Television has the advantage of intrusion value, which as noted earlier, is the ability of a media or advertisement to intrude upon a viewer without his or her voluntary attention. Television ads with a catchy musical tune, sexy content, or motion can grab the viewers' attention.

Television provides many opportunities for creativity in advertising design. Visual images and sounds can be incorporated together to gain the attention of viewers as well as to persuade them. Products and services can be demonstrated on television in a manner not possible in print or using radio advertisements.

It is advisable to match a firm's target audience (market segment) with specific shows. Each television network and each television show tends to attract a specific type of audience. Cable television programming often provides a well-defined, homogeneous audience that matches more narrowly defined target markets.

Clutter remains the primary problem with television advertising, especially on network programs. One episode of NBC's *Law and Order* contained a commercial break lasting more than five minutes. Similar breaks occur on ABC, CBS, and Fox, and they are often packed with eight to fifteen commercials. Many viewers simply switch channels during long commercial breaks. Thus, messages at the beginning or near the end of the break have the best recall. Those in the middle often have virtually no impact. Therefore, clutter makes it difficult for a single message to have any influence.[11]

Television commercials have short life spans. Most ads last 15 or 30 seconds. Occasionally an advertiser purchases a 45- or 60-second ad, but those are rare. Another disadvantage of television is the high cost per ad not only for the media time but also in terms of production costs. Outstanding commercials often are expensive to produce. At the same time, because television ads are shown so frequently, they quickly lose the ability to attract the viewer's interest. Companies are forced to replace the ads with something new before consumers get tired of them and tune them out, while at the same time trying to keep them long enough to recover some of the production costs involved.

Television remains a "glamour" medium. Its wide audience continues to hold a great appeal for companies vending goods and services with more general target markets. This includes most durable goods (washers, dryers, cars, etc.), many staple items (detergent, soap, deodorant), general appeal products (snack foods, beers, soft

Advantages	Disadvantages	**TABLE 8.2**
1. High reach	1. Greater clutter	**Television Advertising**
2. High frequency potential	2. Low recall due to clutter	
3. Low cost per contact	3. Channel surfing during commercials	
4. High intrusion value	4. Short amount of copy	
5. Quality creative opportunities	5. High cost per ad	
6. Segmentation possibilities through cable outlets		

drinks, and Internet sites), and various luxuries marketed to larger groups (cruise ships, theme parks, credit cards).

Business-to-business advertisers use television more frequently for several reasons. First, it is becoming more difficult to reach members of the business buying center, and they do watch television. Second, increased ad clutter in trade journals and traditional business outlets makes televisions spots a more desirable alternative. Third, business advertisements now use more emotional appeals, and television can portray emotions quite effectively. Fourth, because the importance of a strong brand identity is a growing factor in the business-to-business sector, and television ads can be a source of brand identity. Finally, television is an excellent medium to reach members of the buying center when they are not preoccupied with other business concerns. Consequently, they may be more open to advertising messages.

Radio

Radio may not be considered as glamorous as television. This makes it more difficult to attract talented creatives to prepare ads. At the same time, a well-placed, clever ad appeals as being a one-on-one message (announcer to driver in a car stuck in traffic). Many smaller local companies still heavily rely on radio advertising, and most radio ads are produced locally and with small budgets. Table 8.3 summarizes the advantages and disadvantages of radio advertising.

Radio offers several advantages to advertisers. Skillful radio advertisers help the listener remember the message by creating a powerful image to visualize or through repetition. It is important to help the consumer move the ad from short-term to long-term memory. Various sound effects and lively memorable tunes assist in this process. Through repetition a person hears an advertisement often enough to assist in recall; just like repeating a phone number or e-mail address, you remember the numbers or letters.

Radio stations tend to have definable target markets based on their formats. Certain formats (talk radio, lite mix, oldies, etc.) attract similar audiences throughout the United States. This means a firm that wants to advertise on pop stations in the East can find similar stations across the country. Campbell's Soup found radio spots were an effective way to promote its Chunky Soup and its tie-in with the National Football League. The company advertised on radio stations with primarily male audiences and strong sports programming using professional football players praising Chunky Soup.[12]

TABLE 8.3	Advantages	Disadvantages
Radio Advertising	1. Recall promoted	1. Short exposure time
	2. Narrower target markets	2. Low attention
	3. Ad music can match station's programming	3. Few chances to reach national audience
	4. High segmentation potential	4. Target duplication when several stations use the same format
	5. Flexibility in making new ads	5. Overload
	6. Able to modify ads to fit local conditions	
	7. Intimacy (with DJs and radio personalities)	
	8. Mobile—people carry radios everywhere	
	9. Creative opportunities with music and other sounds	

Radio stations offer considerable flexibility and a short lead time. Commercials can be recorded and placed on the air within a few days and sometimes within hours. Ads can be changed quickly. This is especially helpful in violate markets or in the retail sector wherein companies want to change the items featured on sale. Radio also helps a national company that wants to modify each advertisement to fit local conditions. In other words, a manufacturer can develop one national advertisement and change it for each dealer or retailer that carries the manufacturer's merchandise. The modification can be as simple as providing an address, phone number, or Web address for each local outlet.

One major advantage of radio is *intimacy*. Listeners can develop a closeness to the DJs and other radio personalities. This closeness grows over time. Listening to the same individual becomes somewhat personalized, especially if the listener has a conversation with the DJ during a contest or when requesting a song. The bond or intimacy level gives the radio personality a higher level of credibility and an edge to products and services the radio celebrity endorses. No other medium offers this advantage.

Besides intimacy, radio is *mobile*. People carry radios to the beach, the ballpark, work, and picnics. They listen at home, at work, and on the road in-between. No other medium stays with the audience quite like radio.

Radio also has disadvantages. One is the short exposure time of an ad. Like television, most radio advertisements last only 15 or 30 seconds. Listeners involved in other activities, such as driving or working on a computer, may not pay attention to the radio. Further, people often use radio as a background to drown out other distractions, especially at work.

For national advertisers, covering a large area with radio advertisements is challenging. To place a national advertisement requires contacting a large number of companies. Few large radio conglomerates means contacts must be made with multiple stations. Because of this independence, negotiating lower rates with individual stations based on volume or because it will be a national advertisement does not occur. In fact, local businesses can negotiate better rates than a national advertiser because of the relationships the radio stations develop with local firms over time.

In large metropolitan areas, another problem is target duplication. Several radio stations may try to reach the same target market. For instance, in Chicago there are several rock stations. Advertising on every station is not financially feasible, yet reaching everyone in that target market is not possible unless all rock stations are used. The rock music audience is divided among those stations, with each having its own subset of loyal listeners.

Finally, because many ads are locally produced, a common problem with radio ads is putting too much information into one ad. It overloads the consumer and very little is retained.

Radio advertising is a low-cost option for a local firm. Ads can be placed at ideal times and adapted to local conditions. The key to radio is careful selection of stations, times, and construction of the ad. Tests can be created to see if ads effectively reach customers. Immediate response techniques, contest entries, and other devices provide evidence about whether customers heard and responded to ads. Radio *remotes* occur when the station broadcasts from a business location. Remotes are a popular method of attracting attention to a new business (restaurants, taverns, small retail shops, etc.) or to a company trying to make a major push for immediate customers. Effective ratio promotions can be combined with other media (local television, newspapers, etc.) to send out a more integrated message.

For business-to-business advertisers, radio provides the opportunity to reach businesses during working hours, because many employees listen to the radio during office hours. More importantly, radio can reach businesspeople while in transit to or from work. Both radio and television usage has increased for business-to-business marketing.

Integrated Learning Experience

One of the problems with radio advertising is choosing from the large number of stations on the air. Selecting the right ones can be difficult. Access www.100topradiosites.com for a list of the top hundred radio stations, and examine three of these. Why were they selected as top stations? For additional information on radio advertising, access the Radio Advertising Bureau at www.rab.com. Review the menu items in order to get an idea of how much information this site offers. Go to "Media Facts" for information about choosing the various media. Information is listed, about each medium type's advantages and disadvantages. Notice how the benefits change when the medium is combined with radio.

Outdoor

Billboards along major roads are the most common form of outdoor advertising. Billboards, however, are only one form of outdoor advertising. Signs on cabs, buses, park benches, and fences of sports arenas also are types of outdoor advertising. Some would argue that even a blimp flying over a major sporting event is a form of outdoor advertising.

Outdoor advertising has changed its image from "booze and (cigarette) butts" advertising to a legitimate medium over the past few decades. In 1979, tobacco ads accounted for 39 percent of outdoor advertising revenues. Alcohol accounted for another 11 percent. Today those numbers have dwindled to 11 percent for tobacco and only 2 percent for alcohol.

Currently, retailers account for approximately 10 percent of outdoor advertising and media outlets for another 8 percent. Other ads feature upcoming movies, video stores, broadcast television networks, newspapers, and radio stations. Other fast-growing outdoor ad programs are from the fashion industry. The Gap, Calvin Klein, Ralph Lauren, and DKNY regularly buy outdoor space. In Times Square in New York and on Sunset Boulevard in Los Angeles, large outdoor billboards cost as much as $100,000 per month.[13] Table 8.4 lists the basic advantages and disadvantages of outdoor ads.

One primary advantage of billboard advertising is its long life. For local companies, billboards are an excellent advertising medium because the message is seen only by local audiences. Local services such as restaurants, hotels, resorts, service

Outdoor advertising in Times Square. *Courtesy of Liaison Agency, Inc. Photograph by Frederick Charles.*

TABLE 8.4

Outdoor Advertising

Advantages	Disadvantages
1. Able to select key geographic areas	1. Short exposure time
2. Accessible for local ads	2. Brief messages
3. Low cost per impression	3. Little segmentation possible
4. Broad reach	4. Cluttered travel routes
5. High frequency on major commuter routes	
6. Large, spectacular ads possible	

stations, and amusement parks are heavy users of billboards. Billboards provide an effective way to communicate a firm's location to travelers. Individuals who want to eat at a particular restaurant (Wendy's, Shoney's, Burger King) while on the road can normally spot a billboard for that restaurant.

In terms of cost per impression, outdoor advertising is a low-cost media outlet. Outdoor advertising also offers a broad reach and a high level of frequency if multiple billboards are purchased. Every person who travels by a billboard has the potential of being exposed to the message. Many billboard companies provide "rotation" packages in which an ad moves to different locations throughout a town during the course of the year, thereby increasing the reach of the ad.

Billboard ads can be large and spectacular, making them major attention-getting devices. A billboard's large size creates the impression that the product and message are important. Movement and lighting can add to the attention-capturing qualities of billboards.

A major drawback of outdoor advertising is the short exposure time. Drivers must pay attention to the traffic as they speed by an outdoor ad. Most either ignore billboards or give them just a brief glance. Ironically, in large cities along major arteries the cost of billboard spots is increasing. The reason: traffic jams. People stuck in slow-moving traffic spend more time looking at billboards. If this space is not available, a firm can seek billboard locations where traffic stops for signals or at stop signs.

Billboards provide limited opportunities for creativity. The short exposure time means the message must be extremely brief. People usually ignore a complicated or detailed message. Further, billboards offer limited segmentation opportunities because a wide variety of people may view the billboard's message. To help overcome this problem, some companies use geodemographic software technologies to identify the profile of individuals who will pass by a billboard in a specific neighborhood. Such an approach works well on local streets of cities and towns but is not very effective along major interstates, with local and long-distance traffic.

Procter & Gamble uses the most current technology to place billboard advertising for Luvs diapers, by identifying geodemographic segments. P&G uses billboards placed near day care centers and hospitals and in areas with a high number of young marrieds with no children or young marrieds with very young children.[14]

In the past, outdoor advertising was seldom considered in the planning of an integrated marketing communications program or the development of the media plan. Now outdoor advertising is an additional tool to reach consumers. To illustrate, Procter & Gamble as late as 1994 spent virtually no money on outdoor advertising; today, this budget is almost $10 million. Billboard ads can be combined with other advertising media to repeat and reinforce messages for audiences.

stop!

Integrated Learning Experience

One of the leading outdoor advertising companies is the Lamar Advertising Company at www.lamar.com. Under "Rates and Markets," find your home state and local area. What are the company's published rates for outdoor advertising? Compare these rates with those of nearby areas as well as of other states. To understand the different products, access the "Products and Services" section of Lamar's Web site. Finally, access "Why Lamar?" What are the benefits of using outdoor advertising? Why should Lamar be chosen?

communication**action**

Mixing in Internet Advertising

One of the biggest challenges marketing account executives face is integrating and mixing Internet advertising into more traditional advertising programs. Many Internet companies use television spots, designing fast-paced, high-tech, intriguing ads to market their Web sites.

Another potential area for Internet firms is radio advertising, which is less expensive than television. Many Internet companies have small budgets. Therefore radio is an ideal medium. Radio spots can be produced cheaply and quickly. Radio lends itself very well to the branding messages of Internet companies. Radio spots reach potential customers on their way to and from work, at work, and when they are at home on the computer. This makes radio ads ideal for both consumer and business-to-business Internet marketing spots.

As with radio, outdoor advertising is becoming a popular avenue for Web companies. Amazon.com, Excite, and Mothernature.com are three major users of outdoor advertising among the Internet companies. Outdoor advertising requires companies to keep messages short; therefore, many simply promote the Internet address. For instance, Playboy Enterprises has a .com Web site. The company invested $10 million in outdoor advertising aimed at younger, more Internet-savvy readers in New York, Los Angeles, and Chicago. The objective was not promotion of the magazine, but rather the Web site address.

One growth area in magazine advertising are the many dot.com advertisements. Similar to radio, Internet companies find magazines an excellent medium for advertising. Businesses also see magazines as an appealing medium for establishing their Web address. Computer manufacturing companies such as Dell and Gateway invest heavily in magazine advertisements.

Newspapers also are inviting places for Internet companies, because ads can be positioned close to the type of news provided. Thus, e-trade companies can advertise near stock market prices, sports sites can be positioned near the sports page, and so forth. In addition, local companies can advertise their addresses in smaller newspapers.

The least likely outlet for Internet advertising is direct mail. "Snail mail" stands in direct contrast to more high-tech Web sites. Thus, it is less logical to advertise in that way.

Internet advertising already has made a significant impact in the business-to-business sector. It now ranks sixth among the business-to-business marketing media, just behind direct marketing. Annual expenditures are almost $4 billion. The Internet is rapidly becoming the medium of choice for communications with customers and for e-commerce. All estimates are that business-to-business marketing will continue to increase at a very rapid pace.

One question remains as to how individuals and businesses use the Internet. If individuals use it to gather information during the information search stage of the decision purchase process, then it may be difficult to measure the impact of Internet advertising. Through Internet advertising, brand awareness can be increased so, when the time comes for a product purchase, the brand is considered in the person's evoked set. The individual or business may not have considered the brand if it were not for the Internet banner viewed. Tracing the movement of a brand from unawareness to becoming part of a consumer's evoked set is difficult. This is especially true when an advertiser used the Internet, billboards, or any other medium. It becomes unclear which ad caused the product to move to the consumer's evoked set.

In any case, it is certain that many businesses will continue to advertise on the Internet, and Internet companies will continue to promote their sites in other media. Media buyers must consider this interlinkage as advertising campaigns are designed and implemented.

Sources: Carol Krol, "Look Up! Seeing Is Believing," *Advertising Age*, 70, no. 32 (August 2, 1999), p. 2; Alice Z. Cuneo and Ann Marie Kerwin, "Playboy Ads Target Younger Audience," *Crain's Chicago Business*, 22, no. 42 (October 18, 1999), p. 28; "Mediaweek Magazine Monitor," *MediaWeek*, 9, no. 35 (September 20, 1999), pp. 73–77; Laurie Freeman, "Internet Shows Rapid Growth as Communications Tool, Helping to Change Marketers' Use of Traditional Media," *Advertising Age's Business Marketing*, 84, no. 5 (May 1999), p. S6.

Internet

Forty years ago, the newest medium was television. About 15 years ago, it was cable television. Currently, it is the Internet.[15] There is some evidence that television audiences are migrating to the Internet. A study by Forrester Research indicates that 24 percent of Internet users give up time spent eating or sleeping to be on the Web. The vast majority (75 percent) reported that they gave up time watching television to surf the Web instead. A report by the A. C. Neilsen company states that the number of U.S. households watching prime-time television declined by one million viewers in just one year. During that same year, the number of North Americans with on-line Internet services had almost doubled. It is highly likely that the million fewer viewers of prime-time television have shifted some of their attention to the Internet. Table 8.5 presents a brief review of the major advantages and disadvantages of Internet advertising.

As shown, a major benefit of Internet marketing is the creative opportunities available and the short lead time. Creativity is possible because banners can be composed using many different types of graphics. Animation and streaming videos can be incorporated into banner ads. Short lead time is possible because an advertisement can be changed and posted on the Internet immediately, even when ads are placed on other sites.

Segmentation is easy to accomplish with the Internet. The company can track who is clicking on an advertisement and viewing various pages. Engage Technologies records the paths individuals use as they move from site to site. The company uses these data to create a profile of the person and then match it to profiles

TABLE 8.5

Internet Advertising

Advantages	Disadvantages
1. Creative possibilities	1. Clutter on each site
2. Short lead time to send ad	2. Difficult procedures to place ads and buy time
3. Simplicity of segmentation	3. Only for computer owners
4. High audience interest on each Web site	4. Short life span
5. Easier to measure responses directly	5. Low intrusion value
	6. Hard to retain interest of surfers

in a database. Based on the person's profile, appropriate advertisements are then sent. Web surfers are not even aware this tracking takes place and often are amazed that products they like suddenly appear on the screen.[16]

The demographic characteristics of users are fairly well defined. Web surfers are young, well educated, and have relatively high incomes. Women represent about 42 percent of Internet users and men the other 58 percent. The average age is 34.9 years old. Over 65 percent of Internet users have household incomes of $50,000 or more, compared with 35 percent of the U.S. population as whole. In terms of education, 75 percent of the Internet users have attended college compared to 46 percent of the U.S. population. These demographics are beginning to change as more senior citizens get on the Internet to communicate with children and grandchildren. Targeting a specific audience is not too difficult with the Internet, because most companies selling advertising space have a good idea of their audience characteristics.

Audience interest is another advantage of the Internet. Internet browsers normally go to Web sites that attract them. Advertising on these pages is efficient because the audience is already curious about the site. For example, two lucrative places to advertise are on sports-related sites and music sites. Each draws a large number of hits per day, although demographics vary. Sports sites tend to attract males. Music sites tend to attract females. Both have high levels of interest.

The use of the Internet as an advertising medium for business-to-business marketing has increased substantially. Placing ads on business sites is an excellent method of targeting ads to interested buyers. When employees search for information about a particular product, they often will click on Internet ads to see what is offered. Business buyers look for information and consequently pay more attention to ads they see during the search. Internet ads allow individual companies to advertise their own services. For example, an employee gathering information on a vendor's site may see an advertisement for other products the company sells or products from the firm's subsidiary. As more businesses install the Internet for their employees, reaching buying center members through advertising on the Internet should become increasingly productive.

As for disadvantages, Internet clutter is one problem. The explosion of Internet advertising means many sites show numerous ads several layers thick. Web surfers quickly bypass these ads. In addition, a Web site filled with advertisements that delay its loading causes many surfers to become impatient and move on to other sites.

Another major problem for national companies is buying procedures. Almost all advertising spots must be purchased individually from each site. No national buyers that sell Internet space on a set of sites exists as of yet. As Internet advertising matures, it seems likely that entrepreneurs will seize the opportunity to meet this need.

At this time, the Internet is still limited to those who can afford a computer and Internet services. The Internet is a new medium that many who own computers use only for e-mail or other relatively simple services.

Another problem is that Internet ads have short life spans. The wear-out time for Internet ads seems to be even shorter than that of other media.[17] This means advertisers must spend more time updating the advertisements if they hope to gain audience attention.

Unlike television, the Internet tends not to have intrusion value. Web surfers do not have to pause on an advertisement as one would have to do when looking at a magazine or newspaper. To get surfers to stop (i.e., to intrude upon individuals), ad banners feature streaming videos and flashing displays. This approach worked for a while when it was new, but soon became old. To correct this disadvantage, some advertisers have developed what is called *interstitial advertising*, which interrupts a person on the Internet without warning. These type of ads have to be literally clicked off to remove them from the screen and are extremely controversial. Although they have intrusion value, they also are annoying. Interstitial ads can come onto a person's computer even after logging off of the Internet or come on the screen when the next time the person logs on.[18] Although untested at this time, interstitial advertising could prove extremely valuable to business-to-business marketers. Targeted ads could be sent to members of the buying center even after they log off of the computer. The chances of capturing some level of attention increase because these ads must be clicked off. Also, if the business buyer has been searching for information about a product and an advertisement for that product pops onto the screen, the individual will likely study the ad to see what is being offered.

The Internet is the fastest-growing medium in history. It took television 13 years to reach 50 million viewers. It took radio 38 years to reach 50 million. Experts estimate it took only 5 years for the Internet to reach 50 million users.

It is too early to know for sure the full impact of Internet advertising. If it is measured by the number of *click-throughs*, whereby the ad is quickly zapped, Internet advertising appears not to be as successful as advertisers first thought. Studies have shown that Web users tend to ignore banners, and most Internet users can't even remember the last banner they clicked on. Some studies indicate that Internet advertising is ineffective. Other studies reveal the Internet as a successful method of advertising. A study by Millward Brown International concluded that brand awareness using Internet brand banners increased between 12 percent and 200 percent. Compared to brand awareness studies of television and radio ads, Internet banners generated greater ad awareness with a single exposure than did either television or radio.[19]

Internet advertising programs are certain to grow in the future. Chapter 16 is devoted to Internet marketing and e-commerce.

Magazines

The glamour of television has overshadowed magazines for a long time. For many advertisers, magazines have always been a second choice. Recent research, however, indicates that in some cases magazines are actually a better option. A study by the A. C. Neilsen Company revealed that people who viewed ads in magazines were from 2 percent to 37 percent more likely to purchase the product. Also, a study by Millward Brown, examining the cost effectiveness of magazine advertising, revealed promising information for magazines. The study suggested that magazine advertising is three times more cost effective than television.[20] Naturally, the validity of these results have been staunchly debated by television executives. In any case, evidence exists that magazine advertising can be effective. Table 8.6 displays the pros and cons of magazine advertising.

A major advantage of magazines is the high level of market segmentation available. Magazines are highly segmented by topic area. Specialized magazines are much more common than general magazines with broad readerships. Even within certain market segments, such as automobiles, a number of magazines exist.

Advantages	Disadvantages	**TABLE 8.6**
1. High market segmentation	1. Declining readership (some magazines)	**Magazine Advertising**
2. Targeted audience interest by magazine	2. High level of clutter	
3. Direct-response techniques (e.g. coupons, Web addresses, toll-free numbers)	3. Long lead time to ad showing	
4. High color quality	4. Little flexibility	
5. Availability of special features (e.g., scratch and sniff)	5. High cost	
6. Long life		
7. Read during leisure time (longer attention to ad)		

Magazines are so highly differentiated that high audience interest becomes another advantage. An individual who subscribes to *Modern Bride* has some kind of strong attraction to weddings. People reading magazines also tend to view and pay attention to advertisements related to their needs and wants. Often, readers linger over an ad for a longer period of time, because they read magazines in waiting situations (e.g., doctor's office) or during leisure time. This high level of interest, segmentation, and differentiation are ideal for products with precisely defined target markets.

Magazines, both trade and business journals, are a major medium for business-to-business marketing. Businesses can target their advertisements. The copy provides a greater level of detail about products. Readers, if interested, take time to read the information in the ad. Ads can provide toll-free telephone numbers and Web addresses so interested parties can obtain further information.

Magazines offer high-quality color and more sophisticated production processes, providing the creative with the opportunity to produce intriguing and enticing advertisements. Motion, color, and unusual images can be used to attract attention. Magazines such as *Glamour, Elle*, and *Cosmopolitan* use scratch and sniff ads to entice women to notice the fragrance of a perfume or cologne. Even car manufacturers have ventured into this type of advertising by producing a smell of leather in certain ads.

Magazines have a long advertising life, lasting beyond the immediate issue because subscribers read and reread them. This means the same advertisement is often read by more than one person. It is not unusual for an avid magazine reader to examine a particular issue several times and spend considerable amount of time with each issue. This appeal is attractive to advertisers because they know the reader will be exposed more than once and likely pay more attention to the ad. In addition, magazine ads last beyond the current issue. Weeks and even months later, other individuals may look at the magazine. In the business-to-business sector, trade journals are often passed around to several individuals or members of the

An magazine advertisement by Harley-Davidson. Courtesy of Harley–Davidson Motor Company.

An advertisement in *Glamour* for Bijan perfume. Courtesy of Bijan Fragrances, Inc.

buying center. As long as the magazine lasts, the advertisement is still there to be viewed.

One major disadvantage facing magazine advertisers is a decline in readers. The culprit is the Internet. The Leo Burnett Company's *Starcom Report* states that magazines lost 61 million readers from the 18- to 49-year-old age bracket in just one year. Most moved to the Internet. Mediamark Research Inc. recently reported that magazine readerships declined by 5.9 percent for the same year. Of the 200 magazines examined, 56 gained readers while 144 lost readers. The largest gains were in *Vibe, Men's Fitness, Men's Health, Martha Stewart Living*, and *Inc.* magazine. The largest losers were *The National Enquirer, Sports Illustrated, TV Guide, Consumer Reports, Field & Stream, People*, and *Newsweek*.[21] To combat this trend, many of the magazines losing readers have combined with television networks, such as *People* with NBC's *Dateline* program and *Sports Illustrated*'s connection with CNN.

Clutter is another big problem for magazine advertisers. For example, a recent 318-page issue of *Glamour* contained 195 pages of advertising and only 123 pages of content. Ads can be easily lost in those situations. To be noticed, the advertisement must be unique or stand out in some way, such as the advertisement for Bijan perfume showing a woman smoking a cigar.

Long lead times are a major disadvantage of magazines, because advertisements must be submitted as much as six months in advance of the issue. Consequently, making changes in ads after submission is very difficult. Also, because of the long life of magazines, images or messages created through magazine advertising have long lives. This is good for stable products or services, but not for volatile markets or highly competitive markets wherein the appeal, price, or some other aspect of the marketing mix changes more frequently.

Cost is also a major factor with magazines. Because of its high-quality production and long shelf life, magazine advertising tends to be expensive. Ads can run over a million dollars for a single four-color page.

Magazines continue to proliferate even with the problems of declining readership. The wide variety of special interests makes it possible to develop and sell them. Many advertisers still can target audiences and take advantage of various magazine features, such as direct-response Internet addresses and coupon offers. This is especially true in the business market. Although business-to-business marketers increasingly use other media, trade journals and business magazines remain an effective method of reaching their target markets. As a result, the nature of advertising in magazines may change, but individual companies still will find effective uses for the outlets.

Integrated Learning Experience

The primary professional organization for magazines is the Magazine Publishers of America at www.magazine.org. Browse the various sections of the Web site to see what information is available. Examine a few of the articles in the "What's New" section. Review the recent advertising revenues for magazines. To get the feel for one of the many specialty magazines on the market, access the Web site of *Divorce Magazine* at www.divorcemag.com. Scan the various articles in the magazine and current advertisers. Access the "Advertise with Us" section to obtain information about rates and the reasons why a company might wish to advertise in the *Divorce Magazine*.

Newspapers

Upon the launch of *USA Today*, few believed a national daily newspaper could succeed. Obviously it has. The nature of news reporting has changed, many small local papers no longer exist, and conglomerates such as Gannett own most major city newspaper chains. Still, daily readership continues.

For many smaller local firms, newspaper ads, billboards, and local radio programs are the only viable advertising options, especially if television ads are too cost prohibitive. Newspapers can be distributed daily, weekly, or in partial form as the advertising supplements found in the front sections of many grocery stores and retail outlets. Table 8.7 displays the basic advantages and disadvantages of newspaper advertising.

Retailers still rely heavily on newspapers ads, because they offer geographic selectivity (local market access). Promoting sales, retail hours, and store locations is easy to accomplish in a newspaper ad. Short lead time allows retailers to change ads and promotions quickly. This flexibility is a strong advantage. It allows advertisers the ability to keep their ads current. They can modify ads to meet competitive offers or to focus on recent events.

TABLE 8.7	Advantages	Disadvantages
Newspaper Advertising	1. Priority for local ads	1. Poor buying procedures
	2. High flexibility	2. Short life span
	3. High credibility	3. Major clutter (especially holidays)
	4. Strong audience interest	4. Poor quality reproduction (especially color)
	5. Longer copy–message possible	5. Internet classified competition
	6. Cumulative volume discounts	
	7. Coupons and special-response features	

Newspapers have a high level of credibility. Readers rely on newspapers for factual information in stories giving newspaper greater credibility. Newspaper readers hold high interest levels in the articles they read. They tend to pay more attention to advertisements as well as news stories. This increased audience interest allows advertisers to provide more copy detail in their ads. Newspaper readers take more time to read copy, unless simply too much information is jammed into a small space.

Newspaper advertisers receive volume discounts for buying larger *column inches* of advertising space. Many newspapers grant these volume discounts, called *cumulative discounts*, over one-month, three-month, or even year-long time periods. This potentially makes the cost-per-exposure even lower, because larger and repeated ads are more likely to garner the reader's attention.

Many local consumers rely heavily on newspaper advertising for information about grocery specials and other similar price discounts. Many local merchants use newspaper coupons. Newspapers also provide other special-response features ("Mention our ad in today's paper, and receive 10% off").

At the same time, there are limitations and disadvantages to newspaper advertising. First, newspapers cannot be targeted as easily to specific market segments (although sports pages carry sports ads, entertainment pages contain movie and restaurant ads, and so forth). Newspapers also have a short life. Once read, a newspaper normally is cast to the side, recycled, or destroyed. If a reader does not see an advertisement during the first pass through a newspaper, it probably will go unnoticed. Readers rarely pick up papers a second time. When they do, it is to continue reading, not to reread or rescan a section that has already been viewed.

Newspaper advertising suffers from two clutter problems. First, Wednesday papers containing grocery ads are usually larger and more cluttered. Second, holiday season newspapers, especially between Thanksgiving and Christmas hold the most ads of the year. Thus, clutter is at the highest during peak selling seasons.

Newspaper ads often have poor production quality. Few companies buy color ads, because they are much more expensive. Photos and copy tend to be harder to read and see clearly compared to other print media, especially magazines. Newspaper ads tend not to be wild or highly creative. Newspapers editors normally avoid and turn down anything that may be controversial, such as Calvin Klein ads featuring more-or-less naked models. Newspapers are very careful about offending their readers.

Newspapers suffer poor national buying procedures. Many newspapers in small towns are independent or small holding companies own them. For a national advertiser, this means contacting numerous companies. Also, newspapers tend to favor local companies over national firms. Local businesses generally receive better advertising rates than do national advertisers, because local companies advertise on a more regular basis and receive volume discounts. Also, newspapers want to have a strong local appeal. By favoring local companies in ad rates, they can meet this goal and seem more desirable to local patrons.

A new threat to newspapers is the Internet, not a decline in newspaper readership due to movement to the Internet, but rather a shift by advertisers from classified newspaper ads to classified Internet ads. Two large electronic competitors are Microsoft's Sidewalk and CarPoint. Newspapers experience a decline in newspaper ads as retailers move into e-commerce, because retailers are the major advertisers in newspapers. Retail sales via e-commerce is over $8 billion annually.[22] As more households acquire computers and hook to the Internet and consumers become more accustomed to e-commerce, more advertising will shift from newspapers to the Internet.

It is ironic that as newspapers lose advertising, especially classifieds, to the Internet, it is being replaced by advertising for Internet companies. As with the other media, the largest growth category are the dot.com advertisements, especially in the financial and telecommunication industries.

Newspapers counter the trend of classified advertisements moving to the Internet by establishing their own Internet classified sites. Various newspapers own AdOne, CareerPath, Classified Ventures, and PowerAdz. The major obstacle is that the competition is growing faster. Microsoft, America Online, and Yahoo! all have established strong classified ad sections. In one year, the number of classified ad sites increased by 269 percent.[23]

There is even competition in the area of want ads. Monster.com provides help wanted ads on a national scale, which may reduce purchases of local want ad space from newspapers. Thus, newspapers face significant challenges in retaining their advertising revenues.

There is some hope, however. Procter and Gamble now uses newspapers for the first time to promote its Tide detergent. Other national advertisers moving to newspapers include Johnson & Johnson, Kraft, Nestlé, and General Motors.[24] In this uncertain future, newspaper owners must become more creative and resourceful to entice larger companies to advertise locally on a regular basis.

Newspapers have not been a major medium for business-to-business marketers primarily because of their local nature. Most vendors and suppliers seeking the business of local companies do not reside in the same local area. Local companies can use newspapers in efforts to get business from other local companies. Often this approach is not cost effective, because of the inability to target the ad to any given business target market.

Direct mail

Another major advertising medium is direct mail. Many companies send ads directly to target markets of customers through mailing lists or blanket a region for more general products. Wal-Mart, Big K (Kmart), Target, Sears, and other national retail chains often send advertisements to consumers through the mail. Credit card companies are notorious for sending out enticements to apply for their cards, especially to lower-income families and college students. National restaurant chains (KFC, Pizza Hut) also mail directly to potential buyers. These firms mail free samples, coupons, and other special features to potential customers on a daily basis.

The major advantage of direct mail is that it normally lands in the hands of the person who opens the mail, who usually makes a significant amount of family purchasing decisions. Many mail offers include direct-response programs, so results are quickly measured. Direct mail also can be targeted to geographic market segments.

The primary disadvantages of direct mail include costs, clutter, and the "nuisance" factor. To be noticed, direct-mail advertising usually requires a color brochure, making the mailings more expensive to produce. As postage rates continue to rise, so do the costs of direct mail. Mailings tend to clutter post office boxes and become more prevalent during key seasons, such as Christmas. Many people are genuinely annoyed by "junk mail" and actively seek to have their names taken off of mailing lists, especially for catalog-type operations.

Some people find direct mailing to be the least "reputable" form of advertising, because many mail-fraud scams have arisen in the past few decades. Direct mail best suits well-known local or national firms seeking a more immediate response (e.g., coupon redemption) or when the company wants to reinforce ads presented in other media. Direct mail reaches some customers who do not buy newspapers. Record clubs, book clubs, and others have used direct mail effectively over the years. It is likely many firms will continue to use the mail in the future.

Direct mail remains a favorite marketing tool for business-to-business marketers. It provides a method of bypassing gatekeepers when the names of actual members of the buying center can be obtained. Direct mail can be one method of reaching businesses when they are in a rebuy situation and not open to calls by salespeople. Even if the direct mail is ignored when it is received, many people often file it away for future use. Although the cost per contact is high for direct mail, so is the response rate as compared to other media. The key to success for businesses is to make sure that the direct-mail piece gets into the hands of the right person in the buying center and that it is attractive enough to grab attention.

Others

Besides all of the "traditional" and new (Internet) media discussed, numerous new ways are available for companies sending out advertisements. The key, as always, is to make certain the ads reach the right target market with the proper message. Some examples of additional forms of advertising—some that are new and some that have existed for many years—include:

- Leaflets, brochures, and carry-home menus
- Ads on carry-home bags from stores (grocery stores and retail outlets)
- Ads on T-shirts and caps (promotional giveaways and products sold)
- Ads on movie trailers both in theaters and on home video rental products
- Small, freestanding road signs
- Self-run ads in motel rooms on television, towels, ice chests, and so on
- Yellow pages and phone book advertisements
- Mall kiosk ads
- Ads sent by fax
- Ads shown on video replay scoreboards at major sports events
- In-house advertising magazines placed by airlines in seats
- Ads on the walls of airports, subway terminals, bus terminals, and inside cabs and buses

Each of these has additional benefits and problems. For example, small, freestanding road signs effectively gain attention, but many local governments and community citizens consider them eyesores. Yellow page advertising has become more difficult as additional firms enter into the phone book preparation market. Mall kiosk ads are placed in high traffic areas, but are easily defaced by vandals. Ads sent by fax are low cost and can be highly targeted (luncheon specials faxed to local companies just before noon). Still, many business owners become angry when their fax machines are tied up receiving ads. Ads on replay scoreboards have high intrusion values, yet can be ignored or even "booed" by those attending the game. Nonetheless, advertisers must consider all of the possibilities as they prepare advertising campaigns. The goals of reach, frequency, costs, and continuity must all be considered as individual media are selected and groups of media formulated into a campaign mix.

media mix

Selecting the proper blend of media outlets for advertisements is a crucial activity. As campaigns are prepared, decisions must be made concerning the appropriate mix of media. Media planners and media buyers are both excellent sources of information on the most effective type of mix for a particular advertising campaign. It is the challenge of the creative to design ads for each medium that speaks to the audience yet ties in with the overall theme of the integrated advertising campaign. A survey of Table 8.8 shows considerable differences in media mixes that different consumer industries use. Notice that retailers spend more on newspaper advertising (61.1 percent) than they do on any other media. At the same time, all of the other categories spend more on television advertising. Choosing the appropriate advertising channels and then effectively combining outlets requires the expertise of a media planner who can study each outlet and match it with the product and overall message.

TABLE 8.8

Advertising Expenditures by Categories

Category	Magazines	Newspapers	Outdoor	Television	Radio
Retail	4.2%	61.1%	2.0%	27.8%	5.0%
Automotive	14.0	32.7	0.7	50.8	1.8
Services	12.6	36.8	1.6	44.3	4.6
Entertainment	2.3	17.2	1.8	75.8	2.9
Foods	14.9	0.7	0.3	80.5	3.6
Cosmetics	32.5	0.5	0.07	66.2	0.7
Total	11.4	32.7	1.2	51.3	3.3

Jack Nott, "Media Buying and Planning," *Advertising Age,* Vol. 70, no. 32, pp. 1–2.

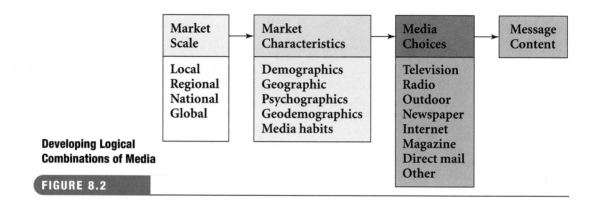

Developing Logical Combinations of Media

FIGURE 8.2

Recent studies by Millward Brown and A. C. Neilsen highlight the benefits of combining different media.[25] Using a telephone survey, Millward Brown found that ad awareness was 65 percent when consumers viewed the ad both on television and in a magazine. It was 19 percent for those who saw only the magazine ad and 16 per cent for those who saw only the television ad. The increased impact of using two or more media is termed the **media multiplier effect**, which means the combined impact of using two or more media is stronger than using either medium alone. Business-to-business firms are just now applying this concept as they use more than traditional trade journals for their advertising dollars. The key is to find effective combinations of media when designing a media mix.

Figure 8.2 shows possible linkages between various media. Consider the many possible options and combinations. Media experts work continually to decide which go together for individual target markets, goods and services, and advertising messages.

media selection in business-to-business markets

Identifying differences between consumer ads and business-to-business ads is becoming more difficult, especially in television, outdoor, and Internet ads. In the past, it was easy to spot business-to-business ads: The content was clearly aimed toward another company, and television, outdoor, and the Internet were seldom used. Currently, about 64 percent of all business advertising dollars are spent in nonbusiness environments.[26]

Several items explain this shift to more nonbusiness media. First, business decision makers are also consumers of goods and services. The same psychological techniques used to influence and gain the consumer attention can also be used for business decision makers.

Second, and probably the most important, business decision makers are very difficult to reach at work. Gatekeepers (secretaries, voice mail systems, etc.) often prevent information flow to users, influencers, and decision makers. This is especially true for straight rebuy situations whereby orders are given to the current vendor. If a company is not the chosen vendor, it is extremely difficult to get anyone's attention. To avoid various gatekeepers, business-to-business firms try to reach the members of the buying center at their homes, in their cars, or in some other nonbusiness venue.

A third reason for this shift to nonbusiness media is that the clutter among the traditional business media has made it more difficult to get a company noticed. Business advertisers realize that to have a chance for a sale, they must have a recognizable brand name. Taking lessons from brand giants such as Nike, Campbell's Soups, Wal-Mart, and Tide, business marketers now know they must establish a strong brand name. A strong brand name helps the company gain the attention of members of the buying center.

W. W. Grainger Company sells industrial maintenance supplies such as motors, tools, lights, sanitary supplies, heating, and air-conditioning equipment to other businesses. Believing that purchasing agents are likely to watch football, Grainger decided to enhance the company's brand name via television rather than use cluttered trade journals. Research conducted by Grainger indicated that the users and influencers for its products, maintenance and repair foreman, are likely to watch sports. Consequently, Grainger purchased advertising space on *Monday Night Football* and other sporting events such as NCAA basketball.[27]

In the past business ads were fairly dull, but now they look much more like consumer ads. Creative appeals and the use of music, humor, sex, and fear, similar to consumer ads, are used. The boldest business ads sometimes include nudity or other more risqué material. In fact, many consumers cannot tell the difference. These firms hope that few business decision makers will notice they are seeing a business ad. When that happens, the business advertiser has succeeded.

Figure 8.3 identifies how business-to-business advertising expenditures are divided among the various media. Figure 8.4 lists the top six business-to-business advertisers. As shown, trade journals remain the number-one media used in business settings. Almost one-third of all advertising dollars are spent here. Trade journals offer a highly targeted audience.

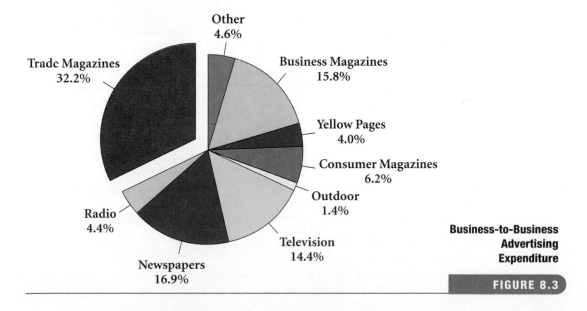

Other 4.6%
Business Magazines 15.8%
Trade Magazines 32.2%
Yellow Pages 4.0%
Consumer Magazines 6.2%
Outdoor 1.4%
Radio 4.4%
Television 14.4%
Newspapers 16.9%

Business-to-Business Advertising Expenditure

FIGURE 8.3

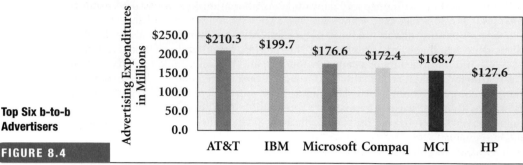

**Top Six b-to-b
Advertisers**

FIGURE 8.4

Trade journals provide an opportunity to reach members of the buying center whom salespeople cannot reach. Gatekeepers cannot prevent trade journals from reaching different members of the buying center. Unfortunately, if the firm is in a straight rebuy situation, it is doubtful the ad will be noticed. If the firm is in a modified rebuy and the buying center is in the information search stage, then the ad has a better chance of success.

Clutter is a major problem in trade journals. Also, business advertisers often fill their adds with too much information. Therefore, ads should be designed to gain the reader's attention, and the copy must be manageable.

In addition to trade journals, business-to-business advertisers also use business magazines such as *Business Week* and consumer magazines. A total of 54.2 percent of the advertising budget goes for magazines. When newspapers and yellow pages are added to this list, print media accounts for about 75 percent of all business-to-

An advertisement for Internet banking
services. Courtesy of WingspanBank.com.

business dollars spent. The primary reasons for these high levels of expenditures in print media are because they have highly selective audiences and the ads have longer life spans in print. Business decision makers and members of the buying center spend more working time examining print media than any other medium. Business will notice the advertisement by WingspanBank.com more if it is located in a trade journal than in a general magazine such as *Time* because readers are more likely to notice and read the advertisement, especially if they have been working or thinking about banking or financial services within their company.

Many goals in business-to-business advertisements are the same as those devoted to consumers. It remains important to identify key target markets; to select the proper media; and to prepare creative, enticing ads resulting in some kind of action, such as a change in attitude toward the company or movement toward a purchase decision. Many of the variables shown in Figure 8.2 apply equally well to business advertising.

Integrated Learning Experience

One of the best sources for business-to-business advertising information is Advertising Age's Net B2B.com. Access this Web site at www.netb2b.com. Under special features, notice "The BtoB 100," which lists the top 100 business-to-business advertisers. Under "BtoB's Best and Brightest" are profiles of the leading media buyers and strategists. The "NetMarketing 200" section ranks the best business-to-business Web sites. What other information is available at this Web site to assist business-to-business advertisers in selecting the right media?

stop!

media selection in international markets

Understanding media viewing habits in international markets is important for successful advertising programs. In the United States, network television has been the primary advertising tool; in other countries, it is not as dominant. For instance, in Europe the best way to reach elite consumers is through magazines. Television and newspapers are second and third, respectively. The most popular magazines in Europe are *Reader's Digest*, *National Geographic*, *Cosmopolitan*, *Marie Clarie*, *Elle*, *Vogue*, *L'Express*, and *Paris Mach*. The most watched European television stations are Eurosport, CNN International, Euronews, and Kabel Eins.[28]

In Asia and Latin America, cable television and satellite are growing in popularity as more homes become hooked to cable or satellite. As a result, more companies buy regional time rather than national and international time. Both Pepsi and Coke have redirected some of their international advertising dollars to smaller regional and local television cable and satellite markets. Companies find this is more effective because of the differences in consumer needs and media habits across the European countries. MTV split its programming into three subregions: (1) the United Kingdom and Ireland; (2) the German-speaking countries of Germany, Switzerland, and Austria; and (3) the Scandinavian countries.[29]

Just as media viewing differs, media buying in other countries often differs. For example, the trend in France is to farm media buying out to international media specialists. France's largest advertiser, PSA Peugeot Citroen, turned over its media buying to Euro RSCG's Mediapolis. Another advertising agency, the Danone Group, chose Carat Media Services France to handle its media buying. Several international companies operating in France follow this trend. Nestlé use to have its own internal company, Societe Publi Edition Distribution Courtage, to purchase media. Now it uses Optimedia, a media specialist firm.[30]

In other countries, the reverse may be true. For example, the top advertising agencies in Brazil fiercely oppose all independent media buying groups. The plan is to push for a change in the law that prohibits the payment of agency commissions and discounts from media buying to any firm that is not a full-service advertising agency. In India, the Advertising Agencies Association passed a stern resolution requiring members to stop handling media-only accounts or risk expulsion from the association. The Advertising Agencies Association of India believes it is critical for the full-service agency to be involved in all aspects of a brand's advertising, including media buying. The resolution and opposition of the Advertising Agencies Association to media buying independents is aimed at Carat Media Services India — India's first independent media buying service. Carat successfully persuaded Charagh Dink, India's largest shirt maker, to move its entire media buying account to Carat while hiring a freelancer to do the creative work. Carat also captured business from BBC World, Cadbury India, and Virgin Music. To prevent expulsion from the Advertising Agencies Association of India, agencies such as Madison DMB&B, which handles media buying for firms such as Coca-Cola, have added small creative assignments.[31]

In Brazil, purchasing media means turning an advertising account over to a full-service agency that also provides creative work. In France, creative work and media buying are seldom done by the same firm. Thus, media purchase varies from country to country.

In international settings, it is important to understand the media habits of consumers as well as their daily lifestyles. McCann-Erickson Worldwide launched a multinational media research effort called Media In Mind in Europe. The goal of this research is improve media effectiveness by matching a firm's advertising to the time of day the audience will be most receptive, as well as to the correct medium. Such firms as Motorola, Johnson & Johnson, General Motors, Coca-Cola, and Boots Healthcare International use Media In Mind. They report their media effectiveness has increased as much as 20 percent over those firms that have not used Media In Mind.

Part of the Media In Mind research in Europe has focused on consumer moods throughout the day. Boots Healthcare International used this research in advertising of cures for headaches. The research found that in Poland the people classified in the "headache" category were more likely to have the headache from the time they woke up until around noon. Thus, Boots Healthcare advertises on billboards that people see on their way to work or at lunch. The company also advertises on radio during the morning hours.[32]

Although outdoor advertising in most countries is primarily billboards, travelers near Riyadh and Jeddah, Saudi Arabia, see unique outdoor advertising. Publi-Graphics transformed two water towers into replicas of Nestlé's Nido brand powdered-milk cans. These two Nestlé powdered-milk can replicas are the largest outdoor advertising of its kind and can be seen for miles around.[33]

In general, many tactics used to develop advertising campaign in the United States apply to international advertising. What differs is the nature of the target markets, consumer media preferences, and the processes used to buy media. Also, companies must carefully attend to cultural mores to make sure the buying process does not offend the cultural and religious attitudes prevalent in any given region. A cultural assimilator must carefully screen clothing, gestures, words, symbols, and other ingredients as a company purchases advertising time or space and prepares ads. Chapter 10 covers additional information about specific issues in advertising design in international markets.

stop!

Integrated Learning Experience

Advertising expenditures across the various media vary widely throughout the world. To see the difference, access the "Top Global Ad Markets" segment through the "Ad Age Dataplace" at www.adage.com. Compare ad spending by medium for the United States and the other countries listed. What differences are there in spending on television, radio, and magazines among the various countries listed? Notice the Web site also lists the top advertising companies, the top ad categories, the largest newspapers and magazines (based on circulation figures), and the ad rates for these particular publications.

Start with the message theme, and finish with the message theme. The IMC approach works best if every activity focuses on the one clear voice of the company.

Decide whether the client is large enough to have a separate media planner and media buyer, or if the two positions should be combined. Remember, the driving criteria should be *service to the client*, not cost savings.

Review the research conducted by the media planner. Make sure the plan is doing an effective job of finding media to match the message, the company, its customers, and the goods or services being advertised.

Review the work being performed by the media buyer. Make sure that purchases do indeed reflect the best available rates for the client. Also make sure the times and schedules are appropriate, and that they will lead to the best possible response.

Develop a strong, positive relationship between the media planner and media buyer, and between those two individuals and the client. The planner and buyer have a large impact on the campaign's success.

Consider hiring a research agency, as needed, to follow up on advertising campaigns to be certain the company effectively reaches its audience.

Review the goals of advertising with every client. Make sure they understand the differences between:

1. Reach (and effective reach)
2. Frequency (and effective frequency)
3. Continuity
4. CPM, GRP, ratings, and CPRP
5. Impressions

Review the advantages and disadvantages of each potential medium with clients. Avoid using the words *always* and *never* when discussing options.

Talk about the potential mixes of media. Note that the Internet probably will be somehow connected to every advertising campaign, even if only to give the company's Web site address.

Ask business customers to think about their intentions in reaching members of the buying center. Remind them of the challenges associated with:

1. Straight rebuys
2. Modified rebuys
3. New task purchases

Consider the differences in mix that exist between business campaigns and consumer campaigns. Make certain creatives are aware of the trade journals and other advertising outlets that should be part of every advertising campaign.

Think SMALL. Remind the creative, media planner, and media buyer of all of the small ways to advertise a product and reinforce a message. These include:

1. Envelopes carrying the company's current advertising message
2. Giveaways in contests whereby the company provides the prize in return for being mentioned
3. Merchandise to be sold or given away carrying advertising—which can include cups, toys, carryout bags, receipts, napkins, towels, packaging, and other containers—and every creative method possible to restate the firm's name

Follow up. Find ways to keep score. Make sure you give prospective clients clear and convincing evidence that your firm knows how to effectively reach a company's ongoing and new customers.

SUMMARY

The traditional view of advertising has been to design a message that will accomplish the intended IMC objective, then find the best media channel. This view is slowly being replaced as the roles of media planners and media buyers have grown in importance. According to Bob Brennan, chief operating officer of Chicago-based Leo Burnett Starcom USA, in the past "95% of your success was great creative and 5% was great media. Now it's much closer to 50–50."[34]

This chapter reviews the role of the media selection process. A media strategy is the process of analyzing and choosing media for an advertising and promotions campaign. Media planners and buyers complete much of this work. The media planner's primary job is to formulate a program stating where and when to place advertisements. Media planners work closely with creatives and account executives. Media buyers purchase the space, and they negotiate rates, times, and schedules for the ads.

The goals of reach, frequency, gross rating points, effective rating points, cost, continuity, and impressions drive the media selection process. Reach is the number of people, households, or businesses in a target audience exposed to media vehicle or message schedule at least once during a given time period. Frequency is the average number of times an individual, household, or business within a particular target market is exposed to a particular advertisement within a specified time period. Gross rating points (GRP) measure the impact or intensity of a media plan. Cost per thousand (CPM) is one method of finding the cost of the campaign by assessing the dollar cost of reaching 1,000 members of the media vehicle's audience. Cost per rating point (CPRM) is a second cost measure, which assesses the efficiency of media vehicle relative to a firm's target market. Ratings measure the percentage of a firm's target market that is exposed to a show on television or an article in a print medium. Continuity is the schedule or pattern of advertisement placements within an advertising campaign period. Gross impressions are the number of total exposures of the audience to an advertisement.

In addition to these basic concepts, advertising experts often utilized the concepts of effective frequency and effective reach. Effective frequency is the number of times a target audience must be exposed to a message to achieve a particular objective. Effective reach is the percentage of an audience that must be exposed to a particular message to achieve a specific objective.

In seeking advertising goals, marketing experts, account executives, and others must assess the relative advantages and disadvantages of each individual advertising medium. Thus, television, radio, outdoor billboards, the Internet, magazines, newspapers, and direct mail should all be considered as potential ingredients in a campaign. Other new media can be used to complement and supplement what the more traditional media outlets delivered. Logical combinations of media must be chosen to make sure the intended audience is exposed to the message. The three-exposure hypothesis suggests that a consumer must be exposed to an ad at least three times before it has the desired impact; other experts believe even more exposures are necessary. In contrast, recency theory suggests that ads truly reach only those wanting or needing a product, and therefore only one exposure is necessary when someone is "on the hot spot" and ready to buy.

In business-to-business settings, companies can combine consumer media outlets with trade journals and other business venues (trade shows, conventions, etc.) to attempt to reach members of the buying center. In many cases, enticing ads using consumer appeals such as sex, fear, and humor have replaced dry, dull, boring ads with an abundance of copy.

When designing business advertising, remember that advertising is just one component of the integrated marketing communications plan. It must be integrated with the sales force, sales promotions, trade promotions, and the public relations in use. Business-to-business advertising using traditional consumer media cannot accomplish all of the communications objectives a business needs to accomplish. They help develop brand awareness and build brand equity, but are usually not the best for providing information the buying center needs.

International advertising media selection is different in some ways from that which takes place in the United States, because media buying processes differ as do media preferences of locals in various countries. At the same time, the process of media selection is quite similar: Marketing experts choose media they believe will reach the target audience in an effective manner.

Media selection takes place in conjunction with the message design and within the framework of the overall IMC approach. Effective media selection means the company spends enough money to find the target audience and does not waste funds by overwhelming them with the same message. Account executives, creatives, media planners, media buyers, and the company's representative must all work together to make certain the process moves as effectively and efficiently as possible.

REVIEW QUESTIONS

1. What is a media strategy? How does it relate to the creative brief and overall IMC program?

2. What does a media planner do?

3. Describe the role of media buyer in an advertising program.

4. What is reach? Give examples of reach in various advertising media.

5. What is frequency? How can an advertiser increase frequency in a campaign?

6. What are gross rating points? What do they measure?

7. What is the difference between CPM and CPRP? What costs do they measure?

8. What is continuity?

9. Describe the three-exposure hypothesis.

10. How is recency theory different from the three-exposure hypothesis?

11. What is effective frequency? Effective reach?

12. What are the major advantages and disadvantages of television advertising?

13. What are the major advantages and disadvantages of radio advertising?

14. What are the major advantages and disadvantages of Internet advertising?

15. What are the major advantages and disadvantages of magazine advertising?

16. What are the major advantages and disadvantages of newspaper advertising?

17. Is the strong intrusion value of television an advantage? Why or why not?

18. Name a product and three media that would mix well together to advertise that product. Defend your media mix choices.

19. What special challenges does media selection present for businesses? What roles do gatekeepers play in creating those challenges?

20. What special challenges does media selection present for international advertising campaigns? What differences and similarities exist with U.S. media selection processes?

KEY TERMS

media strategy the process of analyzing and choosing media for an advertising and promotions campaign.

media planner the individual who formulates the program stating where and when to place advertisements.

media buyer the person who buys the space and negotiates rates, times, and schedules for the ads.

reach the number of people, households, or businesses in a target audience exposed to media vehicle or message schedule at least once during a given time period.

frequency the average number of times an individual, household, or business within a particular target market is exposed to a particular advertisement within a specified time period.

gross rating points (GRP) a measure of the impact or intensity of a media plan.

cost per thousand (CPM) the dollar cost of reaching 1,000 members of the media vehicle's audience.

cost per rating point (CPRP) a measure of the efficiency of media vehicle relative to a firm's target market.

ratings a measure of the percentage of a firm's target market that is exposed to a show on television or an article in a print medium.

continuity the schedule or pattern of advertisement placements within an advertising campaign period.

gross impressions the number of total exposures of the audience to an advertisement.

effective frequency the *number of times* a target audience must be exposed to a message to achieve a particular objective.

effective reach the *percentage of an audience* that must be exposed to a particular message to achieve a specific objective.

intrusion value the ability of media or an advertisement to intrude upon a viewer without his or her voluntary attention.

media multiplier effect the combined impact of using two or more media is stronger than using either medium alone.

ENDNOTES

1. Wilson Bryan Key, *Subliminal Seduction: Ad Media's Manipulation of a Not So Innocent America* (NJ: Prentice Hall, 1973); Jodi Mardesich, "Reading Between the Lines on Subliminal Programming," *Computer Reseller News*, 655 (October 30, 1995), pp. 101–2; Rana Dogar, "Sense & Sellability," *Working Woman*, 22, no. 4 (April 1997), p. 34; Cyndee Miller, "Scent as a Marketing Tool: Retailers — And Even a Casino — Seek Sweet Smell of Success," *Marketing News*, 27, no. 2 (January 18, 1993), pp. 1–2.

2. Jean Halliday, "Porsche Alters Its Media Strategy," *Advertising Age*, 70, no. 34 (August 16, 1999), p. 21.

3. Liz Davis Smith, "90s Require Integrated Marketing Programs," *Birmingham Business Journal*, 12 (March 27, 1995), p. 12.

4. Discussion of media planners and media buyers based on Angela M. Manueal, "Media Planners Rarely Seen, but Play Key Role in Projects," *Business First — Louisville*, 11, no. 42 (May 22, 1995), pp. 42–44.

5. Jack Neff, "Media Buying & Planning," *Advertising Age*, 70, no. 32 (August 2, 1999), pp. 1–2.

6. Arthur A. Andersen, "Clout Only a Part of Media Buyer's Value," *Advertising Age*, 70, no. 15 (April 5, 1999), p. 26.

7. Ibid.

8. R. F. Dyer and E. H. Foreman, "Decision Support for Media Selection Using the Analytic Hierarchy Process," *Journal of Advertising*, 21, no. 1 (March 1992), pp. 59–62.

9. Herbert E. Krugman, "Why Three Exposures May Be Enough," *Journal of Advertising Research*, 12, no. 6 (1972), pp. 11–14.

10. Betsy Tabor, "Is Your Advertising Strategy Obsolete?" *Mississippi Business Journal*, 20, no. 34 (August 24, 1998), p. 28.

11. Chuck Ross, "Now, Many Words from Our Sponsors," *Advertising Age*, 70, no. 40 (September 27, 1999), pp. 3–4.

12. Stephanie Thompson, "Food Marketers Stir Up the Media," *Advertising Age*, 70, no. 42 (September 11, 1999), p. 18.

13. Katy Bachman, "The Big Time," *Adweek, Western Edition*, 49, no. 38 (September 20, 1999), pp. 50–51.

14. Carol Krol, "Look Up! Seeing Is Believing," *Advertising Age*, 70, no. 32 (August 2, 1999), p. 2.

15. "Why Internet Advertising?" *Adweek, Eastern Edition*, 38, no. 18 (May 5, 1997), pp. 8–12.

16. Richard A. Shaffer, "Listen Up! Pay Attention! New Web Startups Want Ads That Grab You," *Fortune*, 140, no. 8 (October 25, 1999), pp. 348–349.

17. Kathy Sharpe, "Web Punctures the Idea That Advertising Works," *Advertising Age*, 70, no. 38 (September 13, 1999), p. 44; Shaffer, "Listen Up! Pay Attention! New Web Startups Want Ads That Grab You."

18. Ibid.

19. "Why Internet Advertising?"

20. Rachel X. Weissman, "Just Paging Through," *American Demographics*, 21, no. 4 (April 1999), pp. 28–29; "The Scoop on Magazine Advertising," *Florist*, 33, no. 5 (October 1999), p. 16.

21. Ann Marie Kerwin, "Magazine Blast Study Showing Reader Falloff," *Advertising Age*, 70, no. 10 (March 8, 1999), pp. 3–4.

22. John Morton, "A Looming Threat to Newspaper Advertising," *American Journalism Review* (May 1999), p. 88.

23. Tony Case, "Reading the Numbers," *Brandweek*, 40, no. 35 (September 20, 1999), Media Outlook, p. 64.

24. Ibid.

25. Lindsay Morris, "Studies Give 'Thumbs Up' to Mags for Ad Awareness," *Advertising Age*, 70, no. 32 (August 2, 1999), pp. 16–17; Rachel X. Weissman, "Broadcasters Mine the Gold," *American Demographics*, 21, no. 6, (June 1999), pp. 35–37.

26. Adrienne W. Fawcett, "Creativity in Other Media Is Raising the Bar in Print," *Advertising Age's Business Marketing*, 82, no. 8 (September 1997), p. 32.

27. Laurie Freeman, "Internet Shows Rapid Growth as Communications Tool, Helping to Change Marketers' Use of Traditional Media," *Advertising Age's Business Marketing*, 84, no. 5 (May 1999), p. S6.

28. Julia Korantang, "European Survey Uncovers the Best Ad Vehicles," *Advertising Age International* (August 9, 1999), pp. 15–16.

29. Joy Dietrich and Normandy Madden, "Multichannel Ad Revenues Up 23% in 98," *Advertising Age International* (June 14, 1999), pp. 21–22.

30. Larry Speer, "Nestlé Joins Trend of Farming Out Media Buys in France," *Advertising Age International* (October 1999), p. 1.

31. Laurel Wentz and Mir Maqbool Alan Khan, "The Backlash Against Indies in Brazil," *Advertising Age International* (October 5, 1998), p. 14.

32. Suzanne Bidlake, "Consumers Under Microscope," *Advertising Age International* (February 8, 1999), p. 21.

33. Korantang, "European Survey Uncovers the Best Ad Vehicles."

34. Neff, "Media Buying & Planning."

35. Bachman, "The Big Time."

36. Noah Liberman, "Web Marketers Use Radio to Net Audience Members," *Atlanta Business Chronicle*, 22, no. 16 (September 24, 1999), p. 73A.

Building an IMC Campaign

Selecting Media for an IMC Advertising Campaign

Following your decision about choosing an in-house approach or an external advertising agency, you must make another set of choices. The media you select to advertise your product need to match the budget, the theme of the IMC program, the specific message, and the product itself. Therefore, carefully consider both traditional media as well as creative ways your company can develop to get your product's message out. Visit the Prentice-Hall Web site at www.prenhall.com/clow or access the Advertising Plan Pro disk that accompanied this textbook and complete the exercise for this chapter. You will be asked to describe both the media you've selected and the ones which were rejected. Also, the reasoning process used to include or exclude media should be identified. Remember that your choices may be affected by local conditions and international considerations.

Critical Thinking Exercises

Discussion Questions

1. To be effective, multiple media should be chosen and integrated carefully. Individuals exposed to an advertisement on combinations of channels selected from television, radio, the Internet, and billboards are more inclined to process the information than if only a solitary media is used. Fill in the following chart by putting in the probability of your being exposed to an advertisement if it were put into each medium. The percentages across each row should add up to 100 percent.

Product	Television	Radio	Newspaper	Magazine	Outdoor	Internet	Direct Mail
Movie							
Restaurant							
Clothing							
Jewelry							
Dry cleaner							

2. Billboard advertising in Times Square is so popular that space has already been sold for 10 years. Coca-Cola, General Motors, Samsung, Prudential, NBC, Budweiser, and the *New York Times* pay rates in excess of $100,000 a month to hold these spaces for the next 10 years. Inter City is building a 50-story hotel at Broadway and 47th Street to accommodate 75,000 square feet of advertising. Even before the completion of the hotel or tower, such companies as Federal Express, Apple Computers, AT&T, HBO, Levi-Strauss, Morgan Stanley, and the U.S. Postal Service have purchased space.[35] Why would companies pay so much for outdoor advertising? What are the advantages and disadvantages of purchasing billboards at Times Square?

3. Repetition and a short, catchy name are the keys for an effective radio spot. Sports equipment retailer Fogdog.com has been very successful with its radio spots. The URL is easy to remember and is reinforced with the sound of a howling dog. People don't have to fumble with finding a pencil to write it down. After a few repetitions, they remember it.[36] Another Web company, Sandbox.com—a fantasy sports game site—wants to develop a radio and billboard campaign. Develop both a radio and a billboard advertisement that will catch people's attention and be easy to remember. What are the advantages of combining a radio campaign with billboards?

4. Xerox has a color printer that sells for $1,200 that it wants to market to businesses. What media mix would you suggest Xerox consider for its $20 million advertising campaign? Justify your answer.

5. Pick either the table of cosmetics companies or the table of clothing companies listed on the next page. Access each firm's Web site. Indicate how many advertisements you have seen in each of the media listed within the last month. Then discuss each company's media plan. Does the company project an integrated message? What target market does the Web site attract? Does the Web site convey the same message broadcast in the other media?

Cosmetics Companies

Company (Web address)	TV	Radio	Newspaper	Magazine	Outdoor	Internet
Estee Lauder (www.esteelauder.com)						
Maybelline (www.maybelline.com)						
Eve (www.eve.com)						
Clinique (www.clinique.com)						
Revlon (www.revlon.com)						

Clothing Companies

Polo (www.polojeansco.com)						
Pepe (www.pepejeans.com)						
Squeeze (www.sqz.com)						
Guess (www.guess.com)						
Lee (www.leejeans.com)						
Wrangler (www.wrangler.com)						

6. The following table provides the population of the top ten Demographic Marketing Areas (DMAs). The target market for a particular company is yuppie boomers, or those 35 to 54 years old who are professionals or managers. Based on the percentage of adults in each DMA that fits the target market profile, calculate the size of the target market in each DMA. Washington has been completed for you. If you had funds to advertise in only five of the ten DMAs, which five would you choose? Why?

DMA	Population	DMA Percent	Number in Target Market
Washington	3,965,200	18.4%	729,600
San Francisco–Oakland	4,824,600	14.2	
Boston	4,495,600	13.6	
Dallas–Ft. Worth	3,669,900	13.3	
Houston	3,251,100	13.1	
New York	14,432,500	12.0	
Chicago	6,483,800	11.7	
Philadelphia	5,655,800	11.6	
Los Angeles	11,391,200	11.3	
Detroit	3,549,600	11.1	

7. A business-to-business firm has decided to expand into Brazil. The company decided to conduct a print advertising campaign and follow it later with a direct-mail campaign. The primary goal of this print campaign is to build brand awareness. The print budget is $250,000. Access the Brazmedia Web site at www.brazmedia.com. Develop a print media campaign based on the information provided. Select the print magazines or newspapers you would use. Also, describe the size of the ad and the frequency of the campaign. Justify your media plan.

Creating a Photo Op

APPLICATION EXERCISE I

Manuel Ortega was placed in charge of an advertising campaign for a new 35 mm camera. His company was going to compete directly with Nikon and Yashica. As the account manager, Manuel was given a $12 million budget for the first phase of the campaign, which was to run for one month.

The objective of the campaign is to explain the firm's version of disk technology. Images recorded on computer disks rather than film are sharper and easier to use. The complexity in conveying the details of the new technology and the benefits to consumers makes the campaign more difficult. Manuel consulted carefully with his media planner, media buyer, and creative after receiving the contract from the company. They agreed to use magazine ads to be followed up with television spots.

Part of their reasoning for choosing magazines was the profile of the target market for this particular type of camera. The company's research indicated that the target buyer is between 18 and 44 years of age, has completed at least two years of college, and has a family income in excess of $30,000. These individuals read magazines at home and subscribe to most of the magazines they read. Manuel knew that individuals who subscribe to a magazine pay more attention to advertisements than do those who purchase the same magazine from a store. The other major characteristic of this group is that they have purchased a 35 mm camera in the past. The company believed those who had not purchased a 35 mm camera in the past were unlikely to buy into this new technology.

The company believed that 20 million individuals in the United States fit the target market profile for the 35 mm camera, and 3.22 million of those individuals read *National Geographic.* Manuel explained to the company's leaders that by dividing the percentage of the total target market by those who read *National Geographic,* the yield is 16.1 percent. In other words, 16.1 percent of the target market for this camera reads *National Geographic* and would be exposed to an advertisement placed in the magazine. As shown in Table 8.9, the percent sign is dropped and the reach for *National Geographic* is listed simply as 16.1. In the advertising industry, this number is the rating for that particular vehicle and can be obtained from commercial sources.

TABLE 8.9

Creating a Photo Op Case Study

Magazine	Cost for Four-Color Full Page Ad	Total Readership (000s)	CPM Total	Target Market (20 M)	
				Rating (Reach)	Cost per Rating Point (CPRP)
National Geographic	$ 346,080	21,051	$16.44	16.1	$21,496
Newsweek	780,180	15,594	50.03	12.2	63,949
People	605,880	21,824	27.76	9.4	64,455
Southern Living	11,370	5,733	1.98	2.4	4,738
Sports Illustrated	965,940	13,583	71.11	10.5	91,994
Time	1,324,282	21,468	61.69	15.9	83,288
Travel & Leisure	183,216	2,205	83.09	2.3	79,659
U.S. News and World Report	100,740	8,929	11.28	8.3	12,137

Table 8.9 indicates that *National Geographic* and *Time* magazines have the largest ratings. *Travel & Leisure* and *Southern Living* have the smallest ratings. Two things explain the difference in ratings: (1) The size of the circulation of the various magazines. For example, the total circulation for *National Geographic* is 21,051,000 readers compared to only 2,205,000 for *Travel & Leisure*; (2) the percentage of the readers who fit the target audience. Not all readers of *National Geographic* fit the target profile for this 35 mm camera. In fact, only 15.3 percent of *National Geographic's* readers fit this profile compared to 20.8 percent of *Travel & Leisure's* readership. (Manuel calculated these percentages by multiplying the rating times 20, then dividing by the readership of the magazine in millions.)

The advertising team decided two primary factors would determine the reach of the campaign. First, was the number and diversity of media being used. A media plan using the eight magazines would have a greater reach than a media plan using only five magazines. Notice that the total reach for the eight magazines is 77.1. Thus, 77.1 percent of the target market for this 35 mm camera would be exposed at least once during the next four-week time period to an advertisement. In addition to the quantity, the diversity of media will have an impact. Magazines that are different from each other tend to overlap less than magazines that are not different. Advertising only in sports magazines, for example, would overlap considerably because the same individuals probably read the various sports magazines. Reach measures the unduplicated percentage of a firm's target market exposed to an advertisement. Ads in media with nearly identical target markets do not reach as many people as advertising in vehicles with different target markets.

TABLE 8.10

Media Plan for Case Study Creating a Photo Op

Magazine	Cost for 4-Color Full-Page Ad	Rating	Number of Insertions	GRPs	Total Cost
National Geographic	$ 346,080	16.1	8	128.8	$2,768,640
Newsweek	780,180	12.2			
People	605,880	9.4			
Southern Living	11,370	2.4			
Sports Illustrated	965,940	10.5			
Time	1,324,282	15.9			
Travel & Leisure	183,216	2.3			
U.S. News and World Report	100,740	8.3			
Total					

Note: The goal is to maximize the GRPs within the $12 million budget. There is a minimum of one insertion per magazine and a maximum of eight per magazine. Based on a linear programming solution, the optimal number of *National Geographic* insertions is eight. *National Geographic's* information has already been completed.

1. Use the information provided in the case and Table 8.9 to develop the magazine media selection plan for the print advertising campaign for Manuel Ortega. Each magazine must have at least one advertisement insertion but no more than eight insertions.

   Use Table 8.10 to calculate the gross rating points for the magazine campaign and the total cost. As noted in the case, Manuel has a $12 million budget to work with. To illustrate how to calculate the gross rating points and total cost, the first magazine, *National Geographic*, has already been completed. The goal is to maximize the gross rating points while staying within the constraints of the $12 million budget. (Those familiar with linear programming can solve this problem using a linear program to maximize the gross rating points. It also can be solved using a spreadsheet and what-if analysis.)

2. Justify the solution, especially in terms of frequencies chosen.

3. Is television a logical medium for the next phase of the campaign? Why or why not? If not television, which medium would be best?

4. If the client wanted to have a fully integrated communications media package, what package of media would be most likely to succeed? Explain the choices.

5. For a long-term project, investigate similar costs for television and radio advertising in your local area. Construct a budget and develop a media buying plan for each medium.

Bass Attacks

Rusty Johnson has had a lifelong love for fishing of all types. He has been on the ocean, on numerous lakes and streams, and occasionally he has made trips to small ponds in the area just to catch small catfish. Having made a fairly significant amount of money in his real estate career, Rusty is looking for a new challenge. He decided to manufacture and sell bass fishing boats in the Lake Ponchartrain area of Louisiana.

Fishing in southern Louisiana takes two forms. First, some anglers like going into the swamps and bayous to get near underwater foliage, where some kinds of bass and crappie hide. Others enjoy getting out on the larger lake, using radar equipment to identify bigger fish resting in the deeper and cooler areas of water in the summertime.

The swamp fisherman requires a maneuverable boat with a small hull, so it does not get hung or scratched in the shallow waters. The large lake fisherman wants more stability and a larger boat to negotiate waves in the deeper open areas. Both wanted a boat that made it easy to pull fish in, with a live well holding tank. Other accessories could then be added depending on the tastes of the fisherman.

Rusty created two kinds of boats in response to the marketplace. He designed the first, the Bass Attack Prowler, for smaller spaces. He named the larger boat the Bass Attack Mastercraft, figuring Bass Attack sounded quite a bit like Bass Tracker, the leader in the field. He also believed the name was unique enough for the seasoned fisherman who would know the difference.

As the company completed the development of a manufacturing site and production of the initial run of boats, it was time to advertise. Rusty knew the real estate advertising market quite well, but he did not feel as confident about reaching fisherman. He faced the problem of geographic dispersion. Beyond the locals in the area, bass fisherman were spread out through the entire state of Louisiana and across the country. They came from a wide variety of backgrounds, some wealthy, some quite poor. Rusty's goal was to get some of the locals to consider his boat instead of the higher-priced, better-known models offered by Bass Tracker.

In the first year of operation, Rusty's company budgeted $200,000 for local advertising and more for "want ads" in some larger outlets, such as Internet sites, fishing magazines, and possibly some travel magazines or newspapers. He also considered billboards and other lower-cost possibilities. He knew he had a quality product, now the goal was to get the word out and generate some sales.

1. Describe the difficulties Bass Attack boats will encounter in its integrated marketing program.
2. Which media should Bass Attack use? Which should the company eliminate? Why?
3. For each of the following media, identify four specific outlets that Bass Attack could use for advertising. For instance, for magazines, a logical outlet would be *Field and Stream*; for television, ESPN fishing shows.
   a. Magazines
   b. Radio
   c. Television
   d. Internet
4. What kind of ad do you think will be successful for this company? Defend your answer.

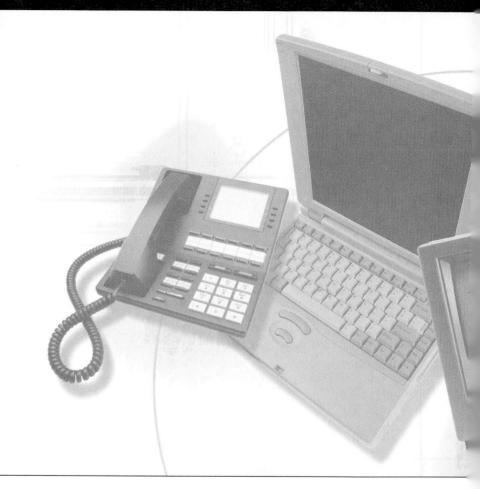

▶ CHAPTER OBJECTIVES

Understand how the hierarchy of effects model explains the process a creative uses to move a viewer from awareness to an eventual purchase decision.

Reconsider the roles attitudes and values play in developing advertising messages.

Recognize how visual and verbal messages are used in ads.

Identify times when each of the major advertising appeals will be effective and when they will not.

Comprehend the difficult task before the creative, as he or she begins to design the advertising message.

IS SILENCE GOLDEN?

An interesting paradox is present in the world of advertising design. On the one hand, the advertiser has so much to say to potential customers in a world full of clutter that companies wonder how they're ever going to be heard. On the other, if the message is jammed too full with information, the message is just as easily lost. Consequently, almost every kind of ad must be framed with some type of *white space*.

White space is the absence of copy in a printed text and the absence of music or sound in a radio or television ad. White space is the area around the pictures and words on a billboard. Advertising creatives know white space is a crucial ingredient in a world cluttered with ads.

chapter**nine**

What you see is what you get.

Introducing New Crest MultiCare Whitening. With every brushing, it removes plaque, fights cavities and dingy tartar build-up, freshens breath, and is so complete it even whitens, for clean and healthy teeth.

NEW
Crest. **MULTI CARE WHITENING**

Creating smiles every day.

In television advertising, a space of silence, without music or some other sound, may quickly attract the viewer's attention. The contrast of sound with white space is an attention-getting factor. It may be a matter as simple as causing the viewer to turn to the television set to see if it has broken. Further, silence research indicates that ads without music often result in higher levels of attention being paid to the verbal message. The same is true for white space, or no sound at all. Viewers tend to pay more attention to the message content following the insertion of white space into the ad.

On the radio, silence is a two-edged sword. On the one hand, "dead air" is a dreaded mistake. If a listener tunes into a station with dead air, the individual quickly changes channels. Consequently, there is very little silence on the radio. The other side of the coin, however, is that a brief pause in a noisy commercial or song has as much attention-getting value as white space on television. The key appears to be to keep the white space so short that the viewer doesn't conclude the station has gone off the air.

Print advertisers must also incorporate white space into ads. In newspapers, ads are often "stacked" on the bottom of a page. To draw the viewer's attention, the ad must be large enough to compete visually and then must be framed enough to differentiate it from other ads. It can be frustrating for an advertiser to pay for column inches of white newsprint, but without the spacing the ad is much less likely to be noticed. Grocery advertisements are the one obvious violation of the white space rule. Grocery ads are routinely jammed with information. Readers expect such clutter and are willing to work through the tangle of products and prices to discover food values and discounts.

Magazine ads can be, in a sense, more artistic. A full-page ad gives the creative the opportunity to arrange the banner, copy, pictures, and tag lines over the full page. White space is still used, but does not necessarily need to frame the ad, because the page is already differentiated from the one next to it. The radical use of white space in the Crest advertisement illustrates the benefit of using Crest toothpaste on a regular basis.

Billboard ads also employ white space to frame the key message, which is normally just a few words. Many billboards have borders around them, often in black, which make the ad seem more like a photo. The border also distinguishes the ad from any background behind the sign.

Cluttered Internet ads are common. Many Web site managers have not yet discovered the importance of white space. Internet surfers are accustomed to flashing past the flood of ads filling the screen when a site is accessed. In the future, don't be surprised to see less screen clutter on many Web sites, unless readers begin to react to Web pages in the same way they do grocery ads.

White space even became an issue in the design of this textbook. As the authors examined the competition, we concluded that several other marketing communications texts were cluttered with copy, figures, sample ads, and other messages. The marketing group decided that this text should be a contrast, with lots of white space to make it easier for students to read and comprehend its various messages. You are now about half finished with this book. How are we doing?[1]

overview

Which advertising message made the biggest impression on you in the last five years? Was it Tiger Woods bouncing a golf ball in time to music? Was it something from the Super Bowl? Was it something sexy, like a Victoria's Secret model being asked to define "desire"? Or did a local commercial get your attention? Did you end up buying a product or using a service because you saw the ad, or was it just entertaining? Do you think business-to-business buyers respond to ads that differ from those oriented toward consumers?

These and other questions demonstrate how the process of designing a set of advertisements for a campaign can be one of the more challenging and interesting components in an integrated marketing communications program. The goal is not only to prepare an ad people enjoy but also to make an ad that changes their behaviors and attitudes. At the least, the goal is to have them remember the goods and services being advertised, so that the next time they consider making a purchase the company will come to mind first.

Chapters 7 and 8 describe advertising from the perspective of the firm and the account executive. The account executive leads the ad agency team in making a pitch for the account, conducts media selections, and works with media planners and buyers. This chapter, which focuses on the actual message design, is largely oriented toward understanding the work of the creative.

Remember, the message design process is not performed in isolation. It is based on the creative brief, which the account executive prepares, and also takes into consideration the media that will be utilized. By combining all of these elements, the creative can design an effective advertisement.

There are two major topics covered in this chapter. The first is to describe three theoretical approaches to advertising design. They are:

- Hierarchy of effects model
- Means–ends theory
- Visual and verbal imaging

The second topic is to review, in detail, the major appeals advertisers use. Many of these approaches will be familiar. The goal of the account executive and the creative is to select the appeal with the best chance of leading to the desired outcome or behavior. From there, the actual message content is developed. Before beginning the process of creating the ad, it is important to remember the steps taken up to this point. These are summarized by noting the items in the creative brief.

the creative brief

Figure 9.1 summarizes the elements of a creative brief, introduced in Chapter 7. This outline directs the creative as he or she prepares various advertisements. Designing an effective advertising message begins with understanding the *objective* of the ad and the *target audience.* Then, the advertising group agrees on a *message theme,* an outline of the key ideas the program will convey. The account executive or client must provide the *support* for the advertising theme or claim as well as the documentation the advertisement needs. The support must match the message theme in the advertisement being designed. Finally, the creative must be aware of any *constraints* that might affect the preparation of the ad. With these key components in mind, the creative moves forward toward designing the actual message. The following section describes three theoretical approaches designed to assist in the process.

advertising theory

In developing an advertisement for an advertising campaign, several theoretical frameworks are useful. The first theory described is the hierarchy of effects model. The second is a means–ends chain. Both the hierarchy of effects model and a means–ends chain can be used to develop leverage points. Leverage points move the consumer from understanding a product's benefits to linking those benefits with personal values. Finally, the third theoretical perspective involves visual versus verbal framework for the ad.

Hierarchy of effects
The **hierarchy of effects model** helps clarify the objectives of an advertising campaign as well as the objective of a particular advertisement. It also aids the marketing team in identifying the best communications strategy (see Chapter 10). The model suggests that a consumer or a business buyer moves through this series of six steps when becoming convinced to make a purchase:

1. Awareness
2. Knowledge

> - **The objective**
> - **The target audience**
> - **The message theme**
> - **The support**
> - **The constraints**

Creative Brief

FIGURE 9.1

3. Liking

4. Preference

5. Conviction

6. The actual purchase

These steps are sequential in nature. Consumers spend a period of time at each step before moving to the next. Thus, before a person can develop a liking for a product, he or she must first have sufficient knowledge of the product. Once the individual has the knowledge and develops liking for the product, the advertiser can try to influence the consumer to prefer a particular brand or company more strongly.

Although the hierarchy of effects model helps creatives understand the impact of an advertisement on viewers, some of its underlying principles have been questioned. For instance, sometimes consumers first make a purchase and then later develop knowledge, liking, preference, and conviction. Shoppers sometimes purchase brands when no or little preference is involved, because coupons and impulse purchase incentives cause them to buy. At other times, someone may not even remember the name of the brand purchased. This is often the case with commodity products such as sugar and flour and even clothing purchases such as socks and shirts.

Still, the major benefit of the hierarchy of effects model is that it is one method used to identify the typical steps consumers and businesses take when making purchases. To encourage brand loyalty, all six steps must be present. A consumer or business is unlikely to be loyal to a particular brand without sufficient knowledge of the brand. Purchasers must like the brand and build a strong preference for it. Next, they must cultivate strong convictions that the particular brand is superior to the other brands on the market. None of this occurs without first becoming aware of the product. Thus, the components of the hierarchy of effects approach highlight the various responses that advertising or other marketing communications must accomplish. This is true of both consumer and business markets.

The hierarchy of effects model has many similarities with theories about attitudes and attitudinal change. Chapter 5 defined the concepts of cognitive, affective, and conative elements of attitudes. The *affective* component contains the feelings or emotions a person has about the object, topic, or idea. The *cognitive* component is the person's mental images, understanding, and interpretations of the person, object, or issue. The *conative* component is the individual's intentions, actions or behavior. The most common sequence that takes place when an attitude forms is:

$$\text{Cognitive} \rightarrow \text{Affective} \rightarrow \text{Conative}$$

It is important to remember that any combination of these components is possible. This means the structured six-step process of the hierarchy of effects model may be more rigid than is actually the case. Keep in mind that sometimes an advertisement that breaks out of the mold, or one that is different, can be very successful because it captures an individual's attention. As a general guideline, however, the cognitive strategies work best for advertising objectives of brand awareness and brand knowledge. Affective advertising strategies are superior in developing liking, preference, and conviction for a product. Conative advertising strategies are best in facilitating actual product purchases. Brand strategies are a mixture of the other three and can be used to accomplish any of the six steps in the hierarchy of effects model.

Means–end theory

A second theoretical approach is a **means–end chain.** An advertisement contains a message or a *means* to lead the consumer to a desired end state. These *end* states include the personal values presented in Chapter 5, and listed in Figure 9.2. The purpose of the means–end chain is to cause a chain reaction in which viewing the ad leads the consumer to believe the product will achieve one of these personal values.

- ❯ Comfortable life
- ❯ Equality
- ❯ Excitement
- ❯ Freedom
- ❯ Fun, exciting life
- ❯ Happiness
- ❯ Inner peace
- ❯ Mature love
- ❯ Personal accomplishment
- ❯ Pleasure
- ❯ Salvation
- ❯ Security
- ❯ Self-fulfillment
- ❯ Self-respect
- ❯ Sense of belonging
- ❯ Social acceptance
- ❯ Wisdom

Personal Values

FIGURE 9.2

Means–end theory is the basis of a model called MECCAS. **MECCAS** stands for **Means–End Conceptualization of Components for Advertising Strategy.**[2] The MEC-CAS model suggests using these five elements in creating ads:

- The product's attributes
- Consumer benefits
- Leverage points
- Personal values
- The executional framework

The MECCA approach is designed to move consumers through these five elements. Thus, the attributes of the product should be linked to the specific benefits consumers can derive. These benefits, in turn, lead to the attainment of a personal value.

To illustrate the MECCAS concept, consider Figure 9.3 below and the milk advertisement shown on the next page. The product attribute of calcium provides the benefits of being strong and healthy. The personal value the consumer obtains from healthy bones is feeling wise for using the product. The leverage point in this advertisement is the white mustache on each female. The white mustache and the message are designed to make the viewer believe that drinking milk is linked to preventing osteoporosis in women.

The MECCAS concept also applies to business-to-business advertisements. As discussed in Chapter 6, members of the buying center can be influenced by social, personal, and political values as well as corporate goals. Consider the advertisement

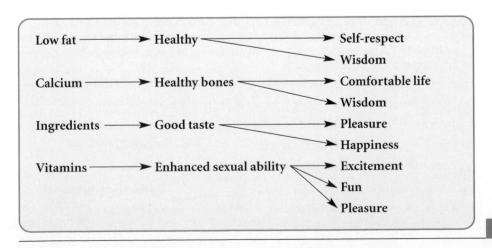

Means–End Chain for Milk

FIGURE 9.3

A Got Milk? advertisement illustrating the use of a means-end chain.
Courtesy of Bozell Worldwide, Inc.

for Greenfield Online on page 303 and the means–end chain in Figure 9.4. Each attribute is presented in terms of the benefits business customers can obtain. Although not explicitly stated, the personal values of members of the buying center choosing Greenfield Online might include job security for making good decisions, self-fulfillment, wisdom, and social acceptance by other members of the buying group.

stop! Integrated Learning Experience

Means–end theory and the MECCAS model are important elements in designing advertisements. Greenfield Online is a Web-based marketing research firm. Access the company's Web site at www.greenfieldcentral.com. Examine the products and services it offers in the "Products and Services" section. What types of custom research help a creative develop a means–end chain similar to Figures 9.3 and 9.4? Next, access Greenfield's "Newsroom." Examine the articles and press releases under each subheading in this section. What types of information presented here would assist an advertising creative in developing a means–end chain?

B-to-B Means–End Chain for Greenfield Online

FIGURE 9.4

Internet ⟶ Robust samples ⟶ Job security
Speed ⟶ Quicker results ⟶ Self-fulfillment
Expertise ⟶ Actionable information ⟶ Wisdom / Social acceptance
Experience ⟶ Reliability ⟶ Job security

ARE YOU STILL BUYING MARKETING RESEARCH DONE THE OLD-FASHIONED WAY?

Do it better on the Internet with the company that pioneered online marketing research.

Our panel of more than one million consumers from all across the Internet is the largest of its kind. It produces robust samples of any demographic or lifestyle you choose. You'll get richer, more actionable information quicker than you can say dot com.

Join the Research Revolution!™ Contact the world's most experienced Internet marketing research company for studies online, on time, on target and on budget.

www.greenfield.com 888 291 9997

Greenfield *Online*
Leading the Research Revolution®

A Greenfield Online business advertisement illustrating the use of a means–end chain in a business ad.
Courtesy of Greenfield Online Inc.

Leverage points

Both the hierarchy of effects model and the means–end chain approach are associated with leverage points. A **leverage point** is the feature of the ad that leads the viewer to transform the advertising message into a personal value. To construct a quality leverage point, the creative tries to build a pathway connecting a product benefit with the potential buyer's value system.

In terms of the hierarchy of effects model, the initial level of awareness begins the process of exposing consumers to product benefits. As the viewer moves through the six stages, he or she eventually develops the conviction to buy the product. At that point, the benefit has indeed been linked with a personal value. In the milk advertisement shown on the previous page used to illustrate the means-end chain, the leverage point is the phrase "There's one person I won't be," which is tied with the copy message "a woman with osteoporosis." The copy goes on to explain that because of calcium (a product attribute), women can have healthy bones (product benefit). Making a conscious decision to use milk to prevent osteoporosis demonstrates the personal values of wisdom and seeking a comfortable life when a woman grows older free of osteoporosis.

In the Greenfield Online business-to-business advertisement above, the leverage point is the picture of an older woman using an old telephone sandwiched between the headline "Are you still buying marketing research done the old-fashioned way?" and the first sentence of the copy explaining that companies can "Do it better on the Internet." The picture creates an excellent mental image of marketing research done the old-fashioned way and the opportunities Greenfield Online can provide.

The means–end chain and MECCAS approaches begin with the product's attributes and the benefits to the consumer. The leverage point is the message in the ad that links these attributes and benefits with consumer values. In the ad itself, the executional framework is the plot or scenario used to convey the message designed to complete the linkage. Chapter 10 presents executional frameworks in detail, in which dramatizations and other methods of telling the ad story help build effective leverage points.

An effective leverage point can also be associated with an attitudinal change, especially when the sequence is cognitive → affective → conative. As the attitude is formed, the individual first understands, then is moved emotionally, then takes action. A leverage point can help the viewer of an ad move through these three stages, thereby tying cognitive knowledge of the product to more emotional and personal values.

Creatives spend considerable amounts of time designing ads with powerful leverage points. Executional frameworks and various types of appeals, as described in the upcoming pages, are the tools creatives use to help consumers make the transition from being aware of a product's benefits to incorporating them with personal value systems.

stop!

Integrated Learning Experience

Examine Figure 9.3, and access the following Web sites the milk industry uses to aim at different target markets.

www.got-milk.com
www.gotmilk.com
www.whymilk.com

What differences exist among these Web sites? Identify the leverage points each site uses. How does each one take the viewer from the advertising message to the personal value being stressed? What product attributes and customer benefits does it highlight? What personal values can you identify? In terms of the means–end chain, which sites are the most effective?

Verbal and visual images

A third theoretical component of advertising design is the decision the creative makes to determine the degree of emphasis given to the visual element of the ad versus the verbal element. Most major forms of advertising have both visual and verbal elements, with the obvious exception of radio. A verbally biased ad places greater emphasis on words. In terms of the ELM model described in Chapter 5, a verbal ad takes the central route (most direct and easily remembered) of information processing. A visually biased ad is processed using the peripheral route.

Visual images often lead to more favorable attitudes toward both the advertisement and the brand. Visuals also tend to be more easily remembered than verbal

This ASICS ad blends visual imagery with the verbal copy.
Courtesy of ASICS Tiger Corporation.

copy. Visual elements are stored in the brain as both pictures and words. This dual processing makes it easier for people to recall the message. Further, visual images are usually stored in both the left and right sides of the brain, while verbal messages tend be stored in the left side of the brain only.

Visual images range from very concrete and realistic to highly abstract. In a concrete visual, the subject is easily recognizable as a person, place, or thing. In an abstract picture or image, the subject is more difficult to recognize. Concrete pictures have a higher level of recall than do abstract images because of the dual-coding process whereby the image is stored in the brain as both a visual and a verbal representation. For example, viewers process an ad with a picture of spaghetti used in promoting a restaurant as both a picture and a verbal representation. Ads with concrete images lead to more favorable attitudes than ads with no pictures or abstract pictures. Research offers many reasons for creatives to include visual images in their advertisements.[3]

Radio does not have a visual component. As a result, radio advertisers often try to create visual images for the audience. Pepsi produced an ad in which listeners hear a can being opened, the soft drink being poured, and the sizzle of the carbonation—an excellent example of creating a visual image. If consumers can see the image in their minds, the effect is greater than actual visual portrayal. An actual visual event requires less brain activity than using one's imagination to develop the image. The secret is getting the person to think beyond the ad and picture the scene being simulated.

Visual imagery is especially important in the international arena. Global advertising agencies try to create what they call *visual esperanto,* a universal language that makes global advertising possible for any good or service. *Visual esperanto* advertising recognizes that visual images are more powerful than verbal descriptions. Visual images also transcend cultural differences.[4] To illustrate the power of a visual image over a verbal account, think of the word *exotic.* To some exotic means a white beach in Hawaii with young people in sexy swimsuits. To others it may be a small cabin in the snow-capped mountains of Switzerland. While to others still, exotic may be a closeup of a tribal village in Africa. The verbal word can vary in meaning. At the same time, a picture of a couple holding hands in front of the Niagara Falls has practically the same meaning across all cultures. A young child smiling after eating a piece of candy also conveys a relatively universal message.

The most important task in creating *visual esperanto* is to create the appropriate visual image. The creative tries to think of an image that conveys the intended meaning or message. The goal is to create a brand identity through visuals rather than words. Then the creative can use words to back up or support the visual image. For example, the creative may decide that a boy and his father at a sports event illustrates the priceless treasure of a shared family moment. In Mexico, the setting could be a soccer match instead of a baseball game in the United States. The specific copy (the words) can then be adapted to the country involved. The difficult part of obtaining a *visual esperanto* is choosing the correct image that transcends cultures. Once a universal image is created, the creatives in each of the countries represented can take the visual image and modify it to appeal to their target audience.

In the past, creatives designing business-to-business advertisements relied heavily on the verbal element rather than visuals. The basis of this approach was the idea that business decisions are made in a rational, cognitive manner. In recent years, more business ads incorporate strong visual elements to heighten the emotional aspects of making a purchase. In summary, all the theoretical models presented in this section provide critical ideas for the advertising creative. They suggest that some kind of sequence must be chosen as the ad is prepared. The endpoint of the ad should be a situation in which the viewer is enticed to remember the product, to think favorably about it, and to look for that product when making the purchase decision. Various kinds of advertising messages, or appeals, can be utilized to reach such key advertising objectives.

stop!

Integrated Learning Experience

Visual images are an important feature of any attempt to market a product globally. Access the Sun Microsystems marketing resource center at www.sun.com/smrc, and the "advertising" section of that center. Next, go to the "International Gallery" part of the site. Examine the advertisements for Sun that appear in various countries throughout the world. What are the similarities? What are the differences? To obtain more information, access the "Outdoor," "Radio," and "TV" sections. To view an ad agency's perspective, access Leo Burnett Agency at www.leoburnett.com. At the "Work" section, look at the examples of the agency's various print, television, or other media advertisements. What are the differences in the ads across the various countries?

types of advertising appeals

Over the years, advertisers have attempted a wide variety of advertising approaches. Seven major types of **advertising appeals** have been the most successful. Advertisers usually select from one of these types of appeals as they develop the advertisement:

- Fear
- Humor
- Sex
- Music
- Rationality
- Emotions
- Scarcity

The particular appeal to use should be based on a review of the creative brief, the objective of the advertisement, and the means–end chain to be conveyed. The actual choice depends on a number of factors, including the product being sold, the personal preferences of the advertising creative and the account executive, as well as the wishes of the client. In determining the best appeal to use, it is often a question of what appeals would be inappropriate. Advertising experts know that certain appeals are less effective at various times. For example, some research indicates that sex appeals are not effective for goods and services that are in no way related to sex.

In any case, this section provides a complete description of the types of advertising appeals that are available. Each has been successfully used and has failed in other ads. The key responsibility of the marketer is to make sure, to whatever degree is possible, that the appeal is the right choice for the brand.

Fear

Advertisers use fear to sell a variety of products. Life insurance companies focus on the consequences of not having life insurance if a person dies. Shampoo and mouthwash ads invoke fears of dandruff and bad breath. These problems can make a person a social outcast. Fear is used more often than most casual observers realize.

Simply stated, advertisers use fear appeals because they work. Fear increases both the viewer's interest in an advertisement and the persuasiveness of that ad. Many individuals remember advertisements with fear appeals better than they do warm, upbeat messages.[5] Consumers who pay more attention to an advertisement are more likely to process the information it presents. This information processing makes it possible to accomplish the ad's main objective.

A theoretical explanation regarding the way fear works is the *behavioral response model* (see Figure 9.5).[6] As shown, various incidents can lead to negative or positive consequences, which then affect future behaviors. For an example of how to use this approach, see the Communication Action Box, "Smoking and Fear: Which Wins Out?"

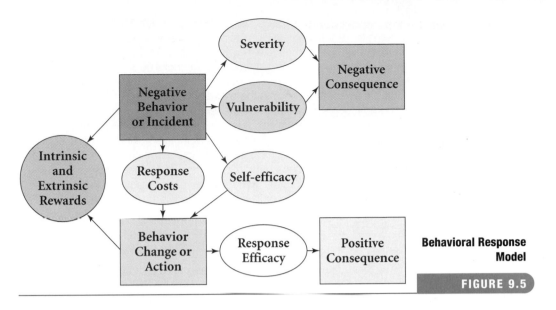

Behavioral Response Model

FIGURE 9.5

communication**action**

Smoking and Fear: Which Wins Out?

For many years, the American Cancer Society has attempted to develop more effective antismoking advertisements. The behavioral response model (Figure 9.5) can be a useful guide in developing such ads. The negative behavior addressed is smoking. The goal becomes to portray negative consequences associated with smoking, such as heart problems, lung cancer, or throat cancer. The severity is the degree of possible physical or psychological harm. The severity should be quite high. Lung cancer often results in death. The vulnerability is the probability that the consequence will occur. Unfortunately, the American Cancer Society knows that many people continue smoking because they do not see themselves as being highly vulnerable.

One side of the behavioral response model includes the intrinsic and extrinsic rewards associated with various activities. Extrinsic rewards are those given by other people. Young people often begin smoking because of the social rewards they obtain such as social acceptance by peers. Intrinsic rewards are internally generated (the ones you give yourself). Teenagers gain an intrinsic psychological reward from smoking when it makes them feel like they are adults.

The fight to curb tobacco usage among teenagers is extremely difficult because of these intrinsic and extrinsic rewards. Recent antismoking ads attempted to tackle the problem by changing the nature of extrinsic rewards. These ads show teenagers who smoke as being undesirable to those of the opposite sex. The idea is that a teenager who believes his or her peers will not accept the smoking behavior is more inclined to quit or never start.

In general, smokers engage in the negative behavior because of the intrinsic and extrinsic rewards they receive and because they either minimize the severity of the consequences or do not see themselves as being vulnerable. To change their behavior requires three things. First is the response cost. In other words, what would it cost to quit smoking? Teenagers can be influenced through fear of losing social acceptance. Adults may worry that if they quit smoking, they will gain weight or become nervous and irritable. These fears must be overcome for a campaign to succeed.

Another element of the behavioral response model is self-efficacy, or a person's ability to change a behavior. Many smokers do not believe they can quit, even when they want to. In a similar fashion, some people who want to lose weight often do not even try because they feel they do not have enough willpower to stick with a diet. To convince a person to quit smoking is to build up enough self-efficacy to make it seem possible. Many recent antismoking ads use phrases such as "The *power* to quit!" to build self-efficacy in the target audience.

Another behavioral response model ingredient is response efficacy. This is the belief that the change in behavior will result in the positive consequence that is being espoused. If a person does not believe that quitting smoking results in better health or a happier life, then there is little incentive to change behaviors.

For both teenagers and adults, antismoking ads must tackle the combined problems of peer pressure, low self-efficacy, and the physical addiction to the product. Therefore, one clear goal should be to use models such as the behavioral response approach to convince young people never to start.

In developing fear advertisements, it is important to highlight as many aspects of the behavioral response model as possible. A business-to-business advertiser offering Internet services tries to focus on the **severity** of downtime if a company's Internet server goes down. Another ad describes the firm's **vulnerability** by showing the high probability that a company's server is going to crash. The Service Metrics advertisement on the next page features a picture of a blindfolded man ready to step into a manhole to illustrate the danger of e-business pitfalls. The goal of the advertisement is to make businesses realize they are more vulnerable than they think and that Service Metrics can help reveal these potential problems before they become disasters.

When using fear, one debate centers on how strong to make the appeal. Most advertisers believe a moderate level of fear is the most effective. A low level of fear may not be noticed, and the fear level may not be convincing in terms of severity or vulnerability. On the other hand, an advertisement with a high level of fear can be detrimental. A message that is too strong causes feelings of anxiety. This leads viewers to avoid watching the ad, by changing the channel or muting the sound.[7] The goal of a fear ad is to be strong enough to get a viewer's attention and to influence his or her thinking, but not so strong that the person avoids seeing the advertisement.

Some recent examples of fear approaches include ads created for the U.S. Census Bureau, New Steel, and Alliance Capital. Recent U.S. Census Bureau television and radio ads pointed out the severity of what happens if census forms are not filled out. Communities might lose neighborhood schools, day care centers, and firehouses. New Steel showed homes not built with steel being destroyed by storms, hurricanes, floods, and tornados. Alliance Capital produced a more subtle type of fear ad. The primary theme suggested that parents and grandparents could be put out on the street because they had not accumulated enough wealth. In one advertisement, the grandfather was forced to leave because of the birth of a baby. There was not enough room or money to support both.

Fear ads match well with certain types of goods and services. Account executives, creatives, and company leaders must decide if fear is a good choice, or if some other type of appeal offers greater promise.

Integrated Learning Experience

To read additional articles about the use of fear in advertising, access Current Issues in Advertising at www.yppa-currentadissues.org. Using the search engine, type in "fear" for a list of articles on the topic. Fear appeals are more common in industries such as insurance, home and vehicle alarm systems, and pharmaceuticals. Pick an industry that is inclined to use fear approaches. Using one of the search engines, locate 10 companies within that industry. Which ones use a fear appeal on their Web page? How effective is the use of fear?

A business-to-business advertisement by Service Metrics using a fear appeal. Courtesy of Service Metrics.

Humor

Clutter is a significant problem in every advertising medium. This makes capturing someone's attention quite difficult. Once an advertiser has the audience's attention, keeping that attention becomes even more challenging. Humor has proven to be one of the best techniques for cutting through clutter. Humor is effective in both getting attention and keeping it. Consumers, as a whole, enjoy advertisements that make them laugh. Something that is funny has intrusive value and can grab attention.

Humor is used in about 30 percent of all advertisements.[8] One reason for the success of humor in advertising may be that the population is aging. According to Abraham Maslow, people tend to develop a more comedic view of life as they mature. Also, humor helps individuals adjust to situations they cannot control and to cope with life's problems. Laughing allows individuals to escape from reality. Comedy Central, improv theaters, and comedy bars have grown in popularity over the past decade. Consequently, humor is an effective approach for reaching a wide audience.[9]

The success of humor as an advertising tactic is based on three things. Humor causes consumers to: (1) watch, (2) laugh, and, most importantly, (3) remember. In recall tests, consumers most often remember humorous ads. To be successful, the humor should be connected directly to the product's benefits. It should tie together the product features, the advantage to customers, and the personal values of the means–ends chain.

Recently, financial and investment companies have begun using humor. In an advertisement for Conseco, Inc., a stocky man walks along a crowded sidewalk wearing scuba gear. He picks up a newspaper and waves to friends on his way to a large water fountain. At the fountain, the man puts on a mask and snorkel and then dives in. A few seconds later, he surfaces with a few coins. The voiceover tag line is "How do you plan to save for retirement?" In another ad, a well-built young man is called in to rub the feet of an elderly woman, who is clearly keeping him as a kind

An advertisement for E∗Trade
using a humorous appeal.
Courtesy of E∗Trade Group, Inc.
Photograph by Will van Overbeek. © 1999
Will van Overbeek, Photographer/Goodby,
Silverstein & Partners, San Francisco, CA.

of gigolo. It uses the same tag line to make the point about retirement planning. An example of humor is the advertisement promoting E∗TRADE shown above. Preliminary results from focus groups watching these ads indicated people saw the company as more caring and personal. In contrast, straight, information-laden ads make financial companies appear boring or stodgy. Consumers who did not use financial services viewed informational ads as being intimidating, because they did not understand the financial lingo in the copy.[10]

Humorous ads pique viewer interest, which can lead to more careful consideration of the message in the ad. A well-done ad increases attention in such a manner that greater comprehension and recall of the message arguments and tag line result. Advertising research indicates that humor elevates people's moods. Happy consumers associate a good mood with the advertiser's products. Humor helps fix the company in the consumer's cognitive structure with links to positive feelings.[11]

Humor captures the viewer's attention, cuts through ad clutter, and enhances recall. Unfortunately, humorous ads can also backfire. Advertisers must be careful to avoid letting the humor overpower the advertisement. When humor fails, it is usually because the joke in the ad is remembered but the product or brand is not. In other words, the ad is so funny that the audience forgets or does not catch the sponsor's name. Although funny ads often win awards, they can fail in terms of accomplishing advertising objectives. To avoid this problem, the humor used in the ad should focus on a component of the means-ends chain. The humor should relate either to a product attribute, a customer benefit, or the personal value obtained from the product. Such ads are the most effective when humor incorporates all three elements.

Further, sarcasm and jokes made at someone's expense are often popular with younger audiences, but are not well received by baby boomer and older generations,

Good or Service	Hints
▶ Beer	▶ Miller Lite, Keystone, Budweiser, Heineken
▶ Restaurants	▶ Wendy's, Shoney's, Long John Silver's
▶ NBA	▶ It's Fantastic!
▶ Telephone	▶ U.S. Cellular
▶ Motels	▶ Holiday Inn, Red Roof Inn

Can you remember an advertisement for each product or service that was funny?

Humorous Ads Quiz

FIGURE 9.6

especially among the more affluent. For example, a recent advertisement by Miller Lite of an elderly couple passionately necking on a sofa was designed to be funny to the young, male beer-drinking audience. Unfortunately, the ad was quite offensive to the older consumers. With age and maturity comes empathy. Put-downs and cruel jokes are not seen as funny by older people. Understanding these different nuances helps advertisers keep from making mistakes in the use of humor.[12]

Another potential danger of humor is offending an ethnic minority. Dinky, Taco Bell's highly visible Chihuahua, received a mixed reaction in the Hispanic community. Although some think the ads are cute, others find them offensive. Most appear to be indifferent. Anytime advertisers utilize ethnicity, they must be extremely careful to avoid offending an ethnic group.

Humorous ads are fun, but difficult to design. One cynic once noted that there are only twelve funny people in the United States. Humor that doesn't work often creates a negative image for the company. Consequently, account executives must be certain the creatives they hire are truly among those who can design and execute funny and effective ads (see Figure 9.6).

Integrated Learning Experience

To read additional articles about the use of humor in advertising, access Current Issues in Advertising at www.yppa-currentadissues.org. Using the search engine, type in "humor" for a list of articles. Humor may be more difficult to find in print and Internet advertising. Choose an industry, and access the Web sites of 10 brands or companies within that industry. Which ones use humor as part of their Web site? Why is it difficult to find humor in print and Internet advertising?

stop!

Sex

First of all, admit it. This is the part of this textbook you've been looking forward to reading. As advertisers look for ways to break through the advertising clutter, they use sexual appeal with increasing regularity. Advertisements in the United States contain more visual sexual themes than ever before. Nudity and other sexual approaches are much more common. Oddly, the actual number of verbal references to sex has decreased over the last decade. Instead, advertisements tend to be more explicitly sexual, showing contact and innuendos and suggest that sex is about to take place. For instance, several recent television ads for jewelry depict a woman wearing a nightgown in the bedroom, looking very passionate and aroused. Then, a ring and the price of the ring are shown with the company's name. Also, the amount of male–female physical contact in advertisements has tripled in the last 30 years.[13]

Sex appeals are one approach to building brand awareness. Shocking viewers is one way to create such awareness. Shock tactics are usually intentional and sometimes are designed to be controversial, such as those Calvin Klein utilized (described in Chapter 2). Why does Calvin Klein continue to push sex and nudity to the limit? The reason is simple: higher sales. Despite being forced to cancel all of the CK Jeans ads showing children in provocative positions, sales of CK Jeans rose from $113 million to $463 million in just one year. As long as sex sells, advertisers such as Calvin Klein will continue to take advantage of its appeal.[14]

Sexuality has been employed in advertising in five ways, including:

- Subliminal techniques
- Nudity or partial nudity
- Sexual suggestiveness
- Overt sexuality
- Sensuality

Subliminal approaches place sexual cues or icons in advertisements to affect a viewer's subconscious mind. In an odd paradox, truly subliminal cues should not be strong enough to be noticed or create any effects. Consumers pay little attention to ads already, and a subliminal message that registers only in the subconscious mind will not be effective. If it did, there would not be the need for such strong sexual content in advertising.

When an advertiser uses a subliminal messages or image, the idea is to have the audience see it. For instance, Smash Advertising used both subliminal seduction and humor in its HeadHunter.net television ad. In the spot, a group of white-collar men stand ogling a computer screen. One man says, "What a package!" Another says, "Look at that figure!" Finally, a female boss shows up to take a look. She comments, "That's a position I could go for." Of course, the group was not looking at porn on the Internet. Rather, they were checking out the salary and compensation package listed for a position on the HeadHunter.net Web site.[15]

The ad on the next page for Bijan perfume features Bo Derek. The location of her arm, the expression on her face, and the line "Bo Derek is wearing Bijan Eau de Parfum and nothing else" provide the subliminal sexual message that she is naked.

A large number of companies use nudity or partial nudity to sell their products. Some ads are designed to solicit a sexual response. Others are not. For example, starting in 1987, underwear companies could use live models in television ads. The first commercials were modest and informational, emphasizing the design or materials used in the undergarment. Still, the first Playtex bra commercials using live models drew strong criticism from organizations such as the American Family Association. Now, advertisements for underwear go much further. Ads do much more than show models wearing undergarments. In a recent issue of *Interview* magazine, the underwear model, Raina, is reclining on a couch, her back arched and pinkie finger tucked below her panty line. Victoria's Secret has launched a number of ads featuring girls in underwear in provocative poses, both on television and on billboards.[16]

Females are not the only ones showing up nude or partially nude in ads. Many men are being displayed in ads. One Diet Coke ad shows women rushing to an office window to see a man pull off his shirt and drink the product. Ads by Calvin Klein often use male nudity.

Instead of nudity, some ads using sex appeals try sexual suggestiveness. The Clairol Herbal Essence Shampoo ads borrowed the "yes, yes, yes!" scene from the movie *When Harry Met Sally* to make the product seem more sensuous.

A recent trend in sexual suggestiveness is to use gay and lesbian themes. Swedish retailer IKEA was the first in the United States to use a gay theme. A television commercial showing two gay men shopping for a dining room table together first appeared in 1994. Now, a number of companies use homosexuality in advertising. New York City–based Daily Soup restaurant ran an advertisement that featured a woman meeting a blind date at a park. She sits next to an attractive man

A Bijan perfume advertisement featuring a subliminal sexual message. Courtesy of Bijan Fragrances, Inc.

whom she thinks may be her date but instead he is met by a biker guy who grabs his butt while giving him a big kiss. Levi-Strauss, in an effort to reach younger consumers, introduced a campaign featuring interviews with real teenagers. In one ad, a young man admits to being gay while explaining that his neighbors didn't like him. Other ads, although not overtly gay, could be interpreted as such. For example, Volkswagen's "da, da, da" television advertisement features two young men riding around in a VW picking up and then discarding furniture. The gay community might see the two men as a couple. Others see them as roommates or friends.[17]

Overt sexuality is becoming more common in advertising. An illustration of this approach was the Levi-Strauss television ads depicting invisible people slowly undressing and getting ready to have sex. No human is in the ad. Only dancing jeans.

Another recent trend in sexual appeals is the use of sensuality. These ads often target women who might respond to more of a sensual suggestion than an overt sexual approach. Instead of strong sexual images, they show an alluring glance across a crowded room. Many view sensuality as a more sophisticated sexual appeal approach because it relies on the imagination. It portrays images of romance and love rather than raw sexuality.

Are sex appeals effective?

A number of studies have investigated sex appeals and nudity in advertising. Almost all of them conclude that sex and nudity do increase attention, regardless of the gender of the individuals in the advertisement or the gender of the audience. Normally, the attention is greater for opposite-sex situations than same-sex situations. That is, a male viewing a female in a sexually provocative advertisement pays more attention than a male viewing another male in a sexually provocative ad.

An advertisement in a woman's magazine using a partially nude male model to sell Stetson cologne.
Courtesy of J. B. Stetson Company.

The same is true for females. To encourage both males and females to pay attention to its ads, Guess often uses both a male and female in a sexually provocative manner in a single advertisement.

Although sexually oriented ads attract attention, brand recall for ads using a sex appeal is lower than ads using some other type of appeal. Thus, it appears that while people watch the advertisement, the sexual theme distracts them from paying attention to the brand name.[18]

In addition to gaining attention, sexually oriented advertisements are rated as being more interesting to viewers. Those ads deemed to be highly controversial in terms of their sexual content were rated as more interesting by both males and females. The paradox, however, is that although the controversial ads are more interesting, they fail to increase the transmission of information. Respondents could not remember any more about the message of the ad than could individuals who viewed the same ad but without a controversial sexual theme.[19]

Advertisements using overt sexual stimuli or containing nudity produce higher levels of physiological arousal responses. These arousal responses have been linked to the formation of both affective and cognitive responses. If the viewer is male and the sexual stimuli is female, such as a naked female in an ad for cologne, then the viewer tends to develop a strong feeling toward the ad based on the arousal response his body experiences. Female viewers of male nudity in an ad often experience the same type of response, although the arousal response tends not to be as strong. The cognitive impression made on the viewers depends on whether they felt the advertisement was pleasant or offensive. If the viewer thinks the ad is in poor taste and is demeaning, then negative feelings and beliefs about the brand result. Such was the case with a television advertisement created by Young and Rubicam, Inc. to promote radio station FM 96.9, a gay–lesbian station in

A Guess advertisement featuring both a male and a female model using a sexual appeal. Courtesy of Guess?, Inc.

Sydney, Australia, which attempted to combine humor with sexuality. The ad portrayed a singing penis dancing and singing the disco tune "Time to Party." Although the ad won a Cannes Silver Lion award for its creativity, the gay and lesbian community found the ad highly offensive. Many felt it perpetuated the stereotype that gays are more perverse than heterosexuals. The heterosexual community found the ad not to be offensive or erotic but instead extremely hilarious. The ad was well known in Sydney area and solicited strong feelings. The trouble was that the ad offended many of the station's target audience.[20]

A common sexual appeal in advertising is to use decorative models. **Decorative models** are models in an advertisement whose primary purpose is to adorn the product as a sexual or attractive stimulus. The model serves no functional purpose in the ad except to attract attention. Automobiles, tools, and beer commercials in the past often used female models dressed in bikinis to stand by their products. Figure 9.7 covers the basic conclusions of studies looking at the impact of decorative models.[21]

When researchers examined the impact of sexual visual stimuli, they found these types of stimuli affected attitudes in four ways. First, consumers tend to form inferences about the advertised brand based on the information presented in the visual part of the ad. In other words, a macho ad infers the product is manly, and so forth. Second, if the visual element is evaluated positively, consumers tend to develop positive attitudes toward both the ad and the brand. If the visual element was evaluated negatively, the reverse was true. Third, in advertising with explicit visual sexual content, the sexual appeal often interferes with message comprehension. The message tends to be interpreted in terms of the ad's visual sexual image. Viewers focused more on the visual component of the ad than on the verbal or written message. Fourth, ads with explicit visual sexual components produce greater

**Factors to Consider
Before Using
Decorative Models**

FIGURE 9.7

> ❱ The presence of female (or male) decorative models improves ad recognition, but not brand recognition.
>
> ❱ The presence of a decorative model influences emotional and objective evaluations of the product among both male and female audiences.
>
> ❱ Attractive models produce a higher level of attention to ads than do less attractive models.
>
> ❱ The presence of an attractive model produces higher purchase intentions when the product is sexually relevant than if it is not sexually relevant.

purchase intentions, which increase if the product advertised is considered sexually relevant.[22]

Sex appeals in the international arena

Although sex is found in advertising worldwide, what is appropriate in terms of sexual appeal varies across countries. Something which is acceptable in one country may not be appropriate in another. For example, in New Zealand a television ad for Rock 93 FM radio station featured a woman wearing a bikini washing a red sports car. The voice-over said, "If you think we'd stoop low enough to use beautiful women and cars to capture your attention, then you're right." The ad was accepted by the Advertising Standards Authority Complaints Board of New Zealand. On the other, a billboard in Wellington promoting billboard advertising showed a woman's cleavage with the caption "Exposure." The Advertising Standards Authority Complaints Board ruled this ad was unacceptable because the woman's cleavage had nothing to do with the product, billboard advertising. Other rulings of the board are more confusing. For example, one ad featured the back view of two young men, pants down around their ankles, standing in a paddock of

In selling their swim and active wear products on the Internet, Jantzen is utilizing a sexual appeal. Courtesy of Jantzen, Inc.

sheep. In most countries, such advertising would not be permitted, but the ad was ruled acceptable in New Zealand.[23]

Religions, cultures, and value systems are the most important factors in determining the level of nudity, as well as sexual references and gender-specific issues. Moslem countries tend to reject any kind of nudity and any reference to sexuality and other gender-related issues. They also do not permit any type of advertising for personal goods, such as female hygiene products, contraceptives, and undergarments. Any hint of sexuality or display of the female body is strictly forbidden.

Moslem countries are not the only ones with restrictive advertising for sex appeals. Many Christian countries such as Ireland, Spain, South Africa, Mexico, and the Philippines have similar standards. In Malaysia, if a man and woman are shown in the same room alone together for more than three seconds, it implies they had intercourse.

In other countries standards on sexually oriented advertising are quite liberal but sometimes confusing. In France sex is everywhere. Advertisers can feature seminude or completely nude models in an advertisement if it can be justified. There must be a relationship between the product and the nude model. It does not take much of a justification in France, where sex is viewed as healthy, innocent, and natural. A strange quirk in France, however, is that sex and humor cannot be mixed. The French do not see sex as silly or funny. On the other hand, Australia, which is conservative in many ways, permitted the singing penis ad used by the gay–lesbian radio station. Such an ad would be prohibited in many other countries.[24]

In many Middle East countries, sex and gender issues are taboo subjects. Sexual appeals are not used in advertising and even sexually related products are difficult to advertise. To get around this, in Egypt, Procter & Gamble hosted a call-in TV show directed toward young girls. The show's panel were health experts and topics ranged from marriage to menopause. The call-in show was followed up with TV talk show called *Frankly Speaking* about feminine hygiene. The goal of the show was to tackle some of the more sensitive issues facing young Egyptian girls. Although the show discussed what happens when a girl becomes a women, it was P&G's policy not to discuss sexuality. P&G sponsored the show and the primary product advertised, P&G's feminine sanitary pads, Always.[25]

Disadvantages of sex appeals

Everyone has heard that "sex sells." Although this may be true, it may be a less powerful weapon than it used to be. How sex sells is changing. The methods for using nudity are not the same. To be effective, nudity must be an integral part of the product being sold rather than a decorative part designed to garner attention. Nudity does not have the shock value it once did. Seeing another naked person in an advertisement is much less likely to cause a viewer to pay more attention to an ad.

One major criticism of sexually based advertising is that it has perpetuated dissatisfaction with one's body. Females in print advertisements and models in television advertising are quite thin. The key to success seems to be the thinner the better. Although the models in advertisements have gotten thinner, the level of body dissatisfaction and eating disorders among women has risen. Research indicates that women feel unhappy about their own bodies and believe they are too fat after viewing advertisements showing thin models. What is interesting is that these same ads have an impact on men, but the reverse. Men feel they are not muscular enough and are too thin or too fat. It does not make any difference if the male is viewing a male model or a female model in advertisements.[26]

In response, some firms have begun using "regular person" models in ads. Wal-Mart and Big K (Kmart) have employees pose in clothing to be sold and with other products. Many positive reactions to this approach have been the result, which means other companies may need to rethink their positions on body image advertising.

Bijan employed an extreme approach in one series of advertisements. Instead of either a superthin model or a regular person, Bijan's advertisement featured a nude overweight female. Several magazine editors refused to carry the advertisement at

An effective use of sex to sell milk.
Courtesy of Bozell Worldwide, Inc.

first but then changed their minds. Of the more than 1,000 e-mails received by Cynthia Miller, the creative who designed the ads for Bijan, only a few were negative. The vast majority were very supportive of the move to think outside of the typical female model stereotype.

The problem with the stereotyping of females in ads takes a different twist in other countries. For example, in Saudi Arabia and Malaysia, women must be shown in family settings. They cannot be depicted as being carefree or desirable to the opposite sex. In Canada, France, and Sweden, sexism should be avoided in any advertising directed toward children. Advertisers refrain from associating toys with a particular gender, such as dolls for girls or GI figures for boys.[27]

In general, the use of sex to make products more appealing is a legitimate tactic for many companies, products, and advertising firms. The goal should be to use sex in a manner that is interesting, germane to the product, and within the ethical standards of the region. From there, taste and other more personalized standards serve as guides. The milk industry advertisement shown above has been very effective. Although the model is dressed in a swimsuit, it is germane to the product. It is a very effective way to persuade women that milk not only is good for healthy bones but also enhances one's appearance. By telling women that bones continue to develop until the age of 35, the ad reinforces the reasons to consume milk.

stop!

Integrated Learning Experience

To read additional articles about the use of sex in advertising, access Current Issues in Advertising at www.yppa-currentadissues.org. Using the search engine, type in "sex" to obtain a list of articles. Sex is common appeal in advertising. Choose an industry to research and locate 10 Web sites of firms in that industry. How many use a sex appeal? What type of sex appeal is used? Now choose an industry that you feel should not use sex appeals. Locate 10 Web sites. Did any of them use a sex appeal?

communication**action**

Using Sex Wisely

Sex appeals have several advantages and disadvantages. The secret to the effective use of sex in commercials is to make sure the approach leads the buyer to the proper desired state, which is arousal to make the purchase, not just arousal in a more general sense. The following guidelines can help.

The first step in maximizing sex appeal is to be as clever as possible with nudity. People in society are accustomed to seeing underwear ads with live models. Consequently, simply trying to create a strong sex appeal does not have the impact it once did. One innovative approach to this problem came from a New Zealand firm selling the "Blendon Bra." The model in the ad has a heart surgery scar near her bra. The message was "This is a bra for real people." The ad proved to be a clever way to get and keep the viewer's attention. Rather than mere sex, it conveyed a feeling of a caring company. The result was a highly effective campaign.

The second step is to make sure the sex appeal does not offend. This is more difficult than it sounds, because any type of sexual appeal is bound to offend someone. Creatives and account executives must consider what level of nudity or sexual suggestiveness is appropriate in a given region. Advertisers must also be careful about ethnicity when creating sex appeals so that specific ethnic groups do not become upset with the company or its ads.

The third step is to consider carefully whether shocking sexuality should be the means of garnering attention. Certainly Calvin Klein has done it and been successful. Still, most experts believe that using sex ads that push the limit and shock viewers is harmful in the long run. Most of the time, strong sexual advertisements are likely to backfire.

The fourth step is to be certain the good or service has a relationship with sex. Most people view using nudity and sex to sell office supplies and household appliances as offensive. Using decorative models in advertisements just to adorn a product no longer works. In fact, some evidence suggests that it may be detrimental to the brand. On the other hand, sexual themes in advertisements for vacations in the Bahamas, perfumes, colognes, and fashionable clothing generally are acceptable and often successful.

The fifth step in maximizing sex appeals is that advertisers must resist perpetuating stereotypes. Females as sex objects is a common problem. For many years, women clad in bikinis were used to sell beer, tobacco, cars, and many other products to the male market. Currently, such advertising alienates many prospective customers.

The sixth step is to be careful that the sex appeal does not overpower the message or the product. When the sex appeal is too strong or too overt, the sex is remembered but not the brand or the message. Visual images of sexuality can easily overpower a message or brand name. Verbal and written messages tend to be less powerful. Verbal messages require the audience to read or listen to the message. When sexuality is involved, it should be part of the context of the advertisement.

The final step in making sex appeals work is to shift to more sensuality and less overt sexuality. Sensuality is especially effective with female target markets and can also be effective for gay or lesbian target markets. A sensuous approach developed by London International Group was quite successful in promoting Durex condoms in the country of Lebanon. Research by London International indicated that young adults need positive encouragement to practice safe sex rather than lectures about the threat of AIDS. Refer back to Figure 9.5 about behavioral responses. The advertising company knew that ads highlighting the threat of AIDS were focused on severity or vulnerability issues associated with not using condoms. As an alternate approach, London International focused on self-efficacy issues combined with the intrinsic and extrinsic rewards of using condoms. The advertisement featured the tag line "Feeling Is Everything." The ad portrays the importance of touching and feeling during sex. The main character in the ad was blind. The ad raises awareness about safe sex, but also emphasizes that there is no need to abandon sensuality.

As with any type of appeal, sex works best when ads are creative and sensitive to the target market. When they are executed poorly, they fail to achieve the desired results.

Source: Kevin Lawrence, "Sex and Marketing," *New Zealand Marketing Magazine,* 18, no. 5 (June 1999), pp. 10–13; Daniel J. DeNoon and Sandra W. Key, "Condom Ad Campaign in Lebanon Focuses on Sensuality," *AIDS Weekly Plus* (August 4, 1997), pp. 9–10.

Musical appeals

Music is an extremely important component in advertising. Music helps capture the attention of listeners and is linked to emotions, memories, and other experiences, especially a song or music that is known. Music can be intrusive, thereby gaining the attention of someone who previously was not listening to or watching a program. Music can be the stimulus that ties a particular musical arrangement, jingle, or song to a certain product or company. As soon as the tune begins, consumers know what product is being advertised because they have been conditioned to tie the product to the music. For example, the song "Like a Rock" is often quickly linked to Chevrolet's trucks for many people, and the Intel "tune" is readily noticed by computer buffs.

Music gains attention and increases the retention of visual information at the same time. For example, think of the McDonald's jingle, "For a good time, and a great place, try McDonald's." Most remember the song along with images of the Golden Arches or Ronald McDonald. Even when consumers do not recall the ad message argument, music can lead to a better recall of the visual and emotional aspects of an ad. Music can also increase the persuasiveness of argument. Subjects asked to compare ads with music to identical ads without music almost always rated those with music higher in terms of persuasiveness.[28]

Musical memories are often stored in long-term recall areas of the brain. Most people can remember tunes even from their childhood days. For examples, consider the musical approaches displayed in Figure 9.8.

Several decisions are made when selecting music for ads. They include answering questions such as these:

- What role will music play in the ad?
- Will a familiar song be used, or will something original be created?
- What emotional pitch should the music reach?
- How does the music fit with the message of the ad?

Music plays a number of roles in advertisements. Sometimes the music is incidental. In others, it is the primary theme of the ad. Occasionally, the use of music misdirects the audience so a surprise ending can be used. For instance, a Volkswagen television commercial showed people on the streets of New Orleans doing things in time to the music (sweeping, bouncing a basketball, unloading a truck) with the end line "That was interesting," and the VW logo followed. The creative must select the correct type of music, from whimsical, to dramatic, to romantic. Just as the wrong plot or wrong actors in an advertisement mean disaster, so does selecting the wrong music. Conversely, a quality match between the music and the ad theme can lead to a strong favorable reaction by the viewer or listener.

Another important decision involves the selection of a familiar tune versus creating original music for the ad. The most common method is to write a jingle or

See if you can think of the tune that matches each of the following tag lines:

▶ Like a good neighbor, State Farm is there.

▶ Feel like a woman (Revlon).

▶ Come see the softer side of Sears.

▶ The ABC News theme (also used in commercials for the news).

▶ I am stuck on Band Aid, cause Band Aid is stuck on me.

Now, ask your parents to sing the tune and identify the products from these jingles.

▶ You can trust your car to the man who wears the Star, the big bright **** Star!

▶ Hold the pickle, hold the lettuce, special orders don't upset us, all we ask is that you let us serve it your way.

▶ Take it off. Take it all off.

▶ My bologna has a first name, it's O S C A R . . . .

▶ **** tastes good, like a cigarette should.

▶ Plop, plop, fizz, fizz. Oh what a relief it is.

▶ It's not how long you make it, it's how you make it long.

▶ Double your pleasure, double your fun, with ****.

▶ Umm Umm good, Umm Umm good, that's **** are, umm, umm good.

▶ From the land of the sky blue waters, **** the beer refreshing.

▶ I'd like to teach the world to sing, in perfect harmony.

Tunes and Tag lines

FIGURE 9.8

music specifically for the advertisement. Background or mood-inducing music is usually instrumental, and advertisers often pay musicians to write music that matches the scenes in the ad. Also, some companies use the same instrumental tune for each commercial, such as United Air Lines, which plays "Rhapsody in Blue" in the background of its television and radio ads.

Using a well-known song in an ad has certain advantages. The primary benefit is that consumers already have developed an affinity for the song. The goal is to transfer this emotional affinity to the product. Brand awareness, brand equity, and brand loyalty are easier to develop when consumers are familiar with the music. They transfer the bond from the song to the product or company. One variation on this approach is to purchase an existing song and adapt the ad to the music.

Using popular songs is often costly. The average price for rights to an established song is $250,000. The Internet company Excite paid $7 million for the rights to Jimi Hendrix's song "Are You Experienced," and Microsoft paid about $12 million for "Start Me Up."[29]

Not all writers and musicians are willing to sell their songs for advertising. Ben McDonald rejected a $150,000 offer from Bausch & Lomb and a $450,000 from Clairol for the Top 40 hit "The Future's So Bright I Gotta Wear Shades." Bruce Springsteen rejected offers in the millions for his hit song "Born in the USA." These and other songwriters feel strongly about preventing their music from becoming part of an ad. To them, it is selling out.[30]

The high cost of established songs, especially top hits, has led advertisers to look for new, less well-known musicians. Unpublished or unrecorded musicians, struggling to survive and establish themselves, can use advertising as a stepping-stone. For example, when singer-songwriter Rufus Wainwright released his first album, no one noticed. Radio did not play his songs and album sales were slow. After Wainwright signed to appear in a Christmas holiday commercial for Gap, he suddenly was in demand and even appeared on *Late Night with David Letterman.* Later he won the *Rolling Stone*'s New Artist of the Year Award. His record label promoted him as, "The Guy on The Gap ad."[31]

The relationship between the advertising and music industries in the United Kingdom is different than in the United States. Artists in the United Kingdom believe that if their songs are played in an advertisement, the attention leads radio programmers to play the song on the air as a single. For many artists, this can be a path to stardom. Ladysmith Black Mambazo reached the U.K. Top 30 with "The Star and the Wiseman" after an appearance in a TV ad for Heinz beans. The idea of ad jingles becoming hits dates back to the 1970s when a Coca-Cola commercial jingle was rewritten and became a hit for the New Seekers. Later David Dundas turned a jingle for jeans into the top song "Jeans On." Now companies such as Virgin Records have special departments dedicated to placing songs with advertising agencies.[32]

A recent musical phenomena swept the United States in the late 1990s. Swing music became popular, and Gap took advantage of the trend by playing Louis Prima's classic "Jump, Jive, an' Wail" in a khaki pants ad. There was some backlash against the ad, as some swing music connoisseurs objected to yuppies using their music to sell clothes they would never wear.[33]

Music is an important ingredient in ads produced for television, radio, and even for the Internet. When a company becomes associated with a popular theme or tune, recall is enhanced and often the firm is seen as delivering higher quality. Creatives must either prepare music themselves or contract for it in some form. Currently, very few organizations use long-standing musical tag lines. Instead, each ad or campaign has its own music. This makes the job of the creative more difficult. He or she must try to "hit a home run" every time a new ad is produced. Other advertising forms, most notably print and billboard, do not use music. Consequently, other appeals become a better match.

Integrated Learning Experience

To read additional articles about the use of music in advertising, access Current Issues in Advertising at www.yppa-currentadissues.org. Using the search engine, type in "music" for a list of articles. How can music be used in Internet advertising? Look for sites that use music either as a primary appeal or to support another appeal.

Rational appeals

Rational appeals are normally based on either the ELM (Elaboration likelihood model) approach (see Chapter 5) or the hierarchy of effects model. The ELM approach assumes consumers use rational thought processes when making purchase decisions. The goal of a rational appeal is to provide the information needed to help make the decision. Automobile advertisements display information about gas mileage, warranties, and other features. The U.S. Postal Service provides information about prices, delivery schedules, and access.

A rational appeal often follows the hierarchy of effects stages of awareness, knowledge, liking, preference, conviction, and purchase. Creatives design ads for one of the six steps. For example, in the knowledge stage, the advertisement transmits basic information. In the preference stage, the ad shifts to presenting logical reasons why one particular brand is superior, such as the superior gas mileage of the automobile or a better safety record. A rational ad leads to a stronger conviction about a product's benefits, so that the purchase is eventually made.

To be successful, rational appeals rely on consumers actively processing the information presented in an advertisement. In other words, the consumer must attend to the message, comprehend the message, and compare the message to knowledge embedded in a cognitive map. Messages consistent with the current concepts in the cognitive map strengthen key linkages. New messages help the person form cognitive beliefs about the brand and establish a new linkage from his or her current map to the new product. For example, a business customer who sees a Kinko's advertisement about videoconferencing services already may have the company in his cognitive structure. The business customer may have used Kinko's in the past but was not aware that the company offers videoconferencing. When Kinko's is already established in this person's cognitive map, it is only a matter of creating a new linkage to entice the customer to try its videoconferencing services.

Print media offer the best outlets for rational appeals. Print ads allow readers greater opportunities to process copy information. They can pause and take time to read the verbal content. Television and radio commercials are so short that it is difficult for viewers to process message arguments. Also, if a television viewer misses the ad, she must wait until the ad is broadcast again to view it.

Business-to-business advertisers use print media extensively. These advertisers take advantage of print's ability to make rational appeals. Many advertising account executives believe trade publications are the best way to reach members of the buying center. Those in the industry read trade publications carefully. Placing an ad in a trade publication means the firm has an excellent chance of hitting its primary target market. Further, trade publications allow advertisers the opportunity to convey more details to potential buyers.

Buying center members who scan trade journals while in the information search stage of the buying process are quite likely to notice the ad, read it, and process the information. Buying center members who are not looking for information about the particular product probably will ignore the same ad. As noted in Chapter 8, magazines do not have intrusion value, and readers can easily skip or ignore an advertisement. A rational appeal usually focuses on a primary appeal, and there are no strong peripheral cues to grab the reader's attention.

Conventional advertising wisdom states that rational appeals are well suited for high-involvement and complex products. High-involvement decisions require considerable cognitive activity and consumers spend more time evaluating the attributes of the individual brands. Thus, a rational appeal is the best approach to reach them. For some consumers, however, emotions and feelings even influence high-involvement decisions. For instance, life insurance involves both rational and emotional elements. Various insurance companies can use both in seeking to influence consumers.

In general, rational appeals are effective when consumers have high levels of involvement and are willing to pay attention to the advertisement. Message arguments and product information can be placed in the copy. Consumers then absorb this information using the central processing route of their mental functioning. Information collected in the central route is more enduring than information gathered through the peripheral route. In terms of cognitive activity, a rational appeal is superior to other appeals in developing or changing attitudes and establishing brand beliefs. This is mainly true when consumers have a particular interest in the product or brand advertised. Otherwise, consumers often ignore ads using a rational appeal. Remember, rational appeals have the lowest attraction appeal and very low intrusive capabilities.

Emotional appeals

Emotional appeals are based on three ideas. First, consumers ignore most advertisements. Second, rational appeals go unnoticed unless the consumer is in the market for a particular product at the time it is advertised. Third, and most important, emotional advertising can capture a viewer's attention and help develop an attachment between consumer and brand.

Most creatives view emotional advertising as the key to developing brand loyalty. Creatives want customers to feel a bond with the brand. Emotional appeals reach the more creative right side of the brain. Visual cues in ads are important in

New Balance uses visual elements in this advertisement to create an emotional appeal of serenity and peace. Courtesy of New Balance Athletic Shoes Inc. Photograph by Paul Wakefield.

emotional appeals. Notice how the visual elements in the New Balance add contribute to a feeling or mood of serenity. Also, peripheral cues such as the music and the actor are crucial. Although individuals develop perceptions of brands based largely on visual and peripheral stimuli, it does not happen instantly. Over time and with repetition, perceptions and attitudinal changes emerge.[34] Figure 9.9 displays some of the more common emotions presented in advertisements.

Research by the Puerto Rico Tourism Company indicated that emotions are the most important factor in the selection of a vacation destination. The emotions specifically identified included tranquility, invigoration, glamour, and enlightenment. To convey these emotional appeals to the U.S. target market, Puerto Rico used singing sensation Ricky Martin in television ads. The campaign was a departure from a more rational approach. Although factors such as price, destination, and amenities were important in choosing vacations spots, they are not as important as the emotional factors.[35]

Emotions Used in Advertisements

FIGURE 9.9

- Trust
- Reliability
- Friendship
- Happiness
- Security
- Glamour–luxury
- Serenity
- Anger

- Protecting Loved Ones
- Romance
- Passion
- Family Bonds
  - *with parents
  - *with siblings
  - *with children
  - *with extended family members

Western Union followed a similar strategy in advertisements targeted to the U.S. Spanish-language television channels and the Latin America countries. The television ads featured testimonials from people reminiscing about their relatives in Latin America whom they left behind when they came to the United States. Using scenes in kitchens, gardens, and local streets, relatives point out they all receive money from their relatives in the United States via Western Union. In one commercial, a mother and daughter make pastries in their kitchen in El Salvador. The mother talks about her son in the United States sending her money each month. Western Union's previous ads focused on product attributes. Customer focus groups in the United States revealed that many had not seen their children, parents, or cousins in Latin America for 10 years. Western Union used this emotional appeal to convey the concepts of trust and reliability, and subsequent sales grew dramatically as a result.[36]

The Effie Awards are sponsored by the New York Chapter of the American Marketing Association. In 1998, of the 34 Effie Gold Awards presented, 21 used emotional appeals. The most common approach winners used was to combine humor with emotions. The second most common approach among the emotional appeal ads focused on the consumer's life and feelings.[37] The MasterCard "priceless" campaign uses this approach.

The priceless campaign used by MasterCard was the invention of the McCann-Erickson Ad Agency. The basic tag line is "There are some things money can't buy. For everything else, there's MasterCard." One of the most popular was of a father and son going to a baseball game together. Mothers responded as favorably as men to the spot. The entire campaign was successful in creating good feelings and it also increased both awareness and usage of the MasterCard. The agency adapted the campaign to international markets, tweaking the commercials to fit the local customs. For example, in Australia, instead of a baseball game, the father and son attend a cricket match.[38]

Business-to-business advertisers are using more emotional appeals. In the past only 5 percent to 10 percent of all business-to-business ads utilized an emotional appeal. Today, that percentage is around 25 percent. A magazine advertisement created by NKH&W Advertising Agency for a product to treat racehorses switched from a rational appeal to an emotional appeal. The target market for the ad was veterinarians. In the past, the ad would have opened with such ad copy as "For swelling in joints use . . ." The emotional ad has the horse thinking, "I will prove them wrong. I will run again. I will mend my spirits."[39]

The rationale for changing to more emotional business-to-business ads is the idea that emotions affect all types of purchase decisions. Members of the buying center utilize product information in making decisions but, at the same time, are just as likely to be affected by the same emotions as regular consumers. Members of the buying center do try to minimize the emotional side of a purchase, but this does not mean that they are unaffected by emotions. As individuals, the affective component of attitudes is as important as the cognitive component. In the past, business-to-business advertisers tended to ignore the affective component.

Television is one of the best media for emotional appeals. Television offers advertisers intrusion value and can utilize both sound and sight. Models in the ads can be "real people." Facial expressions can convey emotions and attitudes. Consumers learn vicariously about a particular product and develop an attitude based on these vicarious experiences. Television ads also are more vivid, more life-like, and they can create dynamic situations that pull the viewer into the ad. Music may be incorporated to make the ad more dramatic. Such peripheral cues are important components of emotional appeals. These peripheral cues (music, background visuals, etc.) also attract a viewer's attention.

As mentioned, emotions can be tied with humor, fear, music, and other appeals to make a compelling case for a product. The same ad can influence a consumer both emotionally and rationally. The goal of the creative is to select the most appropriate emotional appeal for the product and company.

stop!

Integrated Learning Experience

To read additional articles about the use of emotion in advertising, access Current Issues in Advertising at www.yppa-currentadissues.org. Using the search engine, type in "emotion" to find articles. What type of industry uses the emotional appeal? Locate 10 Web sites from an industry of your choice. How many use emotional appeals?

Scarcity appeals

Another appeal that is occasionally used is scarcity. When there is a limited supply of a product, the value of that product increases. Scarcity appeals urge consumers to buy a particular product because of a limitation. The limitation can be a limited number of the products available or, more often, that the product is available for only a limited time. In 1996, General Mills introduced for a limited-time USA Olympic Crunch cereal and Betty Crocker Team USA desserts. Then at the turn of the century, General Mills introduced a Cheerios line called Millenios as a limited-time product. Tiny "2s" were added to the familiar O-shaped cereal Cheerios.[40] McDonald's, Wendy's, and Burger King offer sandwiches (McRib, Hot N' Spicy Chicken, Dollar Whoppers) for limited time periods throughout the year. The scarcity concept is also used for musical compilations, encouraging consumers to buy the product because of its limited availability. By making sure it is not available in retail stores, marketers increase its scarcity value.

The milk industry uses the scarcity appeal, but in a different manner. In their ads, the central figure in the commercial always needs milk to wash down food that was eaten. The disaster is that the milk is gone.

The scarcity appeal is often used with other promotional tools. For example, a manufacturer may advertise a limited price discount offer to retailers who stock up early for Christmas or some other holiday season. Contests and sweepstakes also run for limited times. The primary benefit of scarcity appeals is that they encourage consumers to take action. Creatives normally receive information about scarcity issues in the creative brief, or from the account executive who has consulted with the company.

stop!

Integrated Learning Experience

Choosing an appropriate appeal is an important task in the creative process. Access the Web site of Creative House Marketing at www.creative-house.com. From the main page, access "Samples," "Advertising," and "Brochures." What type of appeal does Creative House use in each advertisement? Access the following company Web sites and study the various sections of each. Identify the types of appeal each firm uses.

Bijan Fragrances (www.bijan.com)
Asics (www.asicstiger.com)
Skechers (www.skechers.com)
Aetna Inc. (www.aetna.com)
Exodus Communication (www.servicemetrics.com)

implications for marketing professionals

Creatives and Marketing Managers Here

Creatives must be certain they understand and utilize the following theories:

1. Hierarchy of needs
2. Means–ends chains

3. Visual versus verbal cues
4. Behavioral response model

Creatives need space. Make sure they have enough freedom to design ads that reflect their best talents and efforts. Let the creative be the first to suggest the leverage point he or she believes most effective.

The marketing team should review the creative brief carefully. Creatives must make sure there is a quality match between the theme, medium, leverage point, and target audience.

When working with clients, make sure they understand the intention of each of the advertising appeals.

1. The primary goal of a fear appeal is to attract attention and create enough cognitive unpleasantness so that the consumer makes a purchase to alleviate concerns.

2. The primary goals of humor are to attract attention, to help the customer remember the product and company names, and to make them feel good about buying the firm's offerings.

3. The main goals of sex appeals are to grab attention and to link the product with the type of sexual appeal being used, from shock value to sensuality. The key is to link the nature of the appeal with the most important element of the product being advertised.

4. Music has many uses. It can be a backdrop, an attention getter, a method to help the consumer remember the product or company, or an overarching theme that runs over a series of commercials.

5. Rational appeals attempt to persuade consumers that a given company's goods and services have some advantage over the competition. The logic of a rational appeal must be sound, and the ad must quickly and convincingly convey the information in a manner the customer can understand.

6. Emotional appeals are based on a wide range of possibilities. The secret is making sure the emotion is appropriate for the advertisement's goals and for the company or products featured.

7. Scarcity appeals are designed to move the consumer to quick action. Conveying a sense of urgency is a key ingredient.

Remember the advantages of combining appeals. Music goes with many media and with other appeals. Humor, sex, and emotions are also logical candidates for combined appeals.

When working with business-to-business clients, make sure they understand print media–rational appeals are not the only choice. Increasingly, creatives are aware of excellent ways to find members of buying centers in other media and to use other appeals.

Discourage clients from using decorative models, except in rare cases.

When developing ads for international advertisers, everyone should remember the importance of *visual esperanto*. Consider the following:

1. The success rates of various appeals vary by country. What works in one culture may not work in another (e.g., sexual appeals).

2. A *cultural assimilator* should examine every ad, to make sure it is not offensive or confusing to patrons in the nation in which the ad will run.

3. Language, slang, customs, and other variables take a long time to learn and understand. A local advertiser may be more successful than a firm trying to be all things to all countries. Know when to farm out work to other companies.

SUMMARY

Developing effective advertisements is the culmination of a series of integrated marketing communications efforts. They include knowing the objective of the ad, the target audience, the message theme used, the type of support needed, and any constraints that apply. Then, a creative must work within the context of key advertising theories in selecting the correct media and designing the leverage point and message appeal that work effectively within each medium.

Three important theoretical approaches drive the development of many advertisements. The hierarchy of effects model suggests consumers move through a series of stages as they are persuaded to make a purchase. The steps are (1) awareness, (2) knowledge, (3) liking, (4) preference, (5) conviction, and (6) the actual purchase. Although the process probably is not a lock-step model that every buyer followers, the hierarchy of effects approach does provide important information about which mental issues to account for in various advertising campaigns. The hierarchy of effects model can be combined with the three main elements present in attitudes: (1) cognitive, (2) affective, and (3) conative components. Ads are designed to influence affective feelings, cognitive knowledge, or conative intentions to act or behave based on an attitude. A means–end chain displays the linkages between a means to achieve a desired state and the end or personal value at issue. Advertisers can select personal values that mesh with the key characteristics of the target market, and then construct ads designed to provide them the means to achieve these ends by purchasing the good or service. These ideas help the creative develop a leverage point to move the buyer from understanding the product's benefits to incorporating those benefits with his or her personal values.

Visual and verbal issues should also be considered in the formation of an ad. Concrete visual images are easily recognized and recalled. Abstract images may be linked with values or emotions the product creates, or the feeling the buyer should experience that may be associated with the product or company. Visual elements are key components in almost every form of advertising. Verbal elements must reach the more rational, central route of the audience's mental processing procedures.

Beyond these components, advertising creatives must form messages using one (or more) of the seven major appeals: (1) fear, (2) humor, (3) sex, (4) music, (5) rationality, (6) emotions, or (7) scarcity. Just as there are logical combinations of media, there are logical combinations of these appeals for various messages. Often, music is the backdrop for messages invoking fear, humor, sex, and emotions. Humor can be linked with sex, music, rationality (by showing how being illogical is silly or funny), and scarcity. Rationality combines with fear in many commercials. The goal of the creative is to design a message argument that takes advantage of the various characteristics of these appeals, breaks through clutter, and convinces the audience to buy the item involved. Mismatches of message tactics are to be avoided, such as combined sex with humor in France, as mentioned earlier.

Business-to-business ads often appear in print, and many times include rational approaches in the copy, as the purchase decision variables are more complex. At the same time, many advertisers have recently discovered that emotional ads can be effective, which expands business-to-business advertising into other venues, such as television, radio, and the Internet.

The process of designing ads for international markets is quite similar to that for domestic ads. The major difference is careful consideration of local attitudes and customers, with due care given to the language, slang, and symbols of the area. For example, Sega recently discovered that its product's name is slang for "masturbation" in Italian, after a major advertising campaign had started. These types of mistakes should be carefully avoided.

Every marketer knows that some ad campaigns, no matter how carefully conceived, still fail. The goal is to try to reach a point where the failure of one specific ad or campaign does not have longlasting effects on the company. To do so, a thoughtfully designed IMC program can build a firm's image in such a manner that brand and product loyalty, along with customer recognition, can reduce the ill effects of one "lead balloon" advertising campaign. In the end, advertising is only one component of an IMC program. Although it is clearly a major and important ingredient, it should be considered in the context of a long-term plan to strengthen the company, its products, and its overall image in the customer's mind.

REVIEW QUESTIONS

1. What are the five main elements of a creative brief? How do they affect the choice of advertising appeals?

2. What are the six stages of the hierarchy of effects model? Do they always occur in that order? Why or why not?

3. How are the three components of attitudes related to the hierarchy of effects model?

4. In a means–end chain, what are the means? The ends? How do they affect advertising design?

5. What is a leverage point? How are leverage points related to the hierarchy of effects model, attitudinal changes, and means–end chains?

6. Why are visual elements in advertisement important? What is the relationship between visual and verbal elements? Can there be one without the other?

7. What are the advantages and disadvantages of fear appeals in advertising?

8. When does humor work in an ad? What pitfalls should companies avoid in using humorous appeals?

9. What types of sexual appeals can advertisers use?

10. When are sexual appeals most likely to succeed? To fail?

11. What should international advertisers consider when thinking about using sexual appeals?

12. Name the different ways music can play a role in an advertisement. Explain how each role should match individual appeals, media, and the other elements in the design of the ad.

13. What are the advantages and disadvantages of rational appeals? Which media do they best match?

14. How can emotions accentuate advertisements? Why are they being used more often in business-to-business advertisements?

15. What is scarcity? How do scarcity ads lead to buyer action?

16. Name four combinations of appeals that are logical combinations for advertisers.

KEY TERMS

white space   the absence of copy in a printed text and the absence of music or sound in a radio or television ad.

hierarchy of effects model   a marketing approach suggesting that a consumer moves through a series of six steps when becoming convinced to make a purchase, including: (1) awareness, (2) knowledge, (3) liking, (4) preference, (5) conviction, (6) the actual purchase.

means–end chain   an advertisement approach in which the message contains a means (a reasoning or mental process) to lead the consumer to a desired end state, such as a key personal value.

Means-End Conceptualization of Components for Advertising Strategy (MECCAS)   an advertising approach that suggests using five elements in creating ads, including (1) the product's attributes, (2) consumer benefits, (3) leverage points, (4) personal values, and (5) the executional framework.

leverage point   the feature of the ad that leads the viewer to relate the product's benefits with personal values.

visual esperanto   a universal language that makes global advertising possible for any good or service by recognizing that visual images are more powerful than verbal descriptions.

severity   part of the behavioral response model that leads the individual to consider how strong certain negative consequences of an action will be.

vulnerability   part of the behavioral response model that leads the individual to consider the odds of being affected by the negative consequences of an action.

advertising appeals   approaches to reaching consumers with ads. The seven major appeals are: (1) fear, (2) humor, (3) sex, (4) music, (5) rationality, (6) emotions, and (7) scarcity.

decorative models   models in an advertisement whose primary purpose is to adorn the product as a sexual or attractive stimulus without serving a functional purpose.

tag line   the final key phrase in an ad which is used to make the key point and reinforce the company's image to the consumer.

ENDNOTES

1. G. Douglas Olsen, "Observations: The Sounds of Silence: Functions and Use of Silence in Television Advertising," *Journal of Advertising Research,* 34, no. 5 (September–October 1994), pp. 89–95.

2. Jerry Olson and Thomas J. Reynolds, "Understanding Consumers' Cognitive Structures: Implications for Advertising Strategy," *Advertising Consumer Psychology,* eds. L. Percy and A. Woodside (Lexington, MA: Lexington Books 1983), pp. 77–90; Thomas J. Reynolds and Alyce Craddock, "The Application of the MECCAS Model to Development and Assessment of Advertising Strategy," *Journal of Advertising Research,* 28, no. 2 (1988), pp. 43–54.

3. Laurie A. Babin and Alvin C. Burns, "Effects of Print Ad Pictures and Copy Containing Instructions to Imagine on Mental Imagery That Mediates Attitudes," *Journal of Advertising,* 26, no. 3 (Fall 1997), pp. 33–44.

4. Marc Bourgery and George Guimaraes, "Global Ads: Say It with Pictures," *Journal of European Business,* 4, no. 5 (May–June 1993), pp. 22–26.

5. Olson and Reynolds, "Understanding Consumers' Cognitive Structures"; Reynolds and Craddock, "The Application of the MECCAS Model to Development and Assessment of Advertising Strategy."

6. Based on Rosemary M. Murtaugh, "Designing Effective Health Promotion Messages Using Components of Protection Motivation Theory," *Proceedings of the Atlantic Marketing Association* (1999), pp. 553–57; R. W. Rogers and S. Prentice-Dunn, "Protection Motivation Theory," *Handbook of Health Behavior Research I: Personal and Social Determinants,* ed. D. Gochman (New York: Plenum Press, 1997), pp. 130–132.

7. Michael S. Latour and Robin L. Snipes, "Don't Be Afraid to Use Fear Appeals: An Experimental Study," *Journal of Advertising Research,* 36, no. 2 (March–April 1996), pp. 59–68.

8. Harlan E. Spotts and Marc G. Weinberger, "Assessing the Use and Impact of Humor on Advertising Effectiveness," *Journal of Advertising,* 26, no. 3 (fall 1997), pp. 17–32.

9. David B. Wolfe, "Boomer Humor," *American Demographics,* 20, no. 7 (July 1998), pp. 22–23.

10. Joel Palmer, "Silliness Sells Securities," *Des Moines Business Records,* 15, no. 12 (March 29, 1999) p. 14.

11. Hillary Chura and Mercedes M. Cardona, "Online Broker Datek Stakes 'Serious Turf' with $80 Mil," *Advertising Age,* 70, no. 10 (October 18, 1999), pp. 1–2.

12. Wolfe, "Boomer Humor."

13. Jessica Severn and George E. Belch, "The Effects of Sexual and Non-Sexual Advertising Appeals and Information Level on Cognitive Processing and Communication Effectiveness," *Journal of Advertising,* 19, no. 1 (1990), pp. 14–22.

14. Robert L. Gustafson, "Shock May Pay Off, but Not in the Long Run," *Indianapolis Business Journal,* 20, no. 14 (June 21, 1999), p. 24.

15. David Gianatasio, "Smash's Sex Appeal," *Adweek,* New England Edition, 36, no. 37 (September 13, 1999), p. 4.

16. Pat Sloan and Carol Krol, "Underwear Ads Caught in Bind Over Sex Appeal," *Advertising Age,* 67, no. 28 (July 8, 1996), p. 27.

17. Laurel Wentz, "Global Village," *Advertising Age,* 68, no. 10 (March 10, 1997), p. 3; Michael Wilke, "A Kiss Before Buying," *Advocate* (Aprll 27, 1999), pp. 34–35.

18. Severn and Belch, "The Effects of Sexual and Non-Sexual Advertising Appeals and Information Level on Cognitive Processing and Communication Effectiveness."

19. D. C. Bello, R. E. Pitts, and M. J. Etzel, "The Communication Effects of Controversial Sexual Content in Television Programs and Commercials," *Journal of Advertising,* 3, no. 12 (1983), pp. 32–42.

20. Based on M. S. LaTour and R. E. Pitts, "Female Nudity, Arousal and Ad Response: An Experimental Investigation," *Journal of Advertising,* 9, no. 4 (1990), pp. 51–63; Bob Garfield, "Pushing the Envelope: The Performing Penis," *Advertising Age International* (July 12, 1999), p. 4.

21. Based on G. Smith and R. Engel, "Influence of a Female Model on Perceived Characteristics of an Automobile," *Proceedings of the 76th Annual Convention of the American Psychological Association,* 15, no. 3 (1968), pp. 46–54; Leonard Reid and Lawrence C. Soley, "Decorative Models and the Readership of Magazine Ads," *Journal of Advertising Research,* 23, (April–May 1983), pp. 27–32; R. Chestnut, C. LaChance, and A. Lubitz, "The Decorative Female Model: Sexual Stimuli and the Recognition of Advertisements," *Journal of Advertising,* 6 (fall 1977), pp. 11–14.

22. Andrew A. Mitchell, "The Effect of Verbal and Visual Components of Advertisements on Brand Attitude and Attitude Toward the Advertisement," *Journal of Consumer Research,* 13 (June 1986), pp. 12–24; Severn and Belch, "The Effects of Sexual and Non-Sexual Advertising Appeals and Information Level on Cognitive Processing and Communication Effectiveness."

23. Kevin Lawrence, "Sex and Marketing," *New Zealand Marketing Magazine,* 18, no. 5 (June 1999), pp. 10–17.

24. Gerard Stamp and Mark Stockdale, "Sex in Advertising," *Advertising Age's Creativity,* 7, no. 6 (July–August 1999), pp. 35–36; Garfield, "Pushing the Envelope: The Performing Penis", Jean J. Boddewyn, "Sex and Decency Issues in Advertising: General and International Dimensions," *Business Horizons,* 34, no. 5 (September–October 1991), pp. 13–20.

25. Elizabeth Bryant, "P&G Pushes the Envelope in Egypt with TV Show on Feminine Hygiene," *Advertising Age International* (December 14, 1998), p. 2.

26. Howard Levine, Donna Sweeney, and Stephen H. Wagner, "Depicting Women as Sex Objects in Television Advertising," *Personality and Social Psychology Bulletin,* 25, no. 8 (August 1999), pp. 1049–58.

27. Boddewyn, "Sex and Decency Issues in Advertising: General and International Dimensions."

28. G. Douglas Olsen, "Observations: The Sounds of Silence: Functions and Use of Silence in Television Advertising," *Journal of Advertising Research,* 34, no. 5 (September–October 1994), pp. 89–95.

29. Michael Miller, "Even Out of Context, the Beat Goes On (and On)," *Pittsburgh Business Times,* 18, no. 18 (November 27, 1998), p. 12.

30. John Marks, "Shake, Rattle, and Please Buy My Product," *U.S. News and World Report,* 124, no. 20 (May 25, 1998), p. 51.

31. Keith Naughton, "Sing a Song of Selling," *Business Week,* no. 3630 (May 24, 1999), pp. 66–67.

32. Paul Sexton, "This is How They Do It in the U.K.," Adweek, Eastern Edition, 39, no. 43 (October 26, 1998), pp. SPS14–SPS15.

33. T. L. Stanley, "The Swing Set," *Brandweek,* 39, no. 37 (October 5, 1998), pp. 38–39.

34. Naughton, "Sing a Song of Selling."

35. Gay Nagle Myers, "Puerto Rico Targets Emotions in New Ad Campaign," *Travel Weekly,* 58, no. 82 (October 14, 1999), p. C4.

36. Joy Dietrich, "Western Union Retraces Roots: The Emotions of Money Transfers," *Advertising Age International* (October 1999), pp. 24–25.

37. Scott Rockwood, "For Better Ad Success, Try Getting Emotional," *Marketing News,* 30, no. 22 (October 21, 1996), p. 4.

38. Hank Kim, "MasterCard Moments," *Adweek,* 40, no. 15 (April 12, 1999), pp. 30–32.

39. Karalynn Ott, "B-to-B Marketers Display Their Creative Side," *Advertising Age's Business Marketing,* 84, no. 1 (January 1999), pp. 3–4.

40. Stephanie Thompson, "Big Deal," *MediaWeek,* 7, no. 44 (November 24, 1997), p. 36; Judann Pollack, "Big G Has Special Cheerios for Big '00'," *Advertising Age,* (June 14, 1999), pp. 1–2.

41. Some of the case information came from the following article: Jay P. Granat, "How to Create an Effective Advertisement," *CPA Journal,* 61, no. 1 (January 1991), pp. 68–80.

Building an IMC Campaign

Choosing the Correct Appeal for an IMC Advertising Campaign

Three key theories should drive the development of your advertising campaign. The hierarchy of effects model, means–end theory, and visual and verbal imaging are important theoretical frameworks from which to proceed. Then, decide if you can make your product somehow sexy, or if you will use fear, scarcity, humor, rationality, or some other approach to capture the customer's attention and persuade him or her to take action and buy your product or service. These factors may vary according to the culture in which you are operating. At the Prentice-Hall Web site at www.prenhall.com/clow, or access the Advertising Plan Pro disk that accompanied this textbook materials for Chapter 9 are designed to lead you through the process of creating the right appeal, given the firm's image and IMC theme.

Critical Thinking Exercises

Discussion Questions

1. Develop a means–end chain similar to the one in Figure 9.3 for each of the following branded products:
   a. Clorox bleach
   b. Durex condoms
   c. Zippo lighters
   d. Kool-Aid
   e. Sony stereos

2. Evaluate the balance of visual and verbal elements of each advertisements shown in this chapter. Which is predominant? Which images are considered appropriate for international advertising, because they have the characteristic of *visual esperanto*? Do they use white space effectively?

3. Try to recall five outstanding television commercials. Identify the appeal used in each one. Why were these five ads effective? Discuss your list with those of other classmates. What was their reaction to your list? How did you feel about theirs?

4. Develop a print advertisement for vitamins using a fear appeal. Be sure to consider the means–end chain prior to starting on the advertisement. After completing the means–end chain and advertisement, to what other media could the advertisement be adapted? How?

5. Borrow a camcorder and develop a 30- or 45-second television spot for one of the following products, using the suggested appeal. Be sure to develop a means–end chain prior to creating the advertisement.
   a. Denim skirt, sex appeal
   b. Tennis racket, humor appeal
   c. Ice cream, emotional appeal
   d. Stockbroker, fear appeal
   e. Dress shoes, musical appeal

6. Record five television commercials using a VCR. Identify which appeal each advertisement uses. Discuss the quality of the advertisement and its best and worst aspects. For each ad, present another possible appeal and how it could be used. What personal values and customer benefits does each advertisement present?

7. Record five television commercials or find five print advertisements that use a sex appeal. Identify which of the five ways sexuality was used. Evaluate each ad using the seven steps presented in the Communications Action Box "Using Sex Wisely."

8. Look up each of the following Internet Web sites. Identify which type of appeal each site uses. Evaluate the quality of that appeal. What other appeals can be used to make the site more appealing? Discuss the balance of visual and verbal elements on the Web site and ad.

   a. Service Metrics (www.servicemetrics.com)

   b. Trashy Lingerie (www.trashy.com)

   c. Navison Software, U.S. (www.navison-us.com)

   d. BMW Motorcycles (www.bmwusacycles.com)

   e. Guess (www.guess.com)

   f. Wonderbra (www.wonderbrausa.com)

   g. Solomon Software (www.solomon.com)

   h. Michael Jordan cologne (www.michael-jordan-cologne.com)

   i. Sweet 'n Healthy (www.sweetnhealthy.com)

Sexy CPAs[41]

APPLICATION EXERCISE I

Jon Johnson came from an unusual background. As an undergraduate at Southwest Missouri State University, Jon studied accounting for one year before changing his major to marketing. His musical talents plus a whimsical creative streak made him an ideal candidate to work in an advertising agency.

The most recent client Jon was asked to serve was a CPA firm called Burns, Connors, and Morris, or BCM, located in St. Louis, Missouri. The firm was quite large but was not affiliated with any of the large national accounting companies. Jon's task was to find a way to compete effectively with the services offered by the major national companies in the local market.

At his first meeting with BCM officials and Jon's account manager, they went over what is known as the AIDA methodology. AIDA stands for Attention Interest Desire Action. Clearly, the ad must garner the prospective client's attention and incite interest. Desire and action are much more difficult to achieve, because a business customer must be moved to consider changing accounting firms or giving some activities to the BCM firm. Jon commented that the AIDA approach seemed quite similar to a hierarchy of effects model.

BCM officials pointed out that their business was more likely to grow by capturing new clients rather than getting long-standing large firms to change. They wanted Jon and his company to stress BCM's areas of expertise (tax accounting and advice) along with the idea that the company has a quality staff, affordable fees, excellent seminars, and the ability to handle international clients. BCM was also proud of its collaborative efforts with prominent local business leaders, politicians in St. Louis, and local law firms and insurance companies.

BCM faced the unique challenge of finding outlets to reach a target market which was smaller and growing firms in need of CPA services. The traditional approach had always been to seek out print media to present ads. Thus, BCM would reach physicians through ads in medical journals (which could be regionally, but not locally, targeted). New businesses might be enticed through ads published in local magazines and specialty journals, insurance companies could be contacted through trade journals, and small businesses through small business magazines and journals. Such an approach was costly, because of the difficulty in reaching all prospective customers in an across-the-board fashion.

In spite of these obstacles, BCM asked Jon and his firm to prepare a series of print ads for a winter campaign. This was a logical time. The key tax season begins in January and ends in April. Jon decided his print ad campaign must have an effective banner or headline. He knew 80 percent of readers read only that part of an ad. Most CPA firms create ads emphasizing the cost savings of using their services. The copy of these ads focused on the advantages each company held in the marketplace. Successful campaigns generally had attractive logos as well as a type of layout that make the company distinct.

Jon prepared the campaign BCM wanted, using the banner, "Small Enough to Know You, Large Enough to Serve Your Financial Needs." The print ad campaign was geared to four primary markets: (1) physicians, (2) small businesses, (3) attorneys, and (4) local restaurants. Each could be reached by magazine–trade journal advertising. The medical campaign centered on special programs and seminars for doctors and featured a photo of a physician meeting with an accountant. The small business ad showed the BCM president working in a storefront setting at a ribbon-cutting ceremony; the same ad was used for restaurants. The attorney ad photo was shot in a law library.

Jon then offered an alternative. He suggested that rather than using such a traditional approach, the company might be able to attract attention and desire with a more sexy and less rational approach. He showed BCM officials a storyboard (six stop frame pictures in sequence used to represent a television ad) for local television and cable outlets. The ad showed BCM's office and people working diligently in it, followed by several local business clients during a regular day of work. The copy featured the same advantages as the print ads. The final board displayed the same businessman from one of the local companies sitting on a beach with a phone–fax–laptop setup. He was working but also sunning himself. Behind the businessman was a woman wearing a skimpy bikini lounging with a drink. The tag line was "We take care of business, so you can take care of yours."

Jon suggested that billboards and print ads could feature the same photo as the final storyboard frame and use the same, more provocative tag line. The same photo and ad could be sent by direct-mail flyer, by fax, and as the main page of BCM's Web site. Jon reported to BCM and to his company that he would be comfortable preparing either approach.

1. Did Jon meet the AIDA model with his television campaign?
2. Did Jon meet the AIDA model with his print campaign?
3. Which campaign would you run for BCM? Why?
4. What other appeal besides sex or rationality might fit BCM?

APPLICATION EXERCISE II

Barry Farber has pretty much "seen it all" in his 30 years of selling used cars. His business, The Auto Advantage, had experienced a series of high and low points related to buyer whims and the nature of the industry. Barry is quick to point out that his strongest ally has always been a local advertising company in Sacramento that has helped him negotiate the troubled waters.

From the beginning, Barry has seen opportunities rise up and drift away. When he opened his modest lot in 1973, the first gas crisis was just emerging. People were dumping gas-hog cars and diligently looking for high-mileage cars and those fueled by diesel. In fact, Barry distinctly remembers offering a practically brand-new Ford LTD II, one of the most popular models of the time, at $3,000 below its "blue book" value, and not being able to find a buyer for weeks due to consumer fears about oil shortages and rising gas prices.

At that time, Barry's new advertising agency manager, Wendy Mozden, pointed out an old technique that had worked wonders for years. She called it *"turning a disadvantage into an advantage."* She learned the tactic by watching old Volkswagen commercials. The original "bug" was promoted as being ugly, but economical. Many restaurants during that era bought ads pointing out that the reason they were so "slow" was due to their higher-quality food, making it "worth the wait."

Consequently, The Auto Advantage placed ads in newspapers and on the radio focusing on the "value" an individual could obtain by trading down or across. Sales reps were instructed to convey to individual buyers that a person would have to buy an awfully big amount of gas at 55 cents per gallon before a large car would actually be costly, especially when mpg (miles per gallon) differences between midsize and smaller cars were so small. The Auto Advantage managed to buy cars that other companies did not want to carry at drastically reduced prices and sell them to the customers they could educate concerning the shift from disadvantage to advantage. Within a few years, those high-priced (and hard to maintain) diesel cars disappeared, and people once again fell in love with larger gas hogs. By then Barry's company was well established in the marketplace.

Barry weathered the invasion of foreign cars into the United States by once again seeing an advantage in the disadvantage. Using patriotic themes, his company subtly pointed out that people buying foreign-made cars hurt the local economy, especially because one of the major manufacturers in the Sacramento area made replacement parts for GM cars. Sales presentations always included the question "Are you in a union?" Those who responded "yes" were easy targets for the company's "Buy American" theme during the early 1980s.

From there, Barry spent a great deal of energy making sure he understood the needs of his aging client base. Those who started families in the 1980s needed minivans in the 1990s. Those who were older and facing retirement often wanted low-maintenance cars. By carefully constructing his original message, that a person would gain an advantage by shopping at his lot, the business continued to succeed.

The next major challenge for The Auto Advantage may become the same one in which the company began. Oil prices started to rise, and the U.S. government created tighter pollution standards for almost every make and model of car. Some consumers again looked for more efficient autos, even hybrid gas–electric models as the new century began. Barry knew he would need to continue to adapt as the marketplace evolved. He continued to look for turnaround situations to find the edge to keep his clients happy with what they bought from The Auto Advantage.

1. Describe an advertisement in which the firm attempts to turn a disadvantage into an advantage.

2. If gas prices double in a one-year time period, how should The Auto Advantage respond? Design an ad to promote fuel economy using the various strategies described in this chapter.

3. Should The Auto Advantage continue to advertise to baby boomer and older clients? How can the company attract Generation X or echo boomer customers to the lot? How would the advertisements differ? Design an advertisement for the Generation X or echo boomer customer.

4. Pick one of the following appeals and use it to design a print advertisement for The Auto Advantage:

a. Fear

b. Humor

c. Sex

d. Emotional

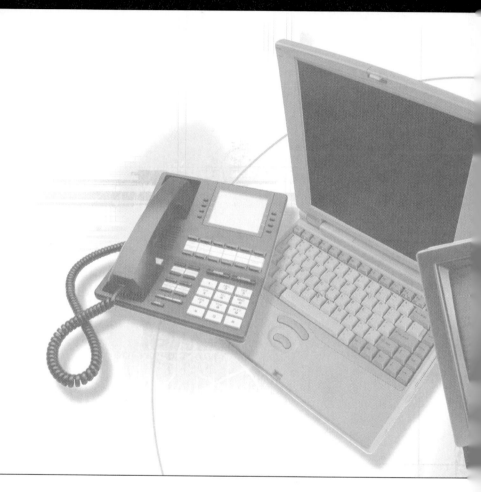

VIAGRA ADVERTISING:
(Place Your Own Joke Here)

When Pfizer first introduced the drug *sildenafil citrate* under the brand name Viagra, a wave of interest swept across the nation, from talk shows to an entire episode of *Mad About You*. Jokes were everywhere. On the other hand, sales of the prescription drug reached more than $180 million in the first two months following the product's launch.

The initial Viagra television ad featured politician Bob Dole and did not name the product nor its manufacturer. Instead, Dole talked about the courage needed to face the

problem of erectile dysfunction. Many viewers believed it was simply a public service announcement and didn't know that Dole was compensated by Pfizer for appearing in the spots. Dole did not name the product. No disclaimers about side effects or the ingredients were necessary as a result.

Following Viagra's release, several incidents generated negative publicity. For openers, at least 30 men died from heart attacks or strokes. These men had taken the pill, and the strain of having sex was the primary cause of death. Further, some women complained that their husbands, who had given up womanizing with advanced age and less interest in sex, had returned to their old habits. The com-

pany scrambled to offset these negative images by producing the second wave of ads showing happy couples who had benefited from the product.

Pfizer's success largely depended on a $35 million first-year advertising budget. In that first year, over 2 million men took the prescription. This generated expected sales of over $1 billion by the second year.

Continuing issues haunted the product. First, Canadian buyers were not able to obtain the drug. Next, on-line purchases made its availability seem far too easy, and fears emerged that unregulated purchases would have a further adverse effect. Also, counterfeiters seized the opportunity to sell fake Viagra pills on-line. Internet problems gave the company a major headache. Also, the high price of the medicine deterred many buyers.

Many HMOs refuse to cover the cost of Viagra, pointing out that it would take away at least $100 million from coverage of other prescriptions, most notably antiviral drugs. Other health care providers expressed concerns about its safety.

The executives selling Viagra remained unfazed. The next generation of ads featured seven reasons to "feel good" about the product, including how it works, when it works, research results, and assurances that most men tolerate the product well. The tag line "Love life again" is now associated with Viagra ads.

In the upcoming years, Pfizer seeks to maintain steady sales and fend off competing products. Time will tell if the product has longlasting users. In the meantime, constructing persuasive, tasteful, and informative ads remains the company's goal. Many approaches, including sensuality, romance, and information, can be used. Which would work for you? For your parents? For your grandparents?

overview

The essence of an integrated marketing communications program is designing a message that effectively reaches a target audience. These messages must be, in a very real sense, quite personal. They are designed to change or shape attitudes. They must be remembered. They should lead to some kind of action, in either the short or long term.

In the most general sense, messages can travel in two ways. First, a personal message can be delivered through a personal medium. Thus, a sales rep closing the deal, shaking the hand of the buyer, giving a reassuring tap on the shoulder, smiling, and talking communicates in an intimate, warm, human fashion. Clearly, personal media (sales reps, repair department personnel, customer services representatives, etc.) must be included as part of the overall IMC program and approach.

At the same time, the various forms of advertising media are impersonal. Television sets are indifferent as to what appears on the screen. Radios deliver any sound that can be transmitted. Computer screens are nothing more than high-tech television screens. The challenge to the marketing account executive, the company, and especially the creative is to design a message that will seem personal, even as it is delivered through an impersonal medium.

Account executives are acutely aware of the importance of effectively reaching a target audience. It is not simply a matter of reach, frequency, and continuity. The message must engage the targeted buyer and influence the individual to the point that he or she will recall and use the advertised or promoted product in some way.

Beyond the goal of making a message personal, many marketers are interested in tangible, measurable results that can be reported to clients and to prospective new customers. Therefore, the relationship between the executive and the creative reaches a critical point at the stage in which an advertisement is designed.

This chapter focuses on several major topics. First, four types of message strategies are described. Each may be used to help convince the consumer to make a purchase, either through reason, emotion, action, or belief in a firm or brand's image. Second, the major types of executional frameworks are noted. These forms of advertising presentation help the creative prepare original, convincing, and memorable ads. Third, four types of sources or spokespersons who appear in various advertisements are described, and the criteria used to select them are reviewed. Fourth and finally, the principles of effective advertising campaigns are noted. These concepts should be combined with the information found in the previous three chapters in order to fully integrate an effective advertising design program. When such a goal is reached, the account executive is able to present the ad to the client with the greatest confidence that the campaign will be successful. When advertisements are combined with other elements of the promotions mix in an integrated fashion, the net result is a stronger company image and a clear IMC theme that will entice consumers to remember the company and take action when they are ready to buy.

message strategies

As noted in Chapter 7, the **message theme,** or the outline of the key ideas in the ad, is a central part of the creative brief. The message theme can be created using a number of message strategies. A **message strategy** is the primary tactic used to deliver the message theme. There are four broad categories of message strategies:

1. Cognitive strategies
2. Affective strategies
3. Conative strategies
4. Brand strategies[1]

The first three represent the components of attitudes, described earlier in Chapters 5 and 9. All four of the message strategies are described in this section. Figure 10.1 lists the four brand strategies along with various forms or approaches from each category.

Cognitive strategies

A **cognitive message strategy** is the presentation of rational arguments or pieces of information to consumers. The advertisement's key message focuses on the product's attributes or the benefits customers obtain from using the product. The product's attributes include a huge range of benefits. Foods may be described as healthful, pleasant tasting, low calorie, and so forth. A tool can be shown as durable, convenient, or handy to use. A drill press machine used in a manufacturing operation may be depicted as reliable or faster than comparable machines on the market. Cognitive message strategies should make these benefits clear to potential customers. There are five major forms of cognitive strategies:

1. Generic messages
2. Preemptive messages
3. Unique selling proposition
4. Hyperbole
5. Comparative advertisements

Cognitive Strategies
- Generic
- Preemptive
- Unique selling proposition
- Hyberbole
- Comparative

Affective Strategies
- Resonance
- Emotional

Conative Strategies
- Action-inducing
- Promotional Support

Brand Strategies
- Brand user
- Brand image
- Brand usage
- Corporate

Message Strategies

FIGURE 10.1

Generic messages are direct promotions of product or service attributes or benefits without any claim of superiority. This type of strategy works best for a firm that is clearly the brand leader and dominant in its industry. The goal of the generic message is to make the brand synonymous with the product category. Thus, Campbell's Soups can declare "soup is good food" without any claim to superiority because the company so strongly dominates the industry. When most consumers think of soup, they think of Campbell's. Nintendo uses similar strategies because the company dominates the video game market with over 70 percent of the market share. Generic message strategies are seldom found in the business-to-business market because few firms dominate an industry to the extent of Campbell's or Nintendo. One major exception is Intel, which controls 75 percent of the microprocessor market. The generic message "Intel inside" has been used for years to convey to both businesses and end users that the processor inside practically any PC is made by Intel. Because the Intel name became synonymous with quality, IBM was forced to display the Intel inside logo to assure buyers that IBM computers contain Intel microprocessors. IBM had always used Intel microprocessors. For several years IBM tried to discontinue displaying the Intel logo, because the IBM marketing team thought it distracted from IBM's name. The return to displaying the Intel inside logo illustrates the power a generic message can have when the firm dominates the market.[2]

Preemptive messages are claims of superiority based on a specific attribute or benefit of a product. Once made, the claim normally preempts the competition from making such a statement. For example, Crest toothpaste is so well-known as "the cavity fighter" that the brand has preempted other companies from making similar claims, even though all toothpastes fight cavities. Thus, when using a preemptive strategy, the key is to be first company to state the advantage, thereby preempting the competition from saying it. Those that do are viewed as "me-too"

An advertisement for Bonne Bell featuring a unique selling proposition. Courtesy of Bonne Bell.

brands or copycats, similar to all of the night time game shows on the air following the instant success of *Who Wants to Be a Millionaire?*

A **unique selling proposition** is an explicit, testable claim of uniqueness or superiority that can be supported or substantiated in some manner. Brand parity makes a unique selling proposition more difficult to establish. Reebok claims it is the only shoe that uses DMX technology, which provides for a better fit. Because of patents, Reebok can claim this unique selling proposition. In the Bonne Bell advertisement aimed at teenagers on the previous page, the company proposes the unique selling proposition that a Bonne Bell Lipshade is the "One and only, one-handed, sleek sweep flipstick."

The **hyperbole** approach makes an untestable claim based upon some attribute or benefit. When NBC claims that its Thursday night lineup is "America's favorite night of television," the claim is a hyperbole. Remember from the discussion about the Federal Trade Commission in Chapter 2 that regulators expect companies to include such puffery. These claims do not have to be substantiated, which makes this cognitive strategy quite popular.

The final cognitive message strategy is a **comparative advertisement.** When an advertiser directly or indirectly compares a product or service to the competition, it is the comparative method. The advertisement may or may not mention the competitor by name. Sometimes, an advertiser simply presents a "make-believe" competitor, giving it a name like product X. This approach, however, is not as effective for comparative advertising stating the actual competitor's name. To provide protection from lawsuits, companies must be sure they can substantiate any claims made concerning the competition.

AT&T and MCI compare rates. VISA brags that many merchants using the card will not accept American Express. Burger King explains the advantages of flame broiling as opposed to frying that McDonald's and Wendy's use. In the business-to-business sector, shipping companies compare their delivery times and accuracy rates.

The major advantage of comparative ads is that they often capture the attention of consumers. When comparisons are made, both brand awareness and message awareness increase. Consumers tend to remember more of what the ad says about a brand than when the same information is in a noncomparative ad format.

The negative side of using comparative ads deals with believability and consumer attitudes toward them. Many consumers think comparative ads are less believable. They view the information about the sponsor brand as exaggerated and conclude that the information about the comparison brand probably is misstated to make the sponsor brand appear superior.

Another danger of comparative ads is the negative attitudes consumers may develop toward the ad. If viewers acquire negative attitudes toward the advertisement, these negative attitudes can transfer to the sponsor's product. This is especially true when the sponsor runs a *negative comparative ad.* The form of advertisement portrays the competition's product in a negative light, such as when Pringles shows someone creating a greasy mess eating regular potato chips. Although the Pringles ad does not create a problem, other negative comparisons may not be as effective.

In psychology, the concept of *spontaneous trait transference* suggests that when someone calls another person dishonest, other people tend to remember the speaker as also being less than honest. When a comparative ad criticizes the comparison brand based upon some particular attribute, viewers of the ad may attribute that deficiency to the sponsor brand as well. This is most likely to occur when the consumer uses the comparative brand, not the sponsored brand.[3]

Companies must be careful in choosing an appropriate comparison firm. In one ad, Nissan compared the Altima sedan to the Mercedes-Benz. Some viewers of the ad said comparing the two cars was like comparing apples to oranges. The improper comparison destroyed the advertisement's credibility. Most advertising experts agree that a more accurate comparison for the Nissan Altima would be the Toyota Camry.[4]

Comparison ads are less common in other countries due to both social and cultural differences as well as legal restrictions. Therefore, it is important to be cognizant of cultural and legal issues. For example, many of the countries of Europe classify comparative advertising as illegal. In Japan, it is not illegal, but it runs against the society's cultural preferences. In Brazil, the advertising industry is so powerful that any attempt to create a comparative advertisement has been challenged and stopped. Many times, international consumers not only dislike the advertisements but often transfer that dislike to the company sponsoring the ad.[5]

The comparative message strategy is beneficial if used with caution. The comparison brand must be picked carefully to ensure consumers see it is a viable comparable brand. Actual product attributes and customer benefits must be used, without stretching the information or providing misleading information. If there are actual differences to compare, then comparative advertising works well. If the comparisons are all hype and opinion, with no substantial differences, comparative advertising does not work as well. Of course, if the comparison is misleading, the FTC can step in to investigate. The largest category of complaints that the FTC deals with is comparative advertising.

In general, comparing a lesser known brand to the market leader seems to work well. On the other hand, comparing a new brand with the established brand is often not effective. Many times, a wise strategy is to simply make the comparison without naming the competitor. This strategy worked well for Avis, which usually does not mention Hertz in ads, yet comparisons are made and consumers know which competitor Avis refers to.[6]

All five of these cognitive message strategies are based on some type of rational logic. They generally are oriented toward the central processing component of the ELM (elaboration likelihood model). In terms of attitudes, the sequence of cognitive → affective → conative is the plan of attack in developing a rational approach. The intention of a cognitive message strategy is first to present consumers with rational information about a product, service, or company, and then to help them develop positive feelings about the same product or company.

Affective strategies

Affective message strategies invoke feelings and emotions and match them with the product, service, or company. They try to enhance the likability of the product, recall of the appeal, or comprehension of the advertisement. Affective strategies elicit emotions that, in turn, affect the consumer's reasoning process and finally lead to action. For example, an emotion such as love can help convince a consumer that a safer but more expensive car is worth the money. Affective strategies fall into two categories: (1) resonance and (2) emotional.

Resonance advertising attempts to connect a product with a consumer's experiences to develop stronger ties between the product and the consumer. For example, use of music from the 1960s takes baby boomers back to that time and the pleasant experiences they had growing up. Any strongly held memory or emotional attachment is a candidate for resonance advertising. Take a look at the advertisement for Cheerios on the next page. This resonance approach shows three generations of a family in the picture combined with the words "Your heart has better things to do than deal with heart disease." Family memories and emotions combine with the product feature of being a heart-smart (low-cholesterol) cereal.

Emotional advertising attempts to elicit powerful emotions that eventually lead to product recall and choice. As described in Chapter 9, many emotions can be connected to products, including trust, reliability, friendship, happiness, security, glamour, luxury, serenity, pleasure, romance, and passion.

As noted in Chapter 9, emotional appeals are not used only in consumer advertisements. They can also be used in business-to-business ads, because members of the buying center are human beings who do not always make decisions based on only rational thought processes. Emotions and feelings also affect decisions. If the

A Cheerios advertisement utilizing a resonance affective message strategy. Courtesy of General Mills.

product's benefits can be presented within an emotional framework, the advertisement is normally more effective, especially in business-to-business ads.[7] When neither reason (cognitive) nor emotional (affective) pitches are the best, an action-based approach or a brand appeal is utilized.

Conative strategies

Conative message strategies are designed to lead more directly to some type of consumer behavior. They can be used to support other promotional efforts, such as coupon redemption programs, Internet "hits" and orders, and in-store offers such as buy-one-get-one-free. The goal of a conative advertisement is to elicit behavior. A conative strategy is present in television advertisements promoting music CDs or cassettes which seeks to persuade viewers to call a toll-free number to purchase the music. They further encourage the action by stating the CD cannot be purchased at stores and is available for only a limited time.

Action-inducing conative advertisements create situations in which cognitive knowledge of the product or affective liking of the product may come later (after the actual purchase) or during product usage. For instance, a point-of-purchase display is designed (sometimes through advertising tie-ins) to cause people to make *impulse buys.* The goal is to make the sale, with affective feelings and cognitive knowledge forming as the product is used.

Promotional support conative advertisements are designed to support other promotional efforts. Besides coupons and phone-in promotions, a company may advertise a sweepstakes that a consumer enters by filling out the form on the advertisement or by going to a particular retailer.

These "Big Sale" signs are a conative strategy designed to encourage customers to make a purchase. Courtesy of PhotoEdit. Photograph by David Young-Wolff.

Brand strategies

The final category of message strategy is not as directly oriented to consumer attitudes. Instead, **brand message strategies** build or enhance the brand or corporate name in some way. Brand strategies can be placed into four categories:

1. Brand user strategies
2. Brand image strategies
3. Brand usage strategies
4. Corporate advertising

Brand user strategies focus on the type of individuals that use a particular brand. One example of a brand user strategy involves celebrity endorsements. When celebrities are present in advertisements, the ad tends to show the user of the brand more than the brand itself. The idea is that consumers who like the celebrity will transfer that liking to the brand itself. Thus, golfers who like Tiger Woods will use the Nike brand, baseball fans who like Nolan Ryan will buy Advil, and so forth. The endorsers who use the product help consumers recall the brand's name and develop a preference for that brand.

Apple Computers used a more common brand user strategy in the company's early years of focusing on educational users. This strategy was so successful that in later years when Apple tried to convince businesses to use Apple's McIntosh computers, business buyers had difficulty perceiving Apple in the business environment. The public still perceives the Apple brand as a computer designed for educational users, not business users.

A **brand image strategy** works toward the development of a brand "personality" (e.g., Mountain Dew). In brand image advertising, the focus is on the brand rather than the user. It generally does not use celebrities in the ads. Often the ad may not even feature a person at all. If a spokesperson appears in the advertisement, it is a typical person rather than a celebrity. The advertisement for Skechers Sport Footwear on the next page is an example of a brand image strategy. Often no verbal copy other than the brand name appears in the advertisement except for the Internet address and toll-free number for a catalog.

The importance of a strong brand in the global business environment has led many businesses to devote more money to brand image advertising. In addition to developing the brand image in trade journals, business advertisers use broadcast media such as television and radio and print media such as magazines. Business advertisers realize that having a strong brand name such as AT&T or Arthur

An advertisement for Skechers Sport Footwear using a brand image message strategy.
Courtesy of Skechers USA Inc.

Andersen gives the company a better opportunity to bid on business contracts and to be considered in modified and new buy situations.

Brand usage messages stress the different uses for a particular brand. A classic example of this approach is the Arm and Hammer baking soda commercials that suggest new uses of the product. When home baking declined, to spur the sales of their baking soda, the company advertised that the baking soda could be used to reduce odors in the refrigerator. Later the company's marketing team promoted the idea that it will freshen carpets and reduce odors in cat litter boxes. Then, building on the brand name, Arm and Hammer developed its own line of toothpaste and another of deodorants.

Corporate advertising promotes the corporate name and image rather than the individual brand. As companies continue to face pressure from the public to be socially responsible, corporate advertising becomes an increasingly important advertising strategy. This is especially true when consumer trust is a key issue. Therefore, banks and financial institutions engage in a great deal of corporate ads.

Companies selling chemical products are also likely to commission corporate advertising to build consumer trust. For instance, many years ago DuPont Chemical realized that corporate advertising was essential. Marketing research indicated a strong distrust of chemical companies because of environmental pollution and chemical spills. DuPont's public efforts were necessary despite the fact that almost all chemical companies sell their products to other companies rather than to individuals.[8]

The primary goal of each of these brand strategy approaches is to develop the brand, including its image, awareness of the brand, and positive reactions to the brand. Whether it is the user, the image, product usage, or corporate image, the nature of a message strategy should be to incorporate the advertising messages conveyed with the overall IMC theme.

Cognitive, affective, conative, and brand strategies can be matched with the hierarchy of effects approach described in the previous chapter. In that model, consumers pass through a series of stages, from awareness to knowledge, liking, preference, conviction, and finally purchase. As shown in Figure 10.2, each strategy can highlight different stages of the hierarchy of effects model.

The message strategy is a key component of every advertising program. To be effective, the message strategy must be matched carefully with the media used, the

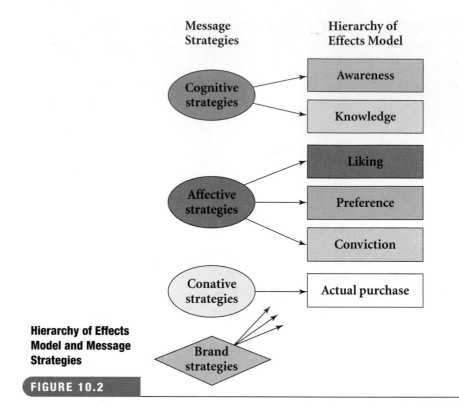

Hierarchy of Effects Model and Message Strategies

FIGURE 10.2

leverage point, and the executional framework. The creative and the account executive must remain in constant contact throughout the process to be certain all the advertising ingredients remain consistent. In the next section, the next element, the executional framework, is described.

---

stop!

Integrated Learning Experience

To observe a large collection of print advertisements, access www.adsGallery.com. Go the "Agencies" section and the "Browse Collection" menu. Pick at least 10 advertisements and see if you can determine the types of message strategy used. Which message strategies are the most common? Look for the type of appeal each ad uses (see Chapter 9). Notice that the site provides information about the ad, the ad campaign, and the agency for each advertisement. You can view additional ads from the same campaign or ads from the same agency. The site also provides Web addresses for each agency so you can explore more ads.

---

executional frameworks

An **executional framework** is the manner in which an ad appeal is presented. The ad appeal is like the script in a movie (e.g., comedy, drama, action film). The ad appeal spells out the overriding format to be used. In Chapter 9, the types of appeals described included: (1) fear, (2) humor, (3) sex, (4) music, (5) rationality, (6) emotions, and (7) scarcity.

If the ad appeal is the script, then the plot of the movie is the actual executional framework. The creative normally decides which executional framework to utilize, however, the media buyer and the account executive also influence the choice. For example, a radio advertisement program as chosen by the executive and purchased by the buyer probably would not feature animation, because it is very difficult to

▶ **Animation**

▶ **Slice-of-life**

▶ **Dramatization**

▶ **Testimonial**

▶ **Authoritative**

▶ **Demonstration**

▶ **Fantasy**

▶ **Informative**

**Executional
Frameworks**

FIGURE 10.3

create. Only well-known voices such as Donald Duck or Bugs Bunny would be useful (and probably expensive).

Figure 10.3 displays the various styles of executional frameworks. This chapter describes each framework in detail. Almost any of them can be used within the format of one of the various appeals. For example, a slice of life can depict fear, as can a dramatization. Informative ads can be humorous, but so can animations. Testimonials or demonstrations are rational or emotional, and so forth.

Animation

Animation is one useful type of executional framework. In recent years animation in advertising has increased, due primarily to the greater sophistication of computer graphics programs. The technology now available to advertising creatives is far superior to the cartoon type previously used. Currently, a technique called *rotoscoping* is accessible to many creatives. Rotoscoping is the process of placing hand-drawn characters digitally into live sequences. As a result, it is possible to present both live actors and animated characters in the same frame. One well-known live action television spot using cell animation features Michael Jordan and Bugs Bunny (and other cartoon characters) in MCI commercials.

Animated characters can be human, animal, or product personifications. Animation was originally a last resort technique for advertisers who did not have money to do a live commercial. Most agencies did not hold it in high regard. In contrast, animation has become the preferred technique for many advertisers. The successful movie *Who Framed Roger Rabbit?* may have sparked this revived interest in animation advertising. Since then, popular Disney films such as *The Little Mermaid* and *The Lion King* have continued the interest in animation advertising.

Besides cartoons, another method of animation, made popular by the California Raisins commercials, is clay animation. Although expensive to create, clay animation has been successful. Another popular product personification is the Pillsbury Doughboy. Computer graphics technology now allows production companies to superimpose these personifications in live scenes.

The computer graphics technology has allowed animation to move beyond personifications into creating real-life images. For example, a recent 30-second Jeep advertisement by Chrysler Corporation opens with a shot of approximately 60 zebras gathered near a water hole in Africa. In the horizon, a Jeep appears. The zebras begin running toward the vehicle, moving into a single line as they run. A lion, perched on a rock watches the whole scene. To television viewers, the zebras look real. They are not. All are computer generated. It would have been impossible to get 60 zebras to run in a single line next to a Jeep.[9]

Animation is used mostly in television spots, although it can also be produced for movie trailers and Internet ads. Single shots of animated characters, such as Tony the Tiger, can also be placed into print ads. Animation was a rarity in

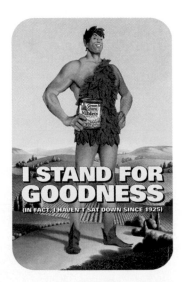

A Green Giant advertisement using animation. Courtesy of The Pillsbury Company.

business-to-business advertising primarily because of the negative view most advertising agencies held about it. Many firms believed animation was appealing to children but was not for businesspeople. These conclusions have changed. More business ads are placed on television because of the availability of high-quality graphics technologies that allow various businesses to illustrate the uses of their products through animated graphics.

stop!

Integrated Learning Experience

The use of animation in advertisements has increased in popularity because of computer technology sophistication. Even the Green Giant and the Pillsbury Doughboy are still popular. Each has a Web site. The Green Giant is available at www.greengiant.com. Be sure to check out "The Green Giant Around the World." The Doughboy is at www.doughboy.com. Notice that Pillsbury created both animations. For the California Raisins, access the Barker Animation Art Galleries, then click on the California Raisins characters. To get an insight into the mind of an animation creative, read Vince Backeberg's 3D Site at www.teleport.com/~v3d/index.html. If you are interested in adding animation to your Web site, or when a business wants to add animation, Animation Factory at www.camelotdesign.com/ad.html contains several thousand free animations. Free animation also is available at the Animation Library at www.animationlibrary.com.

Slice-of-life

In slice-of-life commercials, advertisers attempt to provide solutions to the everyday problems consumers or businesses face. These advertisements normally show common things people experience, especially problems they encounter. Then, the product or service is made available to solve the problem.

The most common slice-of-life format has four components:

1. Encounter
2. Problem
3. Interaction
4. Solution

Actors portray the dilemma or problem and sometimes solve the problems themselves. In others, a voice-over explains the benefits or solution to the problem that the product, service, or company provides.

A typical slice-of-life commercial starts with a child playing soccer and her parents cheering her on (the encounter). Her dirty uniform is then shown with comments by the child that it will never come clean for the championship game or a voice-over stating the same message (the problem). Another parent or the announcer in some form of interaction then introduces the benefits of the new laundry detergent (the interaction). Then the commercial ends with a proud parent taking her daughter to a championship game in a clean uniform (the solution). This commercial can be shot in several ways. The actors can talk to each other in the scenario, making the audience the third party who essentially is "eavesdropping" on the conversation. Or, the commercial can be shot with voice-overs that highlight the problem and solution portions of the commercial, with the announcer speaking directly to the audience.

In print advertisements, slice-of-life frameworks are more difficult to prepare. In a business-to-business advertisement for Messagemedia on the next page, the encounter is the potential female customer. The problem is that the "average single female breaks up with 4.3 men, avoids 237 phone calls, and ignores approximately 79 red lights per year." The interaction occurs through the copy "What are the chances she'll read your e-mail message?" The solution to this problem is Messagemedia's "e-messaging campaign."

The slice-of-life approach was introduced and made popular by Proctor & Gamble. During the 1980s, about 60 percent of all of P&G's advertisements used slice-of-life scenarios. Now P&G uses the slice-of-life method in only about 25 per-

A business-to-business advertisement for Messagemedia.com containing a slice-of-life executional framework.
Courtesy of MessageMedia.

cent of its commercials. Its ads have shifted to more humor, animation, and comparative types of executional frameworks.[10] The major reason P&G and other companies still use slice-of-life executional styles is because it remains an effective method. Studies indicate that the slice-of-life format scores above average in its persuasion ability, which is important in leading consumers into changing their brand preferences.[11]

The slice-of-life executional framework has become popular in Japan in recent years. The slice-of-life style is easily adapted to Japan's more soft-sell approach compared to the more hard-sell approach of the United States. Japanese advertising tends to be more indirect, and the slice-of-life approach allows advertisers to present a product in a typical everyday situation. Benefits can be presented in a positive light without making brazen or harsh claims and without directly disparaging the competition.[12]

Business-to-business advertisements also use slice-of-life commercials heavily. This executional framework is popular because it allows the advertiser to highlight how a product can meet business needs. For example, a typical business-to-business ad begins with a routine business experience, such as a sales manager making a presentation to the board of directors. Then, the projector used does not have a clear picture at the distance the presenter wants to use. Then the ad offers the solution: a projector from Sony. The presentation is made with great clarity, and the board of directors accepts the customer's bid for the account. As with all slice-of-life commercials, disaster is avoided and, by using the advertised brand, a happy ending occurs.

Slice-of-life executional frameworks are possible in most media, including magazines or billboards, because a single picture can depict a normal, everyday situation or problem. The secret is to let one image tell the entire story, with the product being the solution.

Dramatization

A dramatization is similar to slice-of-life executional framework. It uses the same format of presenting a problem, then a solution. The difference lies in the intensity and story format. Dramatization uses a higher level of excitement and suspense to tell the story. A dramatization story normally builds to a crisis point.

An example of a dramatization is a recent Maytag commercial, which appeared after the company abandoned the "lonely repairman" theme the company had used for decades. The commercial was designed for the launch of the Gemini range. Thirty- and 60-second spots featured children carrying pizzas yelling and rushing toward a throng of adults carrying casserole dishes. The groups run toward each other on a battlefield. The two groups are ready to break into battle when the Maytag representative intervenes with the dual-oven range that will accommodate the needs of both groups.[13] This Maytag commercial has all of the critical components of a drama executional framework. It tells a story in a dramatic way leading up to a suspenseful climax wherein the teenagers and adults are just about ready to go to war. Suddenly, from nowhere appears the Maytag product that provides a solution to the crisis.

An effective and dramatic advertisement is difficult to pull off, because it must be completed in either 30 or 60 seconds. Building a story to a climatic moment is challenging, given such a short time period. Not all dramatic executional styles accomplish the high level of suspense required to make them successful. It is often much easier to simply produce a slice-of-life framework. For an example, see the Communication Action Box on the next page.

Testimonials

The testimonial type of executional framework has been successful for many years, especially in the business-to-business and service sectors. When a customer in an advertisement tells about a positive experience with a product, this is a testimonial. In the business-to-business sector, testimonies from current customers add credibility to the claims being made. In many business buying situations, perspective vendors are asked for references. Testimonials provide references in advance. Further, most buyers believe what others say about a company more than they do what a company says about itself. Thus, testimonials by someone else offer greater credibility than self-proclamations.

Testimonials also are an effective method for promoting services. Services are intangible; they cannot be seen or touched. Consumers cannot examine the service before making decisions. A testimony from a current customer is an effective method of describing the benefits or attributes of the service. This matches the method most consumers use in selecting a service. When choosing a dentist, an attorney, or an automobile repair shop, consumers often ask friends, relatives, or coworkers. A testimonial ad for a service simulates this type of word-of-mouth recommendation.

The Bank of Santa Clara created a testimonial advertising campaign to reach small and medium-size business customers. The bank promotes a "hometown banking at its best"–type of message theme. The ads feature a variety of business-people such as lawyers, restaurant owners, motel operators, retailers, manufacturers, and accountants interacting with bank employees. The goal is to depict small and medium-size business owners in a comfortable banking environment.[14] In the various print and television ads, the customers are then interviewed about their relationships with the bank. Print ads change weekly. This allows for more customers to be shown in ads and keeps the ads fresh. Television ads are produced in groups so the ads can be rotated. Typical ads are kept for several months. Business customers especially like being featured in the advertisements because they provide additional exposure for their businesses.

Surveys conducted by the Bank of Santa Clara indicate the testimonial campaign has been successful. More than 75 percent of the bank's customers have seen the ads. More importantly, over 50 percent of the bank's customers indicated that the advertisements influenced their decision when they selected the Bank of Santa Clara.

Drama versus Slice of Life

It is difficult to create a strong drama executional framework. The difference between a drama executional framework and the slice of life is in the power of the story. For example, consider an advertisement for tires. Using the means–ends Chain concept from Chapter 9, the attribute to feature will be the tire's tread and its ability to grip the road in adverse weather conditions. Therefore, the customer benefit is safety and the personal value is a sense of security. In a slice-of-life commercial, the advertisement can feature a vehicle stuck in the snow or skidding around the corner. The solution is then presented, a particular brand of tire that will perform well in those adverse circumstances.

Now consider a drama executional style for the same means–ends Chain, developed by Ogilvy & Mather Ad Agency for Dunlop tires. The commercial opens in the closing seconds of a boys' rugby match. The score is 23–22. The field is muddy. The losing team is awarded a penalty kick right in front of the opponent's own goalpost. Young Rupert Williams has the chance to win the game with one final kick, and, as it is presented in the drama, it looks to be an easy kick. As the boy prepares for the kick, the announcer says, "He could slot this one with his eyes closed, but he's taking his time. He wants to be sure." As the boy approaches the ball, he loses his footing on the muddy field and the ball just dribbles a few feet in the mud. A different voice-over then announces, "Because you never think about grip until you lose it. Think Dunlop tires."

This ad has all of the markings of a great drama ad. It has suspense. It has excitement. It has a crisis. It has a solution. But is it a great drama? Perhaps not. As soon as the announcer says the kick is an easy one, the audience knows he is going to miss. The suspense is deflated before it occurs. Possibly a more dramatic approach would be to set up the story so the audience knows the kick must go through, with the whole season or championship riding on this one kick. The boy should be the smallest player on the team and could be scorned and derided by his teammates. As the audience takes in the scene, they cannot help but cheer for the underdog. The scorned, skinny kid has to win it all for the team so he can be the hero. When it does not occur, the impact is more devastating. The impact of not having tires with grip becomes more convincing. Would this revised ad work, or would it be too frustrating because it ends in failure? Creatives and account executives encounter this type of dilemma on a daily basis.

Source: Bob Garfield, "One Slip, and It's All Over for Almost Great Tire Ad," *Advertising Age International* (May 1997), p. 16.

One major reason companies choose testimonials is that they enhance company credibility. Endorsers and famous individuals do not always have high levels of credibility, because consumers know they are being paid for their endorsements. In testimonials, everyday people, often actual customers, are the main characters. Other times they are paid actors, who look like everyday consumers, not models.

When more dramatic or slice-of-life types of venues are not the best, the creative considers the use of testimonials. He or she can present them in practically every advertising medium, and they can focus on both the product itself and the overall image of the brand or firm.

Authoritative

In using the authoritative executional framework, an advertiser seeks to convince viewers that a given product is superior to other brands. One form is **expert authority.** These ads employ a physician, dentist, engineer, or chemist to state the product's advantages over other products. Martha Stewart and Bob Vila are celebrities with authoritative voices. Firms also can feature less recognized experts such as automobile mechanics, professional house painters, nurses, or even aerobics instructors. Advertising presents each of these as an expert or authority in a particular field. These experts also talk about the brand attributes that make the product superior.

Many authoritative advertisements include some type of scientific or survey evidence. Independent organizations, such as the American Medical Association, undertake a variety of product studies. Quoting their results gives an ad greater credibility. Survey results are less credible. Stating that four out of five dentists recommend a particular toothbrush or toothpaste is less effective, because consumers do not have details about how the survey was conducted. On the other hand, when the American Medical Association states that an aspirin a day reduces the risk of a second heart attack, it is highly credible, and a company such as Bayer can take advantage of the finding by including it in its ads. The same is true when a magazine, such as *Consumer Reports,* ranks a particular brand as the best. Any scientific and independent source not paid by the advertising company can make an ad claim more powerful.

Authoritative advertisements have been widely incorporated into business-to-business sector ads, especially when available scientific findings provide support for a company's products. Independent test results are likely to have a more profound influence on members of the buying center. Members actively look for rational information to help them make decisions. The TWA advertisement below states that J.D. Power rates TWA as "#1 in frequent traveler satisfaction [for] short flights."

The authoritative approach assumes consumers and business decision makers rely on the central processing route from the ELM (elaboration likelihood model) approach. When they do, the authoritative approach works most effectively in print ads when buyers take the time to read the claim or findings the advertisement provides.

TWA uses the independent test results of J.D. Power to support the claim that it is number one. Courtesy of TWA–Trans World Airlines, Inc.

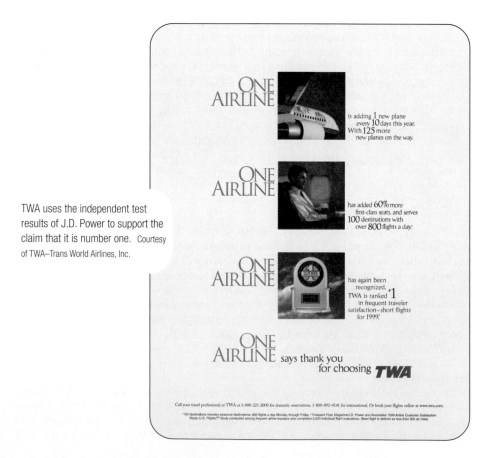

Authoritative ads work especially well in specialty magazines. For example, in a hunting magazine, having an expert hunter discuss the superiority of a particular gun is effective, because readers have an interest in hunting. Brides observe the endorsements of wedding experts in special bridal magazines. Readers notice these specialized advertisements, and the claims made have greater credibility. The same is true in business-to-business magazines. Trade journals in the business world are similar to specialty magazines in the consumer world.

Demonstration

Advertisements using the demonstration executional framework show how a product works. A demonstration is an effective way to communicate the attributes of a product to viewers. Other product benefits can be described as the product is exhibited. For example, one recent advertisement showed how a new form of dust cloth could be attached to a handle or used separately. The demonstration highlighted the product's multiple uses by cleaning a television screen, a wooden floor, a saxophone, and light fixtures on the ceiling. Thus, consumers were shown how to use the product and were able to observe its advantages at the same time.

Business-to-business ads often present demonstrations. They allow a business to show how a product can meet the specific needs of another business. Amway relies heavily on demonstrations to entice retail customers to buy products and to convince individuals to begin selling to company's merchandise. When coupled with magazine and brochure ads, the firm can attract both types of customers.

Demonstration ads are especially well suited to television. To a limited extent, the print media can feature demonstrations, especially when a series of photos shows the sequence of product usage.

Fantasy

Some products lend themselves to the fantasy type of executional framework. Fantasy executions are designed to lift the audience beyond the real world to a make-believe experience. Some fantasies are meant to be realistic. Others are completely irrational. Often, the more irrational and illogical ads are, more clearly consumers recall them. Fantasies can deal with anything from a dream vacation spot or cruise ships to a juicy hamburger or an enticing Digiorno pizza. The Jantzen ad on the next page encourages consumers to fantasize about what the world would be like if they ruled. People are even encouraged to share their fantasies by accessing Jantzen at www.jantzen.com.

The most common fantasy themes, however, are still sex, love, and romance. According to some marketing experts, raw sex and nudity in advertisements are losing their impact. In their place, advertisers show a softer, more subtle presentation of sex. Fantasy fits nicely with preferences for a tamer sexuality, which primarily is found in older members of the population. For some senior citizens, raw sex and nudity simply are offensive. Fantasy is an excellent way to approach older individuals by taking them into a world of romantic make-believe rather than hard-driving sexuality.[15]

One product category that uses fantasy is the perfume and cologne industry. In the past, the most common theme was that splashing on a certain cologne causes women to flock to you. For women, the reverse was suggested. Although used extensively, these ads were not particularly effective, because few people believed them. Currently, perfume advertisers tend to portray the product as enhancing the love life of a couple or even making a man or woman feel more sensuous, rather than turning a man into a "babe magnet" or a woman into a "diva."

A well-done print fantasy ad campaign features Sol Lingerie, created by the TDA Advertising & Design firm. The ads allow the reader to fantasize about the lingerie. No pictures of the product are shown. Instead, only the word *lingerie* appears in the ads, at the bottom of the page. One version shows a man losing his grip on his briefcase as he walks through the doorway with the word *lingerie* as the only clue as to why he is reacting in that manner. The viewer is free to develop his or her own fantasy about what will take place and about the brand itself.[16]

A Jantzen ad utilizing a fantasy executional framework. Courtesy of Jantzen Inc.

Television fantasy ads for cruise lines show couples enjoying romantic, sensuous vacations together, swimming, jet skiing, and necking. The goal is to make the cruise into more than just a vacation—it should become a romantic fantasy trip. Fantasy ads also can show people experiencing the thrill of winning a major sports event or sharing a common product (beer, pizza) with a beautiful model. Effective fantasies can inspire both recall and action.

The business-to-business advertising field has not used fantasy a great deal primarily because of fear that members of a buying center would not take a fantasy approach seriously. As with the other executional frameworks, creatives now use more fantasy in business-to-business ads.

Informative

A common advertising executional framework is an informative ad. Informative ads present information to the audience in a straightforward matter. Agencies prepare informative ads extensively for radio advertisements, because only verbal communication is possible. Informative ads are less common in television and print because consumers tend to ignore them. With so many ads bombarding the consumer, it takes more than just the presentation of information to grab someone's attention.

The most common fantasy themes are sex, love, and romance. Courtesy of Corbis/Stock Market. Photograph by Ariel S. Kelley.

Consumers highly involved in a particular product category pay more attention to an informational ad. Such is often the case when business buyers are in the process of gathering information for either a new buy or modified rebuy. On the other hand, if the business is not in the market for a particular product, buying center members do not pay much attention to informative ads. Thus, informative ads work well only in high-involvement situations. Many advertisers believe that business buyers need detailed information to make intelligent buying decisions. As a result, the informative framework continues to be a popular approach for business-to-business advertisers.

One of the keys to informative advertising is the placement of the ad. An informative advertisement about a restaurant placed on a radio station just before noon is listened to more carefully than if runs at 3:00 in the afternoon. An informative ad about a diet product in an issue of *Glamour* that has a special article on weight control or exercising will be noticed more than if it is placed in the fashion section of the magazine. An informative business ad about lathes works well next to an article about capital cost of equipment. Consequently, informative ads have limited uses but can be effective when placed properly.

Beyond these types of executional frameworks, the creative decides about all of the other ingredients, including music, copy, color, motion, light, and size (see the Application Exercise at the end of this chapter). Finally, one element remains.

communication **action**

The Changing World of the Creative

The advertising landscape is changing. New pressures have affected the role of the creative. For some, the most dramatic shift is in the center of power of the entire industry. For many decades Madison Avenue agencies were viewed as being on the cutting edge of innovation in advertising. Currently, if you believe renowned creatives Bob Kuperman and Roy Grace, the shift has most of the "action" to the west.

Kuperman states that: "The Madison Avenue label may play to middle America. But any client or marketing head knows he doesn't have to go to New York to get what he wants in terms of creativity." Grace is more blunt. He states that too many creative decisions fall within a safety zone of familiar styles, concepts, and sales techniques, especially in the Big Apple.

One of the reasons for the change is the shift to market research–driven advertising development. Focus groups and other forms of testing have made it so that, according to Grace, "There's too much testing and too much research. Advertising is too much of a science and not as much of an art." This frustration appears to be growing throughout the industry. Winston Fletcher notes that every major creative decision is subjected to research. When things get modified, creatives can scream themselves hoarse, but don't win out over the focus group.

To regain control, some creatives have moved into the role of director, splitting their time between commercial development and commercial production. In this new role, creatives limit themselves to one company per industry. For example, one creative noted that he had just prepared a $50 million campaign for Jack in the Box and therefore would not film for clients such as McDonald's or Burger King. The Chicago-based Fusion Idea Lab, which creates a number of Bud Light spots, will not film ads for other breweries.

Taking over the new role of director also puts the creative more directly in the line of fire, in terms of reporting tangible results. Unfortunately, "Creatives are probably the worst judges of their own work," states Don Williams, creative director at the PI Design agency. The new accountability may force some creatives away from directing and back into simple development.

Creative Stuart Burnett concludes that the best route to take is to find a marketing communications firm rather than a simple ad agency. He states that "marketing communications agencies are best responding to the [new] challenges. Their media-neutral, integrated approach is winning more and more fans and is getting them sexier work, bigger budgets, and meatier problems to solve."

No matter who employs the creative, the goal is to keep things original. According to Jeff Goodby, a major creative in San Francisco, "Advertising very quickly turns into formulas, and the real enemy of the creative organization is the formulaic feeling." Consequently, the firm Goodby, Silverstein & Partners is working to make sure the agency's creatives take risks and work to sell themselves to clients.

If you are looking for a dynamic, interesting, and evolving career, the job of creative offers many challenges and opportunities. As the next generation of creatives moves forward, the nature of the advertising "game" will continue to shift with the times, making things exciting for everyone involved.

Sources: Alice Z. Cuneo, "Goody Grows Up," *Advertising Age,* Crain Communications (2000), at www.webinfo@adage.com; Winston Fletcher, "Drop in Creative Tension May Kill Off Imagination," *Marketing,* Haymarket Publishing, Ltd. (August 27, 1998); Stuart Burnett, "Comment," *Marketing,* Haymarket Publishing, Ltd. (December 16, 1999); Kathy Desalvo, "Two-timers," *SHOOT,* BPI Communications (March 26, 1999); Justin Elias, "Now and Then," *SHOOT,* BPI Communications (September 10, 1999); Robert Mcluhand, "Creatives Can Sharpen Focus," *Marketing,* Haymarket Publishing Ltd. (April 20, 2000).

stop!

Integrated Learning Experience

For producing television commercials, access www.commercialtelevision.com to review a three-step approach for developing an advertising campaign. Be sure to look at the "Creative Ideas," "Hollywood Productions," and "Media Planning" sections. To view the latest televison ads, access www.television-commercials.com. Choose 10 commercials from the archives in the "Latest" section. Which appeal does each advertisement use? For more ads, access the "Library." Select "Ad Agencies" to obtain samples of ads produced by particular production houses. You can access "Production" to learn more about the production process.

sources and spokespersons

One other major issue remains for the creative, the company, and the account executive. Selecting **sources and spokespersons** to use in advertisements is a critical decision. Four types of sources are available to advertisers:

1. Celebrities
2. CEOs
3. Experts
4. Typical persons

Approximately 20percent of all advertisements use some type of *celebrity spokesperson.* Payments to celebrities account for around 10 percent of all advertising dollars spent.[17] Celebrity endorsers are used because their stamp of approval on a product can enhance the product's brand equity. Celebrities also help create emotional bonds with the products. The idea is to transfer the bond that exists between the celebrity and his or her audience to the product being endorsed. This bond transfer often is more profound for younger consumers. Older consumers are not as susceptible to celebrity endorsements. Still, many advertisers believe they are effective. Figure 10.4 lists some major brands and their endorsers.

Agencies also utilize celebrities to help establish a "personality" for a brand. The trick is to the tie the brand's characteristics to those of the spokesperson, such as Elizabeth Taylor's love of the finer things in life being attached to her line of scents and perfumes as well as other products. In developing a brand personality, the brand must already be established. The celebrity just helps define the brand more clearly. Using celebrities for new products does not always work as well as with already established brands.

There are three variations of celebrity endorsements: (1) unpaid spokespersons, (2) celebrity voice-overs, and (3) what may be called *dead-person endorsements.* Unpaid spokespersons are those celebrities who support a charity or cause by appearing in an ad. These types of endorsements are highly credible and can

▶ Ace Hardware: John Madden	▶ GMC Trucks: Grant Hill
▶ Adidas: Steffi Graf	▶ Hanes Hosiery: Fran Drescher
▶ American Express: Jerry Seinfeld	▶ Hanes Underwear: Michael Jordan
▶ Amway: Shaquille O'Neal	▶ Kmart: Rosie O'Donnell
▶ AT&T: Whitney Houston	▶ L'eggs: Jamie Lee Curtis
▶ Campbell Soup: Wayne Gretzky	▶ MasterCard: Tom Watson
▶ Compaq Computers: Hakeem Olajuwon	▶ Nintendo: Ken Griffey, Jr.
▶ Converse: Larry Bird, Larry Johnson, Lattrell Sprewell	▶ Outback Steakhouse: Rachel Hunter
▶ Danskin: Nadia Comaneci	▶ Revlon: Cindy Crawford
▶ Fila: Naomi Campbell, Grant Hill, Kathy Ireland, Vendela	▶ Sprite: Grant Hill
	▶ Taco Bell: Spike Lee, Shaquille O'Neal, Hakeem Olajuwon

Celebrity Endorsers

FIGURE 10.4

entice significant contributions to a cause. Politicians, actors, and musicians all appear in these ads. VH1's "Save the Music" ads are a recent campaign of this type.

Many celebrities also provide voice-overs for television and radio ads without being shown or identified. Listeners often respond to the ads and try to figure out who is reading the copy. This adds interest to the ad but may also serve as a distraction, when the individual does not hear the message while trying to identify the speaker.

A dead-person endorsement occurs when a sponsor uses an image, or past video or film, featuring an actor or personality who has died. Because dead persons do not have legal rights, many companies use them in ads without paying high fees. Dead-person endorsements are somewhat controversial but are becoming more common. John Wayne, Fred Astaire, Will Rogers, John Belushi, Elvis Presley, and many others have appeared in ads and even become spokespersons for products after dying. Colonel Sanders has become a spokesperson in animation for KFC.

Instead of celebrities, advertisers can use a CEO as the spokesperson or source. Dave Thomas of Wendy's is possibly the most famous CEO in commercials. For many years, Lee Iacocca was the spokesperson for Chrysler, and Michael Eisner serves as the main voice for Disney. A highly visible and personable CEO can become a major asset for the firm and its products. Many local companies succeed, in part, because their owners are out front in small market television commercials. They then begin to take on the status of local celebrities.

Expert sources include physicians, lawyers, accountants, and financial planners. These experts tend not to be famous celebrities or CEOs. Experts provide backing for testimonials, serve as authoritative figures, demonstrate products, and enhance the credibility of informative advertisements.

The final category of spokesperson are *typical-person sources.* Typical persons are one of two different types. The first category consists of paid actors or models who portray or resemble everyday people. The second is actual, typical, everyday people used in advertisements. Wal-Mart, as already mentioned, features its own store employees in freestanding insert advertisements. Agencies also create many "man-on-the-street" types of advertisements. For example, PERT shampoo recently prepared ads showing an individual asking people if they would like their hair washed. Dr. Scholl's interviews people about problems with their feet that might be resolved with cushioned shoe inserts.

Real people sources are becoming more common. One reason for this is the overuse of celebrities. Many experts believe that consumers have become saturated with celebrity endorsers and that the positive impact today is not as strong as it was in the past. One study conducted in Great Britain indicated that 55 percent of the consumers surveyed reported that a famous face was not enough to grab their attention. Celebrities held a greater appeal for the 15-to-24 year old age bracket. Sixty-two percent of that group stated that a famous person in an ad would get their attention.[18]

Source characteristics

In evaluating sources, most account executives and companies consider five major characteristics. The effectiveness of an advertisement may depend on the degree to which a spokesperson has one or more of the five characteristics, which are:

1. Attractiveness
2. Likability
3. Trustworthiness
4. Expertise
5. Credibility

One reason for using celebrities is that they are more likely to possess at least an element of all five characteristics. A CEO, expert, or typical person probably lacks one or more of them.

Attractiveness has two ingredients, (1) physical characteristics and (2) personality characteristics. Physical attractiveness is usually an important asset for an endorser. Bijan uses Bo Derek's physical attractiveness to promote its line of menswear, perfume, and jewelry. Advertisements with physically attractive spokespersons fare better than advertisements with less attractive people. This is true for both male and female audiences. At the same time, the attractiveness of the spokesperson's personality is also important to many consumers. This personality component helps viewers form emotional bonds with the spokesperson. If the spokesperson is seen as having a sour personality, even if physically beautiful, con-

A Bijan advertisement featuring Bo Derek. Courtesy of Bijan Fragrances, Inc.

sumers are less likely to develop an emotional bond with the individual and the product.

Closely related to the personality component of attractiveness is *likability*. Consumers respond more positively to spokespersons they like. This liking arises from various sources. Perhaps consumers like a movie in which the person acted or the character played by the actor. An athlete gains likability if he or she plays on the consumer's favorite team. Other individuals are likable because they support the favorite charities of consumers. Even though they may never actually meet the spokesperson, consumers can develop a liking or disliking for them based on their exposure to them. As noted earlier in this text, many people know Dennis Rodman as a talented basketball player but dislike his flamboyant personality and fashion choices. When Monica Lewinsky began endorsing Jenny Craig, several local companies pulled the ads over fears of negative consumer reactions. If consumers do not like a particular spokesperson, they are likely to transfer that dislike to the product the celebrity endorses. This is not an automatic transfer, because consumers recognize that endorsers are paid spokespersons. Still, there is almost always a negative impact on brand attitude.

A celebrity may be likable or attractive. But he or she may not be viewed as *trustworthy*. Trustworthiness is the degree of confidence or the level of acceptance consumers place in the spokesperson's message. A trustworthy spokesperson helps consumers believe the message. Two of the most trusted celebrities are Michael Jordan and Bill Cosby. Likability and trustworthiness are highly related. People who are liked tend to be trusted and people who are disliked tend not to be trusted.

The fourth characteristic advertisers look for when examining sources is *expertise*. Spokespersons with higher levels of expertise are more believable than sources with low expertise. Richard Petty and Jeff Gordon are seen as experts when automobile products and lubricants are advertised. Often when expertise is desired in an ad, the ad agency opts for the CEO or a trained or educated expert in the field. American Express features Maria Barraza, a small business owner and designer, to promote its Small Business Services.

A potential negative side to using a CEO as the spokesperson may be present: Although he or she has a high degree of expertise, the individual may lack some of the other key characteristics (attractiveness, likability, or trustworthiness). Expertise can be valuable in persuasive advertisements designed to change opinions or attitudes. Spokespersons with high levels of expertise are more capable of persuading an audience than someone with zero or low expertise.[19]

The final source selection characteristic is *credibility*, which is the sum of the other characteristics. It is a composite of attractiveness, trustworthiness, likability, and expertise. Credibility affects a receiver's acceptance of the spokesperson and message. A credible source is believable. Most sources do not score highly on all four attributes, yet they need to score highly on at least two in order to be perceived as credible.

Matching source types and characteristics

The account executive, ad agency, and corporate sponsor, individually or jointly, may choose the type of spokesperson. They can choose a celebrity, CEO, expert, or typical person, and the specific individual must have the key characteristics. This section matches source types with various characteristics.

Celebrities normally score well in terms of trustworthiness, believability, persuasiveness, and likability. These virtues increase if the match between the product and celebrity is a logical and proper fit. For example, Gabriela Satatini endorsing Head Sportswear is a good fit. An athlete endorsing any type of athletic product fits well. Companies can be creative but also use common sense in making quality matches. For instance, the match of boxer George Foreman to his Lean Mean Grilling Machine is a great success. On the other hand, convincing consumers that celebrities such as Charles Barkley, Sammy Sosa, Dan Marino, and Emmitt Smith eat at McDonald's is more challenging.

Michael Jordan is one of only a few celebrities who can endorse a number of products and maintain a high level of credibility. Courtesy of Bijan Fragrances, Inc.

Several dangers exist in using celebrities. The first is negative publicity about the celebrity caused by inappropriate conduct. In the early 1990s, Pepsi discovered that actions by celebrities such as Mike Tyson, Madonna, and Michael Jackson became a liability. This potential for negative publicity has lead some advertisers to use deceased celebrities, because what was essentially *negative likability* became attached to the company and its products. Many companies concluded that there was no need to risk bringing embarrassment or injury to themselves or the brand. It is also a reason that more ads use cartoon characters. Practically everyone likes cartoons.

The second danger of using celebrities is that their endorsement of so many products tarnishes their credibility. For example, after Sammy Sosa's historic home run chase with Mark McGwire, Sosa signed endorsement contracts with McDonald's, Spanish-language TV network Telemundo, Fila, Fuji Photo Film USA, Chicago clothier Bigsby & Kruthers, a comic book company, Total Sports Concepts, a cereal called Slammin' Sammies from Famous Fixins', and sunglass marketer Native Eyewear.[20] Only a few exceptional celebrities such as Michael Jordan and Bill Cosby can get away with endorsing so many products. Advertisers hope Sammy Sosa's personality, likability, and high level of trustworthiness put him the same class with Cosby and Jordan.

Another problem associated with celebrity endorsements is credibility. Consumers know celebrities are paid, which detracts from their believability. If the celebrity endorses a number of products, consumer evaluations of that person's credibility declines further. Some advertising research indicates that when a celebrity endorses multiple products, it tends to reduce his or her credibility and likability as well as consumers' attitudes toward the ad.[21]

As a result, careful consideration must be given to the choice of a celebrity. The individual cannot simply be famous. The person should possess as many of the characteristics as possible, match the product or service being advertised, not be "spread too thin" or overexposed, and promote a positive image that can be transferred to the product, service, or company.

A *CEO* or other prominent corporate official may or may not possess the characteristics of attractiveness and likability. CEOs should, however, appear to be trustworthy, have expertise, and maintain a degree of credibility. A CEO is not a professional actor or model. Coming across well in a commercial may be difficult. It is important to build some type of angle to help the CEO succeed as a spokesperson. For example, some of Dave Thomas's loyal customers say he is physically attractive, certainly not in a sexy way but rather like a big teddy bear. When combined with the expertise to pitch new sandwiches, Thomas becomes a credible source, especially because Wendy's uses the right mix of humor in its ads.[22]

Companies must be aware of the trustworthiness issue. For example, many times the owner of a local auto dealership represents it as the spokesperson. The primary problem is that many consumers view used car salespeople as those who cannot be trusted. Other local business owners may be highly trustworthy, such as restaurant owners, physicians, eye care professionals, and so forth.

Advertising creatives and account executives should be careful about asking a CEO or business owner to serve as a source. They first must be convinced that the individual has enough key characteristics to promote the product and gain the consumer's interest and trust.

Experts, first and foremost, should be credible. The ad agency should seek out an expert who is also attractive, likable, and trustworthy. Experts are helpful in promoting health care products and complicated products that require explanations. In other situations, consumers will place a degree of trust in the company when purchasing the product or service recommended by an expert. An expert who is unattractive and dislikable cannot convince consumers that he or she can be trusted, and credibility drops as a result. Business-to-business ads often feature experts. The agency should be certain that an expert spokesperson has valid credentials and will be able to clearly explain a product or service's benefits. Then the source's trustworthiness and credibility rises.

Typical person ads are sometimes difficult to prepare, especially when they use real persons. First, typical-person sources do not have the name recognition of celebrities. Consequently, advertisers often use multiple sources within one advertisement to build credibility. Increasing the number of sources in the ad makes the ad more effective. Hearing three people talk about a good dentist is more believable than hearing it from only one person. By using multiple sources, viewers are motivated to pay attention to the ad and to process its arguments.[23]

Real person ads are a kind of two-edged sword. On the one hand, trustworthiness and credibility rise when the source is bald, overweight, or has some other physical imperfections. This can be especially valuable when the bald person promotes a hair replacement program or the overweight source talks about a diet pill. On the other hand, attractiveness and likability may be lower.

Using customers in ads can be difficult, because they will flub lines and look less natural on the screen. These difficulties with actual customers and employees lead many ad agencies to turn to professional models and actors portraying ordinary people. Professional actors make filming and photographing much easier. Also, the agency is in the position to choose a likable but plain person. The desired effects (trustworthiness and credibility) are often easier to create using professional actors and models.

In general, the ad agency should seek to be certain that the source or spokesperson has the major characteristics the ad needs. When the appeal is humor, likability is very important. In a rational or informational ad, expertise and credibility are crucial, especially in business-to-business ads. In each case, the goal is to try to find as many of the characteristics as possible when retaining a spokesperson.

Integrated Learning Experience

Michael Jordan, Dave Thomas, and Martha Stewart are well-known celebrities. What impact does Michael Jordan have on the success of his cologne (www.mjcologne.com) and his automobile dealership (www.michaeljordanlincoln.com)? To find out about Dave Thomas, go to (www.wendys.com), and look at the "Meet Dave" section. For Martha Stewart, access www.marthastewart.com.

creating an advertisement

Figure 10.5 illustrates the process a typical creative uses in preparing an advertisement. The process begins with the creative brief, which outlines the message theme of the advertisement as well as other pertinent information. Using the creative brief as the blueprint, the creative develops a means–ends chain, starting with an attribute of the product that generates a specific customer benefit and eventually produces a desirable end state. This means–end chain is the foundation on which all of the decisions will be made.

Following the development of the means–end chain, the creative chooses a message strategy, the appeal, and the executional framework. He or she also decides about a source or spokesperson at this point, because the choice usually affects other creative decisions. Selection of the leverage point is usually done after the creative begins work on the advertisement. The leverage point takes the consumer from the product attribute or customer benefit to the desired end state. The type of leverage point used depends on the message strategy, appeal, and executional framework.

Although certain combinations tend to work well together, the creative has an almost infinite number of ways of preparing an advertisement or campaign. For example, if the creative wants to use a cognitive message strategy, the most logical appeal is rationality. The creative, however, can use fear, humor, sex, music, or scarcity. The one appeal that would not work as well is emotions. It can be used, but the emotional part of the advertisement can overpower the cognitive message the creative is trying to send to the viewer. If the creative decides to use a humor approach with a cognitive strategy, other logical and illogical combinations emerge. In terms of the executional framework, dramatization and authoritative tend not to work as well with humor. Any of the other executional frameworks are suitable.

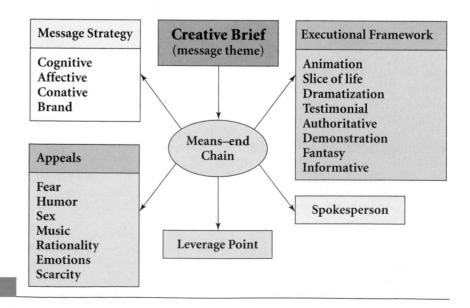

Creating an Advertisement

FIGURE 10.5

This flexibility allows an almost infinite number of advertisements to be possible from a single means—end chain. The combination to use depends on the creative's expertise and experience as well as the creative's opinion about the best way to accomplish the client's advertising objectives.

Integrated Learning Experience

Creating an award-winning advertisement requires skill and knowledge about both advertising and the marketplace. Access DDB Needham Agency at www.ddbn.com, and find the "Work" section. Examine its winning works under "Recognition," along with other advertisements it has produced. Pay close attention to the "State of the Art" section concerning the methods used to create advertisements.

advertising effectiveness

Producing effective ads requires the joint efforts of the account executive, creative, media planner, and media buyer. Working independently can produce some award-winning ads, but often they will not be effective ads that meet a client's objectives. One major problem ad agencies face is producing a commercial to stand out among the thousands of existing ads. If an agency can break through the clutter, half of the battle is won. All that remains is for consumers or businesses to react to the ad in the appropriate manner.

To be effective means creating an ad that accomplishes the objectives desired by clients. The task of making sure the ad meets the IMC objectives requires that creatives and account executives follow the six basic principles described in greater detail next (see Figure 10.6).

The first principle is to maintain **visual consistency.** Seeing a specific image or visual display over and over again helps embed it in long-term memory. Visual consistency is important because consumers, whether individual consumers or members of a business buying center, spend very little time viewing or listening to an advertisement. In most cases, it is just a casual glance at a print advertisement or a cursory glimpse at a television ad. Visual consistency causes the viewer to move the advertising message from short-term memory to long-term memory. Consistently used logos and other long-standing images help fix the brand or company in the consumer's mind. For example, people remember Frosted Flakes because of the visually consistent use of Tony the Tiger. They know Green Giant products by their cartoon spokesperson. Logos such as the Nike swoosh and the Prudential Rock emblem are well established in the minds of many consumers.

The second principle of effective advertising is concerned with *campaign duration.* Consumers do not pay attention to advertisements. This means the length or duration of a campaign is important. Using the same advertisement over an appropriate period of time helps embed the message in long-term memory. Account executives should give careful thought to how long to use an advertisement. The ad

▶ **Visual consistency**

▶ **Campaign duration**

▶ **Repeated tag lines**

▶ **Consistent positioning**

▶ **Simplicity**

▶ **Identifiable selling point**

Principles of Effective Advertising

FIGURE 10.6

> ▶ It's everywhere you want to be.
> ▶ Are you feeling it?
> ▶ Just do it.
> ▶ You're in good hands.
> ▶ The brushing that works between brushings.
> ▶ Driving excitement.
> ▶ A different kind of company. A different kind of car.
> ▶ When you care enough to send the very best.
> ▶ The ultimate driving machine.
> ▶ It takes a licking and keep on ticking.

Which tag lines can you identify?

FIGURE 10.7

Answers: VISA, Reebok, Nike, Allstate, Colgate, Pontiac, Saturn, Hallmark, BMW, Timex.

should be changed before it becomes stale and viewers become bored with it; however, changing ads too frequently impedes the retention process. Reach and frequency affect the duration of a campaign. Higher frequency usually leads to a shorter duration. Low reach may be associated with a longer duration. In any case, typical campaigns last one to two months, but there are exceptions. Marlboro and Camel still use the same visual imagery and have never changed their basic advertisements, but these are rare cases.

The third method used to build effective advertising campaigns is *repeated tag lines.* Visual consistency combined with consistent tag lines can be a more powerful approach. The advertisement can change, but either the visual imagery or the tag line remains the same. The U.S. Army has promoted the tag line "Be all that you can be" for many years, and the Marines are known as "The few. The proud. The Marines." Tag lines help consumers tie the advertisement into current knowledge structure nodes already in their minds. Figure 10.7 contains some of the more common tag lines. See how many you can identify.

A fourth advertising principle is *consistent positioning.* Maintaining a consistent positioning throughout a product's life makes it easier for consumers to place the product in a cognitive map. When the firm emphasizes quality in every ad, it becomes easier to tie the product into the consumer's cognitive map than if the firm stresses quality in some ads, price in others, and convenience in a third campaign. This inconsistency in positioning makes the brand and company appear more confused and harder to remember. The Smith Barney tag line, "We make money the old fashioned way, we earn it!" has been the company's consistent rallying point and position for many years. People easily recall the firm's name as a result.

Simplicity is the fifth principle of effective advertising. Simple advertisements are easier to comprehend than are complex ads. A print ad with a simple tag line and limited copy is much easier to read than an overloaded or complex one. Consequently, advertisers must resist the temptation to relate all of a product's attributes in a single advertisement. This practice is more prevalent in business-to-business print advertisements and should be avoided there as well. Further, consumer ads on radio or television spots often are so verbally overloaded that the announcer is forced to talk faster. This is usually ineffective, because the listener has too much information to grasp in such a short time period.

The principle of simplicity should be applied more carefully to Internet advertising. The primary reason for simplicity with the Internet is load time. Individuals surfing the Internet will not wait more than a few seconds for something to load; if it doesn't load quickly, they move on to another site.

The final principle of effective advertising is the concept of an *identifiable sell ing point.* The emphasis should be placed on all three of the words: (1) identifiable, (2) selling, and (3) point. The advertisement should have a selling point (price, quality, convenience, luxury, etc.) that is easily identifiable to the viewer of the ad. For example, the selling point of a Priceline.com ad is lower airfares. Radio listeners immediately know the focus point of these ads. Remember, the concept is a selling point, not selling *points.* The best advertisements are those that emphasize one major point and do not confuse the viewer by trying to present too many ideas. An advertisement's primary goal is to fix the product into the cognitive map of the viewer through establishing new linkages or strengthening current linkages. An identifiable selling point helps reach that goal.

Beating Ad Clutter

As noted at the start of this section, overcoming clutter is the first step in creating an effective advertising campaign. The presence of a competitor's ad within the same medium or time spot makes the ad clutter problem worse. A recent survey of television advertising revealed that during prime-time programming, 42 percent of the ads shown had one or more of their competitors also advertising during the same hour. Research suggests that the effectiveness of an advertisement is significantly reduced when a competitor advertisement was also shown during the same time slot.[24]

One method advertisers use to overcome this brand interference is repetition. Repeating an ad can increase brand and ad recall. In advertising studies, this repetition is effective in increasing recall if no competitor ads are present. When competitor ads are present, repetition does not help the competitive ad interference problem and does not stimulate greater recall.

Because mere repetition of an ad does not always work, advertisers have begun to take advantage of the principles found in **variability theory**.[25] In this theory, variable encoding occurs when a consumer sees the same advertisement in different environments. These varied environments increase an ad's recall and effectiveness, by encoding it into the brain through various methods. Creatives can generate this effect by varying the situational context of a particular ad. For example, the MasterCard campaign noted previously uses various settings to convey the same basic message, "There are some things money can't buy. For everything else, there's MasterCard." Varying the context of the ad increases recall. This is a very effective method to overcome competitive ad interference.[26]

Another method designed to decrease the negative impact of competing ads is to use a second medium. Using two media to convey a message generally is more effective than repeating an advertisement within the same medium. Using more than one medium also reduces competing ad interference. An ad that appears on television and in magazines works better than one that appears only on television. Consumers seeing an advertisement in a different medium are more likely to encode the ad than if it is always seen in only one medium.

Clutter remains a difficult problem in advertising. Creatives who are able to capture the attention of the audience and transmit messages successfully are in great demand. Companies constantly experiment with various approaches to reach the audience. When the program works, the advertising firm and its client have a great deal to celebrate.

Integrated Learning Experience

At www.zeldman.com is the "Ad Graveyard." This site contains real ads that did not run. Go to this site. Based on the principles you learned in Chapters 9 and 10, identify what is wrong with the ads. What could be done to turn the buried ad into a usable one? Compare these ads to those you observed at www.adsGallery.com and www.televisioncommericals.com.

stop!

implications for **marketing professionals**

Marketing managers must know how to stay out of the way and when to intervene in the creative process. This includes

1. Giving advice and opinions to creatives as needed
2. Waiting until the creative feels the ad is ready for review before passing judgment

Stay in careful contact with clients as the advertising design process goes forward.

Avoid being "starstruck" when considering celebrity endorsers. Think about the bottom line and whether the personality has the characteristics needed to make effective commercials.

Help your clients avoid being starstruck as they encounter potential endorsers.

Learn tactful methods to inform a CEO that he or she is not the right person to be an ad spokesperson.

Set reasonable budgets for advertising projects, and stay within those budgets.

The marketing manager should let everyone know the buck does stop at his or her desk. Final decisions about ads should account for all of the principles described in this chapter, especially noting the importance of maintaining the overall IMC theme.

Be accountable when things do work out. Share credit with the entire team when they do. Remember, advertising is not about building your ego; it's about creating successes for other people, and you can't do that by yourself.

SUMMARY

Advertising is the process of transmitting a personal message across one or more impersonal media. The message should reflect the image which occurs throughout an IMC program. Four types of message strategies are present in advertisements. Cognitive strategies emphasize rational and logical arguments to compel consumers to make purchases. Affective strategies are oriented toward buyer emotions and feelings. Conative strategies are linked to more direct responses, behaviors, and actions. Brand strategies are designed to strengthen the image of the firm or brand. These strategies should be integrated with various types of appeals through the media selected for the campaign.

Executional frameworks tell the story in the ad. Animation has become more sophisticated and provides many new creative approaches in the design of ads. The slice-of-life approach and dramatizations are problem-solving types of ads, leading the consumer to something better by using the product. Testimonials are rendered by individuals who have realized the benefits of a product. An authoritative expert can build consumer confidence in a product or company.

Demonstrations show how products can be used. A fantasy takes people away from the real world to a make-believe place. This makes the product more exotic and desirable. Informative ads render basic information about the product. Each can be used effectively to persuade consumers and business-to-business buyers to consider a company's offerings.

Celebrities, CEOs, experts, and typical persons can be chosen to be "out front" in the advertisement. Each has advantages and disadvantages. The marketing team selects sources or spokespersons based on the individual's attractiveness, likability, trustworthiness, expertise, or credibility. The more of these characteristics that are present, the better off the advertiser will be.

Effective ad campaigns are based on the six principles of visual consistency, a sufficient campaign duration, repeated tag lines, consistent positioning, simplicity, and presenting an identifiable selling point. Creatives and account executives must incorporate these principles into the advertising campaign to enhance the odds of success. Also, clutter must be overcome by repeating ads and showing them in various media, or in some other way.

Dooigning ads is often considered the most glamorous part of the advertising industry, and it is in many ways. Remember, however, that the other side of the glamour coin is hard work and the constant pressure to perform. Many people think being a creative is a burnout-type of job. At the same time, those who have proven track records of success are well rewarded for their efforts. Utilizing the principles presented in this section can be key to success in the highly competitive and exciting business of advertising design.

REVIEW QUESTIONS

1. Name the four types of message strategies creatives can use. How are message strategies related to the message theme?

2. What types of products or services best match cognitive message strategies? Name the five types of cognitive approaches.

3. When will an affective message strategy be most effective? What two types of affective messages can creatives design? Give an example of each.

4. What is the primary goal of a conative message strategy?

5. What does a brand message strategy emphasize? Describe the four forms of brand strategies.

6. How is an executional framework different from an ad appeal? How are they related?

7. List as many uses of animation-based advertisements as possible. What forms of animation are possible with the available technology?

8. How are slice-of-life and dramatization executional frameworks similar? How are they different?

9. How are authoritative and informational executional frameworks similar? How are they different?

10. What types of testimonials can advertisers use? Give an example of each.

11. Which media are best for demonstration-type ads?

12. What kinds of products or services are best suited to fantasy-based executional frameworks? What products or services are poor candidates for fantasies?

13. Name the four main types of sources or spokespersons. What are the advantages and disadvantages of each?

14. Name the five key criteria used when selecting a spokesperson. Which four build to the fifth?

15. Name the tactics available to overcome clutter. How does variability theory assist in this process?

KEY TERMS

message theme   the outline of the key idea(s) that the advertising program is supposed to convey.

message strategy   the primary tactic used to deliver the message theme.

cognitive message strategy   the presentation of rational arguments or pieces of information to consumers.

generic messages   direct promotions of product or service attributes or benefits without any claim of superiority.

preemptive messages   claims of superiority based on a specific attribute or benefit of a product that prempts the competition from making the same claim.

unique selling proposition   an explicit, testable claim of uniqueness or superiority that can be supported or substantiated in some manner.

hyperbole   making an untestable claim based upon some attribute or benefit.

comparative advertisements   the direct or indirect comparison of a product or service to the competition.

affective message strategies   ads designed to invoke feelings and emotions and match them with the product, service, or company.

resonance advertising   attempting to connect a product with a consumer's experiences to develop stronger ties between the product and the consumer.

emotional advertising   attempting to elicit powerful emotions that eventually lead to product recall and choice.

action-inducing conative ads   creating situations in which cognitive knowledge of the product or affective liking of the product follow the actual purchase or arise during usage of the product.

promotional support conative advertisements   ads designed to support other promotional efforts.

brand message strategies   ad messages designed to build or enhance the brand or corporate name in some way.

brand user strategies   focus on the type of individuals that use a particular brand.

brand image strategies working toward the development of a brand "personality."

brand usage messages stressing the different uses for a particular brand.

corporate advertising promoting the corporate name and image rather than the individual brand.

executional framework the manner in which an ad appeal is presented.

expert authority when an advertiser seeks to convince viewers that a given product is superior to other brands.

sources and spokespersons persons in the advertisement who make the actual presentation.

visual consistency occurs when consumers see a specific image or visual display over and over again.

variability theory a theory stating that when a consumer sees the same advertisement in different environments, the ad will be more effective.

ENDNOTES

1. David Aaker and Donald Norris, "Characteristics of TV Commercials Perceived as Informative," *Journal of Advertising Research,* 22, no. 2 (1982), pp. 61–70; Henry A. Laskey, Ellen Day, and Melvin R. Crask, "Typology of Main Message Strategies for Television Commercials," *Journal of Advertising,* 18, no. 1 (1989), pp. 36–41.

2. Bradley Johnson, "IBM Moves Back to Intel Co-op Deal," *Advertising Age* 68, no. 10 (March 10, 1997), p. 4.

3. Dhruv Grewal and Sukumar Kavanoor, "Comparative Versus Noncomparative Advertising: A Meta-Analysis," *Journal of Marketing,* 61, no. 4 (October 1997), pp. 1–15; Mark Dolliver, "So, If You Can't Say Something Nice. . .," *Adweek, Eastern Edition,* 39, no. 14 (April 6, 1998), p. 21.

4. Jean Halliday, "Survey: Comparative Ads Can Dent Car's Credibility," *Advertising Age,* 69, no. 18 (May 4, 1998), p. 26.

5. Naveen Donthu, "A Cross-Country Investigation of Recall of and Attitudes Toward Comparative Advertising," *Journal of Advertising,* 27, no. 2 (summer 1998), pp. 111–21.

6. Grewal and Kavanoor, "Comparative Versus Noncomparative Advertising: A Meta-Analysis"; "Bring Back Brand X," *Advertising Age,* 70, no. 46, (November 8, 1999), p. 60.

7. Karalynn Ott, "B-to-B Marketers Display Their Creative Side," *Advertising Age's Business Marketing,* 84, no. 1 (January 1999), pp. 3–4.

8. Karen Heller, "Responsible Care—Public Outreach: The Stakes Are High," *Chemical Week,* 148, no. 26 (July 17, 1991), pp. 81–84.

9. Barth, "Aargh! Animation Noses into Contract," *Orlando Business Journal,* 16, no. 18 (October 1, 1999), p. 5.

10. Halliday, "Survey: Comparative Ads Can Dent Car's Credibility."

11. Michael L. Maynard, "Slice-of-Life: A Persuasive Mini Drama in Japanese Television Advertising," *Journal of Popular Culture,* 31, no. 2 (fall 1997), pp. 131–42.

12. Ibid.

13. Hillary Chura, "Maytag Airs Epic Drama for $35 Mil Range Intro," *Advertising Age,* 70, no. 28 (July 5, 1999), p. 4.

14. Based on Ronald D. Reinartz, "Testimonial Ads Win Loyalty and Attract Customers," *Bank Marketing,* 28, no. 3 (March 1996), pp. 25–29.

15. J. Levine, "Fantasy, Not Flesh," *Forbes,* 145, no. 2 (January 22, 1990), pp. 3–5.

16. Mark Dolliver, "Sol Lingerie," *Adweek, Western Edition,* 49, no. 39 (September 27, 1999), p. 28.

17. Sam Bradley, "Marketers Are Always Looking for Good Pitchers," *Brandweek,* 37, no. 9 (February 26, 1996), pp. 36–37.

18. Claire Murphy, "Stars Brought Down to Earth in TV Ads Research," *Marketing* (January 22, 1998), p. 1.

19. Roobina Ohanian, "Construction and Validation of a Scale to Measure Celebrity Endorsers' Perceived Expertise," *Journal of Advertising,* 19, no. 3 (1990), pp. 39–52.

20. Wayne Friedman, "Home Runs Kings Still, but Not with Ad Deals," *Advertising Age,* 70, no. 28 (July 5, 1999), pp. 3–4.

21. Carolyn Tripp, Thomas D. Jensen, and Les Carlson, "The Effects of Multiple Product Endorsements by Celebrities on Consumers' Attitudes and Intentions," *Journal of Consumer Research,* 20 (March 1994), pp. 535–47.

22. Cebrzynski, "Dave Thomas: Not Exactly a Sex Symbol, but He Knows How to Sell a Burger," *Nations Restaurant News,* 33, no. 36 (September 6, 1999), p. 14.

23. David J. Moore and John C. Mowen, "Multiple Sources in Advertising Appeals: When Product Endorsers Are Paid by the Advertising Sponsor," *Journal of Academy of Marketing Science,* 22, no. 3 (summer 1994), pp. 234–43.

24. Raymond R. Burke and Thomas K. Srull, "Competitive Interference and Consumer Memory for Advertising," *Journal of Consumer Research,* 15 (June 1988), pp. 55–68.

25. A. W. Melton, "The Situation with Respect to the Spacing of Repetitions and Memory," *Journal of Verbal Learning and Verbal Behavior,* 9 (1970), pp. 596–606.

26. H. Rao Unnava and Deepak Sirdeshmukh, "Reducing Competitive Ad Interference," *Journal of Marketing Research,* 31, no. 3 (August 1994), pp. 403–11.

27. Grewal and Kavanoor, "Comparative Versus Noncomparative Advertising: A Meta-Analysis."

Building an IMC Campaign

Selecting an Executional Framework for an IMC Advertising Campaign

Finally, you are ready to prepare the actual ad. To complete the task, think about the various message strategies to employ, including cognitive, affective, conative, and brand strategies. You also need to decide on an executional framework format, such as animation, slice of life, testimonial, dramatization, or one of the others. Another significant ingredient in your campaign's success level is your choice of a spokesperson. Visit the Prentice-Hall Web site at www.prenhall.com/clow or access the Advertising Plan Pro disk that accompanied this textbook to complete this final stage of your IMC plan. The exercise for this chapter leads you through these decisions. At the end, you need to design and execute the ad for your product. If this is done correctly, the ad will reflect the IMC theme and all of the other components of the IMC program you have completed up to this point.

Critical Thinking Exercises

Discussion Questions

1. Mark 10 advertisements in a magazine. Identify the message strategy, appeal, and executional framework each uses. Did the creative select the right combination for the advertisement? What other message strategies or executional frameworks could have been used?

2. Record 10 television advertisements on videotape. Identify the message strategy, appeal, and executional framework each uses. Did the creative select the right combination for the advertisement? What other message strategies or executional frameworks could have been used?

3. Studies involving comparative advertisements as compared to noncomparative ads produced the following findings.[27] Discuss why you think each statement is true. Try to think of comparative ads you have seen that substantiate these claims.

   a. Message awareness was higher for comparative ads than for noncomparative ads it the brands are already established brands.

   b. Brand recall was higher for comparative ads than for noncomparative ads.

   c. Comparative ads were viewed as less believable than noncomparative ads.

   d. Attitudes toward comparative ads were more negative than toward noncomparative ads.

4. Suppose Charles Schwab wants to develop an advertisement with the message theme that Charles Schwab understands the needs of individual consumers and can design an investment strategy to meet each person's particular needs. Which type of message strategy should Schwab choose? Why? Based on the message strategy chosen, which executional framework should the company use? Why? What type of source or spokesperson should Schwab use? Why? Would the type of media being used for the advertisement affect the message strategy choice? Explain your answer.

5. A resort in Florida wants to develop an advertisement highlighting scuba diving classes. Pick one of the following combinations of message strategy, appeal, and executional framework. Then design an advertisement using those components.

   a. Hyperbole cognitive message strategy, humor appeal, and demonstration.

   b. Emotional message strategy, emotional appeal, and slice of life.

c. Conative message strategy, scarcity appeal, and informative.

d. Emotional or resonance message strategy, sex appeal, and fantasy.

e. Comparative message strategy, fear appeal, and a testimonial.

6. For each of the following executional frameworks, identify a commercial that uses it. Evaluate the advertisement in terms of how well it is executed. Also, did the appeal and message strategy fit well with the executional framework? Discuss why you remember the advertisement. What makes it memorable?

a. Animation

b. Slice of life

c. Dramatization

d. Testimonial

e. Authoritative

f. Demonstration

g. Fantasy

h. Informative

7. Name three influential commercial spokespersons. For each one, discuss the five characteristics to use to evaluate spokespersons. Next, make a list of three individuals who are poor spokespersons. Discuss each of the five evaluation characteristics for each of these individuals. What differences exist between an effective and a poor spokesperson?

8. Find a copy of a business journal such as *Business Week* or *Fortune,* or a trade journal. Also locate a copy of a consumer journal such as *Glamour, Time, Sports Illustrated,* or a specialty magazine. Look through an entire issue. What differences between the advertisements in the business journal and consumer journals are readily noticeable? For each of the concepts that follow, discuss specific differences you noted between the two types of magazines. Explain why the differences exist.

a. Message strategies

b. Executional frameworks

c. Sources and spokespersons

9. Access the following Web sites. For each one, identify the primary message strategy it uses. What executional framework does it use? Does it use any sources or spokespersons? What type of appeal does it use? For each Web site, suggest how the site could be improved by changing either the message strategy or the executional framework or both. Be specific. Explain how the change would improve the site.

a. Georgia Pacific (www.gp.com)

b. Playland International (www.playland-inc.com)

c. MGM Grand (www.mgmgrand.com)

d. The Exotic Body (www.exoticbody.com)

e. Cover Girl (www.covergirl.com)

f. American Supercamps (www.americansupercamp.com)

g. Windmill Hill Place (www.windmillhill.co.uk)

Charitable Competition

John Mulvaney was placed in charge of his company's newest account, the United Way Charities of Savannah, Georgia. This branch of the United Way had never retained the services of an advertising agency, but had gotten caught in the crush of competitive problems in the past decade. Consequently, the organization decided it was necessary to prepare more professional advertisements in order to succeed in the new millennium.

At the first meeting with the organization's leaders, John discovered a world of competition he had never envisioned. First of all, the number of charities competing for contributions had grown exponentially in the past decade. Churches, illnesses, women's shelters, homeless shelters, performing arts facilities (art galleries and community theaters), veterans groups, colleges and universities, minority organizations, Girl Scouts, Boy Scouts, and dozens of other charities were in the marketplace for charitable dollars. Illnesses alone included heart disease, lung disease, AIDS, MD (Jerry Lewis telethon), blindness, and many others. Organizations representing these causes contact small and large donors alike.

Second, bad publicity had tainted the entire industry. Church scams combined with spending abuses by leaders of other charities created a negative impact. Many people believe charities simply fund themselves, with very few of the dollars actually reaching people in need. As a result, contributions declined.

Third, a booming economy had created an odd effect. On the one hand, the number of extremely rich people had grown, especially those associated with Silicon Valley. Many of these individuals were actually trying to be effective altruists. Unfortunately, far too many of these givers wanted to see their names on buildings rather than simply making contributions to operating budgets. Also, prosperity (lower unemployment, fewer people in poverty) has created a kind of complacency in which many regular givers have begun to assume there was simply less need for charity.

The United Way received major support from the NFL for over two decades. Visibility was high, and the organization had a solid base of donations. The goal was to build on this base and combat the problems that had grown. John contacted his best creative, Tom Prasch, to see what could be done.

Tom argued that the primary problem with United Way ads was that they were boring. They typically showed a football player visiting a sick child or shaking hands with some community leader. Viewers could tune them out easily. Tom said the United Way needed something that would recapture the attention of John Q. Public. Tom told John and the United Way that he believed strongly in the use of seven attention-getting factors:

1. Intensity
2. Size
3. Contrast
4. Repetition
5. Motion
6. Novelty
7. Familiarity

Intensity means that bright, loud, strong stimuli capture the attention of the audience. A large-size billboard or full-page newspaper ad is more likely to be noticed than something normal or small. Contrast is the difference between dark and light or loud and soft. Repetition means something repeated has attention-getting value. Motion captures attention, even in print ads where the illusion of movement can be created. Novelty occurs when someone encounters a novel stimulus in a familiar setting (a new piece of furniture in a living room will be immediately noticed). Familiarity means finding something familiar in an unfamiliar setting such as seeing the Golden Arches in a foreign country.

Tom suggested that United Way had only one solid attention-getting factor: its logo. It was highly recognizable from being repeated for so many years. None of the other factors were featured in the ads.

John gave the United Way a major discount in billing for services. He also constructed a very conservative budget. The group agreed that any endorser must volunteer his or her time in order to serve. Then, they turned Tom loose to create a new local campaign.

1. Design a campaign for the United Way of Savannah. Use Tom's attention-getting factors to create the ads.
2. Which media should the United Way use? Why?
3. What kind of message strategy would be best? Why?
4. What kind of executional framework should be used? Why?
5. What kind of source or spokesperson is best for this campaign? Defend your choice.

Kid's Palace

APPLICATION EXERCISE II

Pam Burns loved kids. She had raised three of her own and now had two grandchildren. With an "empty nest" about to emerge, Pam decided it was time to put the two main loves of her life, kids and free enterprise, into one package. With the help of her husband and investment capital from her personal savings and the adventuresome spirit of a few friends, Pam purchased an old building near the largest outdoor mall in Memphis, Tennessee. There she created her new business, Kid's Palace.

Kid's Palace provided a variety of fun activities. Playrooms filled with plastic balls, tunnels, jungle gyms, a video arcade, plus other toys and games were inside. Also, there were tables and chairs set in a crafts area. At one end of the building a snack bar carried not only traditional junk food but also healthier treats such as milk, orange juice, fruit bars, cheese, and crackers.

Pam designed Kid's Palace to be a place children could go to play while under the supervision of several college-age students. Parents could leave older children, and younger children had areas with tables, chairs, and age-appropriate activities, so that parents could watch them in a comfortable setting and socialize with other adults at the same time.

Pam's snack bar area had a section dedicated especially to birthday parties. Parents could bring their own cakes, and Kid's Palace provided plates and plastic forks. The student helpers assisted at the parties. Video screens in the snack bar area ran cartoons and other children's program continuously. Music played in the rest of Kid's Palace at a low volume.

Repeat business was Pam's primary marketing goal. She hoped to entice adults to bring kids to her indoor park and conclude it was a great alternative form of entertainment. Troublemakers and other problem children were quickly escorted out of the building, given a refund, and told they could come back only if they behaved.

Pam went to a local advertising agency seeking advice on the kinds of ads she could run for her new business. She had budgeted enough to support a fairly strong television and radio campaign. She also considered mailing coupons to parents or giving them away at PTA meetings.

The remaining questions were

Should she advertise to parents or to children?

What kind of message should Kid's Palace send?

After a long visit with the agency, the campaign was ready. Pam hoped to have a long and prosperous run providing an alternative form of fun, so that young people could do more than stay home, watch television, and play video games.

1. What kind of message strategy, leverage point, and executional framework should the ads for Kid's Palace provide?
2. What kind of spokesperson or source should Kid's Palace use in its advertisement?
3. Apply the principles of effective advertising to ads for Kid's Palace.
4. Design a print or television advertisement for Kid's Palace.

› **Trade Promotions**

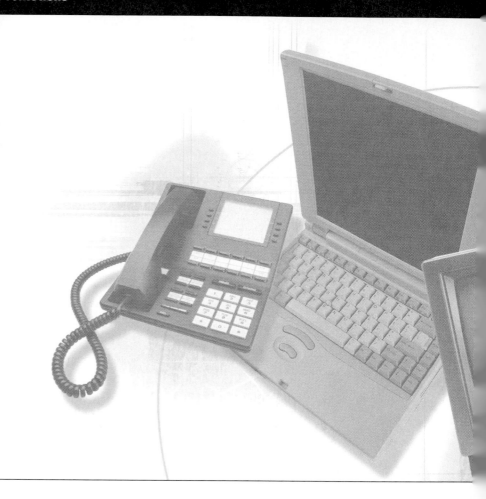

▶ **MARKETING COMMUNICATIONS SKILLS TO LEARN IN THIS CHAPTER**

Recognize the important relationship between advertising programs and the other parts of the promotions mix.

Understand the difference between trade promotions and consumer or sales promotions, and when to use each tool.

Become aware of how trade promotions tools build strong ties with other members of the marketing channel (retailers, wholesalers, distributors, etc.).

Know when and how to use each of the major trade promotions tools.

Overcome the barriers and obstacles to effective use of trade promotions.

WHAT'S GOOD FOR WAL-MART, IS GOOD FOR AMERICA?

It wasn't that many years ago when a prominent citizen proclaimed, "What's good for General Motors is good for America." The quote inspired considerable debate as to what constitutes "good." The domination of the Big Three (Ford, Chrysler, General Motors) in the auto industry was viewed as beneficial by some and essentially an unfair oligopoly by others.

Currently, another version of the Big Three exists, this time in retail. Wal-Mart, Kmart, and Target are dominant forces in the retail industry. These and other megafirms have changed the structures of many marketing programs.

chapter**eleven**

Previously, a series of Mom and Pop–type operations created opportunities for small manufacturers to gain an entryway into retail markets. Now, with so many customers using one-stop shopping, the entire retail game has changed.

First, in many small communities, a number of retail stores have simply been pushed out of business. Many small bookstores, drugstores, and other local entrepreneurial operations simply cannot compete with megastores. As a result, manufacturers and distributors direct less attention to those that remain, instead seeking to capture the "big prize" of a mega-store's account.

Second, megastores offer megadiscounts. Manufacturers are being forced to grant major discounts to these large chains to keep their items on the shelves. Among other things, this creates huge barriers to entry for smaller companies trying to sell to the megagiants, because they simply cannot afford the same price cuts.

Capturing key shelf space on a megastore's main aisle is a major victory for a manufacturer. Each season the process begins again as various companies try to garner favor from large retail outlets. For example, one major new campaign program is found in the back-to-school season (August and September). Everyone from lunch box manufacturers to food suppliers has been forced to adjust to the needs of the megastore.

In one recent back-to-school season, the Kellogg's company created Snack Pack cereals, Kraft made Stove Top meal kits for kids, Quaker prepared Instant Oatmeal Dinosaur Eggs, and Nabisco introduced its Tiger Toys and Snacks line. Each was trying to maintain shelf space in the larger retail operations. Contests, promotions, cooperative advertising programs (shared ad costs between the manufacturer and the retailer), and other incentives were a major part of the plan.

Besides these new products, other companies tried to keep favor with the Big Three through different programs. Dannon Natural Spring Water tried a tie-in with the National PTA program. Campbell's created a Labels for Education Program, and Kraft created a Nickel-O-Zone promotion as a tie-in with Nickelodeon's programming. Each company sought to create attention for its products that would drive the retailers to display its products prominently in key areas of the store.

At the same time, retailers continue to flex their marketing muscles, asking mostly for price discounts rather than other gimmicks. Stores set up in-house displays featuring their own favored products, and the manufacturer can do little to change this policy.

Whether or not large-scale megaretailers are good for the nation's economy remains a major debate. Many smaller community leaders have become frustrated by the negative effects a Wal-Mart or Kmart can cause, because entrepreneurial jobs are lost in favor of shelf stocker/checkout counter positions with lower pay. Regardless of how the trend plays out, it is clear that manufacturers, wholesalers, and distributors must pay careful attention to the role megastores play in the futures of these companies. Incentives and promotions should remain one key element in the process.[1]

overview

Marketing goods and services can seem like a bold and exciting process at times. Creating television advertisements, Internet Web sites, radio spots, and other marketing efforts are attractive to many people interested in highly visible marketing careers. At the same time, however, it is important to remember that effective integrated advertising and *marketing* communications programs include both visible and subtle ingredients. And sometimes, those more subtle elements actually end up enticing the customer to make the purchase. In fact, about 75 percent of all promotional dollars are spent on things other than advertising.

This section explores the other parts of an IMC program. As shown in Figure 11.1, these critical components add significantly to the impact of any IMC effort, especially when they are executed correctly. When the marketing team fails to incorporate the other parts of the promotions mix into the IMC plan, it is incomplete and the odds of success are diminished.

A successful IMC program builds on the foundations established earlier. Consumer markets are defined, business-to-business customers are identified, and various buyer behaviors are studied. Next, advertising campaigns are formulated to reach all key customers. Then trade promotions and the others parts of the promotions mix can be structured to enhance the IMC message and lead to the final purchase decision.

Many marketing account executives recognize the major role the promotions mix plays in portraying the firm's clear voice and message. As noted in Chapter 1, there are four components to the promotions mix:

1. Advertising
2. Trade promotions
3. Sales promotions
4. Personal selling and sales management

Promotional Mix

Ch. 1, 2   Level 1
**Integrated Marketing
  Communications
Ethics and Social Responsibility
  in Marketing Communications**

Ch. 3–6   Level 2
**Promotion Opportunity
  Analysis
Brand and Firm Image
  Management
Consumer Buyer Behavior
Business-to-Business Buyer
  Behavior**

Ch. 7–10   Level 3
**Advertising Management
Advertising Media Selection
Advertising Design: Appeals
Advertising Design: Executional
  Frameworks**

Marketing Plan

Level 4

Level 5

Ch. 11–13
**Trade Promotions
Consumer Promotions
Personal Selling and
  Sales Management**

Ch. 14–17
**Public Relations and
  Sponsorship Programs
Database Programs
Internet Marketing
Evaluation an Integrated
  Marketing Program**

**An Integrated
Marketing
Communications Plan**

FIGURE 11.1

The previous section of this text dealt with the first component in the mix: advertising. This section is devoted to the final three. First, in this chapter, trade promotions are described, with the other elements presented in Chapters 12 and 13.

When the promotions mix is truly integrated, the company's internal and external publics both speak with the same voice. Employees know what the organization tries to achieve with its marketing program, the advertising agency designs messages that portray the company speaking with one clear voice, and individual customers as well as business buyers are aware of the company's products and services. This, in turn, bodes well for the future of the firm.

the nature of trade promotions

Trade promotions are the expenditures or incentives used by manufacturers and other members of the marketing channel to help push their products through to retailers. The best way to understand trade promotions is to note that they are incentives that members of the trade channel use to entice another member to *purchase goods for eventual resale.* In other words, trade promotions are aimed at retailers, distributors, wholesalers, brokers, or agents. A manufacturer can use trade promotions to convince another member of the trade channel to carry its goods. Wholesalers, distributors, brokers, and agents can use trade promotions to entice retailers to purchase products for eventual resale.

The difference between trade promotions and consumer or sales promotions is that the latter involves a sale to an *end user or customer.* When a manufacturer sells products to another business for end use, the enticements involved are consumer or sales promotions tools. On the other hand, when a manufacturer sells to another business for the purpose of having the good resold, then trade promotions tools are being used.

The role played by trade promotions is to build strong relations with other members in the channel. When a retailer stocks the merchandise a manufacturer promotes, consumers have the opportunity to buy the product. The same is true for distributors, wholesalers, brokers, or agents. If they carry the product, they help push it down to retailers.

According to Ernst & Young, between 7 percent and 10 percent of sales revenues received from all branded goods are spent on trade promotions. In other words, for every dollar of sales, seven to ten cents has been spent on trade promotions.[2]

In marketing consumer goods, the same survey indicates that the amount spent on trade promotions has grown from 38 percent of total promotional expenditures in the 1980s to approximately 50 percent today. Although it is difficult to estimate the exact amount spent on trade promotions, there is no doubt manufacturers devote more money to trade promotions than to any other promotional tool. Many manufacturers would like to reduce these expenditures or cut them out entirely. What they find, however, is a situation in which they can do neither because of resistance from retailers, directions from their own sales managers, the effects on profits, and pressures from their competitors that still offer trade promotions.

To be effective, trade promotions should be an integral part of the IMC program. Unfortunately, in most companies, the individual handling trade promotions is not involved in the IMC planning process. These companies often view trade promotions as being merely a means for getting products onto retail shelves or satisfying some channel member's request. To satisfy the administration's demand to increase sales, trade managers often feel greater and greater pressure to use trade promotions to push their products. Little consideration is given to the other components of the IMC program when trade promotions programs are developed.

To solve this problem, the marketing executive must explain the benefits of a systematic approach to all parts of the marketing mix to company leaders. Tie-ins between ad campaigns and trade promotions programs can help companies achieve more "bang" for their marketing bucks. The account executive also has a vested interest in bringing the trade promotions program in line with the other parts of the IMC plan, because the goal is to generate tangible sales and other measurable outcomes.

A variety of trade promotional tools exists. These items are used by manufacturers as well as other members of the trade channel. Figure 11.2 lists the most common promotional tools.

types of trade promotions

Individual companies select trade promotions techniques based on a variety of factors. These include the nature of the business (manufacturer versus distributor), the type of customer to be influenced (e.g., selling to a retailer versus selling to a wholesaler), company preferences, and the objectives of IMC plan being used. Each ver-

> ▶ **Trade allowances**
>
> ▶ **Trade contests**
>
> ▶ **Trade incentives**
>
> ▶ **Training programs**
>
> ▶ **Vendor support programs**
>
> ▶ **Trade shows**
>
> ▶ **Specialty advertising**
>
> ▶ **Point-of-purchase advertising**

Trade Promotional Tools

FIGURE 11.2

oion of a trade promotions program offers various benefits. A review of the major categories follows.

Trade allowances

The first major type of trade promotion manufacturers and others use in the channel is a trade allowance. **Trade allowances** can be packaged into a variety of forms, including the four described in Figure 11.3. The purpose of a trade allowance is to offer financial incentives to other channel members in order to motivate them to make a purchase. The channel member then is in a better position to offer discounts or other deals to their customers. A discussion of the types of trade allowances follows.

An **off-invoice allowance** encourages channel members to place orders, because they receive a financial discount on each case ordered. Companies often use these types of allowances during holiday seasons to encourage retailers to purchase large quantities of various items. Orders must be placed by a specific date to receive a holiday off-invoice allowance. Manufacturers also can place a minimum order size as a further condition. Off-invoice allowances are a common form of trade promotion and are used extensively because they help accomplish many IMC objectives.

A second type of trade allowance is called a **drop-ship allowance.** As defined in Figure 11.3, a drop-ship allowance is money paid to retailers who are willing to bypass wholesalers, brokers, agents, or distributors when making preplanned orders. Passing the middle members of the channel benefits both the manufacturer and retailer. Profit margins can increase for both the manufacturer and the retailer. Instead of keeping the larger margin a drop-ship allowance offers, retailers can pass along the savings to consumers by lowering prices.

There are other advantages to drop-ship allowances. For instance, by shipping merchandise directly to the retailer, a stronger relationship with the retailer results. Also, the manufacturer does not have to rely on the middle person to handle various transactions. The manufacturer also does not need to give additional effort, trying to make sure the middle person will push the manufacturer's brand. When wholesalers represent several manufacturers, they either push all equally or, more likely, push the brand that makes them the most money.

The primary disadvantage of bypassing a wholesaler or distributor is that a wholesaler who handles other products for the manufacturer may retaliate by either dropping the manufacturer or not pushing its other products. Manufacturers must try to avoid damaging relationships with wholesalers when using drop-ship allowances.

Perhaps the most controversial form of trade allowance is a slotting fee. **Slotting fees** are funds paid to retailers to stock new products. Retailers justify charging slotting fees in several ways. First, retailers must spend money to add new products to their inventories and to stock the merchandise. If the product is not

---

▶ **Off-invoice allowance: A per-case rebate paid to retailers for an order**

▶ **Drop-ship allowance: Money paid to retailers who bypass wholesalers or brokers for preplanned orders**

▶ **Slotting fees: Money paid to retailers to stock a new product**

▶ **Exit fees: Money paid to retailers to remove an item from their SKU inventory**

Trade Allowances

FIGURE 11.3

successful, the investment in initial inventory represents a loss, especially when the retailer has stocked a large number of stores.

Second, adding a new product in the retail store means allocating shelf space to it, because most shelves are already filled with products. Adding a new product means either deleting another brand or product or reducing the amount of shelf space allocated to other products. Regardless of the method used, the retailer has both time and money invested when making the adjustment for the new product.

Third, slotting fees make it easier for retailers to finalize decisions about new products. The typical supermarket, which carries 40,000 SKU (stockkeeping units), must evaluate at least 10,000 new products per year. The amount of money a manufacturer is willing to pay to get a product on the shelf indicates the manufacturer's faith in that new product. For some stores, slotting fees are as much as $25,000 per item. Some national chains charge slotting fees in the millions. A manufacturer that does not believe the product will succeed is reluctant to invest millions of dollars in slotting fees. Consequently, retailers contend that slotting fees force manufacturers to conduct careful test marketing on products before introducing them.

The other issues lead to the fourth reason for charging slotting fees. Retailers support slotting fees because they reduce the number of products introduced each year. This, in turn, drastically reduces the number of new-product failures. Fifth, and finally, slotting fees add to the bottom line. Many products have low margins or markups. Slotting fees provide additional monies to support retail operations. It has been estimated that 20 percent to 40 percent of the net profits earned by retailers come from trade promotion monies.[3]

The other side of the argument comes from manufacturers, which claim slotting fees are practically a form of extortion. Many manufacturers believe slotting fees are too high and are unfair in the first place. These fees force manufacturers to pay millions of dollars to retailers that could be used for advertising, sales promotions, or other marketing efforts. Slotting fees virtually prohibit small manufacturers from getting their products on store shelves because they cannot afford them. Although some large retail operations have small vendor policies, getting merchandise on their shelves still is extremely challenging. For example, one small manufacturer experienced a drop in sales from $500 per day to only $50 per day when its shelf space was reduced. A large national manufacturer paid the store a large slotting fee, which took space away from the smaller firm.[4] In addition to keeping small manufacturers out of the market, slotting fees favor incumbent suppliers. New entrants into the market face tremendous investment of up-front money already, and then they must add on slotting fees. Unless they are absolutely sure their brand will compete, a new competitor may decide not to enter a market simply because of slotting fees.

A fourth approach to granting a trade allowance is called an exit fee. **Exit fees** are monies paid to remove an item from a retailer's inventory. This approach is often used when a manufacturer wants to introduce a new size of a product or a new version, such as a three-liter bottle of Pepsi or Pepsi One. PepsiCo already has products on the retailer's shelves. Adding a new version of the product involves lower risk and is not the same as adding a new product. Rather than charging an up-front fee such as a slotting allowance, retailers ask for exit fees if the new version of the product fails or if one of the current versions must be removed from the inventory.

Procter & Gamble uses trade allowances to help place their products such as Pampers wipes at the retail level. Courtesy of Procter & Gamble Company. Used by permission.

stop! Integrated Learning Experience

Slotting fees are a controversial topic not only for retailers and manufacturers but also for governmental agencies. Congress and the Federal Trade Commission are the primary federal agencies involved in the debate. Using a search engine such as Yahoo!, locate Web sites and articles that discuss slotting fees. What arguments do you find supporting slotting fees? What arguments do you find against them? What is the position of Congress? What is the position of the FTC? From your research, what, if anything, should be done about slotting fees?

Disadvantages of trade allowances

Although trade allowances are key incentives used to build relationships with retailers, there are some disadvantages. These include:

1. Failing to pass along allowances to retail customers
2. Forward buying
3. Diversion

First, in extending trade allowances to retailers, manufacturers assume that a portion of the price reduction will be passed on to consumers. This occurs less than 50 percent of the time. In the majority of cases, retailers charge consumers the same price and pocket the allowance.[5] When a portion of the price allowance is passed on to consumers, retailers often schedule competing brands, so they can have at least one deal going at all times. It is not an accident that one week Pepsi offers a reduced price and the next Coke offers a discount. The two products are rarely promoted on-deal (passing along trade allowance discounts) at the same time. By offering only one on-deal at a time, the retailer always has a reduced price competitor for the price-sensitive consumer. The retailer also can charge the brand-loyal consumer full price 50 percent of the time. While accomplishing these goals, the retailer receives special trade allowances from both Pepsi and Coke.

Another problem trade allowances create is the practice of forward buying. **Forward buying** occurs when a retailer purchases excess inventory of a product while it is on-deal. The retailer then sells the on-deal merchandise after the deal period is over, saving the cost of purchasing the product at the manufacturer's full price. Forward buying provides two options to the retailer. First the retailer can choose to extend price savings to customers by selling the product cheaper than its competitors. The second option is to charge full price for the product. This increases the retailer's margin of profit on the product, because the company purchased the merchandise at a reduced price. The disadvantage of forward buying to retailers is the additional costs of holding inventory, which are known as the *carrying charges* associated with the merchandise. The decision to forward buy and how much to forward buy depends on the potential additional profit that can be earned compared to the additional costs and carrying charges for inventory.

Another practice retailers engage in is diversion. **Diversion** occurs when a retailer purchases a product on-deal in one location and ships it to another location where it is off-deal. For example, a manufacturer may offer an off-invoice allowance of $5 per case for the product in Texas. Diversion tactics mean the retailer purchases an excess quantity in Texas and has it shipped to stores in other states. As with forward buying, retailers have to examine the potential profits they can earn compared to the cost of shipping the product to other locations. Shipping costs tend to be relatively high compared to trade allowances offered. Consequently, retailers do not use diversion nearly as much as forward buying.

Although these three disadvantages are important considerations, many manufacturers still conclude that they must grant trade allowances in order to succeed. As a result, they remain a major part of the retail distribution process.

Trade contests

To achieve sales targets and other objectives, manufacturers sometimes use trade contests. Rewards are given as contest prizes to brokers, retail salespeople, retail stores, wholesalers, or agents. These funds are known as **spiff money.** The rewards can be items such as luggage, a stereo, a television, or a trip to an exotic place such as Hawaii. Contests can be held at various levels, such as:

1. Brokers versus brokers
2. Wholesalers versus wholesalers
3. Retail stores within a chain versus one another

4. Retailer store chains versus other retail chains

5. Individual salespersons within retail stores versus one another

In other words, the contest can be between brokers or agents who handle the manufacturer's goods. It can be for wholesalers, or it can be a sales volume contest between individual retail stores. Although contests can be designed between retail organizations (e.g., Kmart versus Wal-Mart), they are seldom used because of conflict of interest policies present in many large organizations. Buyers in large organizations are often prohibited from participating in vendor contests because they create conflicts of interest and unfairly influence their buying decisions. Although this is exactly what a contest is designed to accomplish, many large retail organizations do not want buyers participating, because they may make purchase decisions for 500 to 2,500 stores. This places undue pressure on the buyer.

When conducting a contest at the individual store level, most channel members agree that these contests work best when restricted to a specific region. Many times, they are also limited to exclusive dealerships, such as auto, truck, or boat dealers that sell a particular brand.

The final type of trade contest is among salespeople in various retail outlets. The goal of this type of trade contest is to encourage salespeople to push the manufacturer's brand over competing brands. These types of contests are quite popular among salespeople and are common in many industries such as those producing durable goods (refrigerators, boats, dishwashers, etc.).

Wilson Golf developed a mystery shopper promotion aimed at encouraging golf pro shops to display the Ultra line of golf balls. Prior to the mystery shopper promotion, Wilson offered the Ultra line at a reduced price along with a special display. Mystery shoppers were sent to 2,000 randomly selected pro shops to see if the store had at least three different Ultra balls on display and in stock, and to enter stores that did in the contest. In the 2,000 shops visited, 50 percent were using the manufacturer's display and 70 percent had more than three models in view. The winner of the $50,000 grand prize was Avila Country Club in Tampa Bay, Florida. Wilson was extremely satisfied with the trade contest. Usually no more than 10 percent of retailers ever use a manufacturer's display.[6]

Trade incentives

Trade incentives are similar to trade allowances. The difference is that trade incentives involve the retailer performing a function in order to receive the allowance. Figure 11.4 lists various trade incentives and their definitions. The goals of trade incentives vary. Therefore, the primary purpose for most plans is to encourage retailers either to push the manufacturer's brand or to increase retailer purchases of that brand.

The most comprehensive trade incentive is the **cooperative merchandising agreement (CMA),** which is a formal agreement between the retailer and manufacturer to undertake a cooperative effort. The agreement can involve a certain number of advertisements by the retailer that also mentions the manufacturer's brand. Another approach is to feature the manufacturer's brand as a price leader. Also, a cooperative agreement can be made to emphasize the manufacturer's brand in an in-house offer made by the retail store or a special shelf display featuring a price incentive. The advantage of the CMA agreement in featuring various price breaks is that the manufacturer knows that the retailer passes the price allowance on to the customer. One final form of CMA is a special in-store display that the retailer agrees to use on certain dates or for a specific time period. For example, when Coors beer features a display featuring supermodel Heidi Klum at Halloween, a special cooperative merchandising agreement may be reached with individual liquor stores to get them to set up the displays.

CMAs are popular with manufacturers because the retailer must perform a function in order to receive money. Consequently, the manufacturer retains control over the functions performed. Also, if price allowances are made as part of the

> ▶ **Cooperative merchandising agreement (CMA):** An annual incentive contract to pay retailers for advertisements, special displays, or price features for the manufacturer's brand over a period of time
>
> ▶ **Corporate sales program (CSP):** A promotion across a manufacturer's total brand portfolio with products usually shipped directly from the factory in ready-to-display pallets
>
> ▶ **Producing plant allowance (PPA):** An incentive to a retailer to purchase full or half truckloads directly from the factory
>
> ▶ **Back haul allowance (BHA):** Monies paid to retailers that send their own trucks to the manufacturer to pick up merchandise
>
> ▶ **Cross-dock or pedal run allowance:** Monies paid to retailers for placing full truck orders for multiple stores that can be distributed by a single truck from the manufacturer
>
> ▶ **Premium or bonus pack:** Free cases of merchandise for placing an order within a specified time period or for ordering a specific quantity

Trade Incentives

FIGURE 11.4

CMA, the manufacturer knows that the retailer passes a certain percentage of the price discount on to the consumer. Further, CMAs allow manufacturers to create annual contracts with retailers. These longer-term commitments reduce the need for last-minute trade incentives or trade allowances.

Possibly the most important benefit of a CMA to a manufacturer is that it creates trade incentives designed to support specific marketing objectives and also can be incorporated into an overall IMC plan. Cooperative merchandising agreements allow the manufacturer to plan the trade promotional component of the integrated marketing communications program rather than relying heavily on trade promotions to accomplish short-term, last-minute goals.

CMAs also benefit retailers. The primary benefit of a CMA from the retailers' perspective is that it allows them to develop calendar promotions. **Calendar promotions** are promotional campaigns the retailer plans for customers through manufacturer trade incentives. By signing a CMA, a retailer can schedule the weeks a particular brand will be on sale and offset the other weeks with other brands. By using calendar promotions, the retailer will always have one brand on sale while the others are off-deal. Using calendar promotions allows the retailer to rotate the brands on sale. This arrangement is attractive for the retailer's price-sensitive customers, because one brand is always on sale. For the brand-loyal consumer, the retailer carries the preferred brand at the regular price sometimes and on sale at others. By arranging sales through trade incentives, the margins for the retailer are approximately the same for all brands, both on-deal and off-deal, because they rotate. Retailers can effectively move price reductions given to the customer to the manufacturer rather than absorbing it themselves. A store may feature Budweiser on-deal one week and Heineken the next. Loyal beer drinkers stay with their preferred brand, while price-sensitive consumers can choose the on-deal brand; and the liquor store retains a reasonable markup on all beers sold.

A **corporate sales program (CSP)** is another form of trade incentive. CSPs are offered primarily by highly specialized manufacturers. The CSP is a promotion across a manufacturer's total brand portfolio. The manufacturer ships individual products to the retailer in ready-to-display pallets. As a result, the retailer does not have to prepare the merchandise for display, because it is already on a pallet. These display pallets work well for warehouse stores or retailers such as automobile parts stores in which decor is not a critical issue. By offering the incentive on all of the manufacturer's brand, the manufacturer encourages the retailer to carry all of its brands and not just some of them.

When a manufacturer offers a retailer an incentive called **producing plant allowance (PPA),** the retailer purchases a full or half truckload of merchandise in order to receive a major discount. The high cost of shipping means manufacturers always look for ways to reduce these costs. Making stops at a dozen retail stores costs more than stopping at only one or two. Smaller manufacturers or highly specialized manufacturers that typically sell through a distributor or some other type of middle person use PPAs. For these manufacturers, in addition to saving money on transportation, the retailer and manufacturer can save money that would normally have gone to the distributor. The only time a large manufacturer such as Procter & Gamble uses PPAs is for small retailers that typically purchase small quantities. Grocery stores, furniture outlets, and sporting goods stores may hold "truckload clearance" sales occasionally to raise volume and increase interest in the retail outlet.

Another form of trade incentive is called a **back haul allowance (BHA).** A BHA is granted when the retailer pays the cost of shipping. The primary difference between a PPA and a BHA is that the retailer, instead of the manufacturer, furnishes delivery trucks. With the back haul allowance, the retailer gets a much greater incentive allowance but also absorbs the cost of shipping.

For small retailers with multiple stores, a **cross-dock or pedal run allowance** can be obtained. These allowances are paid to retailers for placing a full truck order, which is then divided among several stores within the same geographic region. For example, if a small grocery chain has 8 stores within a 50-mile radius, the company can order a full truckload of merchandise from a manufacturer and divide the groceries among the stores. One of the keys to the cross-dock allowance is that each store accepts a full pallet. No pallets have to be broken, making it faster to load and unload goods.

The final type of trade incentive is a **premium or bonus pack.** Instead of offering the retailer a discount on the price, the manufacturer offers free merchandise. For example, a manufacturer may offer a bonus pack of one carton for each 20 purchased within the next 60 days. The bonus packs are free to the retailer and are awarded either for placing the order by a certain date or for agreeing to a minimum-size order. Often, to receive the free merchandise, the retailer must meet both stipulations, a specified date and a minimum order size.

Trade incentives are often tied in with consumer sales promotions. For example, to generate interest in the Chrome Visa card developed by Harley-Davidson motorcycles, Harley-Davidson launched the Harley Dream Sweepstakes for consumers and a trade incentive program for retailers. At the consumer level, a new Big Twin motorcycle was awarded each week for 52-weeks. Chrome Visa cardholders received one entry into the sweepstake for each dollar spent, and H-D raised the amount to two entries per dollar spent in participating Harley retail stores. To encourage Harley retailers to push the Chrome Visa credit card and place the display on their counters, Harley-Davidson created a trade incentive. For each customer who filled out the Chrome Visa card application and was subsequently approved, the retailer received a $20 credit toward Harley-Davidson merchandise for the store.[7]

Harley-Davidson launched the Harley Dream Sweepstakes using both trade and consumer promotions. Courtesy of Corbis/SABA Press Photos, Inc. Photograph by Laura Kleinhenz.

stop!

Integrated Learning Experience

The National Promotional Allowance Association (NAPAA) is a not-for-profit national organization that focuses on the development and administration of program allowances provided by manufacturers and suppliers to retail and wholesale customers. Access the Web site at www.napaa.org. What types of services does NAPAA offer? How can the association benefit manufacturers? Would the association be beneficial to retailers?

Training programs

Another type of trade promotions program involves providing training. Manufacturers often provide training programs to the members of the sales staff at a retailer location or to wholesalers. Many retailers and wholesalers sell multiple brands. Manufacturers are willing to provide training to these salespeople, because they learn more about the manufacturer's brand. This makes it more likely that the retail or wholesale sales force will push the manufacturer's brand instead of a competitor's product. Having additional knowledge about one brand over other brands biases salespeople toward that brand.

Savings Bank Life Insurance (SBLI) of Massachusetts decided to add training to a trade promotion package to boost sales of some of the firm's products. SBLI sells annuity and property casualty insurance products through 200 banks in Maine, Massachusetts, New Hampshire, and Rhode Island. Although only 20 percent of SBLI's sales were generated through the bank distribution channel, banks were viewed as a growth market that SBLI wanted to exploit. The problem SBLI and other insurance companies faced was that most bank personnel know little about insurance and therefore not equipped to sell insurance products. SBLI hoped to bolster sales through specialized training for bank personnel combined with lower prices. SBLI set up a Web site dedicated exclusively to the banking industry. Banks could provide customers with the Web address as well as put a hot link to the bank's Web page. The results were an increase in bank sales and a strong new relationship between various banks, their employees, and SBLI.[8]

To compete in the highly competitive software market, Microsoft launched a training program aimed at value-added resellers. The training program was entitled "Helping Clients Succeed." The three-day workshop was designed to help resellers better understand Microsoft software. Traditionally, Microsoft's field representatives concentrated on technology. Resellers tended to focus on providing solutions to customer problems. The primary goal of the training program was to encourage resellers to utilize Microsoft's factory representatives in consultative selling.[9] While SBLI focused on training at the retail level, Microsoft focused on training at the reseller or wholesaler level.

Vendor support programs

Vendor support programs are trade promotions manufacturers offer to support a retailer, wholesaler, or agent's programs. Naturally, vendor support programs are designed to support the vendor's activities that most favor the manufacturer. The two most frequently used vendor support programs are billbacks and co-op advertising. In a **billback** program, the manufacturer pays the retailer for special product displays, advertisements, or price cuts. In this case, the retailer or wholesaler initially pays for the display, advertisement, or price cut. Then the retailer or wholesaler bills the manufacturer for the activity, thus the term *billback*. The primary advantage of the billback to the manufacturer is that the retailer is willing to perform a function on behalf of the manufacturer in order to receive the trade incentive. The second advantage is that the retailer or wholesaler pays full price for the merchandise sold and bills the manufacturer only for the support program.

The more common vendor support program is co-op advertising. In a **cooperative advertising program,** the manufacturer agrees to reimburse the retailer a certain percentage of the advertising costs associated with advertising the manufacturer's products in the retailer's ad. To receive the reimbursement, the retailer follows specific guidelines concerning the placement of the ad and its content. In almost all cases, no competing products can be advertised. In most cases, to receive the reimbursement, the manufacturer's product must be displayed prominently. There may be other restrictions on how the product is advertised as well as specific photos or copy that must be used.

In most cooperative advertising programs, retailers accrue co-op monies based on purchases. This is normally a certain percentage of sales. For example, B.F. Goodrich, a manufacturer of automobile tires, offers a 4.5 percent co-op advertising fund on all purchases. This money can be accrued for one year, then it starts over again. B.F. Goodrich pays 70 percent of the cost of an approved advertisement. Any of the media can be used for the advertisement such as radio, newspaper, magazines, television, and outdoor. This unlimited media choice does not hold true for all manufacturers. For example, Dayton, another tire manufacturer, does not allow magazine advertisements to be used for co-op advertising dollars. B.F. Goodrich allows group ads for co-op monies; Dayton does not. Further, Dayton requires preapproval for some of the media buys and advertisements while Goodyear does not require any preapprovals. Thus, each manufacturer has its own set of restrictions that must be followed if the retailer wants to qualify for co-op monies.[10]

Each year manufacturers offer an estimated $25 billion in co-op money to retailers, of which only about two-thirds is claimed. Why does almost $8 million go unclaimed? Some of the more common reasons include:

1. The manufacturer rejects co-op claims because of errors in filing.
2. Purchase accruals are tracked inaccurately.
3. Retailers are unaware of a co-op program.
4. Restrictions placed by the manufacturer are not followed correctly.[11]

Although errors do occur in the filing of claims, the more common reasons for not collecting are that purchase accrual records were not kept accurately or that retailers simply were not aware that a cooperative program was in place. Figure 11.5 provides examples of common co-op types of situations.

Many cooperative advertising programs allow accrual of co-op monies over a year, however, some manufacturers restrict when the times co-op dollars can be spent. For example, a firm that produces snowblowers probably would provide co-op dollars only during the fall and winter. The rest of the year people rarely buy snowblowers, so the funds would not be spent wisely.

Keeping track of co-op dollars is difficult. One firm, the Archer–Malmo Advertising company, uses the Internet to track co-op dollars for companies such as Samsung Electronics, Pennzoil Corporation, General Electric, and RCA. Each firm reports co-op expenditures on-line. Retailers can then access these statements and view how much money is available in co-op funds along with the deadline (usually annual) by which the remainder must be spent. To make it more user friendly, the firm now makes it possible for retailers to submit claims on-line. Retailers can also download manufacturer's graphics and logos for various ads. This use of the Internet is likely to increase in the future. Using the Internet simplifies the co-op process for both the retailer and the manufacturer.[12]

The Intel Corporation provides probably the largest co-op advertising program in the world. Intel spends about $750 million a year to promote the "Intel inside"

Cooperative Advertising

FIGURE 11.5

▌ **Best Buy and Hewlett Packard**
▌ **Goody's and Dockers**
▌ **Ace Hardware and Tru-Test Products**
▌ **Intel and IBM, Toshiba and HP**
▌ **Motorola and Skytel**
▌ **JCPenney and Reebok**
▌ **Sprint and Radio Shack**
▌ **American Airlines and MCI Worldcom**
▌ **Radisson Hotels and TGI Fridays**

theme. Intel offers a 6 percent co-op fund to all PC makers that place the Intel logo on their computers. Further, Intel allows a 4 percent fund accrual on the cost of print ads featuring the Intel inside logo and provides 2 percent for television and radio ads featuring the Intel video or audio tag. This accrued co-op money can be used to pay up to 66 percent of the cost of a print advertisement or 50 percent of the cost of a broadcast ad. Intel cuts any payment in half for any advertisement that features a third-party logo of any type to ensure it is the only co-op brand featured in an ad. Approximately 1,400 PC makers worldwide as well as the top 10 PC makers take advantage of the Intel co-op advertising program.[13]

Co-op advertising programs benefit most retailers because retailers are able to use manufacturer dollars to expand advertising programs. In a co-op ad, the retailer gains additional ad coverage at minimal cost. Retailers also benefit from the image of a national brand, which can attract new or additional customers to the store. From the retailer's perspective, there is little to lose in co-op programs. The only negative side is that the retailer is reimbursed following the placement of the ad.

Manufacturers also benefit from co-op ads. Manufacturers gain additional exposure at reduced costs, by sharing ad costs with retailers. More importantly, almost all co-op advertising programs are tied to sales. The retailer accrues co-op advertising dollars based on a certain percentage of sales. Thus, to get the co-op money, the retailer must not only promote the brand prominently but also purchase the product for resale. As a result, it is not surprising to see the wide variety of cooperative advertisements appearing so regularly in all media, for both consumer products and business-to-business ads.

Trade shows

In business-to-business marketing, total expenditures on trade shows ranks third, with only advertising and sales promotions receiving greater funding. Over $12 billion are spent on trade shows each year. Manufacturers spend between $70,000 and $100,000 to attend a major trade show; this includes airline fees, hotels, entertainment costs, booth fees, and equipment. Retailers pay about $600 per person for those who attend trade shows.[14]

From a manufacturer's standpoint, a trade show offers the opportunity to discover potential customers and sell new products. Also, relationships with current customers can be strengthened at the show. A trade show often provides the chance to find out what the competition is doing. Many times, trade shows present a situation in which the manufacturer's sales team can meet directly with decision makers and buyers from business-to-business clients. A trade show can be used to strengthen the brand name of a product as well as the company's image.

From the retailer's perspective, a trade show allows buyers to compare merchandise and to make contact with several perspective vendors in a short period of

Over $12 billion are spent on trade shows each year. Courtesy of Liaison Agency, Inc. Photograph by Jeff Scheid.

time. In some cases the retailer can negotiate special deals. Trade shows are an ideal place for buyers and sellers to meet in an informal, low-pressure situation to discuss how to work together effectively.

Some national and international trade shows are attended by thousands of buyers. To be sure the trade show is successful, manufacturers seek out key buyers and try to avoid spending too much time with nonbuyers. Narrowing down the large number of contacts to those most promising is called *prospecting*. Figure 11.6 list five categories of buyers that attend trade shows. It is important to weed out the education seekers who are not interested in buying. Manufacturers should concentrate their efforts on three groups: solution seekers, buying teams, and power buyers. Asking the right questions identifies solution seekers and buying teams. The power buyers are more difficult to identify because they don't want to be identified. They often do not wear badges at trade shows so vendors do not know who they

communication **action**

Making the Most of a Trade Show

Trade shows require a substantial investment of time, money, and personnel. To make sure these funds are spent wisely, one well-known writer recommends several key tasks and ideas to complete and implement.

1. Ask the right questions. Among other things, this means asking open-ended questions to help you find out if the buyer is serious or browsing. Avoid pat questions such as "May I help you?" which usually draws a response of "No, just looking."

2. Spend time with the right attendees. The MAN profile works best, whereby money, authority, and need (in the budget) direct the booth worker to the correct prospect. Make sure the person in the booth can actually afford the products he or she is viewing.

3. Be a careful listener. Keep notes, because most sales do not take place at the actual show, but rather months later. Identify the customer's needs and special circumstances to effectively close the deal in a later follow-up contact.

4. Know the difference between a person who is an actual prospect and someone who is just a "name" on a business card. Instead of spending too much time "pitching" the product, invest your energy in finding out what customers are looking for, and then make sure to follow up later to fill those needs.

5. Do not bombard potential clients with literature. They will probably throw it away anyway. Instead, give a small fact sheet, and send major mailings to their office later, where they are much more likely to actually review the materials you send, especially if they contain a well-written cover letter.

6. Avoid overcrowding a booth with materials. In one 1999 small appliance trade show, a company displaying only 7 products sold more merchandise than the company in the next booth, which offered over 50 items. Keep it simple, so the potential customer can handle the goods and become more interested as a result.

7. Pay attention to matters such as "booth etiquette" and body language. Do not stand with your arms folded, and do not eat, drink, or make phone calls while on duty. Keep the booth area clean and not crowded with briefcases and empty coffee cups. Dress appropriately for the show.

Effective booth management also should tie in with the firm's image and IMC program. The goal is to build sales and long-term relationships as various companies spend the time and energy needed to attend trade shows.

Source: Dale English, "On Displays," *Business First, Western New York,* 16, no. 9 (November 29, 1999), p. 31.

> Education seekers: Buyers who want to browse, look, and learn but are not in the buying mode

> Reinforcement seekers: Buyers who want reassurance they made the right decision in past purchases

> Solution seekers: Buyers seeking solutions to specific problems and are in the buying mode

> Buying teams: A team of buyers seeking vendors for their business; usually are in the buying mode

> Power buyers: Members of upper management or key purchasing agents with the authority to buy

Five Categories of Buyers Attending Trade Shows

FIGURE 11.6

are. The Communication Action Box on the previous page provides more information about how to make the most of a trade show.

In the United States, few deals are finalized during trade shows. Buyers and sellers meet, discuss, and maybe even negotiate, but seldom are buys completed. Instead, manufacturers collect business cards as leads to be followed up later; however, the procedure varies for international customers.

Several differences exist when international companies attend trade shows.[15] The first major difference is that international attendees tend to be senior executives with the authority to make purchases. They fit into the power buyer category listed in Figure 11.6. American manufacturers must understand that the international attendee often wishes to conduct business during the trade show, not afterward. The second contrast is that international attendees spend more time at each manufacturer's booth. They stay longer in order to gather and study information in greater detail. Because of the travel expense involved, the international guest wants more in-depth information than an American counterpart usually needs. The increase in international participants has caused trade show centers to set up more meeting spaces, conference centers, and even places to eat where buyers and sellers can meet to discuss buys.[16] The number of international trade show visitors has increased dramatically in the past decade.

Trade shows have changed in other ways. Large national and international shows are being replaced by niche shows. For example, in the 1990s, many mega-sports trade shows were attended by everybody in the sporting goods business. For instance, the National Sporting Goods Association World Sports Expo in Chicago attracted over 90,000 attendees during the mid-1900s. The number has dwindled to fewer than 40,000 today. Now manufacturers and retailers attend specialty trade shows that focus on only one sport. The smaller shows are cheaper to set up, and individual companies believe they are much more effective in making viable customer contacts. Many have concluded that it is too easy to be lost in the crowd at the bigger shows.[17]

The decision on whether to attend a general national show or a specialty show depends on the objective the firm wishes to accomplish. When the goal is to enhance the firm's brand or corporate name, generally large national shows are the best. When the goal is to expand a market base beyond the regional or current customers, a national show works well. On the other hand, specialty shows are better in three situations, most notably when the goal is to:

1. Establish a client base quickly
2. Establish a new brand
3. Promote a new product

Manufacturers should look beyond the numbers when choosing trade shows. Large trade shows may have a greater number of attendees, but if the attendees do not fit the profile of a manufacturer's customers the show will not be profitable. One easy method of finding out if the attendees match a manufacturer's customer profile is to talk to customers and competitors to discover which trade shows they attend. Before spending thousands of dollars on a show, a manufacturer should find out who attends and how well the show fits with the firm's goals and target market. Trade shows should match with the objectives of the overall IMC program as well as other marketing tools that are being used.

stop!

Integrated Learning Experience

The best resource for trade shows can be found at www.tsnn.com. Information about the overall trade show industry is available as well as articles about trade shows in specific industries. Explore the Web site for items that would benefit manufacturers attending trade shows. What information is available to retailers or other attendees of trade shows? Next, look for trade shows that will be held in your area during the next few months. Another valuable source of information is the *TradeShow Week Magazine* at www.tradeshowweek.com. What additional information is at this site? Read about trade show trends and the article archives available at this site.

Specialty advertising

Specialty advertising, also known as *giveaways,* can be integrated into an IMC program to provide an additional feature designed to impress customers. These gifts, such as pens, coffee mugs, calendars, key chains, and many others, have the name of the firm imprinted on them. The items sometimes include a message, logo, or tag line. These messages are tied in with the advertising theme.

A promotional gift provides the customer with a constant reminder of the company. No other IMC tool can remain with a customer over such a potentially long period of time. A coffee mug with the firm's name and logo might be used every day. A shirt imprinted with the company's logo will be seen by dozens of people. Figure 11.7 displays the top five types of gifts given to customers.

Specialty advertising gifts are often distributed at trade shows, by salespeople, or via direct-mail campaigns. Companies spend almost $12 billion annually on promotional items.[18] The concept behind specialty gifts is **reciprocation.** Whenever someone receives a gift, the human desire is to return a gift or favor. In business, this psychological advantage can be used in a number of ways. At a trade

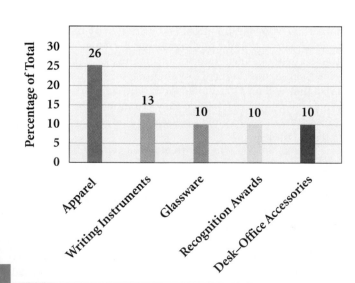

Top Categories in Specialties Advertising

FIGURE 11.7

show, promotional gifts create a positive impression of the business. Care must be taken, however, to ensure the gift conveys the intended message. For example, if one booth hands out a plastic mug to trade show attendees, while the next one gives a porcelain mug, attendees get different impressions of the two vendors. The tendency would be to view the business giving the plastic cup more negatively, meaning the gift actually worked against the company that gave it.

One of the best strategies in selecting advertising specialties is to make sure the item is unique and conveys the company's message. For example, at one trade show a cotton gin company gave away miniature bales of cotton with its logo printed on the bale. The item was not really useful, but it was unique. In another setting, a florist gave a rose to each woman attending a Latino businesswomen's conference. Both times the gift served its purpose by being unique enough to gain attention but also by focusing on the company's product.[19]

Specialty gifts can help reinforce buying decisions. In other words, they can make a customer feel that he or she made a good choice. Gifts can strengthen business relationships and also help stimulate interest from a new potential prospect. In general, specialty gifts can be an important means of strengthening communications with all types of customers.

Point-of-purchase advertising

Point-of-purchase (POP) advertising is any form of special display that advertises merchandise. POP displays are often located near cash registers in retail stores, at the end of an aisle, in a store's entryway, or any other place where they will be noticed. Point-of-purchase advertising includes displays, signs, structures, and devices used to identify, advertise, or merchandise an outlet, service, or product. POP displays should serve as an important aid to retail selling.

The store shelf and point-of-purchase display represent the last chance for the manufacturer to reach the consumer.[20] They can be used to make an impression just before a purchase is made or to leave an impression when the buyer exits the store. More than 55 percent of mass-merchandisers and 60 percent of supermarket shoppers remember seeing a point-of-purchase display immediately following a trip to a retail outlet.

POP displays are highly effective tools for increasing sales. About 50 percent of the money spent at mass-merchandisers and supermarkets is unplanned. Often these purchases are *impulse buys.* When consumers make purchases, they often do not decide on the particular brand until the last minute. For food purchases, 88 percent of the decisions about brands are made in the store at the time of the purchase. For all products, 70 percent of brand choices are made in the store. In many instances, point-of-purchase materials influenced the decision.

Coca-Cola reports that only 50 percent of soft drink sales are made from the regular store shelf. The other 50 percent result from product displays in other parts of the store. American Express found that 30 percent of purchases charged on the American Express card came from impulse decisions by customers seeing the "American Express Cards Welcome" sign. Other research indicates that an average increase in sales of 10 percent occurs when one POP display is used and 22 percent when there are two. Consequently, POP advertising is very attractive to manufacturers.[21]

Currently, manufacturers spend more than $13 billion each year on point-of-purchase advertising materials. The largest users of POP advertising are restaurants, food services, apparel stores, and footwear retailers. The fastest-growing categories are fresh, frozen, or refrigerated foods, and professional services.[22]

Manufacturers view POP displays as an attractive method of getting a brand more prominently displayed before customers. Many retailers have a different perspective. Retailers believe POP materials should either boost sales for the store or draw customers into the store. Retailers are not interested in the sales of one particular brand, but instead want to improve overall sales and store profits. Retailers prefer displays that educate consumers and provide information. As a

POP displays are very helpful when selling products such as cosmetics, perfume, or cologne. Courtesy of Bijan Fragrances, Inc.

result, retailers are most inclined to set up POP displays to match their objectives. Several factors cause retailers to leave POP materials unused. Some of these problems are shown in Figure 11.8.

The most common reason retailers do not use displays furnished by manufacturers is that they are inappropriate for the channel. In other words, a display that works well in a discount store may not be appropriate for a supermarket or a specialty store. Various retailers and channel members have different needs in terms of what they want in a POP display design. Manufacturers should consult with each type of channel member to ensure the display meets these needs.

The size of a display is important to retailers. Store space is limited, and customers do not respond well when freestanding displays at the end of aisles block

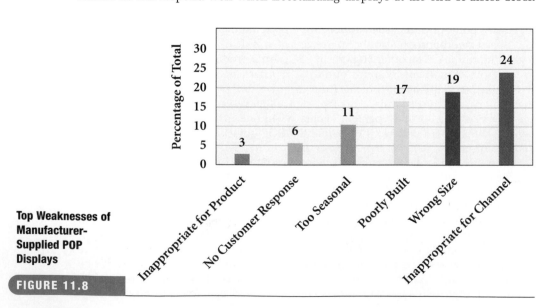

Top Weaknesses of Manufacturer-Supplied POP Displays

FIGURE 11.8

traffic through the store. Consequently, individual retailers normally will use only POP displays that fit the allocated space. Retailers prefer easy to assemble, easy to stock, and adaptable displays. Consequently, manufacturers must remember that if a retailer does not like a display, it won't be used, no matter how great it looks.

Retailers want displays to be durable. Corrugated cardboard (which is often used) tends to wear out and tear. Poorly built displays are often thrown away. Retailers do not have time to repair displays. They also take down worn, shabby looking exhibits. Retailers give preference to manufacturers offering customized displays for individual stores.

The VF Corporation develops customized in-store displays and signs for various lines of jeans. The VF company individualizes the displays for discount retailers such as Kmart and Wal-Mart. The manufacturer of Insignia Crafted resilient flooring learned that high-end flooring purchases are not impulse decisions. Customers want to examine samples of the flooring. Therefore, a display with information pamphlets and a Consumer Style Selection Kit, which contained samples of the different floor materials, were offered to flooring vendors. Customers could then take both the information pamphlet and the selection kit home, and the display was able to positively influence sales.[23] In both cases, the major issue was to offer the retailer the type of display that could be most useful in raising sales.

To be effective, POP displays must communicate the product's attributes clearly. Pricing and other promotional information is also useful. The display should encourage the customer to stop and look, pick up the product, and examine it. A customer who stops to examine a product on display is more likely to buy it. The best POP displays are those integrated with other marketing messages. Logos and message themes used in advertisements should appear on the POP. The POP display should reflect any form of special sales promotion. Customers more quickly recognize tie-ins with current advertising and promotional themes as they view displays.

The POP display should make a clear, succinct offer that customers immediately understand. Many times the POP display only has three-tenths of a second to capture the customer's attention. If it fails, the customer simply moves on to other merchandise. Colors, designs, merchandise arrangements, and tie-ins with other marketing messages are critical elements of effective POP displays.[24] Figure 11.9 lists some additional pointers for point-of-purchase advertising.

Three new trends are present in the use of POP displays:

1. Integration with Web site programs
2. Displays that routinely change messages
3. Better tracking of POP results

▶ **Integrate the brand's image into the display**

▶ **Integrate the display with current advertising and promotions**

▶ **Make the display dramatic to get attention**

▶ **Keep the color of the display down so the product and signage stand out**

▶ **Make the display versatile so it can be easily adapted by retailers**

▶ **Make the display reusable and easy to assemble**

▶ **Make the display easy to stock**

▶ **Customize the display to fit the retailer's store**

Effective POP Displays

FIGURE 11.9

Each of these items represents key changes in POP programs. A review of these issues follows.

The first new trend is integrating POP displays with the Internet site and Web address of the company. For example, Tucker Federal Bank distributed POP materials to its 14 branch banks encouraging people to sign up for a free checking service. The display encouraged people to go to the bank's Web site. The URL, http://www.justrightbank.com, was integrated with the advertising tag line "Not too big. Not too small. Just right." Customers who visited the bank's Web site could complete and submit the application for free on-line checking. Effective integration of e-messages involves more than just printing a Web address on the POP display. The company should encourage customers to go there for a specific reason, such as was the case with Tucker Federal.[25]

The second trend in POP advertising is developing displays with the capability of changing the message. Messages are changed daily, weekly, or, in some extreme cases, several times per day. One method manufacturers use to accomplish these changes is by featuring LED electronic signs, which can be changed via a computer. This allows the manufacturer or retailer to offer new messages more frequently to keep the POP fresh to consumers. To the retailer, the big advantage is that messages can be localized and designed to meet changing local needs. To the manufacturer, it offers an opportunity to partner with retailers in looking for ways to maximize sales.[26]

The third issue is accountability. Both retailers and manufacturers look for methods to measure the effectiveness of POP displays. Retailers have limited space and can set up only a fraction of the displays sent to them. They want to use the most effective displays. Manufacturers invest money into building, shipping, and promoting POP displays. The manufacturer wants its display to be utilized and not set in a storeroom or simply thrown away. Thus, it is in the best interests of both parties to develop methods for measuring effectiveness.

One method to measure results is tying the POP display into a point-of-sale (POS) cash register. Items on the display are coded so that the POS system picks them up. Then individual stores measure sales before and during a POP display

In developing POP displays to promote Preferred Stock for men, Stetson will want to make sure that their Web site and POP displays concide. *Courtesy of Preferred Stock.*

program by using cash register data. The data also help the retailer decide when to withdraw or change a POP display due to slumping sales. This technology allows retailers to identify the POP displays with the largest impact on sales. A retailer even could use this method to test-market different types of POP displays in various stores. The most effective displays can then be rolled out nationally.

From the manufacturer's viewpoint, using POS data can help it improve POP displays. It also provides the opportunity to strengthen a partnership with the retailer. This bond helps the manufacturer weather poor POP showings, because the retailer may stay with a manufacturer that tries to develop displays of benefit to both parties.

Internet trading may have reduced some retail store traffic. Still, many customers shop and window-shop frequently. A POP advertising program remains an important ingredient in selling to the end user and in strengthening bonds with retailers as part of a larger trade promotions effort.

Integrated Learning Experience

Point-of-purchase displays should be an important component of a firm's IMC program. Research indicates that effective POP displays have a positive impact on sales. Access the following firms that produce POP displays.

Melrose Display Inc. (www.melrosedisplays.com)
Visy Displays (www.visydisplays.com)
Vulcan Industries (www.vulcanind.com)
Display Design & Sales (www.displays4pop.com)
Acrylic Designs, Inc. (www.acrylicdesigns.com)

Which firm's site is the most attractive? Which firm would be the best from the standpoint of developing displays for manufacturers? For retailers?

communication**action**

POP Displays and Beauty Products

A point-of-purchase display is the final chance for a cosmetics company to convince the consumer to choose its brands over the competitors'. Almost one third of sales of cosmetics can be linked to noticing and being attracted to a display. Many cosmetics are also, in part, impulse buys. Consequently, the design and placement of POP displays represents a key element of the promotional efforts of cosmetics manufacturers.

Colors are one key ingredient. Colors can create sophistication, fun, and various emotions. Colors are often linked with individual companies. The colors of the display should match the packaging of the product and the IMC theme the cosmetics firm presents in other places.

POP displays should lead the consumer to touch or pick up the product. Once a consumer has touched a product, a purchase almost always follows. Teenagers are more likely to pick up items with bold and bright colors and designs. Global Beauty Concepts targets 12- to 15-year-old girls with its brightly designed Petunia range of cosmetics. On the other hand, Fine Fragrances uses simple lines and colors in the attempt to reach key "high street" retailers and their customers.

Males prefer more neutral colors than do females. Products such as razors and colognes are more likely to sell with more minimalist POPS. Unisex products also sell better with a more subdued approach. Calvin Klein cosmetics has led the way in promoting unisex products in its displays for CK fragrances.

A more recent trend in POP displays is to make them interactive. Clairol Cosmetics pioneered the use of interactive displays. Customers use a keypad or touch screen to select more information about the company's products.

Beyond a sturdy display rank, many factors go into the design of an effective cosmetics POP display. Color, shape, size, positioning of "testers," and other elements of design are key ingredients in the sale of these highly profitable items.

Sources: "First Impressions Count," *Soap, Perfumery and Cosmetics,* Wilmington Publishing Ltd., 72, no. 4 (April 1999), p. 91; Charles Kessler, "Interactive Prompts to Purchase," *Soap, Perfumery and Cosmetics,* 69, no. 4 (April 1996), p. 31; "Designs on Color," *Soap, Perfumery and Cosmetics,* Wilmington Publishing Ltd., 70, no. 4 (April 1997), p. 35.

objectives of trade promotions

The trade promotions manager should be included in the planning stages of the IMC program. This increases the chances that trade promotions and incentives will be effectively coordinated with the other components of the IMC process. Regrettably, the process is more difficult than it appears, because manufacturers and retailers have objectives that differ from each other and from those of distributors.

For manufacturing operations, the primary goal is to increase sales of their brands. Retailers, on the other hand, try to increase the market shares of their stores. Retailers may be less concerned with which brand sells the most. Instead, they promote the brands that have the highest sales or contribute the most to profits. Often retailers play one manufacturer against another to see which one will offer the best deal. Therefore, manufacturers are limited in which trade promotions they can or cannot use by the retailers who sell their products. This problem becomes even more complicated when a wholesaler or distributor is involved. These organizations also have specific goals related to volume and profit.

Figure 11.10 lists the major objectives of trade promotions from the manufacturer's perspective. At times one takes precedence over another, but each one may be a key goal for a given trade promotions effort. These objectives are described next.

Obtaining initial distribution

When a firm begins operations, enters a new territory, or seeks to expand into global markets, one primary concern is finding retail outlets to carry the product. The company must be able to develop a distribution network through either a "pull" or a "push" strategy. *Demand pull* occurs when advertising and publicity causes con-

Objectives of Trade Promotions

- Obtain initial distribution
- Obtain prime retail shelf space or location
- Support established brands
- Counter competitive actions
- Increase order size
- Build retail inventories
- Reduce excess manufacturer inventories
- Enhance channel relationships
- Enhance the IMC program

FIGURE 11.10

sumers to become aware of a product's availability. These individuals then ask retailers if they carry the product, which leads the retailer to become more interested in it. A *push strategy* is the result of aggressive marketing efforts by the manufacturer to entice retailers to consider placing the product on its shelves. One goal of a trade promotions effort is to assist in this form of push strategy. Trade shows, slotting fees, vendor support programs, specialty advertising, and point-of-purchase displays help a manufacturer gain a wider audience for a new product.

Obtaining prime retail shelf space or location

Retail shelf space is critical in selling merchandise. Simply stated, a manufacturer that cannot get its products onto retailer shelves will not sell merchandise. Quality spots of shelf space mean higher sales. A manufacturer who has 24 inches of prime shelf space is likely to do better than a company given only 10 inches of shelf space. To get quality space and more space means manufacturers must be willing to provide incentives to retailers in the form of trade promotions in addition to providing products with high consumer demand. Trade allowances, contests, training programs, and trade incentives can assist in capturing and maintaining quality shelf space.

Supporting established brands

Trade promotions efforts often are used to increase shelf space for current, well-established products. Even in situations where the manufacturer merely tries to maintain current shelf space, trade promotions are needed to keep competitors from taking retail space. More often than not, the competition continually tries to find ways to offer retailers a better deal. This forces manufacturers to make sure they stay on top of what is happening in order to maintain quality shelf space and

Companies such as Keebler often use trade promotions in conjunction with consumer promotions such as coupons. Courtesy of Keebler Company.

lead the retailer to support established brands. For instance, if a new competitor were to enter the potato chip market, that manufacturer would logically spend considerable funds seeking to push out more established brands, such as Lays, Frito-Lay, and Guys. These chip suppliers would be interested in maintaining superior locations on grocery store and convenience store shelves. Every trade promotions tool can be used to support established brands.

Countering competitive actions

Manufacturers often use trade promotions to counter a competitive action. The competitive action may be a trade promotion deal being offered by the competition to retailers, a consumer promotion, an aggressive advertising campaign designed to increase demand pull, or some other promotional effort. To ensure channel members do not emphasize the competition instead of their products, manufacturers offer some type of trade promotion that matches the competition's effort or that is attractive to the channel member. This can become a vicious spiral in which manufacturers pump more and more dollars into trade promotions just to keep up with one another.

On the other hand, failing to fend off competitive threats has even greater consequences. A firm helps its own cause by taking care of other parts of the business relationship, such as by meeting delivery deadlines, providing support services to retailers, accepting returns without problems in crediting retailer accounts, entering into cooperative advertising agreements, and other activities designed to build strong ties between the two organizations. Each time the competition acts, the manufacturer chooses to use either the same trade promotions tactic or another form designed to counteract the competition's efforts.

Increasing order sizes

Another goal of trade promotions programs is to push an individual brand through the channel of distribution in such a way that order sizes increase. Manufacturers primarily use trade allowances and sales contests to increase order sizes. The objective may be to increase the order size from either the retailer or the distributer. Occasionally, a POP will induce a larger order by the retailer, if the display features a major advertising campaign or a key season for the product, such as starter fluid for barbeque grills featured in the summer.

Building retail inventories

Another marketing goal can be to build retail inventories, thus preempting the competition. A large retail inventory of a particular brand should result in the retailer pushing that particular brand over competing brands. Trade allowances that lead to forward buying or diversions may actually help reach the goal of larger retail inventories. Other parts of the IMC plan, such as advertising and consumer sales promotions, also drive the retailer to hold larger inventories in anticipation of increased retail sales.

Reducing excess manufacturer inventories

Trade promotions help manufacturers reduce inventory levels. This often occurs near the end of a fiscal year or near the end of an evaluation period when sales have not met forecasts. To ensure a quota is met, a manufacturer offers retailers an especially attractive trade promotion deal. This in turn helps reduce excess manufacturer inventories.

Enhancing channel relationships

Manufacturers also utilize trade promotions to enhance relationships with other channel members. Contests, allowances, incentives, giveaways, and training all make the relationship between the manufacturer's sales rep and the company's buyers more personal and intimate. Maintaining positive relationships is especially important if the competition also is heavily involved in granting trade promotions.

Enhancing the IMC program

Finally, trade promotions should be used to enhance other IMC efforts. If a manufacturer plans a massive consumer promotion campaign, it makes sense to support the consumer sales promotion effort with trade promotions. The same is true for a major advertising campaign. Manufacturers spending large amounts of money on advertising campaigns want to be sure their products are available in stores. Manufacturers also try to be sure certain retailers promote the product with desirable shelf space or end-of-aisle displays. To obtain these more desirable locations normally requires a more concerted trade promotions effort. It is important to remember that the company's image and theme should be enhanced not only through clever advertisements but also through the other elements of the promotions mix, including trade promotions incentives.

Integrated Learning Experience

Trade promotions are an important element in accomplishing IMC objectives. Many firms turn to speciality agencies or full-service agencies to handle trade promotions programs. The same agency often handles the sales promotion component and manages trade promotions in order to ensure the two mesh together. Look up the following firms to see what type of trade promotion services they offer. What appears to be each agency's strengths? While reviewing the various trade promotions objectives discussed in this chapter, which agency appears to be the best selection, given those objectives?

C-E Communications (www.cecom.com)
Co-op Communications, Inc. (www.coopcom.com)
TradeOne Marketing (www.tradeonemktg.com)
Sable Advertising Systems (www.sableadvertising.com)

concerns in using trade promotions

Beyond manufacturers, every other member of the marketing channel should also work to incorporate trade promotions into overall IMC efforts. This occurs, only if top management buys into the integrated marketing communications concept and insists on including the trade promotion manager on the marketing team. The manager must also make sure all the team members work together with a common marketing agenda.

In most organizations, employee pay structures encourage the use of trade promotions irrespective of the IMC plan. Sales managers face quotas, and if sales fall behind, the easiest way to boost them is to offer retailers a trade deal. Further, companies often evaluate brand managers based on the sales growth of a brand. The easiest way to ensure continuing sales growth is to offer trade deals. The pattern of using trade deals to reach short-term quotas rather than long-term image and theme building will not change until top management adopts a new style. The IMC approach will only succeed when a long-term horizon is considered and the compensation structures change to accommodate this long-term view of success.

To illustrate why a change in management philosophy is necessary, consider the following situation. A sales manager or brand manager has one month left in the fiscal year and is 12 percent behind on a sales quota. To ensure the quota is reached, the sales manager requests a trade deal to encourage retailers to buy excess merchandise. In the short term, the goal has been achieved. In the long run, however, the brand's image may have eroded. It takes a long-term perspective for management to say that increasing trade promotions to meet the quota is not part of the IMC plan and should not be done. Eroding brand image to meet short-term goals is not in the company's best long-term interest. If a strong brand image can be developed, retailers will stock the brand with fewer trade deals because it pulls customers into their stores. For example, Titleist has, for many years, enjoyed a strong brand image. Most golf pro shops will carry these golf balls simply because the company holds such a strong position in the marketplace. This allows Titleist to stay out of trade wars with other manufacturers based solely on trade allowances. Nike may be in the process of building a similar advantage for many of its products.

Meanwhile, as company leaders consider ways to include trade promotions into an overall IMC plan, they need to be aware of potential problems associated with trade promotions programs. These include:

1. Costs
2. The impact on small manufacturers
3. Overreliance on trade promotions to move merchandise
4. The potential erosion of brand image

The first major concern is the cost of trade promotions. Manufacturers spend billions of dollars per year on trade promotions. In turn, these costs are often passed on to consumers in the form of higher prices. It is estimated that 13 cents out of every dollar spent for frozen food items goes directly for the cost of trade promotions. Seven to 10 percent of the price for all brands pays for trade promotions.[27] Therefore, management must try to keep these costs at a reasonable level and make sure the money is spent wisely. Rather than simply getting into "bidding wars" with competitors, the company should use trade promotions dollars to build relationships and achieve key IMC goals.

The second major concern with trade promotions is their impact on small manufacturers. When the cost to get an item initially stocked in a store ranges anywhere from $1,000 to $20,000, large manufacturers have the advantage. They can afford to invest more heavily in trade allowances. Only eight of the top 15 retailers in the United States have programs that allow small vendors opportunities to stock their merchandise. Figure 11.11 displays both types of retailers. Although these retailers have special programs for small manufacturers, there is no guarantee they will get shelf space when a large manufacturer such as General Mills offers millions of dollars in trade incentives such as slotting fees and cooperative advertising programs (including coupon redemption programs).[28] Small-scale manufacturers must discover creative ways to gain shelf space, both in major retail chains and through smaller vendors. It is clearly a challenging part of the process, but one that must be addressed in order to achieve long-term success.

The third major concern is that the use of trade promotions has led to a situation in which merchandise does not move until a trade promotions incentive is offered. In the grocery industry, an estimated 70 percent to 90 percent of all purchases made by retailers are on-deal with some type of trade incentive in place. The

Retailers with Small Vendor Programs	Retailers with No Small Vendor Programs
▸ Wal-Mart	▸ Circuit City
▸ Kmart	▸ Consumer-Electronic
▸ Sears	▸ Office Depot
▸ Sam's Warehouse	▸ Service Merchandise
▸ Price Costco	▸ Wal-Mart Supercenter
▸ Target	
▸ Home Depot	
▸ Toys "R" Us	

Retailers and Small Vendor Programs

FIGURE 11.11

constant use of deals has trimmed manufacturer margins on products and created competitive pressures to conform. If a manufacturer tries to quit or cut back on trade promotions, retailers replace the manufacturer's products with other brands or trim their shelf space to allow more room for manufacturers offering better deals. For example, recently Procter & Gamble cut back on trade promotions in an effort to sell more products off-deal to boost profit margins. In a retaliatory action, Safeway cut some of the less popular P&G sizes and brands from its stores. Curbing trade promotional expenditures is extremely difficult because trade promotions are a critical part of moving goods from manufacturers to retailers. Manufacturers will have to use trade promotions more wisely, to ensure they accomplish the intended IMC objectives.[29]

The fourth major concern with trade promotions is that they can cause the erosion of a brand's image. As more and more money is pumped into trade promotions, less money is spent on advertising. As discussed in Chapter 4, brand image is built through intensive advertising and high product quality. When advertising expenditures are cut, consumers no longer seek out specific brands in their purchase decisions. Instead, they choose from brands viewed as being equal in quality (called brand parity). The situation worsens when trade promotions discounts are passed on to consumers. At that point, brands already seen as being equal are selected only on the price or discount being offered. Instead of choosing a specific brand with superior attributes, consumers make the purchase decision based on price, and brand image no longer has any meaning.

The best way to correct this problem is to spend more on advertising designed to rebuild the brand's image. Unfortunately, to spend more on advertising means cutting trade promotions incentives. The risk becomes that other competitors will move in by offering trade promotions to retailers and shelf space will be lost as a result. Then, the vicious cycle begins again.

These four problems make management of trade promotions programs a challenging part of the marketing planning process. Effective IMC programs achieve a balance between all elements of the promotions mix and identify clear goals and targets for trade promotions programs. Only then is the company able to compete on all levels and not just through a cycle of trade promotions bidding wars.

implications for **marketing professionals**

Trade Promotions Managers

Emphasize brand equity. Work with the account executive and client companies to create a balance between what they spend on trade promotions as compared to the rest of the promotions mix.

Visit retail stores that sell the products of manufacturing companies you represent. Observe how the product is displayed and how retail sales reps treat it. If the manufacturer is not well represented, the company should know.

Design contests that match advertising themes and carry the firm's message to the target level. Each of these has different needs in preferences in contests and prizes.

- Distributors
- Wholesalers
- Retail buyers
- Salespersons in retail stores
- Customers

Help the company establish effective linkages with other firms through cooperative advertising programs. Explain the benefits, and stay involved in the designs of these ads to make sure the client receives the optimal benefit from the expenditures.

Inform the marketing team about all specialty advertising items. Make sure these are useful, tasteful, and carry the firm's message effectively.

Make sure trade promotions items such as POP displays carry the company's major theme and IMC emphasis.

Attend trade shows. Observe how various manufacturers, distributors, and wholesalers represent their goods. Note any competitive advantage a company gains by effectively managing the trade booth.

Help the company set quality goals for trade promotions programs. Link those goals to advertisements and other parts of the promotions mix.

Assist the company, to whatever degree possible, in assessing the effects of trade promotions incentives and discounts as compared to advertising and other promotions items. It is your responsibility to make sure short-term gains are not made at the expense of long-term success.

SUMMARY

The marketing mix consists of four basic components: (1) advertising, (2) trade promotions, (3) consumer promotions, and (4) personal selling. Trade promotions are the primary tool members of the marketing channel use to push products onto retailer shelves. Anytime a product is being promoted for resale, a trade promotions program is being utilized.

A wide variety of trade promotions programs exists, including trade allowances, trade contests, trade incentives, training programs, vendor support programs, trade shows, specialty advertising, and point-of-purchase displays. Several major factors affect the choice of promotional tool, most notably:

- Standard practice in the industry
- Competitive pressures
- Company preferences
- Marketing goals and objectives

Common objectives for trade promotions programs include obtaining distribution for new products, gaining prime retail space, supporting established brands, countering the competition, increasing order sizes, enlarging retailer inventories or reducing manufacturer inventories, enhancing channel relationships, and building on other parts of the IMC program. Various trade promotions tools match with these goals.

The major issue facing marketers who work with promotional programs is making sure the promotions match overall IMC goals. They should be coordinated with advertising expenditures and campaigns and balanced with other parts of the promotions mix. Trade promotions are costly and place enormous pressures on small manufacturers. Many wholesale and retail firms simply will not place orders for merchandise until a trade promotions incentive is offered. Company leaders must work diligently to build and maintain brand image and not fall into the trap of simply engaging in competitive trade promotions bargaining to retain retail space. Instead, brand image and strong relationships with various vendors can counterbalance competitor attempts to steal space merely by offering a short-term price discount.

As with all of the other ingredients of an IMC plan, the primary task is to develop a coordinated and balanced plan of attack to reach the marketplace with one clear message. Trade promotions must be included in the process and not dominate marketing expenditures to the point that other aspects of the marketing mix are neglected. When this balance is achieved, the company can compete in the long term for better position with other members of the channel as well as retail customers. Maintaining the vision to see long-range goals is one key element in managing trade promotions.

REVIEW QUESTIONS

1. What is a trade promotions program? How is it related to other elements of the marketing mix?
2. What is the difference between trade promotions and consumer sales promotions?
3. Describe the four main types of trade allowances and the goals they are mostly likely to achieve. Which is the most "controversial"? Why?
4. What is forward buying? Why is it a problem for manufacturers?
5. What is a diversion tactic? Why are diversions used less frequently than forward buying?
6. What is spiff money?
7. Name and briefly describe the various forms of trade contests. Which is the least likely to be used?
8. Name and briefly describe the major forms of trade incentives. Which ones involve retailers paying some of the costs first, before receiving compensation?
9. Why are training programs considered to be a form of trade promotion? What objectives will a quality training program be most likely to achieve?
10. What is a billback?
11. What advantages do cooperative advertising programs hold for manufacturers? For retailers?
12. Why have smaller specialty trade shows begun to replace larger, more general shows?
13. How are international attendees different from local attendees at a trade show? What should a manufacturer do to meet these differences?
14. What are the five top giveaways associated with specialty advertising? How are they related to the concept of reciprocation?
15. What are the characteristics of a high-quality, effective POP display?
16. What are the major objectives manufacturers try to achieve with trade promotions programs? Are these objectives different than those of wholesalers or distributors? Why or why not?
17. What problems are associated with trade promotions programs? How can manufacturers overcome these problems?
18. How should a retailer respond to trade promotions incentives? Should retailers try to get manufacturers involved in bidding wars? Why or why not?
19. What role should trade promotions play in the overall IMC plan?

KEY TERMS

trade promotions the expenditures or incentives used by manufacturers and other members of the marketing channel to help push their products through to retailers.

trade allowances financial incentives offered to another channel member to motivate it to make a purchase.

off-invoice allowance a financial incentive offered to a channel member to place an order and receive a discount on each case ordered.

drop-ship allowance money paid to retailers who are willing to bypass wholesalers, brokers, agents, or distributors when making pre-planned orders.

slotting fees funds paid to retailers to stock new products.

exit fees monies paid to remove an item from a retailer's inventory.

on-deal when a price allowance is being given as part of a trade promotions program.

forward buying when a retailer purchases excess inventory of a product while it is on-deal.

diversion when a retailer purchases a product on-deal in one location and ships it to another location where it is off-deal.

spiff money rewards given as contest prizes to brokers, retail salespeople, retail stores, wholesalers, or agents.

trade incentives given when the retailer performs a function in order to receive the discount or allowance.

cooperative merchandising agreement (CMA) a formal agreement between the retailer and manufacturer to undertake a cooperative effort.

calendar promotions promotional campaigns retailers plan for their customers through manufacturer trade incentives.

corporate sales program (CSP) a form of trade incentive offered by highly specialized manufacturers.

producing plant allowance (PPA) a trade incentive in which the retailer purchases a full or half truckload of merchandise in order to receive a major discount.

back haul allowance (BHA) a trade incentive whereby the retailer pays the cost of shipping and the retailer, instead of the manufacturer furnishes delivery trucks.

cross-dock or pedal run allowance monies paid to retailers for placing a full truck order that is then divided among several stores within the same geographic region.

premium or bonus pack given by offering the retailer free merchandise rather than a discount on the price.

billback   the manufacturer pays the retailer for special product displays, advertisements, or price cuts.

cooperative advertising program   the manufacturer agrees to reimburse the retailer a certain percentage of the advertising costs associated with advertising the manufacturer's products in the retailer's ad.

reciprocation   a psychological concept that whenever someone receives a gift, the human desire is to return a gift or favor.

point of purchase (POP)   any form of special display that advertises merchandise.

ENDNOTES

1. Stephanie Thompson, "Red Letter School Days," *Brandweek,* 39, no. 29 (July 20, 1998), pp. 22–25; Susan Greco, "Selling the Superstores," *Inc.,* 17, no. 10 (July 1995) p. 54.

2. Jack J. Kasulis, "Managing Trade Promotions in the Context of Market Power," *Journal of the Academy of Marketing Science,* 27, no. 3 (summer 1999), pp. 320–32; Anthony Lucas, "In-Store Trade Promotions," *Journal of Consumer Marketing,* 13, no. 2 (1996), pp. 48–50.

3. Kasulis, "Managing Trade Promotions in the Context of Market Power."

4. Martin Hoover, "Supermarket 'Slotting' Leaves Small Firms Out," *Business Courier: Serving the Cincinnati-Northern Kentucky Region,* 16, no. 25 (October 8, 1999), pp. 3–4.

5. Philip Zerillo and Dawn Iacobucci, "Trade Promotions: A Call for a More Rational Approach," *Business Horizons,* 38, no. 4 (July – August 1995), pp. 69–76; Jack Mohr and George S. Low, "Escaping the Catch-22 of Trade Promotion Spending," *Marketing Management,* 2, no. 2 (1993), pp. 30–39.

6. Malia Boyd, "A Case for Incentives," *Incentive,* 169, no. 2 (February 1995), p. 14.

7. Laurie Watanabe, "Duel at Dawn," *Dealernews,* 33, no. 12 (November 1997), p. 59.

8. Michael Moore, "SBLI of Mass. Unveils Plan to Revitalize Sales at Banks," *American Banker,* 164, no. 152 (August 10, 1999), p. 9.

9. Michele Marchetti and Andy Cohen, "In Search of Microsoft's Softer Side," *Sales and Marketing Management,* 151, no. 12 (December 1999), p. 20.

10. Roger A. Slavens, "Getting a Grip on Co-op," *Modern Tire Dealer,* 75, no. 3 (March 1994), pp. 34–37.

11. Ibid.

12. Dana Blankenhorn, "Memphis Company Solves Co-op Ad Accounting Problem Online," *Advertising Age's Business Marketing,* 83, no. 12 (December 1998), pp. 3–4.

13. Bradley Johnson, "IBM Moves Back to Intel Co-op Deal," *Advertising Age,* 68, no. 10 (March 10, 1997), p. 4.

14. Jim Martyka, "Sports Trade Shows Shrink, Specialize," *City Business: The Business Journal of the Twin Cities,* 17, no. 13 (August 27, 1999), p. 10; Laurie Freeman, "B-to-B Marketing Communications Budgets Grow 14.5% as Overall Spending Reaches $73 Billion," *Advertising Age's Business Marketing,* 84, no. 5 (May 1999), pp. S3–S4.

15. Matthew Flamm, "Alien Influences," *Crain's New York Business,* 15, no. 46 (November 15, 1999), pp. 35–36.

16. Ibid.

17. Martyka, "Sports Trade Shows Shrink, Specialize."

18. Alastair Goldfisher, "Firms Give Away Everything to Capture Trade-Show Traffic," *Pacific Business News,* 37, no. 3 (April 2, 1999), p. 21.

19. Polyack, "Creativity Is Key to Successful Giveaway Marketing Campaigns," *Business Journal Serving Fresno and the Central San Joaquin Valley,* no. 322532 (November 1, 1999), p. 4.

20. Hilary S. Miller, "P-O-P Has High Recall, Survey Shows," *Beverage Industry,* 85, no. 12 (December 1994), pp. 15–16; Matthew Martinez and Mercedes M. Cardona, "Study Shows POP Gaining Ground as Medium," *Advertising Age,* 68, no. 47 (November 24, 1997), p. 43.

21. David Tossman, "The Final Push—POP Boom," *New Zealand Marketing Magazine,* 18, no. 8 (September 1999), pp. 45–51.

22. Ibid.; Martinez and Cardona, "Study Shows POP Gaining Ground as Medium."

23. "POP: Vendors Turn to Specification," *Discount Store News,* 38, no. 10 (May 24, 1999), pp. 9–10.

24. Alf Nucifora, "Point-of-Purchase Advertising Now a Marketing VIP," *Business Journal [Phoenix],* 19, no. 49 (September 17, 1999), p. 32.

25. Dana James, "Seeing Green," *Marketing News,* 33, no. 24, (November 22, 1999), p. 19.

26. Scott Flom and Mark Mitchell, "New Age of P-O-P Indicates Alliances Make for Good Marketing," *Marketing News,* 33, no. 24 (November 22, 1999), p. 22.

27. Richard Merli, "Retailers and Suppliers Agree: Trade Promo Stinks," *Frozen Food Age,* 48, no. 2 (September 1999), p. 51; Anthony Lucas, "In-Store Trade Promotions," *Journal of Consumer Marketing,* 13, no. 2 (1996), pp. 48–50.

28. Greco, "Selling the Superstores," pp. 55–61.

29. Kasulis, "Managing Trade Promotions in the Context of Market Power."

30. "Harley Sweepstakes Kicks Off AgrEvo's DeltaGard Promotion," *Pest Control,* 65, no. 9 (September 1997), pp. 28–29.

Building an IMC Campaign

Matching Trade Promotions Tactics with an IMC Advertising Campaign

With an integrated approach, there will be a tie-in between the advertising campaign you employ and the trade promotions offered. These include all the kinds of discounts that are passed along to retailers as well as other items. Does your product lend itself to a point-of-purchase display? What other incentives can you offer to the retailer to lead the company to prominently display and emphasize the product you are selling? If a wholesaler distributes your product, what incentives should you offer to encourage the wholesaler to push your product through the channel? What kinds of trade promotions can be used for services, if that was the thing you decided to promote? To help you work out these issues, both in domestic markets and internationally, complete the exercise for Chapter 11 by accessing the Advertising Plan Pro software included with this textbook or by accessing the Web site at www.prenhall.com/clow.

Critical Thinking Exercises

Discussion Questions

1. One type of trade show that has received considerable publicity recently is the gun show. While some gun trade shows are restricted to only retailers, others allow anyone to attend. What is your evaluation of gun shows? Should they all be restricted to only retailers?

2. AgrEvo Environmental Health held a trade contest to launch a new line of DeltaGard low-dose formulations. DeltaGard is an insecticide sold to pest control companies and retailers. To encourage pest control companies to purchase DeltaGard, AgrEvo teamed up with Harley-Davidson and developed the DeltaGard Win-a-Harley Sweepstakes. Entry forms were available only to licensed pest control companies and were featured at the annual National Pest Control Association trade show, at official AgrEvo DeltaGard distributors, on the AgrEvo Web site, and in a series of advertisements that ran during the trade contest. First place was a Harley-Davidson motorcycle valued at over $12,000. Second place was a Harley-Davidson leather jacket. Third place was a Harley-Davidson wristwatch.[30] Was this trade contest a good idea? Would every pest control company be motivated by the prizes offered? Could this trade contest be improved to create greater participation?

3. Debate has continued for many years about the use of slotting fees by retailers. Recently, the U.S. Congress examined the practice when it considered them to potentially restrict free trade. Using an academic search engine, locate some recent articles about slotting fees. Should they be permitted, or should laws be passed restricting or even eliminating them?

4. Study a recent Sunday or Wednesday newspaper. How many cooperative advertisements are present? What brands does the retailer's advertisement promote? Are these advertisements effective from the viewpoint of the manufacturer? How effective are they for the retailer?

5. Go to a nearby retail store. How many POP displays are present? Which ones are the most impressive? Why? Which ones did not succeed in gaining your interest? Why? Return to the same store a week later. How many new POP displays are there? Which ones are still up?

6. Interview a retail store manager about trade promotions used at his or her store. Especially discuss POP displays and trade allowances. Find out what percentage of the POP displays received are not used. Why are others not used? What criteria does the store manager use in deciding?

7. From the list of stores in Figure 11.11, pick one that is close by. Interview the manager about the store's small vendor program or lack of a small vendor program. Report the findings to your class.

8. Access the Trade Show News Network at www.tsnn.com. Pick one trade show from each of the following categories:
   a. Apparel
   b. Boating and yachting
   c. Gender specific
   d. Photography
   e. Physical fitness and health

   Find out the following information about each trade show. Evaluate it as being potentially successful or a waste of time for the exhibitor and the attendee.
   f. Type of show
   g. Location of show
   h. Show date
   i. Number of exhibitors
   j. Number of attendees
   k. Names of exhibitors
   l. Names of the attendees

9. Access the Trade Show News Network at www.tsnn.com. Pick one category of trade shows from the list in Exercise 8-1. Assume you are a small manufacturer in that industry. Locate five trade shows that would be feasible to attend as an exhibitor. Evaluate each one. If you could afford to attend only one, which show would you choose? Why?

10. Access the Trade Show News Network at www.tsnn.com. Pick one category of trade shows from the list in Exercise 8. Assume you are a buyer for a retail outlet. Locate five trade shows that would be feasible to attend as a buyer. Evaluate each one from the viewpoint of a buyer.

Waterbed World

Bernice Kepford prepared for an important staff meeting with her clients at Waterbed World, knowing that the next year or two would be crucial in that company's life. Bernice's advertising agency had long served Waterbed World in a fairly simple fashion, preparing print ads for trade journal advertising campaigns. Now, however, the company needed a strong boost to sales.

Waterbed World began as a small "head shop" operation in the early 1970s. At that time, the owner sold posters, black lights, subversive literature, and drug paraphernalia. As a side product, the local company (in Fort Myers, Florida) also carried waterbeds. At the time, the quality of the product was low and it was not the store's main feature. Later, as waterbed quality improved, the owner decided an upscale clientele would be more profitable. He relocated Waterbed World to a freestanding store near a major mall. Salespeople began to wear dresses and suits, and the store sold waterbeds along with quality furniture and other higher-markup items.

In the early 1980s, Waterbed World acquired a mattress manufacturer, and the seamless waterbed mattress became the company's most visible product. Waterbed World expanded to sell its mattresses and frames on a national level. Traveling sales reps visited waterbed stores throughout the country and the firm grew quickly to a major scale. Three primary promotional tools were used: (1) trade shows for furniture and waterbeds, (2) trade journal advertisements, and (3) personal selling techniques of the traveling reps.

As the millennium ended, interest in waterbeds had begun to diminish. The beds had a loyal set of consumers, but the increased quality of regular mattress and air mattresses provided substantial competition. The owner of Waterbed World believed the company needed to move the product into other, more mainstream, markets in order to survive. Specialty waterbed stores were not the answer.

The company asked Bernice to create a trade promotions campaign to go along with consumer ads for Waterbed World's products. The goal was to expand the sales of mattresses and frames into furniture stores, and even into places such as Wal-Mart's Supercenters and Sam's Club outlets. No distributors or wholesalers would be involved. Waterbed World wanted to sell directly to an entire new set of retailers.

Consumer ads would promote two features: (1) better sleep and (2) healthy rest. They would portray other mattresses as less comfortable and harder on the joints and back as the person sleeps. Ads also would emphasize product quality and customer support.

One of Bernice's primary concerns was how the company could convince various retailers that waterbeds would bring in potential customers and generate profits for the stores. She knew retail space was limited, especially for such large items.

1. What trade promotions tools should Bernice recommend? Which ones would not work?

2. How can Waterbed World integrate this new emphasis on retail accounts with consumer sales promotions and advertising?

3. What obstacles will Waterbed World encounter as the firm makes this move into new markets?

APPLICATION EXERCISE II

Musa Pinar, the promotions trade manager for Galactic Toys, knows his firm is in for a new experience. Galactic Toys is a highly successful company in its home country, Turkey. In that region, the toy business is not as strongly dictated by the successes and failures of films and is not quite as dominated by the Christmas season. In an effort to build sales and "test the waters," Musa has been asked to study the U.S. toy market to see if the firm's biggest-selling line, Galaxy Conquest toys, could compete effectively.

In the United States, each year over half of all the toy purchases are made at the retail level during November and December. The summer movie schedule provides some clues as to which "fad" toys are most likely to succeed. Any new *Star Wars* film boosts sales of its figures, and the same is true for *Star Trek, Toy Story,* and many others. A second set of toys has a more annual and traditional base, including Barbie, GI Joe, as well as standard board games and more generic products such as Lincoln Logs and Legos. These products are updated to keep them more current and are staples for several manufacturers in the industry.

Seasonal toys are featured in major trade shows every summer. Major companies set up booths and hold extravagant release campaigns for new products and other innovations. The media are invited and a feature story can become the lifeblood of a new fad product. Cabbage Patch Dolls, Teenage Mutant Ninja Turtles, Tickle Me Elmo, and Furby toys have created near riotous conditions in various retail outlets following successful media campaigns in the pre-Christmas publicity season. Toys tied to movies enjoy the additional benefits of the Halloween costume season ahead of actual toy sales.

Toy buyers can be distributed roughly into four categories. First, those who buy for small children tend to rely on major name brands, such as Fisher-Price and Playskool. At a slightly older age, Tonka toys are big sellers. Second, grade-school-age children constitute the primary market for fad and trendy toys. Parents view many of these products as "status symbols" as much as they are playthings for kids. Thus, owning a Furby represents not only a fun toy, but a major one-upmanship factor for parents who want their kids to have everything. The third set of buyers tends to purchase more staple toys. These shoppers are often lower-income families who cannot afford the more extravagant prices paid for the season's hottest item, or are parents who simply withdraw from the "keeping up with the Joneses" mentality associated with high-status toys. Fourth, junior-high-age kids now buy more sophisticated technology-based toys, especially Nintendo products.

Galactic Toys would normally be placed in the GI Joe–*Star Wars* section of toy store shelves. Individual products are high-quality, but reasonably priced toys for more staple buyers who are less driven by trends and more inclined to seek out items that do not break easily. The problems Musa believes the company will experience are:

- Gaining attractive booths at major trade shows
- Breaking through the publicity campaigns of major fad toys, to build interest by various stores
- Convincing retailers that Galactic Toys are more year-round, and less seasonal, products (e.g., toys for birthday gifts and other minor celebrations or occasions)

To succeed, Musa thinks he should start with the trade shows themselves. He attended a few shows and noticed glamorous women dressed in attractive fashions showing off dominos and checkerboards. He watched the video presentations, saw giveaways, and examined other attention-seeking devices. Next, Musa subscribed to all key trade journals and solicited information about prices, locations in magazines, and other information about ads. Third, Musa has been looking for tie-ins with other products, such as breakfast cereals, T-shirts, and others. Still, in his report to company leaders, Musa wrote that making headway in such a tough marketplace is going to be a challenge, even with the company's best efforts.

1. Assess Musa's report.
2. Design a trade promotions campaign and integrate it with a larger IMC program and theme for Galaxy products.
3. Besides trade shows, are there any other trade promotions tools Galactic Toys can use to increase sales?
4. Are there any other special challenges a Turkish toy company will encounter when trying to compete in the United States? What are they?

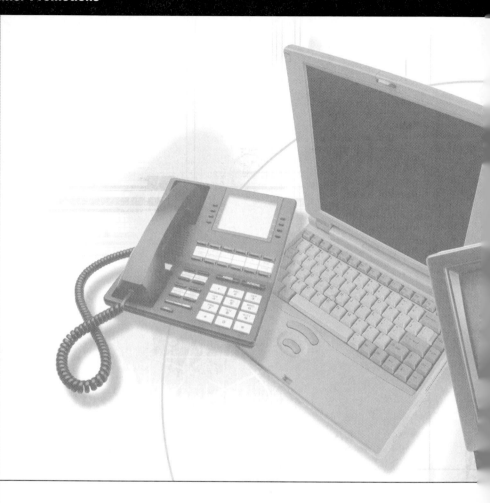

► **CHAPTER OBJECTIVES**

Be aware of the goals, advantages, and disadvantages for each promotions program that can be used in marketing a company or product.

Tie consumer promotions with trade promotions and other elements of the promotions mix and then match them to the overall IMC program.

Seek out quality uses of consumer promotions for sales to business-to-business buyers.

Understand the limitations that are present when consumer promotions programs are developed for international customers.

TIME-SHARE VACATION PROPERTIES:
Half-Product–Half-Service Promotions

Leisure time activities and recreation generate major revenues for the economies of various regions, states, and even nations. Many types of organizations attempt to lure tourists into their areas, through hotels, restaurants, theme parks, and other activities. One of the more lucrative parts of tourism is that vacationers spend money in different ways while on trips. Items ordinarily considered too expensive are more readily purchased.

chapter**twelve**

One set of companies that has taken advantage of the desire for quality leisure time is the time-share industry. Basically, time-share property holders own blocks of time for condominiums, apartments, townhouses, or motel rooms in resort towns. Normally a block is one week long. Time-shares are "products" in the sense that a person buys ownership of the location for the specified time period. A deed is prepared, and usually the ownership can be resold or passed along to heirs when the original owner dies.

Time-shares also are services. The typical time-share agreement includes a clause stating that the owner will pay a "maintenance" fee each year. The fee covers housekeeping, lawn care, and other services the time-share com-

pany provides. More importantly, other aspects of time-shares make them truly unique. These time allocations can be traded across nationwide networks of time-share locations. A person can exchange a week in Santa Cruz, California, for a week in Branson, Missouri. The trade involves paying a fee for the swap to the company running the network.

Various weeks of time have more or less "value," depending on the season. For instance, a time-share week in New England during the autumn, when the leaves are changing to their spectacular colors, has more value than a week in the winter. A week in New Orleans during the Mardi Gras season has more value than a week in the middle of summer. Most firms declare weeks of ownership to have one of three levels: (1) peak, (2) regular, or (3) off-season. Peak season weeks may be traded for all three types, and off-season can usually be exchanged only for off-season times.

Promotion of time-shares involves a variety of tactics. First, the firms advertise heavily in tourist magazines and magazines devoted exclusively to time-share properties. Second, the typical time-share program includes granting a prospective buyer a small period of time (usually one night to a full weekend) to stay free at a time-share property. The prospect must agree to tour the facility and hear the sales pitch in order to receive the free night(s) of lodging. Often, small gifts are given. Meals, fruit baskets, bottles of wine, and other small tokens such as T-shirts and lawn chairs are part of the package.

The tour involves showing the client the property in detail, plus a presentation of all of the additional benefits of time-sharing, including the exchange network. Then, at the close of the sale, the prospect is usually offered a one-time, must-buy-today discount to purchase a week of time.

To beef up prospect lists, members of the time-share community are given gifts for bringing in potential buyers. A member may receive extra days or weekends of time for finding prospects. Some are even given "upgrades" for their weeks (e.g., from off-season to regular) for identifying someone who might visit the area.

The exchange program also offers vacations to non-time-share areas, along with coupons and discounts for tours and other activities in tourist areas, such as coupons for meal discounts and reduced-price boat rides at lake resorts.

There is even an after-market for time-shares. Many can be resold. Firms which resell time-shares can work either separately from or in conjunction with the time-share management team. These properties normally do not offer the free visits and gifts used to entice first-time buyers of the property.

Competition in the time-share market is intense. Locations that do not fill up the time slots for each room quickly face cash flow problems. Some critics argue the free visits are simply "bait and switch" techniques that cause people who cannot afford to make purchases to spread themselves too thin. Those who enjoy time-share privileges argue the programs are among the best investments in leisure time. As the baby boom generation continues to age and accumulate additional disposable income, the odds are high that time-share companies will continue to prosper. At some point, you may find yourself tempted by a free vacation, a few goodies, and a very polished sales rep seeking to lure you into the exciting world of vacation property ownership.

overview

Many methods are available to entice consumers to take the final step and make a purchase. Advertising creates interest and excitement and can be used to offer the deal that brings the consumer into the store. At the same time, marketers use other tactics in conjunction with advertising programs. Besides trade promotion incentives offered to retailers, consumer promotions programs can be highly effective in generating sales and building traffic.

Consumer promotions (sometimes called *sales promotions*) are the incentives aimed at a firm's customers. These customers can be end users of the product or service or they may be other businesses. As noted in Chapter 11, the difference between consumer promotions and trade promotions is that trade promotions are directed at firms that resell the manufacturer's or firm's products. Consumer promotions are directed toward individuals or firms that use the product and do not resell it to another business. Thus, consumer promotions can be used in both consumer markets and business-to-business markets.

- ▶ Coupons
- ▶ Premiums
- ▶ Contests and sweepstakes
- ▶ Refunds and rebates
- ▶ Sampling
- ▶ Bonus packs
- ▶ Price-offs

Types of Consumer Promotions

FIGURE 12.1

As with other parts of the promotions mix, consumer promotions should be tied into the integrated marketing communications plan. Figure 12.1 lists the most common consumer promotions. A review of each type follows.

coupons

A coupon is a price reduction offer to a consumer. It may be a percentage off the retail price such as 25 percent or 40 percent, or an absolute amount ($.50 or $1.00). In the United States, 300 billion coupons were distributed and 4.8 billion redeemed in 1999. This 2 percent redemption rate represents approximately $3.6 billion in savings for consumers, or about 70.2 cents per coupon. Approximately 78 percent of all U.S. households use coupons and 64 percent are willing to switch brands with coupons.[1]

Nearly 80 percent of all coupons are distributed by manufacturers. Figure 12.2 lists the various forms of coupon distribution. Eighty-eight percent of all coupons are sent out through print media, with 80 percent distributed through **free standing inserts (FSI).** FSI are sheets of coupons distributed in newspapers, primarily on Sunday. Another 4 percent of coupons are distributed through direct mail, and 3.5 percent more are distributed either on or in a product's package. The remaining 5 percent are delivered in other ways.[2]

- ▶ Print media
- ▶ Direct mail
- ▶ On or in package
- ▶ In store
- ▶ Sampling
- ▶ Scanner delivered
- ▶ Cross ruffing
- ▶ Response offer
- ▶ Internet
- ▶ Fax
- ▶ Sales staff

Methods of Distributing Coupons

FIGURE 12.2

A manufacturer's coupon from S.C. Johnson encouraging consumers to purchase Vanish Brush Free.
Courtesy of S.C. Johnson & Son, Inc.

Most companies prefer using FSI and print media to distribute coupons for several reasons. First, consumers must make a conscious effort to clip or save the coupon. Second, coupons create brand awareness because consumers see the brand name on the coupon even if they do not actually use the coupon. Third, FSI encourage consumers to purchase brands on the next trip to the store. Manufacturers believe that consumers are more likely to purchase a couponed brand and remember the name when they redeem a coupon. This moves the brand to the consumer's long-term memory. Hopefully, consumers will recall the brand and buy it the next time the need arises, even when they do not have coupons. The S.C. Johnson advertisement above encourages consumers to buy Vanish Brush Free using the coupon in the advertisement.

Types of coupons

Coupons are often distributed in retail stores placed on or in packages. The consumer immediately can redeem the coupon while making the purchase. This type of coupon is called an **instant redemption coupon.** These coupons often lead to trial purchases and purchases of additional packages of a product. Some coupons are given out along with free samples of a product to encourage consumers to try a new brand. Many grocery stores allow a company to cook a new food product and offer free samples of it along with coupon giveaways. Coupons also are placed in dispensers near various products, which provide convenient access for customers. All of these are forms of instant redemption coupons, because customers can use them immediately.

Coupons also can be placed inside packages so that customers cannot redeem them quite as quickly. This approach encourages repeat purchases, and the coupons are called **bounce-back coupons.**

Firms can issue coupons at the cash register. They are called **scanner-delivered coupons,** because they are triggered by an item being scanned. The item being scanned is normally a competitor's product. Firms use this approach to encourage brand switching.

Another way to distribute coupons is cross-ruffing. **Cross-ruffing** is the placement of a coupon for one product on another product. For example, a coupon for a French onion dip placed on a package of potato chips is a cross-ruffing coupon. To be successful, cross-ruff coupons must be on products that fit together logically and usually are purchased and consumed simultaneously. Occasionally, a manufacturer uses cross-ruffing to encourage consumers to purchase another one of its products. For example, the Kellogg company may place a coupon on a Rice Krispies box for another cereal, such as Frosted Flakes or an oatmeal product. This type of couponing tactic encourages consumers to purchase within the same brand or family of products.

Coupons also stimulate trial purchases of new products. Manufacturers send coupons in advance to consumers, making it more likely a trial purchase will follow. Prior to a shopping trip, a consumer may not have decided upon a specific brand to purchase. This means the consumer is more willing to purchase the brand with an introductory coupon mailed to his or her home than if the coupon is available only in the store, where the consumer is less likely to take the time to examine it.

Response offer coupons are issued following requests by consumers. Requests may be from a 1-800 number or an Internet inquiry. Coupons then are mailed to the consumer or sent by Internet to be printed by the consumer. The coupon can also be faxed. In the business-to-business sector, a fax is the most common method of distributing response offer coupons. Office supply companies and other vendors use response offer coupons to invite business customers to make purchases or place orders. Firms also distribute coupons through their sales representatives, which allows for instant redemptions, because the salesperson also takes the order.

Another form of coupon is one that is *electronically delivered.* The first retailer to offer "U-pons" (paperless, Internet-delivered) was Dick's Supermarkets, which used San Francisco–based Planet U to send out coupons to 50,000 Savings Club members in Wisconsin and Illinois. In that program, redemption rates for baby products averaged 36 percent, cheese and peanut butter 30 percent, bread 24 percent, prepared frozen foods 22 percent, and cookies 20 percent in the first year. U-pons can be sent electronically to the retailer's point-of-sales system. The coupon also has a code printed on it to trace it back to the house where it was used. Consumers using this electronic distribution method click on the coupons they want on their computers while at home. The amount of the coupon discount is automatically deducted from the purchase price through the use of a frequent-shopper card presented at the store.[3]

Coupon responses

The typical response rate for a coupon distribution is less than 2 percent. Redemption rates for Internet-delivered coupons average more than 20 percent. Research into coupon redemptions helps retailers understand how consumers respond. For example, coupons are not used equally among various ethnic groups. African Americans and Hispanics tend to redeem coupons less than does the population as a whole, because there is a lower distribution rate to certain ethnic groups. Freestanding inserts in Sunday papers account for 80 percent of the distribution of coupons. Minority groups tend to read ethnically oriented newspapers and magazines and are less inclined to subscribe to publications aimed at the general population. Consequently, the FSI do not reach them. Magazines and newspapers targeting individual ethnic groups contain fewer coupon offers than do more general-appeal print media. Lower redemption rates can make ethnic groups appear to be less attractive and therefore they receive fewer direct-mail coupons. To correct this cycle, manufacturers and other distributors of coupons can improve their targeting approaches by sending out offers through the more ethnic publications.[4]

Problems with coupons

There are a few drawbacks to the use of coupons as a promotional tactic. They include:

- Reduced revenues
- Mass-cutting
- Counterfeiting
- Misredemptions

The first disadvantage is that current brand users who are already brand loyal simply redeem the coupon with their next purchase, thereby reducing full-price revenues. Brand-loyal customers redeem approximately 80 percent of all coupons.[5] Some argue that offering them a price discount when they would be willing to pay full price does not make sense. Manufacturers, however, point out that these consumers may be willing to stock up on the item, which means they won't use the competition's coupons. Consequently, manufacturers recognize that brand-loyal customer redemptions are a "necessary evil" if mass-distribution is used. Some firms use direct mail to distribute the coupon primarily to nonloyal customers. They try to target nonusers and the competitor's customers. The primary disadvantage of this method is the high cost of direct mail, especially in light of the low response rate associated with direct-mail coupons.

The second problem associated with coupons is that, of the $3.6 billion in coupons that are used, between 10 percent and 30 percent are illegally reimbursed. One common form of coupon fraud is called *mass-cutting*.[6] This occurs when coupons are "redeemed" through a fraudulent retail outlet that does not exist, except at a mailbox set up by an illegal "coupon ring." At $.50 to $3.00 per coupon, mass-cutting of coupons is highly lucrative. Many times these rings take advantage of charitable organizations and religious groups that think they are helping a worthy cause by sending in coupons to the mailbox to receive a percentage of the proceeds. Instead, they actually are aiding an illegal activity.

Counterfeiting occurs when coupons are copied and then sent back to the manufacturer for reimbursement. The manufacturer pays for unused coupons. Newspaper-generated black-and-white coupons are the easiest to counterfeit. Color copiers have made other forms of counterfeiting easier to pursue.

Retailers usually are not involved in mass-cutting or counterfeiting of coupons. They can, however, engage in the *misredemption* of coupons. For instance, a coupon for soup often states the size of can for which the discount applies. If the discount is used for another size, such as a 12-ounce can instead of the 24-ounce can, then a misredemption occurs. This may be due to an error on the part of the clerk who did not check the coupon carefully. Or, the clerk might have known it was the wrong-size can but did not want to bother finding the correct size or risk making the customer mad by denying the coupon. Other times, clerks honor coupons for merchandise that was not purchased when they take the coupon and subtract it from the customer's total without matching it to the actual product.

Some misredemptions are performed by retail "clearinghouses" that collect money for coupons even when they were not actually redeemed by customers. Other retailers submit coupons for reimbursement rather than placing them on the shelf or some other location in the store. The typical supermarket redeems more than 1,000 coupons per day. As a result, there is ample opportunity for errors, mistakes, and fraud.[7]

stop!

Integrated Learning Experience

One method of reducing coupon fraud is to use electronic coupon distribution and redemption. Access In Store Media Systems, Inc. at www.ismsi.net to learn about its patented electronic Coupon Exchange Center. What would be the advantage of such a system to manufacturers? To retailers? To consumers? What potential disadvantages are there to this system of distributing and redeeming coupons?

Tactics to improve coupon effectiveness

Three factors influence how attractive a particular coupon appears to consumers. First is the face value of the coupon. The higher the face value, the more attractive the coupon becomes and the more likely it will be redeemed.

Second is the distribution method. Research indicates that FSI are the most attractive to consumers because they can choose coupons in the privacy of their homes. In-store coupons are less attractive because consumers do not want to take time to process information while in the store. Consumers normally do not like making brand choice decisions while shopping. The only exception to this occurs when the coupon is for a brand that is already on a shopping list. Consumers perceive bulk-mail coupons as the least attractive, because the individual has to sort through a series of coupons to find the one he or she might actually use.

The third attractiveness factor is whether the coupon is for a preferred brand or at least for a brand that is already in the consumer's evoked set (readily recalled brands). Coupons for the preferred brand or one from the evoked set tend to be more attractive than those for unknown or unrecognized brand names.[8]

Coupons are likely to remain a popular form of consumer promotion. Many retail establishments enjoy the benefits of manufacturer coupons. The coupons bring customers into the store and have no direct cost to the retailer. Other retailers double and even triple coupon face values as an additional enticement to bring customers into the store. Consequently, stronger bonds develop between retailers and manufacturers when coupon programs are in place.

*communication***action**

Coupons and Condoms

Condom use is one of the best methods for slowing the growth of sexually transmitted diseases and for reducing unwanted pregnancies. Unfortunately, far too many young people use them inconsistently (not every time) because of the embarrassment of making the actual purchase combined with the cost of the condom itself.

One recent research effort indicates that traditional condom sales promotions are not as successful as they could be. The traditional approach is a free condom giveaway in conjunction with an event, or at a booth set up by a family planning or disease prevention agency. Unfortunately, one free use does not lead to a consistent buying pattern.

To entice buyers to consider condom purchases in drugstores and other locations, they first must see the coupon and then be inspired to make the purchase. Coupons for condoms located at the purchase site (the display) are more readily noticed. The higher the value of the coupon, the more likely the coupon will be redeemed. Males are more likely to take the time to examine coupons at purchase sites and to make the purchase.

Thus, the most logical use of sales promotions, rather than giveaways or premiums, may be simply to place the coupon at the site where a person can examine it without further embarrassment. Then, by making the price less prohibitive by offering a coupon-based discount, a greater number of items may be purchased at one time, or at the least the customer will return to make another purchase when needed. Such an approach may be more of a win–win solution to generating sales while preventing unwanted pregnancy and disease at the same time.

Source: Darren W. Dahl and Gerald J. Gorn, "Encouraging Use of Coupons to Stimulate Condom Purchase," *American Journal of Public Health*, 89, no. 12, 1996, p. 4.

Integrated Learning Experience

Coupons are one of the most popular forms of consumer promotions. Many companies will assist a business in a couponing program. To learn about what services these firms offer and how the Internet is being promoted as a new, more effective medium of distribution, access the following companies.

Coupons.com, Inc. (www.coupons.com, look under advertising)
I.A.M. Sales & Design Representative (www.clickoncoupon.com, Look under advertising)
Coupon Country–Kaufman Advertising (www.couponcountry.com)

premiums

A second form of consumer promotion is the offer of a premium. Premiums are prizes, gifts, or other special offers consumers receive when purchasing products. When a company offers a premium, the consumer pays full price for the product or service, in contrast to coupons, which are price reductions. Some marketing experts believe the overuse of coupons damages a brand's image. Conversely, premiums actually can enhance brand image. The key is to pick the right type of premium. Premiums can be used in the attempt to boost sales; however, they usually are not as successful as coupon sales. Nevertheless, premiums remain a valuable consumer promotional tool with over $4.5 billion per year being spent on them in the United States alone.[9]

There are four major types of premiums:

1. Free-in-the-mail premiums
2. In- or on-package premiums
3. Store or manufacturer premiums
4. Self-liquidating premiums

Free-in-the-mail premiums are gifts individuals receive for purchasing products. To receive the gift, the customer must mail in a proof of purchase to the manufacturer, who then mails the gift back to the consumer. Sometimes more than one purchase is required to receive the gift. Review the premiums being offered by The Fisher Boy advertisement shown on the next page. Consumers collect points from the front of Fisher Boy packages to be redeemed for "cool" prizes. To further encourage sales, the advertisement has a coupon attached.

Credit card companies use premiums to entice individuals to sign up for credit cards. Instead of providing a proof of purchase, the consumer needs only to activate the card. First USA–Bank One VISA mailed an offer of a box of Godiva chocolates for customers who requested and activated their card. The tag line used to promote the premium was "We chose Godiva chocolates as our special gift to you, because, like the First USA Platinum Card, Godiva represents excellence." In a campaign to professionals, instead of Godiva chocolates, a Share Electronic Organizer was given. The message to the professional was "You know better than most that successfully managing a hectic professional schedule requires organization and discipline. So to help you keep control, we'll send you the Sharp Electronic Organizer." Both offers required the consumer to actually use the card before the gift would be mailed.[10]

In- or on-package premiums are usually small gifts, such as toys in cereal boxes. Often the gift is disguised or packaged so the consumer must buy the product to find out which premium it contains. The most famous of these may be Cracker Jack's prizes. At other times the gift is attached to the package, such as package of blades with the purchase of a razor.

Store or manufacturer premiums are gifts given by either the retail store or the manufacturer when the customer purchases a product. Fast-food restaurants offer children a toy with the purchase of a child's meal. To entice luxury-car purchases

A free-in-the-mail premium offer by Fisher Boy. Courtesy of Fisher Boy.

and leases, Cadillac dealers developed a unique premium. They offered a personalized video golf lesson featuring Greg Norman to consumers who test-drove Cadillacs. To receive the tape, however, the customer had to come back a second time, which increased the chances of a purchase. During the first visit to the showroom, the customer's golf swing was videotaped. It was then mixed with footage from Greg Norman's golf swing. Customers who came back for the second visit were presented with the videotape.[11]

The last major type of premium is called the **self-liquidating premium,** because the consumer must pay an amount of money for it. For example, the premium may be offered for only $4.99 plus shipping and handling and two proof of purchase from a box of Cheerios. The premium is called self-liquidating because the $4.99 covers the cost of the premium. The manufacturer also receives money for shipping and handling so consumers pay most or all of its actual cost.

One of the most popular self-liquidating premium programs was Pokemon toys and trading cards offered by Burger King. The Pokemon toy and trading cards were offered to consumers for only $1.99 with the purchase of a Kid's Meal or Big Kids value meal. Burger King offered 57 different toys, each one packaged inside a Poke Ball with one of 151 trading cards. The interest in the Pokemon trading cards became so intense that most Burger Kings held trading nights on Tuesdays so children could trade cards. At one point in the Pokemon craze, Burger King had ordered 100 million toys. The company ran a special full-page advertisement in *USA Today* announcing the arrival of a new batch of toys. The toys were gone in just a few days. Many Burger King restaurants began offering Pokemon posters when they ran out of the trading cards. The Pokemon premium program was the most successful in Burger King's history. Many stores experienced a 30 percent increase in business during the promotion's final weeks. Trading nights became so popular in some places that police had to provide crowd control.[12]

Problems with premiums

The two major problems associated with premium programs are: (1) the time factor and the (2) the cost.

Concerning time-related issues, premiums tend to have short life spans. Many companies try to find items that are hot and adopt them as premiums. The problem is that by the time the marketing material is developed and the merchandise arrives, the item no longer is popular. Many companies have warehouses full of premiums that turned out to be busts because either they waited too long to order the merchandise or the product they thought would be a great premium turned out to be ignored by customers. Such was the case with KFC. Knowing of the popularity of Pokemon and seeing Burger King's success led KFC to promote Pokemon bean bags. The program turned out to be a disaster. Most KFC stores still had huge stocks of the bean bags six weeks after the end of the promotion.[13]

The second problem connected to premiums is the cost. A premium exclusively offered often increases the demand for the item. For example, numerous Disney tie-ins with fast-food restaurants are exclusive contracts. In these arrangements Disney promises not to sell the premium to any other vendor or restaurant. Yet it may offer the merchandise to other types of businesses or to retail outlets. This type of deal normally raises the price of the item and cost to the firm. Consequently, a rising scale seems to exist. Lower-cost premiums generate less interest and probably fewer sales. Higher-cost premiums create more sales, but cost more to provide.

Building successful premium programs

Figure 12.3 highlights the primary keys to building successful premium programs.[14] First, and probably most important, is to match the premium to the target market. For a target market such as older, high-income individuals, the premium may be china or fine crystal. If the market is children, a cartoon figure or a character from Walt Disney or Sesame Street would be attractive. The premium should match the desires and interests of target market members.

Next, the best premiums are those that reinforce the firm's image in some way. They should not be cheap trinkets. Offering cheap merchandise insults customers and can damage the image of a firm.

Premiums are more likely to succeed when they are tied into the firm's products. These items can enhance the image of the product as well as the image of the firm. For instance, Sears offered a 20-piece Pfaltzgraft dinnerware set to everyone who purchased a Kenmore microwave. Customers had a choice of four different

> ▶ **Match the premium to the target market**
> ▶ **Carefully select the premiums (avoid fads, try for exclusivity)**
> ▶ **Pick a premium that reinforces the firm's product and image**
> ▶ **Integrate the premium with other IMC tools (especially advertising and POP displays)**
> ▶ **Don't use premiums to increase profits**

Keys to Successful Premiums

FIGURE 12.3

Source: Based on Bon Jagoda, "The Seven Habits of Highly Successful Premiums," *Incentive,* (August 1999), Vol. 173, Issue 8, pp. 104–105.

patterns. In just six weeks, 4,000 premiums were redeemed. Offering the dinner-ware dishes with the purchase of a microwave reinforced Sears products while the high quality of the dishes reinforced the Kenmore brand image.[15]

It is not necessary to link the premium to the product. Premiums perceived to be of high quality and those desirable to consumers can achieve results. A travel magazine recently tested three different premiums:

1. Travel booklet
2. Desktop calculator
3. AM/FM headphone radio

The travel booklet was highly related to the product, the travel magazine. The calculator and the radio were more generic. The results of the test were:

1. A 1.8 percent response rate for the calculator and the radio
2. A 1.3 percent for the travel booklet

The response rate was only 0.1 percent when no premium was offered. This clearly indicates the power of a premium to motivate consumers to action.[16]

As with coupons, it is important to integrate premiums with the other components of the IMC program. Premiums are an excellent means of adding value to a product instead of slashing prices or using coupons. They can reinforce the brand's image. Premiums can serve as a "thank you" to current customers or to attract new customers. *Sports Illustrated* has a rich history of premium programs, from videos to watches to phones, which are presented for either renewing a subscription to the magazine or ordering one for the first time.

Although premiums are an excellent method of adding value or enhancing a brand, they are not as effective at increasing profits. Therefore, a clear relationship between the premium's intention and IMC goals should be established. Logically the goal should be more about image than profit.

contests and sweepstakes

Contests and sweepstakes are popular forms of consumer sales promotions. Both are used in consumer markets as well as business markets. A primary factor in the success of this type of appeal is the prize list. Members of the target market for the contest or sweepstakes must believe the prizes are desirable enough to entice them to participate. Prizes perceived to be of low or no value do not work.

The words *contest* and *sweepstakes* tend to be used interchangeably, yet there are some differences, primarily legal. *Contests* normally require the participant to perform some type of activity. The winner is selected based on who performs best or provides the most correct answers. Often, contests require a participant to make a purchase to enter. In some states, however, it is illegal to force a consumer to make a purchase to enter a contest. It is important in developing contests to know the different state and federal laws that apply.

Contests range from the controversial bikini or suntan contests at local night-clubs to popular television shows such as *Jeopardy* or *Who Wants to Be a Millionaire* game show contestants must answer questions correctly to win prizes. While some contests are mostly chance (e.g., *Wheel of Fortune*), others require skill. For example, a Woodcraft store held a contest for its customers to demonstrate their woodworking skills. Woodcraft gave a prize of $100 to the person who demonstrated the greatest skill in making his or her first piece of furniture with wood purchased from the company.[17]

No purchase can be required to enter a *sweepstakes.* Consumers enter as many times as they wish. It is permissible for firms to restrict customers to one entry per visit to the store or some other location. The chances of winning a sweepstakes are based on a probability factor. The probability of winning must clearly be stated on all point-of-purchase (POP) displays and advertising materials. In a sweepstakes, the probability of winning each prize must be published in advance. This means the firm must know how many winning tickets, as compared to total tickets, have been prepared.

People enter contests and sweepstakes that they perceive as being worth their time and attention. Consumers do not enter every contest or sweepstakes they encounter. Instead, they selectively choose. The decision is often based on the perceived value of the contest or sweepstakes prize combined with the odds of winning. The greater the perceived odds of winning, the more likely a person will play the contest or enter the sweepstakes.

The perceived value of a prize has two components: (1) extrinsic value and (2) intrinsic value. The extrinsic value is the actual attractiveness of the item (a car versus an all-expense-paid vacation). The greater the perceived value, the more likely the person will participate. Intrinsic values are those associated with playing or participating. A contest requiring the use of a skill, such as the one with Woodcraft or an essay contest, entices entry by individuals who enjoy demonstrating a skill. In that case, extrinsic rewards become secondary. Instead, participants enjoy competing and demonstrating their abilities, which in part explains the popularity of fantasy football and baseball leagues and "pick the winner" sports contests.

The impact of a contest and sweepstakes can be enhanced when it is marketed with other elements of the IMC plan. For an example, see the Communication Action Box in this section.

Problems with contests and sweepstakes

The problems associated with contests and sweepstakes are:

- Costs
- Consumer indifference
- Clutter

communication action

Racing to Sell Cereal

Recently, General Mills developed a $10 million IMC Cheerios promotion with a NASCAR tie-in. The NASCAR sweepstakes theme was featured on POP displays in retail outlets as well as on special Cheerios cereal boxes. Although the primary brand for the promotion was Cheerios, General Mills supported the sweepstakes on other brands such as Trix, Lucky Charms, Cinnamon Toast Crunch, Hamburger Helper, SuperMoist cake mixes, Rich & Creamy frosting, and Gold Medal flour.

General Mills used trade promotions to encourage retailers to display the Cheerios POP materials. The sweepstakes was promoted using print advertisements, FSI, and radio advertisements. Consumers could win tickets to the Daytona 500, go-carts, and other merchandise featuring Cheerios car driver Johnny Benson. Thirty-eight percent of NASCAR's fans are females. In the majority of families, the female does the grocery shopping. Consequently, General Mills wanted to make sure female fans would see the in-store displays. To encourage retailers to use the displays, General Mills awarded special VIP treatment at the Daytona 500 for any retailer that increased the volume of Cheerios sold during the promotion by 20 pallets.

The innovative tie-in between two seemingly unrelated products was a great success. Other firms, including Pepsi, have followed with NASCAR promotions. Thus, it has become clear that car races can be used to sell more than just motor oil.

Source: Stephanie Thompson, "General Mills to Pump $10M into 10-Brand Daytona Promo," *Brandweek*, 39, no. 39 (October 9, 1998), p. 6.

Company leaders must seek to overcome these issues in order to create successful promotional programs.

Contests and sweepstakes require companies to provide prizes, entry forms, legal statements, supportive advertising and other promotional activities, and often enticements to retailers to set up POP displays and other contest-related materials. Failure to support a contest fully means the odds of success diminish. Companies must be prepared to undertake all of the necessary expenditures associated with the program.

Consumers are increasingly indifferent to many contests and sweepstakes because of the rising availability of gambling opportunities. State lotteries, casinos, riverboat gambling, and Internet gambling make it possible to play games of chance and skill frequently. As a result, a contest offering a prize of a free dinner or $100 may not seem very exciting.

Clutter results from the number of firms promoting contests at any given time. With so many legal and illegal places to play games of chance, the idea of making a purchase or trip to the store to enter one more contest is less appealing.

Creating successful contests and sweepstakes

One factor in the success level of a contest is finding the right prize. Firms can be creative in trying to reach this goal. For example, instead of money, Lever Brothers' Sunlight dishwasher soap developed a tie-in with Molly Maids to offer housecleaning for a year to 25 prize winners. In a similar contest, Molly Maids teamed up with Maxwell House coffee to offer 30 house cleanings. More than 500,000 people entered these contests.

A second factor in generating a more successful contest is to be able to take advantage of a special event. During the historic home run race between Mark McGwire and Sammy Sosa, Pepsi developed a contest for the fans who flocked to the stadiums to watch. At Pepsi POP displays, consumers could enter the contest by filling out a form and guessing how many home runs would be hit and who would hit them. The grand prize was a trip to the World Series for four. By leveraging this special event, Pepsi developed a winning promotion.[18]

The Internet provides several opportunities for individuals who play contests and sweepstakes for their intrinsic value. The Internet allows for interactive games that can challenge the contestant's ability. Yoyodyne Entertainment has designed over 100 contests and games for companies such as H&R Block, MCI, American Express, Fox TV, and *Rolling Stone* magazine. H&R Block's contest called "We'll Pay Your Taxes" was designed to drive traffic to and through the H&R Block Web site. Through a series of weekly e-mail messages, players were directed to H&R Block's Web site for the answers. Each e-mail message contained brief product messages from H&R Block. The game ran just two months but averaged 46,000 hits per week, more than H&R Block had the entire previous year.[19]

To encourage consumers to continue playing a contest, the extrinsic values of prizes can be increased by allowing small, incremental rewards. A consumer who wins a soft drink or a sandwich in a sweepstakes at Subway is more likely to continue playing. Scratch-and-win cards tend to be effective because the reward is instant. As with coupons, instantly redeemed prizes are more popular with consumers than are delayed rewards. Using special Java technology, scratch-and-win cards can even be used on the Internet so that consumers can win instant prizes.

To fully ensure that the success of the contest or sweepstakes, it is important to coordinate the promotion with the advertising, POP displays, and other marketing tools. All of these elements must be directed toward the same target audience and convey a united message. These features add to the cost of the contest, however such integration is a crucial ingredient in achieving the desired goals.

When the contest or sweepstakes program features a tie-in with another company, the two firms should carefully coordinate their activities. It is a daunting task to include all creatives, trade promotion managers, consumer promotion managers, media buyers, and media planners, but it is also necessary in order to create a successful program.

The primary goals of contests and sweepstakes are to encourage customer traffic and boost sales. There is no doubt that a contest or sweepstakes increases customer traffic. The question is if they actually boost sales. Some do, others do not. Marketers are beginning to realize that intrinsic rewards tend to draw consumers back. This means many Internet games are exciting prospects, because they can be structured to create intrinsic rewards.

Marketing research has demonstrated that brand awareness increases with multiple exposures to an advertisement or contest. Therefore, although contests and sweepstakes may not boost sales in the short run, they can be a driving force behind brand awareness and brand image development over longer periods of time. As a result, they remain another weapon in the marketing arsenals of many organizations.

stop!

Integrated Learning Experience

Sweepstakes and contests are excellent methods for building customer traffic for a retail outlet. Certain firms can assist in the development of sweepstakes and contests. This becomes more important in the case of sweepstakes and contests due to the legal restrictions imposed by various states. Access the following companies to see what types of services they can offer. How could they assist a firm in developing a contest or sweepstakes?

> Sweepstakes Builder (www.sweepstakesbuilder.com)
> Promotions Activators, Inc. (www.promotionactivators.com)
> ADPAC Corporation (www.adpaccorp.com)

What other consumer promotional services can these firms offer? What are the advantages and disadvantages of using one firm for all of a firm's consumer promotions?

refunds and rebates

Refunds and rebates are cash returns offered to consumers or businesses following the purchase of a product. Consumers pay full price for the product but can mail in some type of proof of purchase, and then the manufacturer refunds a portion of the purchase price. A *refund* is a cash return on what are called "soft goods," such as food or clothing. *Rebates* are cash returns on "hard goods," which are major ticket items such as automobiles. Normally refunds are small and rebates are larger. For example, the typical refund offered on a food item may be $1 while the typical rebate on a car may be $500, $1,000, or more, depending on the price and size of the car.

Rebates can be given on services. In an effort to drive traffic to their Web sites, 12 banks developed a tie-in rebate program with Amazon.com. Students and parents could receive the rebate by purchasing books from Amazon.com through each bank's Web site. For each purchase made, a 3 percent rebate was offered to whichever local school the customer designated. The tie-in increased traffic to the banks' Web sites and also provided money for the local schools to purchase books from Amazon.com. The plan turned out to be a great community service project for the banks.[20]

Sometimes rebates from several sources are packaged together. Circuit City advertised a personal computer system valued at $980 for only $300. The $680 savings were in the form of four different rebates. The first rebate was a mail-in rebate to Hewlett-Packard, the computer manufacturer. The second rebate was from Canon for the printer. The third was from Circuit City, and the fourth from CompuServe. To get the CompuServe rebate, the customer had to sign a three-year Internet contract at a cost of $21.95 per month.[21]

Problems with refunds and rebates

The problems associated with refunds and rebates include their costs, the paperwork involved, and diminished effectiveness. The retail outlet must carefully document manufacturer rebates so that the customer is reimbursed. To hold down the paperwork, many automobile dealerships have the rebate assigned to the dealer and deduct the amount from the sales price. This often lessens the "impact" of the rebate, because no check is ever delivered to the customer.

The cost of a refund or rebate is the lost revenue from the sale price combined with the mailing and record-keeping costs involved. Further, a promotional or advertising campaign emphasizing the offer must be developed, or the program goes unnoticed. These extra promotional expenditures further add to the costs of the plan.

Many rebate programs suffer from diminished effectiveness, because consumers have come to expect them. For example, many car dealers find their customers won't buy until rebates are offered. As a result, there is no new purchase activity associated with the rebate, but rather a delay in the purchase as consumers "wait out" auto manufacturers.

Recently Sears eliminated its refund program for credit card purchases. As might be expected, there were complaints from customers who had become accustomed to receiving a refund following a major credit purchase. They felt almost "penalized" by the elimination of the plan.

Creating effective refund–rebate programs

To generate an effective refund or rebate program, the offer must have:

1. Visibility
2. Perceived newness
3. An impact

The refund should be visible. Customers must find out about the program before they can take advantage of it. Refunds and rebates have their greatest successes when they are perceived as being new or original. When they are an entrenched part of doing business, they have simply become an expected discount. Rebates and refunds must have the impact of changing the buyer's behavior, either by leading to more immediate purchases or by causing the customer to change brands.

Retailers tend to like refunds and rebates, because the retailer maintains its margin or markup on the product, because the item or service is sold at full price. Recently, Iomega offered a $50 rebate on its Zip drive that sold for $199. Retailers responded favorably to the Iomega rebate because it was easy for consumers to understand, the display materials were attractive, and implementing the rebate was easy for retailers. Also, the rebate was large enough to stimulate sales and encourage consumers to choose the Iomega brand.[22] Consequently, effective rebate programs are an option for various companies seeking to heighten the buying excitement levels associated with their products.

sampling

One method of encouraging consumers to try new product is sampling. Sampling is the actual delivery of a product to consumers for their use or consumption. Normally, samples are provided free of charge. Often a coupon or price-off incentive then is used to persuade the consumer to make a purchase of a larger version of the product, such as a full-size package.

In business-to-business markets, companies often provide samples of products to potential clients. Sampling also can be used in the service sector. For example, a tanning salon may offer an initial visit free to encourage new customers to try its facilities. Dentists and lawyers use sampling when they offer an initial consultation free of charge.

> ▶ **In-store distribution**
> ▶ **Direct sampling**
> ▶ **Response sampling**
> ▶ **Cross-ruff sampling**
> ▶ **Media sampling**
> ▶ **Professional sampling**
> ▶ **Selective sampling**

Types of Sampling

FIGURE 12.4

Figure 12.4 lists various ways samples are distributed. The most common consumer method is *in-store distribution,* such as when food product companies have personnel cooking the food and passing it out to individuals in the store. *Direct sampling* is a program in which samples are mailed or delivered door to door to consumers. Various demographic target markets can be identified for free samples. In the business-to-business sector, salespeople often deliver direct samples. *Response samples* are made available to individuals or businesses who respond to a media offer on television, on the Internet, from a magazine, or by some other source. *Cross-ruff sampling* plans provide samples of one product on another. A laundry detergent with a free dryer sheet attached to the package is a cross-ruff sample. *Media sampling* means the sample is included in the media outlet. For example, a small sample of perfume can be included in a magazine advertisement. *Professional samples* are delivered by professionals, such as when doctors provide patients with free drug samples. First, the doctor received a package of samples from the drug company. *Selective samples* are distributed at a site such as a state fair, parade, hospital, restaurant, or sporting event. For instance, many times Power Bars are given to people attending football or basketball games. There is a tie-in between the product (nutrition) and the event (athletics).

The target audience determines the best method of sampling to use. Direct sampling is generally the ideal for business-to-business situations. Other methods tend to work better for consumers. For example, women tend to prefer mail samples they can examine at home. Men prefer samples given to them at a store or an

Sampling is an effective method to entice consumers to try a product. Courtesy of PhotoEdit. Photograph by Bill Aron.

event. The advantage of passing out samples at an event is that the person receiving the sample receives the personal touch. A smile, a greeting, and even information can be conveyed along with the sample. Also, if the consumer liked the event, then he or she may transfer the good feelings toward the event to the sampled product.[23]

Internet-based response sampling programs have become popular with both consumers and manufacturers. Bristol-Myers/Squibb was one of the first companies to utilize the Internet for product sampling. The company offered a free sample of Excedrin to individuals who requested the sample and were willing to provide their name, address, and e-mail information. In addition to the 12-pack sample of Excedrin, consumers received coupons for additional Excedrin purchases along with the quarterly Excedrin Headache Relief Update Newsletter.[24] The advantage of this form of response sampling is that only consumers who request the product receive it. By using the Internet, a company gathers additional information to be added to a database.

Problems with sampling

Product sampling is an effective method to introduce a new product and generate interest in that product. The primary disadvantage of this form of promotion is the cost. A special sample-size package must be developed. The package must be very similar to the regular-size pack, so consumers will be able to identify the product after using up the sample. Many times samples are mailed adding to the expense of the program. Even samples given out in stores require either an individual to distribute them or some kind of permission from the store.

To fully cover an area with samples requires careful planning of the distribution. Many times people simply discard the sample without even trying the product. Therefore, careful market research must be employed before undertaking a sampling program.

Effective use of samples

As with the other consumer promotions, sampling must be a central part of the IMC plan. The primary purpose of sampling is to a encourage trial use by a consumer or a business. Sampling is most effective when it introduces a new product or a new version of a product to a market. Samples also help promote a current product to a new target market or to new prospects.

Gillette recently showed how to integrate a sampling plan into an overall IMC program effectively. Gillette used samples as one component of its repackaged line of women's shaving products. The company spent $75 million to roll out the "Gillette for Women Fashion Collection," which combined women's razors, blades, and shaving gels under one umbrella. The rollout included print and television advertisements, in-store displays, and samples.[25]

In one survey, 71 percent of a set of consumers said they would try a new product if they liked a sample. An amazing 70 percent reported that they would be willing to switch brands if the trial use of the product was a positive experience. Many companies have achieved high success levels with sampling programs. For instance, the market share of Colgate-Palmolive's Nourishing Shower Gel doubled after its sampling campaign. Sales for Avon's True Color eyeshadow increased 38 percent after a sampling venture. Thus, sampling can be a successful way to stimulate trials and increase sales.[26]

bonus packs

When an additional or extra number of items is placed in a special product package, it is called a bonus pack. For example, instead of the regular number of bars of soap in a package, the consumer buys four bars for the price of three in a bonus pack promotion. Recently, Rayovac offered three free AA batteries in a bonus pack containing nine batteries. Bonuses range from 20 percent to 100 percent with a 30 percent bonus being the most typical.

Reasons for Using Bonus Packs

▶ Increase usage of the product
▶ Match or preempt competitive actions
▶ Stockpile the product
▶ Develop customer loyalty
▶ Attract new users
▶ Encourage brand switching

FIGURE 12.5

Figure 12.5 identifies the major objectives of bonus packs. Increasing the size or quantity of the package can lead to greater product use. For example, if a cereal box is increased in size by 25 percent, the consumer is likely to eat more cereal, because it is so readily available. This is not true for products that have a constant rate of consumption. For instance, if Colgate increases the size of a toothpaste container by 25 percent, consumers will not use more toothpaste. In effect, what this does is delay the customer's next purchase. Still, manufacturers do offer these types of bonus packs, because they may help to preempt the competition. A consumer with a large quantity of the merchandise on hand is less likely to switch to another brand, even when offered some type of deal, such as a coupon.

A firm's current customers often take advantage of a bonus pack offer. When customers stockpile a quantity of a particular brand it discourages purchasing from a competitor. Bonus packs reward customer loyalty by offering them, in effect, free merchandise.

Bonus packs rarely attract new customers, because the consumer has never purchased the brand before. Obtaining an extra quantity does not reduce the purchase risk. In fact, it adds to the risk, especially when the customer does not like to "waste" a product by throwing it away if dissatisfied with the product.

Bonus packs can lead to brand switching if the consumer has used the brand previously. Facing purchase decisions, consumers may opt for brands that offer a bonus pack at the regular price. These products hold an advantage over competitive brands that do not offer bonus packs.

Problems with bonus packs

Some marketing research indicates that consumers are skeptical of bonus pack offers. When the bonus is small (20 percent to 40 percent), consumers often believe the price has not truly changed. Unfortunately, when the bonus is large, such as two-for-the-price-of-one sale, consumers tend to believe that the price was first increased to compensate for the additional quantity. Even though increasing the size of a bonus catches the consumer's attention, it may not convey the desired message.[27]

Bonus packs are costly because additional amounts of product sell for the same or a similar price. Also, they may incur new packaging and shipping costs. Cash flows may slow down, because customers buy larger quantities and therefore purchase the item less often.

Using bonus packs effectively

Bonus packs tend to be popular with manufacturers, retailers, and customers. A retailer can build a good relationship with a manufacturer that uses a bonus pack to increase brand switching and stockpiling. Retailers gain an advantage because the bonus pack is a "bargain" or "value" offered through the retail outlet.[28] Customers like bonus packs because they get additional product at the same price. For ongoing products with high competition, the bonus pack approach is one way to maintain brand loyalty and reduce brand switching at a minimal cost.

A bonus pack offer for two packages of Lean Slices by Carl Buddig. Courtesy of Carl Buddig & Company.

price-offs

A price-off is a temporary reduction in the price of a product to the consumer. A price-off can be physically marked on the product, such as when a bottle of aspirin shows the regular retail price marked out and replaced by a special retail price (e.g., $4.99 marked out and replaced by $3.99). Producing a label with the price reduction premarked forces the retailer to sell the item at the reduced price. This ensures the price-off incentive provided to the retailer through the trade promotion is actually passed on to the consumer. At other times, the price-off is not on the actual item, but on a POP display, sign, or shelf.

Price-offs usually stimulate sales of an existing product. They work well in the business-to-business area. They also can entice customers to try new products, because they reduce the financial risk of making the purchase. Companies often tie price-off offers with samples of new products.

The retailer can initiate a price-off promotion. Retailers usually offer price-off discounts to draw traffic into the store. The idea is for customers to purchase additional items other than those on sale. During the holidays and other times of the year, price-off sales are very common. Retailers advertise major price-off sales at the holidays of Christmas, Thanksgiving, and Presidents' Day. Many use Presidents' Day sales to reduce inventories of winter clothes and unsold Christmas merchandise.

Problems with price-off promotions

Price-offs are easy to implement and can have a sudden impact on sales; however, they also can cause problems. While a price-off offer may have a large impact on sales, it can be devastating for profit margins because it normally takes at least a 20 percent increase in sales to offset each 5 percent price reduction.

A special price-off offer by Papa John's. Courtesy of Papa John's International.

Perhaps even a greater danger is that price-off programs encourage consumers to become more price sensitive. In the same way that customers respond to rebates, they can either wait for a price-off promotion or choose another brand that happens to be on sale. An estimated 25 percent of consumers base their purchase decisions on price. Price-offs are often necessary because of competitive and trade pressures. Individual firms must be careful not to overrely on price-offs.[29]

Too many price-off offers can create a detrimental impact on the firm's image. Such may be have been the case with Sears' retail operations. In the attempt to lure customers back from category killers such as Wal-Mart, Best Buy, Home Depot, and Target, Sears initiated several price-cutting and sale strategies. Sears used the tag line "The good life at a great price. Guaranteed," and redesigned newspaper ads to focus on prices and price-offs. The words save and sale were shown 44 times in just one advertisement. The ads did bring more shoppers into Sears stores; however, marketing experts are concerned that the ads may have gone too far. The fear is that shoppers will become reluctant to purchase items that are not on sale. If this occurs, instead of the price-offs drawing traffic to the store to boost sales and profits through buying nonsale items, they will draw traffic to the store only to purchase sale items. Such a result would hurt long-term profits.[30]

Using price-off offers effectively

Price-off programs can be used to increase store traffic and generate sales. They work better with higher markup items and for products or services that normally do not offer discounts. The goal should be to create new interest in the product to entice buyers to take a second look. Loyal customers may be attracted to a price-off discount and buy to stock up, but they should not be the primary targets for price-off programs. Instead, new users or customers who have drifted away to other products should be the target market.

Price-offs have proven to be successful trade promotions for two reasons. First, the price-off has the appeal of a monetary savings to consumers. Second, the reward is immediate. Unlike rebates, refunds, contest, sweepstakes, and other promotional incentives, consumers do not have to wait for the reward. As always, price-off programs should be incorporated into the firm's overall IMC program.

Integrated Learning Experience

Many companies offer special consumer promotions on their Web sites. Examine the following company Web sites for consumer promotions.

> Taco Bell (www.tacobell.com)
> Hershey's (www.hersheys.com, look under consumer info)
> Quaker State (www.quakerstate.com)

What types of promotions are available? What are the objectives of the various consumer promotions? Do the promotions on the Web sites mesh with their advertising and consumer promotions at retail outlets?

other issues in promotions programs

The major forms of consumer sales promotions programs are coupons, premiums, contests, refunds, sampling, bonus packs, and price-off offers. Each has distinct advantages and problems. The marketing account executive's goal should be to help the company select a consumer sales promotion approach that matches its trade promotions efforts, advertisements, and personal selling tactics. The entire promotions mix can then be structured to mesh with a more integrated IMC plan.

At times companies combine two or more consumer promotions activities into a single campaign, called an *overlay*. For example, to attract Chinese consumers in Canada, Tropicana combined sampling with coupons. Free samples (50,000 cups of orange juice) were given out along with 30,000 coupons at a Chinese New Year's celebration in Vancouver. Asians who live in the United States and Canada are not typically large users of coupons; however, Tropicana Canada's research showed that the Chinese consider oranges to be harbingers of good luck. A few weeks after the promotion, 40 percent of the coupons were redeemed, and sales of Tropicana orange juice among the Chinese community in Canada increased considerably.[31]

Another common strategy is to develop a consumer promotion with another product or company such as the ad featuring General Mills Betty Crocker brand and Tyson shown on the next page. This is called a tie-in. *Intracompany tie-ins* are the promotion of two different products within one company using one consumer promotion. The more common tie-in is with another company, such as General Mills and Tyson, which is an *intercompany tie-in*. When the Spice Girls reached the peak of their popularity, Pepsi promoted a tie-in offering Spice Girl prizes across nine countries in Europe. Fast-food restaurants often use tie-ins with movies and toys to attract children.[32] Whether a promotion is a stand-alone or an overlay or tie-in program, careful attention must be given to planning the event to maximize its effect.

planning for consumer promotions

In planning the consumer promotions component of the IMC, it is vital that the promotions support the brand image and the brand positioning strategy. To ensure this occurs, it is first necessary to bear in mind the target audience of the program. Then research must be conducted to identify the core values present in the target

An intercompany tie-in by Betty Crocker with Tyson. *Courtesy of Betty Crocker and Tyson.*

audience as well as opinion regarding the firm's products, especially as they relate to the competition. Once this information is gathered, the firm is ready to finalize the consumer promotions plan. In terms of sales promotions, consumers can be divided into three general categories:

1. Promotion prone consumers
2. Brand-loyal consumers
3. Price-sensitive consumers

Promotion prone consumers regularly respond to coupons, price-off plans, or premiums. They are not brand loyal and purchase items that are on-deal. A **brand-loyal consumer** purchases only one particular brand and does not substitute regardless of any deal being offered. Few consumers are completely promotion prone or brand loyal. Instead, buying is more like a continuum anchored at its ends by promotional proneness and brand loyalty. People tend toward one approach or the other, but sometimes lapse into the other approach. The tendency toward being promotion prone or brand loyal may depend on the product being purchased. A beer drinker may be extremely promotion prone, while a wine drinker may be quite brand loyal. The same beer drinker may be extremely loyal to a pizza brand, and the same wine drinker may be quite promotion prone when it comes to buying potato chips.

For the **price-sensitive consumer,** price is the primary if not the only criterion used in making a purchase decision. Brand names are not important and these individuals will not pay more for a brand name. They take advantage of any type of promotion that reduces the price. It is important to identify the set of promotion prone or price-sensitive consumers who will be targeted by a consumer promotions program.

For brand-loyal consumers, sales promotions can be crafted to boost sales and reinforce the firm's image. For example, one small local restaurant has a monthly drawing for a free meal for two. To enter, patrons put a cash register receipt from the last meal at the restaurant in a box upon leaving. Each month the restaurant draws five names. The more often a person dines at the restaurant, the greater the chance of winning. A simple promotion such as this can boost sales for the restaurant by tying chances of winning with additional meals. The additional cost to the restaurant to run this promotion is minimal and can result in excellent goodwill from its customers.[33]

In any event, planning promotions programs should always tie together the theme of the IMC plan with more specific goals associated with the product and the target market being attacked. Building brand image is more of a long-term goal, and generating sales is more short range. Price-based offers normally are designed to: (1) attract new customers or (2) build sales. Other consumer promotions such as high-value premiums can be used to enhance a firm's image.

Sweepstakes, special offers, and rebate programs can be "institutionalized" so that consumers begin to expect them to appear. For example, once a year Burger King offers Whoppers at a two for $2 rate. McDonald's ran its Monopoly game for several years. Hardee's offers two roast beef sandwiches for $2 on a regular basis. When customers begin to recognize and expect these programs, and look forward to them, a stronger and more loyal base is being built.

Integrated Learning Experience

Planning consumer promotions requires considerable expertise. Most firms lack the skills to design cost-effective consumer promotions. The same is true of many advertising agencies that specialize in advertising, not consumer promotions. At the same time, to be effective a consumer promotions program must be integrated with advertising and all of the other forms of marketing communications. Use a search engine to locate some consumer promotion firms in your area. In addition, examine the following Web sites.

> www.savesmart.com
> www.gravesgroup.com
> www.salespromo.com

stop!

business-to-business programs

Sales promotions are used extensively in the business-to-business area. In fact, 18.7 percent of business-to-business marketing budgets are spent on sales promotions. Manufacturers are the most inclined to offer some type of sales promotion to their customers.[34]

Sales promotions are not monies offered to retailers, wholesalers, distributors, or agents who stock the manufacturer's products for resale. Those funds are trade promotions monies. Instead, manufacturers offering some type of special promotion to their customers (another business) are involved in business-to-business sales promotions. For example, a manufacturer needing paper for copy machines may be enticed to buy from a paper company offering a sales promotion incentive. The paper itself is necessary for the company, but is not used in making products and is not resold.

Finance, insurance, and real estate services are the second largest business-to-business users of sales promotions. Although many finance, insurance, and real estate companies service consumers, a large portion of their revenues comes from business-to-business customers. A bank offering a premium or sweepstakes to small businesses uses a sales promotion. The same would be true for insurance companies and real estate companies that use sales promotions aimed at business customers.

Coupons often are used in the business-to-business sector. For example, an office supply company may fax or mail coupon offers to its businesses customers. A pest control business may offer an introductory coupon to encourage businesses to sign up for its services. Microsoft offered a $99 off coupon on its one-day training session about installing and supporting BackOffice SBS, which is designed for small to medium-size businesses. The coupon was made available only to CPAs who were official members of the American Institute of Certified Public Accountants (AICPA).[35]

While FSI and print media work well for consumer promotions aimed at end users, direct mail, fax, or coupons distributed by sales staff work best for business markets. In business-to-business promotions, companies need to be more focused on targeting. Few business buyers would see or use a FSI coupon. To be effective, the coupon must reach the hands of the purchasing agent or someone who has the authority to make the purchase decision or can influence the purchase decision.

Premiums also can be offered in business-to-business markets. They can be additional merchandise given to the firm for making a purchase. For example, a company such as Quaker State can offer a free case of motor oil for placing an order within a specified time period or for a specific size of order. John Deere used Christmas ornaments and John Deere trading cards as premiums with its dealers. Gifts such as these should be aligned with the products being sold.

Contests and sweepstakes can be used to attract purchases in much the same way as they are used in consumer markets. Business buyers are just as interested in winning prizes as are customers in other situations.

Sampling is an excellent method to encourage a business to try a product or service. For example, an office supply store offers a company the use of a copier for a month in an effort to land a contract to supply all of the firm's copiers. The types of products that lend themselves well to sampling in the business arena include:

- Fabricated and component parts
- Maintenance and repair parts
- Process materials
- Operating supplies
- Raw materials

For example, providing a sample in the area of process materials has the advantage of giving the engineers an opportunity to analyze the materials to see if it meets their standards. Through analysis, they may find that the material is actually superior to the product they currently use. Sampling is an effective method of getting a company's products into the hands of the individuals who are the influencers in business purchase decisions.

Bonus packs also can be part of business-to-business marketing. Offering a prospective business a bonus pack may attract new users. The lure of additional merchandise at no additional cost appeals to cost-conscious business buyers.

Price is often a negotiated item in the business-to-business sector. Consequently, *price-off programs* are not used as often. Many business relationships are formalized by a contractual agreement, and the price is fixed by that contract. Price-off discounts can be offered by vendors seeking to obtain a new business contract by enticing the business customer to at least consider the firm making the offer. Also, a vendor can offer a price-off program to tempt customers to purchase additional merchandise. Price-offs can be used to preempt competitive deals. The latter situations occur when there is no formal contract between the firm and the vendor. Firms furnishing operating supplies normally operate without contracts and use price-offs as part of their marketing programs.

As a result, the importance of business-to-business consumer promotions programs will continue. Marketing managers should integrate these efforts into all other parts of the promotions mix, for both business buyers and other customers.

international consumer promotions programs

As first discussed in Chapter 1, to fully integrate marketing communications means the firm must develop an overall, global IMC program. Each country or each region requires some flexibility in order to adapt marketing activities, including consumer promotions, to fit local needs.

Although the desire may be to centralize global consumer promotions programs, this process can be difficult. Customs, laws, and views toward various types of sales promotions differ throughout the world. Even within Europe, the laws governing consumer promotions are not consistent. For example, in France and England, contests offering free prizes are legal; however, in Germany, the Netherlands, and Belgium, they are illegal. Coupons, which are common in the United States, are legal in all European countries except Germany. At the same time, German laws allow on-pack price reductions and gifts inside of a package.

In Japan, the maximum value of a premium is either 10 percent of the selling price or 100 yen (80 cents). Thus, it would not make sense to use a premium in Japan. Although companies would like to utilize the same sales promotional tactic throughout the world in order to gain economies of scale, it is not always possible.[36]

Coupons are not as prevalent in the United Kingdom as they are in the United States. Culturally, coupon redemption is associated with being underprivileged in England. Customers fear that using coupons will cause the cashier to judge them to be poor and needy.[37] Still, coupon redemption rates are higher in Europe than they are in the United States. Table 12.1 compares redemption rates and distribution methods of the United States with three European countries: England, Italy, and Spain. As shown, the overall redemption rates are 14.3 percent in Italy and 16 percent in Spain as compared to only 2 percent in the United States.

A primary explanation for the difference in redemption rates is distribution. In the United Kingdom, 5.4 billion coupons were distributed. Newspapers were the predominant means of distribution, but magazines, door-to-door, in- or on-pack, and in-store distribution methods were also heavily used. In Italy, in- or on-pack distribution accounted for 63.2 percent of the 621 million coupons distributed. When the coupon is already in or on the package, it is easily redeemed, thus creating the highest rate. In Spain, door-to-door and in- or on-pack distribution are the primary methods. A total of 106 million were distributed.[38]

In Japan, restrictions on print media carrying coupons were not lifted until 1990. Retailers and consumers are still reluctant to use coupons. In 1991, Japanese

Media	Redemption Rate				Distribution Method			
	England	Italy	Spain	U.S.	England	Italy	Spain	U.S.
Newspaper	1.9%	—	1.4%	0.8.%	26%	—	10.0%	1.9%
Magazine	2.8	1.4	1.4	0.3	13	5.7	14.7	4.2
Door to door	11.0	13.7	12.9	—	18	2.0	43.0	—
In/on pack	25.1	20.3	30.7	9.2	15	63.2	25.2	2.5
In store	27.7	32.3	28.2	6.8	19	22.1	5.5	1.9
FSI	12.0	—	—	1.4	1	—	—	85.4
Mailing	—	6.6	—	3.6	—	6.5	—	1.1
Overall average	6.8	14.3	16.0	2.0				

TABLE 12.1

Couponing in Selected Countries

Sources: "International Coupon Trends," Direct Marketing, 56, no. 4 (August 1993), pp. 47–49; "FSI Coupon Redemption Rate for Frozen Foods," Frozen Food Age, 47, no. 3 (October 1998), p. 70.

newspapers were allowed to carry freestanding inserts, but the average redemption rate still is only 1.2 percent. To encourage retailers to redeem coupons, Japanese supermarkets are offering checkout coupons. Checkout coupons issued for competing products have had some success.[39]

Contests and sweepstakes are successful in many countries. Marketers must be careful to research the laws, regulations, and most importantly, consumer attitudes toward contests and sweepstakes. A cultural assimilator helps the company assess the potential impact of local attitudes toward the contest.

In order to manage the consumer promotion function within a global market successfully, a company needs an experienced international sales promotion coordinator or manager. Some of the major responsibilities of this coordinator are:[40]

1. Promoting the transfer of successful consumer promotion ideas among the company's brands from one country to another

2. Proposing and soliciting ideas for consumer promotions within and across each region or country

3. Developing and presenting training on consumer promotions planning to each local region that is responsible for developing them

4. Gathering performance data on each sales promotion program and making the information available to each regional sales promotion manager

5. Developing methods for measuring the effectiveness and efficiency of the various consumer promotions

6. Coordinating relationships with all sales promotion agencies that are being used

7. Coordinating efforts between advertising agencies, media buying agencies, and any other agencies or firms they are working with sales promotions in a region or country

8. Making sure all consumer promotions fit into the firm's overall IMC program

Effective management of a global IMC program is one of the keys to long-term success. Using sales promotions tactics wisely is one ingredient in the formula. A truly integrated marketing communications program pulls together all elements of the marketing mix so that the firm's voice is heard clearly in all areas in which it competes.

Integrated Learning Experience

One widely read journal featuring promotional marketing is called *PROMO*. Access its Web site at www.promomagazine.com. Examine the table of contents. Who is the Agency of the Year? What other agencies are listed in the top 25? Read at least two articles from the current issue of *PROMO*. How would *PROMO* be of assistance to a firm designing promotional materials? How would *PROMO* be valuable to promotional and advertising agencies?

implications for **marketing account executives**

Marketing Account Executives

Help the client company establish clear goals for any sales promotion program. Make sure the tactics (coupons, premiums, price-offs) match the goals. Typical goals include:

- Increased sales in the short run
- Higher brand loyalty
- Preempting the competition
- Encouraging larger purchases at the same time
- Enticing buyers to try a new product

■ Selling the same product to new buyers

■ Strengthening relations with retail outlets or manufacturers

Make sure your own company is in the position to work effectively with sales promotions. Either establish a working relationship with a firm that provides these programs, or create an in-house department.

Reexamine the overall IMC program in light of all activities in the promotions mix with clients. Make sure they see the connections between advertising, personal selling, consumer promotions, and trade promotions.

Remind clients that sales promotions can be highly effective tools in business-to-business sales. Remember that the promotions should reach members of the buying center directly. Find creative ways to place enticements into the hands of influencers and decision makers.

Be certain that any international sales promotion campaign has been carefully scrutinized by someone familiar with the customers, laws, and other key features of the targeted country or region.

SUMMARY

An IMC program highlights all four elements of the promotions mix. In the previous section of this textbook, advertising was carefully considered, because it is often the main "voice" of the IMC message. At the same time, the other parts of the mix (trade promotions, consumer promotions, and personal selling) play a crucial role in the success or failure of the overall marketing program.

This chapter reviews the techniques available to attract consumers to the company by using consumer sales promotions. These tactics include coupons, premiums, contests and sweepstakes, refunds, rebates, samples, bonus packs, and price-off deals. These items should be combined with specific promotional goals to have the right impact on customers.

Consumer promotions are often used to boost sales. They can be an excellent short-term method to increase sales or a firm's market share. They can also be an excellent means of introducing new products. Often a consumer promotion prompts consumers to at least try the product where selling it at the regular price will not. Coupons and contests have been successful tactics for attracting new customers. Consumer promotions can boost sales of a particular brand, and evidence suggests that they increase sales of the overall product category rather than just take sales away from competitors.

Sales promotions also can be used to increase the household inventory of the item being promoted. Consumers with more of a particular product in their house experience fewer home "stockouts" and often increase their usage of the product. In other words, having more potato chips on hand means people in the home might consume them at a faster rate.[41]

In many large companies, a consumer or sales promotion manager handles the planning and execution of all of the consumer promotions. In smaller companies, this person may handle both trade and consumer promotions. The same is true for agencies. Full-service agencies often have specialists in the fields of trade and consumer promotions, or they employ subsidiary firms to handle the sales promotions.

The New York–based advertising agency DDB Needham handles advertising for brands such as Budweiser, Volkswagen, American Airlines, and Sony. Louis London, a sales promotion subsidiary agency of DDB Needham, handles the sales promotion aspect of these accounts. Seldom do the large advertising agencies actually do consumer promotions within the agency. Companies that do not have relationships with subsidiary consumer promotions agencies often have a separate internal division to handle consumer promotions. The recent push toward more fully integrated marketing communications programs has led some clients to seek out firms that can manage every aspect of the communications program, including consumer sales promotions.

Just as large advertising firms are branching out into consumer promotions, specialty consumer promotion firms are adding additional services. To be able to meet the advertising needs of their clients, they often utilize freelance creatives. Regardless of which type of agency is used, full-service or specialty, the trend for both is to expand offerings to allow for a greater degree of integration of the consumer promotion component with the other elements of the IMC plan.[42]

Unfortunately, many sales promotions still are not part of the integrated marketing communications plan. They start out being part of the IMC program and may be carefully designed to support the IMC plan and firm's desired brand image. As long as sales increase and the goals of the firm are being met, all is fine. If, however, sales slump and target goals are not met, marketers often turn to additional sales promotion tactics, seeking a quick remedy. Printing and distributing a 50-cent coupon yields results much faster than does increasing advertising. Yet, as was discussed in Chapter 11, money spent on promotions and taken away from advertising often dilutes the brand's image. When the brand image is tarnished, consumers then base purchase decisions on criteria such as price or a promotional offer rather than brand name or perceived brand quality. While increased use of sales promotions techniques often provides a short-term solution to slumping sales, their overuse can damage the brand's image in the long run.[43]

The most crucial step in planning an integrated consumer promotions program is to match the firm's target market, specific marketing goals, and promotional tactics together. Goals range from quick boosts to sales, to increased brand awareness, to improved brand image, and establishing solid relationships between manufacturers and members of the marketing channel, specifically retailers. Consumer promotions pro-

grams also can expand the reach of the company into the business-to-business market. Again, carefully set goals combined with well-chosen tactics are the key.

Internationally, consumer promotions programs can be used when they are chosen based on the characteristics, attitudes, laws, regulations, and cultural nuances of a given geographic region. The primary objective of any promotions program must always be to enhance the message sent forth in other aspects of the IMC program in a manner that helps the company reach its long-term marketing objectives in a cost-effective and positive fashion.

REVIEW QUESTIONS

1. What is a consumer sales promotion? How is it different from a trade promotion?
2. What is an FSI? What kind of sales promotion is distributed through FSI?
3. Name and describe four types of coupons. Which is the most popular with manufacturers? Which has the highest redemption rate?
4. What is a U-pon?
5. What problems are associated with coupon programs?
6. How can companies most successfully utilize coupons?
7. What is a premium? What four types of premium programs can companies use?
8. What are the disadvantages of premium programs?
9. How can companies enhance the odds of success of a premium program?
10. What is the difference between a contest and a sweepstakes?
11. What problems are associated with contests and sweepstakes?
12. What tactics can be used to improve the success rates of contests and sweepstakes? What role might the Internet play in this process?
13. How is a refund different from a rebate?
14. What problems are associated with refunds and rebates?
15. What can be done to make rebate programs more successful?
16. Name and describe six types of samples programs that manufacturers can employ.
17. What disadvantages are there to sampling programs?
18. What can be done to enhance the odds of success of a sampling program?
19. What is a bonus pack? How is it different from samples?
20. What problems are associated with bonus pack programs?
21. What bonus pack plans are most effective?
22. What is a price-off sales promotion?
23. What are the disadvantages of price-off programs?
24. How can manufacturers most successfully employ price-off discounts? How can retailers most successfully use price-off discounts?
25. Describe sales promotion tactics in business-to-business settings.
26. What problems must be overcome when developing international sales promotions programs?

KEY TERMS

consumer promotions (sometimes called *sales promotions*) incentives designed for a firm's customers.

free standing inserts (FSI) sheets of coupons distributed in newspapers, primarily on Sunday.

instant redemption coupon coupon that customers can redeem immediately when making a purchase.

bounce-back coupons coupons that customers cannot redeem instantly but instead must be used at a later purchase.

scanner-delivered coupons coupons issued at the cash register, which are triggered by an item being scanned.

cross-ruffing the placement of a coupon for one product on another product.

response offer coupons coupons are issued (or mailed) following requests by consumers.

free-in-the-mail premiums gifts given to individuals for purchasing products; however, the customer must mail in a proof of purchase to the manufacturer to receive the gift.

in- or on-package premiums small gifts, such as toys in cereal boxes, in which the gift is often disguised or packaged so the consumer must buy the product to find what it is.

store or manufacturer premiums gifts given by either the retail store or the manufacturer when the customer purchases a product.

self-liquidating premiums gifts that accompany purchases where-by consumers must pay an amount of money for them.

promotion prone consumers individuals who are not brand loyal and regularly respond to coupons, price-off plans, or premiums, only purchasing items that are on-deal.

brand-loyal consumer someone who purchases only one particular brand and does not substitute regardless of any deal being offered.

price-sensitive consumer a consumer for whom price is the primary if not the only criterion used in making a purchase decision.

ENDNOTES

1. Kapil Bawa and Srini S. Srinivasan, "Coupon Attractiveness and Coupon Proneness: A Framework for Modeling Coupon Redemption," *Journal of Marketing Research,* 34, no. 4 (November 1997), pp. 517–25; "Coupon Use Seen Growing," *Editor and Publisher,* 129, no. 47 (November 23, 1996), pp. 16–17; "DSN Charts: Coupons," *Discount Store News,* 38, no. 9 (May 3, 1999), p. 4.

2. Corliss L. Green, "Media Exposure's Impact on Perceived Availability and Redemption of Coupons by Ethnic Consumers," *Journal of Advertising Research,* 35, no. 2 (March–April 1995), pp. 56–64.

3. "Net Coupons Deliver High Redemption Rate," *Frozen Food Age,* 47, no. 3 (October 1998), p. 63; "Replace Coupon Clipping with Clicking," *Chain Store Age,* 74, no. 12 (December 1998), p. 226.

4. Green, "Media Exposure's Impact on Perceived Availability and Redemption of Coupons by Ethnic Consumers."

5. Elizabeth Gardener and Minakshi Trivedi, "A Communication Framework to Evaluate Sales Promotion Strategies," *Journal of Advertising Research,* 38, no. 3 (May–June 1998), pp. 67–71.

6. "Coupon Rooks, Sybil Gets a Sole, Just Imitate It, etc.," Adweek, Western Edition, 45, no. 24 (June 12, 1995), p. 24.

7. "DSN Charts: Coupons."

8. Bawa and Srinivasan, "Coupon Attractiveness and Coupon Proneness: A Framework for Modeling Coupon Redemption."

9. Don Jagoda, "The Seven Habits of Highly Successful Promotions," *Incentive,* 173, no. 8 (August 1999), pp. 104–5.

10. Rachel McLaughlin, "Freebies: From the Financial Side," *Target Marketing,* 21, no. 7 (July 1998), pp. 67–68.

11. Kate Bertrand, "Premiums Prime the Market," *Advertising Age's Business Marketing,* 83, no. 5 (May 1998), p. S6.

12. "News Digest," *Nation's Restaurant News,* 33, no. 49 (December 6, 1999), pp. 14–15; "For the Record," *Advertising Age,* 70, no. 51 (December 13, 1999), p. 80; Elbruz Cebrzynski, "Kids Meal Craze: BK's Pokeman Promo a Hit," *Nation's Restaurant News,* 33, no. 47 (November 22, 1999), pp. 1–2.

13. Theresa Howard and Terry Lefton, "KFC Units Buried in Bean Bags," *Brandweek,* 40, no. 4 (January 25, 1999), pp. 4–5.

14. Jagoda, "The Seven Habits of Highly Successful Promotions."

15. Bertrand, "Premiums Prime the Market."

16. Rachel McLaughlin, "Nuts and Bolts," *Target Marketing,* 22, no. 5 (May 1999), pp. 14–17; Nora Wood, "Flawless," *Incentive,* 172, no. 12 (December 1998), pp. 41–44.

17. Allen Fishman, "Sales Promotions Easy Way to Plug Business," *Denver Business Journal,* 49, no. 3 (September 26, 1997), p. 28A.

18. Linda Formichelli, "Scoring Points," *Incentive,* 173, no. 9 (September 1999), pp. 94–98.

19. Rodney J. Moore, "Games Without Frontiers," *Marketing Tools* (September 1997), pp. 38–42.

20. Matt Andrejczak, "12 Banks Help Schools Get Rebates on Books Through Marketing Pact with Amazon.com," *American Banker,* 164, no. 205 (October 25, 1999), p. 18.

21. "Doin' the Rebate Rumba," *Consumer Reports,* 64, no. 11 (November 1999), pp. 62–63.

22. Aaron Ricadela, "Rebates Bundles Promote Margins," *Computer Retail Week,* 167 (April 21, 1997), pp. 41–42.

23. Alison Wellner, "Try It — You'll Like It!" *American Demographics,* 20, no. 8 (August 1998), pp. 42–43.

24. Jennifer Kulpa, "Bristol-Myers Squibb Breaks Ground with Direct Response Product Sampling Website," *Drug Store News,* 19, no. 7 (April 7, 1997), p. 19.

25. Merdedes M. Cardona, "Gillette Turns Attention to Women," *Advertising Age,* 70, no. 51 (December 13, 1999), p. 12.

26. Claire Mahoney, "Because It's Worth It," *Soap, Perfumery and Cosmetics,* 72, no. 7 (July 1999), pp. 61–64; Wellner, "Try It — You'll Like It!"

27. Beng Soo Ong and Foo Nin Ho, "Consumer Perceptions of Bonus Packs: An Exploratory Analysis," *Journal of Consumer Marketing,* 14, no. 2–3 (1997), pp. 102–12.

28. Larry J. Seibert, "Are Bonus Packs Profitable for Retailers?" *Chain Store Age,* 72, no. 12 (December 1996), pp. 116–18.

29. Mike Ogden, "Price-Based Promotions May Hurt Your Bottom Line," *Washington Business Journal,* 18, no. 6 (June 18, 1999), p. 54.

30. Eddie Baeb, "Sears Dumps Softer Side for Hard Sell," *Crain's Chicago Business,* 22, no. 50 (December 13, 1999), pp. 4–5.

31. Showwei Chu, "Welcome to Canada, Please Buy Something," *Canadian Business,* 71, no. 9 (May 29, 1998), pp. 72–73.

32. Allyson L. Stewart-Allen, "Cross-Border Conflicts on European Sales Promotions," *Marketing News,* 33, no. 9 (April 26, 1999), p. 10; Chu, "Welcome to Canada, Please Buy Something"; Howard and Lefton, "KFC Units Buried in Bean Bags."

33. Fishman, "Sales Promotions Easy Way to Plug Business."

34. Christine Bunish, "Expanded Use of Collateral Material, Catalogs Boost Sales Promotions," *Advertising Age's Business Marketing,* 84, no. 5 (May 1999), p. S11.

35. "Microsoft, CPAs Unite on Market," *Computer Reseller News,* no. 766 (December 1, 1997), p. 66.

36. Stewart-Allen, "Cross-Border Conflicts on European Sales Promotions."

37. Allyson L. Stewart-Allen, "Below-the Line Promotions Are Below Expectations," *Marketing News,* 29, no. 19 (September 11, 1995), p. 9.

38. "International Coupon Trends," *Direct Marketing,* 56, no. 4 (August 1993), pp. 47–49

39. "Targeting Supermarket Shoppers," *Target Marketing,* 19, no. 10 (October 1996), p. 44; "International Coupon Trends."

40. Kamran Kashani and John A. Quelch, "Can Sales Promotion Go Global?" *Business Horizons,* 33, no. 3 (May–June 1990), pp. 37–43.

41. Kusum L. Ailawadi and Scott A. Neslin, "The Effect of Promotion on Consumption: Buying More and Consuming It Faster," *Journal of Marketing Research,* 35, no. 3 (August 1998), pp. 390–98.

42. Kenneth Hein, "The New Players," *Incentive,* 173, no. 6 (June 1999), pp. 21–24.

43. Mike Mohammad, "Making All Strands Lead Back to Brand," *Brandweek,* 39, no. 43 (November 16, 1998), pp. 28–29.

44. Liz Parks, "Chains See Today's Wealthy Teens as Tomorrow's Loyal Customers," *Drug Store News,* 21, no. 15 (September 27, 1999), p. 84.

45. Vanessa Friedman, "Planet Clinique," *Elle,* 13, no. 9 (May 1998), pp. 218–19.

46. *The Joplin Globe* "Many Europeans Hostile Toward U.S. companies." (May 10, 2000), p. B-4.

Building an IMC Campaign

Creating Consumer Promotions for an IMC Advertising Campaign

Besides all of the offers your company might make to retailers, other offers go directly to consumers. Coupons, premiums, sweepstakes, and contests and other sales promotions can spice up your IMC approach by appealing to various individuals. When these promotional materials are tied in with the firm's theme, image, and advertisements, the result can be a positive impact on how people view the product and the company. This chapter's exercise is designed to cause you to consider the relationship between consumer promotions and trade promotions for individual purchasers, international customers, channel members, and other businesses. Access this information from your Advertising Plan Pro disk or at www.prenhall.com/clow.

Critical Thinking Exercises

Discussion Questions

1. According to Kim James, sales promotion manager for Eckerd Drug, "The teen and preteen segments are important because they (teens) are developing buying habits and loyalties during these ages and are our future loyal consumers." In addition to established brands such as Cover Girl and Maybelline, Eckerd Drug now stocks brands such as Bonne Bell, Jane, and Naturistics.[44] Which consumer promotions would be the best to attract teens and preteens to the cosmetics in Eckerd Drug? What tie-ins or overlays would you recommend?

2. Many manufacturers believe the best method for differentiating their brands from competitors is advertising. It is true that consumer and trade promotions cannot replace advertising in brand development. At the same time, well-chosen promotional tactics can support brand differentiation. Discuss which consumer promotions

manufacturers should and should not use to develop their brands. Justify your answer.

3. As with the other consumer promotions, international expansion requires understanding the laws and customs of each country and culture. For example, in Saudi Arabia and other Muslim countries, Clinique had to modify its sampling techniques. In the United States and Western cultures, Clinique provides cosmetic samples in retail outlets for customers to try. In the United States, females normally sell retail cosmetics, while in Saudi Arabia males do. At the same time, Muslim custom prohibits a male from touching a female, so female customers must either apply the cosmetics themselves or bring their husbands to the store with them.

   Asking a female customer "What color are your eyes?" constitutes a grave offense in Saudi Arabia, because the eyes are believed to be the gateway to the soul. Asking her about skin tone does not make sense, because females keep their faces covered after they reach the age of 14. Sampling is very important for Clinique in Saudi Arabia.[45] How would you organize a sampling program in light of these cultural factors? What other consumer promotions could be used? If you have someone in your class from a Muslim country, ask your classmate to discuss the use of consumer promotions in his or her home country.

4. Design a magazine advertisement with a detachable coupon or premium for one of the following products. Compare your offer with those of other students in your class. Discuss the differences between the offers.

   a. SunBright Tanning Salon

   b. Dixie Printing

   c. Hamburger Haven

   d. Blue Bell Ice Cream

5. Suppose the Rawlings Sports Equipment Company tries to increase sales of baseball gloves this season. The company intends to use consumer coupons. Discuss the pros and cons of each method of distributing coupons for Rawlings listed in Figure 12.2. Which methods should it use? Why?

6. To maintain its strong brand image, suppose Revlon's marketing team decides to use a premium for each of its lipstick products. What type of premium would you suggest for Revlon for each of the target markets listed below? Which premium would you use? Justify your answers.

   a. Caucasian females over the age of 50

   b. African-American females, ages 14 to19

   c. Hispanic females, ages 25 to 40

   d. Professional females, ages 30 to 50

7. Meet in groups of four to six students. Ask each group member to identify the last contest and the last sweepstakes he or she entered. What enticed them to enter? What was the extrinsic reward? What was the intrinsic reward?

8. Video games generate huge revenues for many companies. One manufacturer decided to use sampling as a method to reach the primary target market, males between ages 15 and 30. The sampling could have been distributed in one of two ways. First, the actual game could be loaded on a computer for targeted individuals. Second, potential customers could be sent an abbreviated version of the game. Which sampling method would be the best? Using Figure 12.4, discuss the pros and cons of each sampling method in terms of this new video game. Which type and method of sampling would you recommend? Why?

9. Consumers can be divided into three broad categories in terms of how they respond to consumer promotions: (1) promotion prone, (2) brand loyal, and (3) price sensitive.

Identify two services or goods that would fit into each category for you personally. For example, you may be promotion prone when you buy soft drinks (your favorite brand is "What's on Sale!") but be very brand loyal when you buy shoes (Nike, Reebok). Compare your completed list with those of other students. Discuss the differences you observe.

10. Interview three people who have lived in another country about the use of consumer promotions in their countries. Make a list of those promotions heavily used and those not used. Present your findings to the class.

Sunny Success

APPLICATION EXERCISE I

Jessica Corgiat faced a difficult challenge as she took over the Sun Products, Inc. account. As a relatively new account executive, Jessica knew it was important to establish measurable results when conducting various advertising campaigns. Sun Products sells items primarily oriented toward beach-related activities, the most successful of which is the company's line of sunscreen products.

The tanning industry faces a unique set of challenges as a new generation of consumers emerge. First, more than ever consumers are aware of the dangerous long term effects of tanning. These include more wrinkles along with vastly increased chances of developing skin cancer in later life. In Australia, where the ozone layer is the most depleted, exposure to the sun is even more hazardous. More importantly, however, is a potential shift in cultural values regarding appearance.

A few generations ago, in Europe, completely white skin was a sign of affluence. Those who were forced to work outside developed tans. Those who lived as royalty or as the wealthy class could show their high social standing by simply keeping out of the sun.

As the new millennium commences, it is possible that a certain set of consumers will begin to believe that tanning is equal to foolishness. Or at the least, that a suntan is no longer as "sexy" as it has been for many years. Beach bums and bunnies continue to run counter to this trend. The question remains, however, whether a national obsession with being browner continues in the general population.

One method to counter this problem is by developing new products designed to screen out the sun rather than enhancing the sun's tanning properties. Lotions with higher SPF (sun protection factor) values generally sell at higher prices. Higher-quality sunscreens do not wash off in a pool or while swimming. Further, items containing herbal ingredients and new aromas are designed to entice new interest. Sun Products with aloe vera and vitamin E may help reduce the pain and heal a sunburn more quickly. Products which "tan" without exposure to the sun are being developed for those who want the beach look without doing time in the sand.

At the same time, to promote more "traditional" products to college students on spring break and others who still enjoy a deep, dark tan requires careful promotion. Advertisements often stress the "fun" aspects of being outdoors.

Hawaiian Tropics, one of the chief competitors in the tanning industry, has taken a unique approach to the promotion of its products. The company holds an annual contest in which the Tropics team of beach girls is chosen to represent the firm. Contestants are female, beautiful, and have good tans. Those who win the contest tour the country promoting Hawaiian Tropics products and appear on television programs such as *Wild One* on the E! channel.

At individual events held at beaches across the United States and in other locations, free samples of Hawaiian Tropics may be given out, along with coupons and other purchase incentives. Giveaways of beach towels and other beach equipment are used to heighten interest in the product at various stores.

Jessica is considering how to respond to this quickly changing marketplace. Besides product development, she needs to describe a "theme" the company can use, either oriented toward "safety" or "sexy" or "safety with sexy." She is considering the entire range of promotional possibilities, from coupons for new products, to premiums as giveaways for existing products, to contests, sampling, bonus packs (with various ranges of SPF values in the same pack), to refunds for higher-priced lotions. She knows the key is to maintain a message and theme for this company, which will help it stand out in the crowd of Coppertone, Ban du Soleil, and Hawaiian Tropics. She realizes to succeed she needs Sun Products' POP displays placed prominently in as many places as possible, from drugstores to swimming specialty stores.

1. Which consumer sales promotions items will be least helpful to Jessica and Sun Products?

2. Which consumer sales promotions items will be most helpful to them?

3. Design an IMC program for Sun Products, Inc., focusing on advertising themes, trade promotions, and consumer sales promotions. Explain how it will differentiate the company from other suntan product companies.

A Sticky European Mess

Irene Freitas knew she faced an uphill battle. Irene has been the marketing director for the highly successful Phil's Fabulous Pastries for the past seven years. Phil's is well known across the East Coast for cinnamon rolls, turnovers, twists, and a variety of fruit-laden pastries. Many of its customers are highly brand loyal, and many smaller cafés and coffee shops (although not Starbucks) feature Phil's pastries.

Phil Diamond, CEO of the company, decided that the firm had saturated the marketplace. Expansion to the Midwest invites competition from many highly successful Chicago and Kansas City–based pastry companies. The idea of moving farther west was not inviting, because Phil was concerned that his company could not compete well there either.

Phil decided to consider the possibility of expanding into Europe. Phil loved to travel to France, Spain, and Germany. He has seen many small bakeries that were thriving, but believed no real major pastry competitor existed in many countries in the European community. He asked Irene to travel there to investigate the opportunity to "go global."

What Irene was afraid to tell Phil was that, most Europeans tended to highly resent U.S. companies. She had seen some recent surveys indicating that the majority of Europeans from many countries believed companies from the United States were driven by profits and nothing more. They also resented the exportation of U.S. "culture" through its films and Internet sites, which many considered to be destructive to the well-being of the youth. Europeans think Americans carry and use too many guns, are racist, and are too materialistic.[46] Irene also hated to think that she would need to tell Phil that he might be a prime example of what Europeans tend to dislike. He was a "bottom line" kind of guy, gruff, and not exactly versed in the ways of other cultures.

Phil's pastries always entered a new local market in the same way. The company would set up a series of sampling sites, where free pastries were given out with coffee or other beverages at restaurants, coffee shops, and grocery stores. Quickly, two-for-one coupons were distributed to those who would fill out free-drawing entries for prizes at the giveaway locations.

Later, Phil's followed up with local newspaper coupons and cooperative television advertising for any location that would carry its pastries. Phil's never set up freestanding retail outlets, instead focusing on simply shipping product to other stores. The net result was low overhead, with a high markup on each item. Phil's shared the costs of coupon redemptions and other giveaways with local stores. Irene was dubious as to whether these tactics would work in the European community.

1. Assess Phil's Fabulous Pastries odds of success.

2. Would Phil's do well in France, where pastries are quite popular? Why or why not?

3. What kinds of consumer promotions programs have the best chances of working when selling pastries in the United States and in other countries?

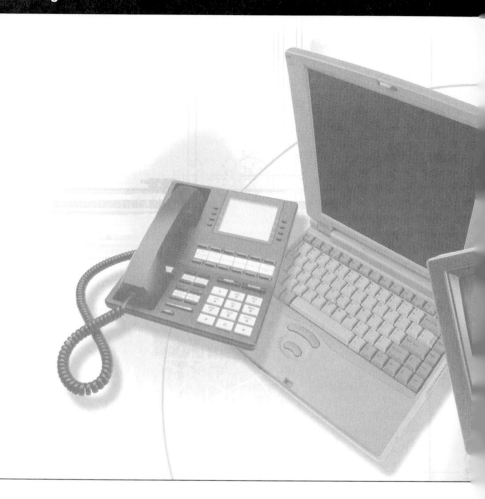

► **CHAPTER OBJECTIVES**

Be fully aware of the role personal selling plays in the success of both retail outlets and manufacturing operations.

Recognize the critical function personal selling plays in business-to-business IMC programs.

Integrate the steps of the buying decision-making processes of both consumers and other businesses with personal selling tactics.

Understand the nature of personal selling in the international marketplace.

Study the role the sales manager plays in developing plans, goals, motives, and compensation packages to realize the full potential of the personal selling component of the IMC program.

HAIR CARE:
The Personal Selling of Personalized Services

Hair care is more than just a cut or a perm. For men, the trend is moving toward exfoliating pores, smoothing skin with moisturizers, and using hair colors, especially in Europe. Even so, sales of men's toiletries exceeded $2.8 billion in the United States in 1998. For women, hair coloring, shampoos, lighteners, treatments, and permanents still are the staples.

Those who dispense both types of products have unique roles. Customers expect the hair care professional to deliver a high-quality style or coloring treatment and also

to function as a fashion adviser. While women often are interested in the cosmetic benefits of products, men tend to focus on the functional performance benefits of a scent or look. The personal service person working in a salon must know how to complete the technical tasks of cutting and shaping hair, and have the interpersonal sales skills needed to vend the outlet's other goods and services.

The second half of the twentieth century witnessed a shift in the nature of personal services. Previously, men went to barber shops and women patronized beauty salons. Unisex trends have changed the traditional structure of hair care, and chains such Prime Cuts, Master Cuts, and others grown in response to demands for places where Mom,

Dad, and the kids could all be served at the same time. Freestanding hair care locations compete with style salons in malls and with those that operate as parts of other retail stores, such as JCPenney. Small individual shops face rugged competition from companies specializing in not only cutting and styling but also other personal care features.

Individual stylists know the keys to personal success include repeat business and good tips. Therefore, while delivering a shampoo or style, the stylist often tries to personalize the contact enough so that a new customer will ask to be served by the same employee on the next visit.

One trend many firms utilize to increase store revenues is to become the sole provider of a supplier's hair care products within a given territory. One shop may feature Nexus conditioners and shampoos, while another sells Wella products. The Wella cosmetic supplier, featuring products such as Koleston Perfect, Viva Color, High Hair, and Wellaflex, became well-established in Germany in the 1990s. Since then, the company has become strong in Europe, Asia, and South America. Wella currently is trying to strengthen its hold on Japan and Malaysia. Many male customers enjoy Wella's mousse and styling gel products.

Salon employees may or may not be happy with the idea that they must sell various products in addition to rendering services. Although a stylist gains commissions and incentives for selling the goods, the same individual does not want to risk alienating a client by "pushing" a given set of products onto the customer. This creates a balancing act between the goals of the job (repeat customers and tips) and the goals of the organization (increased revenues based on product sales). Management must carefully monitor both, with the ultimate goal remaining: to serve a happy and satisfied customer base.

The U.S. trend toward megastores may continue to change not only the selling of personal products but also the venues in which those products are delivered. A full-service boutique offers not only hairstyling and care but also massage, manicure–pedicure, and facial treatment services. Specialists in each area will be expected to continue to provide quality personal care but also to sell store tie-ins with individualized suppliers.

The ultimate winners in this environment may be customers, who can shop around for quality and price in the personal services area. The losers may be the small, old-time barbershops and beauty salons, which must upgrade and add services in order to compete in this new, dynamic, and complex environment.[1]

overview

Personal selling is sometimes called the "last three feet" of the marketing function, because it represents the distance between the salesperson and the customer on the retail sales floor as well as the distance across the desk from the sales rep to the business customer. Personal contact between the sales representative and the prospective buyer can be used to add the final touch to a successful marketing communications program. A bond or partnership between a sales representative and his or her clients can be one of the most valuable assets a company holds in the marketplace.

Quality relationships between salespeople and buyers are crucial ingredients in every marketing program. Intimate, trusting, and friendly interactions create long-term bonds that help a firm build and maintain a strong share of the market. A positive purchasing experience often causes the buyer to provide word-of-mouth recommendations to as many as 6 other people, such as family members or friends.

What makes the process of personal selling more crucial may be what happens when a purchasing experience is not positive. A complaining customer is likely to tell as many as 11 other people when something bad happens. Consequently, any successful IMC program must be designed to build and maintain constructive ties between the sales force and various customers.[2]

In this chapter, the roles that personal selling and sales management play in the overall IMC program are depicted. First, the nature of retail selling is described. Second, business-to-business selling activities are outlined. In the third section, the nature of the sales management process is discussed. Basic information about personal selling is provided throughout this chapter, however, the primary thrust of this discussion is to integrate sales activities with larger promotional and IMC efforts. When this occurs, the company's message reaches the customer through both personal (sales rep) and impersonal (media) channels.

types of personal selling

Personal selling is a marketing communications tool that allows the firm to establish two-way communications with buyers. This communication can take place in the retail store or at the buyer's place of business. It can take place in person, by mail, by e-mail, or over the telephone. From the integrated marketing communications perspective, personal selling can be divided into two major categories:

1. Retail sales
2. Business-to-business selling

In addition, certain selling activities can be oriented toward both retail and business customers, such as Internet Web site sales, telemarketing, and database approaches. These methods will also be described in this chapter. The following section provides some basic information about the nature of retail selling.

retail sales

Sales to consumers often are finalized by retail salespersons. Transactions take place on the sales floor, in cash register checkout lines, on the telephone, and in a variety of other places. Perhaps the most common thread tying all these selling places together is that the sales representative "is" the company, as far as the customer is concerned. The salesperson is many times the only personal contact the consumer ever has with the retail outlet. Therefore, retail selling, and its ties to the overall IMC program, are vitally important to the ultimate success or failure of the organization. Retail selling can be divided into four general categories:

1. Selling in shops and stores
2. Personal selling and services
3. Telemarketing
4. Other retail sales activities

Selling in shops and stores

It is likely that most of you thought of retail sales first when the concept of personal selling was introduced in this chapter. The most common form of retail selling is the **single transaction** type. Single transactions involve a sales rep meeting with a customer and working with that individual until the sale is finalized or until the person decides to shop elsewhere or not make a purchase. Most specialty stores (e.g., jewelry, fashion boutiques, smoke shops, antique stores) feature single transaction sales. Large ticket item goods are also often single transactions, such as when a consumer shops for an automobile or a washing machine.

Unfortunately, many salespeople in single transaction settings use high-pressure techniques to convince buyers to make purchases. Most of the time, however, it is helpful to avoid pressure tactics and instead to try to develop a relationship, even when the sale appears to be a single transaction. Creating favorable relationships during single transactions has several advantages. First, it can lead to more transactions. If a relationship is positive, the customer may go back to the same company in the future. Second, a favorable experience, as mentioned earlier, leads to positive word-of-mouth recommendations, which in turn entices new customers to contact the company. Third, the company's reputation and image is built over time, even when single transactions are the norm.

The type of selling rapidly replacing single transactions in shops and stores is the *order-taker* type of sale. Order takers are individuals who perform tasks as simple as filling an order at Burger King to more involved orders in hardware or lumber stores. Many times order taking in a retail situation overlaps with serving as the

The Good Housekeeping Seal takes the guesswork out of buying a faucet.

While advertising can develop a strong brand name like Peerless, salespeople at a hardware store often influence which brands are purchased. Courtesy of Delta Faucet Company.

Every Peerless® kitchen and bath faucet comes with the Good Housekeeping Seal, and the Peerless pledge that the quality inside matches the quality outside. You have our word on it. And theirs.

PEERLESS
The Do-It-For-Yourself Faucet.®

cashier. Large retail operations such as Big K (Kmart), Target, and Wal-Mart completely separate cashier functions from order taking. In a small store, such as a bookstore, one person performs the order taker and cashier roles at the same time.

Retail salespeople deal primarily with end users. A few also work with business customers. In any case, retail salespeople have direct contact with customers at the point of purchase, so they can have considerable influence on individual purchasing decisions. Courtesy, attentiveness, and a pleasant demeanor are key ingredients in becoming a successful retail store salesperson, no matter the type of store involved. Marketing executives should emphasize to all members of the organization that personal selling is the primary element of the IMC program in which direct human contact takes place. Salespeople often show customers items that have been featured in advertisements or through other promotional activities. Therefore, they become key members of the marketing team executing the final phase of a successful IMC program—completing the sale.[3]

Personal selling and services

Many individuals sell or perform services for retail customers. Lube and Oil shops sell oil and provide oil change services at the same time. As noted earlier in the chapter, many people sell the services they render, such as the personal services of hair care, massage therapy, lawn mowing and gardening services, and so forth.

At the most general level, services can be divided into two categories for the purposes of describing personal selling. First, some services are simply sold by the sales rep, and that is the fundamental element driving the relationship. Insurance sales are a classic example of this kind of selling. An insurance agent primarily provides coverage. The company is responsible for processing claims, especially in the area of health care coverage. This type of selling is often a single transaction, but also can be a **repeat transaction** relationship. Many customers routinely return to the same company and sales representative when they desire additional services. Therefore, this type of selling has a great deal in common with retail sales. Courtesy, attentiveness, and other personal selling skills are needed for the individual and the company to succeed. Both retail selling and services selling are essentially *problem-solving* activities. Individual customers seek to solve problems by making purchases.

The second type of service is one in which the person doing the selling also performs the service. A hair care specialist provides cuts and perms, but also sells shampoo and conditioner. The goal of practically every service provider of this type is *repeat business,* or the occasional (and regular) transaction type. Loyalty and relationships are crucial elements in determining success for these individuals and their businesses. As a result, these individuals must be skilled at the services they provide and also have credible people skills. Bartenders who own their own taverns, shoe shine shops, and many other small businesses live or die based on the talents of a single individual or a few key employees.

Telemarketing

Another form of retail selling takes place using telemarketers. These individuals use the telephone to make sales calls. Telemarketers can be either inbound or outbound. In **inbound telemarketing,** telemarketers handle only inbound telephone calls. They do not make initial contacts with customers but rather respond to telephone orders or inquiry calls. Many 1-800 numbers are designed to attract inbound calls.

Outbound telemarketing is the variety many people encounter on a daily basis. Outbound telemarketers call prospective customers or clients. Long-distance phone services are notorious for making outbound telemarketing calls, and many consumers are quite frustrated by the numbers of telemarketing calls they encounter on a daily basis, especially at the dinner hour. Credit cards are offered, service contracts are suggested for previously purchased appliances, and an endless variety of aluminum-siding to college fund-raising phone calls bombard many households. Many people consider these tactics invasive and annoying. The simple fact is, however, that they work or else companies would abandon them.

Other retail sales activities

Many organizations rely on other forms of retail selling to enhance profits. For example, restaurants sometimes employ an individual whose sole job is to display an attractive array of desserts for customers to consider following a meal. Many bookstores such as Borders offer coffee and small snacks to customers who are examining books. Video stores employ individuals to both stock shelves and make sales. Some also offer movie-renting advice to regulars who frequent the shop.

These seemingly smaller activities, including providing small repair services, advice, and help filling out credit applications, are crucial ingredients in building profitability for smaller retail outlets and chain stores. In a truly *integrated* communications program, these activities are given attention as well as the larger (and seemingly more glamorous) functions that are performed, such as advertising and setting up point-of-purchase displays.

The "good hands" of Allstate usually belong to an individual salesperson. BLOCKBUSTER relies on retail clerks who can handle "rush" periods as well as slower times. The message of personal service and quality, which many retail firms try to stress, must include all forms of selling activities.

sales presentations in retail settings

Many books detail ways to make effective sales presentations. It is important to remember that the prime component of the sales presentation is how it relates to the overall IMC plan. What a salesperson says to a prospect or customer must be the

Consumer Buying Process

FIGURE 13.1

▶ **Problem recognition**

▶ **Information search**

▶ **Evaluation of alternatives**

▶ **Purchase decision**

▶ **Postpurchase evaluation**

same message that the other elements of the IMC plan convey. A different message delivered by the sales rep leads to confusion and dissatisfaction among customers. Many times salespeople are not under the direct supervision of the selling firm. Therefore, it becomes even more critical to spend time acquainting every salesperson with the firm's IMC plan. Rewards should then be structured to reinforce those who enhance the message effectively while making sales presentations.

The typical sales presentation involves more than just trying to close a deal. Another objective is to gather information. At other times, the major goal is to develop a relationship with the buyer and then to request permission to prepare an offer or bid. Therefore, the sales rep should tailor the sales presentation to the major goal. In Chapters 5 and 6, the stages of various purchasing processes were described. It is helpful for the sales team to reexamine these steps or stages prior to making a sales presentation, so that the presentation matches which stage the buyer is in during the visit.

To illustrate how the sales presentation should correspond with the consumer's buying stage, consider the purchase of a refrigerator and Figure 13.1. A retailer's sales presentation should match the stage or step involved. Some customers will be in the *problem recognition* stage, knowing at some basic level that they need a refrigerator. The retail salesperson should focus on determining the specific needs of the customer. Asking the right questions helps the customer define his or her needs more clearly. Thus, the sales rep may ask these questions:

1. What is the size of the space that you have for a refrigerator?
2. How much frozen food do you purchase compared to other food?
3. How much ice do you use?
4. How much cold water do you drink?
5. What type of kitchen decor do you have?

Simply trying to sell the refrigerator to an individual who has not identified his or her needs is not a successful sales strategy. The sales rep who compares a particular brand to the competition or tries to highlight benefits of his or her product is less likely to succeed, because the customer has insufficient information to make an informed judgment about the kind of refrigerator to buy. Unfortunately, many retail salespeople skip the first stage (problem recognition) and even the second (information search) and start immediately highlighting the benefits of a particular brand (the third stage in Figure 13.1, evaluation of alternatives). The net result is often a confused customer who becomes frustrated and walks out of the store.

In the second stage, the *information search* process, the consumer still may not be ready to make a purchase. Instead the customer's goal is to gather information about various brands and models. The salesperson should try to supply this information. Naturally, the sales rep tries to slant the information to make his or her company's products appear to be the best option.

In the third stage, *evaluation of alternatives,* the customer considers the pros and cons of various companies and their products. At this point, the salesperson can openly discuss the benefits each brand offers and even contrast his or her company's models with those the competition offers. Many retail stores carry multiple brands. This makes the salesperson's job easier, because the opportunity exists to help the consumer evaluate several brands at the same location, thus heightening the chances the retailer will capture the sale.

Finally, the *purchase decision* is made. During that stage the rep stops selling the product and starts selling other related items, such as service contracts. This is a delicate time, because the customer may be nervous about the decision itself and does not need to hear right away that the product might break down. Instead, the rep should focus on ideas such as convenience and peace of mind, all the while finalizing the paperwork of the sale of the refrigerator itself.

Finally, the *postpurchase evaluation* stage offers unique opportunities for salespeople to build stronger relationships with customers. Reassurance that a wise decision has been made is always a good idea following the purchase. As the sale is closed, the customer usually provides information on credit applications and applications for warranties that can be used in later selling activities. These are known as cross-selling programs.

Cross-selling involves the marketing of other items following the purchase of a good or service. Banks as well as other businesses have long realized that selling additional products to their current customers is cheaper than soliciting new customers. Banks can offer insurance, loans, and other financial services in addition to checking and savings accounts. The problem is how to successfully cross-sell such additional services. The traditional method has been direct mail, but it has not been very effective. Outbound telemarketing for the purpose of cross-selling often alienates customers. Most do not like being called by their bank or a company using a telemarketer trying to sell them additional services. To be effective in cross-selling means the plan should be fully integrated with the firm's general IMC program. Thus, a firm that has just sold a refrigerator may be able to cross-sell other appliances, as long as the approach does not offend or alienate the family that just has made a purchase.

Inbound telemarketing calls appear to be a better time for cross-selling.[4] First, customers are less defensive because they initiate the call. Second, resolving the problem that prompted the call makes the customer more responsive to cross-selling. Third, the inbound telemarketer has access to customer information that assists the cross-selling effort. It is important to handle such calls with care, however, because cross-selling inbound calls can be a disaster when they are handled poorly. When a customer is already angry or upset about a company's product and places an inbound call, the attempt to cross-sell additional products can cause the customer greater frustration. To understand how a firm, such as a bank, can use incoming calls to a call center to cross-sell, read the Communication Action Box on the next page.

Achieving successful cross-selling following a purchase requires the development and linkage of quality data, integrated information technology, specialized software, computerized decision models, training, and the right type of salespeople. People from the marketing, operations, and information systems departments must work together to create a system that identifies the best cross-selling services to offer customers. Salespeople in the call centers must be given the power to resolve problems quickly and effectively so that the customer is conducive to a cross-sell. It also must be understood that not all customers should be targeted for additional services. In some cases, the call center's role should be to resolve the problem and then let the customer go. Complex and comprehensive decision models must be developed to identify the best prospects and the best products to offer them.[5]

Regardless of which type of sales presentation a firm uses, it is important to integrate the personal selling function into the overall IMC plan. Salespeople should present the same message that advertising, consumer promotions, trade promotions, and every other element of the IMC program uses. This task is more challenging than it might first appear, because many retail salespeople are not often paid very well. This means guaranteeing quality becomes more difficult. Most retail

When consumers evaluate alternatives, salespeople have an opportunity to discuss the benefits of brands such as Keepsake. Courtesy of Keepsake.

communication action

In the past decade, many bankers have discovered what marketers have known for years: It is much easier to sell more things to current customers than it is to solicit new customers. Cross-selling represents one method to increase revenues from current customers. Inbound service calls signal that the customer needs help and, if properly assisted, may be open to suggestions regarding other banking services.

One advantage the bank holds in creating cross-selling programs comes from the extensive record keeping already in place for various account holders. A few simple commands made by a knowledgable computer operator places all relevant information in front of the service clerk as an inbound call takes place. Thus, some-one who has received an overdraft charge for the first time may call the bank to find out why the charge was made, and why it cost so much to process an unfunded check. The phone rep, seeing that the customer has a great deal of money in the bank in other accounts and has never been charged with an overdraft before, can quickly remove the service charge. At that point, the customer, feeling in charge of the situation and satisfied with the result of the call, can be easily guided into considering other banking services, such as automatic overdraft pro-tection, insurance, or other financial services.

The secrets to cross-selling bank services are as follows:

1. Make sure the problem is resolved (the reason the inbound call was made in the first place) before suggesting any new services.

2. Make sure the services being offered are viable to the individual customer. If the suggestion seems "random," the customer may become quickly frustrated.

3. Make sure the "pitch" does not sound "canned." If a customer soon decides the salesperson is simply reading a script, odds are the call will end quickly.

These tactics may work in other service situations. To be effective, the vendor company must have access to key customer information. Inbound telemarketing and cross-selling programs may be expensive to maintain. Only those companies that can be certain the revenues exceed the costs should proceed with this type of personal selling tactic.

Source: David Howe, "The Cross-Sell Connection," *Banking Strategies,* 74, no. 6 (November–December 1998), pp. 120–24.

salespeople work independently, often with very little direct supervision. Thus, while creatives can ensure actors in TV advertisements say the right things, firms have far less control over what a salesperson says. Management is advised to con-sider carefully the importance of the retail sales force in overall company success.

stop!

Integrated Learning Experience

Retail sales are important for both retailers and manufacturers. Just as manufacturers want a retailer to push their products, retailers want their salesclerks to encourage customers to purchase from them rather than another retail outlet. Retailers are not concerned about which brand customers buy as long as they buy it from them. Articles about retail selling are available at "Retailer News" in the Archive sec-tion at www.retailernews.com. To get a feel for companies that offer training to retail salespeople, access Sales Train in Ontario, Canada, at www.retailsalestrain.com. For the United States, Accelerated Performance Training offers a number of products and services for retail sales. Examine the services available under "Programs" and "Products" at its Web site, www.aptretail.com.

The manufacturer's dilemma

From the manufacturer's perspective, one problem continually exists: Retail sales-people have a tremendous impact on final purchase decisions. More than half of the time, a customer finalizes a purchase decision while *in the store.* Therefore, the retail salesperson can strongly influence the purchase choice, yet the manufacturer has little or no influence over the retail employee. For example, a retail salesperson who strongly prefers Amana refrigerators steers customers toward those models, even when General Electric, Coldspot, and others are available. To combat this problem, manufacturers rely on three strategies:

1. Providing retail sales training
2. Extensive advertising
3. Offering contests and incentives

Retail training can orient the sales force of a given retail chain or store toward the manufacturer's products. Trainers can show retailers the advantages and special features of the manufacturer's goods. Advertising can attract the attention of a retail salesperson, who then has the product in mind each day on the job. An ad targeted toward end user customers also can be useful in persuading the retail salesperson to think about the product more carefully. Contests and incentives more directly persuade the salesperson to emphasize the manufacturer's products. Some retail chains won't allow such contests, but for those that do, the prizes offered can keep one manufacturer in the minds of the retailers' sales force.

Many manufacturers utilize **missionary salespeople** to work with retailers. These members of the sales force try to develop goodwill, stimulate demand, and provide the training and incentives needed to enhance the manufacturer in the retailer's mind. Missionary salespeople also are known as *merchandisers* and *detailers.*

business-to-business personal selling

The second major component (often first in terms of sales generated) is personal selling for the business-to-business side of the IMC program. Personal selling is the vital link between a vendor and a client. Companies that develop effective business-to-business marketing programs carefully invest in and study how to make quality sales presentations to client companies. The three primary forms of business-to-business selling are:

1. Field sales
2. In-house sales
3. Telemarketing and Internet (technology-based) programs

Field sales involve a salesperson going to the customer's place of business. In consumer markets, the field salesperson travels to the customer's home or work-place. Amway and Avon utilize consumer field salespeople. The field sales approach also is common in the business-to-business sector. Some of these individuals are **order getters,** because they go out and actively seek new customers and sales.

In-house sales mean a salesperson works from the company's office. Sales reps handle phone-in orders, faxes, and Internet customers. The in-house sales staff does not go to the customer's residence or place of business. The in-house salesperson may make the initial contact with a customer. In most cases, however, in-house salespeople simply respond to or take orders from the customers who contact the company.

Telemarketing and *Internet selling* are similar to retail programs; however, as described in the upcoming section, they can become quite complex. Telemarketing programs involve both inbound and outbound calls. Although outbound telemarketing can be a very good method for business-to-business firms to qualify prospects, many companies consider it invasive and a nuisance. Internet programs and Web sites help firms develop sophisticated linkages between the seller and the buyer. The natures of these programs are outlined in the following section, in which business-to-business relationships are defined.

buyer–seller relationships

Personal selling can play a major role in creating a successful business-to-business component of an IMC program when the marketing team understands the fundamentals of buyer–seller relationships. As Figure 13.2 illustrates, buyer–seller relationships can vary from a single transaction to a strategic partnership.

In the single transaction situation, the buyer and seller interact for the purpose of one individual purchase. In that situation, normally the only objective is to make the sale. Developing or building a relationship is not considered. A real estate salesperson selling a business for someone who is retiring or selling land to a large manufacturer may view such sales as single transactions.

In the business-to-business sector, single transactions are usually found in new-buy situations. The buying firm often calls upon salespeople to help identify a specific need as well as the solution. Team selling and consultative selling are very important in these new-buy situations. Companies sometimes spend months and thousands of dollars to obtain a single transaction bid, especially if the contract is worth millions of dollars.

Occasional transactions are often modified rebuy situations. The consumer or business purchases these products on an infrequent basis. Computers, telecommunications equipment, and manufacturing equipment and machines are business-to-business examples of occasional transactions and rebuy situations. In both cases, the buyer evaluates needs and usually contacts several vendors.

Repeat transactions occur when buyers purchase on a regular basis. Grocery shopping involves repeated transaction for consumers. Raw materials and component parts purchases are often repeated transactions in the business sector. These types of purchases are considered straight rebuys. Both consumers and businesses continue to purchase from specific vendors as long as their needs are being met. These companies switch only when they become dissatisfied with their current vendors.

To ensure a continual supply of a product, firms often enter into a **contractual agreements** with vendors. The contract guarantees that the price and regular delivery of the product or service will remain stable over a given period of time. Repeat transactions and contractual relationships may not create a high level of trust between the buyer and seller. In the case of repeat transactions, the same vendor is used because it is convenient, the company offers low prices, or for some other tangible reason. It is easier for a competitor to attempt to capture these accounts, because no commitment or relationship has been developed. With contractual relationships, the seller does not have to worry about a competitor moving in, as long as the contract remains in force. Only at times of renewal will changes be made.

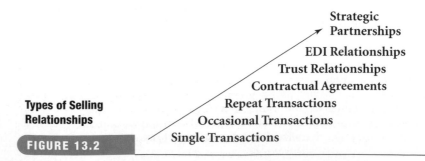

Strategic
Partnerships
EDI Relationships
Trust Relationships
Contractual Agreements
Repeat Transactions
Occasional Transactions
Single Transactions

Types of Selling Relationships

FIGURE 13.2

Unfortunately, many contractual relationships tend to be more adversarial than based on mutual trust. This often leads to dissatisfaction between the parties and a change in vendors at the end of the contractual period.

Trust relationships between buyers and sellers are based on things other than contracts. The two parties have interacted and worked together so well that both parties believe they benefit from the relationship, and each party trusts the other as a result.

An **electronic data interchange (EDI) relationship** expands the level of trust to include the sharing of data. EDI relationships occur when one company provides full access to another business. Firms routinely exchange purchase orders, shipping notices, debit and credit memos, production rates, and other information through some type of electronic format in an EDI relationship. Also, cost figures, sales information, production data, and any other information are shared so that parties can work together more effectively. Sharing information involves a high level of risk and takes place only when a firm fully trusts the vendor to use the information properly. Both trust and EDI relationships are almost always exclusive relationships, whereby buyers purchase from only one supplier or source company. This allows for greater benefit to both parties, which is a critical element of sustaining a long-term relationship.

The most intimate type of selling relationship is a **strategic partnership.** The two parties share information, exhibit high levels of trust, and move to the point where they share a common mission. The goal is to collaborate on plans to benefit both parties as well as the customers of the buying firm. In this type of relationship, the supplier looks for ways to modify or engineer its products to improve the selling firm's position in the marketplace. Strategic partnerships allow two separate firms to work as a team.

The sales staff must consider carefully the types of buyer–seller relationships to be established as IMC plans are developed. Personal sales calls are costly. At the transaction level, relationship building becomes a lower priority. Thus, using field salespeople to actually record sales transactions (e.g., fill out purchase orders) may not be an efficient use of resources. Using in-house sales, telemarketers, and the Internet may be a more efficient way of finalizing simple transactions.

business-to-business relationships

Manufacturers can have a difficult time in building quality relationships between salespeople and clients. Ordinarily, manufacturers sell their products through marketing channel members such as wholesalers and retailers. To develop these relationships requires interpersonal contact, which is not always possible. Instead, manufacturers may use intense advertising to build a strong brand name. Also, high product quality and effective use of consumer promotions can build sales rather than the close interpersonal relationships.

In the business-to-business sector, the potential value of each customer must be evaluated as the firm attempts to build relationships. Those with low potential should be handled through telemarketers, the Internet, or in-house salespeople. Clients with the potential to generate higher sales and profits should cause the company to try to build strong relationships and, if possible, a strategic partnership.

Figure 13.3 outlines the steps in developing a strategic partnership. In the model, the steps from simple awareness to a fully developed partnership normally require a long period of time. At any one of the stages, the relationship can dissolve. Also, any particular relationship may never get beyond a given stage because of reluctance or lack of trust on the part of one or both of the parties. Sometimes the size of the buying organization makes it financially impossible to expand the relationship to the next stage. In any case, the goal remains to expand and build relationships with all business-to-business clients that can expand sales and help the selling firm develop greater financial stability over time.

> **Awareness:** The customer becomes aware of a vendor's capabilities.

> **Exploration:** The initial trial period at the transaction level with no or limited commitments by both parties.

> **Expansion:** The expansion of the interactions, commitments, and profits of both parties. A contractual arrangement may be reached.

> **Commitment:** The agreement by both parties on an exclusive trust relationship that may involve EDI interchanges.

> **Partnership:** The sharing of people, resources, data, and mission to accomplish a unified goal that benefits both parties.

Steps in Developing a Strategic Partnership

FIGURE 13.3

Source: Based on James C. Anderson, "Relationships in Business Markets: Exchange Episodes, Value Creation, and their Empirical Assessment," *Journal of the Academy of Marketing Science*, Vol. 23 (1996), pp. 346–350.

stop!

Integrated Learning Experience

Keeping salespeople excited and energized is a major challenge for every organization. Salespeople experience rejection on a daily basis. Consequently, it is easy for reps to become discouraged. Many companies hire motivational speakers to stir up their sales force. Examine the Web sites of the following firms or individuals who offer motivational services. Which firm or person is the best? Why?

Jesse James (www.wantedjessejames.com)
Milt Simon & Associates (www.miltsimon.com)
Paul Nalle Ph.D. and Associates (www.paulnalle.com)
Tony Alessandra (www.alessandra.com)
Rory Aplanalp & Associates (www.rory.com)

the business-to-business personal selling process

There are major differences between the various types of salespeople listed at the start of this chapter (field sales, in-house sales, telemarketing sales). At the same time, however, the *process* used to make a sale is very similar in all categories. Figure 13.4 lists the steps to follow in a typical selling process. A discussion of each one follows.

Identifying prospects

The first step in the selling process is identifying prospects. *Prospects* are potential customers. For example, for a plastic manufacturer, prospects are all manufacturers that use plastic in their production processes. At any given time, the company can narrow prospects down for a more targeted effort. For example, the same plastics company may decide to target the automotive industry. Consequently, the sales staff would orient prospecting efforts toward firms within that industry. The sales staff would then call on these customers knowing they are supported by other components of an integrated marketing communications plan, such as direct-mail messages, advertising strategies, and trade promotions programs. All of these components emphasize the company's overall theme and also tailor that theme to the automobile industry.

> Identifying prospects
> Qualifying prospects
> Knowledge acquisition
> Sales approaches
> Sales presentation
> Follow-up

Personal Selling Process

FIGURE 13.4

Figure 13.5 identifies some of methods salespeople use in prospecting. The goal of prospecting is to develop a list of companies or individuals that can be approached on a personal level. *Current customers* can be one of the best sources of sales leads. Satisfied customers often are willing to provide names of other potential customers. In many instances, they also provide the names of decision makers, influencers, and purchasing agents. This helps a salesperson to bypass gatekeepers and find the individuals who actually make purchase decisions.

Commercial and government *databases* provide additional prospect lists. For example, a firm selling janitorial supplies may be able to purchase the mailing list from a janitorial trade journal. Commercial sources such as CompuServe, Discloser, Inc., and the *Funk and Scott Index of Corporations and Industries* can be used. Government sources are the Census of Business, the Census of Manufacturers, and the Standard Industrial Classification Code. Also, many marketing and marketing research firms sell information that assists various companies in developing prospect lists.

Trade shows are an excellent method for developing prospects. A vendor can gather names and collect additional information from prospective buyers. It is crucial to keep accurate records from trade show contacts, because excellent prospects can often be identified. Most attendees at trade shows are potential buyers.

Advertising and Internet inquiries are valuable sources of prospects when individuals or companies request additional information after seeing an ad. For instance, a magazine advertisement featuring a toll-free number, an Internet address, or a response card can lead to a new contact. Inquiries also result when television and radio ads provide telephone numbers and Internet addresses. Company Web sites give individuals the opportunity to request further information. The leads obtained from advertisements are usually very solid, because the consumer or business has already asked for additional information about the company. The Sevicesoft advertisement is designed to obtain leads for the company's interactive e-mail software.

The *consumer sales promotions* component of an IMC program can also generate prospects. Contests and sweepstakes often require individuals and companies to fill out forms in order to enter. This provides the basic prospecting information. Rebates, refunds, sampling programs, and coupons or premiums also can yield leads.

An advertisement encouraging prospects to visit the Servicesoft Web site or to call for additional information and to register for a free seminar.
Courtesy of Servicesoft.

> Customer leads
> Databases
> Trade shows
> Advertising inquiries
> Internet inquiries

> Sales promotions
> Vendor leads
> Channel leads
> Networking
> Cold calls

Methods of Prospecting

FIGURE 13.5

Vendors may be willing to identify prospects. Current vendors are normally overlooked as a source of prospects, yet they may deal with other companies in the industry. The concept of reciprocation (as mentioned in Chapter 11) suggests that a vendor may supply the names of prospective customers in return for a firm's business.

In addition to vendors, other *channel members* can be sources of leads. Distributors, agents, brokers, and retailers often will provide names. The key to obtaining prospects from vendors and channel members is to rely on strong relationships that the firm has with other companies. The stronger the relationship, the more likely the channel member will be to provide valuable prospects.

Networking is another way of getting acquainted with potential customers. Professional, social, and business organizations are common places for networking. A real estate salesman, for example, could develop valuable contacts through networking at the Chamber of Commerce, Kiwanis, or other meetings of civic organizations. Business-to-business salespeople often join professional or trade associations to meet potential prospects.

The last (and least) productive method of prospecting is *cold canvassing*. Cold calls mean little is known about the prospect. Cold-call prospects often are companies or individuals found using a source such as the yellow pages. A business-to-business salesperson who writes down the names of companies he or she hears during a normal day of work may use that list for cold calling. An Avon salesperson going door-to-door is also making cold calls. The odds are much lower that these tactics will succeed; other forms of prospecting normally are more effective.

In any case, developing a quality list of prospects is an important initial step in the personal selling process. The cost of making a personal sales call on a business is over $300. Salespeople cannot afford to spend time calling on companies who are not interested or would not make good customers. Over time, the sales force should analyze each source carefully to see which yields the best list of potential prospects. The sources that produce the best prospects should then become the primary ones used.

Developing effective prospecting tactics requires careful planning. Some companies take this function out of the hands of the sales staff for two reasons. First, using salespeople to develop prospects is costly. There are lower-cost and more efficient methods. Second, time spent prospecting is not time spent selling. It makes more sense to use salespeople where their expertise lies—in selling. To locate prospects, many firms use direct mail, direct-response advertising, and telemarketers. These methods are cheaper than using salespeople and tend to be quite effective. Telemarketers can be trained to locate prospects and to qualify the prospects to turn over to the field sales staff.

Qualifying prospects

Qualifying prospects is the process of choosing the individuals or companies holding the highest potential to be customers. It is important to choose the prospects with the greatest potential because sales calls are so expensive. One method of qualifying prospects is to group them into categories based on their potential. Figure 13.6 identifies questions or criteria that can be used for this process.

Questions for Qualifying Prospects

▶ What is the sales volume potential?
▶ Is the prospect dissatisfied with its current vendor?
▶ Does the prospect use single or multiple sourcing?
▶ Is the prospect a good fit with current customers?
▶ Does the prospect fit with the firm's IMC plan?
▶ How difficult will it be to get past the gatekeeper(s)?

FIGURE 13.6

The best category contains those that have the highest potential based on responses to the six questions in Figure 13.6. For example, a particular prospect may buy a large volume; however, if it is satisfied with its current vendor and uses only a single source, it is difficult to get past the gatekeeper. A prospect with a lower sales potential that is dissatisfied with a present vendor is more likely to switch. Also, businesses using multiple sources are often easier to approach. These companies are more willing to purchase from new vendors than are those using single sourcing. Unfortunately, companies using multiple sources tend to purchase smaller amounts and often leverage the various vendors against one another to obtain better prices.

It is important to decide if a particular prospect is a good fit for the selling firm. Often, in an effort to increase sales, every prospect is considered viable, which is not always a good idea. Concentrating sales efforts in specific industries can provide a firm with expertise and economies of scale in that industry. It also helps the company build a strong brand name and brand image in that industry. The image can be leveraged to get past gatekeepers. Therefore, being the major supplier within a specific industry has tremendous advantages. Buyers feel comfortable with a major supplier and are even willing to pay a little more knowing they have a stable supplier. Business buyers normally prefer well-established companies because of their dependability.

Every individual responsible for qualifying prospects should be thoroughly familiar with the firm's IMC plan. If they were not involved in the communication market analysis discussed in Chapter 3, the basic concepts of the communication analysis should be available. The target market analysis and the opportunity analysis conducted during the communication analysis provide valuable information about the target market and the opportunities available to the firm. This information should be used in qualifying prospects. For example, the opportunity analysis for a tool manufacturer may reveal that its primary competitors are not adequately serving small to medium-size independent automobile repair shops. In that situation, small to medium-size repair shops become more enticing prospects.

Advertising plans are another important consideration when qualifying prospects. A financial firm that creates an advertising campaign aimed at hospitals and medical facilities probably does so because those prospects received a higher score than did other prospects, such as physicians or some other totally unrelated group of businesses. The sales force should concentrate its efforts on the same set of potential clients. The next campaign may focus on small businesses. At that point, the sales staff knows where to call next.

Integrated Learning Experience

The high cost of making personal sales calls requires companies to narrow their prospect lists down to the most attractive potential customers. To get a feel for qualifying prospects, assume you are a supplier of fiberglass that is used to manufacture surfboards. Listed below are manufacturers of surfboards. Look at each company's Web site. Then narrow the list down to the best four prospects. Write down the criteria you used to qualify them using the information provided in this textbook as a guide.

Becker Surf Sport (www.beckersurf.com)
Aloha Surf Boards (www.alohasurfboards.com)
Bamboo Surfboards of Australia (www.bamboosurfboards.com.au)
Bruce Jones Surfboards (www.brucejoans.com)
Stickman LLC (www.stickmansurf.com)
Schroedel Surboards and Clothing (www.schroedel.com)
Gordon & Smith (www.gordonsmith.com)

Knowledge acquisition

After prospects have been qualified, the knowledge acquisition stage begins. Figure 13.7 lists typical information that a salesperson obtains about a prospect prior to a sales call. The goal of the knowledge acquisition stage is to provide the

> ▶ Identify current vendor(s)
>
> ▶ Identify prospect's customers
>
> ▶ Assess customer needs
>
> ▶ Determine roles of price, service, and product attributes in the purchase decision
>
> ▶ Determine roles of trade and sales promotions in the purchase decision
>
> ▶ Determine critical customer benefits or product attributes
>
> ▶ Identify risk factors in switching vendors
>
> ▶ Identify buyer's personality type

Knowledge Acquisition

FIGURE 13.7

information needed to make an effective sales presentation. The more specific information a salesperson has about a prospect, the greater the potential for making a sale. The information also can be used to either disqualify a prospect or upgrade the prospect to a higher category. When the knowledge acquisition step suggests the prospect is not a good fit for the company, the prospect should be either dropped from the prospect list or downgraded to a lower priority. The same is true if a competitor is firmly entrenched with that customer. When the information indicates a company has unfulfilled needs and can be influenced by the firm's current trade promotions mix, the prospect can be upgraded to a higher-priority category.

Many salespeople like to skip the knowledge acquisition stage and jump directly into making sales calls. This is not surprising, because they earn commissions for making sales, not for acquiring knowledge. It is possible to spend too much time gathering information; however, in most cases, salespeople tend to spend too little time acquiring this critical information.

Some information about a prospect can be acquired through secondary sources such as trade journals and various databases. Other knowledge, however, can be obtained only from the prospect directly. These efforts are called *fact-finding programs* or *prospect qualification contacts*. Telemarketers sometimes can qualify leads and gather pertinent information for the salesperson. Other times, when the best prospects are involved, a salesperson makes the initial sales call. The goal is to discover the customer's needs along with other critical facts. If the prospect has a current vendor, it is highly likely that the only person the salesperson will see is the gatekeeper or the purchasing agent.

Identifying the vendor(s) who currently serve the prospect is an important first step in knowledge acquisition, as outlined in Figure 13.7. When a firm conducts a competitive analysis and position analysis (as described in Chapter 3), the company's leaders learn about the competition's products and sales approaches. Sales reps can also compare products and sales approaches. These details make it easier to prepare a sales presentation that highlights the advantages of the selling firm over the buyer's current vendor.

Knowing the prospect's customers provides key ideas about the supplies necessary to make an effective sales presentation. Being aware of the prospect's customers demonstrates that the company understands the prospect's situation. It also can help the company modify products or services to better meet the needs of the prospect and the prospect's customers. For example, a supplier of electronic components that understands that the needs of a manufacturer of televisions to be

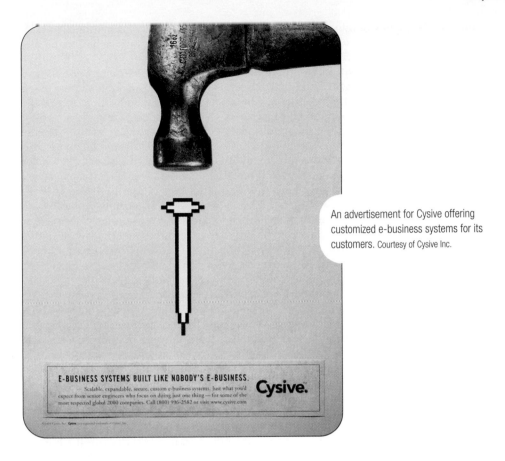

An advertisement for Cysive offering customized e-business systems for its customers. Courtesy of Cysive Inc.

placed in RVs has a distinct advantage, because the RV manufacturer's needs are much different than those that sell televisions to retail stores. Considering the differences in electronic components used in televisions for RVs (as opposed to standard television sets) allows the electronic components supplier to make a better sales presentation. For Cysive's engineers to design an e-business system for their clients, they must understand their clients' customers and what their clients' customers want when placing e-orders. Without this knowledge, the e-business system designed may not meet the need of Cysive's customers.

Buyers look for the best value possible as they examine vendors. For buyers, value can be defined as the best combination of price, service, and product attributes. It is important to know how much emphasis a potential customer places on each factor. A prospect who values service will be impressed most when the service component is stressed during a sales presentation. Understanding the prospect's view of value is critical to successful selling.

Trade and sales promotions are crucial elements of a complete IMC approach. Nearly 75 percent of all promotional dollars are spent on trade and consumer promotions. Therefore, it is important to understand how the prospects view these promotions. Prospects that place a high emphasis on receiving trade promotions should be considered carefully by the selling firm. When the vendor decides these promotions can be part of a synchronized IMC plan, the program is more likely to succeed. Remember, it is illegal to offer trade promotions to one customer without making the same offer to all customers. The best prospects are those who value the current trade and consumer promotions the selling firm offers. Salespeople may be tempted to offer whatever trade or consumer promotion a prospect seeks in order to finalize a sale, but if the promotion is not part of the company's current IMC plan, it sets a dangerous precedent. Identifying the roles that trade and sales promotions play in the buyer's purchasing decision process reveals vital information. The selling firm should make sure that any prospect contacted can be reached using elements of the seller's current IMC plan.

Knowledge acquisition also involves identifying the *customer benefits* and *product attributes* that will be critical in the buyer's decision-making process. Each product sold features core product attributes; these must match the needs of the buyer if the product is going to be considered. Usually all competing vendors offer basic core attributes that are similar or the same. Beyond these basic features are the special attributes or services the company offers. These benefits and attributes differentiate one competitor from another and often are the deciding factors in choices buyers' make. For example, a manufacturer using a just-in-time inventory management system normally is highly concerned about delivery reliability. The most critical factors in the purchase of materials such as steel or aluminum generally are stress strength, thickness, and consistency of sheets. A component parts vendor making transistors knows that most electronics firms are concerned with defect rates, because they cannot test each transistor before it is used. Thus, for each product purchased, the seller identifies the critical customer benefits and product attributes most likely to affect the buyer's final purchase decision.

For buyers, there is a certain level of *risk involved in switching vendors.* The risk may be low when maintenance supply items are being purchased but very high for raw materials and component parts being considered. An extremely high level of risk exists when the current vendor and buyer have a strong relationship and use EDI. Anytime the vendor and customer exchange data and share information, the risk in switching vendors increases. This is one of the techniques vendors use to create barriers to prevent competitors from taking their customers. A strong EDI relationship usually benefits both parties and makes it more risky to change vendors.

The final piece of information used in preparing a sales presentation is discovering the buyer's *personality type.* Several personality typologies have been developed over the years. Perhaps the most useful for sellers to identify during the knowledge acquisition stage is what can be termed the *value orientation of the buyer.* There are three basic types:[6]

1. Intrinsic value buyers
2. Extrinsic value buyers
3. Strategic value buyers

Intrinsic value buyers understand the product, know how to use it, and view the product as a commodity-type item. Normally price is the most important element of the value triad (product attributes, price, and service). Transactional selling is the most common method used in reaching intrinsic value buyers. Salespeople in these situations function as order-takers once they obtain a basic contract. Many times, retail customers are intrinsic value buyers.

Extrinsic value buyers focus more on the product attributes and the solution a particular product can provide. The buyer wants a salesperson who understands the buyer's situation and can adapt the product to fit the buyer's needs. The buyer tries to build a relationship with the salesperson. Extrinsic value buyers prefer the consultative sales approach, because the seller understands the problems they face and works diligently with them to discover solutions. Figure 13.8 compares the differences between consultative selling and transactional selling. Some situations are still best suited to transactional sales; still, most experts believe that in the future successful sales organizations will view themselves as selling consultants.

Strategic value buyers usually seek out partnerships with suppliers. They want more than just advice; they want vendors willing to partner with them to satisfy customer needs. Within the partnership, both parties work to achieve mutually beneficial solutions. Often teams from both companies collaborate in the design and marketing of products and services. These relationships normally involve cross-functional teams from both companies in the partnership. For example, IBM

> Consultants think long term; sales reps think short term.

> Consultants are considered experts; sales reps are considered salespeople.

> Consultants are specialists that make recommendations to help the prospect succeed; sales reps sell, sell, and sell.

> Consultants are a valuable resource; sales reps are there to sell.

> Consultants help solve problems; sales reps present product benefits.

> Consultants offer solutions that benefit the customer; sales reps adapt their product to fit the customer's perceived needs.

> Consultants want to know more about helping; sales reps want to know about how to close a sale.

Consultative Selling vs. Transactional Selling

FIGURE 13.8

Source: Gitomer, "Discipline Yourself and Profit from the Art of Consultative Selling" *Capital District Business Review*, (January 17, 2000), Vol. 26, No. 41, p. 29.

sent a team to Monsanto, a manufacturer of agricultural and pharmaceutical products, to explore research issues for gene mapping of both plant and animal cells. The result of this collaborative effort was a contract between IBM and Monsanto worth several hundred million dollars.[7]

In general, gathering information about prospects can be time-consuming and costly, yet it is essential. Many business-to-business firms either hire individuals to gather this information for the sales force or contract independent agencies to gather it. Either way, firms should spend more money on front-end sales development. Salespeople should not call on prospects until they have accurate information about the potential client. Using trained sales development personnel to gather information offers the following advantages:[8]

- The ability to capture more information about prospects
- The ability to capture information faster
- Better recording, quantification, and transformation of information for salespeople
- Improved sharing of information among salespeople and other members of the sales team
- Reduced biases by salespeople against certain companies, for whatever reason (seems like a low prospect, angry when turned down for a previous sale, etc.)

Firms using trained individuals or subcontracting sales information development experience higher rates of return on their investments.

After the information has been gathered, and a type of selling format has been established (e.g., transactional, contractual, trust, EDI), then the actual process of selling may begin. Various selling approaches are used to persuade the buyer to make the purchase.

Sales approaches

Personal selling textbooks list many types of sales approaches. Almost all of them can be classified into one of these four approaches:

1. Stimulus–response
2. Need–satisfaction
3. Problem–solution
4. Mission-sharing

A discussion and analysis of each type follows.

A **stimulus–response sales approach** uses specific statements (stimuli) to solicit specific responses from customers. Another name for a stimulus–response approach is a "canned" sale pitch. Usually the salesperson memorizes the stimulus statements (the pitch). Telemarketers, retail salesclerks, and new field salespeople often use this method.

The goal of the **need–satisfaction sales approach** is to discover a customer's needs, and then provide solutions that satisfy those needs. This approach requires the salesperson to be skillful and ask the right questions. A good relationship between the sales rep and the customer helps improve the chances of revealing the needs.

The **problem–solution sales approach** requires the selling organization to analyze the buyer's operation. Often a team featuring engineers, salespeople, and other experts interacts with the customer to analyze the customer's situation fully. Once the company's problems are understood, the team can offer feasible solutions. The problem–solution approach is often used in new-buy situations, because the buying organization may not have a solid grip on the problem and may even welcome help in defining its own needs.

The final sales approach involves the strategic partnership concept introduced in Figure 13.2. In a **mission-sharing sales approach,** two organizations develop a common mission and then share resources to accomplish that mission. In some ways, such a partnership resembles a "joint venture" project.

Traditionally, buyer–seller relationships have been considered to be adversarial in some respects. In that model, the buyer questions the seller's motives and often distrusts the statements made by the seller. Such customers believe most salespeople say and promise anything to make a sale. Sellers, in turn, typically assume the buyer is going to resist any sales approach. To overcome this problem, many firms try to move toward stronger partnerships, such as the mission-sharing sales approach.

Using more of a strategic partnership approach means the buyer and seller work together to develop superior products for the marketplace both wish to attack. The salesperson's approach changes, and he or she spends time looking at and understanding the buyer's problems as well as its customer base. This system is quite different from trying to sell someone a product without any knowledge of the buyer's customers or how the product fits into the buyer's overall mission.

The biggest determinant of which type of sales approach to use is the form of buyer–seller relationship that exists. Other major factors in selecting a sales approach are the dollar value of the sale and the role of personal selling in the IMC plan. The mission-sharing sales approach is not the best for all products and all industries. For example, in retail settings and consumer sales situations, the stimulus–response sales approach is the most common. Occasionally, the need–satisfaction model is used, especially when the dollar value of a sale is higher. Items such as a computer systems, automobiles, and financial services may require a need–satisfaction type of sales approach.

The business-to-business sector uses all four sales approaches, depending on the goals of the selling organization. To develop brand loyalty, however, it is necessary to utilize sales approaches that lead to high levels of trust and stronger partnerships.

Business-to-business sales presentations

Sales presentations usually are more complicated in business-to-business transactions than they are in consumer or retail situations. When contacting another business, salespeople often encounter difficulties, because they must get past gatekeepers in organizations in order to reach members of the buying center. This is especially difficult when the company is in the early stages of a purchasing decision-making process and is carefully trying to identify its needs. Only the current vendor is likely to have convenient access at that point. This gives the current

- ❯ **Identification of need**
- ❯ **Establishment of specifications**
- ❯ **Identification of alternatives**
- ❯ **Identification of vendors**
- ❯ **Evaluation of vendors**
- ❯ **Selection of vendor(s)**
- ❯ **Negotiation of purchase terms**

The Business-to-Business Buying Processes

FIGURE 13.9

vendor the advantage of being able to cross-sell other products and services, because the rep already has access to the business. The current vendor's sales team should work hard to help its business customers identify new needs. Figure 13.9 displays the typical business-to-business buying process.

In new-buy situations, a salesperson improves his or her chances of closing a deal by helping the business establish product specifications. Rendering product advice can be beneficial to the selling company in two ways. First, by helping another firm to establish specifications, the salesperson demonstrates a desire to assist the company in meeting its needs. Second, the selling firm's team can structure the specifications in ways that benefit the company rather than its their competitors. In any type of partnership relationship, assisting a firm in establishing objectives is a critical part of the selling process, especially as the purchasing firm tries to specify its needs.

When both the buyer and the seller are interested in developing a strategic partnership, the selling firm should be closely involved in identifying alternatives. The goal of the strategic partnership is to find the best solutions for both parties. As a consequence, the vendor's primary goal is not to make one specific sale, but rather to further the strategic partnership. This approach contrasts a more transactional-type relationship. In that situation, selling is the first, and often only, goal. At times, the buying firm's best solution is to take care of a need internally. In that situation, the selling firm must resist the temptation to push its products as a better solution, because a short-term gain endangers a longer-term, more profitable partnership. There are even moments in strategic partnerships when it is possible that a third firm is subcontracted to provide the needed product or service. Such a show of goodwill by the firm, which ordinarily sells its own products to the client company, builds trust levels in the long range.

Vendor or selling firms are rarely involved when purchasing companies identify potential vendors. A sales rep can attempt to be involved in the evaluation of vendors through the bidding process, but often this does not work. Instead, the salesperson should try to obtain as much information as possible about the buying firm. Then, the seller can gear a sales presentation to the company in the evaluation stage of the buying process. In the evaluation stage, a salesperson can present the advantages of the firm, how the company's product meets specific buyer needs, and also the benefits the specific vendor's brand holds over the competition.

There are similarities and differences between selling to other businesses as opposed to retail customers. Both customers go through a purchasing process that involves identifying needs and comparing alternatives. The primary difference is that, when selling to a retail customer, the individual is in the store and is, in essence, a "captive audience" until he or she leaves. In contrast, when selling to other businesses, the buyer may consider several companies at the same time. The sales rep must take advantage of any private moments in which he or she has the attention of buyers and influencers in order to succeed. A strong case must be made for one company's advantages over others as the purchasing firm considers its options.

WestLB (a financial services firm) recently indicated in a series of advertisements targeted to institutional clients that the company could provide individual solutions to complex financial needs. The ads emphasized that the company understood the unique needs of institutional customers and that it could provide innovative, tailor-made programs with a European bias. WestLB utilized relationship managers and product specialists who worked with individual clients.[9] These points were prominently displayed in WestLB's ads. It was equally important for the sales staff to convey the message in their sales presentations. This consistent message helped ensure that the selling function, advertisements, and other marketing efforts reinforced the same theme. Customers getting the same message from all of these sources remembered the message. The message had the desired impact, and WestLB's share of the institutional marketplace grew as a result.

Follow-up

As crucial as the initial sales presentation is to selling firms, the follow-up provided can be even more critical. Keeping customers happy results in repeat purchases and brand loyalty. Unhappy customers not only defect to a competitor but also spread negative word-of-mouth communications about the firm. It is much more cost effective to retain old customers rather than to entice new ones. Therefore, the critical role follow-up plays in selling cannot be overemphasized.

Unfortunately, successful follow-ups are hard to create. A salesperson paid through commissions may be reluctant to spend very much time following up sales, because follow-ups do not generate additional revenues in the short term. Switching the account to another person to follow up may sound like a good idea, but many customers don't like this approach because they have already developed a relationship with the salesperson. As a result, the best method is to create the proper incentives for regular salespeople to do follow-up work by using these tactics:

1. *Education.* Teach the sales rep that follow-ups create loyalty and therefore are the quickest path to more sales down the road.

2. *Motivation.* Hold back the commission (or part of it), until the sales rep provides information that a follow-up call or communication has taken place.

3. *Indoctrination.* Have more experienced sales reps show new and younger salespeople the value of long-term, repeat-business customers.

It is also important for salespeople to understand the nature of the company's IMC plan. The sales team should reinforce the key message and theme spelled out in the firm's IMC plans, goals, and objectives. The sales manager should assume the responsibility of making sure everyone in the sales department is familiar with the IMC plan and will attempt to use the major message in making sales calls.

Unfortunately, in many organizations the sales manager is not involved in the IMC planning process. Instead, a meeting takes place between the sales manager and the marketing staff later, in which they discuss an IMC plan that has already been formulated. In most cases, this is just an informational meeting. The marketing team expects the sales manager or sales trainers to relay key IMC information to individual salespeople without allowing them to participate in the development of the program. As noted in Chapter 1, to be effective, the IMC plan must permeate the entire organization. Thus, a better approach is to include as many people as possible, including sales managers and even salespeople, in the development of an IMC program. Salespeople have personal contacts with customers. As a result, they can become valuable assets in creating and implementing an IMC plan.

Integrated Learning Experience

Organizations invest heavily in sales training. While some firms use internal personnel for training, most use external firms for at least part of a training program. Examine the Web sites of the following firms. What services and products do each offer that would be beneficial? Refer back to Figure 13.4. Which of the firms listed appears to be the best for each of the steps in the selling process?

Sales Training Institute and STI International (www.salesinstitute.com)
The Sales Bureau (www.salesbureau.com)
Customer Focus, Inc. (www.trainingwireless.com)
Omega Performance (www.omega-performance.com)
The Richardson Company (www.richarsonco.com)
Creative Channel Services, Inc. (www.creativechannel.com)

new trends in business-to-business personal selling

Many recent trends in the marketing arena have affected personal selling. Marketing teams, account executives, and company officials should be aware of these changes as they prepare and implement IMC plans. First, in both consumer markets and business-to-business markets, product parity is becoming the norm. In other words, fewer distinguishable differences exist among the various brands than ever before. Therefore, individual companies must create marketing advantages using nonproduct attributes. The perception of superiority can be built by developing a strong brand name or by actually selling a superior product or service.

Decline in the number of salespeople

Also, as technology continues to evolve, it is possible that the need for salespeople will continue to diminish. Some sources estimate that the number of sales positions present in the United States will decline by as much as 50 percent over the next decade.[10] Those who remain must both be technologically skilled and understand the selling process, making the new job challenging and demanding. Sales managers are likely to conclude that selection of sales reps is a key part of a successful selling program, because there will be fewer sales reps, and each will have more responsibilities. Training and upgrading both technical and selling skills take on a great deal of importance in such an environment. Other trends are expected to affect personal selling in future years; some of these are listed in Figure 13.10.

Expansion of sales channels

A major impact of technology is the expansion of the number of channels buyers can use to purchase products. Most of the time, a buyer no longer needs a salesperson to place an order. In fact, with EDI technology, computers can both place and take orders. Instead of a salesperson, the selling firm relies on customer service representatives, who work with buyers to ensure that deliveries, quality specifications,

▶ **Decline in the number of salespeople**
▶ **Expansion of selling channels**
▶ **Long-term relationships and strategic partnerships**
▶ **Team selling**
▶ **Database customer segmentation**

Trends in Personal Selling

FIGURE 13.10

and orders are maintained at desired levels. The salesperson's primary use is to make the initial sale.

In other business-to-business settings, a similar scenario often takes place in straight rebuy situations. The *order taker* is the company's Internet Web site or a telemarketer. This approach saves the purchasing agent time. Orders can be placed via a secure Internet account, or a staff person can call an inside salesperson from the company that wants to make a purchase. The vendor can utilize customer service reps to check on clients and to make sure clients are satisfied with the products they receive, which is more of a *missionary sales* type of activity. Using technology to place orders reduces costs and increases speed and efficiency considerably.

A typical customer utilizes multiple channels to communicate with a firm. For example, the business customer sometimes talks to a field salesperson, such as when the customer wants to purchase a copy machine. Later, the same customer communicates with the vendor's internal salesperson to purchase accessories and additional products. Then, to order toner or paper, the customer uses the Internet to communicate.

A new selling technique in business-to-business markets is the use of e-mail. Although most businesses and consumers oppose *spamming* (sending unwanted e-mail advertisements), legitimate e-mail selling does take place. For instance, Northern Tool & Equipment, a supplier of light industrial products and tools to small businesses such as auto repair shops and landscapers, has had some recent success using e-mail. Northern contacted all of its 1,600 customers by telephone to determine whether they would mind receiving e-mails before launching a direct e-mail sales program. In preparing the e-mail program, Northern wanted to make sure the company used a unified theme. The idea was to coordinate e-mail with Web site messages, outbound calls, and mailings. The company made sure that every medium conveyed the same message.[11]

While Northern Tool & Equipment used e-mail technology as a direct-marketing tool, Global Crossings used it to qualify prospects and to send potential clients proposals. Prior to using e-mail, Global Crossings averaged 400 telephone calls for one sale. The company sent out literature to 50 of the 400 via FedEx. Now Global Crossings sends prospects a multimedia e-mail attachment, which can be as large as 800 Kb, that provides a full presentation. Using this approach, Global's sales increased from one per 400 telephone calls to four per 400 calls. It also reduced costs, because the presentations were sent by e-mail instead of FedEx.[12]

Long-term relationships and strategic partnerships

The use of technology such as EDI and the Internet has led many companies to reduce the number of *vendors* with which they deal. In exchange for reducing the number, buyers desire long-term relationships and, in many cases, strategic partnerships. These customers believe that by utilizing fewer vendors they can order in larger quantities, which often leads to price discounts and lower costs-per-unit purchased. Still, the key in these situations is developing a trust relationship between the buyer and seller. At times a company eventually deals with only one vendor. In that situation, the vendor must deliver or the client business may be forced to stop operations. A manufacturing assembly line that does not have a critical component part must stop production until that component part arrives. When a manufacturer relies on a single vendor, the company must be sure that vendor can and will deliver on time with sufficient quality.

Ernst & Young trimmed the firm's target customer list from several thousand down to only 300 U.S. firms and 300 international firms. By focusing on these 600 prospects, Ernst & Young experienced a 30 percent growth rate. Square D Company, a manufacturer of electrical, automation, and control products, followed a similar strategy. Rather than try to serve all 4,200 OEM accounts, Square D Company focused on the top 200. The result was a 40 percent growth in revenues from these 200 accounts.[13]

Team selling

The movement toward seeking out fewer vendors and stronger long-term commitments means more companies are using teams rather than individuals to sell. Teams often consist of engineers as well as salespeople. The goal of the team is to be able to better meet the needs of buyers and to ensure that a strong relationship is maintained. Often engineers and other technical people continue a relationship with a client firm long after making a sale. A major difficulty of using engineers on a selling team is that they are not trained to be salespeople. In fact, the approaches of a salesperson and an engineer are often in opposite directions. In trying to make a sale, a salesperson is optimistic things will work and usually has a solution to any problem or objection a prospect may have. On the other hand, engineers tend to be cautious and see all kinds of potential problems. Without training, it often appears that the two are not in sync and that the salesperson is just trying to make a sale and doesn't care whether the product works.

To be a successful team, it is essential that both the salesperson and the engineer are trained in ways to work together. Both need to see their role as consultants and problem solvers. In addition to training, using a three-phase sales approach improves the results of this type of multidisciplinary sales team. In *phase one,* the salesperson and technical person listen to the customer's concerns and try to identify the customer's needs. This phase is a probing exercise designed to make sure the selling team has a clear picture of the difficulties or problems being faced. In *phase two,* the team takes the information back to the office where it can work on a solution out of sight of the prospect. This gives the engineer or technical person an opportunity to question, doubt, and investigate different solutions. Once a feasible solution has been decided upon, it is time for *phase three,* when the team goes back to the client. This three-phase strategy helps engineers arrive at the best solutions for their customers. Also, the team appears to be knowledgeable using this three-phase approach.[14]

The team approach is also effective in a strategic partnership. In these teams, technical people such as engineers are part of the project; however, senior-level management personnel are included in order to solidify a strategic partnership. For instance, at Nalco Chemical, the CEO and other senior-level executives regularly call on their strategic partner customers. When Nalco wins a national account, senior-level executives become part of the account team to oversee the relationship. Nalco pairs its senior-level executive with an executive from the customer's company. In addition to participating in the initial sales process, the executives also serve as evaluators of the partnership. Xerox Corporation uses a similar approach. According to David Potter, director of global account marketing, if senior executives from both companies are involved, "There will be a better understanding of the big picture, not just the sales picture." As with Nalco, these two senior-level executives meet on a regular basis to discuss such things as the customer's markets, financial plans, and quality-control measures. The involvement of higher-level executives ensures the relationship remains a strategic partnership because executives at this level are actively involved in strategic planning for both companies.[15]

Database customer segmentation

Advances in computer technology now allow companies to develop databases that help them segment markets. Based on profiles of their best customers, these companies look at both low- and high-yield customers so that the marketing team can locate firms or individuals that have profiles similar to their best customers. These new prospects are then targeted by either salespeople or telemarketers. The goal is to cultivate stronger relationships with these viable new customers. Also, new products or services can be sold more easily to loyal customers. Instead of spending large sums of money to locate new customers, firms realize that an effective way to increase sales is through selling to members of the bottom 80 percent of their current customers who have the potential to become stronger allies. Bell Canada uses business intelligence software developed by IBM to mine customer data.

communication **action**

Many companies offer products both to retail customers and to other businesses. These firms must work with all forms of personal selling in order to succeed. For example, Dell Computers uses five different ways for customers to place orders: field salespeople, in-house salespeople, retail stores, telemarketers, and the Internet. A customer, as well as the staff at Dell Computers, can choose which channel is appropriate. For consumers, sales are made via the Internet, by telephone, or at a retail store. Once a computer purchase has been made, the customer continues to have these three options for placing additional orders. From a cost-efficiency standpoint, Dell encourages using the company's telemarketers and the Internet to place orders because these customers make only occasional transactions.

Many of Dell's customers are businesses. For small business customers, using a field sales representative would be inefficient. A field salesperson can make an initial sales call, but once the initial sale has been made, in-house sales staff or telemarketers continue servicing the account. The goal with consumers and small businesses is to encourage repeat purchases. Building strong relationships may not bring a profitable return on costs if field salespeople are involved. When the client is a medium to large business, Dell uses field salespeople. By modifying the type of sales staff used based on the type of buyer–seller relationship, Dell reduces personnel costs while at the same time maintaining a high level of sales.

Source: Liam Hegarty, "Winning Market Strategies: How Dell Does It," *Fairfield County Business Journal,* 37, no, 48 (November 30, 1998), p. 7.

Bell Canada's goal is to increase the retention of the company's corporate customers through better meeting their needs. Through data mining, Bell Canada has been able to segment customers into specific groups based on forecasted service needs. Using this information, Bell Canada knows which services are the most likely to match a firm's corporate mission and which firms are the most likely to upgrade services. Rather than cold selling services, the field sales staff at Bell Canada are equipped with a detailed profile of the customer, which identifies which services to sell.[16]

personal selling in international markets

Personal selling in international markets is difficult. A series of boundaries must be overcome in order to succeed, beginning with language and slang issues, customs, morés, regional differences with other nations, doubt, suspicion, and distrust. Even when two companies recognize major advantages will take place if they cooperate, it is still difficult to build the long-term bonds to enable the process to move forward.

For example, Jim Moreli of Allied Signal Europe was assigned to sell nylon in Europe. Calling on a company in Finland, he found himself sipping vodka with the Finnish company's representatives. After hours of negotiation, they took a sauna then plunged naked into a pool of cold water. It was a rude awakening. International selling is not always like it is in the United States. Jim had to adapt to local customs, traditions, and cultural differences. Through his efforts, however, the company adapted it sales methods to match those local customs; Allied Signal built up a $90 million nylon business in Europe in only three years. One of Allied Signal's keys for success was using local sales forces and distributors to supplement and assist the organization's American sales force that was sent to Europe.[17]

There is always a choice to be made when setting up a personal selling system. The firm can hire and manage local members of the community to make sales calls,

- ▶ Provide information about culture, mores, customs, and traditions
- ▶ Ensure instructors have credibility
- ▶ Use instructors with experience in international sales
- ▶ Include in the training individuals native to the countries or regions
- ▶ Encourage salespeople to consider the positive experiences they are about to have
- ▶ Provide benefits that people in international market seek from products being sold
- ▶ Present, discuss, and rehearse sales presentations and closings within cultural context
- ▶ As much as possible, provide language training instead of relying on translators

Tips for Training International Salespeople

FIGURE 13.11

or it can elect to send its own sales force overseas. Each approach has distinct advantages and disadvantages.

When salespeople are used from a different country or culture, the company must provide sound training. Figure 13.11 lists some tips for training an international sales force. The goal must be to orient the salesperson to the vendor company while at the same time taking advantage of the person's expertise in understanding the local culture.

When salespeople are sent to overseas locations, the key to success is making sure they understand the culture, mores, customs, and traditions of the country where they are being sent. A salesperson insensitive to the culture of another country probably won't succeed and can offend individuals from the buying firm. In some cases, the offense may be very difficult to overcome in future sales attempts. Consider just a few of the differences salespeople must know about:

1. In *Bangkok,* touching a person on the head is roughly the equivalent of touching the "private parts" of a person in the United States.
2. In *Hungary,* it is common to throw a massive, expensive party after a deal has been closed, or the customer may be insulted that you did not.
3. In *Buenos Aires,* people may poke fun at the sales rep's wardrobe or weight, which is a sign of familiarity and that they like the rep.
4. In *Galway,* your client is likely to be late for a meeting, but highly complimented when you say you like his or her sense of humor.
5. In *Bermuda,* people really do wear shorts to conduct business, but they are cut like top-of-the line slacks and are worn with knee-high socks.
6. In *Santiago,* it will seem like the client is standing way too close, but if you pull away, he or she might be insulted.
7. *Israelis* are offended by the "thumbs up" sign.

The role of a *cultural assimilator,* as mentioned in earlier chapters, is to help the selling firm understand local practices. To do so increases the chances of building a longer-term relationship with a company in another country.

International competition has forced companies to examine their selling functions closely. Cold calls are difficult to justify because of the high cost per sales calls. Companies spend more time and money qualifying prospects in order to increase the success rates of their salespeople. Some firms hire specialists, freelancers, or other firms to locate and qualify prospects for them.

The secret to managing personal selling in international settings is to carefully plan out the approach, account for the culture, and follow up when difficulties arise. As the world becomes smaller, more and more "experts" are available to assist in dealing with the various nuances present in individual countries.[18]

the role of the sales manager

Careful integration of the personal selling component into an overall IMC program is, in some sense, the "finishing touch" to the IMC plan. Potential customers and other prospects may be enticed to purchase goods and services because of advertisements, trade promotions, consumer promotions, and other communications from the organization. Then, the salesperson can finalize the purchase and begin the process of building a long-term relationship with a single customer and developing the company's image on a larger scale. To do so, the sales manager should address three issues:

1. Planning
2. Goal setting
3. Motivation and compensation

In the area of *planning,* the sales manager should be included in IMC planning process, as noted earlier. Then, the sales manager must be held accountable for developing plans that strengthen the IMC program. Sales meetings should begin with the manager restating company's overall theme and marketing strategy. Selling tactics, ordering systems, and all other parts of the personal sales program must be consistent with the company's marketing communications program. The emphasis on quality communications and an overall theme can be something as simple as Wal-Mart's insistence that its employees are "associates" rather than tellers and clerks. Terms such as *professionalism* can be routinely applied to discussions of methods for working with customers.

A famous furniture company in Texas, led by "Mattress Bob," recently changed its entire selling plan, moving from what he called "man-to-man" selling to a "zone." The essence of the change was to replace the high-pressure one-on-one approach of commission sales with a problem-solving, assistance-rendering method. The company shifted salespeople from commissions to salaries and put *group incentives* in place. Individual associates performed tasks as simple as minding children while customers looked at furniture. The net result was an explosive growth in both sales and reports of customer satisfaction. The entire approach began with an IMC plan in which the company asked itself, "What is our most important activity?" The answer was "satisfying customers," and from there all other ingredients were put into place.

In the area of *goal setting,* individual sales plans are best served when goals are set for the entire company, for individual products, and for individual salespeople. Goal setting creates meaningful targets and can clarify the company's larger objectives. For instance, in a recent speech to the American Booksellers organization, the CEO of Barnes & Noble noted that many book manufacturers had become too complacent and satisfied with increasing revenues, when the source of the increase was simply higher prices. Instead, his argument was book *prices* should be *lowered,* which he believed would have the effect of increasing *unit* (or *individual book) sales* as well as overall revenues in the long run. Careful goal setting helps clarify what types of customer-based performance objectives to seek out. In the case of book sales, more readers may be equal to longer-term stability, especially in the face of competition from electronic media. Further, the salesperson may find the task of selling a little easier, when selling from the manufacturer to the bookstore, and from the bookstore to the individual consumer.

Finally, *motivation and compensation* programs lead sales reps to emphasize the correct components of the IMC program. For instance, when a product such as

ZIMA first hit the marketplace, sales reps were probably compensated for generating new customers, especially bars and liquor stores willing to sell the product in the first place. Later, as ZIMA stabilized and gained market share, new incentives were developed to move selling from the *pioneering* stage (finding new outlets) to a more *competitive* stage, wherein sales increases are more incremental and maintenance of the market share is the most crucial feature. In the pioneering stage, bonuses and other incentives were probably paid for finding new stores. In the competitive stage, incentives are probably based on marginal growth in sales and customer satisfaction. Motivation programs and compensation packages should reflect the overall IMC approach, key goals, and specific performance targets for specific products. The image and brand loyalty of the firm may well rest on the efforts of salespeople. Therefore, they should be compensated in a manner that reflects the importance of those key tasks.

Integrated Learning Experience

The management of a sales force is a difficult and challenging job, but one that is very important to an organization. *Sales and Marketing Executives International* is a journal designed for sales managers. Access this Web site at www.smei.org. What information and resources are available to sales managers? Another source of information is *Sales and Marketing Management* at www.salesandmarketing.com. How can this source help a sales manager?

implications for marketing professionals

Sales Manager

Recognize the differences and similarities between retail selling and business-to-business selling.

Teach the retail sales force the value of quality attention, even in single transactions settings, noting the importance of company image and other longer-term issues.

Continually review the steps of the buying decision-making process with both retail and business-to-business sales reps. Establish methods to make certain they carefully work on each step of the process.

1. Distinguish between prospecting and making the actual sale

2. Highlight the advantages of a product or service at the appropriate time

3. Follow up to make certain the customer is satisfied with the outcome

Work with the marketing manager to develop tactics that lead to longer-term relationships with business-to-business buyers.

1. Employ the correct computer equipment to increase possible EDI relationships

2. Set up purchasing systems to make reorders and rebuys efficient and easy

3. Send out missionary salespeople to continue contacts and develop other types of interpersonal bonds with individual companies

4. Qualify companies that make the best candidates for longer-term connections

Note the differences and similarities between local sales and international clients. Employ the kinds of individuals who work well with foreign cultures.

Insist, as much as you can, on being included in IMC planning processes. Share all IMC message information with your entire sales staff *regularly*.

SUMMARY

Personal selling takes place in several major and important ways. First, manufacturers as well as small companies put products into the hands of end users and customers. Second, many relationships exist between salespeople who sell from one company to another.

In retail sales, almost all buyer–seller relationships are transactional in nature. Although many (if not most) retail stores talk about building relationships with their customers, very few actually do so. Unless the customer shops at the same store on a continual basis or a high dollar value is attached to each transaction, retailers don't ordinarily take the time to develop strong buyer–seller relationships. At the same time, however, many sales managers recognize the importance of repeat business and try to structure incentives to stress customer service and long-term loyalty. In this environment, the other components of the IMC plan (advertising, consumer promotions) are critical and can build success rates in personal selling situations.

Retailers have more options than do manufacturers and business-to-business vendors in terms of developing bonds with customers. Using advertising and consumer promotions, retailers are able to lure customers into the store. Retail clerks can then interact directly with customers. Retailer buyer–seller relationships ordinarily take place on a transactional level, however, effective store employees can influence consumer attitudes toward the retail outlet. Competent, friendly, and helpful store clerks encourage customers to return. Discourteous store employees cause customers to look for other retail outlets or minimize their purchases in the future.

In business settings, it is important to identify key needs and then to sell products that fulfill those needs. Relationships that are strengthened over time move from single or occasional transactions toward more strategic alliances with business customers. The steps of the buying decision-making process should be carefully followed as the salesperson seeks to develop a bond with a client.

An effective sales force works well in international settings. The secret is to establish a selling team that understands the nature of the international customer and that can work effectively within the norms, customs, and laws of a foreign country.

In the future, electronic approaches are likely to reduce the number of actual salespeople who work for companies. At the same time, this interpersonal aspect of a business and transactional relationship never will completely disappear. As the job of selling moves away from pure "sales" into more of a problem-solving, technical skill combined with selling tactics, the salesperson's role will evolve and grow in importance as firms continue to develop communications programs to reach potential customers effectively through both impersonal (television, radio, journals) and personal channels.

REVIEW QUESTIONS

1. What is a single transaction sale? What mistake do sales reps make when finalizing this type of sale?

2. What is the difference between inbound and outbound telemarketing? What problems are associated with outbound telemarketing?

3. How are the steps of the consumer buying decision-making process related to personal selling?

4. What is cross-selling? How is it related to inbound telemarketing calls? Service calls?

5. What problems do manufacturers face when trying to influence retail sales? How can they work toward overcoming those problems?

6. Name and briefly describe the types of selling relationships that exist in business-to-business settings.

7. What can the sales rep do to build strategic partnerships between the vendor and the client firm?

8. What are the steps of the business buying decision-making process? How are they related to personal selling?

9. What methods are available for prospecting clients in business-to-business settings?

10. What is cold canvassing? Is it an effective method for developing potential customers?

11. There are three "personality" types in buying. Describe each one, and how the salesperson should react to each type.

12. Name and briefly describe the four selling approaches. Which is the most intense and interpersonal in nature? Why?

13. Why is follow-up so important to a business-to-business sales transaction? What can be done to make sure sales representatives follow up their various transactions?

14. What trends are present in personal selling? How should marketing managers respond to those trends?

15. What issues, problems, and opportunities exist in international selling?

16. What three things can the sales manager do to improve personal selling tactics and techniques?

KEY TERMS

single transactions occur when the buyer and seller interact for the purpose of only one solitary purchase.

order takers salespersons whose primary tasks are to take and fill orders.

repeat transactions occur when buyers purchase on a regular basis.

inbound telemarketing selling in response to inbound telephone calls, from a 1-800 number or some other type of customer inquiry.

outbound telemarketing selling by making outbound calls to retail customers or other businesses.

cross-selling the marketing of another item following the purchase of a good or service.

missionary salespeople members of the sales force who try to develop goodwill, stimulate demand, and provide the training and incentives needed to enhance the manufacturer in the retailer's mind.

field sales occur when a salesperson travels to the customer's place of business or home.

order getters salespeople who go out and actively seek new customers and sales.

in-house sales occur when a salesperson works from the company's office.

occasional transactions occur when the consumer or business purchases a particular product on an infrequent basis.

contractual agreements a buyer–seller agreement in which the contract guarantees the price and regular delivery of the product or service.

trust relationships purchasing relationships between buyers and sellers are based on things other than contracts, because the two parties have interacted and worked well together in the past.

electronic data interchange (EDI) relationship occurs when one company provides full electronic access to another business, for purposes of sales, inventory control, and other activities.

strategic partnership occurs when two parties share information, have a high level of trust, and move forward to the point where they share a common mission.

networking developing sales contacts and potential customers by attending meetings of professional, social, and business organizations.

cold canvassing (or cold calling) making sales calls on prospects that often are companies or individuals found using an independent source such as the yellow pages, and where no previous buyer–seller relationship exists.

intrinsic value buyers buyers who understand the product, know how to use it, and view the product as a commodity-type item.

extrinsic value buyers buyers who focus more on the product attributes and the solution a particular product can provide.

strategic value buyers buyers who seek out partnerships with suppliers.

stimulus–response sales approach using specific statements (stimuli) to solicit specific responses from customers (sometimes called a "canned" sales pitch).

need–satisfaction sales approach discovering a customer's needs and then providing solutions that satisfy those needs.

problem–solution sales approach the selling organization uses a team to analyze the buyer's operation and offer solutions through various products and services.

mission-sharing sales approach when two organizations develop a common mission and then share resources to accomplish that mission.

ENDNOTES

1. Tara Rummel, "Enduring in a Sea of Instability," *Global Cosmetic Industry,* 166, no. 1 (January 2000), pp. 16–21; Dana Butcher, "More Than a Shave and a Hair Cut," *Global Cosmetic Industry,* 166, no. 1 (January 2000) pp. 45–48.

2. C. W. L. Hart, J. L. Heskett, and E. W. Sasser, "The Profitable Art of Service Recovery," *Harvard Business Review,* 68 (July–August), pp. 148–56.

3. E. Jerome McCarthy, *Basic Marketing,* 7th. ed. (Homewood, IL: Richard D. Irwin, 1981).

4. David Howe, "The Cross-Sell Connection," *Banking Strategies,* 74, no. 6 (November–December 1998), pp. 120–24.

5. Ibid.

6. Alf Nucifora, "Traditional Sales Thinking Doesn't Work Any Longer," *Business Journal: Serving Greater Tampa Bay,* 19, no. 29 (July 16, 1999), p. 37.

7. Ibid.

8. Patricia R. Lysak, "Changing Times Demand Front-End Model," *Marketing News,* 28, no. 9 (April 25, 1994), p. 9.

9. *The Wall Street Journal* (December 28, 1999), p. C9.

10. Dana Blankenhorn, "E-mail Use Shifts from Prospects to Closures," *Advertising Age's Business Marketing,* 85, no. 1 (January–February 2000), pp. 29–30.

11. Ibid.

12. Ibid.

13. Tim Stevens, "A Bird in the Hand," *Industry Week,* 247, no. 5 (March 2, 1998), pp. 39–47.

14. Eric R. Baron, "Adding Engineer to Sales Can Improve Outcome," *Electronic Engineering Times,* no. 1088 (November 22, 1999), p. 65.

15. Tricia Campbell and Geoffrey Brewer, "Getting Top Executives to Sell," *Sales and Marketing Management,* 150, no. 10 (October 1998), p. 39.

16. Steve Del Zotto, "Personal Selling Gives Companies an Edge," *Computer Dealer News,* 14, no. 15 (April 20, 1998), p. 27.

17. Bill Bregar, "When in Rome . . . Execs Detail Global Trade," *Plastic News,* 11, no. 33 (October 4, 1999), p. 33.

18. Charlene Marmer Solomon, "Managing an Overseas Sales Force," *World Trade,* 12, no. 4 (April 1999), pp. 4–6.

19. Rodgers L. Harper, "Sorting Business Customers to Enhance Return on Equity," *American Banker,* 164, no. 159 (August 19, 1999), p. 4.

20. Solomon, "Managing an Overseas Sales Force."

Building an IMC Campaign

Finding Ways to Improve the Sales Force

Which personal selling theories, approaches, and tactics best match the product or service you are offering? Are they the same in retail markets, the distribution channel, and in business-to-business sales? What kind of sales presentation should be made? The answers to these and other questions should help you more effectively manage the sales force that will be marketing your product. It is important to remember that most of the other promotional items are delivered through some kind of "impersonal" media (a television, radio, or point-of-purchase display). This is one chance you have to deliver your IMC message personally to those who might buy the product or service. Go to the Web site at www.prenhall.com/clow or access the Advertising Plan Pro disk that accompanied this textbook and complete the personal selling exercises designed to add more power to your IMC program.

Critical Thinking Exercises

Discussion Questions

1. Personal selling in retail stores varies greatly depending on the type of retail outlet. Discuss the differences in selling approaches between a retail salesperson in a discount store (Wal-Mart) versus a retail salesperson at a high-end department store (Macy's or Saks Fifth Avenue).

2. First Manhattan Consulting Group uses the telephone to qualify current business customers for additional services. Phone calls, in conjunction with proprietary software that captures customer responses, reduces the time it takes to qualify an account from twenty to thirty hours to only five or six. The software analyzes customer responses to specific questions, which are then tied into their current customer data information to create a fact-based perspective on what would work best for each business customer. Based on the types of relationships discussed in Figure 13.2, which type of selling relationship should First Manhattan pursue, because these businesses are already customers? Explain your answer.

3. Visit a nearby local retail store. Ask the manager to describe the tactics that manufacturers use to encourage retail store salespeople and clerks to push a specific manufacturer's brand. Ask individual salespeople to specify the brands they encourage cus-

tomers to purchase. Based on your conversations, discuss the challenges manufacturers have in encouraging sales in the retail store.

4. In relationship marketing, the company concentrates more on one individual potential customer than on trying to gain a large market share within an industry. Relationship marketing focuses on selectivity, whereby firms concentrate their resources on just a few customers, rather than trying to sell to every customer in the industry. Consequently, preferential treatment is given to the valued customers who offer the highest potential for long-term relationships and long-term profits.

   Unlike the typical transactional buyer–seller relationship, which tends to be antagonistic, relationship marketing focuses on loyalty and commitment between the buyer and seller. Using this philosophy means that firms concentrate their efforts on fewer firms, but strive to be more heavily involved with those firms. The goal is to be the only vendor for a smaller number of customers rather than one of several vendors for a large number of companies. What are the advantages to this type of strategy? What are the disadvantages? What dangers are there in concentrating too much of a firm's sales with a few firms? Are there dangers in trying to serve too many customers?

5. Interview a field salesperson in your area. Ask what challenges he or she faces when selling products. What trends does the salesperson foresee in the future for personal selling? Share this information with the class.

6. For each of the following business products or services, discuss the selling approach (stimulus–response, need–satisfaction, problem–solution, mission sharing) that would be best. Explain your answer.
   a. Office supplies
   b. Computer system
   c. Accounting software
   d. Legal services
   e. Pest control services
   f. Land for a new building

7. Electronic data Interchange (EDI) is the direct transmission of information from one organization's computer to another. Benefits include increased productivity, elimination of paperwork, lower lead time and inventory reduction, facilitation of just-in-time inventory management, and the electronic transfer of funds. Identify an e commerce venture that might benefit from EDI. Identify a business to business industry that might benefit from EDI. What are the benefits to the selling firm? What are the benefits to the purchasing firm?

8. ECA International sells worldwide cost-of-living data as well as other marketing information. Customers purchase memberships with ECA International that entitle them to participate in information gathering and provide access to helpful business data. When ECA first expanded into Asia, its salespeople became very frustrated because they could not sell the service. After researching the situation, ECA found out that the Japanese were not accustomed to the idea of a membership but preferred to purchase the pieces of information on an individual basis. Why did ECA experience this problem? What should be done to resolve the problem?

9. For classes that have international students, ask these individuals to discuss retailing in their home countries. Do store clerks sell in the same way as in the United States? Discuss mores or cultural traditions in each country, and try to explain how they would affect personal selling. If any students have experience as a field salesperson or know of someone in their home country who is a field salesperson, ask them to discuss how it is different than field selling in the United States.

**APPLICATION
EXERCISE I**

Jerry Rogers was angry, frustrated, and ready to quit his job. Jerry had been specially trained to become a travel agent. All his adult life he felt as if that were the one position that would fit him best. He believed that he would get the best travel discounts and see the world as part of the job. He found a school that focused on helping people prepare for entry-level travel agency positions.

Upon completing the program, Jerry took his first job with World-Wide Travel, a small but growing enterprise in northwest Arkansas. Many told Jerry the company was in an ideal place, because there were so many retirees close by in Bella Vista, a senior citizen community.

World-Wide Travel consisted of 13 operating locations in a four-state region (Missouri, Oklahoma, Arkansas, and Kansas). Michelle Dutton owned all of the outlets. She believed agents should be hardworking, commission-oriented, customer-centered employees. She also thought setting up goals and incentives would help lead them to higher sales.

Two weeks after taking the job, Jerry was informed about a major contest in which all of the operating locations would be given quotas to meet. Those that exceeded their quotas by the greatest amount (in dollars and by percent of the quota) would receive free airline tickets to be used whenever they wanted. Also, first prize included a $3,000 sum to be divided among all of the winning outlet's agents.

Jerry was immediately in a difficult situation. He just had begun to learn the computer system, even though he was pretty well-versed in booking tickets of all kinds. He still was uncomfortable with World-Wide's paperwork. In addition, Jerry quickly discovered that the older retiree residents in his area were quite loyal to their agents. He was left with "walk-in" traffic to serve on a rotating basis with all of the experienced employees. Walk-ins were much less likely to book something on the spot, instead asking to "think about it" before actually making the purchase. Unfortunately, they would often phone in to make reservations later without specifically asking for Jerry, who had done all of the groundwork on the sale.

It wasn't long before Jerry was receiving snide comments from other agents about "pulling your weight" when it came to sales. His outlet was in fourth place in the contest, and he was nearly last in individual sales.

Michelle Dutton traveled to the northwest Arkansas location three weeks into the two-month-long contest. She sat down with Jerry and asked him how he felt about the job. He told her he loved the work, but he felt the contest was putting him in a bad situation. First, the unit had the highest (and he believed most difficult) quota to reach of all the units, making winning the contest almost impossible. Second, his "failure" to contribute was making it difficult to make friends with people in the location. He had always figured the job consisted of teamwork, not rivalries. Michelle responded that she was certain she could find somebody who would like the job and the pressure if he felt he couldn't hack it.

When the contest ended, Jerry's unit had moved into second place. He was clearly the scapegoat for not winning, although his sales had improved to the point that he was eligible for several company bonuses based on sales. He tried to point out to his office manager the unfairness of the quota system and how he had been forced into the contest before fully learning the job. The officer manager, Marty, was more sympathetic than Michelle had been, because he knew how his particular area worked and the type of clientele Jerry had to attract in order to gain their trust. Marty complained that Michelle was just a "money-hungry boss" who just made people miserable.

The Friday night after the contest ended, Marty invited Jerry to the "Friday afternoon staff meeting," a code phrase for "happy hour." Jerry received the invitation with mixed emotions, hoping it would turn out to be a morale-enhancing, team-building experience but fearing he would just end up catching flak from his colleagues.

Jerry's fears were realized. After about three drinks, the leading representative from the unit announced that Jerry was the guy that cost them their bonus. Jerry was not a confrontational type of person, so he just left.

The next day Jerry received a call at home from Marty. Marty suggested that the two of them start their own agency. They discussed how they could raise the start-up capital needed. Marty figured with his contacts in the community, the Small Business Institute nearby, and luck, they could create the kind of company where cooperation would replace the cutthroat atmosphere at World-Wide.

Michelle soon became aware of their plan. She called a meeting with them both (who had not yet quit at World-Wide), fired them, and showed them their employment contracts where they had signed a "noncompetition agreement" as a condition of employment. She threatened them with a lawsuit if they started a firm in town.

For the first time in his life, Jerry became confrontational. He told Michelle to "shove it" and marched out. Marty and Jerry soon opened their business in southwest Missouri, just a few miles across the border. They quickly stole many of Michelle's customers. It wasn't long before Jerry was completely content, figuring he'd finally gotten the job he wanted in the first place.

1. What kind of selling takes place at the travel agency?
2. How did Michelle's goal-setting program go wrong? Or, do you believe Michelle's program was fine and Jerry and Marty simply did not "fit" with the World-Wide company?
3. What kinds of contests could Michelle create that would encourage competition but less conflict?

Selling a "U" to You

APPLICATION EXERCISE II

The greatest majority of colleges and universities in the United States are nonprofit or governmentally supported organizations. Why, then, do they spend so much time, energy, and money promoting themselves? The obvious answers are (1) competition, (2) funding problems, and (3) new technology. Competition takes the form of the pressure to build and retain a quality student body. Money must come from a variety of sources, not the least of which is happy alumni. Technology has generated an entire new set of options for students, where Internet courses take the place (in theory) of on-campus experiences.

Many university leaders have discovered that simply advertising the school is not enough. Instead, some colleges have been able to effectively promote themselves utilizing the same IMC principles that profit-seeking organizations use. Therefore, a college needs an effective marketing plan. The plan should define the objectives (student body size, key activities, etc.); outline the budget for advertisements and other promotions; and spell out strategies, tactics, and forms of evaluation. Many successful institutions have learned that using a consistent message and clear theme throughout all aspects of the college (catalogs, brochures, advertisements, public relations efforts, and other promotional activities) gives them a major advantage in the marketplace of students, faculty recruiting, and fund-raising.

Any IMC plan should begin with the foundation of promotional and target market analysis, image development, and understanding of buyer behaviors. Target markets consist of the type of student who will be enticed to attend the school. Other target markets are benefactors and businesses that may give money to the institution. Many university presidents find that their primary job is fund-raising, and effective promotions and personal selling tactics can help in this process. University image is a key factor. Colleges must be able to differentiate themselves from their competitors, which can be difficult, because many people

A Pittsburg State University Print ad.
Courtesy of Pittsburgh State University.

remain uninformed about what takes place on campus. Then, "buyers" are identified. These include parents of high school students as well as the students themselves. As might be expected, factors kids use in choosing colleges (access to taverns, fun social life, good-looking student bodies, and, on a good day, choices of majors and postgraduation placement rates) differ from those parents consider (reputation of the school, cost, closeness to home).

In the area of advertising and promotion, IMC programs often make contact with young people as early as the freshman year of high school. Postcards, calendars, and other entice-ments are sent to younger brothers and sisters of students attending the school, as well as brochures mailed to any referral the college receives. Then the process of personal selling begins.

On-campus events are designed to bring potential students to the campus, so the recruiting department endorses any kind of intellectual contest (history day, math quiz) or talent competition (bands, choirs, debates, speeches) that helps make high school students feel familiar with the institution. Transfer students are another source of prospects. Many recruiters make sure posters and other materials are placed in junior colleges and even in rival schools.

To further the school's outreach, entertainers are brought to the campus to provide shows for students attending the university as well as members of the local community. Schools with successful athletic programs have discovered that on-site pregame parties, especially before football and basketball games, can enhance the image of accessibility of the school to businesspeople, members of the community, students, and potential new students.

College leaders employ flyers, newspaper advertisements, brochures, television and radio spots, and Internet Web sites as forms of advertising. The secret is to make sure that the message highlights the school's best attributes. Ads need to help the institution speak with the same clear voice that profit-seeking advertisers design. In the advertisement for Pittsburg State University (where both of the authors of this text were once employed), the motto "Where People Succeed" along with the campus mascot (a gorilla) is supposed to present a memorable image. The overall theme is that the school provides an environment in which both students and faculty can achieve their educational and life goals.

The IMC program also should consist of business-to-business efforts and international programs. In the case of a university, partnerships with business can lead to targeted research, grants and other funds, and opportunities for students such as internship programs and on-campus job interviews. The university's marketing team should pay attention to local businesses, so that they feel included in the university community, to whatever extent possible. International efforts may focus on recruiting international students and faculty members, and also providing international experiences such as travel and faculty member exchanges whenever possible, which highlights the global image of the institution and builds new friendships for the school.

In the fast-paced, highly competitive world of education, many schools are quickly learning that they must compete, in a real sense, with other institutions. Some have discovered this fact of life only recently. Personal selling is one key element in the overall IMC program for individual schools. Where does your college or university stand?

1. How were you recruited for by your current institution?

2. Does your college have a unified theme used in its marketing program? What is it? Did the personal selling rep (college recruiter) highlight this theme when talking to you and your parents?

3. Design an IMC program with an emphasis on personal selling for your university.

> **Public Relations and Sponsorship Programs**

► CHAPTER OBJECTIVES

Clarify the role played by the public relations department and how that role mixes with the functions performed by the marketing department.

Understand the natures of various organizational stakeholders and why public relations programs are critical to keeping these stakeholders happy with the company's operations.

Integrate the four types of communications managed by the public relations department.

Utilize the tools available to the public relations department.

Work with sponsorship programs and event marketing to build the firm's image and consumer recognition of the brand.

HOW DO THEY DO IT?
The WWF Crashes to the Top

In an all-too-cynical world, it may at first seem odd that a contrived, theatrical performance such as that provided by the World Wrestling Federation is able to flourish at such a high level. Yet, no one can deny the dramatic rise in popularity of the WWF. One recent direct competition resulted in the WWF capturing a 4.2 share on cable, when starting at 11:00 P.M., as compared to a 1.0 share for tennis that was aired during prime time on the same station.

How can this be? Cries of "fake," "phony," "contrived," and "violent" have been aimed at pro 'rassling for years.

chapter fourteen

The sport had to overcome concerns about steroid use in the Hulk Hogan era, criticism from family groups opposed to violence on television, and even the death of a major star in a fall during a stunt at a pay-per-view event. In spite of these difficulties, major WWF personalities are now as well known as many television stars.

The WWF's primary audience is from 6- to 17-year-old boys, especially those ages 11 to 15. Other strong groups are 18- to 24-year-old women and 18- to 44-year-old men. High-tech shows and increased theatrics attracted an even wider audience as the new century began. The WWF extends its reach through numerous tactics, each designed to "spin" positive publicity at the general public.

For example, the WWF sponsored a commercial at the end of the 2000 Super Bowl, in which the spokesman notes that wrestling is "a wholesome form of entertainment," while execs smash each other with chairs and trash conference rooms. In the next scene, a couple necks while a buxom woman purrs, "We never use sex to enhance our image." Finally, a man flies out of a window to the tag line, "WWF attitude. Get it?" For people who "get it," says Jim Byrne, the senior vice president for marketing, being aware of the irony of the sport is one key.

WWF celebrities have ventured into the publishing world, with a book by "The Rock" making the best-seller list. Personal appearances, autographs, and other events designed to keep fans up close and personal with wrestling celebrities have been used to broaden the appeal.

Two magazines also promote various extravaganzas, *WWF Raw* and *WWF for Kids.* Clothes carrying WWF trademarks are sold by JCPenney and Wal-Mart. The Undertaker, Shawn Michaels, and Steve Austin are three hot property names, somewhat replacing Hulk Hogan and Governor Jesse "The Body" Ventura.

The single biggest obstacle to overcome may be "overmarketing." Too many shows and too many pay-per-view events may dilute the market. The WWC, owned by Turner Sports, offers an alternative set of characters and television programs. Those in charge seek to maintain a balance between interest and overexposure.

The WWF "soap opera" is a nonstop series of episodes and events. Key characters move through a series of ups and downs, and enthusiastic fans follow via television, Internet, magazine, and personal appearance venues. The popularity of the WWF extends to other products, including those sold by Daily Juice Products of Verona, Pennsylvania, which offers Piledriver Punch, Backbreaker Blue, and Drop Kick Orange, each with a photo and action shot of a wrestler on the package. Tie-ins with individual wrestling events builds recognition for both the WWF and for firms that serve as sponsors for special "cards" featuring more famous wrestling personalities.

Building a manageable public image while keeping a crowd interested in sex, violence, and carnage is a major juggling act. As long as the WWF succeeds, a number of muscle-bound men and women, and their marketing partners, will keep making money-laden trips to the bank.[1]

overview

The traditional marketing mix consists of advertising, consumer sales promotions, personal selling, and public relations efforts. At this point in the textbook, the first three elements in the mix have been presented. This chapter is devoted to the fourth, public relations.

At the same time, to examine all elements of an integrated marketing communications program fully requires more than just the study of the promotions mix. As shown in Figure 14.1, the IMC plan begins with an examination of promotions opportunities, brand and image management, and consumer–business buyer behaviors. From there, the other ingredients can be finalized to build a more integrated system.

In the final section, more than public relations programs are described. In addition, some of the new components of a marketing plan are outlined to give you the most complete picture of IMC possible. Toward that end, database and direct-marketing programs, Internet marketing, and the evaluation of the IMC program are discussed. When these tasks are complete, the marketing team, account executives, and all others involved have done all that is possible to build and deliver an effective communications program that reinforces the theme that guides the company's marketing efforts and establishes the strongest rapport with all types of customers.

public relations programs and sponsorships

In Hollywood, a well-worn phrase is "There's no such thing as bad publicity." Although this may be true for a bad-boy actor trying to get his name before the public, in the world of marketing and communications, bad publicity is *worse* than no publicity. Many business organizations spend countless hours fending off negative news while trying to develop positive and noticeable messages and themes.

Public relations efforts and sponsorships should be part of the overall integrating marketing communications approach. The same unified message should appear

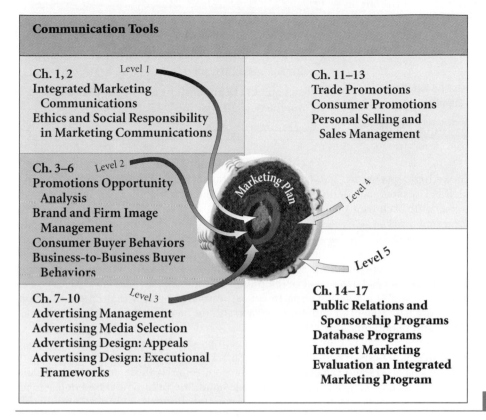

Communication Tools

Ch. 1, 2   Level 1
Integrated Marketing
  Communications
Ethics and Social Responsibility
  in Marketing Communications

Ch. 3–6   Level 2
Promotions Opportunity
  Analysis
Brand and Firm Image
  Management
Consumer Buyer Behaviors
Business-to-Business Buyer
  Behaviors

Ch. 7–10   Level 3
Advertising Management
Advertising Media Selection
Advertising Design: Appeals
Advertising Design: Executional
  Frameworks

Marketing Plan

Level 4

Level 5

Ch. 11–13
Trade Promotions
Consumer Promotions
Personal Selling and
  Sales Management

Ch. 14–17
Public Relations and
  Sponsorship Programs
Database Programs
Internet Marketing
Evaluation an Integrated
  Marketing Program

**An Integrated
Marketing
Communication Plan**

FIGURE 14.1

in every marketing endeavor, from the appearance of the company's letterhead and stationery, to advertisements, promotional items, and any sponsorship program. The goal of an IMC plan is to make sure that each component of a firm's communications plan speaks with one voice. Extending this goal to the public relations function can be difficult, but remains an important challenge for the marketing team.

This chapter is devoted to understanding the roles public relations efforts and sponsorship programs play in the IMC process. First, the nature of a public relations department or function is described, showing how public relations fits in with marketing efforts and various company activities. Second, organizational stakeholders are described, because they constitute the major publics that interact with the public relations department. Methods used to reach stakeholders are also noted. Third, sponsorship programs and event marketing tactics are outlined to show how the company can make quality contacts with existing customers, new prospects, vendors, and other key publics. The goal of these activities must be to reach the general public with the same clear voice that has been developed in all of the marketing approaches, such as advertising and personal selling. When this goal is reached, the firm's image is enhanced and its brands are better known and perceived more favorably in the marketplace.

the public relations department and its functions

The **public relations (PR) department** is a unit in the firm that manages items such as publicity and other communications with all of the groups that make contact with the company. Some of the functions performed by the public relations department are similar to those provided by the marketing department. Others are largely different. One difficulty of moving public relations under the IMC umbrella begins with a major problem: Often the public relations department is separate from the

**Public Relations
Functions**

FIGURE 14.2

▶ **Monitor internal and external publics**

▶ **Provide positive information to each public that reinforces the IMC plan**

▶ **React quickly to any shift by any of the publics from the desired position**

marketing department. The two may cooperate with and consult each other, yet each has a separate role to perform. Bringing the two together can result in "turf wars," with each trying to protect its own area.

Some marketing experts argue that public relations should be part of the marketing department, just as advertising, trade promotions, and sales promotions are under the jurisdiction of the marketing manager. Others suggest that public relations is a different function and cannot operate effectively within a marketing department. Instead, a member of the public relations department should serve as a consultant to the marketing department. Still others contend that a new division, called the department of communications, should be created to oversee both marketing and public relations activities.

In any case, many public relations functions should not be considered typical marketing functions. This is because the marketing department tends to concentrate on customers and the channel members en route to those customers, such as wholesalers and retail outlets. On the other hand, the public relations department focuses on a variety of internal and external stakeholders including employees, stockholders, public interest groups, the government, and society as a whole.

The three key public relations functions are displayed in Figure 14.2. Each represents the tasks given to public relations personnel, whether they are internal employees or members of a public relations company hired to perform those functions.

As a result, one major decision firms must make concerning public relations is who will handle these activities. Most firms have an internal public relations officer or department. Others hire public relations firms to handle either special projects or all of their public relations functions. Still, even when a public relations agency is retained, a firm normally places someone in charge of internal public relations, because most public relations firms deal only with external publics.

The decision criteria used in selecting advertising agencies (as discussed in Chapter 7) can be applied to selecting a public relations firm. It is important to develop a relationship with the public relations agency and to carefully spell out what the firm expects from the agency. In some cases, the goal of a public relations firm is simply to get hits. A **hit** is the mention of a company's name in a news story. Hits can be positive, negative, or even neutral in terms of their impact on a firm. The concept behind getting hits in the news is that the more a consumer sees the name of a company in a news-related context, the higher the brand awareness will become. This may be true, but it is important to consider the type of image that is being developed. It may be a wiser strategy to seek fewer hits and to make sure that those hits project the company in a positive light that also reinforces the firm's IMC theme.

Consequently, when a public relations firm is used, the agency's personnel must be familiar with their client's IMC plan. Then, the public relations firm is able to work on ideas that reinforce the plan. Special events, activities, and news releases can be developed to strengthen the "one voice" concept needed to build a successful IMC program. The following sections describe the targets of various company communications and define the natures of the messages sent out.

types of stakeholders

All of the recipients of company communications are important. Any constituent who makes contact with a company should receive the same unified message. In this section, the stakeholders who are targets of publics relations efforts are described. A **stakeholder** is a person or group that has a vested interest in the organization's well-being.[2] A vested interest can be a variety of items, including:

- Profits paid as common stock dividends
- Loan repayments that a lending institution seeks to receive
- Sales to the company or purchases made from the company
- Community well-being
- A special-interest topic

In other words, any number of items can give a person or another company a stake in the firm's well-being.

To understand the nature of public relations programs, it is helpful to begin by identifying the publics that make contact with various companies. Figure 14.3 identifies the primary internal and external stakeholders that the public relations department should monitor.

In addition to sending communications to each of the stakeholders, the public relations department must closely monitor the actions and opinions of each group. When changes in attitudes, new views, or serious concerns develop, the public relations department should be ready to address the problem. Most importantly, it is the responsibility of the public relations department to be certain that all forms of communications to each of these publics remain consistent with the firm's IMC plan and the image the firm seeks to project.

Stakeholders may be divided into two sets of groups: (1) internal publics and (2) external publics. Both sets of constituents seek out information from the organization regarding various issues, from pay, to ethical concerns, to details about company profitability.

Internal stakeholders

The primary internal stakeholders are the employees of the organization, unions, and corporate shareholders. A brief presentation regarding each follows.

Employees should receive a constant stream of information from the company. Many employees are quite distant from the marketing department, yet they should still be aware of what the company is trying to achieve with its IMC program, even if this means only basic knowledge. Those closest to the marketing department are going to be more acutely aware of the nature of the IMC plan, including how the company's message theme is being sent to all other constituents. Thus, an idea as simple as "Free Internet. All the Time" should be well known by every member of the NetZero organization, along with all advertisers and companies that deal with the firm. Employees who know the main message and image being portrayed by the

▶ **Employees**	▶ **Media**
▶ **Unions**	▶ **Local community**
▶ **Shareholders**	▶ **Financial community**
▶ **Channel members**	▶ **Government**
▶ **Customers**	▶ **Special-interest groups**

Stakeholders

FIGURE 14.3

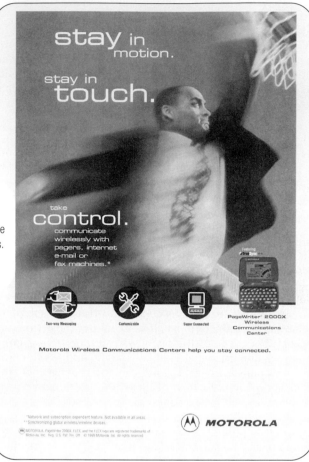

Motorola's theme is that the company's "Wireless communications centers help you stay connected." The theme should be used by employees in all communications.
Courtesy of Motorola, Inc./Personal Communications Sector.© 1999.

company (e.g., "Don't Worry, Drive Happy") have a better sense of how they fit into the company as well as how to perform their individual roles.

The Motorola advertisement above states that the company's "Wireless communications centers help you stay connected." Employees who are aware of Motorola's theme can communicate the same message when dealing with customers, vendors, and other publics.

To work effectively in communicating with employees, the public relations department must keep in close contact with the human resource (HR) department. Publications and communications aimed at employees must be consistent with the image and message that the firm is espousing to customers and other groups. For example, any firm that uses advertising to suggest that employees are always ready to assist customers should make sure those employees are aware of the message. Employee behaviors should then be consistent with the advertising theme that is being conveyed to customers. The HR department should try to hire the kind of worker who is attracted to such an approach, and structure performance appraisals and rewards to favor those who "buy into" the company's overall IMC approach. The emphasis on providing information about company activities must logically extend to every public relations event and sponsorship program.

The company's intended message and theme should also be conveyed to *Unions*. Even though the union may represent employees from a number of organizations, the same unified sense of direction applies. A public relations program aimed at, for example, the hard-core unemployed, should be communicated carefully to the union, which may be interested in cosponsoring any such effort.

Creating a partnership with the union for public relations ventures is likely to build a stronger bond with that organization, which may bode well in future negotiations.

Shareholders also have strong vested interests in company success. Therefore, all communications that go out to them (profit statements, publicity, proxy vote notices) should reflect the company's main strategy and the central idea that guides the organization. Again, a public relations campaign should cause stockholders to "feel better" about the company, which will be helpful in the future.

External stakeholders

Most of the time, the public relations department is able to access internal stakeholders fairly easily. Management can call meetings, send memos and letters, and use numerous other available venues to make contact with these constituents. On the other hand, communications with external publics are more difficult to oversee. In this section, a brief review of the importance of the external stakeholders that company leaders encounter is presented.

Channel members, including wholesalers and retailers, have a direct effect on the success of a firm. Beyond influencing these members with trade promotions and advertising, the company makes contact with them in many other ways. Salespeople can inform the channel member about public relations and sponsorship programs while pitching products and services. The goal is to make sure all marketing efforts present a unified message to these critical links with customers.

Customers may be strongly influenced by promotional campaigns. In some instances, the influence is quite positive. At other times, publicity may seem more like a ruse than a genuine attempt to do something altruistic. Consider, for example, the information provided in the Communication Action Box on the next page regarding the Philip Morris company. Some customers may believe the firm is truly concerned about the community, yet others might be much more cynical.

Overseeing external communications is a daunting task, because the company has little or no influence on how these publics perceive organizational activities. Publicity may or may not be reported by the *media*. The company has little power over how the media report any public relations effort it makes. It is wise to remember that most reporters are looking more for a "story" than to be a shill for a company's publicity machine. Therefore, great care must be given to the release of information to newspapers, magazines, and television and radio stations.

The *local community* may be directly and indirectly influenced by public relations efforts. For example, when McDonald's sends employees out with trash bags to clean up the neighborhoods surrounding a local unit, the city may notice. Customers may or may not buy more Big Macs, but those who live nearby are going to feel much more favorably about having the company in the neighborhood. A grocery store that allows recycling bins to be placed in the parking lot may receive additional business from those who stop by to discard old phone books and make a quick purchase at the same time.

Another key stakeholder is the *financial community,* which lends money to the company. This group is most interested in the firm's financial well-being, but also is interested in any goodwill the company can generate.

Finally, both the *government* and various *special-interest groups* will carefully monitor and watch company activities, especially in the negative areas of pollution, discrimination, harassment, and unfair treatment of employees. A concerted public relations effort may be developed to fend off investigations of anything negative, while at the same time building on the positive elements of the organization's activities. For example, the NCAA spends a portion of its promotions budget attempting to highlight the more positive aspects of athletic programs. Football player Payton Manning was recently featured in an ad, noting the benefits of completing a college program. The publicity machine for the NCAA sends out press releases each time an athlete does something positive for the community, because it bodes well when a counterbalancing bad story or event occurs.

communication**action**

Philip Morris began as a tobacco company. Many of its products remain in that industry. In addition, the company has acquired the Miller Brewing Company and 7-Up over the years. Since many of Philip Morris's products are essentially "vices," the company has a strong vested interest in creating as many positive contact points as possible.

One program devised to generate goodwill is the "We Card" coalition. In conjunction with the Coalition for Responsible Tobacco Retailing, Philip Morris sends out placards to retailers suggesting that they ID any customer who looks to be 27 years old or less. All 50 states have a minimum purchase age of 18, except Alabama, Alaska, and Utah, which require customers to be 19. Philip Morris has heavily advertised its involvement with the We Card effort. This may be, in part, due to complaints that the tobacco industry targets young people to attract new business.

The We Card program also allows Philip Morris to build more positive ties with retail outlets along with local police officers. Combating underage purchases is easier with the We Card kits. In addition, the company provides training to retailers regarding crime prevention.

Another major thrust developed by the public relations team is the food program for the elderly. This venture combines Philip Morris with the National Meals on Wheels Foundation. Again, substantial positive publicity results from this type of effort.

In the area of disaster relief, Philip Morris employees volunteered their time on several occasions to help provide food and water to those who had been flooded or struck by hurricanes or ice storms. Miller Brewing used its facilities to provide fresh water to those whose systems had been contaminated during storms. Advertisements showing Miller beer trucks rushing to deliver fresh water emphasized the company's involvement in helping people during times of personal crisis.

Beyond these efforts, the Marlboro team is linked with programs to reduce domestic violence, as well as disaster relief, hunger, and youth access to tobacco. These may seem like conflicting messages, yet the company, which also relies on humor in its ads, may be able to convince consumers that the company is not out just to push products on unsuspecting members of the public. Doing so may be one of the keys to success in the future, as tobacco suit settlement agreements drive up cigarette prices and continuous negative press bombards the organization.

Sources: "Philip Morris to Provide More Than 1 Million Meals to the Elderly in All 50 States," *Fund Raising Management,* 30, no. 6 (August 1999) p. 1, Philip Morris press releases, December 19, 1995, March 23, 2000; Philip Morris Web site; and Mike Bierne and Aaron Baar, "Burnett Supports New Marlboro Entry," *Adweek,* 40, no. 2 (October 18, 1999), p. 1.

In the attempt to influence each of these external publics, the public relations department performs three tasks. First, the department monitors each group in order to discover how it views the firm. Second, the PR department provides positive information about the firm that reinforces the company's IMC message and one-voice theme. Third, whenever the views of a public stray into the negative realm, the public relations department must immediately embark on moving them back to the more positive aspects of the company's activities. A departure from the desired image is most volatile during a crisis. Figure 14.4 provides some suggestions for handling a crisis. Remember that the concept of crisis management was discussed in detail in Chapter 4.

In general, a totally integrated communications program accounts for all types of messages that an organization delivers to both internal and external stakeholders. Every contact point provides the opportunity for a message to be sent. The mar-

> ▶ Develop a plan and checklist for dealing with a crisis
> ▶ Deploy members of public relations staff as quickly as possible
> ▶ Return calls to media immediately
> ▶ Quickly gather the information needed to communicate to media
> ▶ Designate one person to be the spokesperson
> ▶ Communicate with all employees immediately
> ▶ Provide updates on regular basis
> ▶ Be available 24 hours a day to media
> ▶ Confess when the organization has made an error
> ▶ Convey steps the organization is taking to correct the crisis
> ▶ Empathize with any victims of crisis
> ▶ Keep all publics informed of progress

**Responding
to a Crisis**

FIGURE 14.4

keting department tends to create contact points with customers and potential customers. To complement this effort, the public relations department deals with the myriad of contact points that are not created or planned, yet are just as critical as those that are planned. An unplanned contact point such as a news article or an individual talking to an employee of the firm at a social gathering allows the firm to build a positive image or reduce any negative messages that are being passed along. Naturally, it is more difficult to deal with unplanned contact points, because they cannot always be anticipated. The key is constantly to monitor what is going on around the firm in order to keep constituents as happy and satisfied as possible.

Integrated Learning Experience

Public relations are normally handled within an organization. Still, a number of organizations and publications exist to assist public relations personnel. Although individual companies may hire public relations firms to handle specific issues, almost all companies maintain public relations departments. The Public Relations Society of America (PRSA) at www.prsa.org is one of the major associations that creates PR for individuals. The PSRA produces two publications: *Public Relations Tactics* and *The Strategist.* In Canada, the primary PR association is the Canadian Public Relations Society (www.cprs.ca). For those involved in international corporations, an excellent publication is the *PR Week Magazine* found at www.prweek.net. For organizations wanting to hire a PR firm, the Council of Pubic Relations Firms is an excellent source.

stop!

types of messages

Four types of communications or messages are part of integrating communications to stakeholders.[3] Each of the following plays a role in helping to unify the firm's IMC program into one clear voice:

1. Planned messages
2. Inferred messages
3. Maintenance messages
4. Unplanned messages

The first type of communication sent out includes all of the **planned messages** produced by the marketing department. These are presented through advertising

Store displays and signs are examples of inferred messages. Courtesy of The Image Works. Photograph by M. Siluk.

agencies, trade promotion programs, public relations press releases, and signs. They may also be found on product packages, company stationery, and messages such as shareholder statements.

The second type of communication, **inferred messages**, comes from the *messages stakeholders infer* from the company regarding its brands. An example of this form of communication would be the shareholder's experience of a news report on a local television station. Also, an employee's perception of the salary and benefit package offered by the firm is an inferred message (e.g., "You are valuable to us, so we're paying you top dollar!"). A customer's perception of a retail store in which the firm's products are offered also sends an inferred message. In other words, a product sold at a discount store is going to be perceived differently than one sold at Macy's Department Store. Also, a pair of shoes sold for $200.00 produces a different impression of the company than a pair sold for $19.99.

Maintenance messages are the third type of communication. These messages are delivered primarily by the firm's employees. They include how the company's employees initiate and respond to customer contacts. They also consist of such things as the attitudes portrayed by service personnel, secretaries, and any other employee a customer encounters. Maintenance messages are found in instruction manuals and printed materials that accompany a product inside the package or on the label.

The final type of communication is any **unplanned message.** News reports, announcements by civic or consumer advocacy groups, product recalls, and interactions with the credit department often are unplanned. As noted earlier, managing these unplanned encounters constitutes a major component of successful communications programs.

Integrating all four types of communications within a single firm is a major challenge for the marketing team and public relations department. The public relations department must play a prominent role in designing the total communications package sent out by the organization. These efforts must be intricately intertwined with messages conveyed by not only the marketing department but also the human resource department and all other departments that in any way communicate with stakeholders.

public relations events

There are two main ways in which a firm seeks to change the views of consumers and other stakeholders directly. The first is through various altruistic activities, and the second is known as cause-related marketing. Both are *planned events* designed to draw positive attention to the organization.

Altruistic activities

Altruistic activities are things provided to employees and other internal stakeholders. Examples include sending flowers to employee families who have lost loved ones or have family members in the hospital. Enlightened companies work to build loyalty and commitment from employees, through programs such as drug or alcohol counseling, child care for workers' children, purchase discounts, and numerous other benefits and programs. Beyond simply providing these services, it is helpful for the public relations department to communicate carefully that the department is available to both internal constituents and external publics, when appropriate.

Cause-related marketing

A second form of a planned public relations event is **cause-related marketing.** When a firm ties a marketing program into some type of charity work or program, goodwill can be generated. American businesses spend over $600 million each year to buy the rights to use a not-for-profit organization's name or logo in company advertising and marketing programs. This type of partnership agreement between a not-for-profit and a for-profit business is based on the belief that consumers will purchase from companies willing to help a good cause.

As has been noted many times in this text, brand parity has become the norm for many goods and services. In other words, customers perceive that there are few notable differences between products and the companies that sell them. Many marketers use cause-related marketing to help develop stronger brand ties and to move consumers as well as businesses toward brand loyalty. A recent survey revealed that 66 percent of those who responded said they would be willing to switch brands and 62 percent said they would be willing to switch retailers to a firm associated with a good cause.[4] One difficulty businesses can encounter is that what is a "good" cause to one customer may be disliked by another. For example, Dayton Hudson found a large number of picketers outside company stores objecting to contributions made to Planned Parenthood, even as others praised Dayton Hudson's involvement.[5]

Another survey, conducted by 17 state attorneys general, concluded that consumers place high levels of trust in not-for-profit organizations and prefer products marketed in association with not-for-profit causes. Approximately 75 percent of Americans stated that cause-related programs by businesses were acceptable or highly acceptable. Those responding also believed that brands associated with a not-for-profit organization were superior to brands not tied to a special cause.

Most consumers like the idea of businesses supporting worthy causes. Consumers who react to cause-related marketing can be divided into four groups:

1. Skeptics
2. Balancers
3. Attribution-oriented
4. Socially-concerned

Skeptics tend to believe the motive behind a business's involvement in cause-related marketing is only to generate profits. These negative feelings increase if the firm uses the not-for-profit organization in any type of advertising or promotion of the business. Skeptics think businesses should support causes without resorting to any publicity or advertisements that promote what they are doing.

Balancers try to balance a desire to help a cause while still trying to make product purchases using the traditional purchase criteria. Balancers are pleased when firms support causes, but do not allow this support to overwhelm a logical purchase decision. These consumers are not willing to switch firms only because a business supports a given cause.

The third group, *attribution-oriented* consumers, considers the motives of the business that is involved with a particular cause. This group tries to find out what causes a business supports and why each firm supports individual causes. When an attribution-oriented consumer concludes the firm's support of a particular cause is only to increase sales or enhance a firm's image, then the consumer reacts negatively. On the other hand, a belief that the company is acting out of genuine concern leads this consumer to be fully supportive of the business and willing to purchase its products. The criteria used in making this decision relate to how the firm advertises or promotes its alliance with the not-for-profit organization.

The final group, *socially-concerned* consumers, supports nearly any cause-related marketing efforts. These individuals understand the firm must benefit from the partnership with a not for profit or the support cannot be maintained. A socially concerned consumer concludes that the end justifies the means. As long as good causes receive benefits, the rest is not a crucial concern.[6]

In the past, some companies donated to causes with little thought to the impact or benefit of such gifts. These philanthropic efforts were expected of big business. Currently, most companies want to know what the benefit will be. Although company leaders may be concerned about the environment, supporting environmental

▶ Improve public schools	52%
▶ Dropout prevention	34%
▶ Scholarships	28%
▶ Cleanup of environment	27%
▶ Community health education	25%

Causes Consumers Prefer

FIGURE 14.5

Source: Bevolyn Williams-Harold and Eric L. Smith, "Spending With Heart," *Black Enterprise*, (July 1998), Vol. 28, No.12, p. 26.

causes must, in some way, result in tangible benefits for the company. Otherwise the company will not be able to give support. "Benefits" include:

- Additional customers
- Increased profits
- Consumer goodwill for the future
- Better relations with governmental agencies
- Reduced chances of facing lawsuits

These and other potential benefits lead companies to get involved. Relationships that do not yield positive benefits to the business sponsor do not last long.

A prime example of this kind of mutual-benefit scenario occurred when Kimberly-Clark, which was celebrating its 120th anniversary, helped build playgrounds in 25 cities in which its manufacturing plants were located. The company asked schoolchildren in each area to help design the playgrounds. Employees became part of the actual building process. This effort helped both children and company employees, who felt good about their contributions and the contributions made by the company. Kimberly-Clark experienced heightened goodwill in each of the 25 communities. Many times, causes that have an impact in local neighborhoods are better received than are national or global causes.[7] Figure 14.5 highlights the top five areas consumers want businesses to consider as they seek out causes to support.

In choosing a cause, a company must focus on issues that relate to its specific business. Supporting such efforts is received more positively by consumers. When the company supports an unrelated cause, consumers may feel the business simply is trying to benefit from the not for profit's reputation. This may lead some consumers to stop buying the company's products. Consumers are becoming skeptical about the motives behind the increased emphasis being given to various charities. Even though most people understand that a business must benefit from the relationship, they still tend to develop negative views when they believe that the business is exploiting a relationship with a not for profit.

When a good fit exists, much more positive reactions emerge. For example, a good fit exists between Calphalon, a maker of gourmet cookware, and Share Our Strength (SOS), an antihunger organization. Calphalon raises millions of dollars to help feed hungry people throughout the United States. Twice a year, Calphalon selects one size of pan to feature the SOS logo. The sale of each pan carrying the SOS logo results in a $5 donation by Calphalon to SOS. Sales of pans displaying the SOS logo have averaged 10 times more than sales of pans without the SOS logo. Thus, SOS is a good fit for Calphalon, because Calphalon benefits through additional sales and an enhanced public image.[8]

Cause-related marketing is also important for not-for-profit organizations. Competition has increased in both the business world and the not-for-profit world. An increasing number of not-for-profit organizations currently competes for contributions and gifts. Strategic relationships with businesses can boost contributions for a not-for-profit organization considerably. For example, the American Cancer

Society sold its logo to the Florida Department of Citrus for $1 million per year. The American Cancer Society also endorses the Nicoderm nicotine patch produced by SmithKline Beecham for $1 million per year.

The American Lung Association received $1.25 million per year in a deal with Nicotrol, a patch produced by McNeil Consumer Products that competes with Nicoderm. The American Heart Association receives $2,500 per product the organization certifies as healthy. Each year the Association receives $650 for recertification of the product.[9] These relationships with businesses result not only in direct increases in revenues but also in greater publicity for the not-for-profit organization.

In summary, the goals of both altruistic activities and cause-related marketing are to enhance the standing of the company in the community, to build goodwill with both internal and external stakeholders, and to develop stronger brand equity for company products and services. Beyond simply developing these programs, the company must carefully construct messages that blend the IMC theme together with the positive publicity that the firm desires to create. Thus, when Kimberly-Clark, which sells many items relating to children, builds playgrounds, the overall IMC theme can be integrated with the firm's gestures of goodwill. The next section describes methods to promote these positive activities.

public relations tools

The public relations department has several tools available to make people aware of various public relations programs. Figure 14.6 lists these tools. Each represents the opportunity to make a planned contact with various constituencies, thereby enhancing the image of the firm while providing other information. A review of each of these tools follows.

Most public relations departments produce some type of *corporate newsletter* for the organization's employees, which is an excellent means of communicating important internal information, such as results of sales contests and other company activities. Newsletters also transmit "soft" information, including articles about company picnics, notes about employees who have had babies, and so forth. The concepts developed in the IMC program can be reinforced in a newsletter, both directly and indirectly. Articles about the firm's IMC program and its marketing goals are direct approaches. Other, more indirect stories that note the spirit and concepts of the IMC can also appear. For example, if part of the IMC effort is emphasis on customer service, then articles about customer service in the newsletter support this aspect of the IMC plan. Further, if each newsletter featured an employee who had demonstrated superior customer service, employees would realize that management does recognize good customer service.

Newsletter articles can emphasize the communications program directly and indirectly at the same time. For instance, a plaque or reward given to an employee

> ▶ **Corporate newsletters**
> ▶ **Internal communications**
> ▶ **Media news releases**
> ▶ **Stockholder correspondence**
> ▶ **Annual reports**
> ▶ **Special events**
> ▶ **Collaboration with internal publics**

Public Relations Tools

FIGURE 14.6

may be featured in a newsletter article. In that story, employees learn that management emphasizes quality customer service and that rewards are available for employees who excel in that area. The article may also have an impact on various managers. Department heads and other managers recognized for superior service serve as examples both to other managers and to subordinates. The newsletter can be an extremely valuable tool for mentioning the firm's IMC concept and making the case to support the effort.

In addition to official newsletters, public relations may employ other types of *internal communications,* including bulletin boards, e-mail list server groups, letters, and memos. These venues routinely reach internal publics and are utilized to make sure employees remain informed about events and happenings both within and outside of the organization. When company leaders are about to make a public announcement, it is best for the employees to hear the message first. A company that is the target of bad press or criticism by a consumer special-interest group should alert and inform employees so that they respond in an appropriate fashion, even if it means simply discussing the problem with friends and neighbors while not at work.

A *bulletin board* is another method used to communicate internally. Although the public relations department should not be responsible for everything that appears on a bulletin board, the department's staff must work to make sure all messages sent out match with what the firm wishes to communicate. This is especially true for items targeted to various employee groups. For example, if the company wants to communicate to all its target markets that quality is number one, then bulletin board messages sent out by the PR department should convey and support this theme. A memo encouraging employees to increase output or cut costs might send the wrong message.

Other public relations tools are more oriented to external stakeholders, even though internal groups may also read them. For instance, media **news releases** are messages issued by the company regarding a wide variety of topics, including the release of a new product, a change in corporate leadership, or any other newsworthy item that generates a positive public image. Even though public relations people are anxious to send out news releases, they need to remember that members of the media are selective in what they consider newsworthy. A company or agency that bombards the media with releases eventually may find even the firm's most important news releases will be ignored. Therefore, PR department managers must carefully select the releases that go out. Sending only key releases builds credibility with members of the media. The goals of a news release are to build goodwill with the public and use the news media to gain exposure to the public. Information printed or broadcast by the news media has a higher level of credibility with the public than does advertising.

In most companies, the public relations department prepares the annual report and other *stockholder correspondence.* These documents should speak with the one clear voice found in all other materials. In other words, the IMC theme present in advertising, promotions, and the other IMC components must also be prominently displayed in the *annual report,* proxy vote statements, and other mailings.

Another venue available to develop positive publicity is a company-sponsored *special event.* One of the best examples of this type of approach is Saturn's annual "homecoming," initiated in 1994. Each spring Saturn invites all car owners to a huge outdoor party in Spring Hill, Tennessee, where the company's main factory is located. Over 40,000 Saturn owners attend this festivity annually, along with dealership owners and employees. The goal is to create an image of a "Saturn family," which is then reinforced through advertising and other promotional materials. Advertisements often picture company employees traveling great distances to care for Saturn owners (family members), including one worker who made a trip to Alaska to make sure a car seat was delivered in order to correct a problem.[10] Saturn's homecoming, as well as other Saturn public relations ventures, is handled by an outside group, the Hal Riney agency.

Timing issues

Public relations efforts are often combined with advertising programs, such as in the Saturn approach. Consequently, timing is a critical factor. For instance, a firm may use a press release to announce a new product or advertise the product first. In terms of timing, a sequence must be developed including the point at which employees are informed of the product, ads, and news releases. The objectives of the firm's IMC plan largely determine the order. When the goal is to create brand awareness of an issue or product, advertising goes first followed by public relations.

A goal of building believability about a product claim or corporate viewpoint probably starts with the public relations news release. Therefore, before advertisements were created claiming aspirin can reduce the risk of heart attack, it was important to send out news releases featuring the medical evidence that supports such a claim. Medical evidence has much higher credibility than an advertisement does. As a result, the public relations department and the advertising team must be closely allied to ensure effective timing. Companies that employ separate agencies should have a marketing manager responsible for coordinating the activities of the two agencies (PR and advertising) to guarantee that the timing of news releases and ad campaigns is right for the company.

Each year, Saturn invites all of its car owners to a huge outdoor party in Spring Hill, Tennessee. Courtesy of AP/Wide World Photos. Photograph by John Russell.

Integrated Learning Experience

Many firms hire professional public relations firms to handle part or most of their public relations activities. Listed below are the names of some public relations firms. Access these Web sites to see what types of services they offer. Identify each PR agency's expertise.

> A and R Partners (www.arpartners.com)
> Bain and Associates, Inc. (www.bainpr.com)
> Sandwick International (www.sandwick.com)
> The Weber Group (www.webergroup.com)

stop!

integrating public relations with the IMC process

As mentioned earlier, the public relations department often is separate from the marketing department. Company leaders must work hard to be certain the organization's communications speak with one voice. Figure 14.7 highlights a process for integrating public relations with the IMC process.[11]

> ▶ **Audit pockets of communication-related expenditures throughout the organization**
>
> ▶ **Identify all contact points for company and its products**
>
> ▶ **Analyze internal and external communications that affect the organization**
>
> ▶ **Create compatible themes, tones, and quality across all communication channels**
>
> ▶ **Link the IMC process with participatory management**
>
> ▶ **Create shared performance measures**

Integrating Public Relations & IMC

Source: Based on Matthew P. Gonring, "Putting Integrated Marketing Communications to Work Today," *Public Relations Quarterly*, (Fall 1994), Vol. 39, No. 3, pp. 45–48.

FIGURE 14.7

Beginning a communications audit

As shown, the first step is to conduct an audit of all communication-related expenditures within an organization. These should be combined into a single budget that clearly displays an overview of all communication activities and expenditures. From that budget, allocations are made for advertising, trade promotions, sales promotions, public relations programs, and all other IMC operations. It is important to coordinate all communication activities through one consolidated program, so that money is not wasted and activities are not duplicated.

Identifying contact points

The second step is to identify all potential communication contact points, both internal and external. A **communication contact point** is any place where someone receives a message from or about the organization. The message can be direct or indirect. For instance, a product's package is a contact point with customers, because information appears on the label. A building is a contact point for local community members who enter and leave the organization. Stock exchange listings and information are contacts point with the financial community. Paycheck stubs and bulletin boards inside of a factory are contact points for employees. Memos, phone calls, and e-mails are contact points for vendors. By identifying every potential contact point, the firm has the opportunity to monitor incoming and outgoing communications.

Each contact point should be analyzed carefully to determine how it affects the company. Where is the firm able to project a positive image? Which contact points are weak or provide mixed signals? What messages are being conveyed at each contact point? By examining what occurs at each contact point, company leaders are in a better position to know where to strengthen the messages being sent to both internal and external publics. They should also try to determine if any conflicting messages are being sent to those in contact with the company.

Creating themes and the tone

Once the contact points have been identified and analyzed, the organization is ready to create compatible themes, an effective tone, and quality messages across all communication channels. This means finding themes, such as advertising tag lines, company mottos, and other key phrases. McDonald's was known for years in the business community for two phrases:

1. Location, location, location
2. QSC (quality, service, cleanliness)

These themes set a tone for employees and others who are internal to the firm and project a clear message to outside constituents. Therefore, when Saturn says it is a different kind of car company, and says it often enough, the major publics around the firm begin to believe the message.

Developing a managerial style

To ensure compatible themes are sent through each contact point, the IMC process works most successfully when a participatory management style exists. An autocratic, top-down management system does not foster communication with employees. A participatory management style makes it easier for the various functional areas within a firm to work together and relate the same themes to others. Including various managers within the company in the IMC planning process helps each member to understand the company's direction and proceed with a more unified approach to achieving the company's marketing goals.

Creating shared performance measures

The last and most difficult part of integrating public relations into the IMC process is developing shared performance measures. The public relations department should be evaluated under the same communications umbrella as the marketing department. The same would be true for the other departments and employees who oversee communications contact points. Goals must be expressed in a manner that allows managers to compare successes and identify problem areas in both the marketing and public relations departments, as well as for all other marketing–public relations activities.

In summary, the reason for integrating public relations with other IMC activities is to make certain the program is truly consolidated under one overall theme. Many firms are well known to their external publics because of these well-integrated approaches. For example, the publicity surrounding Sam Walton during the early years of Wal-Mart helped him to build his retailing empire, just as the publicity about the many altruistic activities of a local hospital helps build trust in the community in which it operates. Contacts points can be driven by changes in the firm, such as when Pizza Hut reformulated the ingredients in its main pizzas, while shifting the advertising messages and redesigning its menus and take-home boxes. Members of the company knew the firm was upgrading the quality of the food, and the public saw a great deal of tangible change as the chain moved to aggressively maneuver in the highly competitive pizza marketplace.

There are two other major ways in which individual companies can "get their message out" to consumers and others: (1) sponsorship marketing and (2) event marketing. These subjects are described next.

sponsorship marketing

Sponsorship marketing means that the company pays money to sponsor someone or some group that is participating in an activity. A firm can sponsor a practically unending list of groups and individuals. For years, local firms sponsored everything from little league baseball and soccer teams to adult bowling teams. Other organizations sponsor college scholarship programs, participate in special "days" (such as a Labor Day festivals), as well as individuals who enter various contests. Many local car racetracks feature drivers who are sponsored by various companies. On a national scale, Nike purchases sponsor "exemptions" for golf tournaments. In Tiger Woods's first year on the PGA tour, this meant he could enter a professional tournament without being "qualified" (a top money winner or winner of a tournament in the previous year). A company can sponsor boxers, players, and occasions (a "home run giveaway" at a baseball game).

Sponsorships are used to accomplish many different objectives for organizations. For example, sponsorships can:

- Enhance a company's image
- Increase a firm's visibility
- Differentiate a company from its competitors
- Showcase specific goods and services
- Help a firm develop closer relationships with current and prospective customers
- Unload excess inventory

In choosing a sponsorship, it is important to match the audience profile with the company's target market. Thus, a firm may choose to sponsor a participant at an event attended primarily by females if a company's main market is female. Marketing executives also consider the image of the individual participant or group and how it relates to the firm's image. For instance, a contestant in an "upscale" competition, such as a beauty contest, should be sponsored by a tuxedo or formal gown company. Sponsorships are designed to help the company present a unified message to all audiences, which projects a positive corporate image. If possible, the firm should be the exclusive sponsor of the person or team. It is much easier to be remembered if the firm is the only sponsor compared to being one of many sponsors.

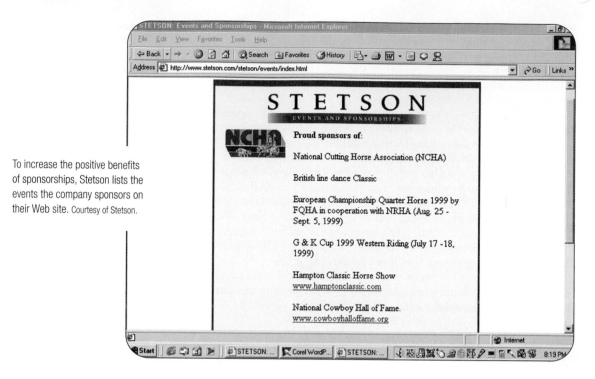

To increase the positive benefits of sponsorships, Stetson lists the events the company sponsors on their Web site. Courtesy of Stetson.

Many sponsorships are related to sports. Sporting events are highly popular and often attract large crowds. In addition to the audience attending the game or competition, many more watch on television. Athletes tend to be idolized by fans and can be effective spokespersons for various products.

The same is true for music concerts. Several companies sponsor bands at rock and pop concerts as a means of reaching loyal listeners and fans. The idea is to take the loyalty associated with the musical entertainer and transfer part of it to the product or company serving as the sponsor of the concert. SmithKline Beecham used this strategy for OXY Balance, an acne treatment. OXY Balance sponsored a recent 'N Sync's 50-city U.S. tour. To maximize the impact of the 'N Sync tour, OXY Balance added a "Face the Music" promotion that included a sweepstakes in which the grand-prize winners received all-expenses-paid trips to Florida, tickets to an 'N Sync concert, and the opportunity to witness a preconcert sound check with the band. At the concert, samples of OXY Balance were given to audience members. Each sample contained a premium offer encouraging the purchase of full-size tube of OXY Balance. In addition to advertising, sweepstakes, sampling, and premium activities, SmithKline Beecham also developed Web site links providing additional information about OXY Balance, ideas about how to treat acne, as well as details about 'N Sync's concert tour.[12] In the past, pharmaceutical companies relied on mostly traditional marketing avenues for promoting products. Intense competition has led to innovations such as this sponsorship program as methods to differentiate companies from their competition.

Some organizations have moved away from sports sponsorships toward more cultural events, such as classical music groups and jazz bands, visual art exhibits by noted painters, dance troupes, and actors for various theater performances. Cultural sponsorships are not a good match for every firm. They are effective for those products sold to the more affluent members of society. Consequently, financial institutions are the primary sponsors of these types of performers. In the past, many institutions provided funds without receiving much recognition. Now these philanthropic efforts are being leveraged by having the name of the company strongly associated with the cultural activity. This includes printing the name of the firm on programs and regularly mentioning the brand or corporate name as being responsible for arranging for the artist to be present at the cultural event. Also, sponsors usually receive choice seats at performances that can be given to key clients. For example, Credit Suisse sponsors the U.S. Equestrian Team and the individual performers for the Lincoln Center Theater. The company uses these cultural activities to help them establish long-term relationships and build goodwill with key clients, who get good seats at horse shows and theatrical performances.[13]

TNN (The Nashville Network) uses a different type of sponsorship approach when the network sponsors groups or performers at music concerts, rodeo cowboys, and car race drivers. TNN sends network celebrities to these occasions in a specialized mobile van. By creating a physical presence at an event being broadcast on TNN, the network believes it can build stronger relationships with viewers. The 30-foot truck is equipped with several entertainment devices including auto racing video games, prizes, T-shirts, hats, and music premiums. The type of merchandise carried on the truck is geared to the event featuring the sponsored person or group. CMT (Country Music Television) has been using the same approach for a number of years and visits over 1,000 sites each summer.[14]

communication**action**

Is NetZero Netting Zero?

One major sponsorship program, undertaken by NetZero, is its association with halftime programs at NBA and WNBA games. The company not only sponsors ads on NBC telecasts but also has a presence in many NBA arenas. The tie-in, between a basketball net and the Internet, is designed to build brand recognition for the provider.

Although the recognition factor is growing, the NBA's difficulties have the potential to be tied to NetZero. First, the departure of Michael Jordan and a strike-shortened season were soon followed by declining fan interest. Television ratings dropped significantly following the strike season.

In addition, *Sports Illustrated* reported a drop in actual attendance at NBA games. Ticket prices have become so high that the regular "fan" can't afford to attend games. Instead, corporations purchase season tickets and many go unredeemed. This means actual attendance is much lower than "reported" attendance, with no-shows counted as being present, because the ticket was sold.

The NBA has responded with a series of tactics. The first was a disaster. The league attempted to convince coaches that they would be "miked" during games, so fans could hear what they were talking about. Most simply refused. The egg on the face of the league lasted for several weeks.

As an alternative, the NBA viewer can now "listen in" to conversations between referees and players on the court. Also, a member of the team leading at halftime is now interviewed about his or her thoughts on the first half of the game.

Just as fan interest began to rebuild, a new threat emerged. During the 2000 season, a series of rumors emerged that the league was involved in a "conspiracy" designed to make sure the Los Angeles Lakers and New York Kicks made the NBA finals. The conspiracy theory drew so much attention that it was reported by CNN-SI and drew comments from Danny Ainge during a telecast. This negative publicity will be difficult to counteract, especially in light of similar charges during the Michael Jordan era. Referees, who are the league's most direct employees, were viewed as changing the outcomes of games by the "calls" they made at key moments.

Facing these and other other public relations incidents undoubtedly caused NetZero to reconsider its investment. Any tie-in with a sport, whether it is professional basketball or professional boxing, runs the risk of bad press aimed at the sport spilling over to the sponsor.

In addition to milk, notice all of the corporate sponsors listed on Jeff Gordon's uniform. Courtesy of Bozell Worldwide, Inc.

At 24, I became the second youngest champion in NASCAR history. Here's another little-known fact. Of the 42 drivers who chase me at more than 200 mph, most don't get enough calcium. My advice? Drink three glasses of milk a day. Preferably while standing still.

MILK
Where's *your* mustache?™

It may be hard to measure the impact of a sponsorship program directly. This can make such a program seem like a dangerous approach for a small, struggling company. For example some marketing experts viewed Rachel's Gourmet Snack's three-year, multimillion sponsorship of two Indianapolis 500 race cars as a dangerous strategy. At the time, the company was struggling financially. Even though it may indeed have been a risky tactic, it worked out exceptionally well for Rachel's. Eddie Cheever, one of the drivers sponsored by Rachel's, overcame 30-to-1 odds and won the Indianapolis 500. Rachel's name was prominently displayed on the car, on Eddie Cheever's uniform, and on the uniforms worn by his pit crew. The name was seen by 300,000 fans at the raceway and by millions on television. The company was immediately flooded with phone calls from customers. Soon, Rachel's opened distribution outlets throughout the United States. Therefore, even though the sponsorship program seemed risky, the return was overwhelming.[15]

To maximize the benefits of a sponsorship effort, it is important to define the primary goals of the program. As with the other marketing tools, the goals of the sponsorships should be integrated with the firm's overall IMC theme. The public should easily recognize the link between the person or group being sponsored, the activity, and the company involved.

To achieve the maximum impact for the sponsorship, the message should be combined with other advertising and promotional efforts, such as the TNN van and the OXY Balance programs mentioned earlier. Normally a company spending $100,000 on a sponsorship should also spend $200,000 to $400,000 leveraging that sponsorship. Advertising the sponsorship prior to the event is essential. Most marketing experts recommend that no more than 10 percent of a firm's marketing budget be allocated to sponsorships. Rachel's Gourmet Snacks gambled on the firm's sponsorship of Eddie Cheever by spending substantially more than 10 per-get employees involved and boost morale, should be met by finding events internal members will enjoy. Many times, the goals of sponsoring an event are to:

1. Help the firm maintain its market share
2. Build strong brand presence in the marketplace
3. Enhance the product or firm's image

To meet these goals means carefully selecting a program to sponsor that matches the firm's *customers, vendors,* or *employees*. For instance, the Pedigree Chum brand is the sponsor of the most prestigious dog show in the world, held annually at Crufts in England. This sponsorship dates back to 1969. Pedigree sets up a large display at the four-day Crufts event. Fifty to 60 Pedigree staff members are present to talk to dog owners, breeders, trainers, and attendees. In addition to Crufts, the Pedigree Chum brand maintains a presence at 450 other dog shows each year. At each show, the goal of Pedigree is to develop relationships with dog breeders, work with dog trainers, and keep in contact with other opinion leaders. By the time a dog gets to Crufts, Pedigree has already made contact, and it is highly likely the dog will have been fed Pedigree products. The breeder often endorses the Pedigree brand. This investment in a physical presence at dog shows is an essential element of the company's IMC theme: "Top breeders recommend Pedigree Chum." Pedigree works diligently to heighten the odds that a breeder will feed his or her dogs Pedigree Chum and subsequently endorse the product. Usually within two hours of the Crufts show, a new ad has been produced featuring the winning dog, the owner, and the trainer.[18]

Matching the event with a segment of the firm's target market helps the company keep in contact with customers and vendors. For 40 years, General Motors has been involved in golfing events, especially the PGA Tour. Buick is the title sponsor at four or five PGA Tour locations each year and also is present at other tournaments. The model emphasized by Buick varies depending on the projected audience for the event. Golf is attractive for GM due to the match between the target audience (golfers and golf fans) and Buick's target market. Golf attracts an upscale, primarily male audience similar to the profile of a typical Buick owner. To support the company's involvement in golf tournament events, Buick offers free tickets to attend through in-store promotions at Buick dealers, sweepstakes, and test-driving campaigns.[19]

Cultural events often target the more affluent and educated members of the local community. For example, in San Francisco 90 percent of those who attend the symphony are university graduates. Sixty-four percent hold graduate degrees or have completed some graduate work. The average age of a symphony audience member is 54, and the average income per person is $80,000. Approximately 17 percent of audience members have annual incomes over $150,000. Another 16 percent have annual incomes between $100,000 and $150,000. As a result, cultural sponsorships are very attractive to certain companies.[20]

Cross-promotions boost the impact of an event marketing program. General Motors developed a tie-in promotion between its Oldsmobile Intrigue sedan and the first *X-Files* movie. The objective of the event marketing program was to attract young, married adults with children to test-drive the Intrigue. Produced by event marketing agency Frankel & Company of Chicago, "*X-Files* Expo" events were held in several major cities. They offered attendees free movie tickets, prizes, and photo opportunities with the stars of the film. The *X-Files* Expo events resulted in 8,554 consumer test-drives for the Intrigue and 10,000 requests for information about the car.[21]

Sponsoring participants in an event should insist on *placement of the company name,* logo, and other product information in every advertisement and brochure for the event. Many attendees of special events keep the program as a souvenir or as something to show others. Placing the sponsor's name and message on the program generates an ad with a long life span. The sponsoring business must work to maximize brand-name exposure by connecting the firm's name with the event's marketing program. Working closely with the event management team is cent of its budget, which is partly what made the approach such a risky strategy for the firm.

Finally, when conducting a sponsorship program, the marketing team should try to incorporate other trade and consumer promotions. At the event itself, sampling is an effective method to encourage people to try a product. Unless a sponsorship is surrounded by some kind of supporting marketing effort, the money invested may not accomplish as much.

Integrated Learning Experience

Sponsorships are big business both for the not-for-profit firms holding events and for the companies providing the support. In Canada, the *Sponsorship Report* is a publication dedicated to fostering successful partnerships between corporations and not-for-profit groups. Access the Sponsorship Report at www.sponsorship.ca to see what services it offers. To assist firms in selecting the best sponsorships that will integrate well with their IMC plans, a number of agencies are available. Access the following Web sites to see what types of services are being offered to companies to assist them in their sponsorship activities.

Performance Research (www.performanceresearch.com)
IEG Sponsorship (www.sponsorship.com)
BDS Sponsorships Ltd (www.sponsorship.co.uk)

event marketing

Event marketing is quite similar to sponsorship marketing. The major difference is that sponsorship marketing involves a person, group, or team. Event marketing occurs when the company supports a specific event. This often includes setting up a booth or display and having some type of physical presence at the event. Almost $8 billion is spent annually on event marketing, with General Motors and Philip Morris as the top two spenders in the past several years.[16]

Many events are sports related. A rodeo sponsored by Lee Jeans or a music concert put on by a radio station are marketing events. In addition, many more segmented events are held. For instance, an Hispanic fiesta funded by a food company or a health fair conducted by a local hospital (e.g., "An Affair of the Heart" wellness program sponsored by Freeman Medical Hospital) is event marketing.

Sponsoring the right event can provide the sponsoring organization with greater brand-name recognition and help to develop closer ties with vendors and customers. Also, events can help boost morale for the employees who participate or attend. Sponsoring local events provides a company with the potential to generate free publicity. These events may also be used to enhance the company's image in the local community.

There are several key steps to take when preparing an event. Therefore, to ensure the maximum benefit from event sponsorships, companies should[17]:

1. Determine the objective(s) of sponsoring events.
2. Match each event with customers, vendors, or employees.
3. Cross-promote the event.
4. Make sure the company is included in all event advertising and brochures.
5. Track results.
6. Evaluate the investment following the event.

The company should determine the key *marketing objectives* to accomplish before becoming involved in a particular event. When the objective is to reward customers, it is crucial to find an event major customers would be interested in attending. Objectives that are more internally oriented, especially those designed to vital to seeing that the sponsor's name receives prominent attention in all materials associated with the event.

Some events turn out better than others for the sponsor. To determine the best events, firms need to *track results*. In addition to sales, the company can monitor how many pieces of literature were given to attendees, the number of samples distributed, and the number of visitors to the sponsor's display booth. Further, marketing research can be conducted to measure brand awareness before and after the event to discover if any new brand recall or brand awareness developed.

Results and marketing information allow the business to *evaluate the investment* in the event. Company leaders and marketing managers then can decide if sponsoring a particular event was beneficial and whether to sponsor the event in coming years or similar events in the future.

Event marketing has increased in popularity during the past decade due to its potential to reach consumers on a one-to-one basis. Many firms have established event marketing departments to plan, execute, and evaluate events. Other firms retain freelance event marketing specialists. One such organization is an agency specialist known as Events Marketing, Inc. The agency, based in Los Angeles, specializes in producing Hispanic-themed events. Events Marketing, Inc.'s client list includes the Bank of America, Coors Brewing Company, Lever Brothers, Polaroid Corporation, the California State Lottery, Western Union, and Safeway.[22]

In the future, event marketing tie-ins with other media, especially the Internet, will rise. For instance, many television programs focused on sports now allow viewers to watch "enhanced programming" by going on-line while watching a game or contest. The NBA championships employ one of the more sophisticated versions of this type of program. Events including rock concerts, boat shows, and other more specialized programs will continue to see an increased interest by marketing firms trying to make contact with customers in personalized ways that do not directly involve a sales call. Event marketing and sponsorship programs make these contacts easier to generate.

Integrated Learning Experience

Event marketing used wisely can enhance the image of a corporation. The key is to choose the right kinds of events. Each one should match the firm's goals and IMC plans. As with other forms of promotions, certain companies specialize in event marketing and others offer event marketing services as part of a wider portfolio of services. Examine the following firms. Study the types of events they offer and the types of services they render in relation to events marketing.

Advantage International, LLC (www.advantage-intl.com)
Pierce Promotions and Event Management, Inc. (www.ppem.com)
Trojan Sports and Event Marketing (www.trojansports.com)
Event Marketing Concepts, Inc. (www.emconcepts.com)
Woolf Associates (www.woolfassociates.com)
RPMC Event Marketing and Promotion Agency (www.rpmc.com)

stop!

implications for **marketing professionals**

Public Relations Department Managers

Get yourself in the loop. Know what is happening in marketing planning meetings. Make sure you can create messages that support the firm's IMC theme.

Regularly pull out a list of stakeholders for your company. Update it when necessary. Ask yourself the following questions:

1. How do we make contact with this group?

2. How does this group make contact with us?

3. What does this group think of us?

4. What can we do to upgrade our image with this public?

Update and examine the methods by which you send messages to various groups. Make sure you are fully utilizing new technologies, such as:

1. The Internet and the firm's Web site
2. Teleconferencing
3. Faxes
4. E-mails

Randomly check contact points where unplanned messages arrive. Make sure employees send out the right messages and respond correctly when someone or another firm contacts your organization.

Go over all altruistic plans and cause-related marketing efforts with the marketing department and top management. *Become a skeptic.* Ask if these programs will be perceived as being based on good intentions, or are simply opportunistic attempts to gain some free publicity.

Carefully consider sponsorship programs. Use a cost–benefit model when evaluating them. Think in terms of:

1. Expenditures
2. Revenues (if any) gained from the sponsorship
3. The number of people exposed to the person or event
4. Opportunities for direct, interpersonal contacts with customers
5. Long-term image and brand equity development potential
6. Benefits of a long-term association with the same event or group

SUMMARY

The public relations department should play a major role in an integrated marketing communications program, whether the department is separate from marketing or combined as part of a communications division. Public relations efforts are primarily oriented to making sure that every possible contact point delivers a positive and unified message on behalf of the company.

There are many stakeholders inside and surrounding a company. Any person or group that has a vested interest in the organization's activities is a stakeholder. Internal stakeholders include employees, unions, and stockholders. External publics include members of the marketing channel, customers, the media, the local community, financial institutions, the government, and special-interest groups.

Whenever possible, the firm sends out planned messages to portray the company and its products in a positive light. Some messages are inferred to customers, such as when the buyer connects a higher price with greater product quality. Maintenance messages are sent to employees through manuals and other printed materials and provide information about how to respond to various publics and how to present the company's products. Unplanned messages require careful monitoring and should be managed to whatever degree possible.

In the attempt to build a favorable image of the company, the public relations department develops special events such as altruistic activities and cause-related marketing programs. Due care must be given to making certain these acts are not perceived with cynicism and skepticism. This means being certain than any good deed matches with company products and other marketing efforts. A natural fit between an altruistic event and the company's brand is more readily accepted by various members of the public.

To reach all intended audiences, the public relations department has a series of tools available. These include company newsletters, internal messages, public relations releases, correspondence with stockholders, annual reports, and various special events. Even the bulletin board in the company's break room can be used to convey messages to internal stakeholders.

Sponsorship programs enhance and build the company's image and brand loyalty. A sponsorship of an individual or group involved in some kind of activity—whether it is a sporting event, a contest, or a performance by an artistic group—can be used to link the company's name with the popularity of the player involved. Sponsorships should match with the firm's products and brands.

Event marketing occurs when a firm sponsors an entire event. A strong physical presence at the event is one of the keys to successfully linking an organization's name with a program. To do so, the firm must determine the major objective of the event sponsorship, match it with company customers and publics, and make sure the firm's name is prominently displayed on the literature accompanying the event.

Managing public relations, sponsorships, and event marketing programs requires company leaders to carefully assess both the goals and the outcomes of individual activities. A cost–benefit approach may not always be feasible, but the marketing team should be able to track some form of change, whether it is increased inquiries, the number of samples passed out at an event, or a shift in the tenor of news articles about the organization. The primary task of public relations is to be the organization's "watchdog," making sure those who come in contact with the company believe the firm is working to do things right and to do the right things.

REVIEW QUESTIONS

1. Describe the role of the public relations department. How is it related to the marketing department? Should both departments be called the department of communications? Why or why not?
2. What is a stakeholder?
3. Name the major internal stakeholders in organizations. Describe their interests in the company.
4. Name the major external stakeholders of organizations. For each one, describe its major interest in the company.
5. Four kinds of messages are sent internally and externally by various companies. Name and describe each type of message. Give an example.
6. What kinds of altruistic activities can an organization provide on a local scale? On a national level?
7. Give three examples of cause-related marketing programs that impressed you with their sincerity. Name and describe three that seemed "phony."
8. Describe the relationships between skeptics, balancers, attribution-oriented consumers, and socially concerned consumers with cause-related marketing programs.
9. Name and describe the internal public relations tools that the department can utilize.
10. Name and describe the public relations tools the department uses to reach external publics.
11. How can the company make sure public relations efforts are being integrated with the larger IMC program?
12. What is sponsorship marketing? Name a pro athlete, musician or musical group, or performer of some other type who has been featured in a sponsorship program. Was the program effective or ineffective? Why?
13. Describe an event marketing program. What must accompany the event in order to make it a success?
14. What are cross-promotions? How are they related to event marketing programs?

KEY TERMS

public relations (PR) department   a unit in the firm that manages items such as publicity and other communications with all of the groups that make contact with the company.

hit   the mention of a company's name in a news story.

stakeholder   a person or group that has a vested interest in a firm's activities and well-being.

planned messages   those produced and sent out by the marketing department.

inferred messages   those that stakeholders decipher independently through contacts with an organization.

maintenance messages   those delivered primarily by the firm's employees in contact with external publics.

unplanned messages   externally generated (media, consumer groups) information about the organization.

altruistic activities   company-sponsored efforts designed to build goodwill with both internal and external publics.

cause-related marketing   matching marketing efforts with some type of charity work or program.

news release   a message sent out by the public relations department regarding an aspect of a company's operation.

communication contact point   any place where someone receives a message from or about the organization.

sponsorship marketing   when the company pays money to sponsor someone or some group that is participating in an activity.

event marketing   when a company pays money to sponsor an event or program.

cross-promotion   a tie-in between a company's product and an event.

ENDNOTES

1. Emily Fromm, "Good, Clean Entertainment," *Adweek,* 40, no. 4 (January 25, 1999), p. 3; Kelly Shermach, "Wrestling on a Peak Keeps One Eye on Valley," *Marketing News,* 31, no. 10 (May 12, 1997), p. 24; John Agoglia and Cory Bronson, "Outside the Ring," *Sporting Goods Business,* 32, no. 3 (February 8, 1999), pp. 68–69.

2. Donald Baack, *Organizational Behavior* (Houston: Dame Publications, 1997).

3. Sandra E. Moriarty, "PR and IMC: The Benefits of Integration," *Public Relations Quarterly,* 39, no. 3 (fall 1994), pp. 38–44.

4. Charles Maclean, "For-Profit–Nonprofit Alliances Benefit Both Sides," *Business Journal Serving Greater Portland,* 16, no. 43 (December 17, 1999), p. 28.

5. Brad Edmondson, "New Keys to Customer Loyalty," *American Demographics,* 16, no. 1 (January 1994), p. 2.

6. Deborah J. Webb and Lois A. Mohr, "A Typology of Consumer Responses to Cause-Related Marketing: From Skeptics to Socially Concerned," *Journal of Public Policy and Marketing,* 17, no. 2 (fall 1998), pp. 226–38.

7. Sarah Lorge and Geoffrey Brewer, "Is Cause-Related Marketing Worth It?" *Sales and Marketing Management,* 150, no. 6 (June 1998), p. 72.

8. Ibid.

9. Brian K. Miller, "Many Companies Give Generously, but with a Catch," *Business Journal Serving Greater Portland,* 14, no. 43 (December 19, 1997), pp. 28–29.

10. Moriarty, "PR and IMC: The Benefits of Integration."

11. Based on Matthew P. Gonring, "Putting Integrated Marketing Communications to Work Today," *Public Relations Quarterly,* 39, no. 3 (fall 1994), pp. 45–48.

12. Jeanie Casison, "Prescription for Success," *Incentive,* 173, no. 5 (May 1999), pp. 77–81.

13. "Cultural Sponsorship Can Help Reach the Affluent," *Bank Marketing,* 26, no. 10 (October 1994), p. 7.

14. Kate Fitzgerald, "TNN Hits the Country Roads," *Electronic Media,* 18, no. 16 (April 19, 1999), p. 50.

15. Harvey Meyer, "And Now, Some Words About Sponsors," *Nation's Business,* 87, no. 3 (March 1999), pp. 38–41.

16. Kate Fitzgerald and Nick Lico, "The Big Event," *Automotive News,* 73, no. 5812 (March 29, 1999), pp. AM24–AM25.

17. Kim Pryor, "Events as Incentives," *Incentive,* 173, no. 8 (August 1999), pp. 102–3.

18. Bhavna Mistry, "Top Pedigree Wins the Show," *Marketing Events* (April 1998), pp. 30–31.

19. Fitzgerald and Lico, "The Big Event."

20. "Cultural Sponsorship Can Help Reach the Affluent."

21. Ibid.

22. Rob Evans, "Events Marketing Incorporated Brings Fiestas to Fairs," *Amusement Business,* 109, no. 40 (October 6, 1997), p. 5.

23. Maclean, "For-Profit/Nonprofit Alliances Benefit Both Sides"; David Kratz, "In Cause-Related Marketing, Make the Product the Means of Giving," *Public Relations Tactics* (May 1999), p. 13; Terry Lefton, "Triple Latte Phenom Makes Cause with McGwire Four-Bangers for '99," *Brandweek,* 40, no. 6 (February 8, 1999), p. 16.

24. Betsy Nichol, "Integrated Marketing: The Cluster-Buster," *Franchising World,* 26, no. 5 (September–October 1994), pp. 15–17.

Building an IMC Campaign

Generating Positive Publicity and Considering Sponsorships

A fully integrated marketing communications program considers all of the means by which customers and other publics make contact with an organization. These messages travel in several directions, including from inside the organization to those outside of the firm, from customers and others to those inside the company, and between members of various departments within the organization. Positive public relations involves all of these publics through planned messages, inferred messages, maintenance messages, and unplanned messages. Publicity campaigns such as cause-related marketing and other altruistic activities can help build the firm's image. Further, event sponsorships that reflect the company's image and theme can be highly valuable. Go to the Prentice-Hall Web site at www.prenhall.com/clow or access the Advertising Plan Pro disk that accompanied this textbook to complete the exercise for this chapter. It will help you learn how to incorporate your public relations department in with other marketing efforts and promotional activities.

Critical Thinking Exercises

Discussion Questions

1. Watch the news on television or read your local paper for news about a local or national business. Was the report positive or negative toward the firm? Did the news report affect your attitude toward the company? Watch one of the many special investigative shows such as *60 Minutes*. What companies did it investigate? If you were the firm being featured, what would you do to counteract the bad press?

2. The public relations officer for a small but highly respected bank in a local community was charged with sexual harassment by a female employee. What type of communications should be prepared for each of the constituencies listed in Figure 14.3? Which of the constituencies would be the most important to contact?

3. How important is the local community for a manufacturing firm that sells 99 percent of its products outside of the area? Does it really matter what the local people say or believe about the manufacturer as long as the firm's customers are happy?

4. What causes do you support or are special to you? Do you know which corporations sponsor or support the causes? If not, see if you can find literature or Web sites that contain that information. Why do you think the corporations choose a particular cause to support? What benefit do you think the corporations receive from their sponsorships?

5. When Starbucks opened its first coffee shop inside of a public library, 10 percent of all proceeds from coffee sold there went to support the operation of the library. Do you think public libraries should allow profit-seeking organizations such as Starbucks to sell their products inside of their buildings? Is this a conflict of interest for governmentally sponsored organizations such as libraries? What if the local doughnut shop wanted to sell doughnuts at the library? Should it be allowed to do so? How does a library decide whom it will and will not partner with?

6. In a another program, Starbucks enlisted the support of home run hitter Mark McGwire. For each home run McGwire hit, Starbucks donated $5,000 to a child literacy program in the city in which the home run was hit. This provided local publicity for Starbucks in each of those cities. The program boosted sales for Starbucks as well as

enhancing its image among the American public as a company that cares about children, literacy, and libraries.[23] How do you feel about this cause-related marketing program? In your mind, is it any different than selling coffee in libraries, as in Question 5? Why didn't Starbucks just donate money to child literacy programs instead of tying it into home runs hit by a baseball superstar?

7. Managers often are the most difficult group for the public relations department to reach. To entice employees to reach departmental goals, managers often communicate using memos or verbal messages. These messages may conflict with the IMC theme. For example, in an effort to trim costs, a manager may send a memo to all employees telling them to use only standard production procedures. Through verbal communications, employees learn that anyone caught violating or even bending the policy to satisfy a customer will be immediately reprimanded. The manager's action suggests that even though he wants employees to provide customer service, in actuality, they had better not do anything that is not authorized. Employees soon get the message that management cares only about costs, not the customer. Employees will perceive any advertising message about customer service as a big joke. Write a memo to employees that supports the IMC goal of high customer service, yet alerts them to the need to follow standard operating procedures. Is there anything else you would do to ensure that this not a conflicting message being sent to employees?

8. Baskin-Robbins recently utilized public relations efforts to reach potential new franchise operators. In each market targeted for expansion, Baskin-Robbins prepared news releases announcing plans to open a specified number of stores. These news articles normally appeared in the business section of the local newspapers, often on the front page. The news articles contained more details than the classified ads that Baskin-Robbins used to attract franchise operators.[24] What advantage does Baskin-Robbins gain by combining the articles with the ads? Why would newspapers print an article about Baskin-Robbins wanting to open franchises? Is this really newsworthy information?

9. Corporate sponsorships are very important to not-for-profit organizations. Without their financial assistance, many causes would not exist. Look up two organizations from the following list of not-for-profit organizations. Who are their corporate sponsors? What benefits do the profit seeking companies receive from these sponsorships?

   a. American Cancer Society (www.cancer.org)
   b. National Alliance of Breast Cancer Organizations (www.nabco.org)
   c. Arthritis Foundation (www.arthritis.org)
   d. Multiple Sclerosis Society (www.mssociety.org.uk)
   e. United Cerebral Palsy (www.ucp.org)
   f. Alliance for the Wild Rockies (www.wildrockiesalliance.org)
   g. National Wildlife Federation (www.nwf.org)
   h. Trout Unlimited (www.tu.org)

Fourth of July Marketing: More Fireworks Than They Needed

Station manager Jim Jefferson decided it was time to pull the plug. For the past 12 years, his television station (KSNN) proudly sponsored the local annual Fourth of July Festival. Until recently, the event had been a solid promotional marketing tool that generated sales and good-will for a variety of vendors. Now, however, Jim has decided the hassles outweigh the benefits.

The first KSNN Fourth of July Festival was a modest affair. One sponsor, a dynamite factory located in the community, chipped in money for a small fireworks display, and the local college allowed the event to be held in an open area of the campus. As time passed, the scale and scope had grown into the single largest attraction in the area each year.

First, corporate sponsors were added. Each provided funding for various aspects of the program. Some paid for the actual fireworks and were rewarded with the company's logo lit up in a display to start each year's show. Other sponsors kicked in money so that relatively famous entertainers could be brought in. Vendors paid money to sell their food and drink products during the course of the event.

When the event initially began, the festivities started at about 7:00 P.M. with only a fireworks display. As the show evolved, the gates were opened at 2:00 P.M., and programs started around 4:00 P.M., led by a welcoming proclamation from the mayor. Bands played, local choirs sang patriotic songs, parachute jumpers swooped into the arena. The local college opened its football stadium to accommodate parking, seating, rest room facilities, and other amenities.

KSNN developed a tie-in with an area radio station. Beginning in the sixth year of the event, the fireworks were set up in time with music piped through stadium speakers with a simulcast on the radio. KSNN even broke into network programming to provide pictures of the fireworks show for the city.

The event generated a considerable amount of money for KSNN. Sponsors were required to buy ads promoting the event for two weeks prior to the Fourth of July weekend. The college was given free advertising time throughout the year in exchange for opening its facilities. By the tenth year, nearly 40,000 people were at or near the school, seeing the ads and visiting the booths and displays set up by the various sponsors.

KSNN also benefited from the football stadium setup. Key sponsors and their guests were given seats inside the air-conditioned press box during the day. KSNN served food and drinks to these individuals as part of their pampered exposure to the show. The guests could then move to the roof of the press box when the actual fireworks display took place. The school's president was thrilled to be able to schmooze with major corporations in the area each year and in fact had generated donations to the college based on these relationships.

Unfortunately, in the eleventh year, vandalism associated with the event reached an all-time high. The school's football field, which was made of AstroTurf, was badly damaged by hoodlums who infested the event. Traffic jams caused so many problems that the local police department began asking to be reimbursed for all the overtime it was forced to pay to keep officers on duty to direct traffic and solve other problems.

Also, some of the sponsors began to object to the rising fees they were being charged to be associated with the event. KSNN's revenues had risen, but the station was also paying higher expenses each year.

The tide turned when the college rejected KSNN's bid to return for a thirteenth show. The president reported that replacing the football field surface made it too cost prohibitive for the college to be involved. KSNN was forced to move the event to a local city golf course, over the objections of golfers and several members of the city council, who feared destruction of the greens, fairways, and tee-boxes would be a major expense.

In the same year, two sponsors dropped out, citing costs as their key concerns. Food and drink vendors expressed frustrations that they would not have good places to set up to sell their products, and the remaining sponsors balked at bad locations for their booths. Many attendees had to ride shuttle buses to get close enough to see the show, and they completely bypassed the booths on the ride.

The growing number of headaches with the city, sponsors, and others caused the local newspaper to write articles about problems the show created. Jim decided the negative publicity was not what his station needed.

Following intense negotiations, KSNN withdrew after the show. Another local television station took over sponsorship of the event, but pared it down to a simple fireworks display at a local auto racetrack, to be held in conjunction with a day of racing.

1. Did KSNN wait too long before pulling out? Should the company's leaders have tried to solve the problems on their own, rather than just giving up?
2. What benefits accrued to KSNN, the sponsors, and the college when the show was going well?
3. Do you think the college was wise to withdraw from the show? Why or why not?

Minor League Team, Major League Problems

APPLICATION EXERCISE II

Drew Burns was excited and depressed at the same time. He had just been named as director of public relations for the Tulsa Mustangs, the newest entry into the Arena Football Association. Arena football has been a relatively successful venture for a number of smaller cities and teams for over a decade. The small field, the fast pace, high-scoring games, and the opportunity to attend football games in the off-season had attracted a number of fans.

Arena football relies heavily on sponsorships to succeed. Various companies provide giveaways at games, from seat cushions to caps and other team memorabilia. Local restaurants provide coupons for price discounts on food when the team wins. Soft drink bottlers from individual cities provide drinks and other enticements to keep fans involved.

Players in arena football are required to stay after the game and make contact with fans. They sign autographs, shake hands, and fans go onto the field so that they may feel more part of the action. Sponsors love the one-on-one contact between individuals.

Drew's problem was trying to become established in his new market. Tulsa has a major college with its own sports teams and, more importantly, minor league baseball. Minor league baseball has experienced a resurgence of interest due to the high ticket prices major league teams charge. Families on budgets find they can go to a game, eat a hot dog, and still have some change left over. A typical family excursion to a major league game may cost over $150 for a family of four, with parking, ticket prices, and concessions being relatively expensive for the normal-size family. A beer at most major league ballparks costs around $4.

With a major competitor for the "Joe Average" sports fan, Drew knew he would have to make a positive impact on the community right away for the team to succeed. Arena football faced two problems as he began the venture. First, the "Kurt Warner effect" was wearing off. The rags to riches story of Kurt Warner's journey from arena football to the NFL Superbowl had lost its impact. Fans did not expect a player from the arena league to regularly become well-known at a higher level, and Warner was viewed mostly as a fluke.

Second, too many football players had made headlines for misbehavior. In one year, two professional players had been accused of murder, and numerous accounts of violence and crime had taken over the sports page. In fact, a book entitled *Pros and Cons* detailed all of the pro players who had some kind of brush with the law. Consequently, the Tulsa team needed to distance itself from those kinds of bad boys and try to establish a more squeaky-clean reputation.

Drew had a very limited budget. He simply could not advertise his way to success. He knew he would need the cooperation of the owners, the league, his players, the local media, and several sponsors to garner the attention his team needed. The players may be his biggest asset. Many had voiced the willingness to appear at promotional events on behalf of local charities to help the team gain an audience. At the same time, many other sports programs (rodeos, little leagues, soccer leagues, etc.) could attract potential customers away from the idea of summer football. Tulsa also had an active social life in terms of band concerts and other summertime events.

1. Will the Tulsa Mustangs succeed in this environment? Why or why not?

2. What kinds of events should Drew schedule for his players who are willing to help the team?

3. How can Drew generate positive publicity for the Mustangs, beyond personal appearances by players? What should the IMC theme be for this team?

4. Most sporting events develop corporate sponsors for giveaways to fans and as a means of attracting fans to the games. What type of corporate sponsors should Drew solicit? What benefits would corporate sponsors expect from Drew?

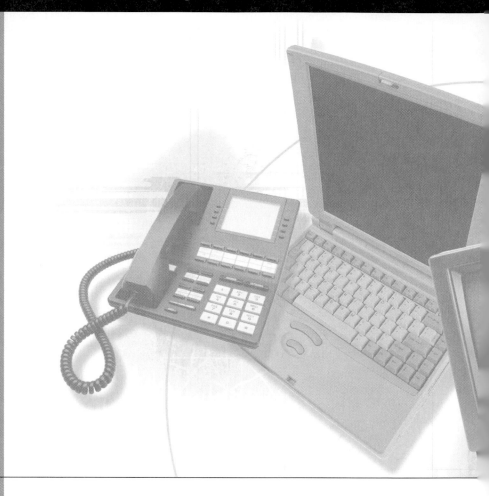

▶ **CHAPTER OBJECTIVES**

Learn how to match a database program with an IMC program.

Develop clear and useful objectives for database programs, such as increased sales, improved brand equity, and discovering ways to reach new customers.

Effectively apply the steps of database program development to meet the company's IMC needs.

Use the database to improve direct-marketing programs.

Apply database management programs to permission marketing systems.

Know how and when to utilize frequency programs and incentives.

DEL MONTE:
When More Than Just Fruits and Vegetables Are at Stake

Del Monte has long been a major competitor in canned foods and other products. When the company launches a new line of canned fruit nationwide, the marketing team first looks for ways to move the product by identifying the best customers and the best stores. The marketing plan includes print and radio advertisements, coupons, free-standing inserts in newspapers, in-store displays, in-store promotions, and pay-for-performance trade promotions. All of these efforts are coordinated through a database that segments Del Monte's customers by buying habits.

chapter fifteen

Del Monte's database can break down stores and customers by geographic regions, buying habits, income levels, and other demographic information that helps company markets determine the best stores for selling the new product. Del Monte's central database has information regarding 55,000 grocery stores, chain drugstores, and mass-merchandisers that are the firm's primary customers. Major stores include Jewel, Safeway, Target, and Wal-Mart. This extensive database helps Del Monte analyze the buying patterns of each store and provides a profile of the store's most frequent customers, whether they are senior citizens, college students, large families, blue-collar workers, or upper-income consumers. In addition to

purchasing information, Del Monte knows which products sell best at which stores and where new products are most likely to do well.

When calling on its customers, the wholesalers and retailers who carry products, Del Monte salespeople are armed with extensive information about what is and is not selling. They can then modify trade promotions and other incentives to boost sales for each individual store. They also can use this information to create consumer promotions to pull the product through the channel. Salespeople from Del Monte are seen more as partners than salespeople because of their extensive knowledge of each store's customers.

In this case, the database available to Del Monte helps the marketing team succeed in the difficult world of slotting fees (see Chapter 11), fickle customers, strong competition, and heavy government regulation. Any company that can gain a competitive edge using a database to understand its end user and business customers is advised to follow the "fruity" approach that Del Monte is working to perfect.[1]

overview

Integrated marketing communications programs are the most successful when they are consistent throughout the entire company. Each activity, no matter how big or small, is part of the overall plan. Consequently, anything the firm sends out, from mailings to plastic or paper bags for carrying items, should reflect the firm's image and theme. This message can be emphasized in other communications efforts.

In this chapter, two major topics are described. **Database management** is the first subject. Effective IMC programs are built on a solid understanding of customers. High-quality marketing teams use information obtained from a database not only to increase sales but also to establish customer profiles for future efforts. The first section of this chapter describes ways to manage a database and support a firm's IMC program within the same framework. The role database marketing plays has changed as firms enter the twenty-first century. In the past, database programs were often considered a minor marketing tool. In this new century, databases are at the core of IMC programs.

The second topic to be described is direct marketing. Direct-marketing programs afford the company the opportunity to make one-on-one contacts with current customers and potential new customers. These contact points are times to spell out, reinforce, and promote the firm's image and theme. Therefore, beyond simply selling goods and services, direct-marketing programs can utilize the information developed in various databases to make sound connections with customers of all types. Direct marketing is especially valuable to the marketing team looking for ways to complement and supplement other IMC efforts, such as advertising, personal selling, and consumer or trade promotions.

A new wrinkle on direct-marketing programs is called permission marketing, a program in which customers give consent to be targeted with direct-marketing mailings and other contacts. Permission marketing programs help generate even more detailed information for a company's database. Also, many firms keep data records so they can create frequency programs. These programs give rewards to customers who make continuing purchases from the same company.

Direct marketing will be most productive when the company's marketing team can work with a solid database. Database management is the use of people and technology to collect and process data to be used in IMC marketing efforts. Database management is discussed first in this chapter, followed by direct marketing, permission marketing, and frequency programs. Each approach allows the company to know its customers better as well as to build stronger bonds with them over time.

developing an IMC database

Developing an IMC database is not the same thing as database marketing. The role of the database in an IMC program is to support the total marketing effort. It is not just another marketing program, such as advertising or personal selling, that just happens to use a database. Figure 15.1 outlines the steps required to develop an IMC database. An explanation of each of these steps follows.

⟩ **Determine obectives**

⟩ **Collect data**

⟩ **Build data warehouse**

⟩ **Mine data for information**

⟩ **Develop marketing programs**

⟩ **Evaluate marketing programs and data warehouses**

Steps in Developing a Database

FIGURE 15.1

Determining objectives

The objectives and role of the database in the marketing program determine much of what will take place as the data is generated. Asking the typical who, what, when, where, why, and how questions provides valuable insights into these objectives. For instance:

- Who will use this information?
- What kinds of data are available?
- When (or how often) will the information be used?
- Where will the data be located or stored?
- Why do we need certain data, and not other types?
- How will the data be used?

Answering these simple questions helps the marketing department design the proper system. Answering these questions is not enough, however. In addition, a larger, more important ingredient is making sure the information helps the company maintain a successful integrated marketing communications plan. Consequently, the database should provide the foundation on which the IMC plan can be built. Typical objectives for an IMC database include:

- Providing useful information about a firm's customers
- Creating information about why customers purchase the products they do
- Sharing information with creatives as they prepare advertisements and other promotional materials
- Revealing contact points that can be used in direct-marketing programs
- Yielding information about the role each member of a buying center plays in a business-to-business transaction and how each individual is involved in the buying decision-making process
- Tracking changes in purchasing behaviors and purchasing criteria used by customers

Knowing the objectives drives the rest of the data collection process. Without them, the firm can waste time and resources collecting information that has no real value for the firm's marketing efforts. These objectives may change or be modified from time to time, however the essential information needed to pursue the company's overall IMC goals should remain relatively constant.

Collecting data

After the objectives of the IMC database have been determined, a firm is ready to decide on potential sources of data. Most firms seek out both internal and externally generated sources of data. The most logical place to look for data within a firm is through customers, an internal source. Unfortunately, most companies have only

Sources of Data

FIGURE 15.2

▶ Internal customer data

▶ Commercial database services

▶ Survey data of customers

▶ Channel members

▶ Governmental data sources

a portion of the data about their own customers they should have, even though they can be a gold mine of valuable information. Other sources of information are called secondary data or external data. External data are essential for developing a quality IMC database. Figure 15.2 lists the major sources of data a firm can use.

Names and addresses of customers are the most common *internal data* available. Modern information technology techniques make it possible for nearly every business to track purchasing information and tie it in with names and addresses. Often, the most critical component of an IMC database is an index of the purchasing behaviors of buyers. This information helps the marketing team identify and profile its best customers. These customers may be targeted to increase the number of purchases they make or to cross-sell other goods and services to them. Purchasing behaviors can be used to create profiles suggesting who may become new customers in the future. When seeking additional customers, a firm that knows the type of individual or business most likely to make a purchase holds a distinct advantage in the marketplace.

For retailers, scanner data can reveal many things about a customer's purchases. If information is kept over time, scanner data become a valuable history of what items the customer buys, which brands are purchased, how often things are purchased, and how much is purchased. Many times this information can be tied directly to a customer's name, address (especially zip code area), age, family size, and other bits of demographic information. The retailers that collect this data from credit reports, surveys, or other instruments, are building valuable databases. This internal data should answer the questions posed in Figure 15.3. If they do not, the

Internal Data Information

FIGURE 15.3

▶ Where are the customers located?

▶ What have they purchased?

▶ How often have they purchased?

▶ How did they initially make contact?

▶ How do they order or purchase (in person, Web, mail, phone, etc.)?

▶ What is known about their families, occupations, payment histories, interests, attitudes, and so forth?

▶ In business-to-business situations, who are the influencers, users, deciders, and purchasers?

▶ In business-to-business, is it a corporate office or branch offices?

firm's marketing team may want to look at ways of expanding the database to gather as much information as possible about current customers.

To illustrate how a retailer can collect information for an IMC database, consider ZCMI, a small 14-store department store chain located in Salt Lake City. ZCMI began building a database through information collected from credit applications filled out by the 165,000 individuals who applied for the ZCMI premiere credit card. The card was the department's store own credit card, which made demographic information easy to obtain.

The next step was to add in information from customers who used different credit cards, such as Visa or MasterCard. This customer information can be purchased from the respective credit card companies. The final piece of the database that ZCMI obtained was information about the company's cash and check customers. By using the name, address, and social security information on checks, ZCMI gathered personal information about each of these customers from commercial database companies.

Collecting information about customers is an essential step in the process of developing a viable database. Courtesy of Corbis/Stock Market. Photograph by Jose L. Pelaez Inc.

For cash customers, retail clerks requested telephone numbers. These telephone numbers made it possible for ZCMI to purchase information from external database services. The only customers ZCMI was not able to put into the database were individuals who paid cash and did not have phones or would not give the retail clerk a phone number. This, however, was only a very small portion of the customers.[2]

Information collected through such sales efforts is not sufficient to meet all of the needs for an effective IMC planning program. Secondary or *external data* are required. Psychographic, lifestyle, and attitudinal information can be valuable external data to supplement information collected from regular customers. Retailers can purchase this type of information from external *commercial database services.* Normally, retailers tend to deal with customers on a transactional basis only and cannot generate other kinds of data without some form of outside help. For consumer businesses, demographic information such as income, age, race, marital status, and household type should be added if it is not already part of the database. The *neighborhood lifestyle cluster,* which depicts purchasing behaviors, media preferences, credit histories, attitudes, and interests, is another type of useful external information.

To supplement information gathered from commercial database services, an organization can gather *survey data* from its customers. The Communication Action Box on the next page illustrates how Levi-Strauss collected this kind of information from customers and how the survey data were used to develop individualized marketing programs for various target groups. To prevent biases, it is often advisable to hire an external marketing research firm to conduct the customer survey. A major advantage of hiring an external firm is that the company can supplement the customer survey data with noncustomer data. In other words, external firms can collect information from companies or individuals who are not customers that can be added to the database or be used in comparison to the firm's regular customer group.

Information obtained from *channel members* is especially important. Channel members are often customers. Consequently, manufacturers should compile a database that includes information about both retailers and wholesalers. This data may be supplemented with end user information. In this case, wholesalers and retailers are the manufacturer's primary customers. Consequently, the manufacturer's database should include every member of the marketing channel, and end user information may, in some ways, be the least vital.

Finally, there are times in which the organization can collect information from *governmental data sources.* The government provides helpful economic information plus other data from the Bureau of Vital Statistics and the Census Bureau to many firms.

Simply collecting data does not place them into a usable form. The next step is to construct a system that makes the information helpful to the marketing team and others involved in the company's operations.

communication**action**

To be effective, a company's database must be much more than a collection of names and addresses. Levi-Strauss & Company, when threatened by a combination of market forces and image problems, was able to respond by developing a strong database marketing program. Old Navy, Calvin Klein, and other brands had made inroads into the marketplace, just as Levi's had become associated with the older generation, possibly not hip enough to suit the younger consumer.

Levi's reacted by emphasizing the concept of *relationship marketing*. This meant trying to understand what consumers want and then giving them a voice to be heard by company leaders. To meet these objectives, the firm identified five consumer groups for a pilot program using a major survey. Using the database that was already in place, the company contacted various shoppers and enticed them to fill out questionnaires. In total, nearly 100,000 consumers completed questionnaires, which were distributed at stores, colleges, the Lilith Fair, and via customer service lines. Levi's carefully recorded the "doorway" each respondent used and tied it to other information, which eventually yielded the five major groups of shoppers. Each of the five groups expressed differing needs when it came to jeans.

Next, Levi's targeted the groups individually. Promotions were structured to match the nature of the customer profile that emerged. For example, one group known as Valuable Shoppers were individuals willing to spend $60 or more on a pair of pants. These patrons were sent thank-you gifts following purchases of custom-fit jeans. The gift was a planter with flower bulbs and a card signed by the clerk who took the fitting. Responses from this group were impressive. A Valuable Shopper who received a gift purchased, on average, 2.3 more pairs of jeans within the next few weeks.

On-line shoppers, who largely came from a group identified as Echo Boomers, or persons ages 15 to 25, were not sent this type of premium. Instead, this group was enticed with fashion messages. The goal was to match the promotional approach with the buyer group's characteristics.

By contacting consumers through questionnaires, gifts, promotions, and service lines, Levi's believed it was able to establish a two-way, more intimate form of communication with its clientele. This, in turn, helped the company combat declining interest in its products. The keys to success started with having a fairly well-established database to begin the program, enhancing the database, and listening to what consumers had to say. Any organization that is willing to utilize the talents and programs made available from an effective database management team may be in the position to reap similar rewards.

Source: Betsy Spethmann, "Can We Talk?" *American Demographics,* 21, no. 3 (1999), pp. 42–45.

Building a data warehouse

Constructing a useful data warehouse requires an understanding of all the various ways the organization might use the data. Some of the more common uses are:

- Targeting customers for a direct-marketing program such as direct mail
- Developing a system so that field salespeople have access to important customer information as they prepare to make sales calls
- Making it possible for internal salespeople to be able to access the database when a customer calls to place an order
- Giving the service department and customer relations department access to customer data as they deal with inquiries and complaints

In the case of customer complaints, a profitable customer may be dealt with differently than a marginal customer who holds little potential earnings for the firm. Although the company does not want to alienate any customer, some obviously receive greater attention than others.

The development of a quality data warehouse begins with identification of any current information that may be available to the firm in some form. External data are then added to allow for better targeting of marketing programs. One method a firm can use to enrich internally generated data is geocoding. **Geocoding** is adding geographic codes to each customer record. This allows the company to plot the addresses of customers on a map. Geocoding is especially helpful as a firm makes decisions about placements of retail outlets.

Further, geocoding makes it possible to incorporate demographic information with some lifestyle information in individual records. Thus, information such as age, income, education, disposable income, net worth, number of children, race, employment, and whether the individual rents or owns a home may be included with each record. Lifestyle data can be developed so that the marketing team can discover media habits, most notably magazine and newspaper readerships along with other pertinent information that applies to specific geographic areas. A number of firms do this through combining addresses supplied to them with other information available through external sources.

A company can either hire an external firm to geocode files or perform the task internally by utilizing geocoding software, one version of which is called CACI Coder/Plus. Based on the individual's address, the CACI Coder/Plus identifies a "cluster" in which the address belongs. For example, if the majority of a firm's customers are classified as 3B, or Enterprising Young Singles in the CACI system, the firm knows that this group dines out frequently and spends money on furniture, small appliances, and apparel. Members of this group like to rent videos and are inclined to use personal computers both at home and at work. Media preferences of the 3B group are *Entertainment Weekly* and the *Wall Street Journal.* By locating the zip codes where 3Bs have a major presence, the retailer can target this group and know where to locate a retail outlet.

A company that is not interested in building another facility could use the information for the purposes of directing mass-mailings instead. A direct-mail program aimed at 3Bs would start by acquiring a mailing list of zip codes containing a large percentage of 3Bs. Mailings are then sent to those zip codes. This saves money and the recipients are more likely to respond to the message.[3]

A data warehouse is built based on the information available at a reasonable cost to the organization and the IMC goals established at the outset. The information not only must be important or relevant but also must be convenient and accessible to those who will work with the database. At that point, effective data mining is possible.

Integrated Learning Experience

Many companies turn to professional firms for assistance when developing a data warehouse. A company in New Zealand called Brains (www.brains.co.nz) has developed a customer relationship management system that allows companies to develop a sophisticated database. U.S. firms that provide similar services are Sagent Technology at www.qmsolft.com and Centrus at www.centrus.com. Access these Web sites to see what types of services they offer. What information can they add to a firm's database that would turn the database into a data warehouse? A major source of commercial data that can be added to a firm's database is provided by Donnelly Marketing at www.donnellymarketing.com. From its "Products and Services" menu, find the types of data a firm can purchase that would help supplement a database.

stop!

Mining data for information

Just as miners panned for gold, market analysts sift through mountains of data for information to help the firm better understand customers. **Data mining** normally involves one of two approaches: (1) building profiles of customer groups or (2) preparing models that predict future purchase behaviors based on past purchases.

First, data mining can be used to develop a profile of a firm's best customers. This profile helps identify prospective customers. It can be used to develop specific marketing programs for the firm's primary ongoing customers.

The profile can be used as a yardstick to evaluate current customers who are not in the high-quality category. Through this effort, customers who are viable prospects for upgrades receive sales calls. The object is to move them from being average customers to being "good" customers or to have a higher value.

A firm that sells several different types of goods or services can develop multiple profiles, one for each product or service group. These profiles identify current customers for cross-selling of other goods or services. To do so, a list of prospects to be called upon by field sales reps is generated. Some customers may be contacted only by mail or a telemarketer program. Others are deleted because they do not match a profile and are not likely to make purchases.

The second use of data mining is to develop models that predict future sales based on past sales activities. For instance, Staples, Inc. used modeling to develop an understanding of the company's catalog customers. The model was designed to examine Staples' current customers in order to identify the specific names of the most frequent catalog buyers. Then, by mailing to only this portion of the list, Staples reduced mailing costs and increased response rates.

According to Tom Rocco, vice president of Rodale Press publishing company, "Response modeling is an important part of the mailing program for many of the companies that rent our lists. They can tighten their mail programs to target the most likely respondents."[4] In the future, more companies will be able to take advantage of modeling procedures to mine their own customer databases and also to select names from commercial sources.

The ability to develop customer profiles through data mining and data modeling has changed the way marketers purchase data. In the past, a firm planning a direct-mail campaign would purchase a list of names and addresses that best matched the company's customers. Currently, many companies refuse to purchase whole lists. Instead, they extract names from a list based on a customer profile or model developed from an understanding of their own customers.

The method that is used to mine the data is determined by specific informational needs. If the firm wants to develop a direct-mail program to current customers, a different process is used than if the firm wants to develop a direct-mail program to attract new customers. Profiles and models assist in designing the database best suited for these programs.

Developing marketing programs

Once the data have been mined for information, the organization is ready to develop marketing programs. The data provide clues about the best approach for each group of customers. Marketers use this data to determine which sales promotions have the best odds of success as well as the ones that will not work. Database information gives insights regarding where to advertise and the type of appeal that might spark heightened interest in a particular group of customers. The information gleaned from a data warehouse puts the firm in a better position to develop a comprehensive IMC program.

To illustrate how data mining assists in the development of marketing programs, think about a department store chain such as ZCMI, mentioned earlier in this chapter. If the store intends to launch a new high-end line of men's clothing, the first step would be to identify names of customers from the company's database who responded to the last marketing promotion featuring similar products. Next, the marketing team would query the system to identify all shoppers who purchased men's apparel during the last year.

Once the list was generated, company leaders would decide if they have sufficient names from internal sources or if more names are needed. If more are needed, the company might seek out external sources. Then the data could be mined by cross-referencing shopping habits. People who purchase specific brands, such as Polo or Tommy Hilfiger, may be enticed to try a new brand, if the marketing appeal were directed properly toward that group of shoppers. Another strategy might be to locate men who purchased expensive shoes within the last year. The idea would be to use the database to produce names to contact for this special promotion.

Using this type of method, ZCMI tested to see how effective a targeted mailing offer would be. In that program, ZCMI mailed out 13,000 pieces of mail. Five thousand ads were sent to specific customers who matched the profile of the best potential buyers. The other 8,000 were sent to a nonfocused group of people who simply had made a purchase at ZCMI. The database technology allowed ZCMI to personalize the ad to the specific group of 5,000. The result was that the response rate for the targeted mailings was 50 percent greater than for the nonfocused mass-mailing. More importantly, the average transaction size was double for the targeted group over the nonfocused mass-mailing group.[5]

Although the primary purpose of a database may be to target certain customers with specific messages, it also can be used to enhance service to all customers. To do so requires that all of the information about each customer be readily available to employees, salespeople, and other customer contact persons who deal with customers.

To illustrate how a database can enhance service and develop loyalty among a firm's customers, consider a business traveler arriving at a hotel in Denver. Typically, upon arriving in Denver, the business traveler would check in with a clerk who would confirm that the traveler wants a nonsmoking room with a queen-size bed. Usually no other significant conversation takes place. On the other hand, if the clerk at the front desk has access to all of the business traveler's information, other conversations might take place after the clerk confirms the reservation. For instance, the clerk could say, "I see you were in Chicago last week at one of our hotels. How was your stay there?"

After the response, the clerk could add, "I made sure your room has a second line and voice mail. We also stocked your refrigerator with sparkling water, which I understand you prefer." Or the clerk could say, "When you were at Chicago, you requested copies of the *New York Times* and *USA Today*. Would you like us to get them for you while you're staying in Denver?"

Training clerks and employees of a hotel to look up information from the hotel's database regularly can lead them to provide better service for regular customers. The hotel would be able to offer a personalized form of service unavailable at other hotels, creating a competitive advantage in the lucrative repeat-business market. This same technology can be used by many businesses to enhance the level of personalized service. The major benefit of this type of program is that it increases brand loyalty or loyalty to a particular service provider.

Database programs are used in other parts of the marketing program as well. Unfortunately, few companies use their data warehouse to provide information to advertising creatives, consumer promotion managers, trade promotion managers, or other communication personnel within and external to the firm. Many advertising firms give creatives basic demographic information about the client's customers. The advertising company then tries to discover the best ways of reaching those customers. Seldom has there been contact between the creatives and the database marketing department.

In the modern marketplace, account executives are increasingly interested in making sure someone from the client's database department is part of the project team. By supplying the creatives with information such as psychographics, attitudes, purchase behaviors, lifestyles, and trends, creatives are better able to design a creative piece with an ideal appeal to consumers. The **creative brief,** as described in Chapter 7, should supply the creative with as much information as possible about customers and potential customers. The company relies on its database to be able to provide this information. Further, the account executive should insist that this information is made available to the team. In many cases, it may be beneficial for the individuals managing the IMC database to meet directly with the advertising agency's creative staff.

A wide variety of marketing programs can result from database analysis. Effective companies are adept at utilizing data in both consumer and business markets. Currently, these same organizations combine old techniques with the endless set of new possibilities yielded by the Internet to develop even stronger ties with customers and potential new clients. To complete the program successfully, it is a good idea to assess the firm's progress toward its marketing goals.

Evaluating marketing programs and data warehouses

A high-quality data warehouse contains information about as many customers as possible. Each transaction is recorded on a continual basis. This allows for the analysis of various purchasing trends among customer groups and even of individual customers. More importantly, by continually collecting information the firm is able to evaluate its overall IMC program. Questions to be answered can be as general or as specific as the ones that follow.

- Do our customers know our overall theme and image? Is this image positive?
- Have we moved toward improved brand equity in the past year?
- Which items are our customers most inclined to buy? Which are not selling well? Do we know why?
- Is our customer base changing? Is this because we changed, or because a new group is best suited to our products?
- What things should be done in the future to improve our position?
- What type of customer can we reach that we currently do not serve? How should we attack this marketplace?

This evaluation is necessary to determine which programs work and which do not. From this evaluation, the marketing program can be modified to better meet the needs of those being targeted.

One application of a customer database is the attempt to market directly to consumers or businesses that purchase the product. A new form of direct marketing is called permission marketing. These and other uses of databases are described next.

stop!

Integrated Learning Experience

One of the major advantages of maintaining a database is the opportunity to mine it for information about current customers and prospective customers. AIM Marketing at www.aim-mktg.com offers predictive modeling and analysis. DB-Marketing at www.db-marketing.com offers both data mining services as well as geomarketing services. From the DB-Marketing Web site, examine what is said about database marketing and geomarketing. A third company you may want to access for information about data mining is Database Marketing Solutions at www.database-marketing.com.

direct marketing

Direct-marketing programs are designed to develop closer relationships with customers. They can enhance loyalty to a brand or company instead of loyalty to retailer. Direct-marketing programs often reap greater profits, because the middle channel members are bypassed. Figure 15.4 identifies the most typical forms of direct marketing. Regardless of the type chosen, it is important to display a toll-free number and a Web site frequently so that consumers can contact the company for additional information.

- ❯ Mail
- ❯ Catalogs
- ❯ Telemarketing
- ❯ Mass-media
- ❯ Alternative media
- ❯ The Internet
- ❯ E-mail

Methods of Direct Marketing

FIGURE 15.4

Mail

The most common form of direct marketing is through the mail. Mail is an effective direct-marketing tool for everything from generating leads to obtaining orders. The impact of direct mail is easily measurable in terms of comparing the number mailed to the number of responses and sales. Direct mail can be easily targeted to various consumer groups. Marketing teams can test every component of a direct-mail campaign, including the type of offer, the copy in the ad, graphics used, color, and the size of the direct-mail packet.

Most consumers and businesses receive several direct-mail offers on a daily basis. The use of database programs allows marketers to decrease the total number of pieces sent. Also, effective database management means the company can increase the number of mailings to those selected. Many credit card companies are quite sophisticated at identifying the best candidates for offers. The down side is that all of the other credit card companies have identified the same set of consumers. The result is that these individuals receive multiple mailings from credit card companies and others. The abundance of offers means most tend not to be opened.

Direct mail is often used by business-to-business operations. Cysive, a developer of e-business systems, developed a very successful direct-mail marketing program. The firm based its marketing approach on how e-business systems are developed by Cysive's experts.

Cysive's e-systems are designed by engineers with input from the company's clients. While looking for a way to market Cysive, John Saaty, the company's vice president of marketing, compared the building of an e-system to that of constructing a building. A firm that wants a state-of-the-art facility would hire professional contractors to do the work. The same should be true for the building of an e-system. It should be constructed by expert engineers. According to Saaty, "70% of all e-commerce projects fail because of lack of expertise of those constructing the Web site."

Using the concept of building an e-system, the Cysive advertisement was designed featuring a hammer hitting an e-nail. The slogan "E-business systems built like nobody's e-business" is supported by ad copy highlighting how senior engineers would build a system that would be scalable, expandable, and secure.

Prior to the direct-mail campaign, Cysive ran the ad shown in select journals and newspapers read by business professionals. Print media such as the *Wall Street Journal, Business Week,* and *Fortune,* were selected. According to Saaty, the two main objectives of the print ad campaign were to "develop brand awareness and produce leads."

The second part of the campaign was a direct mailer. According to Saaty, "The first step is to understand your target market and you must have a specific target market in mind when developing a direct mailer." Using the concept of building an e-business system, Cysive developed a direct mailer aimed at CEOs from large companies, especially Fortune 500 companies. CEOs were targeted for two reasons. First, the type of system that Cysive builds costs in the millions of dollars.

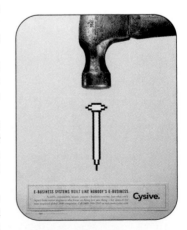

An advertisement used by Cysive to support the company's direct-marketing program. Courtesy of Cysive Inc.

Therefore, it is likely that the CEO would be involved in the decision as well as in the negotiations. Second, if the CEO's attention could be garnered, even if he or she were not involved in the decision process, the CEO might be willing to ask someone in the office to contact Cysive for further information.

Since the target market was Fortune 500 CEOs, Saaty knew the typical direct-mail piece would not work. It had to be something special. Using the concept of building, Cysive developed a direct mailer that included a box with a real hammer. Cysive's logo was placed on the hammer. On the outside of the box were the words "Some e-business systems are held tegether with bubble gum and spit." Inside was the hammer with the phrase, "We take a different approach." The initial survey of CEOs indicated the hammer was well received.

When asked why an actual hammer, which costs the firm much more than a traditional direct-mail piece, Saaty replied, "These were going to CEOs. The traditional approach would not work. We needed something different, something symbolic of building an e-business system. We also wanted something the CEO would not throw away but would be useful. While mailing the actual hammer was 10 times more expensive than the traditional approach, it got the CEO's attention."

Approximately 500 hammers were mailed to CEOs. The response rate was 2 percent to 3 percent. Cysive eventually signed a multimillion dollar contract. According to Saaty, "Just the one contract covered the cost of the direct-mail program." Salespeople followed up every lead generated from the direct mailing. In addition, salespeople contacted those who did not respond. In almost all cases, the hammer opened the door to talk to the CEO or some other high-ranking official.

Cysive plans a second marketing program as a follow-up. Using the same building concept, Cysive plans to mail out screwdrivers, pliers, and other tools. According to Saaty, "Not only can these tools be used around the office, they illustrate very effectively our goal of building e-business systems with senior engineers." The same procedure will be used with national advertising, direct marketing, and then sales calls. It is a well-designed IMC plan providing direct leads for the sales force.

To be effective, firms need quality data warehouses that can help them locate the best prospects. Further, companies need information to assist them in developing messages that are more likely to create enough interest so that consumers read the offer instead of tossing it into the wastebasket. To do so requires companies to do more than simply identify their best prospects based on one characteristic such as location. They must then look closely at other variables, such as attitudes, opinions, interests, and demographics in order to design a message with a stronger appeal.

Although direct mail is frequently sent to whites, it is not as likely to reach some minority groups. According to a recent Hispanic consumer survey, Hispanics average only 10 pieces of direct-mail items per month. Because they receive so much less, 72 percent of Hispanics always read their direct mail and 66 percent respond to direct-mail offers. These positive results have led firms such as Lazos Latinos and Nia Direct to specialize in direct marketing to Hispanic communities.[6]

To develop its African American and Hispanic database, Nia Direct gathers names and information from not-for-profit organizations, minority fraternities and sororities, churches, and civic groups. To obtain this information, Nia offers the not-for-profit organization free advertising and consulting services. The company then combines the information from purchased database information and information from the Bureau of Labor Statistics and U.S. Census Bureau. Once these data are collected, Nia runs a computer regression analysis to determine response patterns among the minorities in its database. The database management team then develops profiles spelling out the type of minority person most likely to respond to a specific offer.

Using this method, Nia Direct has developed an extensive database. To get consumers to open the direct mail, the envelope has been designed with ethnic images or cultural symbols that many recognize. Realizing the opportunity to expand their presence to minorities, companies such as Kraft Foods, JCPenney, and Hallmark Cards have hired Nia Direct to design direct-mail pieces for them. In addition to envelope design, the message, prizes, offers, coupons, and other features must be targeted to the minority and be something of interest to members of the group.[7]

Two trends have enhanced the quality of direct-mail programs. The first is greater sophistication in database management. Companies are able to gather large amounts of data from both internal and external sources. Also, the people managing these databases are more skilled at processing information to refine direct-mail campaigns.

Second, technology has greatly improved, leading to higher-quality execution of direct-mail pieces. The details available from databases make it possible to design one-on-one communications with potential customers. Instead of mass runs of standardized messages, it is now possible to prepare individual pieces addressed to specific customers.

The new technology that takes advantage of these two trends is called **digital direct-to-press.** It is especially attractive in the business-to-business market. Digital direct-to-press instructs a computer to send a specific message to a printer. This gives the marketing team a high-quality one-of-a-kind piece to send to each potential customer, and each one can be adapted to the specific company. In the business-to-business sector, information about the firm's customers and the locations of their customer's offices can be included in the mailing. The specific pitch is designed and customized for each customer.[8]

Digital direct-to-press can also be sent to homes. Thus, one direct-mail piece from a company such as Avon may display the image of a bottle of perfume or lipstick while the next has a picture of products for children. Past purchase information may drive the process, and customers feel that the firm remembers what they purchased last. It is also possible to include the names of children, birthdays, or even hobbies into what is sent to various customers.

The down side to digital direct-to-press is the cost. To personalize each direct-mail piece is much more expensive than running mass offers with only a personalized cover letter. It takes a great deal of expertise to design a computer program that results in these personalized messages, which adds to the cost due to a higher payroll. On the other hand, the advantage is a higher response rate to these special mailings.

The large volume of junk mail received by consumers and businesses has created negative attitudes toward direct-mail marketing similar to the way people react to telemarketing. Many businesses are contacted by direct marketers as frequently as consumers. Consequently, marketing programs must be designed to cut through the clutter.

Catalogs

One direct-marketing approach that has survived is a catalog program. Many consumers tend to be more favorable in their responses to catalogs. Catalogs are viewed at one's leisure. Consequently, they have an impact for a longer period of time than does a direct-mail piece or a telemarketing phone call. Catalogs are low-pressure offers that allow consumers time to consider goods they may want and the prices they are willing to pay. Catalog copy rarely says, "Act today and save 25 percent." Also, catalog copy doesn't sound like a telemarketer saying, "All I need to do is to verify your address for you to have this fantastic product."

Many consumers save catalogs. This means other family members, friends, and acquaintances may all see the same offer. In business-to-business settings, catalogs are often passed along to other members of the buying center or filed for future use, giving them a longer life. Most direct-mail pieces and telemarketing offers are immediately discarded, making catalogs a viable alternative.

The key to successful cataloging is an enhanced database. A company with a solid understanding of its individual and business customers can develop and target catalogs to reach those customers. Most large catalog companies including L.L. Bean, Spiegel, and JCPenney create specialty catalogs geared to specific market segments. Specialty catalogs are smaller, which reduces costs but still displays the goods customers are most likely to purchase. For example, consumers who have purchased camping supplies in the past should receive catalogs containing special coupons for items such as hiking boots. Also, an entry form for a contest in which the prize is a camping trip to Yellowstone National Park or the Smoky Mountains may generate additional interest in the catalog and the items being featured.

For business-to-business customers, catalogs are often essential selling tools. They provide standard information that can be passed on to various members of the buying center. As noted in Communication Action Box below, a Web site is also important. The site can be designed to convey technical information that the buying center's engineer may wish to see. It can provide information about purchasing procedures and prices for the purchasing agent. Thus, the Internet is more flexible than a catalog by itself. Together the two media provide more of the essential information required by various members of the buying center.

Telemarketing

Telemarketing is another tool used for direct marketing. Database information makes it possible for callers to contact the best prospects in order to sell merchan-

communication**action**

Cataloging and Interneting

The Internet has changed the nature of catalog marketing. Although some catalogers have ignored the Internet, most realize that they must find ways to effectively leverage what the Web has to offer. This can be done in several ways. One way is to place an entire catalog on a Web site. Customers can then order either by a typical catalog response (an order form or phone call) or via the Internet. A second approach is to use the Web to advertise the catalog. Only those who make requests at the Web site are sent catalogs. Most companies are somewhere between, which means they place their most requested products on the Internet as well as encourage customers to order directly from the site. For a full listing of products and greater detail, customers can order the complete catalog.

A reverse trend is also occurring. Some companies are placing their Web address on catalogs and encouraging customers to access the Internet for more details and to place orders. When these materials are organized properly, a large number of products can be displayed on the site without making it too slow to access each item.

Companies that use catalogs realize that, in most cases, they are serving a diverse audience. The marketing team should provide both catalogs and a Web page. Some consumers will use only one or the other to place an order; however, more and more individuals use both to examine merchandise. Often, the telephone is still used to place an order, because many consumers are still skeptical about giving out a credit card number over the Internet.

In the business-to-business sector, merging catalogs and the Internet is practically essential for survival. Many businesses want accounts set up on the Internet. These customers want individualized access to that account as well. This is advantageous to the vendor, because prices may vary depending on size of order, past orders, and other factors. As a result, many companies deal with pricing issues by giving individualized entries to their Web sites via passwords. For companies offering cumulative discounts, having a Web site that allows for different pricing is a valuable addition to a marketing program.

For users, the Internet provides information about the benefits, uses, and specifications of various products. In the future, expect to see greater merging of catalogs and Web sites, complete with audio, streaming video, and other new techniques.

Telemarketing companies will need to improve the targeting of their efforts: if they want to continue to succeed. Courtesy of Liaison Agency, Inc. Photograph by Seth Resnick.

dise. Consumers receive a vast number of telemarketing calls from companies each day. These firms offer credit cards, long-distance telephone service, and other products. In the future, telemarketing companies will need to improve the targeting of efforts if they want to continue to succeed.

Inbound telemarketing can be an important component of a direct-marketing campaign. Taking inbound calls helps support messages provided in other media. Consequently, toll-free numbers should be prominently and frequently displayed in all direct-marketing and promotional materials in order make sure consumers know where to go to gather additional information and place orders.

Mass-media

Mass-media are often part of a direct-marketing campaign.[9] The most common forms of mass-media used in direct marketing are television, radio, magazines, and newspapers. Television delivers access to a mass audience. For products with a more general appeal to the masses, network television is an excellent medium to reach many consumers with a single message. Again, an ad should include a toll-free number and a Web site so that consumers are able to place orders quickly. They also can request further information and ask questions about the product or company. Direct marketing through television ads is easier now that both network and cable television have sound statistics reflecting audience characteristics. Both demographic and psychographic information are available from each network, station, and even for individual shows. Cable television is superior to network television for narrower markets. Thus, a sports channel is better for selling subscriptions to *Sports Illustrated* or *ESPN Magazine*. Most companies have excellent opportunities to match a cable television audience with a target profile.

Radio does not have the reach of television but still can be used to convey strong messages. Radio ads can effectively convey direct-marketing messages by utilizing popular spokespersons and slice-of-life vignettes. Toll-free numbers and Web addresses stated in radio ads must be easy to remember and repeated frequently, because consumers may not have the opportunity to write them down. Radio allows marketers to target their audiences to specific types of consumers, usually based on the station's format.

Radio is an excellent method to reinforce direct-marketing campaigns from other media. In fact, most companies use radio to support other direct-marketing media, but seldom use it alone. The primary exception occurs when a direct-marketing campaign is geographically concentrated. Even then, however, radio normally serves best as a supplement to other media.

Print media (newspapers and magazines) are excellent for direct-marketing programs. They can be utilized to target specific audiences. Magazines can be sent to specific market segments, and newspapers can provide coverage in specific geographic regions. Products with a wider appeal can be featured in national newspapers and magazines. Magazines offer detailed information about the demographics and psychographics of subscribers. Therefore, marketing companies can easily identify magazines that fit profiles of key potential customers. Print ads should highlight toll-free numbers and Web site addresses for consumers, so that they are easy to see.

Alternative media

In recent years, direct marketing has expanded to include what are called alternative media. Alternative media offer several unique new ways to reach consumers. The three most common alternative media are:

1. Package insert programs (PIPs)
2. Ride-along programs
3. Card packs

Package insert programs (PIPs) are direct-marketing materials placed in mail-order fulfillment packages. For example, when a BMG Music Club member orders a CD, inserts are placed in the box in which the CD is shipped. Inserts normally sell products related to music, such as stereo equipment, but also can offer other products such as clothes, jewelry, customized checks, and calendars.

Ride-alongs are direct-marketing materials that accompany or are placed along with another company's catalog or direct-mail piece. For example, when BMG Music sends out a monthly catalog featuring the selection for the month, ride-along materials often are included. As with PIPs, the products represented by the ride-along materials are often related to music but can be for any type of product.

PIPs and ride-alongs are low-cost approaches to reaching a well-defined target market. The target market is defined because recipients are customers of the firm. In the case of BMG music, the consumer has already agreed to receive the monthly catalog or the CDs. Both PIPs and ride-alongs are cheaper than direct mail, because fewer are sent and postage costs are lower.

A **card pack** is a deck of 20 to 50 business reply cards, normally 3½ by 5, placed in a plastic pack. While some card packs are directed toward consumers, most are aimed at business-to-business markets. The primary advantage of the card packs is the low cost. The average CPM cost is only $20 to $35 per thousand compared to $40 to $70 for either PIPs or ride-alongs. The disadvantage is that the company's card is only one of the 20 to 50 cards being sent to the business or consumer.[10]

The Internet

The Internet provides a new channel for direct marketing. For most companies, the Internet is a place for consumers and businesses to get more information. For many, using the Internet is less intrusive than calling a toll-free number. Once on the Internet, many consumers are willing to place orders.

Many companies use the Internet to display goods and services customers can order directly. Banner ads from other sites are often used to encourage consumers to access the firm's Web site. Software such as Connectify Direct, NCR's Relationship Optimizer, and Prime Response Prime@Vantage help firms create interactive direct-marketing programs. The software analyzes consumer purchases, click-streams, and other customer interactions. This information is then combined with demographic and psychographic data from either an internal database or an external database firm. Using all of this information, the software suggests the goods and services the consumer is most likely to consider. Often, this can be done while the consumer is still on-line.

Internet direct-marketing programs are not only fast, but the goods and services that are suggested to the consumer can be based on the individual's past purchasing or click-stream behaviors. For example, a consumer who purchases a tent and looks at various camping supplies can be provided ads about camping equipment. A consumer who has a history of using premiums can be given quick access to premiums similar to those he or she has used in the past.

E-mail

In addition to Web site Internet programs, many companies are developing e-mail direct-marketing campaigns. E-mail makes it possible for the company to deliver customized messages or promotions. One recent success story in the area of e-mail direct marketing was generated by Williams-Sonoma Inc., a retailer of cookware and household goods. The firm developed an e-mail campaign with the objective of attracting customers into the store and also to promote Williams-Sonoma's on-line bridal registry. Approximately 5 percent of the customers contacted by e-mail visited a local Williams-Sonoma store. This total was considerably higher than any direct-mail method the company had used before.[11]

International concerns in direct marketing

Direct marketing across international borders provides several unique challenges for firms. In addition to language differences, each country has a different postal system. Even for companies that take orders across the Internet, there is still the problem of shipping merchandise to another country. For American companies, Europe is one of the most attractive markets because of its large population and the move toward one currency.

Most larger companies translate direct-marketing materials and catalogs into the native language of the majority of people in the target country. Then, the company must hire operators who can speak the language of the country to handle inbound telephone orders and to answer questions. Usually the best approach is to use a native call center in each country.

For smaller companies, preparing marketing materials and catalogs in English works well in most markets. Many residents of Europe speak English as a second language. At the same time, when developing English materials for Europe, it is important to keep the language simple. Many potential customers may have difficulty understanding some English terminology.[12]

Integrated Learning Experience

A number of direct-marketing agencies exist offering a variety of services. To locate a direct-marketing agency in your area, access Agency CompPile at www.agencycompile.com. Select agencies with direct-marketing capability or database marketing firms. Select an area and an industry you are interested in studying. What agencies were listed? Examine several of them to get a feel for the types of services they offer. One well-known firm is Direct Marketing Resources at www.dmrdirect.com. Another high-profile association for direct marketing is the Direct Marketing Association at www.the-dma.org. Access this Web page and read some recent articles about direct marketing.

stop!

permission marketing

A new form of database marketing that is growing in popularity is called **permission marketing.** In a permission marketing program, the company sends promotional information only to consumers who give the company permission to do so. The idea behind permission marketing is that the company does not intrude on consumers with unwanted junk mail, catalogs, or telemarketing calls. Response rates are often higher in permission marketing efforts, because consumers have given the company permission to contact them. People who are not interested in the products do not receive marketing materials, thereby reducing overall marketing costs.

Three large auto manufacturers—General Motors, Ford Motor Company, and DaimlerChrysler—have become involved in permission marketing programs.[13]

Each uses a slightly different approach. All three request permission from individuals in their database prior to marketing to them.

GM had information from millions of customers in its database. Consequently, GM wanted to find ways of tapping into that database to increase sales. Realizing customers are not likely to buy another automobile, GM used its huge database to sell other products. The company advertises digital TVs, satellite radios, credit cards, loans, home mortgages, and insurance to permission marketing customers. GM does pitch its cars and trucks in the same contacts; however, the major emphasis is on nonautomotive products.

GM launched a permission marketing program in 1995 by offering incentives to the company's credit card holders. The incentives were designed to get additional information from the customer and attain permission to market to them. Additional information can be gathered this way or it also can be purchased from database marketing firms. Thus, it is not essential to request additional information to develop a permission marketing program. The key however, is to obtain a large bank of information about each customer who has given permission. In the process of requesting permission, GM asked customers the method they preferred:

- Telephone
- Mail
- E-mail

GM assured customers they would not be contacted by salespeople from local auto dealers. GM also assured customers they could discontinue the program at any time.

While GM sells a variety of products, Ford Motor Company limits its permission marketing program to only automotive products. Ford has been slower in developing a program because the company previously maintained twelve different customer databases. After several years, these were sorted down to only three. Within the next few years, Ford should have all of the information in one data warehouse, which is essential to establishing an extensive direct-marketing program. In this one comprehensive database, Ford will have considerable personal information about each customer including a mailing address, e-mail address, and telephone and pager numbers. To reach this point, every piece of information gathered at a local automotive dealer to service a vehicle must be entered into the master data file.

Ford recently purchased 1,900 Kwik-Fit auto repair centers. Kwik-Fit is Europe's largest automobile repair facility. Through Kwik-Fit, Ford is marketing repairs not covered by a warranty. Ford also sells auto insurance and offers Ford vehicle parts over the Internet.

DaimlerChrysler has linked all of its databases into a system called COIN, or the Customer Owner Information Network. The company markets automotive products in its permission program in a manner similar to what Ford Motor Company does. The difference is that DaimlerChrysler concentrates more on marketing vehicles rather than parts, insurance, or repairs.

To understand the potential impact permission marketing can have for a firm, it is helpful to compare it to the more traditional forms of marketing using direct mail or advertising. These traditional approaches suffer the following disadvantages:

- Clutter
- Competition
- Brand parity problems
- A short time period to respond

Permission marketing has several advantages that arise from requesting consent to market to an individual or business. First the agreement makes it possible to

> ❶ **Obtain permission from the customer**
>
> ❷ **Offer the consumer a curriculum over time**
>
> ❸ **Reinforce the incentive to continue the relationship**
>
> ❹ **Increase the level of permission**
>
> ❺ **Leverage the permission to benefit both parties**

**Steps in Developing
a Permission
Marketing Program**

Source: Seth Godin, "Permission Marketing: The Way to Make Advertising Work Again," *Direct Marketing,* (May 1999) Vol. 62, No. 1, pp. 41–43.

FIGURE 15.5

develop a strong relationship with a customer over time. This bond between the consumer and the company helps overcome the clutter, competition, and brand parity problems associated with other marketing efforts. In addition, customers who participate in permission programs often look forward to hearing from the company. The messages sent are normally personally relevant to the customer. GM, Ford, and DaimlerChrysler have only touched the surface in terms of developing a true permission marketing program. Figure 15.5 outlines the steps that should be used in a permission program.[14]

The first step in permission marketing is to *obtain the permission of the consumer.* This usually requires offering the customer an incentive for volunteering, and the incentive must be of value to the customer. Otherwise the offer will be ignored and the result is no different than those obtained from the other offers the consumer receives. The inducement can be information, entertainment, a sweepstakes prize, a gift, or cash. Whatever is selected, the incentive must be overt, it must be obvious, it must be of value to the customer, and it must be easily and quickly delivered to the individual.

Once the consumer has consented, then the marketer is ready to *offer the consumer a full curriculum of information.* There is no longer a need to design advertisements and direct-marketing materials with the primary goal of gaining the consumer's attention, because the person has already agreed to receive information. Instead, the information must be educational and teach the consumer about the products and services being offered. Little by little, the consumer should receive more information about the firm's products and services.

The third step is to *reinforce the incentive.* Over time, the consumer may become less compelled to participate by the initial incentive. Therefore, new or different incentives should be offered to encourage the customer to continue the relationship. Often these incentives are in the form of premiums that require the consumer to make a purchase. At this point, it is important for the business to have an array of incentives from which the consumer can choose. A two-way communication channel should be opened with consumers, so that they believe they have a voice in choosing their incentives.

The fourth step is to *increase the permission level from the consumer.* This step coincides with step three. The goal is to gather more information from the consumer while obtaining a deeper commitment. During this step the marketer can gather information about the consumer's family, life, hobbies, interests, attitudes, and opinions. This information allows the firm to do a better job of marketing products to specific individuals. It also gives them additional information to identify them as part of a market segment that is the most likely to respond to certain permission marketing techniques.

The final step is to *leverage the information* gathered in step four to provide for the needs of the customer more effectively. During this stage brand loyalty is developed as both parties benefit from the relationship. The firm has a customer willing to purchase additional goods and services. The person also provides new personal information to the company. The customer benefits from having a source of reliable products. Incentives, special promotional offers, and direct communication with the company help customers feel special. A win–win situation for both parties results.

The most well-known permission marketing programs are probably record and book clubs. These clubs seek permission from consumers to send them either a record or book offer each month. In the past, most record clubs sent the offer and if the consumer did not respond, the record of the month was automatically sent. More recently, however, this practice has been discontinued because of too many customer complaints about receiving unwanted items. Members of the Book of the Month Club receive a book that is automatically selected and sent. Members trust the Book of the Month Club to make selections for them.

Permission marketing can be performed through various channels and the Internet appears to be one of the most promising new avenues. The types of consumers who have computers and the Internet match the profile of consumers who are more likely to respond to permission marketing offers. This makes it easier to develop two-way communication between the company and the customer.

Direct mail and the telephone are the other two channels that are often used for permission marketing. Direct mail works for some consumers, yet it is more difficult to develop a strong relationships with these customers. The telephone is better at developing two-way communication but is also more expensive. Marketing managers must carefully choose the venue that reaches members of the target market most effectively.

stop!

Integrated Learning Experience

Permission marketing has gained considerable popularity on the Internet. Access the following firms with permission marketing services to see what types of services each offers. Compare and contrast the firms. Which firms do you like and which ones do you not like?

E@symail (www.easymailinteractive.com)
TKL Interactive at (www.tkinteractive.com)
United Marketing Group, Inc. (www.united-marketinggroup.com)
Focalex, Inc. (www.focalex.com)
Targetmails, Inc. (www.targetmails.com)

frequency programs

A **frequency program** is an incentive plan designed to cause customers to make repeat purchases. Many companies try to build brand loyalty for the products, but in reality repeat purchase behavior is the best they can hope for. This is especially true for product categories where considerable brand parity exists and consumers see very little difference between the brands. The airline industry faces this situation. Both leisure and business travelers tend to choose the airline with the best schedule and best fare. Little brand loyalty exists. To gain repeat purchases, several airlines started frequent-flyer clubs. The primary goal of most frequent-flyer programs is to encourage consumers to continue patronizing a particular airline. The customer earns points on each flight, which can be used for a free upgrade or a free ticket. Figure 15.6 lists various reasons for developing a frequency program.

Companies develop frequency programs for two primary reasons. The first is to develop loyalty among their own customers. The second is to match or preempt the competition. Marketing experts have known for years that it is cheaper to retain customers than to try to win new ones. Seeking to keep a customer can help to

> **Maintain sales, margins, or profits**

> **Increase loyalty of existing customers**

> **Preempt or match a competitor's frequency program**

> **Induce cross-selling to existing customers**

> **Differentiate a parity brand**

> **Preempt the entry of a new brand**

Frequency Program Objectives

FIGURE 15.6

Source: Grahame R. Dowling and Mark Uncles, "Do Customer Loyalty Programs Really Work?" *Sloan Management Review* (Summer 1997). Vol. 38, No. 4, pp. 71–82.

increase sales to the person over time while creating a stronger bond with the individual. This bond makes it possible for the company to cross-sell other goods and services.

Frequency programs were first developed as a method to differentiate one brand from its competition. Unfortunately, the differentiation soon disappeared as competitors responded with their own frequency programs. In the airline industry, all carriers have frequent-flyer programs. The same is now occurring in the lodging industry. Most of the major hotels have developed frequency programs. Those who are resistant to the idea must follow suit or risk losing customers.

In Japan, the idea of a frequency program is in its infancy. The Japanese culture dictates a high level of service and courtesy within the business environment. The economic crisis of the 1990s, deregulation, and increased global competition have caused some Japanese firms to shift to a new strategy.

One of the first data-based loyalty programs in Japan was launched by Oura Oil, a giant gasoline retailer. Oura Oil built its market share by providing outstanding service, much higher than is customary in the United States.[15] From the moment a customer arrived in an Oura station until the person departed, attendants dressed in starched, white uniforms catered to his or her every need with courteous bows offered on numerous occasions. Service employees would pump the gas, clean the windshield and lights, check tire pressure, and handle the payment.

When the government deregulated some industries, self-service pumps were allowed in Japan. With the rise of hypermarts and self-service retailing in Japan, the culture was beginning to change, and a high level of customer service was not sufficient to keep customers anymore. Oura estimated that 30 percent of its customers would prefer cheaper gas prices. To combat these competitive forces, Oura developed a loyalty database program called the "Five-Up Club." The program offered customer rewards. The Five-Up Club program was modeled after the best retail loyalty programs in the world, such as those created by Zellers in Canada and Superquinn in Ireland.

A membership in the Five-Up Club is activated when the individual completes an application form that provides the firm with key demographic information. The customer submits his or her name, address, telephone number, fax number, birth date, as well as the make and model of the individual's car. Since half of the Japanese households have fax machines, the fax number is also used in the development of the loyalty program. As a reward for enrolling in the Five-Up Club, consumers received membership cards and "welcome" gifts such as a Five-Up Club coffee mug. Certificate points are earned for each purchase. These points can be redeemed for gift certificates or merchandise. The gift certificates can be redeemed at Oura stations and in some department stores. Other retailers such as Kentucky Fried Chicken, SOGO Department Stores, and the Japan Travel Bureau purchased

> ▶ **Design the program to enhance the value of the product**
>
> ▶ **Fully cost the loyalty program**
>
> ▶ **Design a reward structure that maximizes a customer's motivation to make the next purchase.**

Building a Loyalty Program

FIGURE 15.7

Source: Grahame R. Dowling and Mark Uncles, "Do Customer Loyalty Programs Really Work?" *Sloan Management Review* (Summer 1997), Vol. 38, No. 4, pp. 71–82.

certificate points from Oura and gave them to their customers. These types of partner relationships increased the usage and prestige of the Oura Five-Up Club account.

Stronger bonds with Oura are developed through special offers made to club members via mail or fax. Also, each year a birthday gift is sent to members giving them special thanks for previous purchases. The type and value of the birthday gift varies depending on the amount of purchases the member has made during the year. Each member also receives a newsletter that has a questionnaire to complete. The newsletter is a device Oura uses to develop a dialogue between Oura and its customers. Oura has developed a mail-order business for the club members offering imported merchandise. This frequency and loyalty program helped Oura not only to maintain its market share but also to generate a slight increase in sales.

Building a frequency or loyalty program involves the three principles identified in Figure 15.7. The first principle is to *design the program to enhance the value of the product.* Unfortunately, some frequency programs neglect this element. For low-involvement products, where the consumer does not have a strong sense of loyalty, the incentive used in the frequency program is often the reason for the purchase instead of the product itself. When this situation occurs, the consumer will switch to another brand as soon as a competitor offers a more attractive incentive or when the incentive being offered is no longer attractive or is discontinued. Often gasoline company frequency programs become caught in this trap. Consumers use a particular gasoline card or credit card because they want the incentive that is being offered, but drift away quickly when the incentive loses value.

For high-involvement purchases, consumers usually place more value on the product than they do on the incentive. This is normally the case with the automotive frequency programs discussed earlier and with many of the credit card frequency programs that tie into a particular cause. For example, many college graduates receive a credit card sponsored by their alma mater. These individuals are willing to use the card to make purchases so that the college can receive money for scholarships. The same is true for those who use a General Motors credit card or purchase other products offered through General Motors direct-marketing program. Because they like their GM vehicle, the incentives are a desirable bonus.

When designing a frequency program, it is important to *calculate the full cost of the program.* Most frequency programs are more expensive to operate than companies estimate. In addition to the cost of the incentives, firms must allow for database costs, record keeping, mailings, and redemption of incentives. The airlines estimate that frequent-flyer clubs cost between 3 percent and 6 percent of their revenues. Costs are much higher than they first estimated, because most travelers are frequent-flyer members but do not accumulate enough points to receive free tickets. Consequently, keeping records and mailing out status reports add to the costs of the program. These expenses are higher than the actual free tickets given out by many airlines.

The third principle in establishing a loyalty program is to *design a frequency program that maximizes a customer's motivation to make the next purchase.* The goal is to keep the individual from switching to another firm. Providing the proper incentives requires an understanding of the value of a customer. Light users or buyers may join the frequency program to obtain incentives. Unfortunately, a program is not cost effective until the firm is able to increase revenues by cross-selling other products to list users. The cost of maintaining a frequency account is often higher than the profits earned from that account, such as is the case in airline frequent-flyer programs. At the same time, the firm must be careful to not alienate light users, because their future purchase intentions are not readily known.

At the opposite extreme are the firm's heavy users. This group is also unattractive for a frequency program, but obviously for a different reason. It is difficult to offer rewards to heavy buyers that are attractive enough to cause them to purchase more. In fact, most may already be at the maximum.

Consequently, the best target for a frequency program is the group in the middle. Incentives can encourage this group to continue to buy, because these individuals often make purchases in order to redeem incentives. When this group increases the rate of purchases, the program tends to generate greater profits than are found in the other two segments.

Frequency programs range from highly complex to very simple. The most successful programs are those that are simple for customers to understand and use. For example, video rental stores offering members a free movie for every ten rentals is a frequency program that encourages the member to rent more movies from them. This type of frequency program is not attractive to light movie users, but it does encourage midrange users to rent more movies and to stay loyal to one store. The same type of frequency program can be used by almost any type of business. Some national hair-cutting chains offer one free haircut for every ten purchased, which encourages more frequent repeat business.

Frequency programs are also found in the business-to-business sector. For example, the Philadelphia-based Bell Atlantic company developed a frequency program for corporate customers called "Business Link." Members saved approximately 15 percent on direct dial calls when their monthly usage exceeded a minimum amount. They also earned points that were redeemed for various rewards. While many companies have policies that restrict employees from receiving gifts, Bell Atlantic's rewards are business-related goods or services as well as gift certificates from restaurants and tickets to shows. Bell Atlantic used the information it gathered from its corporate customers to cross-sell other products and to evaluate its marketing programs. One major advantage of Bell Atlantic's Business Link is the marketing team was able to identify the buying center's key decision maker within each company.[16]

The key to successful frequency programs is the development of a database that allows for accumulation of purchase and personal data. One method to add information to a database is requiring members to use a card that can be swiped electronically at every purchase. This ensures that every purchase will be recorded. The information can then be used for newsletters and targeted mailings to encourage additional purchases or cross-selling. These goals of frequency programs are highly compatible with the elements of most IMC plans.

Airlines and hotels were among the first industries to develop frequency programs. Courtesy of PhotoEdit. Photograph by Tom Pettymen.

Integrated Learning Experience

To obtain the latest news concerning loyalty and frequency marketing programs, access Colloquy at www.colloquy.org. Be sure to look at the "News by Industry" page to see what is happening in particular industries. For companies that specialize in frequency or loyalty programs, examine SerengetisSoftware at www.serengetisoftware.com and Martix Inc. at www.mpic.martiz.com. For both companies, locate their products and services. What types of frequency and loyalty programs does each offer?

stop!

implications for **marketing professionals**

Insist on the right equipment to do your job. This includes

1. Computers
2. Scanners for cash registers
3. Software packages such as CACI Coder/Plus (for geocoding)

Develop a high-quality staff. Train and retrain employees frequently. Stay on the cutting edge of technology and information management techniques.

Get to know the entire marketing department. Generate discussions in which you spell out the items you can provide, including:

1. Customer locations by geographic area
2. Demographic information about key buyers
3. Buyer profiles
4. Attitudinal tendencies of buyers
5. Characteristics of businesses most likely to make purchases
6. Tendencies of business buyers, especially the decision maker

Attend meetings and ask to be invited into discussions where data can be applied, including:

1. Advertising creatives
2. Promotions managers
3. Advertising account executives
4. Conversations with others in the market channel (wholesalers and retailers)

Constantly remind yourself of the goals of the database program. Make sure they are consistent with the firm's IMC goals and major theme.

Constantly reevaluate the effectiveness of various direct-marketing programs. Be innovative. Try new approaches and new media.

- Make sure your database management program is carefully aligned with the firm's Web site. Use the Web site in direct-marketing programs, whenever possible.
- Consider the use of permission marketing programs for your organization. Make sure the data you would receive are unique and valuable.
- Seek out cost information for frequency programs. Develop techniques to see who collects incentives, and whether the benefits of the program outweigh the costs, especially with regard to competitive efforts.

SUMMARY

Database management may, in some ways, seem like a mundane task. Numbers and statistics are not normally considered glamorous, yet their power in helping the marketing department reach key IMC goals should not be underestimated. IMC is a *communications*-based marketing approach, and customers often are willing to communicate fairly important information that can be used to enhance brand loyalty, increase sales, and develop long-term relationships when buyer characteristics and purchasing behaviors are clearly understood by the marketing team.

Managing a database begins with establishing clear goals for the program. Data sources, both internal and external, must be evaluated so that those offering the most vital information are used. Then, a data warehouse can be built to store and recall consumer information efficiently. Data mining means the company knows the profile of its main customers. These current customers can be targeted in future promotions, and potential new customers may be discovered, especially when they have similar characteristics to those who currently make purchases. Marketing programs may be enhanced as the database team helps creatives, account executives, promotions managers, and others understand and meet the needs of various buyers.

One of the most important applications of a database program is direct marketing. These efforts, whether via mail, catalogs, phone, fax, mass media, the Internet, e-mail, or some other method, should target the most viable potential customers. Geocoding identifies individuals with the right attributes by zip code. Others may identify themselves when they contact the firm by telephone or through the company's Web site.

Permission marketing is a new approach in which the customer agrees to receive promotion materials in exchange for various incentives. Permission marketing generates customer loyalty and helps the firm develop stronger bonds with patrons over time. Mining a database can help the company identify the strongest candidates for joining a permission marketing program.

Frequency marketing programs are incentives customers receive for repeat business. Moderate-purchase-level customers are of most value in frequency programs. These individuals may increase purchases in a manner that covers the costs of the program. Low-use purchasers create paperwork, and high-use purchasers probably cannot be enticed to buy any more. Either way, many organizations find it necessary to create frequency programs in response to those being offered by the competition.

The new millennium has witnessed an explosion of information that is available to various organizations. Database management in the future always will involve the decision of what information to retain and what to ignore. The firm cannot be caught in the position of not having enough data to market effectively, but also must be wary of being swamped with too much unnecessary and trivial information. A well-defined IMC program bonds well with database management. Both processes involve identifying key buyers and establishing an image and theme that will be attractive to those buyers. When the entire marketing team is "on the same page," data collection and management should be a powerful tool for building and maintaining a strong voice and competitive advantage in the cluttered world of marketing promotions.

REVIEW QUESTIONS

1. How is an IMC database different from database marketing? Is this a key difference? Why or why not?

2. Name the steps involved in developing an IMC database.

3. What kinds of objectives should be established in an IMC database program?

4. What is the primary source for internal database information? How can this data be collected?

5. Name and describe the external sources of database information.

6. What are the most common uses for information in a data warehouse?

7. What is geocoding? What role does it play in database programs?

8. When mining data, what are the two most common activities?

9. What benefits are associated with direct-marketing programs?

10. What are the advantages and disadvantages of direct-mail programs? How can an IMC database be used to enhance the advantages?

11. What is digital direct-to-press? Describe how such a program can be used in both consumer and business-to-business markets.

12. What advantages do catalogs hold over telemarketing calls and direct-mail programs?

13. How can mass-media programs be incorporated into direct-marketing efforts?

14. Name and describe three forms of alternative media that can be used in direct-marketing programs.

15. What are the benefits and challenges associated with international direct-marketing programs?

16. Describe a permission marketing program. What are the key benefits of this approach?

17. What are the steps involved in developing an effective permission marketing program?

18. Describe a frequency program. What are the major benefits of frequency programs?

19. Which type of user pays off the best (to the company) in a frequency program, light users, medium users, or heavy users? Why?

KEY TERMS

database management the use of people and technology to collect and process data to be used in IMC marketing efforts.

geocoding adding geographic codes to customer records when developing a data warehouse.

data mining developing a process to sift through information to help the firm better understand its customers.

direct marketing developing and maintaining direct contacts with customers, for the purposes of selling items, enhancing brand loyalty, and meeting service needs.

digital direct-to-press a program that instructs a computer to send a specific message to a printer, which can be used to individualize marketing materials sent to consumers and business buyers.

package insert programs (pips) direct-marketing materials placed in mail-order fulfillment packages.

ride-alongs direct-marketing materials that accompany or are placed along with another company's catalog or direct-mail piece.

card pack a deck of 20 to 50 business reply cards, normally 3½ by 5 inches, placed in a plastic mail pack.

permission marketing a form of database marketing in which the company sends promotional materials only to consumers who give the company permission to do so.

frequency program a marketing plan designed to cause customers to make repeat purchases by offering them incentives.

ENDNOTES

1. Richard Cross and Janet Smith, "The New Data Game," *Marketing Tools,* 5, no. 2 (June 1998), pp. 20–22; John F. Yarbrough, "Putting the Pieces Together," *Sales and Marketing Management,* 148, no. 9 (September 1996), pp. 68–74.

2. Leo Rabinovtich, "America's 'First' Department Store Mines Customer Data," *Direct Marketing,* 62, no. 8 (December 1999), pp. 42–45.

3. Eric Cohen, "Database Marketing," *Target Marketing,* 22, no. 4 (April 1999), p. 50.

4. Ibid.

5. Rabinovitch, "America's 'First' Department Store Mines Customer Data."

6. Eileen P. Gunn, "Direct & Database Marketing," *Advertising Age,* 70, no. 10 (October 18, 1999), pp. 1–2.

7. Ibid.

8. Patrick Totty, "Direct Mail Gets a New Lease on Life," *Credit Union Magazine,* 66, no. 4 (April 2000), pp. 36–37.

9. Based on Jay Klitsch, "Making Your Message Hit Home: Some Basics to Consider When. . . ," *Direct Marketing,* 61, no. 2 (June 1998), pp. 32–34.

10. John Ahern and Rachel McLaughlin, "What You May Not Have Known, but Were Afraid to Ask," *Target Marketing,* 21, no. 9 (September 1998), pp. 14–15.

11. Jeff Sweat and Rick Whiting, "Instant Marketing," *Information Week,* no. 746 (August 2, 1999), pp. 18–20.

12. Rolf Rykken, "List Serve in the Real World," *Export Today's Global Business,* 15, no. 11 (November 1999), pp. 34–37.

13. Based on David Sedgwick and Mary Connelly, "GM Sees Dollars in Its Mountain of Buyer Data," *Automotive News,* 73, no. 5819 (May 17, 1999), pp. 3–4.

14. Based on Seth Godin, "Permission Marketing: The Way to Make Advertising Work Again," *Direct Marketing,* 62, no. 1 (May 1999), pp. 40–43.

15. Richard Cross, "High-Octane Loyalty," *Marketing Tools* (April 1997), pp. 4–6.

16. Sarah Lorge and Chad Kaydo, "How to Build a B-to-B Frequency Program," *Sales and Marketing Management,* 151, no. 4 (April 1999), p. 80.

17. Michael Barrier, "The Language of Success," *Nation's Business,* 85, no. 8 (August 1997), pp. 56–57.

Building an IMC Campaign

Establishing Effective Database Programs

What kinds of customers are most likely to buy your product? Who may use it heavily? Which ones are light or moderate users? Where can your key customers be contacted via advertisements and promotional campaigns? Those of you who know the answers to these questions have strong databases and have effectively mined the information that is available. The exercise for Chapter 15 at www.prenhall.com/clow or the Advertising Plan Pro disk that accompanied this textbook is designed to lead you through two major issues: (1) managing a database program and (2) direct marketing. You will be asked to consider whether a direct-marketing program will work for your product, service, or organization.

Critical Thinking Exercises

Discussion Questions

1. What is the difference between a database marketing program and a data warehouse? What are the advantages of a data warehouse for business-to-business operations? What are the advantages for business-to-consumer operations?

2. Can databases be developed for institutional and governmental customers? What types of information would be placed in the database? More importantly, how would the data be used? Discuss these issues in the context of a company that sells copy machines and other office equipment to both institutional and government agencies.

3. Assume you are the account executive at a database marketing agency. A music retailer has asked you to develop a database for the company. How would you go about building a data warehouse? What type of data mining would you do for the music retailer?

4. Examine the methods of direct marketing highlighted in Figure 15.4. Evaluate each method for the following types of businesses. Which ones would be the best? Which ones would not work as well? Justify your answers.
   a. Shoe store
   b. Printing service
   c. Internet hosiery retailer (sells only by the Internet)
   d. Manufacturer of tin cans for food processing companies
   e. Tractor parts dealer

5. For two weeks, collect every piece of direct mail you receive. Examine each one. What type of offers did each make to you? Compare your direct-mail pieces to those gathered by someone else in your class. Compare your direct mail to those of your parents or someone else in a different age bracket. If possible, compare yours to

those sent to a person you know who is from a different ethnic background. What similarities and what differences did you detect?

6. Form a group of four to five classmates. Ask each person to list the catalogs that came into his or her home during the last two weeks. Have each person discuss why he or she receives certain catalogs. Next, discuss how often each of you order something out of a catalog and how the order was placed. Is anyone in the group accessing the Internet for information given in a catalog or ordering from a catalog after accessing a Web site? Discuss how important the catalog market is to you and what you see as the future of catalog marketing.

7. Early in their careers, Helen and Marty Shih realized the importance of keeping a database containing information about their customers. They started their operation selling flowers on the street corner. When they moved into their first store, they started collecting information about their customers. Their first database was developed before they even owned a computer. It was done manually, in notebooks.

   The first use of the database was to remind customers of special dates such as birthdays and anniversaries. Then as the database grew, they discovered the potential to sell for other firms.

   Today, the Shihs' database holds 1.5 million individual names and 300,000 business names, all Asian American. Companies such as Sprint and DHL Worldwide Express hired the Shihs to telemarket their services. The Shihs' currently employ 800 telemarketers selling a wide variety of goods and services to individuals and businesses. All of the entries in their database are Asian immigrants. The telemarketer can speak to them in a native tongue such as Japanese, Korean, Vietnamese, Mandarin, or Cantonese Chinese.[17] For firms that want to use telemarketing to reach minorities, what advantages do the Shihs offer over traditional telemarketing firms? What types of firms would be interested in using the Shihs' telemarketing services? Could the Shihs' database be used for direct-marketing programs? If so, how? What other potential uses do you see for the Shihs' database?

8. What frequency programs have you tried? Why did you participate? Do they affect your purchase behavior? What types of products or services are the most effective matches with frequency or loyalty programs? Why? What types of rewards should be given for each of the products and services you listed?

9. Almost all hotels have some type of frequency or loyalty program. Look at the loyalty programs of the following hotels. Critique each one. Which ones are best? Why?

   a. Best Western (www.bestwestern.com)
   b. Days Inn (www.daysinn.com)
   c. Double Tree Inn (www.hilton.com/doubletree/index.html)
   d. Holiday Inn (www.basshotels.com/holiday-inn)
   e. Marriott (www.marriott.com)
   f. Radisson (www.radisson.com)
   g. Wyndham Hotels & Resorts (www.wyndham.com)

Lincoln Medical Supply

Sara Holmes has just taken on a unique dual role in her job at Lincoln Medical Supply. She was to be in charge of the marketing database for the company and also would serve as liaison with the advertising firm and marketing group that provided promotions for the organization. Sara was told her input would be heavily counted on to help with key decisions to build the size and scope of the company in the next several years.

Lincoln Medical Supply was located in Lincoln, Nebraska. The company served both retail and business-to-business markets by selling and servicing various types of medical equipment, from items as basic as ankle braces to those as sophisticated as fetal monitors. The company had achieved a great deal of success simply through the sheer demand for various products, but the management team was concerned that no coherent marketing plan had ever been developed.

Sara was told that the company had three basic customer groups:

1. Retail walk-in buyers
2. Physicians' offices
3. Hospitals

Retail customers purchased the lower-cost, less intricate items such as braces, bandages, and cold packs. Physicians bought more elaborate equipment and also provided referrals for patients. Hospitals ordered the big-ticket items. Each customer type generated a solid source of revenue for the organization.

Sara's first challenge was to develop a database for each type of customer. Her potential sources for retail customers were insurance forms (many filed for insurance to pay for the items involved) and sales ticket information requested from each person. Doctors' offices could be sources of a great deal of information, but the company often had to "push" the staff to provide statistics on numbers of patients, types of expenditures, and other key facts. Hospitals could be assessed through internal company reports and as well by accessing data from external sources.

Following the simple generation of data, Sara would need to decide if all of this information should be compiled into one overall data warehouse, or if it should be separated by customer type. Clearly the needs of each group were different, and therefore it seemed plausible that the marketing tactics used for each customer type would also vary. At the same time, Sara wanted a consistent message sent out that Lincoln Medical Supply stood for consistent, high-quality, and excellent service advantages. She knew the name "Lincoln" didn't help, because so many companies in the city also used the name (e.g., Lincoln Electric Supply, Lincoln Party Favors, and so forth).

Sara held a meeting with the marketing team. The group told her the primary goal was to build greater brand equity in the name, as a new medical supply house had just opened near one of Lincoln's biggest hospitals. Next, the company's leaders wanted to know how to get walk-in buyers to purchase more items, and how to expand purchases from the other two segments of the business at the same time. The leaders discussed the use of catalogs and an Internet site to widen the scope of product offerings. They also considered the possibility of opening satellite locations in Omaha (50 miles away), Grand Island (90 miles west), and North Platte (400 miles away). They wanted to develop an understanding of the type of individual who would venture into a medical supply store, what the person might buy, and what the person would not buy. They also needed to know if they were meeting the needs of physicians and hospitals. With all of these challenges in mind, Sara took a deep breath and started working.

1. Name the sources of internal and external data for all three types of customers.
2. What types of data should Sara collect from each type of customer?
3. How can Sara meet the goals imposed on her by the marketing group?
4. What kinds of marketing programs could be developed from the data Sara generates? Should the data be separated by customer type or combined into one major database? Why or why not?

Bonus Plan or Major Pain?

APPLICATION EXERCISE II

The grocery store business is rapid moving and risky. Customer preferences can evolve slowly or develop quickly. Hot new items can capture the fancy of some customers, while others remain staunchly devoted to old "standbys." The entry of Wal-Mart into the grocery business has also changed the dynamics of the industry. Smaller stores find they must create and dominate a niche if they want to remain in business.

In each major city, one or more grocery chains continually battle to retain a base group of loyal customers while enticing others to at least occasionally visit the store. Heavy promotion of loss-leader pricing has been the standard in the industry for many years. At the same time, various chains and local stores have tried other gimmicks to keep and build a share of the market.

Bobby's Market was associated with an independent grocer chain. Bobby Mulvaney inherited the store from his father, Bobby Senior, 20 years ago. Bobby had watched as stores opened and closed, and fretted as Wal-Mart's Supercenter, located on the edge of town, began taking away business from his store and others in the area.

The grocer chain associated with Bobby's Market was wary of magnet-card, VIP programs that several groups had tried. These programs, which provided a great deal of data about individual customers and their purchases, seemed to create a kind of "backlash" effect. Those who didn't have the cards wondered why they couldn't receive the more favorable discounts given to VIP cardholders, and those holding the cards soon were bombarded with extra promotions besides the regular weekly ads placed in the newspaper and on television. Consequently, this chain decided not to become involved in any kind of VIP card promotion.

Instead, Bobby was sent a series of materials for a "Bonus Buy" club promotion. Each customer was given a punch card that contained a series of dollar amounts. As the individual bought items from the store, the value of the total purchase was hand-punched into the card. A fully punched card was an entry into a contest, where the prizes ranged from $1 to a $1,000 grand prize, given out each week. To make the process more enticing, various items throughout the store were marked as "Bonus Buy" items, and dollar values on the punch card were increased by $1, $5, or $10, depending on the item. Thus, a package of T-bone steaks was marked with a $10 bonus punch, so the customer received the value of the total purchase plus $10 for that trip to the store, meaning the person was going to gain more entries into the contest for frequently shopping at Bobby's Market. The person gained an even greater advantage if he or she were willing to buy larger numbers of bonus buy items.

One main feature of the contest was that cashiers would give punch cards to every shopper, unless the individual said he or she did not want one. A person who forgot his or her card was allowed to "combine" punches from a series of cards to gain an entry in the sweepstakes. Therefore, even absent-minded customers could still win.

Two negatives were associated with this program. First, the company could not collect any data from those who did not participate. The punch cards did not require the customer to disclose anything until an entry was redeemed. Then, the individual was asked to add his or her address and phone number to the punch card. Still, this meant many people did not provide information, and their actual purchases could not be tracked. Only increases in sales of bonus buy items could be studied.

Second, punching each individual card dramatically slowed the checkout times for all shoppers. Those who didn't want to mess with the contest became increasingly annoyed as cards were being punched and cash prizes were given by cashiers, who weren't ringing up items or sacking groceries while they took care of contest details. Even contest participants shopping at peak hours noticed the lines were longer and checkout times were rising.

As the contest wound down, Bobby wondered if it had been a good idea. He tried to figure out ways to discover if he should try the Bonus Buy plan again in six months. The grocery chain liked the program, because the marketing team could offer bonus buy points for overstocked items. Yet Bobby needed to know how all of his customers were reacting.

1. What kinds of data was Bobby unable to collect from the Bonus Buy promotion?

2. How could Bobby discover whether the contest was a good idea?

3. What goals are associated with the Bonus Buy promotion? Are these goals compatible with those of a small independent grocer trying to compete with Wal-Mart and other larger chains?

4. What other types of data should Bobby collect from the Bonus Buy plan and how could he collect it?

5. How would you restructure Bobby's data collection project so that he could use the information to boost sales and retain customers?

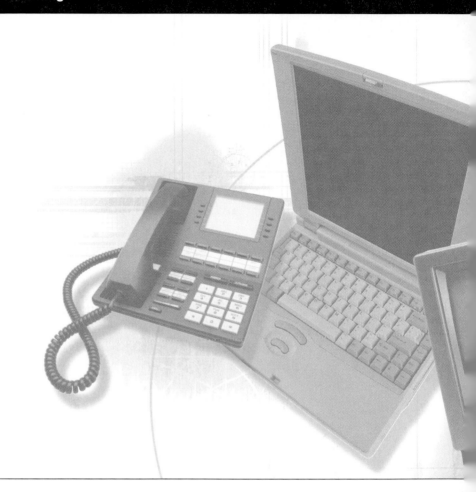

Understand who uses the Internet and how it is used.

Adapt all of the marketing communications functions to Internet programs.

Develop a strong e-commerce program to complement and supplement other selling and promotional activities.

Make sure every component of an e-commerce approach is carefully integrated and designed to attract customers to a Web site and to eventually make purchases.

Be aware of the ramifications of Internet programs for business-to-business customers and for international marketing efforts.

Finalize an IMC program in such a way that it meshes smoothly with all Internet marketing efforts.

FOGDOG SEEKS TO TAKE A BITE OUT OF THE SPORTS EQUIPMENT INDUSTRY

Where do you go when you need a new tennis racquet or golf club? How about a soccer ball or running equipment? Can you go to one store that sells all of these items as well as health food? The answer, as of 1998, is a resounding "Yes," if you go on-line to Fogdog.com.

Fogdog began operations in 1994. The company name was chosen to portray a "light" in the "fog" of sports equipment. By combining the products from a variety of manufacturers into one site, the company, originally known as the Cedro Group, tried to build a strong pres-

ence on the Internet in a manner comparable to Amazon.com. The firm raised $30 million in investment capital and spent heavily to entice customers to shop on-line. In 1999, Fogdog spent 15 to 20 cents of every dollar of revenue on marketing.

When the initial launch occurred, customer interest was relatively strong. To attract more visitors to the company's site, Fogdog created a series of commercials for ESPN, ESPN-2, Lifetime, and later the major networks. The fog-dog character (a man in a dog suit) appears with a celebrity offering quick access to a piece of sports equipment. Soulful singer Isaac Hayes served as one spokesperson, and the company's visibility was enhanced with the sum-mer 2000 release of the movie *Shaft* featuring an updated version of the film's theme song. Fogdog largely relies on humor to vend its products.

One primary advantage held is the brand name. Consumer recall of the name is quite high, which helps the company cut through the clutter of new e-commerce businesses. Major competitors include Global Sports Interactive, and the MVP.com site launched by Wayne Gretsky, John Elway, and Michael Jordan.

Analysts believe Fogdog held a competitive edge in the year 2000, with sales of over $5 million and an average transaction size of $70. The firm believed it would become profitable by the end of 2001.

One major challenge to Fogdog was the downturn in optimism about e-commerce regarding the stock market and a variety of e-businesses as the new century began. Many e-commerce businesses seemed to be "quick hit" ventures designed to attract capital, make a few sales, and leave the marketplace. Many e-companies, including Amazon.com, were not reaching profit goals, and investors were becoming disenchanted. It seems the potential for long-term survival was not great for a number of e-businesses. In other words, the glitz of the Internet was wearing thin, and many companies had not "done their homework" to ensure long-term stability and profitability. Fogdog was determined to overcome this obstacle.

To make sure buyers knew Fogdog would be around, the company hired a series of sports consultants to help with operations. These experts, who came from numerous sports, served under the Fogdog umbrella. By 2000, the site was achieving 40,000 visits per day. The company expected to triple visits by the end of the following year and reach revenues of $1 billion per year within three years.

One major effort is to gain return business. A customer who has made one purchase should experience satisfaction to the degree that the person will come back and buy again. Logistics, service, and ease of purchase are key ingredients in that part of the formula.

New product lines have also been added. For example, food supplements such as creatine, vitamins, and performance supplements (whey, egg whites, and other protein-based items) are available, as well as optics, watches, and memorabilia. The growth in product offerings should make it possible to attract and keep more customers.

Finally, in the attempt to build an even stronger base, Fogdog launched an effort in Europe to support U.S. operations. The company's leaders believe that it will be only a few years before more than half of all sporting goods are purchased on-line. Fogdog is determined to be the industry leader when that change takes place.[1]

overview

Two inventions have had a profound impact on the nature of business in the latter half of the twentieth century: (1) the computer and (2) the Internet. Through the Internet, a business of any size can compete in the global marketplace. In fact, on the Internet, the size of an organization's operation makes little difference, because the Internet is an open environment. Similar companies compete against one another while being only a click of the mouse away. In other words, a buyer can locate numerous sellers offering similar merchandise, similar prices, and similar offers in a very short time period. As more people and businesses become comfortable with the Internet, the marketing landscape will continue to evolve quickly in the coming years.

The influence of the Internet on various businesses and industries has been noted throughout this text. In practically every chapter, some kind of impact or implication has been described. The presence of the Internet and e-commerce is so sweeping that the various applications of Web technology are now essential elements of a fully integrated marketing communications program.

Consequently, this chapter explores the Internet and e-commerce in greater detail. The specific topics to be addressed begin with an examination of the nature of Internet users as well as marketing functions on the Internet. Next, a description of e-commerce and the elements necessary to build a successful e-business, including the types of incentives required to build a base of customers, is provided. Then, an analysis of various IMC topics, such as brand development, brand loyalty, sales support, service efforts, and promotional programs, is presented. In each of these areas, implications for business-to-business marketing programs as well as international concerns are presented.

Upon completion of this chapter, all of the topics associated with constructing an IMC program will have been described. In the final chapter of this section (and this textbook), methods to evaluate IMC programs are outlined. The goal of providing a complete picture of a total IMC program is to help you understand all of the implications and activities associated with marketing communications. When these fundamentals are successfully applied, the company should be in the best position to know and understand its customers, and to meet their needs efficiently and effectively. The Internet is the final piece of the complete marketing puzzle. IMC tactics should be applied to it in conjunction with all other forms of promotion and communication.

who uses the internet?

Use of the Internet has exploded during the last few years in both the consumer and business-to-business markets. Although the experts still debate the future of the Internet, no one doubts it will have an impact on how business will take place in the twenty-first century. The histories of two companies, Dell Computers and Cisco Systems, can be used to portray the evolution of the Internet. Dell Computers reports daily Internet sales of $18 million while Cisco Systems has $28 million per day in Internet sales. Here are some facts about the Internet that highlight its tremendous growth and presence in society:

- The Internet population is now 110 million. Forty-one percent of Americans have access to the Internet.
- There are over 4 million Web sites. Over 235,000 are added each month.
- There are 200 million e-mail boxes in the United States.
- Seven trillion e-mails are sent each year in the United States.
- Nearly 50 percent of the U.S. population (135 million) communicates via e-mail.
- The average e-mail user receives 31 e-mails per day.
- Business-to-business e-commerce in the United States totaled $1.3 trillion in 1999.
- Businesses placed orders totaling $3 trillion worldwide via the Internet in 1999.
- Twenty-five percent of all business-to-business purchases are placed through some type of Internet connection.
- The five top business-to-business e-commerce products are computers and electronics, motor vehicles, petrochemicals, utilities, and paper and office products.
- By 2004, 10 percent of business-to-business advertising dollars will be spent on the Internet. The total amount spent will be $8.7 billion.
- About 54 percent of the e-mail users have responded to an e-mail advertisement. Almost half purchased a product.
- Internet retail sales account for almost 2.5 percent of all retail sales.[2]

In one recent survey, the respondents indicated that 22 percent of Internet users were preteens and teens. An additional 35 percent of the users were college age. Generation X accounted for another 35 percent, and 8 percent were baby boomers or seniors.[3] These statistics will undoubtedly change as more older people become comfortable with the technology.

Business-to-business marketers were among the first companies actually to make profits using the Internet. In today's marketplace, the Web is becoming the communication tool of choice for many business-to-business companies. The Internet provides opportunities for communication, customer service, sales support, collaboration, and e-commerce. Some companies use the Internet for every

> ◗ Building databases for e-mail campaigns
>
> ◗ Designing e-mail campaigns linking customers to Web site information
>
> ◗ Creating fun and innovative games to attract and keep customers coming back to the Web page
>
> ◗ Creating incentive programs
>
> ◗ Translating printed documents, catalogs, brochures, and newsletters for the Internet
>
> ◗ Adding graphics to the Web site

Internet Services Offered by Marketing Agencies

FIGURE 16.1

Source: Ellisor, "Business-to-Business Offer WWW Opportunities," *Houston Business Journal,* (September 17, 1999), Vol. 30, No. 7, p. 18B.

aspect of their business including taking orders, inventory control, production scheduling, communications plans, sales programs, service departments, and support programs. The change from traditional communication channels such as salespeople, telephone, and "snail mail" to the Internet and e-mail happened quickly in some companies and more slowly in others. Now, convincing top management of the benefits of Internet marketing is essential. There is a still a lack of Internet expertise in the business community. As a result, many companies are turning to marketing agencies for guidance. Figure 16.1 identifies some of the Internet services marketing agencies now provide.

stop!

Integrated Learning Experience

To get a feel for who is using the Internet as well as current Web news, the best source may be the CyberAtlas at cyberatlas.com. The "Stats Toolbox" page contains a large volume of statistics concerning Internet usage, top Web advertisers, and major e-retailers. Access this part of the CyberAtlas to discover the large number of categories listed. The sections entitled "Demographics," "Geographics," and "Traffic Patterns" reveal the "big picture," in terms of who is using the Internet. Then, to examine various markets, review the subcategories B-to-B, Finance, Small Biz, Retailing, and Travel.

marketing functions on the internet

To illustrate the impact the Internet can have on an industry, consider airline travel. In the past, airline tickets were normally purchased from the airline or a travel agent. Prices were quite expensive for casual travelers. In the 1980s, governmental deregulation of the airline industry caused prices to fall. Traveling for leisure became a viable option for more people.

Currently the Internet is reshaping the industry. Travelocity, Expedia, and TravelWeb offer consumers and businesses the opportunity to book flights while saving money. To compete with these discounts, the major airlines were forced to start their own Web sites. These sites make it possible to book flights directly.

In addition to airline tickets, Travelocity and other companies help consumers make hotel reservations, rental car reservations, and numerous other types of travel-related bookings at the same time and on the same site. The goal of Travelocity (to be the one-stop shopping location for travelers) has created a new type of customer, an e-shopper. Even though these Web sites were originally designed for leisure travelers, many business travelers take advantage of them to finalize travel plans. Although many leisure and business travelers still use travel agents, others are switching to the Internet. Consequently, companies without a strong Internet presence in the travel industry may have a tough time succeeding in the future.

In general, the greatest impact of the Internet is on sales, marketing, and distribution systems for various businesses. These three activities typically account for 20 percent to 30 percent of the final cost of a good or service. What makes the potential of the Internet so exciting is that e-commerce companies have the potential to save 10 percent to 20 percent of these costs. Thus, instead of paying for packing, shipping, and transporting the product to a retail site, the firm has the option to send it directly to customers and can pocket the markup a retailer would receive. Also, the company can choose to mark down the price of an item, saving customers money and enticing more purchases. Shipping costs may be charged to customers for e-commerce purchases. As a result, the manufacturer does not need to absorb these costs, which are normally part of the price charged to retailers.[4]

A Travelocity ad encouraging consumers to make travel arrangements using the Internet.
Courtesy of Visa USA, Inc.

This section describes the various marketing activities that can be served by the Internet. Figure 16.2 identifies the primary functions a business Web site can provide. A discussion of each of these items follows.

The design of a Web site should be guided by the IMC plan and the specific objective the site seeks to accomplish within the overall IMC program. A flashy Web site designed to attract attention is created when the goal is *advertising.* Many firms use Web sites to promote individual products as well as the overall company. For instance, most movies now are advertised through traditional media (television, magazines) but also have Web sites for e-moviegoers to view.

Still, advertising is rarely presented by itself without being incorporated with other marketing functions. Some Web sites are for *sales support.* In those instances, information about the products should be accessible through either a salesperson or a direct link from the Web page. These types of Web sites are used more routinely for the business-to-business customers rather than retail consumers. Effective sales support sites must be useful for engineers and other members of the buying center who need additional product information. The actual sale is normally made via a salesperson. Then, the price and terms can be negotiated separately.

A *customer service* Internet site provides a different function. The goal of a customer service Web site is to support the customer after the sale. In this instance, documentation and operating information are provided. Customers who have questions can use the e-mail function to obtain information or scroll through the **FAQs,** or **frequently asked questions** people have about various items or services. Portions of these sites may be password protected in order to ensure that only customers who have purchased products can access certain information.

Another purpose for a Web site is to create a positive *public relations* image. Some companies place information about not-for-profit and philanthropic causes they support on their Web sites. Individuals not only see what the company is doing but also may be able to volunteer for or donate money to a cause. At times

▶ **Advertising**

▶ **Sales support**

▶ **Customer service**

▶ **Public relations**

▶ **E-commerce (retail store)**

Functions of the Internet

FIGURE 16.2

these sites are separate from the company's primary site. In others, a link within the site is developed. Preparing a public relations site may be used by a firm in order to react to bad publicity. This gives the firm the opportunity to refute a charge or to explain the company's side of the story.

These marketing functions clearly indicate the potential of the Internet to be a valuable component of the company's IMC program. The next section provides a more complete description of the final item in Figure 16.2, e-commerce.

e-commerce

Many times a Web site is designed for **e-commerce,** or selling goods on the Internet. E-commerce can take on many different forms. A retail store can vend items to consumers through the Internet when there is no handy outlet nearby or simply as a convenience for some shoppers. E-commerce also can be a retail operation that sells entirely on the Internet without any physical store or even inventory. Services are offered, deals are mediated, and products are shipped through this range of e-commerce operations. Instead of investigating all of the various forms of e-commerce, the purpose of the section is to provide a short synopsis of why and how setting up an e-commerce site benefits an organization.

Individual businesses have approached e-commerce in various ways. At one extreme is the business that jumped into e-commerce immediately, because the organization's leaders decided it was the trend of the future. These individuals concluded that the day would come when there would be no retail stores, and everything would be purchased over the Internet or through an interactive television setup. The other extreme includes those who decided that e-commerce is a fad that soon will pass away. These business leaders believe that consumers prefer dealing with people and therefore always will go to retail stores to make purchases. In reality, neither extreme seems very likely.

To the established retail operation, e-commerce offers customers an alternative mode for making purchases. Not every customer uses the Internet, but many do. As time passes, more people will become more comfortable with Web site shopping. Without an e-commerce site, these customers are lost to other retail operations who have established retail on-line sites.

Many times consumers make purchases at retail stores after first using the Internet to gather information. For example, a shopper may research stereos on the Internet and then go to the store with a list of "finalists." Another person may get on the Internet and find a fishing rod with a special set of features. Using the Internet store locator, the individual identifies the closest store offering the product to make the actual purchase. In that case, even though the customer did not make the purchase via e-commerce, he or she has used the Internet as part of the buying decision-making process. Consequently, the leaders of most established businesses know they must develop high-quality e-commerce sites in order to remain competitive in the twenty-first century.

E-commerce components

All e-commerce sites have three components. The first is some type of *catalog.* A catalog can vary from just a few items to a complex presentation of thousands of products. The nature of the firm's operation determines the type of catalog required. In every case, customers should be able to find the products of interest. Photos and product information are important in creating appealing on-line catalogs.

Second, each site must have some type of **shopping cart** to assist consumers as they select products. Again, the shopping cart can range from just checking a circle for an item when only a few products are offered to more complicated shopping carts that keep records of multiple purchases.

Third, each site must establish some way for customers to make *payments* for the things they purchase. For consumers, this normally is a credit card system. For business-to-business operations, payments are normally made through a voucher system. In other situations, a bill is generated or a computerized billing system is used so that the invoice goes directly to the buyer. In more trusting relationships, the invoice is added to the customer's records without a physical bill ever being mailed.

Remember, many consumers are still wary of purchasing products over the Internet. There are two reasons for this reluctance: (1) security issues and (2) purchase behavior habits.

Security issues

Consumer fears about security are based on worries about a credit card number being stolen. Others are concerned about fraud, where a retailer takes the money but does not ship the merchandise. Both can cause people to resist making Internet purchases.

To resolve these problems, a review of the past may be helpful. When telephone orders were first encouraged by mail-order firms, people were hesitant because of fears about giving out a phone or credit card number to a stranger they couldn't see. Now, nearly everyone is willing to provide the information while placing orders on the phone. Also, it wasn't that many years ago that credit card holders expressed anxiety about various store employees stealing those numbers. Originally, customers were instructed to "take the carbon" from a credit card purchase to make sure it was torn into shreds in order to prevent an employee from using the credit card number later.

The same pattern is likely to follow with Internet shopping. As consumers become accustomed to using the Web, fears about giving out credit card information will be no greater than they are for telephone orders or credit card sales. IBM and MasterCard have created a series of independent television commercials designed to calm and reassure people about the quality of their Internet security program; however, these efforts are set back each time a major virus is turned loose.

Purchasing habits

The second issue has strong ramifications regarding the ultimate success of e-commerce. Currently, many consumers are most comfortable when they buy merchandise at retail stores. Some are also comfortable buying through catalogs. It will take time to change these habits, especially the preference for retail shopping.

At the retail store, consumers can view and touch the merchandise. They can inspect it for defects and compare brands. Clothes can be tried on to make sure they fit. In addition, the customer can see how the clothing item looks while being worn. Changing these habits requires the right kinds of incentives. Consumers and businesses must have valid reasons for switching to making purchases via e-commerce instead of through traditional methods (at the retail store or following a call from a salesperson). To overcome this handicap, many e-commerce firms are trying to develop incentives that will attract customers to make purchases in this new format.

e-commerce incentives

Three incentives must be present for consumers to consider making a purchase online. They are the same incentives that lead people to use ATMs and to phone in mail-order purchases. The three incentives are: (1) financially based, (2) convenience based, and (3) value-based.

Financial incentives

First, persuading an individual or business to change to buying via e-commerce requires some type of financial incentive. The first-time purchaser may be attracted to a price incentive, which can be in the form of a reduced price, an introductory price, or an e-coupon. Financial incentives are profitable for most firms because of the reduced costs of doing business on-line. Once the individual or company makes the switch, continuing the financial incentive may not be necessary because of the convenience or added-value features of an e-commerce program.

When consumers or businesses buy over the Internet, the company often can save both time and money. The e-company is then able to pass along savings. Customers placing orders via the Internet save the firm money in several ways, such as:

- Lower long-distance telephone bills
- Reduced shipping costs, because they are passed along to the buyer
- Decreased labor costs associated with stocking shelves
- Lower personnel costs (sales force) paid for waiting on in-store customers

In business-to-business settings, purchases via e-commerce also make it possible to offer financial incentives. The company may be saving the cost of a sales call, which often runs over $300 per call. Passing these savings on to customers can be a very effective means of encouraging customers to switch from their current mode of purchasing to e-commerce.

One special type of financial incentive is known as cyberbait. **Cyberbait** is some type of lure or attraction that brings people to the Web site. The bait may be a special offer such as a pair of jeans that is sold as a loss leader. It may be a game that consumers can play, or it can be a weekly or daily tip on some topic. For example, for a business-to-business health site, a weekly tip on how to reduce health risks and job-related injuries may be a cyberbait that attracts prospects to the site. To entice consumers and businesses to return to the site on a regular basis, additional cyberbait is needed. E-shoppers find it easy to surf the Internet and search competing sites. Therefore, these individuals need some reason to return on a regular basis.

Convenience incentives
The second incentive to encourage customers to switch to e-commerce is convenience. Instead of making a trip to a retail store, a consumer can place the order while remaining at home. More importantly, the order can be placed at any time, which is a major reason why ATMs became so popular. Looking for information about various products can be quicker and easier on the Internet than using *Consumer Reports* or talking to salespeople. For businesses, ordering merchandise, supplies, and materials over the Internet can save purchasing agents considerable time. In addition to ordering, businesses can check on the status of an order, shipment information, and even billing data. In most cases, doing so on-line is considerably quicker than making a telephone call. In the fast-paced world of business, convenience is a highly attractive incentive for many consumers and businesses.

To get consumers to return, a Web site must be updated and changed regularly. It is important to keep the site current. Prices and product information must always be up to date. In addition, the appearance of the site should be routinely changed so consumers will return to see what is new. The front page of a Web site should be revised just as a display at a retail store is regularly altered. The difference, however, is that in changing the Web site, the marketing team must be careful not to change links or location of merchandise. Consumers become accustomed to finding things on the site. It is best not to make it hard for them to locate familiar items. Just as a grocery store seldom moves merchandise around just to create a different look, designers also must be aware that shoppers will become annoyed if they can't find their favorite products. Consequently, convenience remains an important feature as a Web site is being redesigned.

communication**action**

Getting Involved with Soap and Sauce

Most people see a logical connection between the Internet and companies that can sell products directly to consumers. Products such as music CDs, books, and airline tickets sell well over the Internet. But what about low-involvement products such as Tide or Ragu spaghetti sauce? These products would not be purchased over the Internet, because it is not financially feasible for the consumer or the company to offer them. No one particularly needs a box of detergent shipped in by FedEx or UPS. Still, the Internet can be a valuable tool for both products in terms of brand development.

Tide has sites at www.clothesline.com and www.tide.com. Instead of offering information about Tide and using the Internet site as an advertisement for Tide, Procter & Gamble uses the Tide Web site to assist consumers. The Web site provides helpful hints on removing stains from garments as well as other laundry tips. Consumers can ask the "Stain Detective" for help on specific stains by providing information about the type of fabric, color, and other information.

Ragu spaghetti sauce, on the other hand, has a highly entertaining site where a made-up personality known as "Mama" nags you about eating right. Browsers have the option of giving their e-mail address so they can receive coupons, updates on the site, and information about new products that are introduced.

The key, in both cases, is creativity. Firms that can discover ways to augment their communication programs with quality Web sites gain a major advantage in the marketplace. Thus, even soap and sauce are quality candidates for an Internet presence.

Value-added incentives

Financial incentives are often used to encourage customers to switch to e-commerce. At the same time, however, to completely change their purchasing habits in the long term will require some kind of value-added incentive. The added value may be personalization, whereby the firm becomes acquainted with the customer and his or her purchasing behaviors. Further, specialized software can be used to inform customers about special deals. These offers are based on past purchase behaviors or the customer's search patterns. For example, a consumer going through the mystery section of an on-line bookstore may see a banner pop up advertising a special deal on a new mystery novel. In addition to instant banners, consumers and businesses also may receive e-mails offering new information and other special deals that are available. Again, these are based on past purchase behaviors contained within a database. These tools can make it much easier for e-commerce programs to created added values for customers.

Integrated Learning Experience

An excellent Internet advertising and promotion resource is Ad Resource at adres.internet.com. Read the headlines at this Web site. Next, access the various sections such as "Advertising," "Articles," "Business," "Events," and "Marketing." What types of information are provided to help a company with a Web site?

business-to-business e-commerce

For business-to-business organizations, e-commerce may be as critical as it is in consumer markets. For routine rebuy situations, purchasing agents can go to the Internet and compare prices and product information. Once a business account is established, a business customer finds it very easy to place orders. This type of situation works well for products such as office supplies, maintenance supplies, as well as for repair and operation products. These orders are simple, because the product does not have to be modified for the buyer. Also the dollar cost per item is relatively low. For these purchasing situations, a strong brand name may be the one factor that will swing purchases when all other factors are considered equal. Companies are willing to purchase from strong brands that they know provide superior service, on-time delivery, and other more intangible attributes. As a result, to compete in e-commerce, business-to-business firms not only must provide strong e-commerce sites but also must develop strong brand names that stand out among competitors.[5]

Just as with consumers, to encourage businesses to use the Internet for e-commerce involves offering financial, convenience, or value-added incentives. In the iGo.com Internet advertisement below, a 10 percent discount is offered for orders placed via the Internet or by telephone. Also, there is a 10 percent discount on any product or service purchased through the Web site employeesavings.com.

A growing field of e-commerce in the business-to-business sector is on-line exchanges and auctions. These exchanges allow businesses to purchase a variety of commodities and goods at bargain prices. Businesses now use the Internet to enable them to speed up time to the market, to sell directly to other businesses, and to cut transaction and inventory costs. Companies can buy nonproduction goods such as office supplies but also purchase production-related supplies, raw materials, and equipment. There are also sites where companies can purchase oil, natural gas, electricity, coal, chemicals, steel, coal, and other raw materials. Commodity-type

An Internet advertisement for iGo.com featuring a financial incentive to encourage business or consumer purchases. Courtesy of iGo.com.

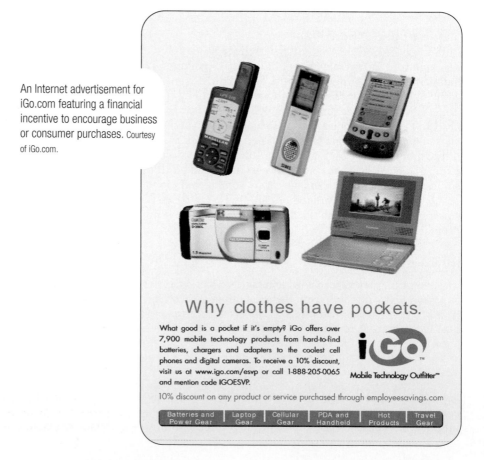

products especially have become popular on the Internet. For example, the average business-to-business sale through a salesperson costs about $300. In the process of wining and dining, a company can spend several thousand dollars to get the sale and then spend additional money on sales commissions. These costs can be greatly reduced through the Internet. Still, it is very important to maintain sales support staff for Internet programs. In-house salespeople are often needed to handle on-line negotiations.[6]

Many of the on-line markets are neutral companies that simply match buyers and sellers. For example, PaperExchange.com recently arranged the sale of 250 tons of container-board grade paper. The paper was owned by a Finnish firm. It had been made for a Japanese firm but was being stored in Kansas City, where it was shipped to its final destination in Tokyo.

PaperExchange receives about 15,000 hits a day from prospective buyers and sellers. This means these types of transactions occur almost daily for various companies. PaperExchange receives 1 percent to 3 percent of the transaction costs for arranging sales.[7]

New York–based E-Steel Corporation opened a similar site for the buying and selling of steel. E-Steel lists both prime, made-to-order steel, and secondary steel products. The goal is to expedite deals between established supply chains that range from large steel mills to small, one-person shops. E-Steel charges a commission of 1 percent. Benefits to its members include faster deals, lower inventories, lower transaction costs, and new customers and suppliers. The advantage of using E-Steel can be illustrated by assuming a firm needed an extra 100 tons of a particular type of steel. After contacting a current supplier, the firm can put out a bid on E-Steel to see if this extra 100 tons of steel can be purchased cheaper from another vendor on the open market.

There are other advantages to e-commerce operations. For example, most consumers still want to make purchases at an actual, physical store. Therefore, it is important to provide store information for buyers. Vicinity Corporation is a company that dispenses store location information to consumers.

A similar process takes place in the business-to-business marketplace. Many businesses want merchandise to be shipped quickly when they use the Internet to obtain information and choose products. Vicinity Corporation's SiteMaker and Business Finder software display locations of the closest store for these businesses, complete with a map and directions showing how to get to there. A business needing specialized parts, supplies, or maintenance equipment is able to access the Vicinity Web site in order to find the nearest location where the merchandise is sold.[8]

For manufacturers such as Hewlett-Packard, Vicinity SiteMaker refers business customers to resellers. HP refers 100,000 customers each month to its closest reseller. This strategy not only has increased the loyalty of the reseller to HP but also has reduced the load on HP's call center. This results in major cost savings, because a human operator locating information and providing it to the customer is both slower and much more expensive. It is also convenient for customers. They can simply type in a zip code or address to gain access to location information. Further, a company can access the information at any time of the day, and no caller is forced to wait on hold for the next available HP company operator.

Many other innovations are part of the business-to-business landscape. For instance, a new form of software makes it possible for firms to track shoppers on the Internet as they move to retail stores. To do so, consumers are presented with special offers and promotions. The offers are purchased on the Internet using credit cards. They then must be picked up at a store within a specified period, which creates the path from the Web to the store. In a variation of this approach, the consumer reserves the item on the Web site and then pays for and picks it up at the retail store. Again, the firm can track the consumer from the Internet to the store. Also, these programs generate excellent feedback regarding the types of promotions that work best on the Internet.

Several manufacturers are also involved in e-commerce. The actual methods used by the manufacturer depend on the distribution channel structure. Retailers and wholesalers become concerned if too many manufacturers establish e-commerce sites, because they sell products directly to consumers. Manufacturers must be aware that bypassing other channel members can cause an alienation that is difficult to overcome if the manufacturer wants channel members to support their brand. Some manufacturers set up an e-commerce site and sell directly to consumers. Others develop sites that enhance the brand but then refer customers to the retailers and wholesalers actually selling the product. Establishing a link to these sites where the customer can continue with an on-line order is important to tying the customer to the brand.

In all of these applications, it has become clear that e-commerce is a major force in business-to-business marketing programs. It seems highly likely that there will be continual growth in the uses of the Internet in business-to-business transactions.

stop!

Integrated Learning Experience

Two business-to-business sites mentioned in this section were PaperExchange at www. paperexchange.com and E-Steel at www.e-steel.com. Access both Web sites. What types of services does each provide for sellers? What types of services are provided for buyers? Which member(s) of the buying center would utilize these Web sites? For Web sites that wish to provide retail outlet information, a prominent firm is Vicinity at www.vicinity.com. For a company looking for specific products and for companies trying to sell products to other businesses, BusinessFinder.com provides a database for both buyers and sellers. Access both of these Web sites and review the types of business-to-business services provided.

international e-commerce

One of the major advantages of e-commerce over the brick and mortar of a retail store is the ability to reach consumers everywhere, even in other countries. Still, almost 46 percent of the current Internet companies turn away international orders because they do not have processes in place to fill them. Therefore, although the Internet makes it possible for a company to sell items in an international market-place, many companies are not prepared to go global. Many obstacles to selling across national boundaries exist. They include communications barriers, cultural differences, global shipping problems due to a lack of sufficient infrastructure, and varying degrees of Internet capability in countries.[9]

Companies preparing to launch global e-commerce sites should keep in mind that a key step is to prepare for international shipments. Smaller products mean air transport is affordable, and DHL Worldwide Express, FedEx, and UPS offer excellent shipping options. Larger merchandise normally is shipped by some type of freight forwarder. Both express delivery and freight forwarding companies usually will be of assistance in shipping to countries they serve. These companies offer specialized logistics software and also provide the proper documentation and forms to meet the regulations of each country.

Making shipping arrangements is not all that must be done. Internet companies must examine both export and import laws in the countries involved. After working on the shipping, payment mechanisms must be installed. Each country differs not only in terms of type of currency but also in methods of payment. For example, in Europe, debit cards are preferred to credit cards. Europe also has a high rate of credit card theft, which increases the risks associated with accepting them.

Another challenge in the international arena is developing Web sites that appeal to the audiences of each country. This entails adding information that some-

> ▶ Using black in backgrounds and graphics has sinister conntations in Asia, Europe, and Latin America.
>
> ▶ The thumbs up sign and the waving hand are rude gestures in Latin America and the Middle East, respectively.
>
> ▶ Showing a woman with exposed arms or legs is offensive in the Middle East.
>
> ▶ Using a dog as a company logo is not successful in Korea because dogs are used for food.

Cultural Disasters to Avoid in International Internet Marketing

Source: Lynda Radosevich, "Going Global Overnight," *InfoWorld,* (April 19, 1999), Vol. 21, No. 16, pp. 1–3.

FIGURE 16.3

one in another country would need, such as the country code for telephone numbers. It also requires removing or changing any colors, words, or images that might be offensive to a particular group of people in another country. Figure 16.3 identifies some cultural disasters to avoid. As has been discussed previously, simply translating an English site into another language is not sufficient. The company must have someone who understands both the language and the culture of the target area in order to insure no one is offended by a company's marketing efforts. Also the cultural assimilator should check to make sure the proper meaning is being disseminated for each communication effort. Using local firms to translate the Web pages often prevents these types of communications problems from occurring.

Probably the most difficult challenge companies face in the international market is the technical side of the e-commerce site. Software compatibility is major technical issue that has not yet been resolved. Countries vary in terms of how they handle e-commerce and these various technologies must be merged into one system. Also, the bandwidth for handling Internet traffic varies considerably. Information technology (IT) people must be involved in every step of an internationalization process.

Another major key to successful global e-commerce is a coherent IMC strategy utilizing local input from the various countries involved. The branding on the Internet site must be consistent from one country to the next and must leverage the brand's main marketing message. For IBM, this meant using local companies in each country to design the Web site and provide the information used on the site. To insure consistency, IBM designs the main marketing messages at its central office, but then local companies translate the messages and add reseller contact and pricing information.

A unique aspect of e-commerce is that small companies can compete as effectively as large companies. For example, Trebnick Systems is a printing business located near Dayton, Ohio. Trebnick employees 10 people, yet its Web site has attracted customers from Japan, Germany, Spain, and Ireland. Similarly, Greyden Press employs only 25 people but uses the Internet as a primary tool of operation. Customers can request quotes and submit jobs on-line. Most customers Greyden serves are not located in Columbus, Ohio, where the organization's facility is physically located. E-commerce allows small companies like this to expand their customer bases beyond their local regions.[10]

In the future, the growth of international e-commerce is likely to be explosive. Firms that "get in on the ground floor" may have a major marketing advantage in the years to come.

IMC and the internet

The Internet should be an important component of the integrated marketing communications plan. As the Internet continues to grow in usage in both consumer and business-to-business markets, its importance will continue to rise. The most critical decision facing businesses is what function the Web site should serve. It is extremely difficult to design a Web site that provides all of the functions mentioned earlier in Figure 16.2. If multiple functions are to be served, it may become necessary to create separate Web sites. These different sites can be connected by links, but a company must resist the temptation to create a Web site that attempts to be everything to everyone.

In addition to incorporating the Internet into the IMC plan, it is vital that the information technology (IT), human resource, production, and shipping departments are included as the marketing team develops the program. If they are not, disasters can happen. For example, marketers at a major consumer goods company launched a highly successful Web site that created 3,000 customer queries a day. The problem was that no one was hired by HR to handle these queries. Victoria's Secret announced its Internet fashion show during the Super Bowl. The site drew more than one million hits. The problem was that no one told the IT department the commercial was going to air. In fact, members of the IT department found out about the Internet fashion show while they were watching the Super Bowl themselves. The result was that the Victoria's Secret system crashed. This type of disaster illustrates why it is essential to communicate with other departments within the company when formulating an Internet strategy.[11]

Coordination between the IT department and other areas involves a variety of activities. Changes can be made quickly on individual Web sites within hours, and marketers must think about how each change can impact other activities in the company. The marketing department should coordinate each advertising campaign with the IT department, so that software capabilities are addressed to ensure smooth operations. The company must work hard to avoid glitches that affect operations. Also, members of the call center need to know when additional telephone calls and e-mail inquiries may result from a special Internet offer. It takes time and effort to coordinate marketing changes with IT and other departments, but any delay in implementation will be offset by a smoother, more efficient operation.

A recent research poll, called the World Wide Internet Opinion Survey, examined the factors that drove people to Internet Web sites for the first time. These results are highlighted in Figure 16.4. As shown, a search engine is the primary method consumers use to discover new Web sites. As a result, it is important for companies to make sure they are listed under as many search engines as possible and also the correct keywords. Notice that television and print ads are the least successful in driving someone to an Internet site for the first time, finishing far behind word of mouth.

▶ Internet content search	38%
▶ Word of mouth	30%
▶ Internet banner	20%
▶ Television ad	7%
▶ Print ad	5%

What Drives People to a New Site?

FIGURE 16.4

Source: Don Jeffrey, "Survey Details Consumer Shopping Trends on the Net," *Billboard*, (May 29, 1999), Vol. 111, No. 22, p. 47.

Many experts believe the traditional banner ad has little influence on people. Not surprisingly, Web designers are trying to attract attention through fancier banners. Graphics, flashing images, and streaming videos are used to garner attention. Interstitial or popup ads were created that forced Web browsers to react. Unfortunately, these types of ads have become highly controversial and many view them as offensive. The truth, however, is that these popup ads work significantly better at attracting buyers than do traditional banner ads. This success has led many Internet companies to develop superstitials that work after a person leaves a Web site or even shuts off the computer. The ad appears the next time the person logs onto the Internet. E-mail advertisements also are being created with full graphics and videos that are sent overnight to customers who were on a particular Web site. Although the ethical implications of such advertising tactics are being debated, the fact is that they work. Since they do, their use will continue to increase.

As part of the World Wide Internet Opinion Survey mentioned earlier, respondents were asked to cite the most offensive form of advertising. Only 24 percent stated that no form of Internet advertising was intrusive or a turnoff. The biggest turn-off was popup ads, named by 40 percent of the respondents. Next most disliked were e-mail ads at 28 percent. Banner ads bothered only 8 percent of the sample.[12]

In business-to-business markets, the number of hits at a B-to-B Web site is directly related to the amount of off-line advertising and sales promotions. A large business-to-business company went from 20,000 visits per month to 80,000 visits per month during a six-month period by doubling the company's annual Internet advertising budget for print, direct mail, and trade shows. A small company went from 2,000 to 6,000 hits per month by increasing their budget for print ads from $25,000 to $65,000 per year. Dynamic Web, a high-tech Web company, saw company Web site traffic increase 250 to 300 hits per week immediately following participation in a trade show featuring the company's Web site.[13]

The Internet affects a firm's IMC program in numerous ways. In this section, the nature of Internet activities in response to various parts of the IMC program are described, including the impact on:

- Branding
- Brand loyalty
- Sales support
- Customer service
- Consumer promotions

These and other topics highlight the value of bringing the firm's Internet programs in line with the rest of its marketing communications efforts. A review of the various IMC topics follows.

Branding

In Chapter 4, the importance of brand image was discussed. Powerful brands are vital to Internet success. The design of a Web site and the information it provides are key variables that affect perceptions of the brand. An IMC plan that emphasizes brand quality should maintain the same theme on the Web site. Also, a Web site should reinforce the integrated communications theme that is presented in other media. When this is accomplished, the Internet becomes a valuable tool in the development of the brand.

Creating an effective brand presence on-line requires more than a Web site with an e-commerce capability. Cyberbranding involves integrating on-line and off-line branding tactics that reinforce each other and that speak with one voice. The most common method of building an on-line brand presence is through an off-line technique called brand spiraling. **Brand spiraling** is the practice of using traditional media to promote and attract consumers to an on-line Web site. From television,

A magazine advertisement for WeddingChannel.com designed to encourage visits to its Web site. Courtesy of Della.com.

radio, newspapers, magazines, and billboards to simple shopping bags, consumers are encouraged to visit the firm's Web site. One goal of each advertising campaign should be to encourage traffic to the site and enhance brand recognition. The interactive nature of the Internet makes it possible for a firm to learn more about each customer. This information can then be used to target more specific messages. The magazine advertisement above by WeddingChannel.com is designed to encourage traffic to the Web site. Once there, WeddingChannel.com requests information from viewers in an effort to learn more about them and their particular needs.

Adobe, a desktop publishing software company, uses billboard, Internet, and print ads to drive traffic to its Web site. Adobe uses print ads in magazines such as *Details, Spin, Wallpaper, and Wired* to target young, 20- to 25-year-old professionals who do not have strong backgrounds in graphic arts but, for some reason, have jumped into desktop publishing. Once at the site, a person can test and try different versions of Adobe's products.[14]

Figure 16.5 identifies some of the techniques business-to-business firms use to advertise their Web sites. As shown, the most common method is displaying the Web address on all printed and promotional material. Next is placing ads promoting the Web address in various trade publications. Over 70 percent of the companies register keywords with search engines, because business buyers often look for a specific product. The odds of making a sale increase substantially when a firm's Web site is cited after a keyword is typed into the search engine. The least used method is placing banners on other sites. Seldom do business customers go to a site when they are at another site. The primary effect of placing banners on other sites is to develop brand awareness and brand knowledge rather than to attract customers.

▶ Putting the Web address on printed materials and promotional items	91%
▶ Advertising in trade journals	74%
▶ Registering the Web site with search engines for keywords	72%
▶ Buying banners on other sites	25%

B-to-B Techniques to Boost Web Site Awareness

FIGURE 16.5

Companies with strong off-line brands benefit from what is called a **halo effect.** A well-received brand leads more customers to try new products and services that are being offered by the company on the Internet. These same customers are also more willing to provide information that can be used for greater personalization of messages. This halo effect results from the credibility of the firm's brand being transferred to an individual's evaluation of the Web site. Barnes & Noble and Toys "R" Us were late entrants into e-commerce. Still, both companies built successful Internet businesses because of the strong brand names transferred to their Web site programs.

A company such as Amazon.com, which was an Internet start-up, is likely to use traditional advertising media to help develop a brand name. Brand-name power cannot be created solely through advertising on the Internet. To achieve a strong brand name, Amazon.com invested a half billion dollars in traditional media. The Internet must be one component of the total IMC program if a strong brand name is to emerge.[15]

Brand loyalty and IMC internet programs

A series of benefits may be realized when a firm effectively utilizes the Internet. For example, the Internet makes it easier for firms to communicate with loyal consumers. This makes it possible to solidify the relationships they have with the company. To secure this advantage, the process begins by identifying the heavy product users. Remember, being a heavy user is not always synonymous with feeling strong brand loyalty. Some individuals or companies are heavy users because of price or convenience or for some other reason. When another firm emerges offering a better price or an improved delivery schedule, the heavy user often will switch while the brand-loyal consumer will not.

Brand-loyal consumers make purchases for reasons beyond the price, the convenience, or the product itself. Often they experience a type of "psychic" or affective feeling toward the brand or company. Also, in nearly every instance of brand loyalty, consumers believe the brand is superior in quality. Inferior items are not likely to create brand loyalty. Lower quality products are more likely to capture repeat purchase behavior rather than loyalty.

The experience or feelings a consumer develops toward a brand are often the result of marketing communications between the firm and the consumer. Although advertising is a major component or communication channel used to develop brand loyalty, the Internet is becoming increasingly valuable.

The Internet provides two opportunities that are not possible with advertising. First, the Internet can be designed to make shopping and other contacts more pleasurable experiences. Buyers return to the Web sites because they enjoyed the experience previously. These feelings may be similar to what a customer encounters at Starbucks. Consumers are loyal to Starbucks because of the total experience and atmosphere of the establishment. True, the coffee is good, but there is much more involved in the feelings of loyalty toward the company.

The second opportunity the Internet provides is the ability to establish one-to-one communication between the consumer and the firm. As discussed in the previous chapter, database technology permits the company to retain a detailed history of groups of consumers as well as information about individual shoppers. Using these data, the company can develop a one-on-one relationship that ties the consumer to the firm. These communications (special offers, customized ads, etc.) often move heavy users toward brand loyalty.

Three companies that have learned to pamper their customers through their Internet programs are Harley-Davidson, Saturn, and Amazon.com. Both Harley-Davidson and Saturn maintain open channels of communication with their customers. Harley encourages buyers to become part of the Harley family by inviting them to motorcycle rallies. Saturn owners are invited to attend a yearly gathering and to meet employees and other Saturn owners. Amazon.com rewards its best buyers with e-mails notifying them of new books of interest. These types of communication create brand-loyal consumers, and the Internet is a simple and inexpensive method to maintain contact.

In communicating with consumers, it is important to provide rewards for loyalty. These rewards are not promotions, but actual rewards. The gift or offer may be the same as for a promotion, but the dialogue with the consumer is different. For loyal consumers, these rewards are mentioned as a way to say "thank you" for that loyalty. On the other hand, consumer promotions are merely used to entice the price-sensitive consumer or the light user to make a purchase. A reward helps the firm to say that the person or business is important, and the psychological impact of this type of message can be very strong.

Sales support on the internet

One key feature of any IMC program is sales support. The Internet can be used in various ways to help with this effort. Manufacturers that sell their products through retailers and wholesalers must be careful to avoid having a Web site that is viewed as a threat. Many retailers and wholesalers are wary of manufacturing Web sites where customers can place orders. To prevent damaging relationships with retailers, manufacturers can offer product information, but actual orders for merchandise should go through the retailer or wholesale vendor.

The strategy of using a Web site for information only rather than for direct sales is found more frequently in the business-to-business sector. In that arena, each manufacturer has fewer customers. Therefore, it is critical for a manufacturer to maintain positive relationships with its retail or wholesale vendors. When a manufacturer sells through multiple vendors, it may be wise to offer a locator on the manufacturer's Web site that shows customers the nearest vendor. For example, a manufacturer of a depth finder for fishing boats could list the retail stores where that particular brand can be purchased. Through locator software, customers can find the closest retail store.

Often, the most important use of the Internet in the area of sales support is providing information about clients and products to the sales staff. The salesperson should be able to access all of the information the company has in its database about any given customer. In addition, data can be collected regarding which products are being examined by individual customers on a Web site. This gives the salesperson insight regarding what product to pitch and how to make the sales approach. The information also helps the company when a number of customers are accessing details about specific products. The **Web master** can then add materials regarding that product in order to increase the odds of making a sale.

Further, the sales staff can utilize the Internet as a valuable resource tool in another way. Although experienced salespeople may have complete knowledge of all of the products sold, new salespeople may not. The salesperson can use the Internet to provide the information a client requests. Often this can be done in the client's office or within a short period of time while on the phone. The Internet also can be used when a customer is ready to place an order. The order can be sent immediately and the salesperson with access to the firm's database can inform the customer of the shipping date. If the item is out of stock, the salesperson informs

Combining Web-tailing with Retailing

One of the more intricate functions of Internet marketing is to make sure it complements and supplements what takes place in the retail store. When these two forces are combined, the potential to build a stronger business rises dramatically.

One success story is found at Gymbore Corporation of Burlingame, California. Gymbore is a children's apparel vendor with 550 retail stores. The company's Internet site offers customers personalized service and suggests matching outfits based on customer selections. The goal according to Susan Neal, VP of business development, ". . . is to provide service at least as good as customers get in our stores." To build the organization's database, Gymbore asks each customer to register on the Web site. Individuals are asked to provide demographic data such as the age and sex of children. To obtain this information, Gymbore offers discounts and other incentives.

Using the Blue Martini E-Merchandising software, Gymbore can analyze the purchase history of each customer and compare it with the demographic data provided. The analysis helps Gymbore customize the Web page for each shopper. For example, a customer who has a five-year-old girl sees a Web page with merchandise for a five-year-old girl. In addition to customizing Web sites, Gymbore reviews what is selling and what is not. Inventory adjustments can then be made in individual retail stores based on Internet traffic. This combination of Internet with retail gives Gymbore a competitive edge over many firms that are still in the "stone age" of Internet usage.

Source: Jeff Sweat and Rick Whiting, "Instant Marketing," *Information Week*, no. 746 (August 2, 1999), pp. 18–20.

the customer that the item must be back ordered. Being given this information at the time the order is placed is much better than receiving a phone call or note later.

Customers can go on-line and receive another kind of sales support. As noted previously, it has the advantage of being available 24 hours a day, 7 days a week. Customers can access a Web site to obtain product information at the time that best suits them. A Web site can provide extensive sales support that can be transmitted to customers and prospects even when the salesperson is not available.

Both prospecting for and qualifying prospects can be facilitated through the effective use of the Internet. A salesperson can locate companies that may be interested in a certain product. For example, Trebnick Systems, a printing service near Dayton, Ohio, discovered customers in Japan, Germany, Spain, and Ireland from examining 160 Web sites. Trebnick made contact and obtained orders. Once prospects have been located, whether through the Internet or through the traditional channels, the Internet can help qualify prospects to see if they are good candidates for sales calls. If they are not, the salesperson may want to try an e-mail contact or turn the lead over to telemarketers to explore.

The Internet provides valuable information for preparing a sales call. By examining a prospect's Web site first, the salesperson can discover information about the company, its products, and the personnel at the firm. Also, the sales rep can use a search engine to locate articles and press releases about a prospect or company. Financial information is available for publicly held corporations. All of this information can be useful in the preparation of a sales call, as the sales rep is able to individualize and personalize a presentation.

Customer service and the internet

The Internet is a very efficient and cost-effective way for companies to provide customer service. Examples that illustrate how well this can be done are found at

FedEx, the U.S. Postal Service, and Visa. Customers of FedEx and the USPS can track packages they have sent through the Internet. It is more efficient to use the Internet, and the costs of telephone calls are reduced, because fewer human operators are needed. Visa provides an ATM finder program for its consumers. Those who use the card are given directions to the closest ATM when one is needed.

The key to using the Web effectively to enhance customer service is found in the design of the Web site. The site must be easy for the consumer to use and provide some benefit over using the telephone. Speed is one primary benefit the Internet offers. Making it easier and faster to get the information encourages consumers to use a Web site. Providing additional information that is not normally given over the telephone can be another advantage.

A major part of customer service is answering questions. Designed properly, a Web site can be a valuable resource for responding to common consumer inquiries. One method is to provide a series of responses to FAQs. They must be indexed or arranged by topics so customers can access answers quickly. Otherwise, consumers become frustrated and call a toll-free number instead. Asking users to go through a long list of FAQs does not work well. This is because customers often look for specific information. Consequently, it is important to provide as much information as possible on the Internet.

An option that should always be available to customers is e-mail. Consumers who have specific questions should have the option of sending an e-mail. If these e-mails are answered immediately and completely, it saves the company from making a telephone call.

Another approach some companies use to enhance customer service on the Internet is to put together discussion groups or chat rooms. Many public relations people dislike chat rooms, even though they provide the opportunity for customers to interact with each other and with the firm in a somewhat controlled environment. One of the best ways for a firm to react to negative comments by consumers is through replying to the complaint directly. Everyone reading the chat conversation sees the response. A discussion group also allows consumers to interact with each other and may provide solutions to problems that the company had not considered. This type of situation can occur with computer software and highly technical products. Such open communication with customers tends to build a stronger bond between the customer and the firm.

For business-to-business marketing, granting access to information within the seller's database can be especially beneficial. Each company with access has a password to gain entry. Providing information in this manner can save everyone considerable time, especially when there is a strong bond between the two companies. For example, a shipping company may allow its customers access to all of its database information concerning location of shipments and availability of trucks, trains, and ocean vessels. In scheduling shipments, this information is helpful to the logistics coordinator responsible for planning and coordinating movement of goods from the manufacturer to the retailer or wholesaler. Thus, by knowing that an ocean vessel currently has capacity for a 25-ton shipment, a logistics manager can reserve the space to ensure a large shipment of merchandise arrives on time. Without the Internet, the logistics manager must make a series of telephone calls to obtain the needed information.

Many retailers now give entrance to their databases to manufacturers using the Internet. Manufacturers study which products are selling. They also can see which colors, sizes, and styles are the most popular. They even can find out which stores have the highest levels of sales. Then the manufacturer can modify or set production schedules in order to make sure retailers have a steady supply of just the right size, color, and so forth.

Customer service is an important part of an IMC program. Quality service conveys key information to the customer that the company cares. Servicing programs also help every member of the marketing channel build strong bonds with its constituents.

Consumer promotions and the internet

A popular cyberbait used in attracting consumers to a site is some type of consumer promotion. To build traffic, a firm must decide whether to have one major event or many smaller events. It is the difference between giving one person $100,000 or 500 people cash or merchandise worth $200. The large promotion attracts the type of person who enters a lottery or contest with the hope of winning the big prize. In contrast, smaller promotions often draw individuals who are more interested in the company's merchandise. For example, a music site could offer every person who buys a CD a chance of winning $100,000, and the odds of winning may be one in a million. On the other hand, the same company can offer free CDs as prizes with the chances of winning being only one in ten. These two promotions would attract different types of potential customers. Consequently, the choice of the promotional form should be based on the goals of the firm's IMC plan and oriented toward the type of person the company seeks to attract to the site.

It is important to change promotions on a regular basis. For example, one month individuals who purchase merchandise may receive 10 percent off. The next month, they may have a one in ten chance of winning a free gift. In the third month, the promotion may change to receiving a third item free if the person buys two. Changing promotions encourages consumers to return to the site. Each promotion may also appeal to slightly different consumers. Thus, a coupon may appeal to one consumer while a premium may be more appealing to another.

A major advantage of offering promotions is the opportunity to build a database. Contests and sweepstakes are effective means of building a database, because no purchase is required. Consumers receive a chance at winning simply by entering. With the lure of a prize in place, most individuals are willing to provide information about themselves. This basic information can be used to start a database. The company can then build records of individual purchases and even the items on the Web sites consumers browse.

An example of an effective marketing program using promotions is the 1-800-Flowers.com approach. The company uses specially designed software to devise Web site promotions. Promotions are based on inventory levels. When the inventory reaches a certain level, a prewritten promotion is automatically put onto the Web site. At the other end, when a promotion results in sales and inventories drop to specified levels, the promotion is pulled off the Web site. This prevents a stock-out situation that might make customers angry.

Instead of automatic promotions controlled by inventory levels, DiscountDomain.com does spot promotions. DiscountDomain.com is an apparel Web site that caters to 12- to 24-year-olds. Using real-time inventory data and real-time data from teen chat groups, DiscountDomain.com designs and puts a promotion up on its Web site within just a few hours. If teens are talking about a specific product that is in DiscountDomain.com's inventory, marketers design a promotion on that item and immediately offer it on the Web site.[16]

In summary, it should be apparent that e-commerce and the Internet now play a vital role in the marketing successes and failures of numerous businesses. Company leaders must account for the role the Internet plays as they develop overall IMC programs. A Web site should reflect the image and theme portrayed in all other marketing communications efforts. A consistent message strengthens the brand and builds the potential for greater brand loyalty. Promotions, sales efforts, advertisements, and every other marketing activity should constantly remind the consumer of the major theme that drives the company. When this is accomplished, the Internet is more likely to fulfill its potential of becoming a strong new channel in the marketplace. Beyond these more general IMC efforts, direct sales to consumers can be used to build traffic and increase profits. These types of programs are presented next.

---

direct marketing on the internet

As noted in Chapter 15, the Internet is an ideal medium for direct marketing. Consumers and businesses now order directly from numerous companies through the Internet. Internet patrons can also be sent e-mails promoting specific products. Businesses, however, have to be careful about sending unsolicited e-mails, because many consumers and businesses are frustrated by the practice of spamming, or sending out mass unwanted e-mails. Spamming on the Internet is equivalent to sending out junk mail to an untargeted audience. Instead, the firm should develop a more targeted Internet e-mail direct-marketing program. To do so, the first step is to get the customer's permission. Obtaining this permission is easier when some type of reward is offered.

In the iGo.com direct-mail piece shown on the next page, notice the box customers can check in order to receive the free iGo e-newsletter. Also, individuals making purchases can receive two months' free service. To get more details about Pocketmail, individuals are encouraged to visit the iGo.com Web site at www.igo.com/pocketmail. This direct-mail piece is designed to encourage consumers to act quickly. Also, from the firm's perspective, the mailing is designed to obtain names for a database, which may then be used in later direct-mail and e-mail marketing programs.

Some florists have been successful using e-mail to encourage direct sales. These companies obtain the client's permission and then send reminders about anniversaries, birthdays, and other important dates. Many customers find these personalized e-mails to be beneficial. It takes time to develop this type of program, because the company needs a great deal of information from customers. When the plan is established, however, it can be a very strong direct-marketing technique.

The most recent trend in direct marketing via the Internet is **interactive marketing.** Interactive marketing is individualizing and personalizing everything from the Internet Web content to the products being promoted to e-mail messages. NCR produces a software called Relationship Optimizer and Prime Response that uses powerful data analysis techniques to personalize direct offers. The NCR software analyzes customer interactions such as click-stream data traffic, any type of customer interaction with the firm, and combines it with demographic information from external or internal direct-marketing databases. As the data are being

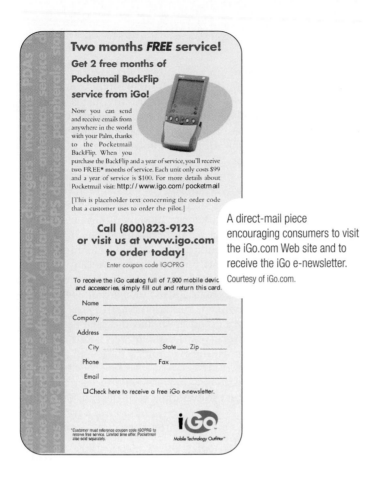

A direct-mail piece encouraging consumers to visit the iGo.com Web site and to receive the iGo e-newsletter.
Courtesy of iGo.com.

processed, the software can launch complex interactive and personalized Web and e-mail campaigns.

Levi-Strauss uses a similar software, called Blue Martini E-Merchandising, to customize both the Levis.com and the Dockers.com Web sites. The Home Shopping Network uses Edify's Smart Options software to track user preferences and suggest products based on the customer's past activities and current purchases. These technologies blur the line between selling and marketing because the messages and products a customer sees are based on past purchasing activities. These programs are designed to increase the odds that the customer will see something he or she wants rather than being forced to wade through scores of products he or she has no interest in purchasing at a more standardized Web site.[17]

As the technology improves and grows, other forms of direct-marketing programs through the Internet will emerge. Also, as more people access the Web while on the move (through pagers and other carry-around devices), Web marketers undoubtedly will develop methods to reach customers with on-demand goods and services. It is likely that direct marketing has only scratched the surface of the potential the Internet offers.

Integrated Learning Experience

Customer interactive software is becoming an important component of many Web sites. Access the Blue Martini Software Company at www.bluemartini.com and Edify at www.edify.com. What types of services do these companies offer? How can their services be used in conjunction with an e-commerce Web site?

stop!

viral marketing on the internet

Today's technology has created a new form of marketing. **Viral marketing** is preparing an advertisement that is tied to an e-mail. It is also a form of advocacy or word-of-mouth endorsement marketing. In other words, viral marketing takes place as one customer passes along a message to other potential buyers. The name *viral* is derived from the image of a person being infected with the marketing message then spreading it to friends like a virus. The major difference, however, is that the customer voluntarily sends the message to others.

Viral marketing messages include ads for goods and services, hyperlinked promotions that take someone immediately to a Web site, on-line newsletters, and various games. Statistics indicate that 81 percent of recipients who receive a viral marketing message pass it along to another person. Almost 50 percent pass it along to two or more people. The marketing message can be more deliberate such as when an individual recommends something to a friend. It can also be transmitted passively, when the message is simply attached to an e-mail. Viral marketing allows a firm to gain rapid product awareness at a low cost.[18]

Blue Marble, a viral marketing company, created a program for Scope mouthwash. Consumers were able to send a customized, animated e-mail "kiss" to their friends. The attached marketing message reinforced the brand message that Scope brings people "kissably close." People who received the e-mail kiss could then forward the message to someone else. Scope's tracking technology indicated most did forward the message.

Some viral messages include incentives to encourage people to pass the message along. Travel site GreenTravel.com enters individuals who pass on the firm's newsletter an opportunity to win an Osprey backpack. The GreenTravel.com newsletter has a prominent, highly visible call to action that many consumers responded to by passing along the document.[19]

The term *viral* may connate the negative image of a computer *virus.* Consequently, care should be given when offering to create such a program for a firm. Company leaders may want to find some other term to describe the technique to the general public so that no undue suspicion or fear arises.

internet design issues

The primary issue in the design of Web site is to make sure it functions properly. e-commerce companies spend an average of $100 to acquire each new customer, and some companies spend up to $500.[20] It may appear that developing an effective Web site is cheap. In reality it is not. As a result, it is essential that the firm specify the key function to be served by the Web site before it is created. In addition, the site should then be designed to support the function, but from the user's point of view. For example, if the function is to *support e-commerce,* then the site needs to be designed so it is easy for customers to navigate, select products, and order them. If the key function is to *support selling,* then the person designing the Web site needs to talk with salespeople and determine their needs.

Companies spend almost $20 billion per year on Internet advertising of Web sites. Just as with the other components of advertising, consideration must be given to where these advertisements will be placed. One approach is to focus on targeted Web sites with similar customer profiles. For example, a Web site for John Deere may also advertise on other agriculture-related Web sites. Another approach is to advertise on a broader array of sites to develop brand awareness. For example, a company can advertise on a variety of Web sites in order to encourage different people to visit its Web site. Even if a person does not go to the site, the ad enhances brand awareness.[21]

- ▶ Clueless banners
- ▶ Slow loading front pages
- ▶ Forcing people to go through numerous screens
- ▶ Too much verbal information
- ▶ Too many technical terms
- ▶ Sites that are hard to navigate

Clues to Poor Design

FIGURE 16.6

A Web site should match the constituency it will serve. Too often, a site is designed by a computer whiz who likes fancy graphics and images, the users of the site hate it because they cannot find what they are looking for or the pages take too long to load. To summarize these kinds of flaws, Figure 16.6 provides some clues to poor Web site design. A discussion of each item follows.

Clueless banners

Banners are often used to advertise a Web site. Web masters should make sure the banners provide sufficient information about what the company sells. Tricking people to come to a site through clever banners can frustrate consumers and often has a negative impact on the brand's image. In other words, rather than being deceptive, the banner should provide a reason for the consumer or business to click on it.

Slow loading front pages

Graphics and videos are great to look at and make a site enticing. Unfortunately, most consumers are not patient enough to wait a long time for a front page to load. After a few seconds most people move on to another site. Therefore, the Web designer should put videos and fancy graphics on other pages. Once the consumer has accessed the site, he or she can choose whether to stay and look at longer loading images. Even then, however, bear in mind that many consumers may stay at the site but become agitated at the same time. This type of frustration has a negative impact on brand image. If streaming videos are used, consumers should be given the option of bypassing the video to go directly to the Web site main page.

Numerous screens

Another source of aggravation surfers experience is being forced to go through numerous screens. Instead, indexes should be developed that help consumers quickly locate the part of the Web site they want to browse, and links should take them directly to the desired page. Also remember that although it looks nice to have moving icons and graphics, if consumers find the Web site difficult to navigate, they become frustrated and quit. Links to other sites and pages within the Web site should be easy to locate.

Too much verbal information

Too many graphics usually cause a site to load slowly. Too much verbal information on a page is cumbersome for viewers. Most do not want to take time to read paragraph after paragraph of information. To correct this problem, verbal copy should be short, precise, and to the point. Additional links can be provided for consumers seeking more detailed verbal information, a video illustration, or graphic demonstrations.

Too many technical terms

Another Web site design flaw occurs when the company uses too many technical terms. Technical terms are more useful when the site is designed for internal

> The Web site should follow a strategic purpose such as to acquire new customers, serve existing customers, cross-sell, and so on.

> Make the Web site easy to access and quick to load.

> Written content should be precise with short words, short sentences, and short paragraphs.

> Content is the key to success, not fancy graphics and design.

> Graphics should support content, not detract from it.

> Make some type of marketing offer to encourage a response.

> Ask for site evaluation.

> Provide easy-to-use navigation links on every page.

> Use gimmicks such as moving icons or flashing banners to gain attention at the beginning but do not use them deeper in the Web site.

> Change the Web site on a regular basis to keep individuals coming back.

> Measure results continually, especially designs and offers.

Tips to Creating Winning Web Sites

FIGURE 16.7

Source: Based on Ray Jutkins, "13 Ideas That Could Lead to Successful Web Marketing," *Advertising Age's Business Marketing,* (June 1999), Vol. 84, No. 6, p. 27.

purposes, but not for customers or the general public. Most consumers are not looking for sophisticated technical information. This type of information can be developed on additional pages and linked to the site. Engineers or users of the product should have access to technical information while other more casual viewers should not.

Sites that are hard to navigate

Finally, any Web site that is hard to navigate creates a negative image of the firm and its products. Consumers may conclude the company doesn't know how to design a Web site and therefore probably doesn't design products that are all that great. Thus, great care should be given the creation of a site that is "user friendly," even for casual Internet customers.

In summary, the proliferation of e-commerce Web sites is a challenging problem by itself. The marketing team should avoid as many pitfalls as possible to achieve the goal of building a stronger company through Internet activities. In contrast to the don'ts listed in Figure 16.6, Figure 16.7 highlights some tips for creating winning Web sites.

stop!

Integrated Learning Experience

A very interesting site is the Cool Site of the Day at www.coolsiteoftheday.com. Access the Web site each day for at least a week. Read the cool site of the day. Write down why you thought it was chosen as the cool site of the day. What winning strategies outlined in Figure 16.7 did it follow? What other interesting pieces of information are available at this site? How could a small business trying to develop a Web site use this site?

implications for **marketing professionals**

Web Masters

Consider yourself to be a major player on the company's marketing team.

Ask to be included in marketing meetings involving the sales staff, promotions, advertising programs, and any other item that might touch a company's Web site.

Keep up with the technology. Techniques for developing greater Internet sophistication routinely appear, and your company should try to stay on the cutting edge.

Avoid the pitfalls of bad Web sites.

Carefully study the marketplace to know where to advertise on the Internet, and who can offer your company quality link options. The marketing team may be less informed about Web information and know more about traditional advertising venues. It is your job to educate everyone about how to effectively use the Internet effectively. Take this responsibility seriously.

Build a strong relationship with the database manager. The two of you can combine to provide extremely valuable information to the company and the marketing department.

Be willing to show the company how to expand sales through direct-marketing programs, combination approaches with retail operations, and business-to-business selling plans. Build Web sites that accommodate business needs for information with efficiency and ease of selling.

Investigate every opportunity to move into international e-commerce. Build toward a future in which national boundaries do not inhibit the growth and expansion of your firm's business.

SUMMARY

Increased usage of the Internet by both consumers and businesses has led most marketing teams to develop some type of Internet site. Sometimes Web designers are being asked to design a Web page because it's the "thing to do," and little or no thought is given to the functions the Web site should perform. This chapter is designed to explain how an Internet Web site can be integrated into the overall integrated marketing communications plan and why it should.

The primary goals of various Web sites are for advertising, sales support, customer service, public relations, and e-commerce. E-commerce ventures normally require a catalog, a shopping cart, and a method to collect payments. In e-commerce and other Internet ventures, customers must feel the process is secure and be enticed to change their buying habits. Three incentives that help people alter buying patterns are financial incentives, greater convenience, and added value.

The Internet changes the traditional ways that buyers and sellers deal with each other. In business-to-business markets, field salespeople have traditionally called on customers and prospects. Information is

shared, prices are negotiated, and orders are taken. On the Internet, buyers can purchase directly from suppliers. Middlemen can be eliminated. Buyers can obtain quotes from a number of vendors and obtain product information from each, all on the Internet. While it saves the selling company money in terms of sales calls, it also risks losing customers. Loyalty and strong relationships are endangered as buyers search the Web to meet their corporation's needs.

International markets may also be served by e-commerce enterprises, especially when cultural differences, shipping problems, and Internet capability problems can be solved. Information technology departments will play a key role in solving the Internet problems. Taxation issues and language differences also require attention in this lucrative and growing marketplace.

The Internet blurs many internal functional boundaries. An effective Internet Web site can advertise, send sales messages, provide public relations announcements, offer press releases to the media, talk about the company, provide answers to frequently asked questions, provide information to investors, dispense product catalogs complete with product descriptions and prices, take orders from customers, process payments, receive e-mail messages, handle customer service queries, and entertain Web viewers.

As always, the primary goal of an Internet program is to expand and enhance the message portrayed by the company's IMC plan. Careful attention must be paid to issues of brand image and loyalty, and Web sites must be designed to support selling efforts and customer service

programs, and deliver consumer promotions of value to potential buyers. Brand spiraling may be used to combine the Internet program with advertising in traditional media. The quality of a Web site is a primary factor in the success of the entire Internet program. Many company leaders are beginning to grasp the potential of these marketing efforts, as interest and activity on the Web continue to grow. In the end, the capacity of the Internet may be limited only by what the company decides to do.

REVIEW QUESTIONS

1. Which age group is most likely to use the Internet? Which is the least? Does this have implications for IMC programs?
2. Name the five marketing functions that can be provided on the Internet that were described in this chapter.
3. Define e-commerce. What are the three common components of e-commerce programs?
4. What two issues must e-commerce providers overcome in order to build successful businesses?
5. Name and describe the three main incentives used to attract shoppers to e-commerce Web sites.
6. What is cyberbait? How must it be used over time to maintain it as an effective marketing tactic?
7. In business-to-business e-commerce operations, what obstacles occur? How can they be overcome?
8. What problems exist for international e-commerce operations? What can companies do to resolve them?

9. How can the Internet affect a brand? Brand loyalty?
10. What is brand spiraling? What is the primary goal of brand spiraling programs?
11. How can the Internet be used to provide sales support?
12. How can the Internet be used to provide customer service?
13. How can consumer promotions be offered over the Internet? What is the goal of a major prize giveaway as opposed to smaller prizes given to larger numbers of consumers?
14. How can direct marketing be used most effectively to reach customers?
15. What is interactive marketing?
16. What is viral marketing? What is the goal of a viral marketing program?
17. What tactics should companies avoid in designing Web sites? What should they do to make effective Web pages?

KEY TERMS

FAQs (frequently asked questions) questions people have about various items or services.

e-commerce selling goods on the Internet.

shopping cart a component of e-commerce operations that allows the individual to mark items to purchase later as part of a complete order.

cyberbait some type of lure or attraction that brings people to a Web site.

brand spiraling the practice of using traditional media to promote and attract consumers to an on-line Web site.

halo effect occurs when a well-received brand leads customers to try new company products and services that are being offered over the Internet.

Web master the person who manages a firm's Web site.

interactive marketing individualizing and personalizing Web content and e-mail messages for various consumers.

viral marketing preparing an advertisement that is tied to an e-mail in which one person passes on the advertisement or e-mail to other consumers.

ENDNOTES

1. Mike Troy, "E-tailers Liven Up Super Show," *Discount Store News*, 3, no. 4 (February 21, 2000), p. 3; John Angoglia, "Fogdog.com Adds Nutrition," *Sporting Goods Business*, 23, no. 4 (February 14, 2000); Chris McEvoy, Matt Powell, and Kellee Harris, "Fogdog.com," *Sporting Goods Business*, 32, no. 11 (July 6, 1999), p. 58.

2. Alf Nucifora, "There Are Lots of Good Reasons for All the Internet Hype," *Pittsburgh Business Times*, 18, no. 42 (May 7, 1999), p. 20; Al Nucifora, "Are You Preparing for the e-Business Revolution?" *Business First*, Louisville, 16, no. 28 (February 11, 2000), p. 17; Don Jeffrey, "Survey Details Consumer Shopping Trends on the Net," *Billboard*, 111, no. 22 (May 29, 1999), pp. 47–48.

3. Jeffrey, "Survey Details Consumer Shopping Trends on the Net."

4. Alan Mitchell, "Marketers Must Grasp the Net or Face Oblivion," *Marketing Week*, 22, no. 3 (February 18, 1999), pp. 30–31.

5. Bob Donath, "Web Could Boost Branding in B-to-B Marketing," *Marketing News*, 32, no. 10 (May 11, 1998), p. 6.

6. John Evan Frook, "Trading Hubs Drive Changes," *B to B*, 85, no. 4 (April 24, 2000), p. 33.

7. Edward Teach, "World Wide Bazaar," *CFO*, 15, no. 5 (May 1999), pp. 113–116.

8. Karen E. Hussel, "New Service Helps Brand Clicks with Bricks," *Advertising Age's Business Marketing*, 84, no. 11 (November 1999), pp. 40–41.

9. Lynda Radosevich, "Going Global Overnight," *InfoWorld*, 21, no. 16 (April 19, 1999), pp. 1–3.

10. Todd McCollough, "Online Services Make Ordering, Billing, Printing a Snap," *Business First*, Columbus, 15, no. 24 (February 5, 1999), pp. 19–20.

11. Julia King, "Online Marketing Tools Can Cause IT Disasters," *Computerworld*, 33, no. 46 (November 15, 1999), p. 49.

12. Jeffrey, "Survey Details Consumer Shopping Trends on the Net."

13. Carol Patton, "Marketers Promote Online Traffic Through Traditional Media," *Advertising Age's Business Marketing*, 84, no. 8 (August 1999), p. 40.

14. Beth Snyder, "Adobe Drive Aims to Build Image as a Web Company," *Advertising Age*, 70, no. 41 (October 4, 1999), p. 28.

15. Robert Harvin, "In Internet Branding, the Off-Lines Have It," *Brandweek*, 41, no. 4 (January 24, 2000), pp. 30–31.

16. King, "Online Marketing Tools Can Cause IT Disasters."

17. Jeff Sweat and Rick Whiting, "Instant Marketing," *Information Week*, no. 746, (August 2, 1999), pp. 18–20.

18. Alf Nucifora, "Viral Marketing Spreads by 'Word of Net,' " *Business Journal*, Central New York, 14, no. 18 (May 5, 2000), pp. 25–26.

19. Ibid.

20. Donna L. Hoffman and Thomas P. Novak, "How to Acquire Customers on the Web," *Harvard Business Review*, 78, no. 3 (May–June 2000), pp. 179–85.

21. Mie-Yun Lee, "Goal-Based Strategy Can Make Banner Ads Click," *Puget Sound Business Journal*, 30, no. 21 (October 1, 1999), p. 18.

22. Tobi Elkin, "Best Buy Takes Cue from Retail Shops," *Advertising Age*, 71, no. 10 (March 6, 2000), p. 8.

23. Hussel, "New Service Helps Brand Clicks with Bricks."

Building an IMC Campaign

Creating Internet Marketing Plans

Advertising PlanPro !

How does the Internet apply to your company, product, or service? You should be able to discover how to use e-commerce effectively as part of an overall IMC program. Or, will you use your Web site for other purposes? Individual products may have local as well as international distribution points. Therefore, they should be effectively promoted on the Web and sold using e-commerce tactics whenever possible. The exercise provided for Chapter 16 on the Advertising Plan Pro disk that accompanied this textbook or at www.prenhall.com/clow is to design your product or company's Web site and to consider all of the potential e-commerce possibilities for the item you are vending. Consideration must also be given to understanding the ways selling your product through the Internet may affect relationships with wholesalers and retailers who also are selling the item.

Critical Thinking Exercises

Discussion Questions

1. What types of goods or services have you purchased over the Internet during the last year? Have your parents purchased anything using the Internet? If so, compare your purchases and attitudes toward buying over the Internet to theirs. If you or your parents, or both, have not used the Internet to make purchases, why not?

2. Access four different Web sites for one of the following products. Locate the FAQ section. Was the FAQ section difficult to find? How is the FAQ section organized? Does it provide effective answers for questions? Do the four sites have similar questions listed?

    a. Antivirus software

    b. Cosmetic surgery

    c. Automobile parts

    d. Cameras

    e. Financial services

3. Best Buy Company was a late e-commerce entry, but has developed a strong e-commerce retail businesses. The key to Best Buy's success, according to Barry Judge, VP of marketing, is, "We do a lot of one-to-one marketing. We're not overly focused on where the consumers buy." The Web site carries every product that Best Buy stocks. It uses personalized services, along with convenient pickup and solid return policies to entice consumers to shop. The consumer can purchase items on the Internet and either have them shipped directly to them or pick them up at the closest store. Shoppers can use the Internet to see if Best Buy stocks a particular item, what the item costs, and to gather product information.[22] What is the advantage to this philosophy? Access the Web site at www.bestbuy.com. Evaluate it in terms of ease of use, product information, and then locate the Best Buy closest to you. Next, access Circuit City's Web site at www.circuitcity.com. Compare it to Best Buy's site. Select one product such as a camcorder to compare the two Web sites.

4. Ironox at www.ironox.com is a business-to-business Internet auction service. Access the Web site to see what types of products it sells. Examine the buyer's corner. What tips are given for buyers? What services does Ironox offer to buyers? What tips and services are listed on the Web site for sellers? What are the advantages and disadvantages of using Ironox for buyers? For sellers? Which members of the buying center would be the most likely to use Ironox?

5. First Energy Corporation, the nation's twelfth largest utility, purchases about 30 percent of its coal over the Internet. The purchasing process that normally took sixty days to complete has been compressed to just two weeks. Bidding takes place on one day, and suppliers know within two to three days whether they have won the order.[23] What risks does First Energy take in purchasing coal over the Internet? How can those risks be minimized? Why would a supplier want to sell coal over the Internet instead of developing a strong personal relationship with First Energy Corporation?

6. Credit card security is an issue with many people. Interview 10 people you know of various ages and genders. Does age or gender make any difference in the person's feelings, especially about the fear of using a credit card over the Internet? Are there specific products or Web sites that people do not trust? More importantly, how do you judge whether a Web site provides the necessary credit security?

7. Pick one of the following product categories. What types of financial incentives are offered on the company's web site to encourage you to purchase? What about the

other two types of incentives: greater convenience and added value? What evidence do you see for them?

   a. Contacts or eyeglasses

   b. Water skis

   c. Jeans

   d. Computers

   e. Camping supplies

8. The primary companies businesses use to ship small packages either overnight or two-day delivery are FedEx, UPS, and the U.S. Postal Service. Access each of these Web sites (Federal Express at www.fedex.com; UPS at www.ups.com; U.S. Postal Service: at www.usps.com). What guarantees do they make about delivery? Which site is the most user friendly? Which site appears to offer the best customer service? In looking at the different functions of a Web site discussed in this chapter, indicate the function for which each Web site was designed?

The Circulation Game

William Johnson was about to embark on a major new phase of his publishing career. He had begun as a writer for a small newspaper in New York oriented to a black readership. From there, William had become an editor and eventually a publisher of a chain of small town newspapers in Georgia. The cities the chain served also were predominantly black. Now, however, William's company had just made a successful bid to acquire newspapers in six cities in the upper Midwest. Suddenly William was about to become one of the largest minority owners in the United States.

The newspaper business has changed dramatically in the past half century. From a time when papers were the primary source of news for most Americans until the new millennium, where citizens are bombarded with news formats of all types, a major shake-out of news chains had occurred. Smaller local papers were forced to compete with national offerings, such as *USA Today* and The *Wall Street Journal*. Readership has changed as well. In the latter half of the twentieth century, editors knew their readers were largely over 18 and reasonably well educated.

Currently, newspapers appear in several formats: tabloids, traditional papers, weekly magazines, and Internet news. They compete with radio news stations, network news, and cable news stations such as CNN, ESPN, and other more specific program formats. Blacks also can tune in to one cable channel devoted more exclusively to them, with the BET (Black Entertainment Channel) offering some news programming. Satellites allow breaking news stories to appear instantly around the world, and people can access news via the Internet when a television is not nearby.

William's company, like most other paper chains, derives income from several sources. First, the "old-fashioned" subscriber forms the basis of the company's circulation numbers. Businesses buy advertising space, and many individuals and companies run classified ads. Weekly newspapers sell additional advertising space in these magazine-type papers. The newest source of revenue is advertising on Internet editions of the paper.

The biggest change in the newspaper business is the partnerships involved. Most papers are owned by media giants that also own radio and television stations. There is a cross-mix of reporting, polling, and other activities. In addition, most newspapers, even in small towns, find they must advertise their product in other markets. Thus, newspapers buy ads on television and on the radio promoting readership. The circulation department conducts telephone sales campaigns designed to entice homeowners to buy papers. Others are distributed in vending machines and in newsstands throughout each city.

In this complex marketplace, William looks for ways to expand the reach of the paper and to compete with other media. He knows the future will witness increasing use of the Internet by most households, but there will continue to be a strong base of readers who want to wake up in the morning, go out to the front yard, pick up a paper, and read it over coffee or breakfast.

1. How can William's company cater to various minorities in its Internet division of the newspaper? Or, should he avoid this type of tactic?
2. What special marketing and IMC challenges affect newspapers in both circulation (retail) and business-to-business (advertising) areas?
3. Look up your local city's newspaper on the Internet. How is it different from a traditional "paper" newspaper? How is it similar?
4. Design an advertising program for William Johnson's local newspaper's Internet edition.

Contract Haulers

APPLICATION EXERCISE II

Mike Testman has served as the computer operator for a local trucking company, Contract Haulers, for the past 10 years. His job is to help the company keep track of inventories, deliveries, and billings for companies served by the firm. These companies are located in a 500 mile region and are considered short trips. Contract Haulers does not perform cross-country deliveries.

Mike knows that 40 percent of the customers who utilize his company ask for less than a full trailer load shipment. This means the driver must combine two to five customers to complete a trailer load. His compamy can charge more per customer because the service is more specialized. The primary target markets for Contract Haulers are small manufacturers and small distributors. A secondary target market is larger manufacturers that need to make shipments to small businesses.

George Coffman, the CEO of Contract Haulers, recently stated that he believes the firm needs a Web site. He convened a meeting of his marketing team to decide what the Web site should feature. At the meeting, the marketing manager spoke first. She stated that the site should help promote the company's name and image. Her argument was that even though it was a short haul server, not enough businesses in the area knew about it. Building the name and image would increase sales due to visibility and loyalty.

The VP of sales spoke next. He believed the site should be used primarily to provide sales support for his 18 person sales force. He said his reps could use the site when making sales calls. If the Web site were properly set up, customers could get information regarding price rates, availability of trucks, and special deals. Contract Hauler's customers would also be able to arrange shipments on the spot while the sales rep was in the prospective customer's office. This would give Contract Haulers a unique competitive advantage in the local market.

The logistics manager then spoke up. He said there is no way the company can do what the sales manager was suggesting on the Internet. Only his office knows where each of the 125 company trucks are located at any given time and which ones are available for shipments. He stated that it would be far too complicated to provide that information on the Internet.

Then the VP of operations suggested that the primary purpose of a Web site should be additional customer support. Customers could access the Web site at any time to find out where a shipment is and when it will arrive. The salespeople could use it to see where trucks are and how soon a truck could come by. In other words, in his mind the site should be used for both sales support and customer service.

The VP of marketing responded. She did not believe the Web site should be so oriented to such an operational use. Instead, sales support and customer service should be handled over the phone with human operators. She emphasized that Contract Haulers had developed a reputation for personalized service. This advantage would be lost using the Internet instead of real people.

Mike was confused and concerned. He watched as the various individuals in the meeting become more engaged in a heated argument over how to use the Web site, and he knew he was going to have to keep many people happy as he designed the site. As the debate appeared to be getting out of hand, George, the CEO, called the meeting to a halt. George told Mike to "do his best" and to "bring me a proposal within the next couple of weeks."

1. What should be the primary purpose of Contract Hauler's Web site?

2. Does the VP of marketing have a valid point? Are logistics issues better handled in person? What are the advantages and disadvantages of doing all scheduling over the telephone or in person at the office?

3. Using a search engine, access at least four Web sites of shipping companies that Mike could take to the next meeting to show what other companies are doing. Make sure Mike is prepared to justify the selection of Web sites as comparable companies.

4. Outline the functions of the Contract Hauler's Web site and how it should be designed.

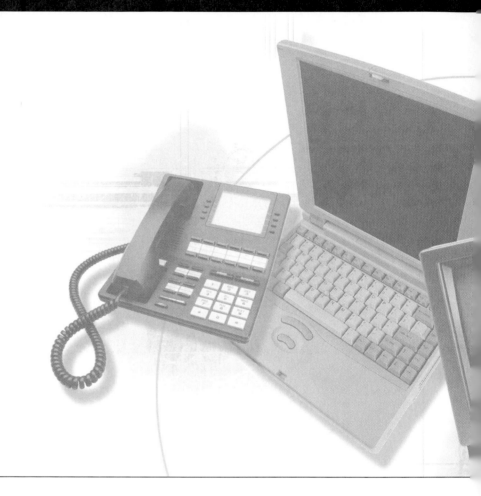

▶ **CHAPTER OBJECTIVES**

Recognize the various levels at which IMC programs should be assessed, from the successes of individual ads and coupon campaigns to long-term survival and growth of the company.

Develop both evaluations of messages and measures of behavioral responses when marketing tools are used.

Assess the quality of public relations efforts in conjunction with studies of other marketing programs.

Develop a series of short- and long-term goals that are linked to the company's voice and theme.

PRETESTING FOR EFFECTIVENESS:
The New High-Tech World of Advertising Design

For many years, management and marketing specialists have known that the easiest way to fix many problems is to prevent them from occurring in the first place. The "rocket" analogy usually follows. If a rocket is off course in the first few minutes of the ride, it will drift much farther off course as the trip proceeds. A correction right away puts the rocket back on track, and the ride goes much more smoothly.

The same is true in advertising design. If the ad is off course right at the beginning, the company spends addi-

chapter**seventeen**

tional funding to develop a campaign that is doomed from the start. One new approach to making ads more effective is to send them through a series of pretests before the campaign begins. A company known as Decision Analyst is the leading international marketing firm in the world of advertising testing.

One program the company uses is based on Internet research. It is called CopyScreen™. To test an ad, a sample is drawn using 200 to 300 target audience consumers who are identified by the Internet. The subjects are shown preliminary versions of print ads and asked for opinions in four areas: (1) attention value, (2) Internet value, (3) purchase propensity, and (4) brand recognition. The responses are

given mathematical scores, and a total is generated for the test ad. Those who go beyond a threshold score are deemed worthy of further development.

The ads moving on to the next stage may be tested through a program called CopyCheck® This program provides more specific feedback concerning the ad's probable effectiveness. Questions CopyCheck attempts to answer include:

1. Will the ad capture the viewer's attention?
2. Will the brand name be noticed and remembered?
3. Does the ad increase the consumer's interest in buying the brand?

4. Does the ad trigger the intent to purchase?
5. How memorable is the brand name?
6. What are the key ideas in the ad?
7. What is missing from the ad (things viewers would like to know)?
8. What did viewers like about the commercial?
9. What did viewers not like about the commercial?
10. How could the commercial be improved?

The Decision Analyst company provides ad feedback in about a week after an advertiser purchases the CopyCheck program. This type of program gives the company preparing the ad two major advantages. First, money is not wasted on ineffective ads. Second, the final ads have a much greater chance of inducing the desired response.

The same company provides feedback regarding the potential for effectiveness of a completed ad as well as tests of recall for ads that have run. Even a rocket that is "in orbit" occasionally needs to have its course adjusted.

The use of computers, the Internet, and more sophisticated research techniques have made it possible for many companies to spend their advertising dollars more wisely. In a world where marketing departments and advertising account managers are being asked to produce tangible results, the use of these types of programs is likely to continue to rise.[1]

overview

John Wanamaker, a well-known nineteenth-century department store owner, was one of the first to use advertising to attract customers to his store. He once remarked, "I know half the money I spend on advertising is wasted, but I can never find out which half." It is difficult to evaluate advertising effectiveness.

Millions of dollars are spent each year on marketing communications programs. Consequently, it is very important for each company to attempt to evaluate these efforts. To spend a major amount on a marketing campaign without trying to find out if it had positive impact does not make sense. The problem, however, as pointed out by John Wanamaker, is figuring out how to evaluate the effectiveness of a marketing communications plan.

This final chapter is devoted to the various methods available for evaluating components of an IMC program. At the most general level, two broad categories of evaluation tools can be used to evaluate IMC systems:

- Message evaluations
- Evaluating respondent behaviors

An overview of these two broad categories of evaluation programs is presented next.

Message evaluations

Message evaluation techniques are used to examine the creative message and the physical design of the advertisement, coupon, or direct-marketing piece. Message evaluation procedures include the study of actors in advertisements as well as the individuals who speak in radio ads. A message evaluation program is designed to consider both the cognitive components associated with an ad (recall, recognition, etc.) as well as the peripheral cues (emotions, attitudes). In Chapter 5, cognitive and peripheral cues were explained in detail.

Evaluating respondent behaviors

The second category, evaluating **respondent behaviors techniques,** addresses visible customer actions including making store visits, inquiries, or actual purchases. This category contains evaluation techniques that are measured using numbers.

In today's IMC marketplace, many advertising companies are being asked to deliver compelling proof that the ads they design actually work. Respondent behaviors provide such evidence. Changes in sales, coupons redeemed, increases in store traffic, and other numbers-based outcomes appeal to many managers. Consequently, both forms of evaluation help the marketing manager try to build both short-term results and long-range success.

matching methods with IMC objectives

When methods of evaluation are being chosen, they should match the objectives being measured. For example, if the objective of an advertising campaign is to increase customer interest in and recall of a brand, then the level of customer awareness should be measured. Normally this means the marketing team measures awareness before and after the ads are run. This procedure is commonly known as *pre-* and *posttest* analysis. At other times objectives vary. For instance, redemption rates measure the success of a campaign featuring coupons, so the behavior (purchasing) rather than the cognitive process (recall) is being tested. Redemption rates can be studied to discover how many items were purchased both with and without coupons.

Several levels of analysis should be identified when evaluating an advertising program. They include the following factors:

- Short-term outcomes (sales, redemption rates)
- Long-term results (brand awareness, brand loyalty or equity)
- Product-specific awareness
- Awareness of the overall company
- Affective responses (liking the company and a positive brand image)

It is important to remember that many marketers can fall in love with only the first factor, short-term outcomes, without considering the long-term impact of a campaign. The company must maintain a voice that carries across campaigns over time. For example, consider the "I love you man" Budweiser ads of the late 1990s. The short-term success was indeed attractive because so many people thought it was funny. Over the years Anheuser-Busch has built a strong voice using humor to sell products, from the Budweiser frogs and lizards to the "Whazzup" team.

In light of these overall goals, then, the marketing manager can consider the various options for evaluating the advertising program. Often it is necessary to think about the evaluation procedure prior to launching a particular campaign. An ad placed in a trade journal may contain a code number, a special telephone number, or a special Internet site that can be used to track responses to a particular campaign. For coupons, premiums, and other sales promotions, code numbers are printed on each item to identify where it came from.

When assessing the effectiveness of an ad, even something as simple as the date or time the advertisement appeared is important. For example, an Internet banner ad campaign should be reviewed by keeping a record of inquiries or hits associated with the banner. In the same way, the dates a magazine reaches the newsstands and when subscribers receive copies are important items used in evaluating magazine ads.

In general, careful planning prior to initiating an advertising program makes evaluation of the campaign easier and more accurate. At the same time, the evaluation of a specific advertisement is difficult, because many factors affect the outcome being measured.

For instance, a retailer may run a series of newspaper and radio ads to boost store traffic. In order to measure the impact of the ads, the retailer keeps records of store traffic before, during, and after the ad campaign. Unfortunately, the traffic count may be affected by other factors, even something as simple as the weather. If it rains for two days, the traffic count will probably be lower. Further, the store's chief competitor may be running a special sale during the same time period. This would also affect traffic. A TV program, such as the season finale of a major series, or even a special program (commencement, all-school play) at the local high school could have impact. In other words, many extraneous factors have an effect on results. Thus, in reviewing an advertising program, it is important to keep these external factors in mind.

More importantly, perhaps, is that one specific analysis does not assess the influence the ad may have had on the larger company image. For example, even though store traffic was low, the ad may have been recalled and stored in the buyer's long-term memory. At some future point, this may make a difference. Conversely, the same ad may have been awkward or in some way offensive, and the store owner may believe the weather affected the outcome instead of a poor advertising design. Consequently, company leaders must be reminded to consider both short-term consequences and long-term implications when they assess overall IMC programs.

message evaluations

Evaluation or testing of advertising communications can occur at any stage of the development process. They can be analyzed at the concept stage before an ad is ever produced. This testing normally involves soliciting the opinions of either a series of experts or from "regular" people. The ad can be tested after the design stage has been completed but prior to development. For example, a television ad may be produced using a story board. A **story board** is a series of still photographs or sketches that outlines the structure of a television ad. After the television commercial is produced, then experimental tests can be used to evaluate the ad. At that point, a group of consumers can be invited to watch the ad in a theater-type setting. When this is done, the test ad is placed in a group of ads to disguise it. Viewers are then asked to evaluate all of the ads (including the test ad) to see if it had the desired effect.

Before launching the campaign, the agency may show the ad in a test market area. Several tools can then be used to measure the quality and impact of the ad. These instruments will be presented in detail later in this chapter. The final stage of evaluation takes place after the marketing communication has been used. Information collected at this time helps the company's leaders and the advertising agency to assess what worked and what did not. These findings are then used in the development of future marketing campaigns.

Companies have several methods to investigate the message content of an advertisement or marketing communication piece. These methods are listed in Figure 17.1. While most of the methods deal with the verbal or written components of the communication piece, peripheral cues are also important and should be part of the message evaluation.

The best method to use in a message evaluation scheme depends on the objective of the communication plan. Most companies prefer to use more than one method to make sure the findings are as accurate as possible. Therefore, while each evaluation tool is discussed separately in this section of the text, in reality multiple measures of evaluation are often used. Also, as mentioned earlier, pre- and posttests normally are used for the purposes of making comparisons before and after a series of ads has run.

▶ **Concept testing**

▶ **Copytesting**

▶ **Recall tests**

▶ **Recognition tests**

▶ **Attitude and opinion tests**

▶ **Emotional reaction tests**

▶ **Physiological arousal tests**

▶ **Persuasion analysis**

**Message Evaluation
Techniques**

FIGURE 17.1

Concept testing

Concept testing is aimed at the actual content of the ad and the impact that content has on potential customers. Many advertising agencies conduct concept tests before spending money to develop an advertisement or promotional piece. A television ad may cost thousands of dollars to produce. Consequently, it is more cost effective to test a concept at the early stages of an ad's development rather than after the actual commercial is taped. Also, if changes must be made, it is less costly to complete them during the planning stage rather than after the marketing piece has already been created. More importantly, once the marketing communication item is finished, creatives and others who worked on the piece tend to take ownership and become more resistant to making changes.

The most common procedure used for concept testing is a focus group. *Focus groups* normally consist of eight to ten people who are representative of the target market. These individuals are paid in cash or are given financial incentives such as gift certificates to entice them to participate. In most cases, it is wise to use independent marketing research firms to conduct focus groups. The goal is to prevent biased results. An independent company is more likely to report that a certain advertising approach did not work than is someone who developed the approach and has a vested interest in it.

The number of focus groups used to study an issue varies greatly. It can be as many as fifty or as few as one. Focus group reactions can be quite different. Results are affected by the makeup of the group and the way the session is conducted. As a result, it is risky to base a decision on just one focus group's final opinion. For example, a humorous ad may have a great deal of appeal to one group, yet another might not think the ad is funny or might even find it offensive. Therefore, it is a good idea to study the responses of several groups to see the impact of the humor on a series of individuals. Even trained focus group leaders experience varying results due to the composition of the group, the questions the group is asked to answer, and the degree of formality used in conducting a session. Also, one person's opinions may strongly influence the rest of the group. Therefore, most agencies use more than one group in order to ensure reliable results. When four different focus groups arrive at the same conclusion, the findings are probably reliable.

Several components of a marketing communications plan can be evaluated with concept tests. They include:

■ Copy or verbal component of an advertisement

■ Message and its meaning

■ Translation of copy in an international ad

■ Effectiveness of peripheral cues, such as product placement in the ad and props used

■ Value associated with an offer or prize in a contest

Two common testing instruments are called comprehension and reaction tests. *Comprehension tests* are used when participants in a study are asked the meaning of a marketing communication piece. The idea is to make sure viewers comprehend the message as intended. The moderator can then explore the reasons why the intended message was not comprehended correctly by the individual or the group.

Reaction tests are used to determine overall feelings about a marketing piece, most notably whether the response is negative or positive. If the focus group reacts negatively to an ad or particular copy in an ad, the agency can make the changes before it is too late. It is possible for an advertisement to be correctly comprehended but elicit negative emotions. Therefore, exploring any negative feelings provides creatives with input to modify the marketing piece.

Copytesting

A second form of message evaluation is copytesting. **Copytests** are used when the marketing piece is finished or in its final stages of development prior to production. They are designed to solicit responses to the main message of the ad as well as the format in which that message will be presented. For a television ad, a copytest could be conducted using a story board format or a version that is filmed by agency members rather than professional actors.

The two most common copytesting techniques are portfolio and theater tests. Both tests place the marketing piece in with others. A **portfolio test** is a display of a set of print ads, one of which is the ad being evaluated. A **theater test** is a display of a set of television ads, including the one being evaluated. The individuals who participate in these studies do not know which piece is under scrutiny. Both techniques mimic reality in the sense that consumers normally are exposed to multiple messages, such as when a radio or television station plays a series of commercials in a row or when a set of newspaper ads appears on a single page. The tests also allow researchers the opportunity to compare the target piece with other marketing messages. For these approaches to yield the optimal findings, it is essential that all of the marketing pieces shown are in the same stage of development (e.g., a set of story boards or a series of nearly completed coupon offers).

Copytesting can utilize focus groups as well as other measurement devices. An ad or coupon that is in the final stage of design can be tested with a **mall intercept technique.** The approach involves stopping people who are shopping in a mall. They are then asked to evaluate the item. The mall intercept technique can incorporate a portfolio approach. To do so, subjects are asked to examine the marketing piece, which is mixed in with others, normally six to ten ads, coupons, or other marketing communications tools. This may be a better approach than showing an item by itself. The disadvantage of displaying only one item is that people tend to give it a more positive evaluation than if it is mixed in with others. Comprehension and reaction tests are commonly utilized in a mall intercept setting.

For television commercials, the theater tests mentioned earlier are used. The test ad is placed among other ads within a television documentary or a new show, such as a pilot episode of a new comedy or drama. The advantage of using a new show is that it is better able to hold the subject's interest. At the end of the program, the individuals participating in the study are asked for their reactions to the ads that were shown. For more valid results, those participating in the study should not know which ad is being tested.

Copytests are valuable instruments in the sense that they can help an agency or company avoid using an ad or marketing tool that isn't "quite ready" or one that receives negative reactions. They also help the advertiser understand if an ad is going to compete favorably when shown in a cluttered setting.

Recall tests

Another popular method used to evaluate advertising is called a **recall test.** This approach involves asking an individual to recall what ads he or she viewed in a given setting or time period. Then, in progressive steps the subject is asked to iden-

A mall intercept technique is often used for copytesting of advertisements and other communication pieces.
Courtesy of The Image Works.
Photograph by Bob Daemmrich.

tify information about the ad. Figure 17.2 lists some of the parts of an advertisement that can be tested for recall.

The most common form of recall test is the **day-after recall (DAR)** test. The DAR method is often used to evaluate TV advertisements. Individuals who participate in the study are called by phone the day after the advertisement first appears. Normally, they are tested using an approach called **unaided recall.** In other words, the subjects are asked to name, or recall, the ads they saw or heard the previous evening, without being given any prompts or memory jogs. For magazines and newspaper ads, there are two approaches. In the first, consumers are contacted the day after the ad appeared. The individuals name the ads they recall and then are asked a serious of questions to discover the features of the advertisements they remember. In the second, an individual is given a magazine for a certain period of time (normally one week) and instructed to read it as he or she normally would during leisure time. Then, the researcher returns and asks a series of questions about which ads became memorable and what features the individual could remember. In the business-to-business sector, the second method is a popular way to test ads for trade journals.

The day-after recall method works best when the objective is to measure the extent to which consumers have learned or remembered the content of an ad. DAR is perceived to be a valuable test because advertisers know that increased recall enhances the probability that the brand is becoming a part of the consumer's

▶ **Product name or brand**

▶ **Firm name**

▶ **Company location**

▶ **Theme music**

▶ **Spokesperson**

▶ **Tag line**

▶ **Incentive being offered**

▶ **Product attributes**

▶ **Primary selling point of communication piece**

Items Tested for Recall

FIGURE 17.2

evoked set, or the primary choices that are remembered when purchase alternatives are being considered. A brand that is part of the evoked set is much more likely to be chosen when the purchase is made.[2]

The second type of recall test is the **aided recall** method. Aided recall means that consumers are prompted by being told the product category and, if necessary, names of specific brands in that category. The respondent still does not know which brand or ad is being tested. When the consumer states that he or she does recall seeing a specific brand being advertised, the person then is asked to provide as many details as possible about the ad. At that point, no further clues are given regarding the ad content.

Most researchers believe the unaided recall approach is superior to other evaluative tests because it identifies the times that an advertisement has become lodged in the person's memory. Unaided recall is also better than aided recall, because some people may respond to a prompt by saying they do indeed remember an ad, even when they are uncertain. Recall scores are almost always higher when the aided recall method is used. Some ad agencies use both methods. First, they use unaided recall to gather basic information. Then, the researcher follows up with prompts to delve deeper into the memories that are present, even if it takes a little help to dig them out.

In both aided and unaided recall tests, if incorrect information is provided, the researcher continues the questioning. Individuals are never told they have given inaccurate answers. Incorrect responses are important data to record. Memory is not always accurate in both aided or unaided recall situations. Consequently, people give incorrect answers. In other words, they may mention commercials that did not actually appear during the test period, but rather one that was viewed at some other time. Although this may seem strange, bear in mind that the average person sees between 50 and 100 ads on a typical night of television viewing. It is easy to become confused.

An incorrect response is often triggered by exposure to a similar ad. For example, a person may remember seeing a commercial for Firestone tires when it was actually presented by Uniroyal. Seeing the Firestone ad triggered the recall of the Uniroyal brand because the individual is more familiar with Uniroyal or holds the brand in higher esteem. This type of error is more common in aided recall tests. In that situation, the individual is being provided with potentially incorrect responses from a particular product category, which increases the odds of remembering the wrong brand.

Recall tests are used to evaluate many types of ad as well as other forms of sales promotions. The design of the recall test varies from one medium to another and from one type of promotional approach to another.

Recall tests are used primarily after ads are aired or have been shown in print. At the same time, however, they can be used in the early stages of communication development. In these instances, participants in the study are recruited and the test is more of the standard experimental design variety. For example, an agency that has created a new business-to-business ad may wonder if the ad would work when aired with consumer ads. Using a theater lab setting, the new ad can be placed in a documentary with other ads. At the end, either the aided or unaided recall method can be used to measure ad and brand awareness.

It is important to take into consideration the age of the respondent used in the study when conducting recall tests. Recall scores tend to decline with age. This is because older people do not remember ads as well as those who are younger. Table 17.1 displays average recall scores for different age segments using both DAR and brand recall instruments.[3] There are several explanations for lower recall scores in older people:

- They have reduced short-term recall capacity.
- Older persons are more fixed in terms of brand choices, making them less easily influenced by advertisements.
- The TV ads used to develop Table 17.1 may have been targeted more toward youth.

Day-After Recall		Brand Recall	
Age Segment	Average Recall	Age Segment	Average Recall
12–17	34%	13–17	70%
18–34	29%	18–34	53%
35–49	24%	35+	36%
50–65	22%		

TABLE 17.1

Impact of Age on DAR and Brand Recall

Source: Based on Joel S. Debow, "Advertising Recognition and Recall by Age—Including Teens," *Journal of Advertising Research,* 35, no. 5 (September–October 1995), pp. 55–60.

For whatever reason, it appears that age does affect recall scores. Still, recall tests are valuable instruments used in testing to see if the ad has the potential to move into a person's long-term memory and affect future purchase decisions.

Integrated Learning Experience

A leading provider of advertising research is Decision Analyst, Inc. at www.decisionanalyst.com. Examine the various sections, including "Published Articles" and "Published Data." Study the previous research conducted by Decision Analyst. Next, go to the "Advertising Research" section under "Company Services" to examine some of the research services such as CopyScreen, CopyCheck, CopyTest, CopyTrack, and CopyRecall. How does Decision Analyst conduct concept and copy testing? What type of organizations would utilize these services? How would they help a creative in designing an advertisement?

stop!

recognition tests

A **recognition test** is a format in which individuals are given copies of an ad and asked if they recognize it or have seen it before. Those who say they have seen the ad are asked to provide additional details about when and where the ad was encountered (e.g., specific television program, the name of the magazine, the location of the billboard, etc.). This information is collected to validate that it was indeed seen.

Next, the individual is asked a series of questions about the ad itself. This helps the researcher gather information and insights into consumer attitudes and reactions to the ad. Recognition tests are best suited to testing for comprehension of and reactions to ads. In contrast, recall tests tend to work well when testing brand and ad awareness. Recognition tests help when the advertiser is more concerned about how the ad is received and what information is being comprehended. This is especially important for ads using a cognitive message strategy, in which some type of reasoning process is invoked in persuading the consumer about the value of a product.

Recognition tests tend to measure how many people saw an advertisement while recall tests tend to measure how many saw the ad and were also sufficiently interested to take the time actually to view or read the ad. Since recognition and recall tests measure different things, many firms and research teams do both with the same subject. First, recall measures are used to start the interview, and then recognition tests are given at the end of the session. For instance, a subject may have viewed an ad during a particular TV show but does not mention the ad when undergoing a recall test. In this situation the respondent can then be given a recognition test to see if he or she remembers seeing the ad. There are many similarities between recognition and recall tests, which means there is a high level of correlation between items identified in both tests. In a study of magazine recall and recognition tests, the average recall score was equal to 0.33 times the average recognition score. In other words, about one-third of those who recognized seeing a commercial

Using celebrities such as Spike Lee increases recall and recognition through greater interest in and liking of the ad.
Courtesy of Bozell Worldwide, Inc.

Here's the direction. You thought milk was just a kid thing. But the plot thickens and you discover your bones are still growing until you're 35. You're on a mad quest for calcium. AND... ACTION. You open the fridge, you grab the lowfat milk, you drink it. CUT. Not from the carton. TAKE 2. Let's use a glass.

MILK
Where's *your* mustache?

when it was shown to them also recalled seeing the ad when asked in an unaided recall test. For newspapers, the average recall was equal to 0.32 times the average recognition score. With aided recall, the percentage is slightly higher because the respondent is given a cue.[4]

Many ingredients affect the degree of recognition of an ad. For print media, the size of the advertisement has a major impact. The larger the ad, the higher the level of recognition. For example, a full-page magazine ad is twice as likely to be noticed as a one-eighth-page ad.

Further, when the consumer uses the brand being displayed in the ad, the likelihood of recognizing the ad rises. A person who uses a brand is about 50 percent more likely to recognize the ad than an individual who does not use the brand. It is not surprising that people tend to notice ads for products they use.

Similar results occur when the test is used to determine if the ad is liked or deemed interesting. An ad that a person likes is about 75 percent more likely to be recognized than an ad the individual did not like. This is one reason celebrities are selected for ads, such as the milk ad above featuring Spike Lee. If an individual likes the celebrity in the advertisement, then he or she will be more likely to recognize the ad. For ads the respondent thought were interesting, the odds of recognition were about 50 percent higher than for ads that were not deemed interesting. Although percentages vary, similar results occur in recall tests.

Therefore, in using recognition (and recall) tests, it is important to consider these key factors that can affect the results of the study. Firms must look beyond the number of respondents who recognize a particular ad. Questions should be asked about which brands the subjects normally buy in the product category, if they liked the ad, and if they found the ad to be interesting. Also, the size of the print ad and the length of the broadcast ad will impact recognition. Larger print ads and longer broadcast ads tend to boost recognition.

Over time, recall and recognition help to establish the brand in the consumer's mind. Loyalty and brand equity are more likely to result. Therefore, even though recall and recognition are more oriented toward the short-term impact of a given ad or campaign, the long-term consequences of a series of successful and memorable ads should be considered.

Attitude and opinion tests

Many of the tests used to measure advertisements are designed to examine the attitudinal components. These types of instruments may be used in conjunction with recall or recognition tests. Attitude tests deal with both the cognitive and affective reactions to an ad. They are also used to solicit consumer opinions. Opinions are gathered from surveys or focus groups. They can also be obtained as part of a mall intercept plan or even in laboratory settings.

The content and formats of attitude tests vary widely. Sometimes specific responses are requested in what are called **closed-end questionnaire** formats. Scales such as *1 = highly unfavorable* to *7 = highly favorable* are often prepared for respondents to answer. In others tests, the individual is allowed to discuss whatever comes to mind regarding some aspect of a product or its advertisements. These are called **open-ended questions.**

Roper Starch Worldwide developed a testing system called ADD+IMPACT. It was created to study consumer reactions to advertisements before they are launched. As part of the testing process, Roper conducts one-on-one interviews with 60 or more consumers. Each participant responds to open-ended questions as well as more standardized closed-ended attitudinal questions. The results of the test, transcripts, and a quantitative analysis of the numbers-based responses are provided to clients within two weeks of the test. By testing the ad prior to a launch, advertisers are more likely to know what people think about the ad and what type of reaction to expect. Changing an ad at this point is much less costly than after a campaign has been launched.[5]

Attitude and opinion studies also can be used to evaluate sales promotions devices such as direct-mail pieces. Although most companies use response rates to measure effectiveness levels for direct-mail programs, one company, de Kadt Marketing and Research, Inc., of Ridgefield, Connecticut, has developed an alternate method. The goal of de Kadt Marketing is to identify the best direct-mail design, not just the design that produces the largest response rate. The firm tries to find out why some direct-mail pieces work and others do not.[6]

De Kadt Marketing begins by recruiting the same types of consumers that would be found in a typical focus group. Subjects are selected based on demographics matching the target market characteristics for the products and the firm being studied. The subjects are asked to collect and classify all of the direct mail coming into their homes for 10 days. During this period, the test piece is mailed to them. The subjects do not know which piece is the test piece. Sometimes more than one test piece is mailed to test different designs.

To complete the test, the subjects are given four large envelopes and instructed to place each piece of direct mail into one of the four envelopes. In the first envelope they place the letters that they normally would have thrown away without even opening. The second envelope holds direct-mail offers that the subjects would have opened but then discarded. The third envelope is for pieces that were opened and read, but then would have been discarded. The difference between the second and third envelopes is that the third envelope contains pieces that were read while the second does not. The fourth envelope is used to collect direct-mail pieces that were opened and either acted upon or kept to be acted on later.

At the end of the 10 days, the respondents bring all four envelopes to the research site. One-on-one interviews are then conducted. Each respondent is asked questions about the types of direct-mail pieces that were typically discarded as well as the ones that were read. Then the moderator goes through each envelope and discusses each item with the subject, seeking the reasons why the piece was placed

communication**action**

There is one new area that requires evaluation: Internet advertisements. Several methods may be used to evaluate Internet banner ads, including standard recall and recognition tests. Unfortunately, these techniques are not as effective for studying Internet viewers. Consequently, a new method of evaluation was developed by Accipiter of Raleigh, North Carolina. Accipiter contacts approximately 400 viewers per ad. The subjects are randomly selected. While the person browses the site, a series of questions about banner ads and the test ad in particular pop up on the screen. The questions are concerned with ad awareness, brand image, viewer attitudes toward the ad, and purchase probability (the odds that the ad will lead the viewer actually to make a purchase). Some critics argue that popup questions are intrusive. Others believe they are an excellent method of encouraging people to participate. In response to the criticism, computer publisher CMP asks for viewer participation through e-mail requests rather than popup ads. To encourage involvement, subjects are entered into a raffle for $100.

In the international arena, Neilsen Media Research developed one of the first global industry standards for measuring the effectiveness of Internet ads as well as Internet audiences with a service called Neilsen/NetRatings. The service is targeted to international marketers, Web site owners, and on-line media buyers. Neilsen/NetRatings provides data regarding advertising effectiveness, e-commerce sales, audience reach and activity, plus demographic profiles of customers. Neilsen/NetRatings is available in 30 countries in Europe, Asia, Latin America, the Middle East, and Africa.

Both programs recognize the importance of assessing Internet ads in a manner that best understands the medium. This makes sense, because many Internet surfers have differing characteristics when compared to magazine and newspaper readers, and even to those listening to the radio or watching television.

Sources: "Accipiter Tests New Ad Research Service; Will It Anger Web Users?" *Electronic Advertising and Marketplace Report,* 12, no. 6 (March 24, 1998), pp. 8–9; Juliana Koranteng, "AC Neilsen to Offer Data on Net Ad Effectiveness," *Advertising Age International* (October 1999), p. 44.

where it was. When the moderator arrives at the test piece, a few additional questions are asked to discover more detail about why it was placed in a particular envelope. The results not only help the firm to understand how consumers react to various direct-marketing pieces but also provide the firm with information about its specific mailing. This means reactions to the test piece can be compared to other direct-mail offers.

As noted in Chapter 5, there are many parts of a consumer buying decision-making process. Attitudes and opinions are connected to short-term behaviors and longer-term assessments of a company and its products. Therefore, in addition to simply remembering that a firm exists, advertisers and IMC planners should try to understand how people feel about the company in the context of larger, more general feelings.

Emotional reaction tests

Many ads are designed to elicit emotional responses from consumers. Emotional ads are based on the idea that ads that elicit positive emotions are more likely to be remembered. Also, consumers who have positive attitudes toward ads would logically develop more positive attitudes toward the product. This in turn should result in increased purchases.[7]

It is difficult to measure the emotional impact of an advertisement. The simplest method is to ask questions about an individual's feelings and emotions after viewing a marketing communication piece. This can be performed in a laboratory setting theater test or the ad can be shown to focus groups. In both circumstances the test ad should be placed with other ads rather than by itself.

A **warmth monitor** is an alternative method developed to measure emotions. The concept behind the warmth meter is that feelings of warmth are positive when they are directed toward an ad or a product. To measure warmth, subjects are asked to manipulate a joystick while watching a commercial. The movements track reactions to a commercial by making marks on a sheet of paper containing four lines. The four lines are labeled:

1. Absence of warmth

2. Neutral

3. Warmhearted or tender

4. Emotional

The warmth meter was developed to evaluate TV ads. It can be adapted to radio ads.[8]

A more sophisticated warmth meter was developed by the University of Hawaii. Individuals watch advertisements in a theater-type lab featuring big screen television. Those who feel negatively about what they are seeing pull a joystick downward. Those who feel more positively push the joystick in the opposite direction. Thus, as they are watching the commercial, they are constantly moving the joystick forward or backward, thereby conveying their feelings at every moment of the ad. The results of the 20 participants are tallied into one graph and then placed over the commercial. This technology allows an advertiser to see which parts of the ad elicit positive emotions and which parts elicit negative emotions. After graphing the test results, the group can then be used as a focus group to discuss the ad and why group members felt the way they did at various moments during the viewing.[9]

A similar technology has been developed by DiscoverWhy. The major difference is that DiscoverWhy provides the service on the Internet. DiscoverWhy can poll 1,000 or more people who look at an advertisement as it is shown on the Internet. As they watch the ad on streaming video, participants use a mouse to move a tab on a sliding scale from one to ten. If they like what they see, they slide the scale toward the ten. Those who don't slide the scale toward the one. After the data have been collected, a graph can be superimposed over the advertisement. This shows the advertiser the likable and nonlikable parts of the commercial. A major advantage of using the Internet is that subjects selected for the study can provide their ratings at any time that is convenient. If the agency needs a focus group to discuss the ad, subjects can be selected from the participants. The focus group session can even be held on-line.[10]

Most of the time, emotions are associated with shorter-term events, such as the reaction toward a given advertisement. At the same time, emotions are strongly held in the memory banks of most consumers. Therefore, an ad that made a viewer angry may be retrieved, and the anger recreated, every time the individual remembers either the ad or the company. As a result, it is wise to attempt to discover emotional responses to various ads before they are released to be shown to the general public.

Integrated Learning Experience

Roper Starch Worldwide is one of the leaders in advertising research. Access its Web site at www.roper.com. In the "Products and Services" section, examine the various industries in which Roper has expertise. Examine the services it provides, especially the ADD + IMPACT. How would Roper's services help an advertising department or advertising agency? While Roper is a worldwide, full-service research agency, Datum Analysis focuses only on the Hispanic market. Access its Web site at www.d-source.com to see the types of ad and concept tests it offers.

stop!

Physiological arousal tests

Emotional reaction tests are *self-report* instruments. In other words, individuals report their feelings as they see fit. Although this may or may not be a flawed instrument, many marketing researchers were interested in finding ways to measure emotions and feelings without relying on the person to report how he or she feels.

Physiological arousal tests measure fluctuations in a person's body functions that are associated with changing emotions. The primary physiological arousal tests are:

1. The psychogalvanometer
2. A pupillometric test
3. Voice-pitch analysis

A **psychogalvanometer** measures a person's perspiration levels. As an individual reacts emotionally to a situation (in this case an advertisement), the amount of perspiration present changes. Perhaps you have noticed that you sweat quite a bit more when watching an exciting movie or sports event. This arousal indicates you are interested and involved emotionally. An ad producing these effects may be more memorable and powerful than one that is boring or receives no emotional response.

The psychogalvanometer works by evaluating the amount of perspiration located in the palm and fingers. A very fine electric current is sent through one finger and returns to the galvanometer through another finger. Remember, a reaction can be negative or positive. The galvanometer simply measures the individual's physiological reaction. One benefit of the psychogalvanometer is that it can be used to assess emotional reactions to many different types of marketing communication pieces including television commercials, consumer promotions, and trade promotions.

A **pupillometric meter** measures the dilation of a person's pupil. Dilation levels also change with emotional arousal. A person who is frightened displays much wider pupils, as does someone who is excited. Pupil dilation can be studied as the subject views a television or print advertisement. Pupils dilate more when the person reacts positively to the ad or marketing communication. Pupils become smaller when the subject reacts negatively.

When conducting a test, the subject's head can be set in a fixed position. The dilation of the pupil can then be measured throughout the ad. In this way, each aspect of the message can be evaluated for positive or negative responses. A graph can be superimposed on the commercial to show evaluators how each person responded to the advertisement.

The **voice-pitch meter** examines changes in the pitch of a person's voice as he or she reacts with emotion. A more shrill or higher-pitched voice indicates a stronger response. A voice-pitch device utilizes special computer software. A person's voice pitch is monitored as the individual answers a series of questions. Vocal chords tighten and pitch is higher when a person is emotionally affected. The amount of change in the pitch is an indicator of how strongly the person has been affected.

All three of these tests are based on the theory that emotions affect people physiologically and that these physical responses can be measured. Some researchers believe physiological arousal tests are more accurate than emotional reaction tests, because physiological arousal cannot easily be faked.

To demonstrate how physiological tests work, consider an advertisement with a sexually attractive male or female. In a focus group, respondents may enjoy the ad but cover up these feelings, stating the ad is sexist and inappropriate. These reactions may be due to social pressure or because the subjects want to be accepted by those around them. The same individual may not move the joystick to report his or her true feelings when participating in a study using the warmth monitor. The stigma attached to sex in advertising often affects self-reported reactions. Thus, a physiological arousal test may be a better indicator of a person's true feelings.

Emotions are short-term reactions that also are stored in long-term memory. Therefore, a feeling of love or affection associated with a song returns each time the song is played. If the relationship goes sour, the same song may elicit strong negative feelings. Therefore, advertisers must continually be aware of the emotions associated with brands and products. It is not surprising, for example, that ValueJet eventually changed its name to AirTran. This may be in part due to negative emotions that continually surfaced following reports of unsafe maintenance practices that eventually led to a crash in Florida.

Persuasion analysis

The final type of message evaluation tool is designed to appraise the persuasive ability of a marketing communication item. While other measures evaluate awareness, emotions, liking, and physical reactions, they do not measure the ability of the marketing piece to persuade the consumer. Persuasion techniques require a pre- and posttest assessment.

A researcher analyzing the persuasiveness of a television ad would start by gathering a group of consumers in a theater. Measures of brand attitudes and purchase intentions are then gathered for the test brand and other brands put in the study. A series of commercials is shown as part of a program. Next, measures are taken to see if any changes in attitude or purchase intentions resulted from exposure to the ads. The amount of change indicates how well the persuasion in the advertisement worked.

One company that conducts persuasion analysis programs is called ASI Market Research. The company normally recruits a sample of 250 consumers to attend a new television program. Once they are in the ASI theater, the consumers are informed that prizes will be given away through a drawing. These individuals are asked to identify the specific brand they prefer in each product category. The subjects are then shown two new TV programs complete with commercials. At the end, the subjects are told that a product was inadvertently left off of the initial survey, and they are asked to fill the form out again in order to enter the drawing. ASI compares before and after responses to the same questions in order to see if there was any changes in attitudes, and the subjects are not aware of the intention of the study.[11]

Knowing the ad actually has persuasive power is a major advantage for the advertiser. Attempts to assess the impact of such ads before they are released to a wider audience are solid investments of marketing dollars.

Integrated Learning Experience

DiscoverWhy offers ad testing through the warmth meter technology discussed in this chapter as well as through Internet interactive services. Access the "Product" section of its Web site at www.discoverwhy.com. Examine the virtual client room to see how DiscoverWhy conducts research. Examine the other products and services offered by DiscoverWhy. Next, access the "Products and Services" section of Ipsos-ASI at www.ipsos-asi.com. Under ad testing, examine the Ipsos-ASI Next TV. What types of services are offered and how is ad testing conducted? Do the same for some of the company's other products such as Ipsos-ASI Next Print. Compare this to the methodologies used by DiscoverWhy.

stop!

evaluation criteria

For all of the programs mentioned thus far, it is important to establish quality evaluation criteria. One program helpful in doing so is called **PACT**, or **positioning advertising copytesting**. PACT was created to evaluate television ads. It was formulated by 21 leading U.S. advertising agencies.[12] Even though PACT was designed to examine the issues involved in copytesting television ads, the principles can be used for any type of message evaluation system and all types of media. Figure 17.3 lists the nine principles that were developed. They should be followed when a written or verbal marketing communication piece is being tested. A discussion of these principles follows.

> ▶ Testing procedure should be relevant to the advertising objectives.
> ▶ In advance of each test, researchers should agree on how the results will be used.
> ▶ Multiple measures should be used.
> ▶ The test should be based on some theory or model of human response to communication.
> ▶ The testing procedure should allow for more than one exposure to the advertisement, if necessary.
> ▶ In selecting alternate advertisements to include in the test, each should be at the same stage in the process as the test ad.
> ▶ The test should provide controls to avoid biases.
> ▶ The sample used for the test should be representative of the target sample.
> ▶ The testing procedure should demonstrate reliability and validity.

Copytesting Principles of PACT

FIGURE 17.3   Source: Based on PACT document published in the *Journal of Marketing*, (1982), Vol. 11, No. 4, pp. 4–29.

First, no matter which procedure is used, it should be *relevant to the advertising objective being tested.* For example, if the objective of a coupon promotion is to stimulate trial purchases, then the test should evaluate the coupon's copy in order to determine its ability to stimulate trial purchases. On the other hand, an evaluation of attitudes toward a brand would require a different instrument.

Researchers should agree on how the results are going to be used when selecting test instruments. They should also agree on the design of the test in order to obtain the desired results. This is especially true for the preparation stage in an advertisement's development, because many tests are used to determine whether the advertisement eventually will be created.

The research team should also decide on a cutoff score to be used following the test. This will prevent biases from entering into the findings about the ad's potential effectiveness. Many ad agencies use test markets for new advertisements before they are launched in a larger area. A recall method used to determine if people in the target market remember seeing the ad should have a prearranged cutoff score. In other words, the acceptable percentage may be established so that 25 percent of the sample should remember the ad in order to move forward with the campaign. If the percentage is not reached, the ad has failed the test.

Using multiple measures allows for more precise evaluations of ads and campaigns. It is possible for a well-designed ad to fail one particular testing procedure yet score higher on others. Consumers and business buyers who are the targets of marketing communications are complex human beings. Various people may perceive individual ads differently. As a result, advertisers usually try to develop more than one measure so that there is greater agreement on whether the ad or campaign will succeed and reach its desired goals.

The test to be used should be *based on some theory or model of human response to communication.* This makes it more likely that the test will be a predictive tool of human behavior. The objective is to enhance the odds that the communication will actually produce the desired results (going to the Web site, visiting the store, making a purchase, etc.) when the ad is launched.

Many testing procedures are based on a single exposure. Although in many cases this is sufficient for research purposes, there are times that *multiple exposures* are necessary to obtain reliable test results. For complex ads, more than one exposure may be needed. The human mind can comprehend only so much information in one viewing. It is vital to make sure the person can and does comprehend the ad in order to determine whether the ad can achieve its desired effects.

For testing complex ads such as this Weight Watchers ad, multiple exposures will be necessary.
Courtesy of Weight Watchers International, Inc.

Often ads are tested in combination with other ads to disguise the one being examined. Placing the test marketing piece in with others means the test subjects do not know which ad is being evaluated. This prevents personal biases from affecting judgments. To ensure valid results, *the alternative ads should be in the same stage of process development.* Thus, if ad copy is being tested prior to ad development, then the alternative ads should also be in the ad copy development stage rather than established ads.

Next, adequate controls must be in place to *prevent biases and external factors from affecting results.* To help control external factors, experimental designs are often used. When conducting experiments, researchers try to keep as many things as constant as possible and manipulate only one variable at a time. For instance, in a theater test, the temperature, time of day, room lighting, television program, and ads shown can all be the same. Then, the researcher may display the program and ads to an all male audience followed by an all female audience. Changing only one variable (gender) makes it possible to see if the ad, in a very controlled environment, is perceived differently by men as opposed to women.

This does not mean field tests are ineffective. Testing marketing communications in real-world situations is extremely valuable because they do approximate reality. Still, when conducting field tests, such as mall intercepts, those doing the testing must try to control as many variables as possible. Thus, the same mall, same questions, and same ads are shown. Then, age, gender or other variables can be manipulated.

As with any research procedure, sampling procedures are important. It is crucial for the *sample being used to be representative of the target population.* For example, if a print ad designed for Hispanic Americans is to be tested, the sample used in the test must be Spanish.

Finally, researchers must continually try to make tests *reliable and valid.* Reliable means "repeatable." In other words, if the same test is given five times to the same person, the individual should respond in the same way over time. If a respondent is "emotional" on one iteration of a warmth test and "neutral" when the ad is shown a second time, the research team will wonder if the test is reliable.

Valid means "generalizable." Valid research findings can be generalized to other groups. For instance, when a focus group of women finds an ad to be funny, and then a group of men reacts in the same way, the finding that the humor is effective is more valid. This would be an increasingly valuable outcome if the results were generalizable to people of various ages and races. Many times an ad may be reliable, or repeatable in the same group, but not valid or generalizable to other groups of consumers or business buyers.

The PACT principles are helpful when designing tests of short-term advertising effectiveness. They are also helpful when seeking to understand larger and more long-term issues such as brand loyalty and identification with the company. The goal is to generate data that documents what a company is doing works. When this occurs, the company and its advertising team have access to invaluable information.

communication**action**

A Quick Quiz

Knowing what works, and what doesn't, is the key to assessing any IMC promotional piece effectively. A magazine entitled *Tested Copy* appeared on a monthly basis for several years. It was oriented toward discovering the best methods for reaching customers. In one issue, the following quiz appeared. See if you can select the correct answers, which appear at the bottom of the page.

Question 1: Which of the following does *Tested Copy* most consistently find as a failure in print advertising? The failure to:
a. Animate the product and bring it to life
b. Thoroughly describe the characteristics of the product
c. Tell the readers what the product will do for them
d. Give the readers sufficient information about the advertisers

Question 2: Which type of advertising is the most believable?
a. Ads that feature real people who have used the product
b. Ads that cite the results of user surveys
c. Ads with a money-back guarantee
d. Ads that name the competition and make comparisons

Question 3: What proportion of readers of women's magazines agree with this statement: *I like the way scented ads make magazines smell?*
a. 29%
b. 44%
c. 68%
d. 80%

Question 4: On average, an ad with sans-serif type is more likely to earn higher readership scores than an ad with serif type.
a. true
b. false

To learn more about this type of marketing information, go to the Web site of Roper Starch Worldwide. Information about the *Tested Copy* magazine is also available on-line.

Source: Alan Rosenspan, "ROPER *Starch* Worldwide, Inc.," *Direct Marketing,* 61, no. 4 (August 1998), p. 4.

Answers: c, c, d, a

behavioral evaluations

The first part of this chapter has been devoted to message evaluations. These techniques provide valuable insights into what people think and feel. Still, some marketing reports contend that the only valid evaluation criterion should be *actual sales.* To these critics it is less important for an ad to be well liked. If an ad does not increase sales, then it is not effective. The same type of argument is often presented regarding the other marketing communication tools such as sales promotions, trade promotions, personal selling, and direct marketing. There is some validity to this position; however, not all communication objectives can be measured using sales figures.

A company with low brand awareness may be most interested in the visibility and memorability aspects of a communication plan, even though a marketing program designed to boost brand awareness may not result in immediate sales. Further, measuring the results of a sales promotion campaign featuring coupons using sales figures is easier to do than measuring the results of an advertising campaign on television. Consequently, effective promotions evaluations should involve the study of both message and behavioral elements. In this section, various behavioral measures are discussed. Figure 17.4 lists these techniques.

Sales and redemption rates

Measuring changes in sales following a marketing campaign is easier now than it was in the past. Universal product codes and scanner data are available from many retail outlets. These data are available on a weekly basis and, in some situations, on a daily basis. Some retail outlets even have access to sales information on a real-time basis, and the information can be accessed at any point during the day.

Scanner data make it possible for companies to monitor sales and help both the retailer and the manufacturer discover the impact of a particular marketing program. Bear in mind, however, that extraneous factors can affect sales. For instance, in a multimedia advertising program, it would be difficult to know which ad moved the customer to action. Further, a company may be featuring its fall line of jackets, and a cold snap may affect the region. If so, which caused the customer to buy, the ad or the weather? Firms utilizing trade and consumer promotion programs must account for the impact of both the promotion and the advertising when studying sales figures. Sales are one indicator of effectiveness, however, they may be influenced by any number of intervening factors.

Advertisements are probably the most difficult component of the IMC program to evaluate, for several reasons. These include:

1. The influence of other factors
2. A delayed impact of the ad
3. Consumers changing their minds while in the store
4. Whether the brand is in the consumer's evoked set
5. Brand equity considerations

First, as just discussed, it is difficult to distinguish *the effects of advertising from other factors.* This is because ads have short- and long-term effects, and consumers

> ▶ Sales
> ▶ Redemption rates
> ▶ Test markets
> ▶ Purchase simulation tests

Behavioral Measures

FIGURE 17.4

and businesses see ads in so many different contexts. Thus, the direct impact of one ad or one campaign on sales is difficult to decipher.

Second, *advertising often has a delayed impact*. Many times consumers encounter ads and are persuaded to purchase the product, but will not actually make the buy until a later time, when they need the item. Thus a woman may be convinced that she wants to buy undergarments due to a sexy and effective presentation by Victoria's Secret. Still, rather than buying them herself, she leaves several well-placed hints for her husband before her next birthday, which could be several months later. The problem is that her husband may have purchased another brand or a different gift. So, then she must wait until Christmas or Valentine's Day, but still the ad worked and led to a purchase. Measuring the impact of an ad in that setting is almost impossible.

Third, many times consumers may decide to make purchases based on an advertisement but *change their minds when they arrive at the retail store*. A competing brand may be on sale, the store could be out of the desired brand, or the salesperson could persuade the customer that another brand is better. In each case, the ad was successful on one level but another factor intervened in the purchase.

Fourth, *the brand being advertised may not be part of the consumer's evoked set*. Upon hearing or seeing the ad, however, the brand is moved into the evoked set. Thus, even when the brand is not considered at first, it will be in the future when the need arises or when the consumer becomes dissatisfied with a current brand.

Fifth, advertising is an essential component of building brand awareness and brand equity. Although sales may not be the result immediately, *the ad may build brand equity,* which in turn will influence future purchases.

It is easier to measure the effects of trade and consumer promotions, direct-marketing programs, and personal selling on actual sales. For example, manufacturers can study the impact of trade promotions by observing changes in sales to the retailers at the time the promotions are being offered. The same is true for consumer promotions such as coupons, contests, and point-of-purchase displays. Many manufacturers push retailers to use their POP displays. At the same time, the retailer will be interested in the effects of the display on sales. Using scanner data, both the retailer and the manufacturer can measure the impact of a POP display. Retailers normally use POPs that have demonstrated the ability to boost sales.[13]

To track the impact of POP displays, Anheuser-Busch, Frito-Lay, Procter & Gamble, and Warner-Lambert joined together as initial sponsors of a program developed by *Point-of-Purchase Advertising International (POPAI)*. In the initial study, POPAI tracked 25 different product categories in 250 supermarkets nationwide. Sponsors paid between $50,000 and $75,000 to receive customized data about the POP displays featuring particular brands. One advantage of using POPAI data is that each firm not only can see the impact of the POP for its brand but also receives comparative data showing how well the display fared against other displays. The major advantage of the POPAI program is its low cost. Sponsors of the POPAI program attained valuable data at a much lower cost than if they had sought the information on their own.[14]

There are a wide variety of responses to marketing communications programs besides sales. Figure 17.5 lists some of the responses that can be tracked. These items are described in the remainder of this section.

One method of measuring the impact of an advertisement, direct mailing, TV direct offers, or price-off discounts to a business customer is to assign a *toll-free number* to each marketing piece. A great deal of information can be collected during an inbound call. Sales data can be recorded and demographic information gathered. Psychographic information then can be added by contacting various commercial services.

In business-to-business situations, a toll-free number provides contact names to help the vendor discover who is performing the various functions in the buying center. As a result, a toll-free number provides sales data to determine which marketing program is the best and also can be used to generate valuable customer

▶ Changes in sales

▶ Telephone inquiries

▶ Response cards

▶ Internet inquiries

▶ Direct-marketing responses

▶ Redemption rate of sales promotion offers

   —Coupons, premiums, contests, sweepstakes

**Responses to
Marketing Messages
That Can Be Tracked**

FIGURE 17.5

information that can be tied to the sales data. Knowing who is responding to each offer helps a firm better understand its customers and the approach that should be used for each target group.

Another method for measuring behaviors comes from *response cards.* These customer information forms are filled out at the time of a purchase. The primary disadvantage of response cards is that less data are obtained. Consequently, commercial sources will be needed to obtain additional demographic and psychographic information. This is because response cards solicited from current customers contain information the firm is already likely to have in its database.

Internet responses are excellent behavioral measures. By using "cookies," a firm can obtain considerable information about the person or business making the inquiry. Many times the person or business responding also is willing to provide a great deal of helpful information.

To evaluate Internet advertising campaigns, AdKnowledge introduced an on-line management tool called MarketMatch Planner. The MarketMatch Planner software includes two components: (1) Campaign Manager and (2) Administrator. Campaign Manager records traffic to a site as well as performing postbuy analysis. Administrator integrates Web ad-buy data and performance analysis with the firm's accounting and billing systems. In addition, MarketMatch Planner has the capability of integrating third-party data including audience demographics from the following sources:

- MediaMetrix for basic demographics
- NetRatings for GRP and other ratings instruments
- Psychographic data from SRI Consulting
- Web site ratings and descriptions from NetGuide
- Web traffic audit data from BPA Interactive.

All of this means that a firm can now quantitatively analyze Internet advertising. An e-company can see exactly how many hits an ad brings to a site. The company also can identify how many sales result and how much is spent per sale. Thus, individual e-businesses can identify demographic and psychographic information about each customer. Internet advertising is much easier to evaluate with hard numbers than is any other advertising medium because of the computer technology contained within individual computers.[15]

Individual companies must be careful how they use Internet data. They should be reviewed in light of the IMC objectives present. An IMC objective of building brand awareness requires something other than Internet sales data to be assessed. Further, an Internet ad can bring awareness to a brand yet not lead to an on-line purchase. This might occur, for example, when a consumer or business uses the Internet to gather information but then makes the actual purchase at a retail store, over the telephone, or by fax. When that happens, the impact of an

By using technology such as MarketMatch Planner, a company such as McCormick can track who goes to its Web site for recipes. Courtesy of McCormick & Co., Inc.

Internet advertising campaign may not be able to reflect all of the brand awareness or sales that the campaign generated.

Various kinds of redemption rates can be used as behavioral effectiveness measures. *Coupons, premiums, contests, sweepstakes,* and *direct-mail pieces* are marketing communications devices that can be coded to record redemption rates. Comparing a current campaign with previous campaigns makes if possible for a firm to examine changes made in the design or execution of an ad. The results are reviewed in light of positive or negative changes in redemption rates.

As an example, consider a consumer goods manufacturer that offers a 50 cent coupon for a product. If the 50 cent coupon results in a 2.3 percent redemption rate compared to a 1.7 percent for a 40 cent coupon, then the marketing team knows the 50 cent coupon was more attractive. Comparisons also can be made between coupons, premiums, and other marketing communication tactics. When making these comparisons, it is important to measure the impact in terms of profitability. For example, it may take a 3 percent redemption rate on a coupon to match the impact on profits of a 1 percent redemption rate for a premium. The difference is that the coupon allows the customer a price reduction on the product, while with the premium requires the same customer to pay full price. The cost of the gift may be lower than the price reduction, and therefore the premium is more profitable per sale.

Immediate changes in sales and redemptions are one form of behavioral evaluation. It is tempting for the advertiser and company to use them and fail to see "the forest for the trees." One campaign, advertisement, or promotions program should be viewed in the context of all other marketing efforts. Behavioral measures are best when the team sees them as part of the "big picture."

stop!

Integrated Learning Experience

Tracking Internet traffic is an excellent method of measuring the effectiveness of Internet advertising. AdKnowledge is a leader in this technology. Access this Web site at www.engage.com. What type of services does AdKnowledge offer? Review the Media Metrix Global Landing Web site at www.media-metrix.com. How can AdKnowledge use the information provided by Media Metrix to develop a more complete profile of the Internet customers being tracked? How can these two firms measure the effectiveness of an Internet ad campaign?

Test markets

A second form of behavioral response can be studied using a test market. Test markets are used when a company examines the effects of a marketing effort on a small scale before launching a national or international marketing campaign. The primary advantage of using a test market is that an organization can examine several elements of a marketing communication program. If the test market is successful, then it is likely that the national or global campaign also will be effective. It is also an excellent method of testing a campaign in a new country before launching it full scale. Test market programs are used to assess:

1. Advertisements
2. Promotions and premiums
3. Pricing tactics
4. New products

When one of these is tested and is not successful, the communication program can be changed. A product may be pulled before it is even released. For instance, McDonald's decided not to go forward with plans to sell onion rings, steak sandwiches, and a sandwich called a McFeast, because sales in a test market program did not warrant a national launch.

Test markets are cost-effective methods to analyze and make changes in marketing efforts before millions of dollars are spent on something that will not accomplish the intended objectives. Ads can be modified, premiums revised, and pricing policies revisited before a more widespread program is undertaken.

One major advantage of a test market is that it resembles an actual situation more than any of the other tests discussed thus far. The key is to make sure that the site selected for the test market strongly resembles the target population. For example, if a product is targeted toward senior citizens, then it is important to conduct the study in an area that has a high concentration of senior citizens.

It is also important to design the test marketing campaign as close to the national or full marketing plan as possible. A long time lapse may cause a company to experience differing results. The goal is to make sure the test market is a mirror image of the actual marketing program.

A test market can be as short as a few days or as long as two to three years. The longer the test market program runs, the more accurate the results. A test that is too short may yield less reliable results. On the other hand, if the test market is too long, the national market situation may change and the test market may no longer be a representative sample. The greatest fear, however, is that the competition is able to study what is going on, giving them time to react to the proposed marketing campaign.

A competitor can respond to a test market program in one of two ways. First, the competition may introduce a special promotion in the test market area in order to confound the results. This may reduce the sales for the product or campaign, making it appear less attractive. The second approach is not to intervene in the test market, but to use the time to prepare a counter marketing campaign. Firms that use this tactic are ready when the national launch occurs and the impact may be that the test market results are not as predictive of what will happen.

Scanner data make it possible for results from test market campaigns to be quickly available. The figures can be studied to determine if test market results are acceptable. A firm also can design several versions of a marketing campaign in different test markets. Through scanner data, the firm can compare the sales from each test market to determine which version is the best. For example, in test market one, the firm may present an advertising campaign only. In test market two, the firm may add coupons to the ad program. In test market three, a premium and advertising can be used. Examining the results from each market helps the firm grasp which type of marketing campaign to use. Other test markets can be used with different prices in different regions to determine the price to charge and the elasticity associated with that price. It is also possible to vary the size of the coupon or premium to discover the impact. Rather than making a change at the national level, a firm can modify the consumer promotion in selected markets to see what happens.

Through test marketing, firms have the opportunity to test marketing communication ideas in more true-to-life settings. Test markets work best for trade and consumer promotions, direct marketing, and other marketing communication tools. They are not quite as accurate when assessing advertising because changes in sales take longer, and the test market program may not be long enough to measure the full impact. In any case, test markets are valuable instruments to use when examining specific marketing features and more general communications campaigns.

Purchase simulation tests

A third behavioral approach available is purchase simulation tests. Consumers can be asked in several ways if they would be willing to buy products. For instance, they could be asked about purchase intentions at the end of a laboratory experiment. In this situation, however, intentions are self-reported and tend not to be an accurate predictor of future purchase behaviors. Test markets examine actual purchases, but are more costly because the marketing piece must be completed first. TV commercials cost from several thousand to over a million dollars to prepare. Even then, the impact of purchasing intentions and behaviors is hard to measure.

A feasible and cost-effective approach to examine purchase behaviors is called a simulated purchase test. A leading marketing research firm that specializes in purchase simulation studies is Research Systems Corporation (RSC). RSC tests commercials by studying consumer behaviors in a controlled laboratory environment.

RSC does not ask consumers to render opinions, describe their attitudes, or even if they plan to purchase the product. Instead, RSC creates a simulated shopping experience. Subjects are able to choose from a variety of products they would see on a normal store shelf. After completing a simulated shopping exercise, the subjects are seated and watch a television preview containing various commercials. The participants are asked to watch the TV preview as they would watch any TV show at home. The test ad is placed in with other ads, and the subjects do not know which ad is being tested.

When the preview is over, the subjects are asked to participate in a second shopping exercise. Researchers then compare the products chosen in the first shopping trip to those selected in the second. Shifts in brand choices are at least partly due to the effectiveness of the advertisement because it is the only variable that has changed.

A major advantage of this methodology is that the test procedures do not rely on opinions and attitudes. Among other things, this means that RSC's procedure can be used in international markets as well as domestic markets.[16] In some cultures, subjects tend to seek to please the interviewer who asks questions about opinions and attitudes. As a result, the answers are polite and socially acceptable. The same subjects may also seek to provide answers they think the interviewer wants to hear. By studying purchases instead of soliciting opinions, subjects are free to respond in a more accurate fashion.

Any methodology designed to tap into behaviors rather than emotions and feelings has a built-in advantage. Opinions and attitudes change and can be quickly affected by other variables in a situation. Observing behaviors and changes in behaviors gets more quickly to the point of the experiment, which is, can the buyer be influenced in a tangible way by a marketing communications tool?

In summary, the three systems designed to examine respondent behaviors are response rates, test markets, and purchase simulation tests. Many of these programs are used in conjunction with one another and also with the message evaluation techniques described earlier. None of these approaches is used in a vacuum. Instead, the data generated and findings revealed are tested across several instruments and with numerous groups of subjects. In that manner, the marketing departmental manager and the advertising agency can try to heighten the odds that both short- and long-term goals can be reached through the ads, premiums, coupons, and other marketing communications devices used. Even then, the job of evaluation is not complete.

evaluating public relations activities

Most public relations can be studied using one or more of the evaluation techniques that have already been described. Many times, however, company leaders use three additional methods. These evaluation techniques are:

1. Counting clippings
2. Calculating the number of impressions
3. The advertising equivalence technique

Counting clippings occurs when a company subscribes to what is called a *clipping service.* The service scours magazines, journals, and newspapers looking for a client company's name. The number of clippings found is then compared to the number of news releases that were sent out. A firm that sends out 400 news releases and is told there are 84 clippings would conclude that the *percent return* is 21 percent.

The second approach, which became popular in the 1990s, is to calculate impressions. *Impressions* are counted as the total number of subscribers and purchasers of a print medium in which the client company's name has been mentioned. For example, when a company's name is mentioned in a newspaper article with a circulation of 800,000 and a newsstand sales of 150,000, then the total number of impressions is 950,000.

There are some problems associated with counting clippings and impressions as methods for evaluating public relations efforts. Clippings ignore whether the article spoke positively or negatively about the company. Any clipping is counted when the company's name is mentioned no matter the context. Unfortunately, this means an article criticizing the company counts as much as one praising the company. With impression counts, everyone who subscribes to or buys a magazine or newspaper is part of the total. No effort is made to see what percentage of those who bought the paper or magazine actually saw the company name or read the article.

Firms that continue using clippings and impressions should modify these techniques when possible. Clippings should be sorted into piles of positive and negative articles in order to see which occurs more frequently. Also, readers should summarize what was said in the article rather than simply noting that the company's name was mentioned. It is also wise to note if the article, whether negative or positive, appeared in a setting that would reach the company's customers, or if it is "buried" somewhere with less importance.

For impressions, surveys should be conducted to indicate the percentage of the total audience (readership of a magazine) that saw the company's name. This can be accomplished by using recall or recognition tests, or both. In addition, attitude questions can be posed to see how people reacted to what was in the story. Again, merely counting impressions does not provide adequate feedback about a PR campaign.

The problems associated with clippings and impressions have led to a third method used to measure public relations effectiveness. The approach, called *advertising equivalence,* involves finding every place the company name was mentioned in print and broadcast media. Then, the market researcher calculates the cost of the time or space if it was a paid advertisement. For example, if the company is discussed in an article that occupies one-half page of a magazine, the firm finds out the cost of a half-page ad. A similar approach is used for TV publicity. The cost of an ad running for the amount of time the company was discussed on the air is calculated. Again, this method makes the most sense only if positive publicity stories are counted.

The least used but best method involves examining the public relations piece in comparison to the company's PR objectives. Many times, the objective of a particular PR campaign is to increase awareness of the firm or product's name. Evaluation includes developing an index of awareness before a PR campaign begins. Then, after the PR event, awareness is measured a second time to see if it actually increased. This kind of information is valuable in the motion picture industry. When celebrities make personal appearances and visits to talk shows in the effort to generate publicity, awareness should increase.

In other situations, the goal of a PR campaign is to build a positive image for the company because of bad publicity or some other negative event. Again, the image should be measured before and after the PR campaign. The goal is to see if the image changed, and, if so, to what degree. This approach is time-consuming and difficult. It may take time for a PR campaign to have a full impact. Still, many firms are interested in knowing if their public relations efforts are working.

Each of these methods is based on the goal of discovering the impact of the PR program. When combined with assessments of the effectiveness of advertisements and behavioral responses, the company has a fairly solid grasp regarding what is going on in the current marketplace. Completion of a full IMC evaluation involves one more crucial process.

evaluating the overall IMC program

Many years ago, Peter Drucker outlined a series of goal areas that are indicative of organizational health. In other words, the goals shown in Figure 17.6 are solid measures of the overall well-being of a company. These goals match very well with the objectives of an IMC program.[17]

- **Market share**
- **Level of innovation**
- **Productivity**
- **Physical and financial resources**
- **Profitability**
- **Manager performance and development**
- **Employee performance and attitudes**
- **Social responsibility**

**Measures of Overall
Health of a Company**

FIGURE 17.6

Source: Peter Drucker, *Management: Tools, Responsibilities, Pratices,* New York: Harper and Row, 1974.

Market share has long been linked to profitability. It demonstrates consumer acceptance, brand loyalty, and a strong competitive position. A promotions opportunity analysis, as described in Chapter 5, should help the marketing team understand both its market share and the relative strengths and weaknesses of the competition. IMC programs are designed to hold and build market share.

Innovation is finding new and different ways to achieve objectives. This applies to many marketing activities, including new and unusual trade promotions devices (Chapter 11), consumer promotions (Chapter 12), public relations events and sponsorships (Chapter 13), Internet and e-commerce programs (Chapter 15), and, of course all of the firm's advertising efforts.

Productivity is reflective of the industry's increasing emphasis on results. IMC experts are being asked to demonstrate tangible results from IMC campaigns. Both short- and long-term measures of the effects of advertisements and promotions demonstrate the "productivity" of the organization, in terms of gaining new customers, building recognition in the marketplace, by sales per customer, and through other measures.

Physical and financial resources are also important to an IMC program. Physical resources include the most up-to-date computer and Internet capabilities. The firm must provide sufficient financial resources to reach this goal. Scanner technologies and other devices that keep the firm in contact with consumers are vital elements in the long-term success of an IMC plan.

Profitability is vital for the marketing department and the overall organization. Many IMC managers know that more than sales are at issue when assessing success. Sales must generate profits in order for the company to survive and thrive over time.

Manager performance and development is possibly an overlooked part of an IMC program. Effective marketing departments and advertising agencies must develop pipelines of new, talented creatives, media buyers, promotions managers, database Web masters, and others in order to succeed in the long term. Also, new people must be trained and prepared for promotion for more important roles over time.

Employee performance and attitudes reflect not only morale within the marketing department but also relations with other departments and groups. As noted in Chapter 1, an effective IMC plan consists of building bridges with other internal departments so that everyone is aware of the thrust and theme of the program. Satisfied and positive employees are more likely to help the firm promote its IMC image.

Social responsibility was described in detail in Chapter 2. It is clear that the long-term well-being of an organization rests, in part, in its ability to eliminate negative activities and expand its positive programs. Brand equity and loyalty hurt when the firm is known for illegal or unethical actions. Therefore, marketing leaders should encourage all of the members of an organization to act in ethical and socially responsible ways.

When these goals are being reached, it is likely that the firm's IMC program is working well. Beyond these targets, IMC plans continually should emphasize the evolving nature of relationships with customers. Retail consumers and business-to-business buyers should be constantly contacted to find out how the company can best serve their needs.

Simply stated, every chapter in this book implies a series of key performance targets for IMC programs that should guide the actions of the marketing department and the advertising agency both in the short term and over the long haul. Firms that are able to maintain one clear voice in a cluttered marketplace stand the best chance of gaining customer interest and attention as well as developing long-term bonds with all key publics and stakeholders. An effective IMC program helps set the standards and measure performance, and in the end becomes the model for marketing success for the entire organization.

implications for marketing professionals

Department Managers and Advertising Account Executives

Always remember that a plan is never complete until goals are set and performance is measured. In the case of integrated marketing communications programs, goals are generated as the company considers:

1. Promotions opportunities
2. Brand image
3. Consumer buyer behaviors
4. Business-to-business buyer behaviors
5. Advertising design
6. Trade and consumer promotions
7. Personal selling programs
8. Public relations efforts
9. All other selling and promotions activities

Match the goal to the level of analysis. Short-term goals should be measured more frequently and in more detail. Longer-term objectives are studied in light of overall trends and more general criteria.

Don't overemphasize the short term at the expense of the long range. The lasting impressions that marketing communications make are as much of an asset as plant and equipment. These include

1. Image and reputation of the brand and of the company
2. Brand loyalty
3. Having one clear voice with a strong message heard in the marketplace
4. Quality interactions and communications with all types of customers
5. Effective internal communications between the marketing department and other departments within the organization
6. Innovative people and quality technologies
7. The ability to adjust and adapt to a changing marketplace while maintaining the winning image and theme the company has developed

Select tools to measure advertising effectiveness at every stage of development. Don't get your ego so involved that you move forward with a bad idea.

Match the type of assessment with the type of message. Some ads tap emotions, others logic. Make sure the instrument you choose is best for the ad or marketing piece being developed.

Examine the success rates of ads as compared to the tools that were used to assess them as they were being created. Revise those instruments if needed. Avoid becoming too attached to any one approach.

Let experts make decisions. When a researcher with credible credentials tells you an ad probably won't work, believe him or her.

Always look to the future for new opportunities rather than to the past to play "what if" or the blame game. Even the best-laid plans sometimes fail. Learn from your mistakes and move on.

SUMMARY

Assessing an IMC program often involves examining the effects of individual advertisements. These efforts are conducted in two major ways: (1) message evaluations, and (2) evaluating respondent behaviors. A wide variety of techniques can be used. Most of the time marketing managers and advertisement agencies use several different methods in order to get the best picture of an ad's potential for success. Advertisements are studied before they are developed, while they are being developed, and after they have been released or launched.

The guiding principles for any marketing tool include agreement on how test results will be used, preestablishing a cutoff score for a test's results, using multiple measures, basing studies on models of human behaviors, using multiple exposures, testing marketing instruments that are in the same stage of development, and preventing as many biases as possible while conducting the test. Many times it is difficult for certain members of the marketing team to be objective, especially when they

had the idea for the ad or campaign. In these instances, it is better to retain an outside research agency to study the project.

Public relations programs should be assessed in light of not only how many times a company is mentioned in the media but also what various ads and stories said about the company. Also, public relations efforts should be compared with the goals for the department in order to see if the company is achieving the desired effects with its publicity releases and sponsorship efforts.

IMC plans are general, overall plans for the entire company. Therefore, more general and long-term criteria should be included in any evaluation of an IMC program. When the IMC theme and voice are clear, and company is achieving its long-range objectives, the principles stated in this book are being applied efficiently and effectively, and the company is in the best position to succeed at all levels.

REVIEW QUESTIONS

1. What is the difference between a message evaluation and respondent behaviors, when assessing the effectiveness of an advertisement?

2. What does a concept test evaluate? How are story boards and focus groups used in concept tests?

3. Describe the use of portfolio tests and theater tests in copytesting programs.

4. What is DAR? How are aided and unaided recall tests used in conjunction with DAR evaluations? What problems are associated with both types of tests?

5. What is a recognition test? How is it different from a recall test?

6. How are closed-ended questions and open-ended questions used in attitude and opinion tests?

7. What is a warmth monitor? What does it measure?

8. Describe how psychogalvanometers, pupillometric meters, and voice-pitch analysis techniques are used in evaluating advertisements.

9. How do the positioning advertising copytesting principles help advertisers to prepare quality ads and campaigns?

10. What are the three forms of behavioral evaluations that can be used to test advertisements and other marketing pieces?

11. Name the measures of behavioral responses described in this chapter.
12. What items can be evaluated using test markets?
13. Describe a purchase simulation test.
14. Describe counting clippings and calculating the number of impressions as methods for assessing public relations effectiveness. What problems are associated with these two techniques?
15. Describe the advertising equivalence approach to assessing public relations programs.
16. Name and describe the criteria that can be used to assess the impact of the overall IMC program, as noted in this chapter.

KEY TERMS

message evaluation techniques   methods used to examine the creative message and the physical design of the advertisement, coupon, or direct-marketing piece.

respondent behaviors techniques   methods used to examine visible customer actions including making store visits, inquiries, or actual purchases.

story board   a series of still photographs or sketches that outlines the structure of a television ad.

concept testing   an evaluation of the content or concept of the ad and the impact that concept will have on potential customers.

copytests   tests that are used to evaluate a marketing piece that is finished or is in its final stages prior to production.

portfolio test   a display of a set of print ads, one of which is the ad being evaluated.

theater test   a display of a set of television ads, including the one being evaluated.

mall intercept technique   a test where people are stopped in a shopping mall and asked to evaluate a marketing item.

recall tests   an approach in which an individual is asked to recall ads he or she has viewed in a given time period or setting.

day-after recall (DAR)   individuals participating in a study are contacted the day after an advertisement appears to see if they remember encountering the ad.

unaided recall   subjects are asked to name, or recall, the ads without any prompts or memory jogs.

aided recall   consumers are prompted by being told the product category and, if necessary, names of specific brands in that category to see if they recall an ad.

recognition tests   a format in which individuals are given copies of an ad and asked if they recognize it or have seen it before.

closed-end questionnaire   subjects are asked to give specific responses to questions, and the answers are usually rated using some type of scale.

open-ended questions   subjects are allowed to discuss whatever comes to mind in response to a question.

warmth monitor   a method to measure emotional responses to advertisements.

psychogalvanometer   a device that measures perspiration levels.

pupillometric meter   a device that measures the dilation of a person's pupil.

voice-pitch meter   a devices that examines the pitch of a person's voice as he or she reacts with emotion to an advertisement or situation.

positioning advertising copytesting (PACT)   principles to use when assessing the effectiveness of various marketing instruments.

ENDNOTES

1. www.decisionanalyst.com; Patricia Riedman, "DiscoverWhy Tests TV Commercials Online," *Advertising Age,* 71, no. 13 (March 27, 2000), pp. 46–47.
2. David W. Stewart, "Measures, Methods, and Models in Advertising Research," *Journal of Advertising,* 29, no. 3 (1989), pp. 54–60.
3. Joel S. Debow, "Advertising Recognition and Recall by Age—Including Teens," *Journal of Advertising Research,* 35, no. 5 (September–October 1995), pp. 55–60.
4. Jan Stapel, "Recall and Recognition: A Very Close Relationship," *Journal of Advertising Research,* 38, no. 4 (July–August 1998), pp. 41–45.
5. Christina Merrill, "Roper Expands Testing," *Adweek, Eastern Edition,* 37, no. 45 (November 4, 1996), p. 6.
6. Jack Weber and Mary Ann Morgan, "Why It Is Important to Assess Direct Mail Effectiveness," *Marketing News,* 32, no. 9 (April 27, 1998), p. 11.

7. Steven P. Brown and Douglas M. Stayman, "Antecedents and Consequences of Attitude Toward the Ad: A Meta-Analysis," *Journal of Consumer Research,* 19 (June 1992), pp. 34–51.

8. Douglas M. Stayman and David A. Aaker, "Continuous Measurement of Self-Report or Emotional Response," *Psychology and Marketing,* 10 (May–June 1993), pp. 199–214.

9. Freddie Campos, "UH Facility Test Ads for $500," *Pacific Business News,* 35, no. 23 (August 18, 1997), pp. A1–A2.

10. Riedman, "DiscoverWhy Tests TV Commercials Online."

11. David W. Stewart, David H. Furse, and Randall P. Kozak, "A Guide to Commercial Copytesting Services," *Current Issues and Research in Advertising,* ed. James Leigh and Claude Martin Jr. (Ann Arbor: Division of Research, Graduate School of Business, University of Michigan, (1983), pp. 1–44.

12. Based on PACT document published in *Journal of Marketing,* 11, no. 4 (1982), pp. 4–29.

13. James Heckman, "Better Measures Could Make a Noise in Retail," *Marketing News,* 32, no. 25 (December 7, 1998), p. 6.

14. Amanda Beeler, "POPAI Initiates Study Tracking Effectiveness of Displays," *Advertising Age,* 71, no. 15 (April 10, 2000), p. 54.

15. Kim M. Bayne, "AdKnowledge Rolls Out Web Ad Evaluation Tool," *Advertising Age,* 69, no. 23 (June 8, 1998), p. 38.

16. Tim Triplett, "Researchers Probe Ad Effectiveness Globally," *Marketing News,* 28, no. 18 (August 29, 1994), pp. 6–7.

17. Peter Drucker, *Management Tools, Responsibilities, Practices* New York: Harper & Row.

Building an IMC Campaign

Evaluating Your IMC Program

There are several levels to consider when evaluating the success of your advertising and promotions activities. They include short-term outcomes (sales, redemption rates), long-term results (brand awareness, brand loyalty, or equity), product-specific awareness, awareness of the overall company, and affective responses (liking the company and a positive brand image). In the exercise for this chapter, various approaches such as counting coupon redemptions, reviewing viewer responses to advertisements, and others are considered as possible methods to evaluate outcomes. It is possible that you may have to go back and modify a component of your IMC program because of inability to evaluate it effectively. Go to the Web site at www.prenhall.com/clow or access the Advertising Plan Pro disk that accompanied this textbook to complete this final stage of your IMC plan.

Critical Thinking Exercises

Discussion Questions

1. Create an idea for advertising one of the following products. Put that idea down in three or four sentences. Organize a small focus group of four other students in your class. Ask them to evaluate your advertising concept. What did you learn from the exercise?
   a. Retail pet store
   b. Baseball caps
   c. Computers
   d. Sweaters
   e. Watches

2. A very popular form of recall testing is the day-after recall (DAR). Write down five advertisements you remember seeing yesterday. In addition to writing down the product and brand, note whatever else you can remember. Form into groups of four students. Compare your lists. How many commercials were recalled? How much could each of you remember about the commercial?

3. Pick out five advertisements you like. Conduct an aided recall test of these five ads. Ask ten individuals, independently, if they saw the commercial. Mention only the brand name. If so, ask them to recall, in an unaided fashion, as much about the ad as they can. If they do not remember the ad immediately, give them cues. Be sure to record how much each person remembers unaided and how much each person remembers with aided information. Report your results to the class.

4. Form into a group of five students. Ask students to write down two advertisements they really like and their reasons. Ask students to write down two advertisements they dislike and their reasons. Finally, ask students to write down an advertisement they believe is offensive and their reasons. Ask each student to read his or her list comparing ads that were liked, disliked, and offensive. What common elements did you find in each category? What were the differences?

5. How important are sales figures in the evaluation of integrated marketing communications? How should hard data such as redemption rates and store traffic be used in the evaluation of marketing communications? In terms of accountability, how important are behavioral measures of IMC effectiveness?

6. In some Asian countries it is improper to talk about oneself. Therefore, questions about feelings and emotions would be too embarrassing for citizens to answer. Those who answer the questions tend to provide superficial answers. Explain the advantages of a simulated purchasing test methodology in this situation. What other methods of evaluating feelings and emotions could an agency use in Asian countries?

7. From the viewpoint of a marketing manager of a large sporting goods manufacturer, what types of measures of effectiveness would you want from the $500,000 you pay to an advertising agency to develop an advertising campaign? Knowing that evaluation costs money, how much of the $500,000 would you be willing to spend to measure effectiveness? What type of report would you prepare for your boss?

8. A clothing manufacturer spends $600,000 on trade promotions and $300,000 on sales promotions. How would you measure the impact of these expenditures? If an agency were hired to manage these expenditures, what type of measures would you insist the company should utilize?

9. Look through a magazine. Record how many advertisements have a method for measuring responses. How many list a code number, a toll-free number, or a Web site? Just listing a toll-free number or a Web site does not ensure the agency or firm will know where the customer obtained that information. How can the ad agency or firm track the responses from a specific advertisement in the magazine you examined?

10. Pick five print or television advertisements that provide Web sites. Go to each site. Was the Web site a natural extension of the advertisement? What connection or similarities did you see between the Web site and the advertisement? Do you think your response was tracked? How can you tell?

Cruising for Increased Profits

Adventure Cruises owns a fleet of ships that tour the Caribbean and the Bahamas, and make trips to Hawaii. The company has been in operation for over 20 years. Recently, there has been a drop in passengers on each voyage. Adventure's leadership believes increasing competition in the cruise ship industry combined with additional new leisure time activities have led to the decline. Some worry that cruise ship tours are viewed as something "old people" do, and that Disney has taken away the family cruise business.

To combat these problems, Adventure Cruises has decided on two tactics. First, the marketing department will present a new ad campaign highlighting the advantages the company holds over other lines. Second, a new type of passenger will be recruited, a "working business vacationer."

Adventure rebuilt the state rooms on 10 of its ships to accommodate business travelers. These individuals can be members of a company or guests of the company. The idea is to get the customer alone on a ship to conduct business over a series of days, all the while being able to enjoy the many features of cruise travel, including fine dining, gambling, shows, and stops at various ports. The advantage to the company is that it has essentially a "captive audience" when a customer is given a free cruise in exchange for doing business with the company footing the bill. Adventure intends to take out ads in business magazines and journals, selling these new packages to various business buyers. Adventure president Henry Crouch points out, "Lots of companies pay really big bucks to rent luxury boxes in football stadiums. They get the customer for what, four or five hours? We can offer them a chance to keep a customer for four or five *days*."

Henry hired a large international advertising agency to prepare ads for both regular passengers and the new business-to-business market. Lauren Patterson was the account executive who signed the deal, by emphasizing that she would follow the Roper Starch test copy principles. For cruise ship passengers, the ads would pass muster only if they met the following criteria:

1. *The eyes have it.* The ads must be clear and easy to follow.
2. *Never place copy above an illustration.* People see the picture first, so if the copy is higher, it's ignored.
3. *Great visuals work.* The idea is to capture attention and interest.
4. *Make sure the headlines and visuals blend with the copy.* Don't confuse the reader.
5. *Don't use confusing visuals.*
6. *Don't use confusing headlines.*
7. *Testimonials increase believability and readership.*
8. *Size matters.* The ad must be big.
9. *Keep it simple.* Readers are not as interested in the product as you are, so make the ad easy to follow.
10. *Break the rules.* Be creative.

In the business-to-business marketplace, three problems routinely occur. Lauren is going to insist that the ads avoid these problems. She calls them the ABC sins in business-to-business marketing. The problems are:

A. Ads that are not visually appealing
B. Ads that are abstract rather than designed with a human appeal
C. Ads that fail to emphasize the benefit to the business buyer

Henry realizes that these two markets (regular passengers and business customers) are somewhat distinct. Still he believes Adventure Cruises should speak with one voice. He believes his company has three major advantages over the competition: better food, unusual entertainment, and excellent service. He wants to be sure Lauren incorporates those three elements into the ads that appear on television and in the trade journals that they select.

1. Design a print ad for Adventure Cruises' regular passengers.
2. Design a print ad for Adventure Cruises' business customers.
3. What type of testing should be done during the design phase of the advertisement?
4. What type of testing should be done after the ad is designed but prior to placing it in a magazine or other print media?
5. What type of testing should be done after the advertisement is launched? How can the effectiveness of the advertisement be measured?

Long-Distance Success in the Cellular Marketplace

When Judy Mims was assigned the account for a major midwestern cellular phone company, she knew the task would be both exciting and challenging. Cellular service was rapidly moving into the mature stage of the product life cycle. There had been many early entries and explosive growth in sales during the past decade, and the shake-out was beginning. Costs, economies of scale, technological advantages, and superior marketing programs were forcing some companies to the sideline.

Clear Voice had been able to set up services in a five-state region, including Missouri, Kansas, Oklahoma, Arkansas, and Texas. The company provided high-quality service at a competitive price. Roaming charges were low, and many long-term contracts had been signed. The company had built alliances with other major providers, giving them national access for the confirmed cell phone user.

Judy knew several issues were currently dominating the industry. First, each company needed a "voice" in the marketplace. The question Judy asked her client to answer was "Why do people use cell phones? And, how do we speak to them as a result?" Cell phones can be used for convenience, for safety reasons, and as status symbols, though the latter was rapidly losing its appeal, because so many people could now afford the phones and the service. "Is the cellular lifestyle different than a noncellular style?" Judy continued. "If so, how do we win over the nonusers? And how do we keep them from signing on with another company?"

Two other issues were daunting the cell phone marketplace. The first was health. There were disturbing reports of links between extensive cell phone use and cancer of the brain, which is not an appealing prospect. The second, flying just "under the radar screen," as Judy put it, is the backlash factor.

There was little doubt that some people hold cell phone users in contempt. They interrupt lunches in restaurants and annoy the patrons trying to have a quiet meal. Cell phone users seem to go deaf when airline flight attendants announce that the phones must be turned off so that a plane can take off. Every flight now involves a trip down the center aisle of the plane just to shut down cell phone fanatics. Further, insurance agencies and law enforcement departments have begun to question the safety of driving a car while talking on the phone. Nearly every driver has had a near miss or accident because someone was more distracted by a phone call than attentive to driving. A few municipalities have even made it a traffic offense to drive while talking on a cell phone.

Against this backdrop, cell phone purchases continue to rise and user fees offer lucrative sources of revenue for various companies. Judy knew an effective campaign would be one that differentiated Clear Voice from other servers as offering a noticeable advantage. Although the short-term prospects of Clear Voice were good, Judy was being asked to develop and maintain an IMC and advertising program to build a strong company over the long term.

1. Name four major goals that Clear Voice should emphasize in the next decade.

2. Define the theme that will drive Clear Voice during those 10 years.

3. Develop an immediate advertising campaign for the company. Select the methods of assessment for the ads to evaluate the advertising campaign. Justify the choices.

4. How should Clear Voice deal with the "negatives" associated with cell phone use? How would you measure the effectiveness of such an effort?

Credits

Chapter 1
Courtesy of PhotoEdit. Photograph by Michael Newman.

Chapter 2
Courtesy of The Image Works. Photograph by Bob Daemmrich.

Chapter 3
Courtesy of Woodfin Camp & Associates. Photograph by C. Nacke.

Chapter 4
Courtesty of PhotoEdit. Photograph by Jose Galvez.

Chapter 5
Courtesy of Woodfin Camp & Associates. Photograph by Bernard Boutrit.

Chapter 6
Courtesy of Sun Microsystems, Inc.

Chapter 7
Courtesy of The Image Works. Photograph by Nancy Richmond.

Chapter 8
Courtesy of PhotoEdit. Photograph by Spencer Grant.

Chapter 9
Courtesy of Procter & Gamble Company. © The Procter & Gamble Company. Used by permission.

Chapter 10
Courtesy of Liaison Agency, Inc. Photograph by Joe Polillio.

Chapter 11
Courtesy of AP/Wide World Photos. Photograph by Chris O'Meara.

Chapter 12
Courtesy of Corbis/Stock Market. Photograph by R. B. Studio.

Chapter 13
Courtesy of Corbis/SABA Press Photos, Inc. Photograph by Greg Smith.

Chapter 14
Courtesy of Liaison Agency, Inc. Photograph by UPN.

Chapter 15
Courtesy of Woodfin Camp & Associates. Photograph by C. Nacke.

Chapter 16
Courtesy of The Image Bank. Photograph by W. Sallaz.

Chapter 17
Courtesy of Toshiba America Information Systems, Inc.

Name Index

Subject Index

END-USER LICENSE AGREEMENT FOR PRENTICE HALL SOFTWARE

READ THIS LICENSE CAREFULLY BEFORE OPENING THIS PACKAGE. BY OPENING THIS PACKAGE, YOU ARE AGREEING TO THE TERMS AND CONDITIONS OF THIS LICENSE. IF YOU DO NOT AGREE, DO NOT OPEN THE PACKAGE. PROMPTLY RETURN THE UNOPENED PACKAGE AND ALL ACCOMPANYING ITEMS TO THE PLACE YOU OBTAINED THEM [[FOR A FULL REFUND OF ANY SUMS YOU HAVE PAID FOR THE SOFTWARE]]. THESE TERMS APPLY TO ALL LICENSED SOFTWARE ON THE DISK
EXCEPT THAT THE TERMS FOR USE OF ANY SHAREWARE OR FREEWARE ON THE DISKETTES ARE AS SET FORTH IN THE ELECTRONIC LICENSE LOCATED ON THE DISK:

1. GRANT OF LICENSE and OWNERSHIP: The enclosed computer programs ("Software") are licensed, not sold, to you by Prentice-Hall, Inc. ("We" or the "Company") and in consideration of your payment of the license fee, which is part of the price you paid and your agreement to these terms. We reserve any rights not granted to you. You own only the disk(s) but we and/or our licensors own the Software itself. This license allows you to use and display your copy of the Software on a single computer (i.e., with a single CPU) at a single location for academic use only, so long as you comply with the terms of this Agreement. You may make one copy for back up, or transfer your copy to another CPU, provided that the Software is usable on only one computer.

2. RESTRICTIONS: You may not transfer or distribute the Software or documentation to anyone else. Except for backup, you may not copy the documentation or the Software. You may not network the Software or otherwise use it on more than one computer or computer terminal at the same time. You may not reverse engineer, disassemble, decompile, modify, adapt, translate, or create derivative works based on the Software or the Documentation. You may be held legally responsible for any copying or copyright infringement which is caused by your failure to abide by the terms of these restrictions.

3. TERMINATION: This license is effective until terminated. This license will terminate automatically without notice from the Company if you fail to comply with any provisions or limitations of this license. Upon termination, you shall destroy the Documentation and all copies of the Software. All provisions of this Agreement as to limitation and disclaimer of warranties, limitation of liability, remedies or damages, and our ownership rights shall survive termination.

4. LIMITED WARRANTY AND DISCLAIMER OF WARRANTY: Company warrants that for a period of 60 days from the date you purchase this SOFTWARE (or purchase or adopt the accompanying textbook), the Software, when properly installed and used in accordance with the Documentation, will operate in substantial conformity with the description of the Software set forth in the Documentation, and that for a period of 30 days the disk(s) on which the Software is delivered shall be free from defects in materials and workmanship under normal use. The Company does not warrant that the Software will meet your requirements or that the operation of the Software will be uninterrupted or error-free. Your only remedy and the Company's only obligation under these limited warranties is, at the Company's option, return of the disk for a refund of any amounts paid for it by you or replacement of the disk. THIS LIMITED WARRANTY IS THE ONLY WARRANTY PROVIDED BY THE COMPANY AND ITS LICENSORS, AND THE COMPANY AND ITS LICENSORS DISCLAIM ALL OTHER WARRANTIES, EXPRESS OR IMPLIED, INCLUDING WITHOUT LIMITATION, THE IMPLIED WARRANTIES OF MERCHANTABILITY AND FITNESS FOR A PARTICULAR PURPOSE. THE COMPANY DOES NOT WARRANT, GUARANTEE OR MAKE ANY REPRESENTATION REGARDING THE ACCURACY, RELIABILITY, CURRENTNESS, USE, OR RESULTS OF USE, OF THE SOFTWARE.

5. LIMITATION OF REMEDIES AND DAMAGES: IN NO EVENT, SHALL THE COMPANY OR ITS EMPLOYEES, AGENTS, LICENSORS, OR CONTRACTORS BE LIABLE FOR ANY INCIDENTAL, INDIRECT, SPECIAL, OR CONSEQUENTIAL DAMAGES ARISING OUT OF OR IN CONNECTION WITH THIS LICENSE OR THE SOFTWARE, INCLUDING FOR LOSS OF USE, LOSS OF DATA, LOSS OF INCOME OR PROFIT, OR OTHER LOSSES, SUSTAINED AS A RESULT OF INJURY TO ANY PERSON, OR LOSS OF OR DAMAGE TO PROPERTY, OR CLAIMS OF THIRD PARTIES, EVEN IF THE COMPANY OR AN AUTHORIZED REPRESENTATIVE OF THE COMPANY HAS BEEN ADVISED OF THE POSSIBILITY OF SUCH DAMAGES. IN NO EVENT SHALL THE LIABILITY OF THE COMPANY FOR DAMAGES WITH RESPECT TO THE SOFTWARE EXCEED THE AMOUNTS ACTUALLY PAID BY YOU, IF ANY, FOR THE SOFTWARE OR THE ACCOMPANYING TEXTBOOK. BECAUSE SOME JURISDICTIONS DO NOT ALLOW THE LIMITATION OF LIABILITY IN CERTAIN CIRCUMSTANCES, THE ABOVE LIMITATIONS MAY NOT ALWAYS APPLY TO YOU.

6. GENERAL: THIS AGREEMENT SHALL BE CONSTRUED IN ACCORDANCE WITH THE LAWS OF THE UNITED STATES OF AMERICA AND THE STATE OF NEW YORK, APPLICABLE TO CONTRACTS MADE IN NEW YORK, AND SHALL BENEFIT THE COMPANY, ITS AFFILIATES AND ASSIGNEES. HIS AGREEMENT IS THE COMPLETE AND EXCLUSIVE STATEMENT OF THE AGREEMENT BETWEEN YOU AND THE COMPANY AND SUPERSEDES ALL PROPOSALS OR PRIOR AGREEMENTS, ORAL, OR WRITTEN, AND ANY OTHER COMMUNICATIONS BETWEEN YOU AND THE COMPANY OR ANY REPRESENTATIVE OF THE COMPANY RELATING TO THE SUBJECT MATTER OF THIS AGREEMENT. If you are a U.S. Government user, this Software is licensed with "restricted rights" as set forth in subparagraphs (a)-(d) of the Commercial Computer-Restricted Rights clause at FAR 52.227-19 or in subparagraphs (c)(1)(ii) of the Rights in Technical Data and Computer Software clause at DFARS 252.227-7013, and similar clauses, as applicable.

Should you have any questions concerning this agreement or if you wish to contact the Company for any reason, please contact in writing: Director of Media, Higher Education Division, Prentice Hall, Inc., 1 Lake Street, Upper Saddle River, NJ 07458.